PENGUIN BOOKS

DRAWING DOWN THE MOON

Margot Adler has been a radio producer and journalist since 1968, pioneering live, free-form talk shows on religion, politics, women's issues, and ecology. She lectures on the subject of Paganism and earth-centered traditions and leads workshops on the art of ritual, celebration, and song. She is currently the New York Bureau Chief for National Public Radio as well as a well-known correspondent on NPR's *All Things Considered* and *Morning Edition*. She is also the host of *Justice Talking*, a national radio show on constitutional issues. Her most recent book is *Heretic's Heart: A Journey Through Spirit and Revolution*.

MARGOT ADLER

Drawing Down

Witches, Druids,

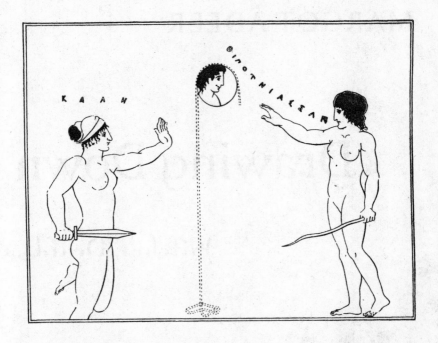

Drawing down the moon: one of the few known depictions of this ancient ritual, from a Greek vase probably of the second century B.C.E.

(New York Public Library)

the Moon

Goddess-Worshippers, and Other Pagans in America

The Classic Study Revised and Updated
with a New Resource Guide: Over 300 Listings of
Groups, Festivals, Publications, and Web Sites

PENGUIN BOOKS

PENGUIN BOOKS

Published by the Penguin Group

Penguin Group (USA) Inc., 375 Hudson Street, New York, New York 10014, U.S.A.
Penguin Group (Canada), 90 Eglinton Avenue East, Suite 700, Toronto, Ontario,
Canada M4P 2Y3 (a division of Pearson Penguin Canada Inc.)
Penguin Books Ltd, 80 Strand, London WC2R 0RL, England
Penguin Ireland, 25 St Stephen's Green, Dublin 2, Ireland (a division of Penguin Books Ltd)
Penguin Group (Australia), 250 Camberwell Road, Camberwell, Victoria 3124, Australia
(a division of Pearson Australia Group Pty Ltd)
Penguin Books India Pvt Ltd, 11 Community Centre, Panchsheel Park, New Delhi – 110 017, India
Penguin Group (NZ), 67 Apollo Drive, Rosedale, Auckland 0632, New Zealand
(a division of Pearson New Zealand Ltd)
Penguin Books (South Africa) (Pty) Ltd, 24 Sturdee Avenue,
Rosebank, Johannesburg 2196, South Africa

Penguin Books Ltd, Registered Offices: 80 Strand, London WC2R 0RL, England

First published in the United States of America by The Viking Press 1979
Revised edition published by Beacon Press 1986
Edition with an updated Appendix III (Resources) published in Arkana 1997
This edition with an expanded Appendix III published in Penguin Books 2006

23rd Printing

Cult evaluation guide reprinted by permission of Isaac Bonewits

LIBRARY OF CONGRESS CATALOGING IN PUBLICATION DATA
Adler, Margot.
Drawing down the moon : witches, Druids, goddess-worshippers,
and other pagans in America today / Margot Adler.
p. cm.
"The classic study revised and updated with a new resource guide:
over 300 listings of groups, festivals, publications, and Web sites."
Includes bibliographical references and index.
ISBN 978-0-14-303819-1
1. Witchcraft—United States. 2. Cults—United States. 3. Goddess religion—United States.
4. Women and religion. I. Title.
BF1573.A34 2006
299'.94—dc22 2006043786

Printed in India
Set in Adobe Garamond
Designed by Francesca Belanger

Contents

IV. The Material Plane

Illustrations follow page 155

Preface to the New Edition

ON ALL HALLOWS EVE, 1979, *Drawing Down the Moon* was published in New York City. On the same day, Starhawk's *The Spiral Dance* was published in California. These two books continue to be many people's introduction to modern Paganism, Wicca, and Goddess spirituality. These books have different perspectives, but they both envisioned a Pagan movement much larger than the one that existed when the books were first published. That larger movement has come to pass, although it is different than either author dreamed or expected.

When *Drawing Down the Moon* was published, modern Pagans, Heathens, Druids, and Wiccans in the United States numbered less than one hundred thousand people. Today many estimates are four to seven times that number, with more than a million worldwide.

In the more than twenty-five years since *Drawing Down the Moon* was published, the world is much changed, but strangely, although many of the details have altered, and some of the early organizations no longer exist, the root ideas in *Drawing Down the Moon* seem more relevant now than they did in 1979.

The message of *Drawing Down the Moon* has always been that the spiritual world is like the natural world—only diversity will save it. Just as the health of a forest or fragrant meadow can be measured by the number of different insects and plants and creatures that successfully make it their home, so only by an extraordinary abundance of disparate spiritual and philosophic paths will human beings navigate a pathway through the dark and swirling storms that mark our current era. "Not by one avenue alone," wrote Symmachus sixteen centuries ago, "can we arrive at so tremendous a secret."

The dominant spiritual trend of our time is militant fundamentalism. Suicide bombers die as martyrs in Palestine and Iraq. In this country, fundamentalists fight to change textbooks and ban books. Like corporations that reduce developing countries to poverty by turning all acreage to a single crop, the belief that there is one word, one truth, one path to the light, makes it easy to destroy ideas, institutions, and people. Almost a hundred years ago, the historian James Breasted wrote this controversial sentence worth contemplating: "Monotheism is but imperialism in religion."

If you go far enough back, all our ancestors were Pagans. They practiced religions that had few creeds or dogmas. There were no prophets. There were myths and legends, but no scriptures to be taken literally. These religions were based on the celebration of the seasonal cycles of nature. They were based on what people *did,* not what people *believed.* It is these polytheistic religions that are being revived and re-created by Neo-Pagans today. This book is the story of that Pagan resurgence.

Drawing Down the Moon is grounded in the view that reality is multiple and diverse. It stands against the totalistic religious and political views that dominate the world. It says, "strive to be comfortable in chaos and complexity. Be as a shaman who walks in many worlds." The book's basic assumption is that your own spiritual path is not necessarily mine. In fact, even the most extreme and authoritarian religions can be seen as appropriate *individual* spiritual paths—but they are only one flower in a garden.

Now, there are many anti-authoritarian religious groups, and many Christian, Muslim, and Jewish groups among them, not to mention Quakers, Bahais, Unitarians, and countless others. What's unusual about modern Pagans is that they remain anti-authoritarian while retaining rituals and ecstatic techniques that, in our time, are used mostly by dogmatic religions or indigenous tribal groups.

Since Pagans are a very diverse group, it is wrong to say all Pagans believe this or that, but here are some beliefs that many people in this book share:

The world is holy. Nature is holy. The body is holy. Sexuality is holy. The imagination is holy. Divinity is immanent in nature; it is within you as well as without. Most spiritual paths ultimately lead people to the understanding of their own connection to the divine. While human beings are often cut off from experiencing the deep and ever-present connection between themselves and the universe, that connection can often be regained through ceremony and community. The energy you put out into the world comes back.

There are now many good books on modern Paganism, Witchcraft, and Goddess spirituality, and many important scholarly works. But this book is still the only detailed history of the origins of Neo-Paganism in the United States. So, in preparing this new edition, there was a constant tension between keeping the book as a piece of history and detailing the journey that modern Paganism has made over the last twenty years, the time that's passed since the last real revision of this book. Many people have asked me to only put in additions, not changes. In the end I have taken a middle course, the same one I took in 1986—leaving most of the book intact, making some changes, cutting out some parts of chapters that seemed overly long ("Living on the Earth"), putting one chapter that seemed really outdated into an appendix ("Scholars, Writers, Journalists, and the Occult"), expanding greatly the sections on Pagan Festivals, Heathenism, Gay Spirituality, the Erisians, and Wiccan Traditions, and adding some new pages on Pagan studies. I also created a much larger up-to-date resource guide to Pagan groups, festivals, and publications and Web sites, more than three hundred listings, with many more Druid and Heathen groups, as well as more entries from Europe, Australia, Canada, and South Africa. Despite this, the explosion of Pagan festivals (more than 350 in the United States), Web sites (at least 5,000, probably more), and groups means that the Pagan movement is becoming so large it is much more difficult to chart.

While some of the early organizations that helped create the Neo-Pagan revival are not dominant organizations today, it is important to remember that they originated and developed key concepts that created a Neo-Pagan viewpoint—concepts like the difference between a tribal and a credal religion, between religions of immanence and transcendence, between a polytheistic and monotheistic outlook, between religions based on words and religions based on experience.

And one fascinating aspect of the rise of Paganism on the Internet has been that some of these early organizations—groups that seemed moribund fifteen years ago—are having a new life, today, on the Web.

Finally, although some scholars may argue this, no one converts to Paganism or Wicca. You will find no one handing you Pagan leaflets or shouting at you on a street corner. Many people came across this book, or one of hundreds of other books, in some isolated corner of America or the world. Often they found it in a small-town library, or in a used bookstore, or stashed away on a friend's bookshelf, or even in a prison. Upon opening its pages, they often experienced a homecoming. Perhaps they said, "I never knew there was anyone else in the world who felt what I feel or believed what I have always believed. I never knew my religion had a name." To these people this book is dedicated.

Preface

"PAGANISM IN AMERICA" . . . This simple phrase stirs deep responses in many people.

A book on Paganism could be many things—since *pagan* has been defined as everything from decadence to sensuality, to return to the primitive, to a stance against religion. It might be yet another book on narcissism in our time, or a book on atheism or hedonism. No matter how precisely the word is defined—and it is defined precisely in the pages that follow—the word *pagan,* like *anarchist* or *communist,* calls forth complex and often negative expectations in readers.

At least several hundred thousand people in the United States call themselves Pagans or Neo-Pagans today, and they use the word *pagan* in a very different way. These people—the subject of this book—consider themselves part of a religious movement that antedates Christianity and monotheism. By *pagan* they usually mean the pre-Christian nature religions of the West, and their own attempts to revive them or to re-create them in new forms. The modern Pagan resurgence includes feminist Goddess-worshippers, modern Witches, new religions based on the visions of science-fiction writers, and attempts to revive ancient European religions—Norse, Greek, Roman, Druid, and Celtic, among others.

The Pagan movement does not include most Eastern religious groups. It includes neither Satanists nor Christians. And it stands in marked contrast to many other alternative religious movements that have received massive coverage in the press—from the Hare Krishnas to the Unification Church. The groups within this book are largely non-authoritarian. The Pagan view is one that says that neither doctrine nor dogma nor asceticism nor rule by masters is necessary for the visionary experience, and that ecstasy and freedom are both possible. It fits well with our pluralistic society.

Part I gives some basic definitions and philosophy. Chapter 1 describes the broad outlines of this movement and defines troublesome words like *pagan* and *witch*. Chapter 2 describes my own entry into this world thirty-five years ago as an observer-participant, and discusses how entry into most of these groups differs from the conversion process so familiar in many religions. Chapter 3 is about the Pagan worldview: how the polytheistic perspective of many Pagan groups demands—at least in theory—a stance against authoritarianism.

Part II describes the Witchcraft revival, its history, its links with Britain and certain British folklorists, and its current practices, "beliefs," and traditions. One chapter describes the role of magic and ritual in these groups; another discusses feminist Witchcraft covens and the broader intersection of feminism and Paganism.

Part III looks at other Neo-Pagan groups: the revivals and reconstruction of ancient European religions—Druids, Heathens, as well as ancient Greek and Egyptian revivals. There is also a section on Gay spirituality. There are also religions based on fantasy and private visions, as well as a potpourri of groups that originated as satire, from the Reform Druids of North America to the worshippers of Eris, goddess of chaos.

Part IV considers the relationship of all these things to the "real world." It looks at Pagans' attitudes to the environment, politics, work, technology, and science. It also looks at the broad changes that have occurred in the movement over the last twenty-five years.

This book could not have been written without the help of hundreds of people. Many of their names appear within.

For the most recent edition, the Internet was a blessing. Thanks to: Andras and Dierdre Arthen, Z Budapest, Chas Clifton and the Nature Religions Scholars Network, Jennifer Culver, Selena Fox, Sally Miller Gearhart, Judy Harrow, Ronald Hutton, Willow La Monte, Michael Lloyd, Aidan Kelly, Morgan McFarland, Patricia Monaghan, Harold Moss, Jean Mountaingrove, Fritz Muntean, Sparky T. Rabbit, Oberon Zell-Ravenheart, Victoria Slind-Flor, Volkhvy, Ben Waggoner, Dale Wallace, Don Wildgrube, and hundreds of others who passed me from one person to another, e-mail to e-mail.

The original book would never have happened without the comments and critiques by friends, scholars, and a diverse group Neo-Pagans, including Isaac Bonewits, Sharon Devlin, Aidan Kelly, Morgan McFarland, Penny Novack, Theodore Roszak, Jeffrey Burton Russell, and my husband, John Gliedman. Others, whose conversations or ideas helped inspire the book included Lindsay Ardwin, the late Bruce Kenyon, Zana Miller, Arnie Sacher, Kathleen Pullen, John Schaar, Ursula Le Guin, Ernest Becker, and Ernest Callenbach. All mistakes are my own.

Volunteers transcribed almost two hundred hours of taped interviews. Special thanks go to Patricia Holub and Elena La Pera. Also, Susan Advocate, Doug Berk, Arlene Coffee, Alice Elste, Mary Joiner, Melvin Jones, Jackie Kelly, Jean Kononowitz, Herb Penmen, and Maureen Scherer.

I traveled thousands of miles doing research for the first edition. I visited hundreds of people and attended rituals at groves and covens across the United States and in England. Often I was housed and fed by strangers, who quickly became friends. Special thanks to Doris and Vic Stuart, Morgan McFarland, Mark Roberts, the Zell-Ravenhearts, Athena and Dagna, Gwydion Pendderwen, and my dear friend, the late Alison Harlow.

The Neo-Pagan journal *Green Egg* published my long questionnaire and I received hundreds of pages in response.

The second edition in 1986 would not have been possible without the help of Larry Cornett, Selena Fox, Christa Heiden, and Bob Murphy. I also received advice or help from Judy Harrow, Oz, Starhawk, Isaac Bonewits, Ginny Brubaker, and Doreen Valiente.

I handed out four hundred questionnaires at three Pagan festivals in 1985, for the 1986 revision, at Rites of Spring, COG MerryMeet, and Pagan Spirit Gathering. I also interviewed people at The Festival of Women's Spirituality. The questionnaire was also published in the Pagan journal *Panegyria*. One hundred and ninety-five responses arrived by hand or in the mail. For this newest 2006 edition, I conducted interviews at Rites of Spring and Pagan Spirit Gathering, and talked and corresponded with representatives of more than three hundred different groups—on the Internet, by phone, and by mail.

As for libraries and institutions, thanks to the Institute for the Study of American Religion and J. Gordon Melton; the Lesbian Herstory

Archives in New York City; the C. G. Jung Foundation in New York and its library; and the New York Public Library, especially the Frederick Lewis Allen Room at the Library—a wonderful room for writers—where all editions but this one were written.

A special thanks goes to the late Mary Card—who taught twelve-year-olds at The City and Country School—a whole year devoted to ancient Greece. Without that experience, this journey might not have been taken. Thanks also to professor Gilbert Rose, who provided me with the rudiments of the ancient Greek language in college, allowing my thoughts to continue in unusual directions.

And thanks to the group of women who meet every weekday at Juliano's coffee house, for keeping me sane.

This book has had several different publishers and many different editors during its four editions. Thanks to Edwin Kennebec, Alida Becker, Joanne Wycoff, and my newest editor at Penguin, Rakia Clark. And deepest thanks to Jane Rotrosen and Donald Cleary of the Jane Rotrosen Agency.

Here is the true story. It was a chance encounter in a bar that is most responsible for *Drawing Down the Moon*. A friend introduced me to an agent, Jane Rotrosen, way back in 1974. Her eyes got wide as I started to talk about my experiences with Pagans and Witches. "Have you ever thought about writing a book," she asked? "No," I said. I hadn't, and I added, "Unlike radio, the written word is so eternal." Thank you, Jane—thirty-one years after that first meeting, here's the latest edition.

Acknowledgments

The author is grateful to the following publishers for permission to reprint excerpts: From *Religious and Spiritual Groups in Modern America,* by Robert S. Ellwood, Jr., © 1973 by Prentice-Hall, Inc. By permission of Prentice-Hall, Inc., Englewood Cliffs, N.J. From *Occultism, Witchcraft and Cultural Fashions,* by Mircea Eliade, © 1976 University of Chicago. By permission of the University of Chicago Press. "The Occult and the Modern World" originally appeared in *Journal of the Philadelphia Association for Psychoanalysis,* Vol. 1, No. 3, September 1974. From Edward J. Moody, "Magical Therapy: An Anthropological Investigation of Contemporary Satanism"; Marcello Truzzi, "Towards a Sociology of the Occult: Notes on Modern Witchcraft"; and Harriet Whitehead, "Reasonably Fantastic: Some Perspectives on Scientology, Science Fiction, and Occultism," in *Religious Movements in Contemporary America,* eds. Irving J. Zaretsky and Mark P. Leone, © 1974 by Princeton University Press. By permission of Princeton University Press. From *Europe's Inner Demons: An Enquiry Inspired by the Great Witch-Hunt,* by Norman Cohn, © 1975 by Norman Cohn. By permission of Basic Books, Inc., Publishers, New York. From *An ABC of Witchcraft Past and Present* and *Natural Magic* by Doreen Valiente, © respectively 1973 and 1975 by Doreen Valiente. By permission of St. Martin's Press, Inc., New York. From *Eleusis and the Eleusinian Mysteries,* by George E. Mylonas, © 1961 by Princeton University Press. By permission of Princeton University Press. From "The Religious Background of the Present Environmental Crisis," by Arnold Toynbee, originally published in *The International Journal of Environmental Studies,* 1972, Vol. III, Gordon and Breach Science Publishers Ltd., 41/42 William IV Street, London WC2, England. By permission of the publishers and the Estate of Professor Toynbee. From "The Witch Archetype," by Ann Bedford Ulanov, originally published in *Quadrant,* Vol. X, No. 1, 1977. By permission of the C. J. Jung Foundation for Analytical Psychology, Inc., New York, NY. From "Witchcraft: Classical, Gothic and Neopagan," by Isaac Bonewits, © 1976 by *Green Egg,* St. Louis, Missouri. From *The Druid Chronicles (Evolved),* ed. Isaac Bonewits, Berkeley Drunemeton Press, Berkeley, California, 1976. From *Real Magic,* by P. E. I. Bonewits, Creative Arts Book Company, © 1979 by P. E. I. Bonewits. From *Green Egg,* © 1968–1976 by *Green Egg,* St. Louis, Missouri. From *Gnostica,* © 1973–1975 by Llewellyn Publications, St. Paul, Minnesota. From "The Rebirth of Witchcraft," unpublished manuscript by Aidan Kelly, © 1977 by Aidan Kelly. From "Why a Craft Ritual Works," "Palengenesia," and "She Touched Me . . ." in *Essays Toward a Metatheology of the Goddess,* by C. Taliesin Edwards (Aidan Kelly), © 1975 by C. Taliesin Edwards. From "I.D.," poem by Barbara Starrett, © 1974 by Barbara Starrett. Frontispiece illustration by permission of the Art and Architectural Division of the New York Public Library (Astor, Lenox and Tilden Foundation).

A Note on Names and Language

A number of those whose names appear within are using "Craft" or "Pagan" names instead of their given names. This may be for reasons of job security, because of the community in which they live, or because, for any one of a number of reasons, they do not wish to be "public" about their religion. Their wishes have been honored.

Throughout the book I do not use "man," "mankind," or "he" as generic terms. At the present time these terms mean "male" rather than being truly generic. Many of those I quote do use these terms and their quotes are left intact. There are also several quotations that contain words with intentionally unconventional spellings, such as "womin" and "thealogy."

I. Background

. . . the Thessalian witches who draw down the moon from heaven . . .
—PLATO, *Gorgias*

If I beheld the sun when it shined, or the moon walking in brightness; and my heart hath been secretly enticed, or my mouth hath kissed my hand: this also were an iniquity to be punished by the judge: for I should have denied the God that is above.
—*Job*, XXXIII, 27–8

I.

Paganism and Prejudice

IN THE LAST FORTY-FIVE YEARS, alongside the often noted resurgence of "occult" and "magical" groups, a diverse and decentralized religious movement has sprung up that remains comparatively unnoticed, and when recognized, is generally misunderstood. Throughout the United States there are thousands of groups in this movement, each numbering anywhere from several to several hundred. Eclectic, individualist, and often fiercely autonomous, they do not share those characteristics that the media attribute to religious cults. They are often self-created and *homemade;* they seldom have "gurus" or "masters"; they have few temples and hold their meetings in woods, parks, apartments, and houses; in contrast to most organized cults, the operations of high finance are rare; and entry into these groups comes through a process that could rarely be called "conversion."

While these religious groups all differ in regard to tradition, scope, structure, organization, ritual, and the names for their deities, they do regard one another as part of the same religious and philosophical movement. They have a common name for themselves: Pagans or Neo-Pagans.* They share a set of values and they communicate with one another through a network of newsletters[1] and Web sites, as well as regional and national gatherings.

Most Neo-Pagans sense an aliveness and "presence" in nature. They are usually polytheists or animists or pantheists, or two or three of these things at once. They share the goal of living in harmony with nature and they tend to view humanity's "advancement" and separation from

---

*"Pagan" and "Neo-Pagan" are capitalized since the words are used here to describe members of a religion, in the same way as one would describe a "Christian" or a "Jew." "Witch" will be capitalized when it is used to refer to members of the modern Witchcraft religion, Wicca or the Craft.

nature as the prime source of alienation. They see *ritual* as a tool to end that alienation. Most Neo-Pagans look to the old pre-Christian nature religions of Europe, the ecstatic religions, and the mystery traditions as a source of inspiration and nourishment. They gravitate to ancient symbols and ancient myths, to the old polytheistic religions of the Greeks, the Egyptians, the Celts, and the Sumerians. They are reclaiming these sources, transforming them into something new, and adding to them the visions of Robert Graves, even of J.R.R. Tolkien and other writers of science fiction and fantasy, as well as some of the teachings and practices of the remaining aboriginal peoples.

Most of these groups have grown up in cities, where the loss of enrichment from the natural world is most easily perceived and where, also, the largest number of intellectual tools to enlarge such a perception exist. Fueled by romantic vision, fantasy, and visionary activities, empowered by a sense of planetary crisis and the idea that such a nature vision may be drowned in an ecocidal nightmare, Neo-Pagans have often allied themselves with other philosophical and political movements.

Since 1972, I have moved freely among a large number of Neo-Pagans. I have visited groves and covens across the country and have attended many festivals and gatherings. I have also visited groups in Canada and the United Kingdom. This book charts the resurgence of these contemporary nature religions.

In the late 1960s it was fashionable to characterize the counterculture and the psychedelic movement as a visionary, "neo-sacral," "neo-transcendental"[2] movement which joined a mystical view of the cosmos to a countercultural lifestyle and worldly politics. In the last decade that movement has virtually disappeared and its place has been taken by large well-financed religious groups usually characterized by authoritarianism and asceticism. The Unification Church of Sun Myung Moon and the International Society of Krishna Consciousness of Swami Prabhupada are two examples among many.

In contrast, the Neo-Pagan groups described in these pages have something of that original "neo-sacral" impulse of the 1960s. They do not regard pleasure as sinful, nor do they conceive of this world as a burden. While many of their members lead quite ordinary, and often successful, lives in the "real world," they are able to detach themselves from many of the trends of the day, maintaining a sense of humor, a gentle anarchism, and a remarkable tolerance of diversity.

I have noticed that many intellectuals turn themselves off the instant they are confronted with the words *witchcraft, magic, occultism,* and *religion,* as if such ideas exert a dangerous power that might weaken their rational faculties. Yet many of these people maintain a generous openness about visionaries, poets, and artists, some of whom may be quite mad according to "rational" standards. They are fascinated by people of diverse professions and lifestyles who have historical ties with, let us say, the Transcendentalists or the Surrealists, as long as the word *occult* is not mentioned.

If Neo-Paganism were presented as an intellectual and artistic movement whose adherents have new perceptions of the nature of reality, the place of sexuality, and the meaning of community, academics would flock to study it. Political philosophers would write articles on the Neo-Pagans' sense of wonder and the minority vision they represent. Literary critics would compare the poetic images in the small magazines published and distributed by the groups with images in the writings of Blake and Whitman. Jungian psychologists would rush to study the Neo-Pagans' use of ancient archetypes and their love of the classics and ancient lore.

But words like *witch* and *pagan* do not rest easily in the mind or on the tongue. Although reporting on Paganism and Wicca has improved in the last decade, pop journalists often still present a Neo-Paganism composed of strange characters and weird rites.[3]

The reality is very different. This *religious* movement of people who often call themselves Pagans, Neo-Pagans, and Witches is only partly an "occult" phenemenon. Often it is interwoven with the visionary and artistic tradition, the ecology movement, the feminist movement, and the libertarian tradition.

A few scholars and specialists have studied and come to understand Neo-Paganism, but the public continues to have an inaccurate picture of it. Misunderstandings begin at the most basic level, with the meanings of words used to describe beliefs and attitudes. Let us take the word *magic.* Most people define it as *superstition* or *belief in the supernatural.*

magic + the supernatural

In contrast, most magicians, Witches, and other magical practitioners do not believe that magic has anything to do with the supernatural.*

Here's an example that illustrates the depth and complexity of these differences. During my travels I came across a coven of Witches living on a farm in the plains of Colorado.[4] This small group was led by a couple who called themselves Michael and Judy. On their farm livestock were raised and sold, goats were milked, pigs were slaughtered, vegetables were grown, canned, and put away. The seasons turned and work proceeded. Michael and Judy were Witches—that is they were members of a polytheistic nature religion who worshipped a goddess and a god and regarded themselves as priests and priestesses of the Earth-Mother. Outside of this, they lived quite ordinary lives, like their neighbors, who also grew crops and raised animals. Unlike most of their neighbors, however, they had no television and spent their few hours of spare time each day studying music and reading books on mythology, Celtic history, or the history and philosophy of magical practice.

Their rituals marked the seasonal turnings of the year and provided a focus for various creative activities—from the writing of poetry and drama to a large number of activities that, in this society, are usually the work of artists, not farmers.

They planted by the phases of the moon (as do thousands of farmers), they used herbal remedies to heal wounds in their animals, they used ritual to unite themselves with the natural world. They experienced the deaths and births of animals and plants.

Now, what did *magic* mean to this group of Witches? And how would their definition differ from the notion commonly held by the public and from the views of scholars? What, in fact, was a real instance of magic at the farm?

Although this group has now disbanded, I visited the farm in 1974 and 1976. On a hot and dry day, four of us—myself, two weekend volunteers who were studying with the coven, and one full-time member—

---

*An entire chapter could be written on the several definitions of the word *magic* that can be found in dictionaries. The *Oxford English Dictionary*, for example, calls it "The pretended art of influencing the course of events . . . by processes supposed to owe their efficacy to the power of compelling the intervention of spiritual beings, or of bringing into operation some occult controlling principle of nature," then adds what amounts to a brief historical essay implying that yesterday's magic is often today's science.

were asked to go down to the river, which habitually dried up in the late summer until, by September, nothing remained but a cracked riverbed. Each year as the river dried up, the fish inhabitants died. Our project was to catch the dying fish in two buckets and fill an entire small truck with the creatures, which would then be used as composting materials for an organic garden.

A few of the fish were floating on the surface, but most were still quite lively and dashed away to survive a few more hours, perhaps days. It was slimy, messy, and unsuccessful work. At the end of three hours we were caked with mud up to our thighs. We returned with only two buckets of fish. It seemed an impossible task.

When we arrived back at the farm, Michael said that he would go back with us to the river, that the job *was* possible, and that, more to the point, the fish were needed. I was skeptical. In the truck on the way to the river he spoke a few words about magic (this may have been the only time I heard the word during my stay at the farm). "Magic," he said, "is simply the art of getting results." He noted that the fish were dying and that they might as well be put to good purpose fertilizing the earth. He impressed upon us the necessity for our actions.

Michael then began to describe how bears catch fish with their paws. He asked us to visualize ourselves as bears, to place ourselves in the position of a hungry bear in need of food. I began to imagine the essence of a bear's life. In such a mood, we waded to the middle of the river, where the water came up to our waists, and began slapping our hands together very quickly, catching the fish between our hands and throwing them over our heads and onto the beach. We continued this process of slapping and throwing until the beach was covered with fish. An hour later, we gathered them up in buckets and took them to the truck, which was soon filled almost to the top. *Def. of Magic*

If I may presume to broaden Michael's definition of magic, it might read something like this: Magic is a convenient word for a whole collection of techniques, all of which involve the mind. In this case, we might conceive of these techniques as including the mobilization of confidence, will, and emotion brought about by the recognition of necessity; the use of imaginative faculties, particularly the ability to visualize, in order to begin to understand how other beings function in nature so we can use this knowledge to achieve necessary ends.

This magic did not involve the supernatural. It involved an understanding of psychological and environmental processes; it was a kind of shamanism, a knowledge of how emotion and concentration can be directed naturally to effect changes in consciousness that affect the behavior of (in this case) humans and fish. It is important to stress that this naturalistic definition of magic was not unique to the farm in Colorado, but is common in one form or another to the other groups mentioned in these pages.

Interestingly, traditional occult definitions of magic have rarely included the supernatural. For example, in Aleister Crowley's famous definition, magic is "the Science and Art of causing change to occur in conformity with Will,"[5] and more recently Isaac Bonewits has defined magic as "folk parapsychology, an art and science designed to enable people to make effective use of their psychic talents."[6] Most of these definitions link magic to an understanding of the workings of the mind. Actually, the idea of the supernatural, of something outside nature, is a thoroughly modern notion unknown to the ancients.

Magic is only one of many terms about which there is misunderstanding. Others are *Pagan* and *Witch*. *Pagan* comes from the Latin *paganus,* which means a country dweller, and is itself derived from *pagus,* the Latin word for village or rural district. Similarly, *heathen* originally meant a person who lived on the heaths. Negative associations with these words are the end result of centuries of political struggles during which the major prophetic religions, notably Christianity, won a victory over the older polytheistic religions. In the West, often the last people to be converted to Christianity lived on the outskirts of populated areas and kept to the old ways. These were the Pagans and heathens—the word Pagan was a term of insult, meaning "hick."

Pagan had become a derogatory term in Rome by the third century. Later, after the death of Julian, the last Pagan emperor, in 362 C.E.,* the word Pagan came to refer to intellectual Pagans like Julian. Gore Vidal, in his extraordinary novel *Julian,* wrote a fictional description of this event in which the Pagan orator Libanius, after attending the funeral of

---

*C.E. (Common Era) is used throughout this book to replace A.D.; B.C.E. (Before Common Era) is used to replace B.C. This is fairly common usage among scholars. See *Webster's New International Dictionary,* 2nd ed. (F. C. Merriam Company, 1958), pp. 540 and 866; *Encyclopedia Judaica,* Vol. I (New York: The Macmillan Company, 1972), p. 73.

a Christian notable, writes in his journal: "There was a certain amount of good-humored comment about 'pagans' (a new word of contempt for us Hellenists) attending Christian services. . . ."[8] Julian, by the way, has long been one of Neo-Paganism's heroes, and an early Neo-Pagan journal was called *The Julian Review.*[9] Centuries later the word *Pagan* still suffers the consequences of political and religious struggles, and dictionaries still define it to mean a godless person or an unbeliever, instead of, simply, a member of a different kind of religion.

Pagan is also often associated with hedonism. This makes some sense, since many ancient pagan religions incorporated sexuality into ecstatic religious practice. Open attitudes toward sexuality play a part in some, but by no means all, Neo-Pagan groups, and the old Pagan religions had their share of ascetics.

I use *Pagan* to mean a member of a polytheistic nature religion, such as the ancient Greek, Roman, or Egyptian religions, or, in anthropological terms, a member of one of the indigenous folk and tribal religions all over the world. People who have studied the classics or have been deeply involved with natural or aboriginal peoples are comparatively free of the negative and generally racist attitudes that surround the word *Pagan.*

Isaac Bonewits uses the term *Neo-Paganism* to refer to "polytheistic (or conditional monotheistic) nature religions that are based upon the older or Paleopagan religions; concentrating upon an attempt to retain the humanistic, ecological and creative aspects of these old belief systems while discarding their occasional brutal or repressive developments, which are inappropriate. . . ."[10] Another Neo-Pagan writer, Oberon Zell-Ravenheart of the Church of All Worlds, has written that Neo-Pagans see divinity manifest in all the processes of nature. According to his view, Neo-Paganism is a constantly evolving philosophy that views humanity as a "functional organ within the greater organism of all Life. . . ."[11]

Since many of the groups I interviewed for this book consider themselves to be Witchcraft covens of one description or another, it will be impossible to understand their nature if one is burdened by stereotyped notions about Witches. There mere words *witch* and *witchcraft* unlock a set of explosive associations that inspire unease if not fear.

Dictionaries define Witches as (primarily) women who are either seductive and charming (bewitching) or ugly and evil (wicked). In either case, the women are supposed to possess a variety of "supernatural" powers. The lexicographical definitions of *witch* are rather confusing and bear little relation to the definitions given by Witches themselves. Participants in the Witchcraft revival generally use *Witch* to mean simply an initiate of the religion Wicca, also known as the Craft.

Followers of Wicca seek their inspiration in pre-Christian sources, European folklore, and mythology. They consider themselves priests and priestesses of an ancient European shamanistic nature religion that worships a goddess who is related to the ancient Mother Goddess in her three aspects of Maiden, Mother, and Crone. Many Craft traditions also worship a god, related to the ancient horned lord of animals, the god of the hunt, the god of death and lord of the forests. Many Neo-Pagan Witches, and Neo-Pagans generally, see themselves as modern-day heirs to the ancient mystery traditions of Egypt, Crete, and Eleusis, as well as to the more popular peasant traditions of celebratory festivals and seasonal rites.

The word *Witchcraft* comes from the Old English *wicce* and *wicca,* referring to female and male practitioners, respectively. Many Witches have said that these two words derive from the root "wit" or wisdom. Others (including myself, in a previous edition of this book) have said the word derives from the Indo-European roots "wic" and "weik," meaning to bend or to turn. According to this view, a Witch would be a woman (or man) skilled in the craft of shaping, bending, and changing reality. This definition would apply well to what happened with the fish in Colorado. Although this definition emphasizes the flexible and non-authoritarian nature of modern Wicca, most dictionaries say something quite different. *The American Heritage Dictionary of the English Language,* for example, says that the word "witch" is derived from the Indo-European root "weik^2," which has to do with religion and magic, and this differs from "weik^4," to bend. Many Wiccans define *Witchcraft* as the "Craft of the Wise," and anyone who reads the literature of modern Wicca will come across this definition. Whether or not this idea is etymologically correct, it is understandable since Witches identify with village elders and healers—those skilled in healing and the practical arts.*

*There is also a huge debate over the term *Wicca,* with some arguing that the term should only be used for British traditional groups. I take a broader view; I consider any group *Wiccan* that is indebted to Gardnerian forms and European sources—that includes most Dianic and eclectic Wiccan groups.

In this book *Witch* refers to the followers of the Craft unless otherwise stated. Neo-Pagan Witchcraft is seen here as one of a number of modern polytheistic religions. I use the word "religion" broadly, to refer to any set of symbolic forms and acts that relate human beings to ultimate conditions of existence, cosmic questions, and universal concerns. Most people in the West tend to associate the word *religion* with the type of religion they are used to. They assume that religion must contain "beliefs" and "dogmas" and must involve a remote and transcendent deity, usually male, though occasionally neuter, and often removed from human interaction. The idea of a "nature religion" seems a contradiction in terms.

Neo-Pagans look at *religion* differently; they often point out that the root of the word means "to relink" and "to connect," and therefore refers to any philosophy that makes deep connections between human beings and the universe.[12] The science fiction writer Joanna Russ once told a convention that science fiction was a "religious literature." Many Neo-Pagans would agree. Similarly, the literature of ecology—for example, the work of writers like Loren Eiseley, René Dubos, Marston Bates, John Muir, and Henry David Thoreau—is seen by many Neo-Pagans as religious. Also, Neo-Paganism returns to the ancient idea that there is no distinction between spiritual and material, sacred and secular. We generally think of spiritual concerns as apart from mundane concerns. This idea is entirely opposed to the Pagan perception. A group of women in a feminist Witchcraft coven once told me that, to them, spiritual meant, "the power within oneself to create artistically and change one's life." These women saw no contradiction between their concern for political and social change and their concern for "things of the spirit," which they equated with the need for beauty or with that spark that creates a poem or a dance. Mirth and reverence coexist as they do in many indigenous cultures.

People who want a convenient box to place these groups in frequently ask me whether they are "occult." Usually this question is asked by people who do not wish to consider them at all, and if I say yes, they feel relieved that they don't have to. The real answer is yes or no, depending on the definition of occult. Yes, because many of these groups deal with hidden or obscure forms of knowledge that are not generally accepted, and no, because a number of groups regard themselves as celebratory rather than magical or occult.

Harriet Whitehead, in an article on Scientology, science fiction, and the occult, makes the point that, contrary to the popular assumption, most occultists have an intellectual style, "a process of sorting, surveying, analysing and abstracting." One of the hallmarks of that style is lack of dogmatism. "The occult world," she writes, "offers to the individual a 'free market' of ideas. . . ." What this resembles, "and not by coincidence, is the intellectual democracy of the scientific and academic communities." She writes that the difference between these two communities and the occult world is that occultists refuse "contentment with the finite" (the phrase comes from William James). Occultists continually affirm that "certain experiences do not cease to exist simply because there is no place for them in our customary order." Occultists display an extraordinary ability to shift from one dimension of reality to another with ease, feeling that the whole world "hangs together in one unified piece."[13] While some Neo-Pagans consider themselves occultists and others do not, Whitehead's characteristics seem to hold true for the groups I've observed. So, as you read, I hope your customary stereotypes will dissolve.

2.

A Religion Without Converts

How do people become Neo-Pagans? Neo-Pagan groups rarely proselytize and certain of them are quite selective. There are few converts. In most cases, word of mouth, a discussion between friends, a lecture, a book, an article, or a Web site provides the entry point. But these events merely confirm some original, private experience, so that the most common feeling of those who have named themselves Pagans is something like "I finally found a group that has the same religious perceptions I always had." A common phrase you hear is "I've come home," or, as one woman told me excitedly after a lecture, "I always knew I had a religion, I just never knew it had a name."

Alison Harlow, a systems analyst at a large medical research center in California, described her first experience this way:*

"It was Christmas Eve and I was singing in the choir of a lovely church at the edge of a lake, and the church was filled with beautiful decorations. It was full moon, and the moon was shining right through the glass windows of the church. I looked out and felt something very special happening, but it didn't seem to be happening inside the church.

"After the Midnight Mass was over and everyone adjourned to the parish house for coffee, I knew I needed to be alone for a minute, so I left my husband and climbed up the hill behind the church. I sat on this hill looking at the full moon, and I could hear the sound of coffee cups clinking and the murmur of conversation from the parish house.

"I was looking down on all this, when suddenly I felt a 'presence.' It seemed very ancient and wise and definitely female. I can't describe it any closer than that, but I felt that this presence, this being, was looking

*Alison Harlow died in 2004. She was a priestess in the Faery tradition of Wicca.

down on me, on this church and these people and saying, 'The poor little ones! They mean so well and they understand so little.'

"I felt that whoever 'she' was, she was incredibly old and patient; she was exasperated with the way things were going on the planet, but she hadn't given up hope that we would start making some sense of the world. So, after that, I knew I had to find out more about her."

As a result of her experience, Harlow began a complex journey to find out about the history and experience of goddess worship. This search led her, through various readings, into contact with a number of Craft traditions, until she ended up writing a column on feminism and Witchcraft for the Neo-Pagan magazine *Nemeton* (now defunct). It is perhaps only fair, at this point, to describe my own entry into this same world.

When I was a small child, I had the good fortune to enter an unusual New York City grammar school (City and Country) that allowed its students to immerse themselves in historical periods to such an extent that we often seemed to live in them. At the age of twelve, a traditional time for rites of passage, that historical period was ancient Greece. I remember entering into the Greek myths as if I had returned to my true homeland.

My friends and I lived through the battles of the *Iliad;* we read the historical novels of Mary Renault and Caroline Dale Snedeker[1] and took the parts of ancient heroes and heroines in plays and fantasy. I wrote hymns to gods and goddesses and poured libations (of water) onto the grass of neighboring parks. In my deepest and most secret moments I daydreamed that I had become these beings, feeling what it would be like to be Artemis or Athena. I acted out the old myths and created new ones, in fantasy and private play. It was a great and deep secret that found its way into brief diary entries and unskilled drawings. But like many inner things, it was not unique to me.

I have since discovered that these experiences are common. The pantheons may differ according to circumstance, class, ethnic and cultural background, opportunity, and even chance. There are children in the United States whose pantheons come from *Star Wars,* while their parents fantasize about *Star Trek*[2] and their grandparents remember the days of Buck Rogers. The archetypal images seem to wander in and out of the fantasies of millions of children, disguised in contemporary forms. That I and most of my friends had the opportunity to take our archetypes from the rich pantheon of ancient Greece was a result of class and opportunity, nothing more.

What were these fantasies of gods and goddesses? What was their use, their purpose? I see them now as daydreams used in the struggle toward my own becoming. They were hardly idle, though, since they focused on stronger and healthier "role models" than the images of women in the culture of the late 1950s. The fantasies enabled me to contact stronger parts of myself, to embolden my vision of myself. Besides, these experiences were filled with power, intensity, and even ecstasy that, on reflection, seem religious or spiritual.

As I grew up, I forced myself to deny these experiences of childhood. At first I missed them; then I did not quite remember what I missed. They became a strange discarded part of youthful fantasy. No one told me directly, "People don't worship the Greek gods anymore, much less attempt to become them through ritual and fantasy," but the messages around me were clear enough. Such daydreams did not fit into the society I lived in, and even to talk about them was impossible. It became easier to discuss the most intimate personal, emotional, or sexual experiences than to talk of these earlier experiences. To reveal them was a kind of magical violation.

Religion had no official place in my childhood world. I was brought up in a family of agnostics and atheists. Still, feeling that there was some dimension lacking in their lives, I embarked on a quasi-religious search as a teenager. I felt ecstatic power in the Catholic mass (as long as it was in Latin); I went to Quaker meetings and visited synagogues and churches. Today it seems to me I thirsted for the power and richness of those original experiences, though I found only beliefs and dogmas that seemed irrelevant or even contradictory to them. I wanted permission for those experiences, but not if it would poison my integrity or my commitment to living and acting in the world.

I remember coming across the famous words of Marx on religion: "Religion is the sigh of the hard-pressed, the heart of a heartless world, the soul of soulless conditions, the opium of the people. . . ."[3] And having no place to put this experience of Goddess nor freedom enough to continue the ancient practice I had stumbled on, I gradually left it behind, and set my sights on the soulless conditions. It was 1964, I was in

Berkeley, and there were many soulless conditions with which to concern myself.

In 1971, while working as a political reporter for Pacifica radio in Washington, D.C., I became involved in various environmentalist and ecological concerns. During that year John McPhee wrote a series of articles for *The New Yorker* called "Encounters with the Archdruid," later published as a book. The articles narrated three wilderness journeys made by David Brower (president of Friends of the Earth and former head of the Sierra Club) in the company of three of his enemies on environmental issues. Two passages from this book come to mind as emotional springboards to the events that followed. The first was Brower's statement that the ecology movement was really a spiritual movement. "We are in a kind of religion," he said, "an ethic with regard to terrain, and this religion is closest to the Buddhist, I suppose." In the second quote, one of Brower's enemies, a developer, spoke against the practices of conservationists and called Brower "a druid." I began to search for an ecological religious framework. I started by searching for Druids.[4]

Around that time two noted historians, Arnold Toynbee and Lynn White, wrote essays in which they said that there *was*, in fact, a religious dimension to the environmental crisis.

Toynbee's article appeared in 1972, in the *International Journal of Environmental Studies*. Its main point was that worldwide ecological problems were due in part to a religious cause, "the rise of monotheism," and that the verse in Genesis (1:28), "Be fruitful and multiply and replenish the Earth and subdue it," had become biblical sanction for human beings to assert their rights over all nature. Toynbee felt that his education in pre-Christian Greek and Latin literature had had "a deeper and more enduring effect on my *Weltanschauung*" than his Christian upbringing:

> In popular pre-Christian Greek religion, divinity was inherent in all natural phenomena, including those that man had tamed and domesticated. Divinity was present in springs and rivers and the sea; in trees, both the wild oak and the cultivated olive-tree; in corn and vines; in mountains; in earthquakes and lightning and thunder. The godhead was diffused throughout the phenomena. It was plural, not singular; a pantheon, not a unique almighty super-human person. When the Graeco-Roman World

was converted to Christianity, the divinity was drained out of nature and was concentrated in one unique transcendent God. "Pan is dead." "The oracles are dumb." Bronsgrove is no longer a wood that is sacrosanct because it is animated by the god Bron. . . .

The Judeo-Christian tradition gave license for exploitation. Toynbee advised "reverting from the *Weltanschauung* of monotheism to the *Weltanschauung* of pantheism, which is older and was once universal."

> The plight in which post-Industrial-Revolution man has now landed himself is one more demonstration that man is not the master of his environment—not even when supposedly armed with a warrant, issued by a supposedly unique and omnipotent God with a human-like personality, delegating to man plenipotentiary powers. Nature is now demonstrating to us that she does not recognize the validity of this alleged warrant, and she is warning us that, if man insists on trying to execute it, he will commit this outrage on nature at his peril.[5]

While Toynbee stopped short of advocating a return to polytheism, and implied that many of the pre-Christian deities were too crude for our age, his basic perception was strikingly similar to the impulse that led to the creation of many Neo-Pagan groups.

The article by Lynn White had appeared several years earlier in *Science* and had begun quite a controversy. While much of White's article, "The Historical Roots of Our Ecologic Crisis," dealt with changes in methods of farming and agriculture over the centuries, a few of its points were strikingly similar to Toynbee's. White observed that "the victory of Christianity over paganism was the greatest psychic revolution in the history of our culture."

> Christianity in absolute contrast to ancient paganism . . . not only established a dualism of man and nature but also insisted that it is God's will that man exploit nature for his proper ends. . . . In antiquity every tree, every spring, every stream, every hill had its own *genius loci*, its guardian spirit. . . . By destroying pagan animism, Christianity made it possible to exploit nature in a mood of indifference to the feeling of natural objects.[6]

In the following years I searched in books and articles for an ecological-religious framework compatible with my own politics and commitment to the world. I soon entered into a lengthy correspondence with a coven of Witches in Essex, England. Being no less a victim of stereotypes than most, I pictured the couple who led this group as in their thirties and middle class. But Doris and Vic Stuart turned out to be in their late forties and fifties. He was an old unionist and socialist and she was a factory worker.[7] At this period, I also contacted a Pagan group in Wales. Frankly, at the time I thought that corresponding with Witches was bizarre and even amusing. I certainly had no thought that there might be any link between these groups and my own experience of Goddess, which still came to me, unbidden, at odd moments.

One day the coven in Essex sent me a tape recording of some rituals. The first one on the tape was called "The Drawing Down of the Moon." I did not know it then, but in this ritual, one of the most serious and beautiful in the modern Craft, the priest *invokes* into the priestess (or, depending on your point of view, she *evokes* from within herself) the Goddess or Triple Goddess, symbolized by the phases of the moon. She is known by a thousand names, and among them were those I had used as a child. In some Craft rituals the priestess goes into a trance and speaks; in other traditions the ritual is a more formal dramatic dialogue, often of intense beauty, in which, again, the priestess speaks, taking the role of the Goddess. In both instances the priestess functions as the Goddess incarnate, within the circle.

I found a quiet place and played the tape. The music in the background was perhaps by Brahms. A man and woman spoke with English accents. When it came time for the invocation, the words came clearly:

> Listen to the words of the Great Mother, who was of old also called Artemis, Astarte, Melusine, Aphrodite, Diana, Brigit and many other names. . . .[8]

A feeling of power and emotion came over me. For, after all, how different was that ritual from the magical rituals of my childhood? The contents of the tape had simply given me *permission* to accept a part of my own psyche that I had denied for years—and then extend it.

Like most Neo-Pagans, I never converted in the accepted sense. I simply accepted, reaffirmed, and extended a very old experience. I allowed certain kinds of feelings and ways of being back into my life.

I tell these stories in a book that contains little personal history in order to respond to the statement I frequently hear: I don't *believe* in *that!* This is the standard response to many of the ideas and people with which this book is concerned. But *belief* has never seemed very relevant to the Neo-Pagan movement.[9]

In my fifteen years of contact with these groups I was never asked to *believe* in anything. I was told a few dogmas by people who hadn't ridded themselves of the tendency to dogmatize, but I rejected those. In the next chapters you will encounter priests and priestesses who say that they are philosophical agnostics and that this has never inhibited their participation in or leadership of Neo-Pagan and Craft groups. Others will tell you that the gods and goddesses are "ethereal beings." Still others have called them symbols, powers, archetypes, or "something deep and strong within the self to be contacted," or even "something akin to the force of poetry and art." As one scholar has noted, it is a religion "of atmosphere instead of faith; a cosmos, in a word, constructed by the imagination. . . ."[10]

My own role has been that of observer-participant. I began by trying to find reasons for my involvement and then traveled across the country to visit hundreds of people in order to contrast my own experiences with theirs. By the end of my travels I found that many of my early assumptions were incorrect.

For example, I found that Neo-Pagan groups were very diverse in class and ethnic background. My first experiences brought me in touch with a much broader spectrum of people than I had known in the student movements of the 1960s. The first three covens I encountered in New York and England were composed largely of working-class and lower-middle-class people. Later, I met covens and groups composed predominantly of upper-middle-class intellectuals. Then I met groups whose members worked as insurance salesmen, bus drivers, police, and secretaries. All my class stereotypes began to fall by the wayside.

Another assumption, and one I was slow to drop, was that the Neo-Pagan resurgence was, fundamentally, a reaction against science, technology, progress. My own involvement had come through a kind of

Luddite reaction, so I assumed it was typical. But in many interviews Neo-Pagans and Witches supported high technologies, scientific inquiry, and space exploration. It is true that most Neo-Pagans feel that we abuse technology; they often support "alternative" technologies—solar, wind, etc.—and hold a biological rather than a mechanistic world view.

In general, I have tried to be aware of my own biases and to make them clear so that, if you wish, you can steer between the shoals.

Lastly, a few words about the reasons for this Neo-Pagan resurgence. One standard psychological explanation is that people join these groups to gain power over others or to banish feelings of inadequacy and insecurity. Obviously (some of the studies referred to later show this) some people do join magical and religious groups in order to gain self-mastery, in the sense of practical knowledge of psychology and the workings of the psyche, so they can function better in the world. But this reason was not among the six primary reasons that Pagans and Witches gave me in answer to the questions "Why is this phenomenon occurring?" "Why are you involved?" Many of their reasons are novel, and completely at odds with common assumptions.

Beauty, Vision, Imagination.   A number of Neo-Pagans told me that their religious views were part of a general visionary quest that included involvement with poetry, art, drama, music, science fiction, and fantasy. At least four Witches in different parts of the country spoke of religion as a human need for beauty.

Intellectual Satisfaction.   Many told me that reading and collecting odd books had been the prime influence in their religious decision. This came as a surprise to me. In particular, most of the Midwesterners said flatly that the wide dissemination of strange and fascinating books had been the *main* factor in creating a Neo-Pagan resurgence. And while class and profession vary widely among Neo-Pagans, almost *all* are avid readers. This does not seem to depend on their educational level; it holds true for high-school dropouts as well as Ph.D.s.

Growth.   A more predictable answer, this ambiguous word was given frequently. Most Pagans see their lives not as straight roads to specific goals, but as processes—evolution, change, or an increase in understanding. Neo-Pagans often see themselves as pursuing the quests of the mystery traditions: initiations into the workings of life, death, and rebirth.

Feminism. For many women, this was the main reason for involvement. Large numbers of women have been seeking a spiritual framework outside the patriarchal religions that have dominated the Western world for the last several thousand years. Many who wanted to find a spiritual side to their feminism entered the Craft because of its emphasis on goddess worship. Neo-Pagan Witchcraft groups range from those with a mixture of female and male deities to those that focus on the monotheistic worship of the Mother Goddess.

Environmental Response. Many of those interviewed said that Neo-Paganism was a response to a planet in crisis. Almost all the Pagan traditions emphasize reverence for nature, and many believe that only by understanding the earth as sacred will human beings be able and willing to protect the planet. Some Pagans told me that a revival of animism was needed to counter the forces destroying the natural world.[11]

Freedom. Another unexpected answer. The Frosts, who run one of the largest Witchcraft correspondence courses in the country, described the Craft as "religion without the middleman." Many people said that they had become Pagans because they could be themselves and act as they chose, without what they felt were medieval notions of sin and guilt. Others wanted to participate in rituals rather than observe them. The leader of the Georgian tradition told me that freedom was his prime reason for making an independent religious decision.

This last reason seemed most remarkable. The freedom that is characteristic of the Neo-Pagan resurgence sets the movement far apart from many other religious revivals. Why have these groups refused to succumb to rigid hierarchies and institutionalization? And how is it possible for them to exist in relative harmony, in spite of their different rituals and deities? These groups can exist this way because the Neo-Pagan religious framework is based on a *polytheistic* outlook—a view that allows differing perspectives and ideas to coexist.

3.

The Pagan World View

We gaze up at the same stars, the sky covers us all, the same universe encompasses us. What does it matter what practical system we adopt in our search for the truth? Not by one avenue only can we arrive at so tremendous a secret.

—SYMMACHUS, 384 C.E.[1]

Monotheism is but imperialism in religion.

—JAMES HENRY BREASTED[2]

WHILE MOST NEO-PAGANS disagree on almost everything, one of their most important principles is polytheism, and this is generally understood to mean much more than "a theory that Divine reality is numerically multiple, that there are many gods."[3] Many Pagans will tell you that polytheism is an *attitude* and a *perspective* that affect more than what we consider to be religion. They might well say that the constant calls for unity, integration, and homogenization in the Western world derive from our long-standing ideology of monotheism, which remains the majority tradition in the West. They might add that monotheism is a political and psychological ideology as well as a religious one, and that the old economic lesson that one-crop economies generally fare poorly also applies to the spiritual realm.

If you were to ask modern Pagans for the most important ideas that underlie the Pagan resurgence, you might well be led to three words: animism, pantheism, and—most important—polytheism. Neo-Pagans give these words meanings different from the common definitions, and sometimes they overlap.

Animism is used to imply a reality in which all things are imbued with vitality. The ancient world view did not conceive of a separation between "animate" and inanimate." All things—from rocks and trees to dreams—were considered to partake of the life force. At some level Neo-Paganism is an attempt to reanimate the world of nature; or, perhaps more accurately, Neo-Pagan religions allow their participants to reenter the primeval world view, to participate in nature in a way that is not possible for most Westerners after childhood. The Pagan revival seems to be, in part, a response to the common urban and suburban experience of our culture as "impersonal," "neutral," or "dead."

For many Pagans, *pantheism* implies much the same thing as animism. It is a view that divinity is inseparable from nature and that deity is immanent in nature. Neo-Pagan groups participate in divinity. The title of this book implies one such participation: when a priestess becomes the Goddess within the circle. "Drawing down the moon" symbolizes the idea that we are the gods, or can, at least, become them from time to time in rite and fantasy. This idea was well expressed in the quotation at the beginning of the *Whole Earth Catalog*: "We *are* as gods and might as well get good at it."[4] The Neo-Pagan Church of All Worlds has expressed this idea by the phrase: "Thou Art God/dess."*

The idea of *polytheism* is grounded in the view that reality (divine or otherwise) is multiple and diverse. And if one is a pantheist-polytheist, as are many Neo-Pagans, one might say that all nature is divinity and manifests itself in myriad forms and delightful complexities. On a broader level, Isaac Bonewits wrote, "Polytheists . . . develop logical systems based on multiple levels of reality and the magical Law of Infinite Universes: 'every sentient being lives in a unique universe.'"[5] Polytheism has allowed a multitude of distinct groups to exist more or less in harmony, despite great divergence in beliefs and practices, and may also have prevented these groups from being preyed upon by gurus and profiteers.

In beginning to understand what polytheism means to modern Pagans we must divest ourselves of a number of ideas about it—mainly, that it is an inferior way of perceiving that disappeared as religions "evolved" toward the idea of one god.

*In recent years, some Pagans are using the word *panentheism* to describe their religious perspective: a belief that there *is* a transcendent source—that divinity is manifest in the material world, but also elsewhere. Some Pagans involved in mystery traditions will tell you they believe in one source, which some could call God, but which embraces all gods and faiths.

The origin of this erroneous idea can be traced to the eighteenth century. We can see it, for example, in the works of the philosopher David Hume, who wrote that just as "the mind rises gradually, from inferior to superior," polytheism prevails "among the greatest part of uninstructed mankind"; and the idea of a "supreme Creator" bestowing order by will is an idea "too big for their narrow conceptions. . . ."[6] Until recently many writers labeled tribal religions "superstition," while dignifying monotheistic beliefs (usually Christianity, Judaism, and Islam) with the term "religion." These notions are usually not stated so boldly today, but they persist.

Many anthropologists have long disrupted the notion that religions "evolve" in linear fashion. Paul Radin more than fifty years ago wrote that monotheism exists in some form among all primitive peoples. Ethnologists must admit, he said, that "the possibility of interpreting monotheism as a part of a general intellectual and ethical progress must be abandoned. . . ." He showed that monotheism often existed side by side with polytheism, animism, and pantheism. Radin regarded monotheism and polytheism merely as indicators of those differences in philosophical temperament that exist among all groups of people.

As for monotheism in our society, Radin observed, "The factors concerned in the complete credal triumph of monotheism in Judaism, Christianity and Mohammedanism have never been satisfactorily explained, but they are emphatically of an individual historical and psychological nature." He added that no progress in solving this riddle will be made "until scholars rid themselves, once and for all, of the curious notion that everything possesses an evolutionary history," and that the great mistake lies in applying Darwinian thinking to analyses of culture. Radin considered primitive societies to be as logical as modern ones, often having a truer, more concrete sense of reality. Most primitive societies exhibit all types of temperaments and abilities: "The idealist and the materialist, the dreamer and the realist, have always been with us."[7]

Harold Moss, a Neo-Pagan writer and priest of the Church of the Eternal Source, once wrote that monotheism existed in many tribal societies; many later societies developed a polytheistic theology as they became more complex and sophisticated. "Today," he said, "in place of a single Christianity with multiple Gods, we see a shattered Christianity, each sect worshipping a slightly different God."[8]

Another problem confronts us when we attempt to look at old and new Pagan religions with fresh eyes: the notion of "idolatry" and the image of dull natives abasing themselves before a stone idol. I remember seeing this image often in books I read as a child—*The Story of Chanukah* is one that I recall vividly. It was easy to feel pity for the poor heathens, as well as a patronizing superiority. Monotheistic religions have long assumed that the worshipper who stands before a statue or a grove of trees can see no further than that statue or grove, that such a worshipper invests divinity in those things and nothing more, and, contrarily, that other people's worship of neutral, omnipotent, and unknowable deities is necessarily pure and sublime.

The best refutation of these notions is in Theodore Roszak's *Where the Wasteland Ends*. The statue and sacred grove were transparent windows to experience, Roszak says—means by which the witness was escorted through to sacred ground beyond and participated in the divine. The rejection of animism, first by the Jews and later, most dogmatically, by certain Christian groups, resulted in a war on art and all imaginative activities. Roszak finds no evidence that the animist world view is false. He notes that none of us has entered the animist world sufficiently to judge it existentially.

> Prejudice and ethnocentrism aside, what we know for a fact is that, outside our narrow cultural experience, in religious rites both sophisticated and primitive, human beings have been able to achieve a sacramental vision of being, and that this may well be the wellspring of human spiritual consciousness. From that rich source there flow countless religious and philosophical traditions. The differences between these traditions— between Eskimo shamanism and medieval alchemy, between Celtic druidism and Buddhist Tantra—are many; but an essentially magical worldview is common to them all. . . . This diverse family of religions and philosophies [represents] the Old Gnosis—the old way of knowing, which delighted in finding the sacred in the profane. . . . I regard it as the essential and supreme impulse of the religious life. This is not, of course, religion as many people in our society know it. It is a visionary style of knowledge, not a theological one; its proper language is myth and ritual;

its foundation is rapture, not faith and doctrine; and its experience of nature is one of living communion.[9]

Our idea of idolatry is therefore a kind of racist perception grounded in ignorance. For Roszak, if there *is* any idolatry, it exists in our society, where artificiality is extolled and religion viewed as something apart from nature, supernatural. Roszak has called the modern view "the religion of the single vision."

Much of the theoretical basis for a modern defense of polytheism comes from Jungian psychologists, who have long argued that the gods and goddesses of myth, legend, and fairy tale represent archetypes, real potencies and potentialities deep within the psyche, which, when allowed to flower, permit us to be more fully human. These archetypes must be approached and ultimately reckoned with if we are to experience the riches we have repressed. Most Jungians argue that the task is to unite these potentialities into a symphonic whole. One unorthodox Jungian, James Hillman, has argued for a "polytheistic psychology" that gives reign to various parts of the self, not always leading to integration and wholeness.

In theological circles an early champion of a new polytheism in the 1970s was David Miller. Miller relies heavily on Jungian ideas. For him, polytheism is the rediscovery of gods and goddesses as archetypal forces in our lives. Miller's arguments, set forth in *The New Polytheism,* are similar to the views of many Neo-Pagans. Yet at the time of publication Miller was apparently unaware of the widespread emergence of Neo-Pagan groups. At the time he was a professor of religion at Syracuse University and reported that his students had become deeply drawn to the Greek myths, at the same time that theologians and psychologists were reappraising the idea of polytheism. Theologian William Hamilton, for one, had said at a conference that students are now seeking access to all the gods, "eastern and western, primitive and modern, heretical and orthodox, mad and sane." These gods are "not to be believed in or trusted, but to be used to give shape to an increasingly complex and variegated experience of life." Hamilton added, "The revolution does not look like monotheism, Christian or post-Christian. What it looks like is polytheism." This remark was the beginning of Miller's journey.

By the end of it Miller had come to believe that the much talked of "death of God" was really the death of the one-dimensional "monotheistic" thinking that had dominated Western culture from top to bottom, influencing not only its religion but its psychology and politics as well. Polytheism, by contrast, was a view that allowed multiple dimensions of reality.

> Polytheism is the name given to a specific religious situation . . . characterized by plurality. . . . Socially understood, polytheism is eternally in unresolvable conflict with social monotheism, which in its worst form is fascism and in its less destructive forms is imperialism, capitalism, feudalism and monarchy. . . . Polytheism is not only a social reality; it is also a philosophical condition. It is that reality experienced by men and women when Truth with a capital "T" cannot be articulated reflectively according to a single grammar, a single logic, or a single symbol system.[10]

Far from being merely a religious belief, polytheism, for Miller, is an attitude that allows one to affirm "the radical plurality of the self." In psychology, for example, it would allow one to discover the various sides of one's personality. Beyond that, it becomes a world view that allows for complexity, multiple meanings, and ambiguities. Like Roszak's "Old Gnosis," it is at home with metaphors and myths. Yet this new polytheism is "not simply a matter of pluralism in the social order, anarchy in politics, polyphonic meaning in language"; the gods, for Miller, are informing powers, psychic realities that give shape to social, intellectual, and personal existence.

Miller disagrees with a number of theologians who espouse monotheism—in particular, H. Richard Niebuhr, who says that the central problem of modern society is that it *is* polytheistic. Niebuhr, defining gods as value centers, sees modern polytheism as the worship of social gods such as money, power, and sex. Against this social polytheism Niebuhr opposes a radical monotheism that worships only the principle of being.

Miller's reply calls for a deeper polytheism. He sees the gods not as value centers but as potencies within the psyche that play out their mythic stories in our daily lives.

Miller believes that we can experience multiplicity without jeopardizing integration and wholeness. He observes that polytheism *includes* monotheism, but the reverse does not hold true. For most people, religious practice comes down to a series of consecutive monotheisms, all within a larger polytheistic framework.

Here Miller is close to the modern Neo-Pagans who devote themselves to one of a number of gods and goddesses or one of a number of traditions, without denying the validity of other gods or traditions.[11]

Miller relies heavily on James Hillman's essay "Psychology: Monotheistic or Polytheistic." Hillman said that psychology had long been colored by a theology of monotheism, especially in its view that unity, integration, wholeness, is *always* the proper goal of psychological development and that fragmentation is always a sign of pathology. Hillman argued that the images of Artemis, Persephone, and Athena collectively formed a richer picture of the feminine than the Virgin Mary. Carrying this idea to the extreme, Hillman suggested that the multitude of tongues in Babel, traditionally interpreted as a "decline," could also be seen as a true picture of psychic reality. He then argued that some individuals might benefit from a therapy that, at times, led to fragmentation.

In the end Hillman advocated a "polytheistic psychology" that would allow many possible voices:

> By providing a divine background of personages and powers for each complex, it would find a place for each spark. . . . It would accept the multiplicity of voices, the Babel of anima and animus, without insisting upon unifying them into one figure. . . .[12]

Hillman's contention that Jung always stressed the self as primary and considered all exploration of archetypes as preliminary to something higher is open to dispute. His views have not been accepted by most Jungians. Still, his question, "If there is only one model of individuation, can there be true individuality?" is close to the Neo-Pagan religious and social critique.

Miller's and Hillman's ideas about polytheism at times seem too much like the liberal notion of pluralism, a kind of competition of factions. Most Neo-Pagans that I know see polytheism not as competitive factions but as facets of a jewel, harmonious but differing. Many Neo-

Pagans *do,* however, see the gods in Jungian terms. The late Gwydion Pendderwen, one of the best-known bards in the Craft, told me, "The gods are really the components of our psyches. We are the gods, in the sense that we, as the sum total of human beings, are the sum of the gods. And Pagans do not wish to be pinned down to a specific act of consciousness. They keep an open ticket."

Miller writes that the task at hand is to incarnate the gods, to "become aware of their presence, acknowledge and celebrate their forms."[13] These gods, he observes, are worlds of meaning; they are the comings and goings, the births and deaths within our lives. They are generally unrecognized because our culture is not in harmony with them.

He notes that the old ways of knowing (such as mysticism, alchemy, and gnosticism) still exist, but most of us are divorced from them. The recent widespread interest in occultism is, in part, a wish to reclaim them. These systems are richer in imagery than the Judeo-Christian tradition as it has come down to most of us. Despite this, both Miller and Hillman worry about a Pagan revival. Hillman is apprehensive about a "true revival of paganism as *religion,*" fearing that it would bring dogmas and soothsayers in its wake. He advocates a polytheistic psychology as a substitute.[14]

Miller advocates a return to Greco-Roman polytheism because we are "willy-nilly Occidental men and women" and other symbol systems are inappropriate.[15] Much of the remainder of Miller's book is an attempt to use Greek mythology to explain modern society. He sees the problems of technology as the playing out of the stories of Prometheus, Hephaestus, and Aesculpius; the military-industrial complex is Hera-Hephaestus-Heracles; the outbreak of the irrational is Pan; and so forth. This may be fine for students of ancient Greek polytheism, but most Neo-Pagans diverge from him at this point.

When Miller's *The New Polytheism* appeared, one Pagan journal called it a "stunning victory for our point of view." Harold Moss, on the other hand, wrote that Greco-Roman polytheism was not a suitable framework for today.[16] And one of the strongest criticisms of Miller's book came from Robert Ellwood, professor of religion at the University of Southern California, in his *Religious and Spiritual Groups in Modern America.*

Ellwood accurately picked up the Neo-Pagan complaint about Miller when he wrote, "One may feel he [Miller] gives our revitalized heritages in Celtic (Yeats), Nordic (Wagner), African (LeRoi Jones), and Amerindian (many names) polytheistic religions short shrift."

Ellwood is no proponent of Paganism, but unlike Miller he spent some time among Pagans and Neo-Pagans. He asks, "Is Polytheism in practice what Miller makes it out to be? What would a serious polytheistic stance in modern America be like?"

Ellwood first looks at the practice of Shinto in Japan and sees polytheism there as a binding, structured system, a reaction, in fact, to increased multiplicity, a means of structuring it into an empire, a cosmos. He argues that polytheism in the past appealed to organizers of the official cults of empires and that the fervent cults of the dispossessed were, largely, monotheistic—the mystery religions, Christianity, and the new religions of Japan.

As for Neo-Pagans in the United States, he acknowledges their "reverence for sun and tree," their sincerity, and the reality of their experience. "The personal vision of some of the Neo-Pagans is deep and rich; they are seers if not shamans," he says. But he sees these groups as unstable, and concludes that "polytheism puts a severe strain on group formation and continuity," and that it "can only be an intensely personal vision," the vehicle for the subjective. Each group is "tiny, struggling, and probably ephemeral"; he finds it difficult to believe that Neo-Paganism as a religious view can deal adequately with human alienation. He claims that polytheism has never been a cause, only a backdrop against which causes have moved.

Ellwood considers the great spiritual problem of the day to be "dealing with multiplicity," but implies that Miller's position, and polytheism in general, lead ultimately to a life of "anchorless feelings," constant changes in lifestyles that will eventually precipitate a backlash. One such form of backlash, he notes, can be seen in the Jesus Movement with its slogan "One Way," and of course there are many other new monotheistic movements. Certainly one would have to agree that Neo-Paganism is a minority vision, struggling amid the majority trend toward authoritarian cults.

Ellwood sees polytheism in the United States as the "polytheism of the lonely poet" rather than that of the temple priest. It is epitomized by the lonely shaman, withdrawn from common feelings and goals. Such images are already staked out, Ellwood says; they can be seen in the personages of Ged in Ursula Le Guin's Earthsea trilogy, Gandalf in J.R.R. Tolkien's *Lord of the Rings* trilogy, and Don Juan in the series of books by Carlos Castaneda. These are all persons who form no lasting groups, have no lasting friends; they share an intuitive knowledge and wisdom, but ultimately remain alone and sad.[17]

For Ellwood, polytheism can never provide social cohesion, nor can it increase multiple options except in private ways. He implies that it is fundamentally antipolitical and antisocial.

Practicing Pagans might say to Ellwood that their religion is not at odds with the experience of wholeness. And while there are always groups that end, and new ones that begin, the Pagan community is much more cohesive today than when Ellwood was writing. Since the 1990s, modern Pagans have begun to form lasting communities—not only legally recognized religious organizations, a trend that has been occurring for thirty years, but seminaries, nature sanctuaries, and organizations and gatherings with a twenty-five year track record.

Most Neo-Pagans would agree with Ellwood that "only monotheistic or monistic religions 'convert' nations. We are not likely to see a temple to Hera, Heracles or Hephaestus on the lawn of the Pentagon." Most would also regard this as a great strength of polytheism—that it does not lend itself to holy wars. Even David Hume's fierce condemnation of polytheism as idolatry and superstition was mitigated by his acknowledgment of polytheists' tolerance of almost any religious practice, in contrast to the intolerance shown by almost all monotheistic religions.

In practice, Neo-Pagans give a variety of reasons for their polytheism.[18] "A polytheistic world view," wrote one, "makes self-delusion harder. Pagans seem to relate to deities on a more symbolic and complex level. Personally I think all intellectualizing about deities is self-delusion." Others told me that polytheism was more likely to encourage reverence for nature. A woman wrote to me: "Polytheism and particularly animism demand the cherishing of a much wider range of things. If you are a monotheist and your particular god is not life-oriented, it is easy to destroy the biosphere you depend on for sustenance—witness where we are right now."

A third reason given to me is the one most emphasized by Miller: diversity and freedom. Alkemene, a Craft priestess in New York, wrote to me:

A monotheistic religion seems analogous to the "one disease—one treatment" system still prevalent in modern medicine. When worshippers view deity in a single way this tends to feed back a homogenous image. The worshippers begin (1) to see homogeneity as good and (2) to become homogenous themselves. Eccentricity becomes "evil" and "wrong." Decentralization is seen as a wrong since what is wrong for "A" cannot possibly be right for "B." A polytheistic world view allows a wider range of choices. A person can identify with different deities at different times. Differences become acceptable, even "respectable."

The old pagan religions did not have much trouble seeing that many different names were "at heart" the same. Of course, their cultures and politics clashed, but they had relatively few holy wars. All of our wars seem to be holy wars of one kind or another.

This idea of diversity and tolerance was also stressed by Isaac Bonewits, who told me, "The Pagans were tolerant for the simple reason that many believed their gods and goddesses to be connected with the people or the place. If you go to another place, there are different gods and goddesses, and if you're staying in someone else's house, you're polite to their gods; they're just as real as the ones you left back home." Bonewits called monotheism an aberration, but "particularly useful in history when small groups of people wanted to control large numbers of people." In *The Druid Chronicles* he observed that monotheism, "far from being the crown of human thought and religion as its supporters have claimed for several bloody millennia, is in fact a monstrous step backwards—a step that has been responsible for more human misery than any other idea in known history."[19]

Many other Neo-Pagans emphasized that polytheism allowed for both unity and diversity, and several asserted that they were monotheists at some moments and polytheists at others. Penny Novack, a Pagan poet, once wrote that glimpses of the One could make her happy, awed, and excited, "but I can't imagine a religion based on it."

Still another wrote to me:

I do not believe in gods as real personalities on any plane, or in any dimension. Yet, I do believe in gods as symbols or personifications of universal principles. The Earth Mother is the primal seed—source of the universe. . . . I believe in gods perceived in nature; perceived as a storm, a forest spirit, the goddess of the lake, etc. Many places and times of the year have a spirit or power about them. Perhaps, these are my gods.

And those Neo-Pagans in the Craft, the followers of Wicca, might well be considered "duotheists," conceiving of deity as the Goddess of the Moon, Earth, and sea, and the God of the woods, the hunt, the animal realm. Feminist Witches are often monotheists worshipping the Goddess as the One. Morgan McFarland, who headed the Dallas convenstead of Morrigana, told me, "I consider myself a polytheist, as in the statement Isis makes in *The Golden Ass* when she says, 'From me come all gods and goddesses who exist.' So that I see myself as monotheistic in believing in the Goddess, the Creatix, the Female Principle, but at the same time acknowledging that other gods and goddesses do exist through her as manifestations of her, facets of the whole." One male polytheist said that certain portions of the Craft were afflicted with "the curse of Goddess monotheism which is apparently driving so many Witches mad."[20] Of the many answers to the question "What does it mean to you to be a Pagan and a polytheist?" the answer that I like best came from the late Wiccan priestess Alison Harlow:

I am confronted very often with trying to explain to people what I mean by Paganism. To some people, it seems like a contradiction to say that I have a certain subjective truth; I have experienced the Goddess, and this is my total reality. And yet I do not believe that I have the one, true, right and only way.

Many people cannot understand how I find Her a part of my reality and accept the fact that your reality might be something else. But for me, this in no way is a contradiction, because I am aware that my reality and my conclusions are a result of my unique genetic structure, my life experience and my subjective feelings; and you are a different person, whose same experience of whatever may or may not be out there will be translated in your nervous system into something different. And I can learn from that.

I can extend my own reality by sharing that and grow. This recognition that everyone has different experiences is a fundamental keystone to Paganism; it's the fundamental premise that whatever is going on out there is infinitely more complex than I can ever understand. And that makes me feel very good.

That last sentence struck me profoundly. What an uncommon reaction to people's differences and how unlike the familiar reactions of fear and hostility! What kind of a person is able to say this—to celebrate differences? This is the question I struggle with. Who are those who can embrace polytheism, accepting a bit of chaos in their spiritual perspective without denying rational modes of thinking? Who are those who are able to suspend belief and disbelief at will and are equally comfortable with scientific discourse and magic ritual? Who, in short, can afford a nonauthoritarian religion? Are we talking about a broad-based phenomenon in this country? Surely not. Are we talking about ways of being that are available only to those strong enough to break with certain aspects of the dominant culture?

My own experience with the Pagan resurgence has made me reluctant to categorize Neo-Pagans according to simple age and class divisions. I am not comfortable with the "radical" analysis that says that the recent rise of occult groups is a white middle-class phenomenon. It is too simple, although many of those I subsequently met did fall into this category.

My tentative conclusion is that Neo-Pagans are an elite of sorts—a strange one.[21] The people you will meet here may be some of those few who, by chance, circumstance, fortune, and occasionally struggle, have escaped certain forms of enculturation.

Most Pagans are avid readers, yet many of them have had little formal education. Few are addicted to television. They are, one priest observed to me, "hands-in-the-dirt archeologists," digging out odd facts, "scholars without degrees." They come from a variety of classes and hold down jobs ranging from fireman to Ph.D. chemist. But as readers, they are an elite, since readers constitute less than twenty percent of the population in the United States.

The paradox of polytheism seems to be this: the arguments for a world of multiplicity and diversity are usually made by those few strong enough and fortunate enough in education, upbringing, or luck to be able to disown by word, lifestyle, and philosophy the totalistic religious and political views that dominate our society. Perhaps in my own fascination with the Neo-Pagan resurgence I am hoping that these attitudes can become the heritage of us all.

Here's the big question: Has the polytheistic affirmation of diversity come at a time when most people increasingly fear complexity and accept authoritarian solutions? Neo-Paganism is a growing movement. According to some sources,[22] there are a million Neo-Pagans around the world. In previous editions of this book, I wondered if Neo-Paganism was doomed to be a delicacy for the few. I am still convinced contemporary Paganism will remain a minority religious phenomenon; but I am more convinced today that it has staying power.

II. Witches

4.

The Wiccan Revival

What can we learn of this witch figure? . . . She takes energies out of consciousness and pulls them toward the unconscious to forge a link between the two mental systems. . . .

We know the roots of our consciousness reach deep into the nonhuman, archaic unconscious. . . . The witch archetype makes visible to us the very depths of what is humanly possible, the great silences at the edge of being. . . .

She stirs up storms that invade whole communities of people. She conducts vast collective energies to our very doorstep. . . . These undirected unhumanized spirit forces are symbolized for us as ghosts, dead ancestors, gods and goddesses come up from the world below. . . .

What do we gain from this vision? A sense of perspective. . . . The witch-seer makes us see into the proportions of life. . . .

The radical impact of the witch archetype is that she invades the civilized community. She enters it. She changes it. . . . She heralds the timeless process of originating out of the unconsciouss new forms of human consciousness and society.

—DR. ANN BELFORD ULANOV[1]

THE WORD *witch* is defined so differently by different people that a common definition seems impossible. "A witch," you may be told, "is someone with supernatural powers," but revivalist Witches do not believe in a supernatural. "A witch," you may be told, "is anyone who practices magic," but revivalist Witches will tell you that Witchcraft is a religion, and some will tell you that magic is secondary. "A witch," you may be told, "is a worker of evil," but revivalist Witches will tell you that they promote the good. The historian Elliot Rose observed that the word *witch* is "free to wander, and does wander, among a bewildering variety of mental associations,"[2] and the occultist Isaac Bonewits has asked:

Is a "witch" anyone who does magic or who reads fortunes? Is a "witch" someone who worships the Christian Devil? Is a Witch (capital letters this time) a member of a specific Pagan faith called "Wicca"? Is a "witch" someone who practices Voodoo, or Macumba, or Candomblé? Are the anthropologists correct when they define a "witch" as anyone doing magic (usually evil) outside an approved social structure?[3]

Bonewits does away with some of this confusion, as we shall see, by dividing Witches into many types, including Classical or cunning folk, Neodiabolic, Familial, Immigrant, Ethnic, Feminist, and Neo-Pagan. And in this book we are (mostly) talking about Neo-Pagan Witches—the revival, or re-creation, or new creation (depending on your viewpoint) of a Neo-Pagan nature religion that calls itself Witchcraft, or Wicca, or the Craft, or the Old Religion(s). This religion, with its sources of inspiration in pre-Christian Western Europe, has a specific history—clouded though it may be—and a specific way of being in the world.

We saw that the word *witch* comes from the Old English *wicce, wicca,* and these words derive from a root *wic,* or *weik,* which has to do with religion and magic. We saw that many practitioners of Wicca will tell you that Wicca means *wise,* although that is etymologically incorrect. Others will tell you that Wicca comes from a root meaning to bend or turn, and that the Witch is the bender and changer of reality.

But etymology does not help one to confront the confusing feeling that lies behind the word *witch.* The very power of the word lies in its imprecision. It is not merely a word, but an archetype, a cluster of powerful images. It resonates in the mind and, in the words of Dr. Ulanov, takes us down to deep places, to forests and fairy tales and myths and friendships with animals. The price we pay for clarity of definition must not be a reduction in the force of this cluster of images.

Witches are divided over the word *witch.* Some regard it as a badge of pride, a word to be reclaimed, much as militant lesbians have reclaimed the word *dyke.* But others dislike the word. "It has a rather bad press," one Witch told me. Another said, "I did not plan to call myself Witch. It found me. It just happened to be a name—perhaps a bad name—that was attached to the things I was seeking." One Neo-Pagan journal stated that the term *Witchcraft* is inappropriate as "it refers to a decayed version of an older faith."[4]

Some witches will tell you that they prefer the word *Craft* because it places emphasis on a way of practicing magic, an occult technology. And there are Witches—the "classical" ones of Bonewits's definition—who define Witchcraft not as a religion at all, but simply as a craft. Others will say they are of the "Old Religion," because they wish to link themselves with Europe's pre-Christian past, and some prefer to say they are "of the Wicca," in order to emphasize a family or tribe with special ties. Still others speak of their practices as "the revival of the ancient mystery traditions." But when they talk among themselves they often use these terms interchangeably, and outsiders are left as confused as ever.

Sadly, it is only poets and artists who can make religious experiences come alive in telling about them. Most descriptions of mystical experiences are monotonous and banal—unlike the experiences themselves. And that is why, after all other chapters lay finished, this one remained unwritten. I had stacks of notes lying in piles on tables: descriptions of Witchcraft by Witches; definitions of Witchcraft by scholars; theories on the origin of Witchcraft by historians, the theories of modern Neo-Pagan writers like Aidan Kelly and Isaac Bonewits; a hundred stories and anecdotes.

But Ed Fitch, a Craft priest in California, told me, "To be a Witch is to draw on our archetypical roots and to draw strength from them. It means to put yourself into close consonance with *some ways that are older than the human race itself.*" I felt a slight chill at the back of my neck on hearing those words. And then I remembered a quotation from Robert Graves's *The White Goddess* that the true "function of poetry is religious invocation of the Muse," that all true poetry creates an "experience of mixed exaltation and horror that her presence excites." Graves said that one must think both mythically and rationally, and never confuse the two and never be surprised "at the weirdly azoological beasts that walk into the circle."[5]

So perhaps the best way to begin to understand the power behind the simple word *witch* is to enter that circle in the same spirit in which C. G. Jung consulted the I Ching before writing his famous introduction to the Wilhelm-Baynes translation. Do it, perhaps, on a full moon, in a park or in the clearing of a wood. You don't need any of the tools you will read about in books on the Craft. You need no special clothes, or lack of them. Perhaps you might make up a chant, a string of names of gods and goddesses who were loved and familiar to you from child-hood myths, a simple string of names for earth and moon and stars, eas-ily repeatable like a mantra.

And perhaps, as you say those familiar names and feel the earth and air, the moon appears a bit closer, and perhaps the wind rustling the leaves suddenly seems in rhythm with your own breathing. Or perhaps the chant seems louder and all the other sounds far away. Or perhaps the woods seem strangely noisy. Or unspeakably still. And perhaps the clear line that separates you from bird and tree and small lizards seems to melt. Whatever else, your relationship to the world of living nature changes. The Witch is the changer of definitions and relationships.

Once on a strange and unfamiliar shore a group of young and igno-rant revivalist Witches were about to cast their circle and perform a rite. They were, like most modern Wiccans, city people, misplaced on this New England beach. They had brought candles in jars and incense and charcoal and wine and salt and their ritual knives and all the implements that most books on the modern Craft tell you to use. The wind was blow-ing strongly and the candles wouldn't stay lit. The charcoal ignited and blew quickly away. The moon vanished behind a cloud and all the im-plements were misplaced in the darkness. Next, the young people lost their sense of direction and suddenly found themselves confronting the elemental powers of nature, the gods of cold and wind and water and wandering. The land—once the site of far different ancient religious practices—began to exert its own presence and make its own demands upon the psyche. Frightened, they quickly made their way home.

The point of all this is simple. All that follows—the distinctions, the definitions, the history and theory of the modern Craft—means noth-ing unless the powerful and emotional *content* that hides as a source be-hind the various contemporary forms is respected. This content lies in the mind. There is something connected with the word *witch* that is atemporal, primordial, prehistoric (in *feeling,* whether or not in *fact*), something perhaps "older than the human race itself." The story of the revival of Wicca is—whatever else it may be—the story of people who are searching among powerful archaic images of nature, of life and death, of creation and destruction. Modern Wiccans are using these im-ages to change their relationship to the world. The search for these im-ages, and the use of them, must be seen as valid, no matter how limited and impoverished the outer forms of the Wiccan revival sometimes appear, and no matter how contested its history.

The Myth of Wicca

Many have observed that myths should never be taken literally. This does not mean that they are "false," only that to understand them one must separate poetry from prose, metaphorical truth from literal reality.

The Wiccan revival starts with a myth, one that Bonewits used to call—much to the anger of many Witches—"the myth of the Unitarian, Universalist, White Witchcult of Western Theosophical Britainy."

It goes something like this: Witchcraft is a religion that dates back to paleolithic times, to the worship of the god of the hunt and the goddess of fertility. One can see remnants of it in cave paintings and in the figurines of goddesses that are many thousands of years old. This early religion was universal. The names changed from place to place but the basic deities were the same.

When Christianity came to Europe, its inroads were slow. Kings and nobles were converted first, but many folk continued to worship in both religions. Dwellers in rural areas, the "Pagans" and "Heathens," kept to the old ways. Churches were built on the sacred sites of the Old Religion. The names of the festivals were changed but the dates were kept. The old rites continued in folk festivals, and for many centuries Christian policy was one of slow cooptation.

During the times of persecution the Church took the god of the Old Religion and—as is the habit with conquerors—turned him into the devil of the new one—the Christian devil. The Old Religion was forced underground, its only records set forth, in distorted form, by its enemies. Small families kept the religion alive and, in 1951, after the Witchcraft Acts in England were repealed, it began to surface again.[6]

At this point the Wiccan Myth branches in many directions. Different Wiccan traditions (or sects) have a different story to tell. Many will mention the work of Margaret Murray, whose *Witch-Cult in Western Europe* (1921) popularized the idea that Witchcraft is the surviving pre-Christian religion of Europe. Many will mention Charles G. Leland, whose books, written at the turn of the century, described a surviving Pagan religion in Italy, including a Witch cult that worshipped Diana, and a host of ancient Etruscan survivals. Others will mention Gerald B. Gardner, a retired British civil servant who said he was initiated into one of the surviving ancient English covens in 1939. Convinced that the Witch cult was dying from lack of knowledge about it, Gardner published some of what he had learned in a novel, *High Magic's Aid*, and after the repeal of the Witchcraft Acts in 1951, published *Witchcraft Today* and *The Meaning of Witchcraft*. British Witches will often mention the work of the Witchcraft Research Association and its short-lived magazine *Pentagram*, which did much to aid the revival.

The elements of this Myth of Wicca can be found—in much lengthier form—in almost all the introductory books on the modern Craft that were circulating prior to 1980, including works by Gardner, Doreen Valiente, Justine Glass, Patricia Crowther, Stewart Farrar, and Raymond Buckland. Many elements are unquestionably true—such as the idea of pre-Christian survivals in Europe. Others are sharply contested by scholars—in particular, Margaret Murray's theory of a *universal, organized* Old Religion.

Until several decades ago most Wiccans took almost all elements of the myth literally. Few do so today, which in itself is a lesson in the flexibility of the revival. Many scholars refuted the literal accuracy of the myth and then wrongly dismissed the modern Craft itself as a fraud. One cannot really understand the revival of Witchcraft today without first becoming familiar with some of the sources that formed the Wiccan Myth and gave birth to the revival. These sources include the matriarchal theorists, such as J. J. Bachofen and Friedrich Engels; the British folklorists; Margaret Murray's theory of Witchcraft in the Middle Ages; and the books of the revival, in particular Gerald Gardner's writings in the 1940s and 1950s.

The Murrayite Controversy

While modern Wicca has very little to do with the witchcraft of the Middle Ages or the sixteenth and seventeenth centuries, the revival was strongly influenced by Margaret Murray's writings.

Although there have been many different approaches to the study of medieval European witchcraft, until about eighty years ago there were two main opposing theories, humorously called by the historian Elliot

Rose the "Bluff" school and the "Anti-Sadducee" school.[7] The former, reflecting the rationalism of the late nineteenth and early twentieth centuries, concluded that witchcraft was a delusion invented by the Inquisition. Rationalist scholars said that "supernatural elements" in reports of the trials—accounts of flying through the air and transformations into animals—made them totally suspect. In addition, the use of torture to obtain these accounts rendered them useless as evidence. Opposing scholars, such as Montague Summers, believed in the reality of Satan and accepted all trial reports as accurate and literal.

In 1921 Margaret Murray published *The Witch-Cult in Western Europe*. Murray was foremost an Egyptologist and secondarily a folklorist and anthropologist. After reexamining the trial documents of the Inquisition, she argued that witchcraft could be traced to "pre-Christian times and appears to be the ancient religion of Western Europe" centered on a deity which was incarnate in a man, a woman, or an animal. One of its forms was the two-faced horned god known to the Romans as Janus or Dianus. Murray wrote that the feminine form of the name—Diana—was found throughout Western Europe as the leader of the witches. Because of this, Murray called the religion the Dianic Cult, although she wrote that the god rarely appeared in female form and a male deity had apparently superseded a female one. This "organized religion" was, according to Murray, primarily a fertility cult, in the tradition described by Sir James Frazer in *The Golden Bough*. It was a cult of the god who dies and is reborn, and whose birth and death are reflected in the cycle of the seasons and the cycle of crops. According to Murray, this cult had originated with an aboriginal British race of small people who were the reality behind the fairy faith. The cult had participants in all classes from the peasantry to the nobility. The two main festivals of the cult, on May Eve and November Eve, were described as "pre-agricultural," having more to do with the fertility of animals than of crops.

Murray wrote that witches practiced a joyous religion. They met at the eight great festivals (sabbats) and at more general meetings (esbats) in covens of thirteen. They feasted and danced and had shamanistic visions. She argued, in fact, that the trial reports of accused witches describing themselves as flying through the air and changing their shape into animals were "ritual and not actual," a "clear account of the witch herself and her companions believing in the change of form caused by the magical object in exactly the same way that the shamans believe in their own transformation by similar means." Murray also argued that the coven, the sabbat, and all other aspects of the accusations made against witches had a reality behind them. The Inquisition had simply turned the god of the witches into their devil and substituted evil for good.[8]

Murray's later books, *The God of the Witches* (1933) and *The Divine King in England* (1954), were even more controversial, particularly the latter. In that book she argued that the idea of the sacred king was a reality in Britain and that many English kings had been ritually murdered; she contended that most of Britain's royalty had been members of the Dianic Cult. Most scholars dismissed this book as the work of a crackpot who had the audacity to publish at the age of ninety. (Murray was a remarkable woman who lived to be a hundred. She published her autobiography, *My First Hundred Years,* in 1963, the same year she died.[9])

Murray's theories were well regarded for some time. In the last forty-five years, however, they have been discredited. The arguments against her were many: that she took as true stories that may have been fabricated under torture; that, while she gave good evidence for Pagan survivals in Britain, she did not give evidence that an *organized* Pagan religion survived, or that this religion was universal, or that covens or sabbats existed before they appeared in trial reports.

The primary value of Murray's work was her understanding of the persistence of Pagan folk customs in Britain and her realization that Witchcraft could not be examined in isolation from the comparative history of religions or from the study of anthropology and folklore. But most scholars today dismiss most of her work.

Studies of European witchcraft, particularly of what has come to be called the witch craze of the sixteenth and seventeenth centuries, are so vast that to summarize scholarship after Murray would be impossible in a book of this nature. Also, the scholarly landscape has changed completely since *Drawing Down the Moon* was first published.

Norman Cohn: Witchcraft as Delusion

The late historian Norman Cohn was the author of *Europe's Inner Demons* (1975). Cohn argued that the stereotype of the witch comes from a specific fantasy that originated in antiquity. This fantasy—that there exists in the midst of the larger society a small clandestine society engaged in antihuman practices, including infanticide, incest, cannibalism, bestiality, and orgiastic sex—was an age-old tradition. It was first used by the Romans to characterize Christians, and later by the Christians to characterize Jews as well as heretical Christian sects such as the Cathars, the Waldensians, the Manichaeans, the Montanists, and groups such as the Knights Templar.

Cohn doubted that a sect of witches ever existed; therefore his book is the history of a "fantasy." He argued that folklorists Jacob Grimm and Girolamo Tartarotti—long considered the originators of the view that witchcraft is a pre-Christian religion—merely drew attention to the persistence of pre-Christian folk beliefs that later contributed to the stereotype of the witch. Karl Jarcke in 1828 first stated that witchcraft was the former Pagan religion of Germany, surviving among the common people. Ten years later Franz Joseph Mone described German Witchcraft as an underground esoteric cult. Cohn believed neither theory was convincing; neither Jarcke nor Mone could show that the worship of ancient gods was "practised by organized, clandestine groups in the Middle Ages." Cohn's next victim was the historian Jules Michelet, whose famous book on witchcraft, *La Sorcière,* appeared in 1862. He characterized Michelet as an "aging romantic radical with neither time nor desire for detailed research." He argued against Michelet's view that witchcraft was a protest by medieval serfs against an oppressive social order and that those serfs came together in secret to perform ancient Pagan dances and satires of their oppressors. Such a view, wrote Cohn, was prompted by "a passionate urge to rehabilitate two oppressed classes—women, and the medieval peasantry," but there was no evidence behind it.

Next, Cohn took on the idea of witchcraft as the survival of a fertility cult. He wrote that Frazer's *The Golden Bough* "launched a cult of fertility cults," and in 1921, when Murray's theory of the Dianic cult appeared, "the influence of *The Golden Bough* was at its height." He was completely contemptuous of Murray. Because she was sixty years old when she put forth her theory, he was convinced that her mind was rigidly "set in an exaggerated and distorted version of the Frazerian mould." (In fact, throughout the book Cohn uses age as a reason to dismiss a scholar or an idea.) He argued—like many other scholars—that

Murray could not prove the existence of an organized cult. But his main criticism was that she eliminated the fantastic features of the witch trial reports and gave a false impression that realistic accounts of the sabbat existed. If there are parallels between the descriptions of the sabbats and fertility rites, they are, he observed, meaningless. For him the sabbats were a complete delusion, a fiction. He rebuked such historians as Elliot Rose and Jeffrey Burton Russell for still being under Murray's influence despite their criticism of her work; and he expressed dismay that Murray's work had "stimulated the extraordinary proliferation of 'witches' covens' in Western Europe and the United States during the past decade, culminating in the foundation of the Witches International Craft Association, with headquarters in New York."

Cohn's main point was that no story with "impossible elements" should ever be accepted as evidence. "Nobody has ever come across a real society of witches," he wrote adding:

> Taken as a whole, that tradition itself forms a curious chapter in the history of ideas. Over a period of a century and a half, the non-existent society of witches has been repeatedly re-interpreted in light of the intellectual preoccupations of the moment. The theories of Jarcke and Mone were clearly inspired by the current dread of secret societies; that of Michelet, by his enthusiasm for the emancipation of the working classes and women; those of Murray and Runeberg, by the Frazerian belief that religion originally consisted of fertility cults; those of Rose and Russell, maybe, by the spectacle of the psychedelic and orgiastic experiments of the 1960s.[10]

According to Cohn, scholars had simply been "grossly underestimating the capacities of human imagination." He wrote that the many "fantastic" notions about witches had a long history in folk beliefs—that they practiced evil, that they changed shape and flew through the air—but were never significant until new Inquisitorial procedures began to investigate ritual magic. At that point, small-scale trials of individuals accused of consorting with demons took place. These were minor affairs, and most of the accused were priests. It was not until all parts of the "fantasy" were put together and believed by those in authority that the witch persecutions could really begin. For most peasants, witches were simply those—mostly women—who harmed by occult means. The other notion, that witches were members of a secret sect headed by Satan, came from educated Church leaders and Inquisitors when the Inquisitors themselves had become convinced of the *reality* of the sabbat and nocturnal flights. (Murray, as we have seen, never considered the nocturnal flights to be real, but believed them to be shamanistic visions similar to those reported by religious visionaries around the world.)

At the end of *Europe's Inner Demons* Cohn, unfortunately, adopted, whole hog, the most popular witchcraft religion of our day—psychiatry. The origins of witchcraft in the Middle Ages lie in our unconscious, he wrote: It is a fantasy at work both in history and the writing of history. The witch hunts would never have taken place without "the fantasy of a child-eating, orgiastic, Devil-worshipping sect." The only continuity is in the fantasy. And where did those fantasies come from? Cohn's answer was that they represented "the innermost selves" of many Europeans, "their obsessive fears, and also their unacknowledged, terrifying desires." These fantasies of cannibalism and infanticide were in all folklore, and their roots were in childhood, part of the "wishes and anxieties experienced in infancy or early childhood, but deeply repressed and, in their original form, wholly unconscious." The creation of a society of witches was, therefore, an unconscious revolt against Christianity as too strict and repressive.

One of the problems with Cohn's argument was his limited conception of the possible. For example, he considered all reports of orgies to be fantasy. He stated, "Orgies where one mates with one's neighbour in the dark, without troubling to establish whether that neighbour is male or female, a stranger or, on the contrary, one's own father or mother, son or daughter, belong to the world of fantasy." Here he is surprisingly ignorant of the history of sex and ritual. Orgiastic practices were a part of religious rites in many cultures of the ancient world. And while most modern group sexual encounters lack a religious dimension, one has only to read reports about modern sex clubs to know that orgiastic experiences are not merely a product of fantasy.

Mircea Eliade: Witchcraft as an Archaic Pagan Survival

In 1976, the historian Mircea Eliade wrote an essay, "Some Observations on European Witchcraft," that noted that although Murray's work was filled with errors and unproven assumptions, more recent studies of Indian and Tibetan documents "will convince an unprejudiced reader that European witchcraft cannot be the creation of religious or political persecution or be a demonic sect devoted to Satan and the promotion of evil."

> As a matter of fact, all the features associated with European witches are—with the exception of Satan and the Sabbath—claimed also by Indo-Tibetan yogis and magicians. They too are supposed to fly through the air, render themselves invisible, kill at a distance, master demons and ghosts, and so on. Moreover, some of these eccentric Indian sectarians boast that they break all the religious taboos and social rules: that they practice human sacrifice, cannibalism, and all manner of orgies, including incestuous intercourse, and that they eat excrement, nauseating animals, and devour human corpses. In other words, they proudly claim all the crimes and horrible ceremonies cited ad nauseam in the Western European witch trials.[11]

Eliade pointed to the cult of the *benandanti,* unearthed by Carlo Ginzburg. On the four great agricultural festivals of the year these Italian wizards fought a battle (in trance) against a group of evil wizards, the *stregoni.* They went to their assemblies *in spiritu,* while they slept, and their central rite was a ceremonial battle against the *stregoni* to assure the harvest. "It is probable," wrote Eliade, "that this combat between *benandanti* and *stregoni* prolonged an archaic ritual scenario of competitions and contests between two opposing groups, designed to stimulate the creative forces of nature and regenerate human society as well." The persecution of the *benandanti* took place in Italy in the sixteenth and seventeenth centuries and in most of the trials the accused were charged with adhering to a cult of Diana. The Inquisitional model pressed upon the accused had an effect and "after fifty years of Inquisitorial trials, the *benandanti* acknowledged their identity with the witches (*strighe* and *stregoni*)." They began to speak of the sabbat and pacts with the devil. Eliade argued that though this example gives no evidence for Murray's horned god or for her organized system of covens, it was nevertheless, "a well-documented case of the *processus* through which a popular and archaic secret cult of fertility is transformed into a merely magical, or even black-magical, practice under pressure of the Inquisition." Incidently, Norman Cohn dismissed the *benandanti* because their experiences were all under trance and therefore, to him, illusory.

Eliade also described parallels in Romanian studies, significant because there was no systematic persecution of witches in Romania, no institution analagous to the Inquisition, and the "archaic popular culture" was therefore under "less rigid ecclesiastical control." Romanian witches were reported to change their shape, to ride on brooms, and to fight all night at specific festival times until they became reconciled. The Romanian Diana was connected with the fairies, and the Queen of the Fairies came to be associated in name with Diana, Irodiada, and Aradia— "names," Eliade wrote, "famous among western European witches."

Eliade concluded that "What medieval authors designated as witchcraft, and what became the witch crazes of the fourteenth, sixteenth, and seventeenth centuries, had its roots in some archaic mythico-ritual scenarios comparable with those surviving among the Italian *benandanti* and in Romanian folk culture."[12]

Modern Wicca, while retaining the use of such terms as *esbat, sabbat,* and *coven,* bears no resemblance to the European witchcraft that the scholars have discussed. There are no beliefs in Satan, no pacts, no sacrifices, no infanticide, no cannibalism, and often not even any sex. Still, the theories of Margaret Murray were strongly influential in stimulating the revival of Wicca, and it can be argued that her work alone generated a number of British covens.

In the last twenty years, the entire landscape of scholarship has changed. Scholars have made meticulous studies of trial records in scores of European communities. A good summary of current scholarship is *Witchcraft and Magic in Sixteenth- and Seventeenth-Century Europe* by Geoffrey Scarre and John Callow (2nd edition). Most scholars now put the number of people killed for the crime of witchcraft from the late fifteenth century through the seventeenth century at between forty and fifty thousand, not millions or even the one million figure I used in the first edition of *Drawing Down the Moon*. With an unknown number of others who "received a more random form of justice at the hands of their neighbors, through common assaults, lynchings and social ostracism."[13] Scarre and Callow argue that it will never be possible to know with complete certainty how many people in Europe were prosecuted for witchcraft and how many suffered death, since records were not always kept, and even where they were, some were lost. But they still say a reasonable figure for executions between 1428 and 1782 is forty thousand. Other scholars put the figure at fifty thousand. The worst persecutions were in the 1590s, and during the period between 1630 and the 1660s. Some of the worst persecutions took place in Germany, with far fewer trials in Italy and Spain, "the heartlands of the Inquisition."[14]

About 80 percent of the victims were women, although in some places (Moscow, for example) male victims predominated. Often the women were poor, and a large number were over fifty. Murray's theory is given short shrift here, as is Jules Michelet's thesis that witchcraft was a protest against repressive social conditions. Scarre and Callow also believe there is little evidence for the 1976 groundbreaking feminist work by Barbara Ehrenreich and Dierdre English, *Witches, Midwives and Nurses,* that argued that the suppression of witchcraft was the suppression of midwives and healers by the emerging male medical establishment. The authors argue that while clearly misogyny played a role, this theory cannot explain why some of the most vociferous voices for persecution came from the peasantry.

Scarre and Callow also say there is little evidence for the thesis of H. R. Trevor-Roper, who argued that the Catholic Church used the stereotype of the witch in local struggles against groups it would not or could not assimilate. Trevor-Roper wrote that the stereotype of the witch might have died had it not been revived in the century of the Black Death and the Hundred Years War, and had it not received new strength from the struggle between Reformation and Counter-Reformation, which "revived the dying witch-craze just as it had revived so many other obsolescent habits of thought: biblical fundamentalism, theological history, scholastic Aristotelianism." He asserted that every major outbreak of the witch persecutions in the 1560s and after took place in the frontier areas between Catholics and Protestants. For example, persecution in England was fiercest in Essex and Lancashire, where Catholicism was strong. In Catholic France most of the witches were Protestant and often came from "Protestant islands" like Orléans and Normandy.[15] Scholars like Scarre and Callow counter this position and argue that witchcraft trials happened in many places where there was little or no interdenominational strife. And in a few cases, Catholic and Protestant lands exchanged information on witchcraft activities.[16] In addition, many prosecutions were spurred on by popular demands not by secular or religious authorities. In fact, many scholars today argue that the persecutions were strongest where the church was weakest, and those accused of witchcraft had a better chance of acquittal in ecclesiastical courts.

Historians who emphasize class, like the English historian Christopher Hill, theorized that witchcraft persecution was used for social control, and for control of the peasantry by the monied classes. Starhawk develops this idea further in her beautiful essay "The Burning Times" in which she argues that "the persecution of Witches undermined the unity of the peasant community."[17] By destroying village healers, one could fragment community and make it easier to enclose the common lands. But Ronald Hutton argues that Hill has been pretty much discredited today, since he often relied on literary works that provided a distorted view of reality. Most scholars today do not believe there was a mass dispossession of common people by enclosure. Hutton writes:

> What we have found instead is a more complex picture of competition between different sorts of commoners, and of landlords, for the use of resources in a time of unprecedented economic opportunity. In other words, it wasn't a straightforward class struggle, and commoners were less often victims and more often opportunists, than the traditional polemics have held. On the other hand there was plenty of class consciousness around, and working people were often very good at protecting their interests and deeply involved in politics.[18]

Other Sources of the Witchcraft Revival

Many of those most responsible for the revival of Witchcraft were influenced by many authors other than Murray and Frazer. They were knowledgeable about classical sources, such as Lucius Apuleius's classical witchcraft romance, *The Golden Ass*[19] (in which Apuleius becomes a priest of Isis after the goddess appears in a beautiful vision), and Charles G. Leland's *Aradia, or the Gospel of the Witches,* published in 1899.[20]

If scholars have contested Murray's thesis, they have totally dismissed Leland by saying either that he was the victim of a bad joke or, since he had written satire in the past, he could not be taken seriously. Jeffrey Burton Russell, author of *Witchcraft in the Middle Ages,* has said that *Aradia* does not contain useful evidence.[21] Elliot Rose has called it a product of art rather than a folk product. One interesting discussion of C. G. Leland can be found in Leo Martello's *Witchcraft: The Old Religion;* another is in Ronald Hutton's *The Triumph of the Moon.*[22]

Charles Godfrey Leland (1824–1903) was an American writer and folklorist who, according to the accounts of his niece and biographer, Elizabeth Robins Pennell, was a political rebel, an abolitionist, an artist, an occultist, and a folklorist. He lived with native American tribes; he studied with gypsies; he compiled gypsy lore, learned Romany, founded the *Gypsy Lore Journal;* he learned the Celtic tinkers' language, Shelta; he became president of the first European folklore congress in 1899; he went to Italy and wrote a series of remarkable books that traced the persistence of Pagan religious beliefs. One of these books, *Etruscan Roman Remains* (1892), is a gem. In it Leland traces the names of Etruscan deities as they degenerated through time into lesser sprites and spirit beings who persisted in chants, rhymes, and incantations.[23] He achieved a measure of fame for writing a series of satiric verses about German-American immigrants, the *Hans Breitman Ballads* (1872), but few scholars have taken him seriously as a folklorist.

The controversy that surrounds Leland concerns his meeting with a woman named Maddalena who claimed descent from an old Witch family. She brought Leland what she said was the local Witches' book, a mixture of myths and spells. Leland called it a translation of an early or late Latin work. The myths tell of Diana (or Tana), Queen of the Witches, and two different versions of her union with Lucifer, the sun. From this union was born a daughter, Aradia, who was to go to earth as the messiah of Witches and teach the arts of Witchcraft to oppressed humanity. Leland wrote that this was a sacred gospel of the Old Religion *(la Vecchia Religione).* He said this religion still prevailed in entire villages in the Romagna in Italy.

Elliot Rose dismissed the book and wrote that "The whole work reads much more as if one of its authors was consciously seeking to establish that the witch-cult was a cult of this particular nature, and grafted material calculated to prove it onto an existing straightforward book of incantations."[24] To this day no one has established whether Maddalena made up the story, or Leland did, or whether there are elements of truth mixed with exaggeration—whatever the case, Aradia was used by Gardner and others and several beautiful stanzas from *Aradia* appear little changed in the rite known as "The Charge of the Goddess." In *Aradia* this appears as follows:

> Now when Aradia had been taught, taught to work all witchcraft, how to destroy the evil race (of oppressors), she (imparted it to her pupils) and said unto them:
>> When I shall have departed from this world,
>> Whenever you have need of anything,
>> Once in the month, and when the moon is full,
>> Ye shall assemble in some desert place
>> Or in a forest all together join
>> To adore the potent spirit of your Queen
>> My mother, great *Diana*. She who fain
>> Would learn all sorcery yet has not won
>> Its deepest secrets, them my mother will
>> Teach her, in truth all things as yet unknown.
>> And ye shall all be freed from slavery,
>> And so ye shall be free in everything;
>> And as a sign that ye are truly free,
>> Ye shall be naked in your rites, both men
>> And women also: this shall last until
>> The last of your oppressors shall be dead. . . .[25]

In the modern Wiccan rite "The Charge of the Goddess," as published, for instance, in *The Grimoire of Lady Sheba*, this is only slightly changed and depoliticized.

> Whenever ye have need of anything, once in the month and better it be when the Moon is Full, then shall ye assemble in some secret place and adore the Spirit of Me, who am Queen of all the Witcheries. There shall

ye assemble, who are feign to learn all sorceries who have not as yet won my deepest secrets. To these will I teach that which is as yet unknown. And ye shall be free from all slavery and as a sign that ye be really free, ye shall be naked in your rites and ye shall sing, feast, make music and love, all in my presence. For mine is the ecstasy of the Spirit and mine is also joy on earth. For my Law is love unto all beings.[26]

Interestingly, many writers took *Aradia's* political references as a sign of the degeneration of the text. The historian T. C. Lethbridge said that *Aradia* was "much distorted by political propaganda."[27] Craft priest and writer Raymond Buckland concurred.[28] Doreen Valiente noted that "Its sexual frankness—which Leland has toned down in his translation—its attacks on the Christian Church, its anarchistic attitude toward the social order, all contributed to make it a book that was pushed aside."[29] Leland was himself a political radical. The more modern Wiccan version was written by Doreen Valiente, who kept some of Leland's phrases and added some of her own poetry.

Still, it is in *Aradia,* and in Leland's other books, that the phrase *"la Vecchia Religione"*—the Old Religion—appears. And that is where the term, now used so often among Witches, may have originated. And *Aradia's* importance in helping to create the revival cannot be stressed enough. In contrast to Murray, Leland as far back as the 1890s said that women were given an equal, perhaps superior, place in the religion. He wrote that whenever "there is a period of radical intellectual rebellion, against long-established conservatism, hierarchy, and the like, there is always an effort to regard woman as the fully equal, which means superior sex." And he noted that in Witchcraft, "it is the female who is the primitive principle." Leland's book became very popular with feminist groups within the Craft, partly because the myth of the creation of Aradia and Diana placed the feminine principle first and partly because feminist Witches—the most political Crafters—have always been very sympathetic to the idea of a link between Witches and oppressed peoples. In the appendix to *Aradia* Leland wrote:

The perception of this [tyranny] drove vast numbers of the discontented into rebellion, and as they could not prevail by open warfare, they took their hatred out in a form of secret anarchy, which was, however, intimately blended with superstition and fragments of old tradition. Prominent in this, and naturally enough, was the worship of *Diana* the protectress. . . . The result of it all was a vast development of rebels, outcasts, and all the discontented, who adopted witchcraft or sorcery for a religion, and wizards as their priests.[30]

Along with Murray and Leland, Robert Graves has been very influential in the Witchcraft revival. *The White Goddess* and some of Graves's lesser-known works, particularly such novels as *Watch the North Wind Rise* and *King Jesus,* had an enormous impact on people who later joined the Craft. Several noted that after World War II a number of books put forth the idea of goddess worship as a way to turn humanity from its destructive course.[31]

Bonewits told me, "Graves is a sloppy scholar. *The White Goddess* has caused more bad anthropology to occur among Wiccan groups than almost any other work. It's a lovely metaphor and myth and an inspirational source of religious ideas to people, but he claimed it was a work of scholarship and that people were to take what he said as true. There are still a few groups of Neo-Pagans who use Graves and Murray as sacred scripture."

It is likely that certain members of the Craft have interpreted Graves too literally. Graves himself said that he wrote the first draft of *The White Goddess* in a few weeks, in a storm of passion, and from the beginning it was very clear in his mind that the book was poetic metaphor.[32] His attitude toward Wicca was always one of bemusement. In 1964, writing in *The Virginia Quarterly Review,* he attributed the spread of organized Witch covens to Margaret Murray's anthropological works. He argued that Witches existed in Britain from early times and that several covens had survived, but that Murray's "sympathetic reassessment of organized witchcraft made a revival possible." Graves looked at the Craft with some amusement, finding it numbered among its members idealists as well as "hysterical or perverted characters." "Yet the Craft seems healthy enough in 1964, and growing fast," he wrote. "It now only needs some gifted mystic to come forward, reunite, and decently reclothe it, and restore its original hunger for wisdom. Fun and games are insufficient."[33]

If much modern scholarship has dismissed Murray as a crank, Leland as a satirist, and Graves as a writer of poetic fancy, Gerald B. Gardner is usually put down as a "fraud" or a "dirty old man." And yet it is impossible to understand the revival of Witchcraft without coming to terms with Gardner and his influence—an influence that is much greater than one would think from reading about his life or reading his works.

The most sympathetic accounts of Gardner's life have been J. L. Bracelin's poorly written biography, *Gerald Gardner: Witch,* Doreen Valiente's beautifully written account in her *The ABC of Witchcraft Past and Present,* and the accounts of various Gardnerians, neo-Gardnerians, and ex-Gardnerians including Patricia Crowther, Stewart Farrar, and Raymond Buckland.[34] The most negative accounts can be found in the works of the occult writer Francis King and the historian Elliot Rose.

Here is the story as put forth by Bracelin, Valiente, Buckland, and others. Since certain parts of it are in controversy, this story can be thought of as part of the Wiccan myth.

Gerald B. Gardner (1884–1964) was an amateur anthropologist and folklorist who lived much of his life in the Far East, working as a rubber planter and tea planter in Ceylon and Malaya and later as a British customs officer. He wrote a book on Malay weaponry in 1936 (*Keris and Other Malay Weapons*) and went into retirement that same year, settling in Hampshire, England, with his wife. He joined a naturist society, apparently having become a nudist early in life.

It was in 1939 that Gardner, according to the story, contacted the Witch cult in England. Valiente, who, according to her own account, was initiated into the Craft by Gardner in 1953, writes that Gardner joined an occult society, the Fellowship of Crotona, which had constructed a community theater called "The First Rosicrucian Theatre in England." Among the members of this occult fraternity was the daughter of Annie Besant, the Theosophist and founder of Co-Masonry, a masonic movement for women.[35]

Bracelin writes that Gardner noticed among the members of the Fellowship a group that stood apart from the others.

> They seemed rather browbeaten by the others, kept themselves to themselves. They were the most interesting element, however. Unlike many of the others, they had to earn their livings, were cheerful and optimistic and had a real interest in the occult. They had carefully read many books on the subject: Unlike the general mass, who were supposed to have read all but seemed to know nothing.[36]

According to Bracelin, Gardner was taken to the house of a wealthy neighborhood woman named "Old Dorothy" and in 1939 was initiated by her into Wicca. Until recently little was known about "Old Dorothy" and many scholars assumed she was a fiction. Valiente wrote that the lady was known to her, but to tell the public who she is would "be a breach of confidence."[37] In an appendix to *The Witches' Way,* Doreen Valiente described her long and ultimately successful search for the birth and death certificates of Dorothy Clutterbuck.[38] Ronald Hutton, in *The Triumph of the Moon,* pretty convincingly demonstrates that Dorothy Clutterbuck existed, but may well have had nothing to do with Gerald Gardner or Witchcraft. Hutton writes that a woman named Dafo, the stage director of the Rosicrucian Theatre, *was* a close friend of Gerald Gardner throughout most of the 1940s, and may well have been his main partner in ritual.[39] In Bracelin's account, Gardner was halfway through the initiation ceremony "when the word Wica was first mentioned: 'and then I knew that that which I had thought burnt out hundreds of years ago still survived.'"[40]

Gardner wanted to write about the Craft openly, but could not because of the Witchcraft Acts in Britain (the last of these acts was repealed in 1951, largely through the efforts of the spiritualist movement). In 1949 Gardner published *High Magic's Aid* under the pen name "Scire." It was a historical novel about the Craft and contained two initiation rituals, but there was no reference to the Goddess.[41] After the last Witchcraft Act was repealed, Gardner came out with two books under his own name, *Witchcraft Today* (1954) and *The Meaning of Witchcraft* (1959). In 1951 Cecil Williamson set up a museum of Witchcraft at Castletown on the Isle of Man. Gardner joined Williamson as the resident Witch and began creating quite a bit of publicity. Valiente writes:

> G.B.G. decided that the time had now arrived for members of the Craft of the Wise to come out into the open and speak out to the world about their rituals and beliefs. . . . Whether or not he was right in this decision is still a matter of controversy among present-day witches, and seems likely to continue to be so.
>
> There is no doubt that G.B.G.'s action was a complete break with the witch tradition of silence and secrecy. I have reason to think that it was also contrary to the wishes of his associates. Today, many persons inside

the witch cult regard G.B.G. as having done far more harm than good by his publicising of witchcraft. Furthermore, they do not agree that G.B.G.'s version of the Craft is an authoritative one. . . . [42]

Gardner's version of the Craft was very different from that described by Murray. To him, Witchcraft was a peaceful, happy nature religion. Witches met in covens, led by a priestess. They worshipped two principal deities, the god of forests and what lies beyond, and the great Triple Goddess of fertility and rebirth. They met in the nude in a nine-foot circle and raised power from their bodies through dancing and chanting and meditative techniques. They focused primarily on the goddess; they celebrated the eight ancient Pagan festivals of Europe and sought to attune themselves to nature. [43]

Valiente wrote that some of Gardner's critics felt the publicity he generated was undignified, but, "looking back," she decided that Gardner was "sincere." Gardner's coven "was mostly composed of elderly people" and he was afraid the Craft "was in danger of dying out." She writes that many considered his insistence on nudity to be his own invention and that, while a very old and valid magical idea, it was unsuitable in the cold and damp of England. She also noted that many other Witches regarded much of Gardner's writings as "a reflection of his own ideas." She noted the use of Masonic phraseology in Gardnerian rituals and the use of quotations from Aleister Crowley.* She wrote:

> When I pointed out to him that I thought this inappropriate for the rites of witchcraft, as it was too modern, he gave me to understand that the rituals he had received were in fact fragmentary. There were many gaps in them; and to link them together into a coherent whole and make them workable, he had supplied words which seemed to him to convey the right atmosphere, to strike the right chords in one's mind. He felt, he said, that some of Crowley's work did this.

---

*Valiente, in her book, *Witchcraft for Tomorrow*, notes with amusement that she is the author of two Craft poems that have appeared in many published (and unpublished, I might add) versions of Craft rituals. She writes that she and Gerald Gardner wrote "Darksome Night and Shining Moon" (a poem used in countless rites that already has numerous spinoff versions) in 1954 or 1955. Her poem "Invocation to the Horned God" has been misquoted in *Lady Sheba's Book of Shadows*, where it appears as part of an ancient rite. Valiente notes that the poem was published in *Pentagram* in 1965 under her name and copyright mark.

From my own study of these rites and traditions, I believe that this old coven which Gerald Gardner joined has fragments of ancient rituals; but fragments only. These were in the hands of the few elderly members that were left. Gerald Gardner, believing passionately that the old Craft of the Wise must not be allowed to die, gathered up these fragments and, with the assistance of his own knowledge of magic, which was considerable, and the result of many years' study all over the world, pieced them together, and added material of his own, in order to make them workable. In doing so, he of necessity put the imprint of his personality and ideas upon them.[44]

The controversy surrounding Gardner is over whether he was initiated into an authentic surviving coven, and how much of revivalist Wicca is his own invention or Crowley's or Doreen Valiente's or anyone else's. Most writers who are not members of the Craft or sympathetic to it dismiss the entire revival as "a fraud" created by Gardner.

Francis King, the English writer, wrote a brief chapter on the Witchcraft revival in *The Rites of Modern Occult Magic* (1970). He estimated that between one and two thousand people in Britain were, at the time he wrote, members of covens that "are practicing, or believe that they are practicing, traditional witchcraft, which they suppose to be the still-surviving fertility religion of prehistoric Europe." King said that he believed that pre-Gardnerian covens did exist (although they may date no further back than the publication of Murray's thesis), but he attributed the growth of the movement to Gardner's writings. King argued that Gardner *was* initiated into a coven; that he did not find "their simple ceremonies to his liking," and so decided "to found a more elaborate and romanticised witch-cult of his own." To do this, he "hired Crowley, at a generous fee, to write elaborate rituals for the new 'Gardnerian' witch-cult and, at about the same time, either forged, or procured to be forged, the so-called *Book of Shadows,* allegedly a sixteenth-century witches' rule-book, but betraying its modern origins in every line of its unsatisfactory pastiche of Elizabethan English."[45]

In fact, there has never been any evidence that Aleister Crowley was hired to write the Gardnerian rituals. There are elements of Crowley in the rituals, just as there are elements of Ovid, Leland, and Kipling. Still, this idea was floating around in the 1970s, and one priestess, Mary Nesnick (who worked in both the Gardnerian and the Alexandrian traditions before creating her own combination tradition known as Algard Wicca), wrote to me:

> Fifty percent of modern Wicca is an invention bought and paid for by Gerald B. Gardner from Aleister Crowley. Ten percent was "borrowed" from books and manuscripts like Leland's text *Aradia*. The forty remaining percent was borrowed from Far Eastern religions and philosophies, if not in word, then in ideas and basic principles.

Eliot Rose wrote a devastating critique of Gardner in his lively book *A Razor for a Goat*. Rose admits his biases. He is an Anglican who believes Witchcraft is foolish, and while it was "once rational to fear witchcraft," it has "never been rational to admire it."

Rose considered the Witchcraft revival to be a sort of literary production by a group of English men and women who were "sorry to see England going to the dogs" after World War II, and felt that a return to goddess worship would prevent this. The Witch cult, wrote Rose, "would happily combine the more aesthetically tolerable *motifs* of several former creeds and the least controversial ethical statements of all ages. Gods with Persian names and Greek bodies would prove, on examination, to have thoroughly Bloomsbury minds."

Rose described Murray's Witch cult as "male-oriented." The myth of the Goddess, he said, "reeks of twentieth-century literary fashion," and was not easily available before 1930. He wrote: "I doubt if at any date much before 1930 enough of the appropriate literature yet existed for many people to feel that to be truly pagan one must be 'matristic.'" He dismissed Engels and Bachofen. He described Apuleius's *Golden Ass* as "syncretistic" goddess religion and Paganism "of a very literary kind." As for Leland's *Aradia*, which was published in London in 1899, he dismissed it as another literary production. He called the book "post-Christian," "not very pagan," and "not very religious at all." He took the position that the Italian Church had so thoroughly taken over the old festivals that it had "quite as good a claim to represent the old paganism as a cult that talks about Diana. . . ." As for Gardner, Rose said his version of Witchcraft was "syncretic," full of Greek names and no Celtic ones, and he even described Graves's contention that goddess worship is a part of the British heritage as a Nazi view.

Since Rose judged the revival of Wicca on the basis of its claim to "old traditions," he could become quite acerbic, as when he observed:

> Those who seek here for a mystical profundity hidden from common men will seek in vain, and wander in the same fog hand-in-hand with the eager latter-day necromancer on their left and on their right the Comparative Religionist spying out the elder gods. If they should pick up ten moonstruck companions, let them form their own coven to prove their own points; it will be as traditional, as well-instructed, and as authentic as any there has been these thousand years.[46]

While various writers were dismissing the revival, within the Craft the debate for many years focused on the question raised by Valiente: Was Gardner's version *authoritative?* Or was he merely an "upstart" and was there some other, older Craft that was authoritative? The second issue of *Pentagram,* the newsletter put out by the British Witchcraft Research Association, reprinted an address to the association in which Valiente paid tribute to Gardner and observed that many people assumed wrongly that he had invented the religion. *Pentagram,* she said, was beginning to contact surviving traditions that had had no contact with Gardner; the Craft had "survived in fragments all over the British Isles," and each group had its own ideas and traditions of ritual and practice. And sure enough, other traditions, declaring themselves to be older, generally calling themselves "traditionalist" or "hereditary," began to provide a counterpoint to the revivalist Craft described by Gardner. Various members of hereditary covens criticized the followers of Gardner and disagreed that Witchcraft was "a simple religion for simple folk."[47]

Almost all the writers in *Pentagram* took the view that the old traditions were fragmented, that these fragments once formed a coherent whole. They saw the Witchcraft Research Association as a kind of "United Nations of the Craft" that would open the way "for a truly great work to be performed; namely, the piecing together of all the true parts of the ancient tradition. . . ." In other words, *Pentagram* accepted the idea that Witchcraft was once the *universal religion,* which had been driven underground to survive in secret, with much being lost. Many articles encouraged the joining of traditions "before it is too late," as the heritage was in danger and time was running out.[48]

A Revisionist History of the Craft

How is one to reconcile all this controversy with the idea of Wicca as a serious movement? Did Gardner simply make it all up? Are there hereditary Witches? Are there covens that predate Murray and Gardner? Did Gardner have access to an older coven?

As we have seen, until a few years ago most scholars dismissed all segments of the modern Craft as a hoax. Some Witches said they were of very old traditions that existed long before the time of Gardner. Others said that Gardner's version of the Craft was a "pure" tradition. And in America descendants of European immigrants insisted that they were Witches through family tradition, and that their Witchcraft didn't resemble Gardner's in the least. What's more, many of them said that Witchcraft was first and foremost a *craft* and only secondarily a *religion*. At the same time, covens sprang up in many places, and coven leaders declared themselves to be heirs of traditions that were thousands of years old. Many of these were soon discovered to be liars. One Wiccan priestess told me, "I've never seen a really old Book of Shadows. I'm not saying they don't exist . . . but like unicorns and hippogryphs, I've never seen one!"

What does this controversy have to do with the reality of the modern Craft? Fortunately, not much. Over the last thirty years, while some writers and scholars were dismissing the Craft as "silly" or "fraudulent," Neo-Pagans and Wiccans began to reassess who they really were and what the Craft was really about. And during this time a number of Neo-Pagan American writers tried to piece together a revisionist history of the Craft.

In the beginning of this chapter it was noted that Isaac Bonewits had divided Witches into several categories. Now is the time to look at his arguments more closely, particularly as they are related to the origins of the Craft and the place of Witches outside the revival.

The history of Bonewits's interaction with the Craft is a stormy one. He is a magician and occultist, who was for many years a priest of the

New Reformed Druids of North America. He then founded a revivalist Druid group called Ár nDraíocht Féin. From the beginning, when he wrote *Real Magic* (1971), Bonewits has always been a bit snide about Wicca. He dismissed the "Myth of Wicca" a little too bluntly, a little too easily, and a little too *early*, and thereby angered many in the Craft. At the time of *Real Magic* and his later article, "Witchcult: Fact or Fancy?" most Witches accepted literally the idea of a universal Old Religion such as that described by Murray. Since Bonewits's views were close to those of more inflexible scholars, he was branded by some as unfriendly to the Craft community. In the book, written when Bonewits was barely out of college, he argued (as he still does) that there never was a unified European-wide Old Religion. There were Pagan religions—many of which were very vital—and many European communities retained Pagan beliefs and even, perhaps, groups well into the Christian era; but Bonewits argued that the "Unitarian Old Religion of White Witches" existed in fancy, not in fact, "the product of local cultural egotism and bad ethnography."[49] His final sally in *Real Magic* caused even more friction:

> Some of the witch groups claim to be Christian, and except for the fact that they often do their rites in the nude, you could find more paganism and witchcraft at a Baptist prayer meeting. Other groups claim to be revivals or remnants of the nonexistent "Witch-Cult of Western Europe" (made so popular by author Margaret Murray). They get their "authority" from their Secret Beliefs Handed Down for Generations of Witches in My Family, etc. This sort of witchcraft tends to be a mishmash of half-forgotten superstition, Christian concepts, and Hindu beliefs. Thus, their "fertility rites" are done for "spiritual fertility" rather than physical fertility, though they like to hint that their ceremonies are really very exciting (they're not—they are hideously boring to anyone who's been to a good love-in).[50]

Several years later Bonewits addressed a meeting of Witches in Minneapolis. His remarks were later published in *Gnostica* as "Witchcult: Fact or Fancy?" He later refined these arguments in a series of articles that appeared in *Green Egg* in 1976–1977 under the title "Witchcraft: Classical, Gothic and Neopagan." He has changed these categories slightly in recent years.

Bonewits's division of Witches into categories is meant to clear up some of the confusion surrounding the word *Witch*. For example, the "classical witch" or cunning folk, would be defined as:

> a person (usually an older female) who is adept in the uses of herbs, roots, barks, etc., for the purposes of both healing and hurting (including mid-wifing, poisoning, producing aphrodisiacs, producing hallucinogens, etc.) and who is familiar with the basic principles of both passive and active magical talents, and can therefore use them for good or ill, as she chooses.

This "classical witch" would be found among most peoples. In Europe this woman (or man) would be an old peasant, perhaps, "a font of country wisdom and old superstitions as well as a shrewd judge of character." For this kind of witch, writes Bonewits, *religion* was fairly irrelevant to *practice*. Some considered themselves Christians; some were Pagans. In Ireland many said that their powers came from the fairies. Relatively few classical witches exist today in Europe. But Bonewits thinks that most people who call themselves "witches" today are "Neoclassical"— that is they use magic, divination, herbology, and extrasensory perception without much regard for religion. According to Bonewits, 70 percent of the Witches in America today are "Neoclassical."[51]

Bonewits's "gothic witches," now called "diabolic witches," are those who appear in trial reports between 1450 and 1750. They represented a reversed version of Roman Catholicism, including pacts with the devil, the devouring of babies, and other pieces of propaganda that the Church used during the Inquisition. Gothic witchcraft, according to Bonewits, is a Church fiction. He refutes the Murrayite thesis of a universal Old Religion with the contention that witchcraft in Europe was a creation of the Inquisition, complete with descriptions of the sabbat, covens, and orgies. He regards contemporary Satanism as neogothic witchcraft because it descends from the gothic witchcraft created by Christianity. Most modern Satanists pattern themselves on the ideas created by the Church and proceed from there. (I would amend this to say that a few modern Satanists seem to be misplaced Neo-Pagans who have not been able to get beyond Christian terminology and symbolism.)

Bonewits does accept the survival of Neo-Pagans into the Christian era, although he is convinced that by the eleventh century most of them had gone underground or had been destroyed. Essentially he takes the orthodox scholarly position that until the middle of the fourteenth century witchcraft simply meant sorcery—the attempt to control nature— and was never an organized survival of Paganism; that the word acquired a new meaning in the fourteenth century, when it was identified as a heresy and was elaborated upon and spread by the Inquisition for its own political ends. We have met his arguments before: official Church policy that witchcraft was illusion was reversed; a new form of witchcraft was created by the Church to root out heresy; many of the old charges against Jews and Gypsies were "dusted off" and combined with the new inventions of the witches' sabbat and the Black Mass.

Bonewits believes that some European families may have kept Pagan traditions alive (he notes that rich families often don't get persecuted) but that there is no evidence of an underground organized religious movement during the European Middle Ages.[52]

Bonewits uses the term "Neopagan Witchcraft" to refer to Wicca. He estimates that of the many thousands of people in America who consider themselves Witches, a statistical breakdown might look something like this:

Neopagan	15 percent
Feminist	10 percent
Neogothic	2–3 percent
Neoclassical	55 percent
Classical	1–2 percent
Family Traditions	1–2 percent
Immigrant Traditions	1–2 percent
Ethnic (Voodoo, Amerindian, etc.)	10 percent[53]

Like many others, Bonewits believes that folklore and literature gave birth to Neo-Pagan Witchcraft: the folklore of Frazer and the theories of mother-right, and Leland's studies of Pagan survivals among the Italian peasantry. He says that the fields of folklore, anthropology, and psychology really began to develop between 1900 and 1920, as did psychical research and ceremonial magic. He speculates:

Somewhere between 1920 and 1925 in England a group of social scientists (probably folklorists) got together with some Golden Dawn Rosicrucians and a few Fam-Trads [see below] to produce the first modern covens in England; grabbing eclectically from any source they could find in order to try and reconstruct the shards of their Pagan past.[54]

Bonewits attributes most Neo-Pagan Witchcraft in the United States to Gerald Gardner's influence, and writes that Gardner took "material from any source that didn't run too fast to get away."

Family Traditions

Bonewits is most illuminating when he talks about the reality of Family Traditions (Fam-Trads). He accepts the idea that some "Classical witches" could have preserved folk traditions and agricultural festivals. While this was no organized universal cult, isolated and powerful families may have preserved many traditions, each family suffering contamination over the years. "There is plenty of evidence," he writes, "of ancient Pagan traditions surviving under thin Christian veneers in isolated parts of Christendom," but "there is almost nothing logical to suggest that the people leading these traditions were in touch with each other or shared more than the vaguest common beliefs."[55] These families often call themselves Witches now, but whether they did a short while ago, or whether they have anything in common with modern Wiccans, remains in question.

Bonewits stresses the contamination of the European family traditions, as well as of those families that immigrated to the United States (Immigrant Traditions). Classical witches were becoming fewer in number, and "Scientism was rapidly becoming the supreme religion in the West."

Most members of Fam-Trads made efforts to conceal their "superstitious" beliefs and Pagan magical systems. Instead they became involved in Freemasonry and Rosicrucianism in the 18th century, Spiritualism and Theosophy in the 19th; for all of these movements were considered more respectable than witchcraft, and still allowed the Fam-Trads to practice occult arts. . . . So as the years went by, members of the Fam-

Trads absorbed more and more from non-Pagan magical sources and handed their new information down to each generation, often carelessly letting the descendants think that a Rosicrucian spell or alchemical meditation was a legitimate part of their Pagan heritage. So even today we have Fam-Trad witches who are far closer to being Theosophists or Spiritualists than to being Classical or Neoclassical witches.[56]

Almost everyone who has met members of family traditions notes that their Craft is far different from the Witchcraft of the revival. They far more easily fit Bonewits's description of "Classical witches." As one Midwestern priestess observed to me, "I know about family traditions— there are lots of people who have been taught how to do various things. But it's rarely called *Witchcraft*. Later on, of course, these people begin reading and they say to themselves, 'I was taught to do *that*, and here they say it's Witchcraft!'"

In Bonewits's analysis, the Family Tradition Witches are essentially "Classical witches" who changed with the times. As he told me, "In order to stay unpersecuted, they had to use a lot of protective coloration. When Rosicrucian terminology was in, they would train their kids with that terminology. When Theosophy was in, they were Theosophists. When Spiritualism was in, they were Spiritualists. And this means that from an anthropological point of view, the Fam-Trads are extremely contaminated. The later generations don't know what's from the family and what's been inserted.

"There may have been Family Traditions who read Frazer and Murray and said, 'Oh, that's what we've been doing,' and copied down all this stuff, thinking, 'This is our long-lost tradition brought back to us by this anthropologist or this folklorist.'

"And when a Family Tradition comes to the United States—an immigrant tradition—they'll start to mishmash their family belief system with the folk customs of the people they're living with. Today, many of these people are sitting on the borderline between being a neoclassical witch and a modern Wiccan Witch."

Do the Witches of these Family Traditions speak about themselves as Bonewits describes them? The answer is, pretty much, yes, as we will see from a few examples.

Lady Cybele is a Witch who lives in Madison, Wisconsin. Her roots are Scots and Welsh, and the main family magical traditions come from her father's side. Both her father's parents were from Craft traditions. After arriving in New York, most of the family settled in Wisconsin and Minnesota.

Cybele told me of family gatherings of over two hundred people at which a small group would get together on the side and talk about "the old ways" or "the way we used to do things." Her family was wary about letting the neighbors know that they had any unusual practices. And to them Witchcraft was a *practice*. She said, "The religious aspect was very simple—worship of Mother Nature. God was in Nature and Nature was female. The Goddess was the earth. The oak tree, not the sun, manifested the male principle. That was about all the theology.

"When I was growing up, the spiritual aspects were not stressed as they are now. The Craft has taken a lot of influences from high magic. I think that's a fine thing, but it's fairly new to the Craft."

Cybele's tradition did not contain written laws. "If the Fam-Trads have a law," she said, "that law would be: 'If it works, do it; if not, throw it out.' The Craft has always borrowed from every culture we've come in contact with." Since the family lived close to the land, she was taught primarily agricultural magic—weather working and crop magic.

"I was shown how to do certain things, practical things. How do you make your garden grow? You talk to your plants. You enter into a mental rapport with them. How do you call fish to you? How do you place yourself in the right spot? How do you encourage them?"

For most of her life, Cybele was unaware of the Wiccan revival. "It wasn't until college that I found out there were other people in the Craft, and I didn't know there were many of us until 1964, when my husband came running home from the library where he worked, bubbling with excitement, saying, 'There are more of us in the world.' He had Gerald Gardner's book and we read it through and he said, 'This is incredible! They're not like us completely, but, *yes,* we do this, and we do that, and whoever heard of *that?*'"

Cybele said that in her experience most Fam-Trads were loners who had difficulty working in covens. Occasionally Fam-Trads would work together, but seldom would it be a formal ritual gathering. More likely it would be a series of telephone calls: "Hey, did you hear about Sam Smith, who is going in for cancer tests Tuesday at eight o'clock? Think about it!" Cybele said that most of the Fam-Trad Witches she knew worked in street clothing and used common kitchen implements for tools. "I've added things from other traditions," she said, "because I think they're fun."

I also talked with Bonnie Sherlock, a Craft priestess in Lander, Wyoming, before her death in 1976. She described the teachings of her Irish immigrant grandmother in similar terms.

"Her beliefs were Pagan, although her room was full of Roman Catholic statues and pictures. She never used the terminology that's used in the Craft today. She called a pentagram a 'star.' If you had the ability, she referred to it as 'the power.' She did not use the term 'aura,' she would say 'light.' She never called it 'Witchcraft,' but simply 'having the power.' She called the summer solstice 'the Middle of the Summer,' and Beltane [May 1st] was 'May Basket Day.' Yule was 'Yule' and Samhain was 'Hallows-een.' She made incense from ground cinnamon in the pantry and pine needles.

"I learned from her that the Craft is a religion of hearth and fireside. The tools of the Craft are kitchen utensils in disguise. It's a religion of domesticity and the celebration of life."

Despite having these teachings, Bonnie Sherlock needed an impetus to begin working in the Craft. As with Cybele, that impetus came from outside and sounds strikingly similar.

"I got an advertisement in the mail and it had a list of books by Gerald Gardner. I decided to subscribe to the British magazine *Pentagram*. Then I saw a letter from Leo Martello in *Fate* magazine, setting up a method of getting Craft people together. Through Leo, I began corresponding with a man who became my High Priest."

But this was still not enough. "You just can't go around saying, 'I'm a Witch.' Perhaps it all boils down to the idea that you have to prove yourself to yourself before you can prove yourself to anyone else. I felt I had to have some kind of initiation. And so I went to a Native American Medicine Man. I went through a ritual, a three-day fast and vision quest. In creating our Delphian tradition, I used a combination of traditions, including Celtic and Native American material as well as things I remembered from my grandmother."

Here is yet another story from a Family Tradition Witch, this one a man from Minnesota:

"I was brought up with a sort of old-fashioned American Pagan-occult background. Mostly, I've revolted against this in much the same way most Neo-Pagans and other counterculture people have revolted against their Judeo-Christian backgrounds. Only a couple of members of my family were people I consider even remotely Aquarian, and they're dead now.

"I was raised as a Pagan. My whole family are 'old-fashioned witches.' This doesn't mean they're anything like the Neo-Pagans or the Pagans of ancient Europe. Mostly it means they're *not* Christians, Jews, Moslems, or modern intellectual atheists.

"Other than reference to 'Mother Nature' and the like, I was never exposed to the Pagan deities as described by Robert Graves and others, and the 'magic' my grandmother, mother, aunts, et cetera, practiced was derived from a wide variety of sources, mostly modern Masonic and Rosicrucian techniques, Spiritualism, 'Gypsy' card reading and divination, Theosophy, and so on. I have an idea the whole thing is rooted somewhere in the past in the Celtic Old Religion, but if so, the elements are so worn down as to be impossible to identify for sure.

"Most of the ways in which my upbringing differed from a standard American one are little nonverbal details. Like being put to nurse on a sheep-dog bitch when my mother ran short of milk, instead of being put on a bottle filled with cow's milk and refined sugar. Cutting my teeth on meat gristle instead of a plastic pacifier. *Lighting* instead of blowing out the candles on my birthday cakes. Bringing home a 'Christmas tree' in a tub, roots intact, and planting it again in the spring. Those are the only things that I remember, but my personality turned out radically different from those of the kids I went to school with. For instance, I *never* had any true understanding of the Christian concepts of 'sin' and 'guilt.' As long as I can remember I've simply realized that if you do something 'wrong,' you get 'punished,' maybe by other people, maybe by the workings of Nature, but never by yourself.

"My family used the word 'Witch' rather loosely for anyone who practiced 'magic'—it had nothing to do with going through any particular *religious* rituals, only operational rituals [spells]. The 'magic' I learned as a child was mainly what you might call 'extrasensory perception'—knowing if an outsider was friendly or hostile, lying or telling the truth, having flashes of knowledge about the future or past of a person or object, locating lost things. As I got older, my aunt and uncle started teaching me from all sorts of 'standard' magical sources: the holy books of a dozen or more religions, the occult and spiritualist books of the last century and this. They also taught me their 'personal' system, which was a hodgepodge from many different magical systems, as well as a lot more that wasn't magic at all but all the con-man tricks necessary to make my living as a magician if I wanted to. (They spent about thirty years traveling around the country calling themselves 'Gypsies' and supporting themselves mostly by doing various kinds of divination. They also gave people 'profound spiritual experiences' by turning them on with peyote without telling them what they were doing.) So I'm really not a 'Witch' in the sense the term is used among modern groups calling themselves by that name, even though I've used that term all my life. 'Magician' would be more descriptive, and it's what I now use to describe myself, leaving 'Witch' to apply to the people who practice Pagan religions loosely derived from Celtic and other Indo-European Old Religions."

As a final example, here is the story of Z Budapest, the feminist Witch of Los Angeles. This is what she told me of her childhood in Hungary:

"I was a Witch before I was a feminist. My family kept a book of who had lived and who had died, starting in 1270. There were quite a few herbalists in my family. At one point our family had a small pharmacy in a little town. My father was a doctor and many people in my family were healers.

"I observed my mother talking to the dead. I saw her go into trance and feel presences around her. She is an artist and her art often reflects Sumerian influences. She presents it as *peasant,* not *Pagan,* and so she gets away with it in Hungary. And in Hungarian, the word is the same.

"Many country folk buy my mother's ceramics. She uses ancient motifs, such as the tree of life, flower symbology, and the idea of the Goddess holding a child within a circle of rebirth. She does spontaneous magic and chants, and rhymes. She tells fortunes and can still the wind."

When Z was sixteen the Hungarian uprising occurred and she became a political exile.

"In one day I saw a total change occur. Suddenly the people of my country came out and loved each other. Hungarians usually hate each other. It was my first initiation into revolution. It made me decide to change my life. I wanted to live. I wanted to thrive. I decided my country was wiped out. I decided to check out the West."

But when Z came to New York she discovered a new form of oppression. The Ford and Rockefeller foundations were giving scholarships to refugees. Men would get a reasonable income, but women could get very little money. They had to become waitresses to even get through high school. She ended up in a traditional role: wife and mother. After twelve years, feeling limited and enslaved, she was driven to make a suicide attempt. During this attempt she had a vision in which she died and death was not fearful. She told me:

"After this vision, I regained my true perspective of a Witch, how a Witch looks at life—as a challenge. It is not going to last forever, and it's all right on the other side, so what are you going to *do?*

"And once that happened inside me, I just packed up and stuck out my thumb and hitchhiked from New York to Los Angeles. And I picked up a paper and there was a women's liberation celebration on March 8th. And I thought I would check out these people. And I knew them. They looked like me. Some of them had my wounds; some of them had different wounds.

"I began to talk about the Goddess. I knew a lot of Pagan customs that my country had preserved, but which had lost religious meaning—although not for me. I also began to read about Dianic Witchcraft, the English literature. A year later I began, with several other women, to have sabbats. In 1971, on the Winter Solstice, we named our coven the Susan B. Anthony Coven."

The pattern is clear. The family tradition begins quite close to Bonewits's definition of "Classical Witchcraft": a heritage of magical teachings, mostly oral. The religion is simple. There are no elaborate initiations. Ritual is at a minimum. It is a *craft*. Then there is contact with revivalist Wicca, in many cases with the "English literature"— Margaret Murray and Gerald Gardner, among others. From this comes a new outward direction toward activity, and in some cases the adoption of more formal structures, initiations, and rituals.

The literature of the revivalist Craft had influenced almost everyone I met. And whatever Gardner had done in England for good or ill, his books had served as a catalyst or springboard for many covens and traditions that did not necessarily "look" Gardnerian. These covens had little of the minor trappings of Gardner's Craft—the nudity, the scourge, the use of particular rituals. But the influence was there.

My interview with the poet and shaman Victor Anderson is a case in point. This was among the most mysterious of my encounters. His was the only story I heard that was clearly from the land of faery. It was pure poetry.

Anderson, the author of a beautiful book of Craft poems, *Thorns of the Blood Rose,*[57] told me of his meeting with a tiny old woman who said to him, at the age of nine, that he was a Witch. He was living in Oregon when he came upon her sitting nude in the center of a circle alongside a number of brass bowls filled with herbs. He said that he took off his clothes, knowing instinctively what to do, and was initiated "by full sexual rite." He then told me of the vision he had in that circle.

"She whispered the names of our tradition and everything vanished; it was all completely black. There seemed to be nothing solid except this woman and I held on to her. We seemed to be floating in space. Then I heard a voice, a very distant voice saying 'Tana, Tana.' It became louder and louder. It was a very female voice, but it was as powerful as thunder and as hard as a diamond and yet very soft. Then it came on very loud. It said, 'I am Tana.' Then, suddenly, I could see there was a great sky overhead like a tropical sky, full of stars, glittering brilliant stars, and I could see perfectly in this vision, despite my blindness.* The moon was there, but it was green. Then I could hear the sounds of the jungle all around me. I could smell the odors of the jungle.

"Then I saw something else coming toward me out of the jungle. A beautiful man. There was something effeminate about him, and yet very powerful. His phallus was quite erect. He had horns and a blue flame came out of his head. He came walking toward me, and so did she. I realized without being told that this was the mighty Horned God. But he was not her lord and master or anything like that, but her lover and consort. She contained within herself all the principles and potencies in nature.

"There were other strange communications, and then the darkness disappeared. We sat in the circle and she began to instruct me in the ritual

*Anderson became almost totally blind as a child.

use of each one of the herbs and teas in the circle. Then I was washed in butter and oil and salt. I put my clothes back on and made my way back to the house. The next morning when I woke up, I knew it had really happened, but it seemed kind of a dream."

After the description of this vision had settled, I asked Anderson, "When did you decide to form a coven?" And he replied, "It was when Gerald Gardner put out this book of his, *Witchcraft Today.* I thought to myself, 'Well, if that much is known . . . it all fits together.'"

On the other side of the country I questioned another Neo-Pagan leader, Penny Novack, one of the early leaders of the Pagan Way, a Neo-Pagan group that in theology was closely allied with Wicca. She described her entry into a religion of goddess worship.

"I was working as a cleaning lady for a small college in Vermont. There was a terrible snowfall and I was out on the road, hitching. The moon was up, a beautiful full moon, and I was walking along the road.

"Now, me and God had this relationship. I always yelled at God and God always said, 'If you get off your ass and do something, it will straighten out.' And sometimes it would and sometimes it wouldn't.

"So I'm walking along this road, shaking my fist at the moon and saying, 'Why am I not growing any more? What am I supposed to do?' And I'm furious and I'm shaking my fist at the moon and getting more freaked by the whole situation when I get this message. I didn't hear a voice. I just got this message: 'Your problem is that your concept of the Eternal One is masculine, and until you can know the One as Feminine, there's no way you're going to grow.' So I said to myself, 'That's weird. I never would have thought of that, but I'll give it a try.'"

When Penny and her husband, Michael, moved to Philadelphia, Michael began to get interested in Witchcraft. Penny told him, "I'm *not* interested in magic. I want something that deals with *goddesses* and *spiritual* growth.

"And Michael is saying, 'I read these books by Gerald Gardner, and it sounds like a real nature religion,' and I'm saying 'Don't talk to me about *Witchcraft.*'

"A week later, in December of 1965, the local Republican committeeman came to call and, in passing, mentioned some Witches he'd like us to meet. He brought over a Gardnerian pamphlet, and things took off from there."

Gardner in a New Light

In the late 1970s, Aidan Kelly, a founder of one of the most vital and beautiful Craft traditions in America—the New Reformed Orthodox Order of the Golden Dawn (NROOGD)—began to write about the origins of the Gardnerian tradition.

The early versions of his manuscript were titled "The Rebirth of Witchcraft: Tradition and Creativity in the Gardnerian Reform." Within this work, Kelly did something quite new. He labeled the entire Wiccan revival "Gardnerian Witchcraft." "I refer to this current religious movement as 'Gardnerian,'" he writes, "because almost all the current vitality in the movement was sparked by Gerald B. Gardner, a retired British civil servant who instituted a reform (and I use this word very precisely) in the 1940s."[58]

Most modern Witches use the term "Gardnerian" to refer either to those specific covens that derive through a chain of apostolic succession from Gardner's coven on the Isle of Man, or to those covens that use Gardnerian rituals, a large number of which have been published in books. NROOGD fits into neither category. But Aidan was saying something different—that the influence of Gardner on the modern Craft revival is much greater than most people realize, and that many groups have, often unknowingly, assimilated his main contributions.

The manuscript focused on the problems we have been considering— the Wiccan movement's claim to historical continuity—since many members of the Craft (at least until recently) have said that their practices descend in a direct line from the pre-Christian religions of Great Britain and Northern Europe. As Aidan observed, most Witches see their religion as a "native Pagan religion of Britain and northern Europe that, according to Margaret Murray's theory, underlay the politico-religious struggle that culminated in the witch trials of early modern time." But, as we have seen, most scholars dismissed Murray's theory and the entire movement as fraudulent. The truth, wrote Aidan, in the late 1970s, lies somewhere in between.

Kelly's manuscript went through many revisions. Part of his work on Gardner was finally published in 1991 as *Crafting the Art of Magic*. One of his most important contributions was finding the earliest version of Gardner's Book of Shadows in the Toronto collections of Gardner's

materials: *Ye Bok of Ye Art Magical.* It is the earliest version of the Gardnerian Book of Shadows, or the Gardnerian liturgy. The material found
its way to Canada after Monique Wilson sold Gardner's museum on the
Isle of Man to Ripley's International Ltd.

At the beginning of his research, when *Drawing Down the Moon* was
first published, Kelly argued that there was no way of proving whether
a New Forest coven actually existed. He wrote that if it did, its procedures
were so rudimentary that new ones had to be invented. And whether he
had traditional information, or simply took information out of books,
Gardner transformed the concepts "so thoroughly that he instituted a
major reform—that is, as has happened so many times in history, he
founded a new religion in the apparently sincere belief that he was merely
reforming an old one" and although this religion may have elements of
the Old Religion, it is "no more the same religion than the first Buddhists were still just Hindus, or the first Christians were still just Jews."[59]

The concepts that were new—the focus of Gardner's reform—were:
the preeminence of the Goddess; the idea of the woman as priestess; the
idea that a woman can *become* the Goddess; and a new way of working
magic that was particularly accessible to small groups. The last was a
combination of the "low magic" common to folklore the world over
(spells and recipes) and the "high magic" of the ceremonial *grimoire.*
Added to this was the idea of the circle as a place to contain power.
Sources used by Gardner included Ovid, Crowley, Kipling, Leland, and
the Order of the Golden Dawn.

Aidan wrote that it *really makes no difference* whether or not Gardner
was initiated into an older coven. He invented a new religion, a "living
system," and modern covens have adopted a lot of it because it fulfills
a need. This new system has little to do with the rituals that are labeled
"Gardnerian." It has little to do with the few covens that "are part of the
'orthodox apostolic succession' of Gardnerian initiation." The reform
consists of these new concepts, the primary ones being the worship of
the Goddess and a new way of working magic, a kind of middle-class
magic (although Aidan did not use that term). The appeal of the Goddess makes the movement more significant than its size would indicate.

Aidan observed that Gardner's reform took place during the same
period in which Robert Graves published *The White Goddess* and
Gertrude Rachel Levy wrote *The Gate of Horn.*[60] He wrote that

the essence of Gardner's reform is that he made the Goddess the major deity of his new movement, and it is the Goddess who captures the imagination, or hearts, or souls, or whatever else they are caught by, of those who enter into this movement. It is as if western civilization were ready to deal again (or finally) with the concept of Deity as Female. Whatever the reasons may be why this readiness exists, it is this readiness which justifies and sustains the Gardnerian movement, not a pseudohistory traceable to the Stone Age.[61]

It was Aidan's view that Gardner had never been given credit for creative genius. He had a vision of a reformed Craft. He pulled together pieces from magic and folklore; he assimilated the "matriarchal thealogy" set forth in Graves and Leland and Apuleius. With these elements he created a system that grew.

Kelly argued that the Craft is valid on its own terms. Why? Because it is a religion based on experience. The Craft is a religion that allows certain experiences to happen. It doesn't need dogma. Its covens are linked by their focus on the pantheons of pre-Christian Europe, by their ethic of "An ye harm none, do what ye will," and, primarily, by their worship of the Goddess.

In later years, after analyzing Gardner's notebooks, Kelly came to believe that there was no basis at all for the claim that Gardnerian Witchcraft derived from the ancient Pagan religion of Europe. Looking at *Ye Bok of Ye Art Magical*, Kelly noted that many things were copied into it, including passages from the *Greater Key of Solomon* that appear in Gardnerian rituals and the initiation rituals that are found in Gardner's novel *High Magic's Aid*. Kelly contended that the book did not start out as a "Book of Shadows" but "had become one—in fact, the very first one—by the time it was filled up and retired." Kelly argued that by looking at the documents it is clear that up until 1954 all the rituals were adapted from the Cabalistic procedures in the *Greater Key of Solomon*. There was, in his view, no emphasis on the Goddess as a major deity and on the high priestess as the central authority in the coven until after 1957, "when Doreen Valiente became the first such 'Gardnerian' high priestess and began to adopt Robert Graves's 'White Goddess' myth as the official thealogy of her coven." According to Kelly, it was only after the publication of *Witchcraft Today*, in 1954, that the

Goddess and the priestess became dominant. Writes Kelly: "Valiente's major work from 1954–7 was the creation of a Pagan theology on which rituals could be based; she also created rituals based on this theology by adapting the cumbersome procedures of the HOGD (Holy Order of the Golden Dawn) system to the needs of a small group. As such things go, I must consider this a major advance in magical technology."[62]

In the summer 1985 issue of *Iron Mountain,* Doreen Valiente replied to his arguments. She said that she did contribute many things to the present-day Book of Shadows of "what has come to be called Gardnerian Witchcraft," but she said her contribution was by no means as extensive as Kelly believed. She said she was not the first Gardnerian priestess and that Gardner already had a working coven when she was initiated in 1953. Valiente said the existence of a pre-1939 coven in the New Forest area did not stand or fall on an analysis of the Gardnerian documents, that independent testimony about such a coven was given to the occult writer Francis King by the writer Louis Wilkinson. Valiente then described her own search for "Old Dorothy," the high priestess who supposedly initiated Gerald Gardner in 1939. After a long search, Valiente found copies of her birth and death certificates and she asserted that her background corresponded to the account given of her in Bracelin's biography of Gardner, and that she was living in the same area on the edge of the New Forest as were Gerald Gardner and his wife in 1939. As we have seen, Ronald Hutton asserts Dorothy Clutterbuck did live in the area but probably had nothing to do with Gardner or the Craft. Valiente also asserted that Kelly was simply wrong to say that there was no emphasis on the Goddess as a major deity and on the high priestess as the central authority in the coven until 1957. "The worship of the Goddess was always there," she wrote, "and according to Gerald always had been there."[63]

In the last years of her life, Doreen Valiente revealed various pieces of information. Some can be found in her book *Witchcraft for Tomorrow,* and the Farrars' *The Witches' Way* reveals more. But there are many questions that remain unanswered. I asked Valiente, "What do you think did exist in 1939?" In a series of letters over the summer and fall of 1985, Doreen Valiente wrote that she believed Gardner did not invent the basic skeleton of the rituals. "I base this belief," she wrote, "on what old Gerald told me, and on the rather disjointed state of the rituals which he had when I first knew him. They were heavily influenced by Crowley and the O.T.O., but underneath there was a lot which wasn't Crowley at all, and wasn't the Golden Dawn or ceremonial magic either—and I had been studying all three of these traditions for years." She wrote that she believed the initiations were more or less as they are today, as were the concepts of the Goddess and the God and the role of the Priest and the Priestess. "Yes, I am responsible for quite a lot of the *wording* of the present-day rituals; *but not the framework of those rituals or the ideas upon which they are based.* On that I give you my word."

Valiente also said she never believed "Gardnerian" or any other Witchcraft rites had "a direct line to the paleolithic." On the contrary, she said, "I think that our present-day rituals bear the same sort of relationship to the ancient days that, for instance, the Sacrifice of the Mass in a present-day cathedral bears to the little ritual meal that took place under dramatic circumstances in the upper room of a tavern in Palestine somewhere around 33 A.D." She wrote that she was intrigued by Isaac Bonewits's suggestion that a group of folklorists in the 1920s got together with some Fam-Trads and some Golden Dawn Rosicrucians to produce the first modern covens in England.

Valiente also had some words that modern American Gardnerians would find surprising. Noting the tendency to use the titles of "Queen," "Lord," and "Lady," within some American covens, she wrote: "All this bowing and scraping to 'Queens' and 'Ladies' makes me sick! The only Queen whose authority I acknowledge lives in Buckingham Palace!" She claimed such ideas were introduced into America by Monique Wilson.

In 1985, the priestess she was most impressed with was Starhawk. "Some years ago," she wrote, "I did some scrying at a Sabbat, in the course of which I predicted that a new young priestess would arise who would do a great deal for the Craft in the future. When I read Starhawk's book I felt that my prediction was coming true." So I asked Valiente, "How do you assess 'validity'? What makes someone valid?" She wrote back, "Well, to paraphrase Gertrude Stein, 'a witch is a witch is a witch is a witch.' If someone is *genuinely* devoted to the ways of the Old Gods and the magic of nature, in my eyes they're valid, especially if they can use the witch powers. In other words, it isn't what people know, it's what they are."[64]

Before moving on, it should be said that some people involved with Gardnerian Witchcraft have been looking at other sources for the Craft. Donald Frew, in a 1999 article in the scholarly Pagan journal *The Pomegranate* wrote that he now believes "that a direct line of transmission can be traced from the Hermetic and Neoplatonic theurgy of late antiquity to the beginnings of the modern Craft movement in the 1930s."[65] Frew and Anna Korn went to the ancient city of Harran in Turkey, to conduct research. Frew argues that Paganism and Neo-Platonism remained active in Harran until the twelfth century, more than five hundred years after Paganism ended in the Roman Empire, and many Neoplatonists fled east. What's more, Gardner, in his writings, mentions a short Neoplatonic work by Sallustius, a friend of the Pagan emperor Julian, *On the Gods and the World.* (In some translations it's called *Concerning the Gods and the Universe.*) Frew writes that Gardner saw this text as explaining the basic theology of the Craft.

The Primary Craft Tradition: Creativity

Today most revivalist Witches in North America accept the universal Old Religion more as metaphor than as literal reality—a spiritual truth more than a geographic one. And while the first issue of *Pentagram* (in 1964) proclaimed that the old traditions were once a coherent whole that only needed to be pieced together again, many Witches never viewed Wicca monolithically and only a few dogmatists would view it so today. Bonewits's old definition of Neo-Pagan Witchcraft would now be disputed by most Wiccans. And he himself has modified his views. But he once wrote:

> "Neopagan Witchcraft" refers to people who also call themselves "followers of Wicca," "Wiccans," and "Crafters." These people are Neopagans who have a duotheistic theology (a Goddess and a Horned God), who believe firmly that once upon a time everybody in Europe worshipped the same way they do now, that the Witches were the priests and priestesses of the Universal Goddess Cult driven underground by the Christians, and that someday every ordained Witch will become the leader of a congregation of Neopagans just as their predecessors supposedly led congregations of Paleopagans.[66]

Bonewits, of course, was describing the Myth of Wicca early in its development in America, at a time when most Wiccans were newly initiated or were obsessed with re-creating "traditions." But already by 1975 this had all changed. Many Witches no longer accepted the Murrayite thesis totally. While some still talked of "unbroken traditions," few of them thought Gardner—or anyone else—had a direct line to the paleolithic caves. And people in the Craft were beginning to regard the question of origin as unimportant. Most had become comfortable with the idea of creativity and originality as the springboard to the Craft. As more and more of the Wicca came to see that there was no such thing as a totally unbroken or uncontaminated tradition, they began to reassess the meaning of their movement.

Today many Witches will speak forcefully about Pagan survivals. Many will talk about different traditions of ancient Pagan peoples and of a rich Pagan past. Many will speak of ancient mythology and folk traditions or about goddesses throughout the world. But they do not accept the Wiccan Myth as it was commonly described thirty years ago.

Many of them feel no link with the witchcraft of the Middle Ages or the seventeenth century, preferring to look farther back to the ancient Greeks, the Celts, and even the Egyptians. If they organize in "covens," it is certainly not primarily because "covens" appear in some descriptions of sixteenth- and seventeenth-century witches, but rather because groups of seven to twelve people have proved over time—in encounter groups, therapy groups, and consciousness-raising groups—to be the best size for like-minded people to work together effectively. Modern Wicca descends *in spirit* from precisely those fragments of pre-Christian beliefs and practices that nobody denies: myths, poetry, the classics, and folk customs.

The comments of Witches are instructive. Ed Fitch, creator of the Pagan Way rituals, Gardnerian priest, and one of those who was attacked in the past for adhering dogmatically to the Wiccan Myth, told me:

"I think all of us have matured somewhat. After a while you realize that if you've heard one story about an old grandmother, you've heard six or seven just like it. You realize that the hereafter must be overpopulated with grandmothers.

"People like Raymond Buckland and myself used to believe that the Craft was very ancient. For a while I think I believed the Gardnerian

Craft literally descended from rituals depicted in the paleolithic cave paintings in the Caverne des Trois Frères at Ariège, France.

"I think all of us went through this sort of thing. I know I did. But now, of course, the realization has come around to everyone that it doesn't matter whether your tradition is forty thousand years old or whether it was created last week. If there is a proper connection between you and the Goddess and the God in the subconscious, and other such forces, then that's what matters."

Ed Fitch's former wife, Janine Renée, said she felt that Murray's chief contribution was to show the prevalence of Pagan survivals in Europe. She felt the Craft was connected to horticulture and that its origins were pre-Germanic and pre-Celtic.

Gardnerian priestess Theos told me:

"I do not personally subscribe to the idea that cavemen were Witches, as many seem so eager to attempt to prove. Nor do I feel that those many later societies who related to those forces were Witches; nor am I certain that those who were accused of being Witches in the seventeenth century were into the same thing we are into in modern Wicca."

Carl Weschcke, a Craft priest in the American Celtic Tradition and the publisher of Llewellyn Press, told me that the universal Old Religion may not have existed geographically, but it existed in the Jungian sense that people were tapping a common source. "We are reaching back; we're trying to rediscover our roots. Nobody I've met seems to have a truly living tradition. Everyone seems impoverished. But it's coming to life, coming to life."

Moria, a priestess from northern California, told me:

"What good is a lineage? You either have the energy or you don't.

"I've seen a lot of people in the Craft get hung up on fragments of ritual and myth. Some people accept these fragments as a dogma. And dogma is the worst thing you can have in the Craft. The Craft has to be a living, breathing religion, something that is alive, and growing."

Many Witches expressed these same feelings. Dianic priestess Morgan McFarland of Dallas said that goddess worship had "an ancient universality about it," but that it had appeared in different places at different times, changing from place to place. Still, she said, "at this point it really doesn't matter whether or not it existed. If not, invent it! The people I know in the Craft are so desperate to bring back some balance to the Mother before she is totally raped and pillaged that we are, through that desperation, creating it or re-creating it."

The late priestess Alison Harlow took a similar position. "It doesn't matter if the Craft is ancient. What does matter is learning to accept the process of intuition that occurs, that rings a bell. When you are doing a ritual and you suddenly get the feeling that you are experiencing something generations of your forebears experienced, it's probably true.

"I don't think we will ever find a *true* history of the Craft, simply because too much time has gone by and all history is lies, often received second or third hand."

Leo Martello put it this way: "Let's assume that many people lied about their lineage. Let's further assume that there are no covens on the current scene that have any historical basis. The fact remains: they do exist *now*. And they can claim a *spiritual* lineage going back thousands of years. All of our pre-Judeo-Christian or Moslem ancestors were *Pagans!*"

A few Witches were downright cynical. Herman Slater, formerly a Craft priest in New York City and the proprietor of the occult shop The Magickal Childe told me a number of years before he died:

"I have been initiated into several traditions. All their origins are questionable. The coven I practice with *now* is democratic. We are oriented toward celebration. We are Gardnerian in outline of rituals with a lot of bullshit thrown out. We are Welsh in background and mythology. Personally, I think Murray and Lethbridge were pretty good propagandists for the movement, but that's as far as it goes."

Almost all Witches stressed the value of creating *new* rituals as opposed to being handed a lot of *old* ones on a plate. "I always stress very strongly the improvisational part of the Craft," Z Budapest said to me. "It's not rigid. Our Book of Shadows is a pattern for others to get inspired and create their own books." A Witch from Minneapolis began to describe to me "the beautiful creativity which is happening in us, which is more important than all the old texts." She said thoughtfully, "If we could really get hold of an old Book of Shadows, it probably wouldn't fit where we're at now. Today, when we have a festival, we first sit down and talk about what that festival means and how can we apply it in terms of how we live now. It makes you think. Those groups that go strictly by somebody's book are really very impoverished."

Glenna Turner, priestess of NROOGD, said, "Following traditions may be a mistake. It's more important for the Craft to answer needs we have today." And Tony Andruzzi, a Sicilian Witch from Chicago, mused, "Yes, my mother taught me a few things. But maybe she got them out of the blue! Who knows if she got these things from *her* grandmother. The important thing is that I'm *working* with a fragment. I'm not just accepting it, putting it in my pocket, burning a candle to it, or wearing it around my neck on a gold chain."

One of the most impressive statements came from the late Gwydion Pendderwen, songwriter, bard, and Craft priest. He said, "We make up all of our grandmothers. We make them up whether or not we actually had a grandmother who taught us anything or not. It doesn't matter whether the grandmother was a physical reality, or a figment of our imagination. One is subjective, one is objective, but we experience both."

Gwydion said that he did not feel the Craft was ever a single entity. "What has come down is so minimal, it could be thrown out without missing it. Objectively, there's very little that has gone from ancient to modern in direct succession. But subjectively, an awful lot is ancient. It is drawn from ancient materials. It represents archetypal patterns."

As I talked to Gwydion and heard him sing some of his songs, I remembered the long piece by him that had appeared in Hans Holzer's *The Witchcraft Report*[67] several years ago. It was on the traditions of Coeden Brith, the two hundred acres of land held by the Neo-Pagan group Nemeton. I had read those pages and had known from my own experiences there that parts of the essay were pure fantasy. "What about that fantasy?" I asked. "What do you feel about that essay now? Does it bother you? Was it a lie?"

Gwydion replied, "Yes, I wrote a fantasy. It was a desire. It was something I wished would happen. Perhaps that's why there are so many of these fantasies running around in the Craft today, and people trying to convince other people that they're true. It is certainly so much more pleasant and 'magical' to say 'It happened this way,' instead of 'I researched this. I wrote these rituals. I came up with this idea myself.'

"So I sent it to Hans Holzer and I didn't think he would print it without checking the facts. And then I began to regret it. And when it came out, I regretted it again. And I began to get inquiries from sincere people and from friends.

"Then I had a long talk with Aidan Kelly. I told him I shouldn't have done it—that Holzer was a fool and a bad journalist for not even checking the facts. But then Aidan said a most extraordinary thing. He said it didn't really matter because the *vision* I had had was a valid Craft tradition."

About thirty years ago, the sociologist Marcello Truzzi wrote:

Basically, witchcraft constitutes a set of beliefs and techniques held in secret which the novice must obtain from someone familiar with them. The normal, traditional means for obtaining such information is through another witch who knows these secrets. Traditionally, this can be done through initiation into an existing witch coven or by being told the secrets of the Craft by an appropriate relative who is a witch. Any other means of obtaining the secrets of witchcraft, such as through the reading of books on the subject or obtaining a mail-order diploma, is not a traditional means and is not considered to be legitimate by traditional witches. Because most witches today have not been traditionally initiated into the Craft, they often create other links to the orthodox as a means of gaining legitimacy. Thus, many of today's witches claim hereditary descent from some ancient witch or claim to be the current reincarnations of past witches.

In general, ascertaining the source of legitimacy in witchcraft groups is very difficult, especially since almost all claim ancient, traditional origins. However, intense investigation usually reveals that the group's secret sources are not as claimed.[68]

But just a few years later one priestess told me, "It's better to get training from experienced people, but lacking that, we just stole it out of every book we could!" And another Witch observed, "Recently, I've begun to see personalities which were once dominant in the Craft recognizing their own inadequacies, being able to admit them and become students again."

Traditionally, religions with indefensible histories and dogmas cling to them tenaciously. The Craft avoided this through the realization, often unconscious, that its real sources lie in the mind, in art, in creative work. Once people became comfortable in the Craft, the old lies began to dissolve. That they did so quickly is an insight into the flexibility of Wicca.

In a brief period many Craft leaders did complete turnarounds. Perhaps the most noteworthy of these leaders is Raymond Buckland, who, along with his wife, Rosemary, brought the Gardnerian tradition to the United States in the 1960s. In 1971 Buckland published *Witchcraft from the Inside*. Speaking as a Witch, he snubbed all "homemade" traditions:

> It says much for the success of Gerald Gardner in obtaining recognition for the Craft as a religion, for its imitators are those who, unable to gain access to a coven, have decided to start their own. These do-it-yourself "witches" would, on the face of it, seem harmless but on closer scrutiny are not so. They are causing considerable confusion to others who, seeking the true, get caught up in the false. The majority of these latter-day "witches" have usually read, or heard of, at least two books—Gardner's *Witchcraft Today* and Leland's *Aradia*. From these they pick out as much information as they feel is valid and make up whatever is missing. . . .
>
> Why do people start such "covens"? Why not wait and search? For some it is just that they have no patience. They feel so strongly for the Craft that they *must* participate in some way. By the time they eventually do come in contact with the true Craft it is too late.[69]

A mere two years later Buckland, in conflict with his own tradition, his marriage broken, created a new tradition—Seax Wicca or Saxon Wicca, a tradition that would be accessible to anyone who opened his new book, *The Tree* (1974). He now believed that there were many valid paths and that he had been guilty of a limited view "in earlier days." Writing in *Earth Religion News,* Buckland said, "While others fight over which is the oldest tradition, I claim mine as the youngest!"[70] And when *The Tree: The Complete Book of Saxon Witchcraft* appeared, it contained these words:

> Those searching for the Craft *can* have ready access to at least one branch, or tradition, of it. . . . With this, and the explanatory material, it is now possible to do what I just said, above, cannot generally be done: to initiate yourself as a Witch, and to start your own Coven.[71]

As Buckland later developed it, Seax Wicca became an accessible tradition available to anyone, and it was the first book of public Craft rituals to appear since Lady Sheba had published what were essentially (with a few modifications and a number of omissions) the Gardnerian rituals. Sheba had said the Goddess told her to do it. Her action was greeted with intense anger by many Witches, particularly Gardnerians. Reaction to Buckland's action ranged from pleasure (expressed by those who had fruitlessly searched for admittance into an existing tradition) to indifference (by most others).

Buckland wrote in *Earth Religion News* that the new tradition was created as an answer to internal conflicts in the Craft. Since most Wiccans were "tradition-oriented," he had given his tradition some historical background, a Saxon background. But: "By this I most emphatically do *not* mean that there is any claim to its liturgy being of direct descent from Saxon origins! As stated above, it is brand new."[72]

Buckland was just one example of the trend away from musty old Books of Shadow and dubious claims of ancient lineage. It could be said that he was following the most authentic and hallowed Gardnerian tradition—stealing from any source that didn't run away too fast.

5.

The Craft Today

Validity

I know of one instance where, some years ago, a person obtained the Book of Shadows of an existing coven after he had been turned down for membership in that coven. Based upon that Book of Shadows, he then established himself as a Witch, performed initiations and the people he initiated went forth into the world and formed their own covens, . . . initiating others in turn. If the first person of this pyramid were not "initiated" does this make all of the initiations invalid? I don't think so. Despite the original fraud those people went through the ceremony with sincerity and apparently received the illumination that comes with true initiation.

—JOSEPH WILSON[1]

IF ANYONE can become a member of the Wicca by reading books, if people can create their own "tradition," if one comes to the Craft out of a sense of homecoming, if the Craft works because of the archetypal content of the human mind, is there such a thing as a "valid" tradition or an "invalid" one? Is any tradition that *feels* right appropriate? How does one decide on validity in such a religion? Does one need an initiation to become a Witch? Here is a true story that may serve to illustrate this problem and provide a key to its solution.

More than thirty years ago, only two years after the beginning of my own Craft journey, I went to England and looked up Alex and Maxine Sanders. Alex Sanders had founded the Alexandrian tradition of Wicca. He claimed that in 1933, at the age of seven, he found his grandmother standing nude in a circle in the kitchen. She then initiated him into the Craft. An account of this tale can be found in June Johns's *King of the Witches* and also in Stewart Farrar's *What Witches Do.*[2]

Alex and Maxine Sanders became celebrities in London. Their pictures appeared in dozens of popular books on the occult. Many of the Alexandrian rituals have been published, and they so resemble the Gardnerian rituals that Alex's story of their origin is often questioned.

At the time I visited London, in the summer of 1973, Alex had left Maxine and she was running the coven alone, as well as conducting a training group and several occult classes. I called her up with some trepidation. I was newly initiated into the Gardnerian tradition and tended to tread softly in strange pathways. I told Maxine I was "in the Craft" and she quickly invited me to attend a circle that night. I expected her to check me out and was surprised that she did not. She asked the name of my "tradition," but little else.

I put my athame and a necklace in my bag and proceeded to the Sanders home. One entered by way of a long foyer that was quite dark. A rather prim woman in a black dress asked me my purpose. I told her I had been invited by Maxine to attend the circle, that I was an initiate from another tradition, and that I was here to see Maxine. "Maxine is very busy now," the woman told me brusquely, "but just go back and change in the loo." I was also informed that I, as a guest, would not have to pay the normal fee of fifty pence to attend the circle.

I was beset by a variety of strong emotions. Here I was, a stranger to this Wiccan circle of another tradition, invited by this priestess who, when I arrived, did not even have the time to greet me and take me in hand. And the money . . . that seemed a violation of every Craft principle I had been taught. I had brought food and wine to many circles, but had never seen a coin change hands. But, undaunted, I went into the bathroom and took off my clothes. The Alexandrians, like the Gardnerians, worked "skyclad."

As I undressed, a woman opened the bathroom door and entered. Let us call her Jane. She is the real heroine of our story. Jane easily weighed over two hundred pounds. She was young, perhaps eighteen. As she undressed, it became painfully obvious that she was nervous and scared and shy and upset about her figure. She was so heavy that her stomach hung down, making her vagina invisible. Since I myself was thirty pounds overweight, her appearance, I regret to confess, cheered me immeasurably. Here was a comrade-in-arms. I suddenly felt calm, cool, an experienced Craft priestess, a woman of the world.

Jane told me that tonight was her initiation into the Craft. She was excited and nervous. "Do you know what's to happen?" she asked me. She had been to three previous circles and a certain number of classes. I told her that I was an initiate of a tradition similar to this one and that she should not be worried; she would have a beautiful experience. Together we walked out of the bathroom—both of us completely nude except for a necklace. I had a sheathed athame in my hand. Together, we walked into this strange and darkened hall.

Everyone else had disappeared, except for the prim woman in black. "Where do we go?" I asked.

"Stay here a minute," said the woman.

Then, two young men appeared. They had taken off their shirts, but they were wearing pants. They blindfolded Jane and bound her hands behind her back. In this way, according to the Alexandrian tradition, she would be brought into the circle. I waited. "Who's the High Priestess?" one of the boys asked the woman in black. At this point I began to feel a sense of unease. Wasn't Maxine Sanders the priestess? And where *was* Maxine, anyway?

In response to the man's question the lady in black turned to him, pointed to me (standing nude in the darkness), and said, "She is."

"What?" I said, not believing her words.

"She is," the woman repeated.

I reacted with absolute amazement. "Wait a minute!" I said. "I've just stepped off the street from another country, from another tradition. I have never been in an Alexandrian circle in my entire life. I have no idea what you even *do!* I just don't think this is right at all, and anyway, I don't know how you conduct your rituals!" I was babbling by this time.

"Oh, it's all right," she replied. "It's all in the book, just follow the book!"

"No," I replied. "I won't do it. I just don't think it's right." And I began to repeat my arguments. "Here I am, a complete stranger, I just don't think this is right."

Meanwhile Jane was standing against the wall, bound and blindfolded, awaiting her sublime experience of initiation and hearing this unbelievable exchange. All of a sudden Maxine Sanders appeared, almost out of nowhere. She was dressed in a long white gown; her blond hair flowed down past her waist. She looked even more beautiful than any of the pictures I had seen of her. "What's the matter?" asked Maxine.

"She won't do it," said the woman in black, pointing at me.

I repeated my arguments to Maxine who told me, "None of the other women have shown up."

Soon several things became clear. The circle-to-be was Maxine's training coven and, within their tradition, first-degree initiations took place in this training group. The priestess of the training group had apparently left after a tantrum over some minor matter. Jane, myself, and six or seven men remained. Jane, by the way, was still standing bound and blindfolded while this explanation was going on. I still refused. Maxine accepted this and said they would make do without a priestess.

One strange event superseded another. For a few moments after we entered the room where the circle was to be held there didn't seem to be an available priest for this training group either, until Maxine threw a small fit. "What kind of Witches do we have here?" she shouted at the seven men in the room. "Why is it always the same person who volunteers?" Finally, someone put his hand up, and everything could begin.

Finally the circle was cast and the ritual was begun. Maxine Sanders listened from outside, on the other side of the room. Power was raised through dancing and chanting: "Eko, eko Azarak, Eko, eko Zamilak, Eko, eko Karnayna, Eko, eko Aradia."

The circle was fairly monotonous. The energy level seemed low, as one might imagine after the disputes. Lines were read and chants chanted without much feeling. If I hadn't still been in a state of shock, I would have been slightly bored.

Then Jane was led through the initiation ceremony. She was consecrated in the names of the God and the Goddess of the tradition: Karnayna and Aradia. She was asked if she wanted to go through with it. She did. She was welcomed with the passwords, "Perfect love and perfect trust." She was ceremonially scourged. She was given an oath. She was anointed with water and wine. She was presented each of the circle tools and welcomed into the coven. The details of this ritual can be found in Stewart Farrar's book.

At the end of the ritual everyone dressed and convened at the local pub, which seemed a much livelier place than the circle. But there was Jane, dressed once more, and her eyes positively glowing in that peculiar and extraordinary way that betokens—as sure as anything—a powerful experience inside oneself, an experience that may have begun a process of great change in her life.

And so we come to the peculiar fact that even if Sanders's story is bogus, even if there was no priestess to cast the circle, even if all the "traditions" were violated, even if untalented students botched the event, still Jane may have gone through a true rebirth.

Many in the Craft have come to see initiation as an inner process. Leo Martello, writing in the *WICA Newsletter,* notes that whereas European traditions say, "A Witch is born, not made," Anglo-American covens say, "A Witch is made, not born." Martello has often observed that a valid initiation depends more on the one receiving it than on the initiator.³ And New York City Craft priest Myrdden wrote:

> I don't think that our Goddess would deny worship . . . to someone . . . just because they were not initiated by an initiated witch. . . . Also who can tell whether the "witch" doing the initiating has really been initiated herself? . . . Many of our origins are obscure and documentary evidence . . . is not usually available, . . . [Sometimes it is] extremely difficult to locate someone who will initiate.
>
> Initiation is primarily a method to protect the institution of the Craft from people calling themselves "witches" who are insincere, "evil" or would give the Craft a bad name. But does it really stop anyone from calling himself a witch? No. . . . The mysteries and secrets of the Craft can be discovered independently of the Craft: we do not have the only way. The Gods can be discovered independently of the Craft. . . . The Gods, only, can make a witch; man can only confirm it.⁴

And Craft priest Phoenix made a similar observation:

> I have come across those who have carefully and proudly constructed their own "Traditions," initiated themselves, and have gone on to keep their secrets and to function with inspiration, sincerity and effectiveness. On the other hand, I think we have all, from time to time, had contact with those who are apparently well able to substantiate a so-called "valid

initiation" (in fact, more than likely a dozen initiations, the majority being "honorary" or otherwise non-working and non-learning) but to whom the Wicca means little or no more than a publicity gimmick, or a way of supporting themselves, a power/ego excursion. . . . Who of these, then, is *truly* of the Wicca?[5]

Who Defines the Wicca?

How do modern Witches define themselves?

Since the Craft is decentralized and each coven is autonomous, no single definition applies to all Wiccans. In the United States most attempts to create a common set of principles and definitions have met with failure, with the exception of adherence to "the Wiccan Rede." Most of those who join the Wicca do so, in part, because of its implicit autonomy—"It is religion without the 'middleman,'" to repeat the words of one Craft priest. Despite this, there have been several attempts by United States Witches to meet and define this slippery term *Witch*. One early attempt to create an ecumenical definition of modern Wicca that would be acceptable to many traditions began in the fall of 1973 when Llewellyn Publications, the occult publishers, sponsored a meeting of Witches in Minneapolis. Seventy-three Witches from different traditions attended. They formed the Council of American Witches and, during the winter of 1974, began collecting statements of principle from various groups. These were printed in the Council's newsletter, *Touchstone*.

Carl Weschcke, publisher of Llewellyn, wrote in *Touchstone* that many Witches felt that a common definition was necessary as a "self-policing" mechanism "to protect ourselves from misunderstanding brought about by those whose personal power trips have exposed all of us to ridicule and injury."[6] It was also felt that a common statement would help dispel the sensationalist image pushed in the media, which continued to link Wicca with satanism.

It turned out that there were many differences among Wiccan groups, a few of them conflicting. Here are some of the answers to the question, "What is a Witch?"

A Witch above all *worships the Triple Goddess and her Consort, The Horned God, in one form or another. A Witch works Magick within a definite code of ethics. A Witch acknowledges and uses the male-female polarity in his/her rites. A Witch takes* total *responsibility for her actions, herself, and her future.*

—NROOGD (New Reformed Orthodox Order of the Golden Dawn)

Witchcraft is an initiatory mystery religion whose adherents seek, through self-discipline, to live a life dedicated to the pursuit and practice of knowledge, wisdom and compassion under the guidance of the Gods.

—COVEN OF GWYNVYD, St. Louis, Missouri

A Witch is a member of a religion which by its own internal definition is monotheistic. [This definition was obviously in conflict with the others.]

—SCHOOL OF WICCA

Wicca can be defined as a pagan mystery religion with a polarized deity and no personification of evil.[7]

—LADY CYBELE

Some Witches refused even to take part in this process of defining the Craft, feeling that a common statement of principles implied an unacceptable degree of centralization. One Witch wrote to *Touchstone:*

> In the early days of the Church, we of the Wicca were persecuted for not joining with the common belief of the church fathers because we refused to join, be baptized or pay our tithes to their God. We were tortured, burned, hanged and placed in vats of ground glass. We preferred to live simply, worshipping our old Gods of Harvest, and doing as we had for years before, and as our fathers had done. . . .
>
> The Church sent in spies who reported on us into our worship circles, and those of us who were caught were humiliated and killed because we were as we were . . . and of course the Church wanted the money and wanted to oppress the people.
>
> Now it seems to us old Wicca that that is what you younger's are doing . . . oppressing us, trying to force us to join in an organization, and criticizing us for wanting our freedom and our belief in freedom. . . .
>
> Let us not quarrel among ourselves. Leave us be and we shall do the same for you. Worship as you see best and allow us also the same right. This is the true Wicca way . . . and the free way.
>
> —From an anonymous Witch (because it is my right to be so)[8]

Other conflicts arose between people bound by strict oaths of secrecy and others who wished to share their information openly. Some felt that little should be "secret" except for the names used for deities and initiation rituals, so that their psychological impact would not be lost. Another problem was "validity." Many felt that initiation was an internal process and that one could receive a valid initiation in a dream or vision, or even at the hands of frauds. Others felt that only certain traditions were "valid."

The groups were closest on ethics. All agreed with the basic Wiccan Creed—"An ye harm none, do what ye will." Most affirmed Aleister Crowley's famous statement: "Do what thou wilt shall be the whole of the Law. Love is the law, love under will." Most agreed that it was unethical to "forcefully violate a person's autonomy." Most affirmed the divinity of all living beings. NROOGD's statement was the strongest.

An it harm no one, do you as you will.
You may not alter another's life/karma without his permission.
Solve the problem, no more, no less. All power comes from the Goddess.
You must help your brothers and sisters in the Craft as best you can.
If you stick your hand in a flame, you'll get burned.[9]

The Council of American Witches, meeting April 11–14, 1974, in Minneapolis, finally did hammer out a statement of principles:

PRINCIPLES OF WICCAN BELIEF

The Council of American Witches finds it necessary to define modern Witchcraft in terms of the American experience and needs.

We are not bound by traditions from other times and other cultures, and owe no allegiance to any person or power greater than the Divinity manifest through our own being.

As American Witches we welcome and respect all Life Affirming teachings and traditions, and seek to learn from all and to share our learning within our Council.

It is in this spirit of welcome and cooperation that we adopt these few principles of Wiccan belief. In seeking to be inclusive, we do not wish to open ourselves to the destruction of our group by those on self-serving power trips, or to philosophies and practices contradictory to those principles.

In seeking to exclude those whose ways are contradictory to ours, we do not want to deny participation with us to any who are sincerely interested in our knowledge and beliefs, regardless of race, color, sex, age, national or cultural origins or sexual preference.

1. We practice Rites to attune ourselves with the natural rhythm of life forces marked by the Phases of the Moon and the Seasonal Quarters and Cross Quarters.

2. We recognize that our intelligence gives us a unique responsibility toward our environment. We seek to live in harmony with Nature, in ecological balance offering fulfillment to life and consciousness within an evolutionary concept.

3. We acknowledge a depth of power far greater than that apparent to the average person. Because it is far greater than ordinary, it is sometimes called "supernatural," but we see it as lying within that which is naturally potential to all.

4. We conceive of the Creative Power in the Universe as manifesting through polarity—as masculine and feminine—and that this same Creative Power lives in all people, and functions through the interaction of the masculine and feminine. We value neither above the other, knowing each to be supporting of the other. We value Sex as pleasure, as the symbol and embodiment of life, and as one of the sources of energies used in magical practice and religious worship.

5. We recognize both other worlds and inner, or psychological, worlds—sometimes known as the Spiritual World, the Collective Unconscious, the Inner Planes, etc.—and we see in the interaction of these two dimensions the basis for paranormal phenomena and magical exercises. We neglect neither dimension for the other, seeing both as necessary for our fulfillment.

6. We do not recognize any authoritarian hierarchy, but do honor those who teach, respect those who share their greater knowledge and wisdom, and acknowledge those who have courageously given of themselves in leadership.

7. We see religion, magick, and wisdom-in-living as being united in the way one views the world and lives within it—a worldview and philosophy-of-life which we identify as Witchcraft, the Wiccan Way.

8. Calling oneself "Witch" does not make a witch—but neither does heredity itself, or the collecting of titles, degrees and initiations. A Witch seeks to control the forces within him/herself that make life

possible in order to live wisely and well, without harm to others, and in harmony with Nature.

9. We acknowledge that it is the affirmation and fulfillment of life, in a continuation of evolution and development of consciousness, that gives meaning to the Universe we know, and to our personal role within it.

10. Our only animosity toward Christianity, or toward any other religion or philosophy-of-life, is to the extent that its institutions have claimed to be "the only way" and have sought to deny freedom to others and to suppress other ways of religious practice and belief.

11. As American Witches, we are not threatened by debates on the history of the Craft, the origins of various aspects of different traditions. We are concerned with our present, and our future.

12. We do not accept the concept of "absolute evil," nor do we worship any entity known as "Satan" or "The Devil" as defined by the Christian tradition. We do not seek power through the suffering of others, nor do we accept the concept that personal benefit can only be derived by denial to another.

13. We acknowledge that we seek within Nature for that which is contributory to our health and well-being.[10]

After the statement of principles was adopted, additional differences surfaced. The Council soon became moribund.

A more successful attempt to form an alliance of Wiccan groups took place in northern California on the Summer Solstice in 1975. Thirteen covens and several solitary Witches ratified the Covenant of the Goddess (COG) after a number of covens in California expressed the desire to build closer bonds, in part out of a concern over harassment and persecution.

When the meeting to form the Covenant was called in the spring of 1975, several months earlier, representatives of forty covens appeared. Many never joined. As the late Alison Harlow, an officer of COG at the time, told me, "Many came out of a desire to make sure that nothing was going to be pulled on any of their covens behind their backs."

The Covenant, like the Council, came face to face with the decentralism of the Craft. As Alison said, "How could we build an organization that, in fact, did not dictate to anyone? How could we create a charter and bylaws we could file with the state as a legal religious organization without giving away the reality of what we're doing?"

The Covenant wisely accepted the basic anarchism of Wicca as not only inevitable, but desirable. They could not define the religion:

> We could not define what a Witch is in words. Because there are too many differences. Our reality is intuitive. We know when we encounter someone who we feel is worshipping in the same way, who follows the same religion we do, and that's our reality, and that has to be understood, somehow, in anything we do.

When the Covenant of the Goddess organized, Aidan Kelly suggested that it base its structure on the bylaws and charter of the Congregational Churches, so that it would be a religious body governed by autonomous congregations—in other words, covens—and not by ruling popes or bishops (or priests and priestesses, for that matter). This suggestion was adopted and Aidan wrote many of the bylaws. Originally, the "members" of the Covenant were covens and each coven got two votes on the Covenant's council. When there were enough covens (five) in a local area, a local council was formed to handle its own affairs.

Some of the items in COG's philosophy are instructive in understanding the eclectic nature of modern Wicca. For example, take the Preamble to the Covenant, as summarized by Alison Harlow in *The Witches' Trine:*

> We establish this Covenant to bring us closer together and to help us serve the Craft and the Pagan Community.
>
> We define ourselves: (1) We all worship the Goddess, and may others honor other deities. (2) We are bound by Craft law, not necessarily identical in all traditions. (3) We recognize each other as being in the Craft.
>
> We are not the only Witches. Witches who do not choose to join us are nonetheless Witches.
>
> Each coven is autonomous. Any authority given to the covenant is by the choice of each coven, and can be withdrawn.[11]

In addition, the charter made clear that the Church or Covenant could not dictate policy, belief, or practice; that it could not, by itself, create a coven or initiate a Witch. Its board of directors had to consist—at all times—of members of more than one tradition.

Its code of ethics was also illuminating:

1. An ye harm none, do as ye will.
2. No one may offer initiations for money, nor charge initiates money to learn the Craft.
3. Any Witch may charge reasonable fees to the public.
4. Witches shall respect the autonomy of other Witches.
5. All Witches shall respect the secrecy of the Craft.
6. In any public statement Witches should distinguish whether we are speaking for ourselves, our coven, or our Church.
7. All these Ethics are interwoven and derive from Craft Law.*

Today COG has more than one hundred member covens and fifteen local councils, and continues to be an important organization.

When you ask Witches for their personal definitions of Witchcraft, they are much richer than these more formal statements. In answering the questions, "What does it mean to be a Witch? What does it feel like?" almost everyone stressed that it was, more than anything, an attitude toward life—a way of living.

Z Budapest told me, "I relate to the Goddess every day, in one way or another. I have a little chitchat with Mommy. I love my freedom. I love my independence. I like to be silent. I can go for days by myself. I like to reach out to crowds. I see the presence of the Goddess everywhere, how she's given me this or that—even hamburgers. I've gotten a whole lot of nourishment from this religion; it has maintained me through difficult times.

"A Witch's approach to life is one that says, 'When evil comes upon you, turn it around, make it work for you.' It means to bend; to be wise.

"Also, the past is a mirror. And the Craft presents women with their past. They look into this mirror and say, 'Look at what we did back

---

*Several lists of Craft Laws—such as those that come by way of Gardner and Sanders—have been published. Several versions of these laws are in Aidan Kelly's "The Rebirth of Witchcraft: Tradition and Creativity in the Gardnerian Reform," unfortunately unpublished. Published versions can be found in many places, including *The Grimoire of Lady Sheba* and Stewart Farrar's *What Witches Do.*

then! We are strong.' They look into this mirror and they like what they see and, eventually, they say, 'Let's do something *more!*'

"And being a priestess of the Craft means responsibility for the collective experiences of the circles I am serving. It means being sensitive to those in the circle. I can touch on my divinity and, also, I can be a tool for others' growth."

Alison Harlow told me that Wicca implies a "sense of connectedness, of cherishing all the forms in which life manifests." Janine Renée said that being a Witch means "trying on the archetypes within you and *becoming them,* by taking on these archetypal powers, expanding the ego until it stands with the gods, and drawing strength from these roots, now, in a world where so much strength has been atrophied by depersonalization."

Others did not stress such cosmic goals—some even found them objectionable. "I'd be happy if most Witches stopped trying to become like the gods," said the late Leo Martello, "and simply developed as human beings." Many stressed that the Craft was a lifestyle. Cybele told me, "It's a way of viewing yourself as a very natural being. You are at one with the stones and at one with the stars. It stresses practical knowledge, not blind belief. It's practical. It permeates absolutely everything I do. Craft people haven't lost touch with what's real. They haven't allowed themselves to be bombarded with stimuli, or, if they have at one point in their lives, they've found their way back." Bran Tree, a Witch, said, "A Witch is someone who sees more than the mundane things of life, who can become excited over the feel of a pebble or the croak of a frog," and Aidan Kelly told me, "What really defines a Witch is a type of *experience* people go through. These experiences depend on altered states of consciousness. The Craft is really the Yoga of the West." Morning Glory Zell-Ravenheart said that a Witch is a type of European shaman, and being a Witch involves being a priestess or priest, a psychopomp, a healer, a guide. "It is the sum of those things. You sense a community. The community may be the whole world or a handful of people."

Most Witches stressed that the goal of the Craft was helping people to reclaim their lost spiritual heritage, their affinity with the earth, with "the gods," with the infinite. Most said it was not a religion for everyone. Many felt the religion would always be small. Many felt the "fad of the occult" was ending; their response to that was relief. Some emphasized the pragmatic side of the religion—practical magic to get various jobs done. Others emphasized the experience of ecstasy and joy. Still others expressed larger goals: responding to the needs of the planet in crisis, or actualizing the divinity within oneself.

How Many Are the Wicca?

How many Wiccans are there in the United States? Again, the decentralism of the Craft makes all estimates suspect. The Witch Sybil Leek estimated that there were "several thousand covens in the United States" in 1971.[12] Sociologist Marcello Truzzi put the figure at three hundred.[13]

Susan Roberts wrote in *Witches U.S.A.:* "Witches don't know how many of them there are—much less where they are. There is no census, no master mailing list. Anyone who claims to have such a list is either lying or deluded."[14] At most, one can make an estimate from the number of people who subscribe to Neo-Pagan and Craft publications, or attend Pagan festivals, but both would be a fraction of the total number. Most of the people I have met who are in covens don't subscribe to *any* Neo-Pagan journals, and most don't attend festivals. And I am continually surprised to find new covens who have created themselves after reading a few introductory books or hearing a few lectures. Since most covens are autonomous, there is no way to compile accurate statistics. While such and such a tradition with a line of apostolic succession may have a record of thirty or forty covens, and another tradition a record of fifty, there is no way to estimate the frequency of the spontaneous creation of new covens and new traditions through the reading of books. It is impossible to know how many people have, let us say, heard a radio interview, gone to their local library and emerged two years later with a "tradition" or started a coven. There may be many groups that have no links with what we have been calling the Neo-Pagan movement. Many may not even have heard the term. Since some of the most vital Craft traditions—NROOGD, for one—started this way, it is a valid route.

In 1985, I estimated that there were fifty thousand to one hundred thousand self-identified Pagans and Wiccans in the United States. By the year 2000, I had doubled the larger number and was saying that I thought the figure was closer to 200,000. I now think that there are double that number, although no one really knows.

There have been numerous attempts to figure how many Pagans there are, most of them are flawed, including my own. More than twenty-five years ago, J. Gordon Melton, who heads the Institute for the Study of American Religion, posed an odd question in a survey of Pagans: Do you own a copy of *The Golden Dawn?* Since only fifteen thousand copies of this book had been published, Melton used the percentage that said yes as a base to then extrapolate the number of Neo-Pagans in the United States. He came up with the number, forty thousand, and doubled it within five years. Today, you can find a number of academics and other writers who have attempted to give better figures for Wicca and for Paganism, both in the United States and worldwide. You can find many of their attempts on a Web site called Adherents.com. There you can find various figures for more than four thousand religious groups. As they say on the Web site, it's the kind of place you go to if you want to know how many Lutherans there are in Florida. On one page they list the top twenty-two religions by number of adherents. Christianity tops the list at 2.1 billion. Islam is 1.3 billion. Neo-Paganism is a surprising number nineteen at one million adherents. That's a lot bigger than I would have guessed. If you look further on the site, you get all kinds of estimates by writers and scholars. And although there are some that are clearly questionable—estimates of ten thousand and five million—most estimates of the number of Wiccans in the United States range between two hundred thousand and seven hundred thousand. Some of the estimates are for Neo-Pagans, others are for Witches, and in some cases it's not clear. Many scholars give estimates somewhere in the middle of that range (Helen Berger, Aidan Kelly), between one hundred and fifty thousand and three hundred thousand. The American Religious Identification Survey (ARIS), a telephone poll taken in 2001, estimated, after factoring in a large number who refused to disclose their religion, and then adding children, that there were about 750,000 Wiccans in the United States (www .religioustolerance.org/wic_nbr3.htm). I will talk more about numbers in Chapter 13, but that's a very large increase since the last edition of *Drawing Down the Moon.*

Sabbats and Esbats—How Covens Work

A coven simply means a group of people who convene for religious or magical or psychic purposes. Not all Witches form covens. Certainly the "Classical Witches" of Bonewits's description were most often solitary, and many scholars would argue that the idea of covens was an invention of those who persecuted Witches that was later adopted by the revival. Among the Gardnerian and Alexandrian Craft laws is one that states, "Ye May Not Be a Witch Alone." So, one would think that at least there are no solitary Gardnerian or Alexandrian Witches, but even that isn't true—many Gardnerians and Alexandrians have decided to function without covens. (In this religion there is an exception to *everything*.)

Whether the word and concept of *coven* was invented by Witches or by Witch hunters, it works. A traditional coven in Wicca is twelve or thirteen, but in practice it is any number from three to twenty, depending on the group's philosophy, the size of the working circle (if it's nine feet in diameter, twelve is a crowd!), and the available members. Again, the coven works, not because of its mysterious nature, but because small groups, working together, are effective.

Some covens work in couples, emphasizing male/female polarity. These will be even-numbered. Other covens do not emphasize polarity and may be more flexible in number and size.

Most Wiccan covens work within a circle, "a portable temple," as one Witch wrote to me. Certain groups in England have been known to set up a psychic "castle," and many Witches will tell you that their circle is really a sphere. The circle is the declaration of sacred ground. It is a place set apart, although its material location may be a living room or a backyard. But in the mind the circle, reinforced by the actions of casting it and purifying it, becomes sacred space, a place "between the worlds" where contact with archetypal reality, with the deep places of the mind—with "gods," if you will—becomes possible. It is a place where time disappears, where history is obliterated. It is the contact point between two realities. It is common for Witches to contrast their circle with the circle of the ceremonial magician. The Wiccan circle is not a "protection from demons" but a container of the energy raised.

Craft ritual usually starts with casting and creating this magical space and ritually purifying it with the ancient elements: fire, water, earth, and air. The circle is cast with a ritual sword, wand, or athame (a small, usually black-handled and double-bladed dagger that is used by almost all covens, whatever their tradition). Different covens have different symbologies, but often the sword represents air, the wand represents fire, the cup water, and the pentacle—a round, inscribed disk of wax or metal—earth.[15] When the circle is cast, often the gods and goddesses are invoked.

Some covens use music, chanting, and dancing to raise psychic energy within the circle. Psychic healing is often attempted, with varying degrees of success. The most common form of "working" is known as "raising a cone of power." This is done by chanting or dancing (or both) or running around the circle. The "cone of power" is really the combined wills of the group, intensified through ritual and meditative techniques, focused on an end collectively agreed upon. Usually a priestess or priest directs the cone; when she or he senses that it has been raised, it is focused and directed with the mind and shot toward its destination.

Many covens also engage in more "spiritual" or "religious" workings. Many of the revivalist covens have rituals in which the Goddess, symbolized by the moon, is "drawn down" into a priestess of the coven who, at times, goes into trance and is "possessed by" or "incarnates" or "aspects" the Goddess. Similarly, there are rituals where the God force is drawn down into the priest who takes the role of the God in the circle. In these rituals Witches *become* the gods within the circle, actualizing that potentiality. When done well, these can be among the most powerful experiences. I have seen people really change in such rituals. I have also seen these rituals become shams.

This is perhaps the place to talk about sexual rites, which are often described in popular books on Wicca. I have found very few covens that engage in explicitly sexual rituals. Many use sexual symbolism and poetry, but rarely is the sex act actualized. The reason for this is a strange one. Most coven leaders I have talked to feel that incorporating sex into rituals is playing with explosive chemicals, because the people in their covens are simply not ready for it. Of course, there are some groups that do use sex in ritual. And, in its highest form, the "Great Rite," often alluded to by the media, is a sublime religious experience. Properly understood, it is not—as the press would have us believe—the carryings on of bored suburban swingers. The idea behind the "Great Rite" is that a woman who, through ritual, has "incarnated" or *become* the Goddess, and a man who, through ritual, has "incarnated" or *become* the God—in other words, two people who have drawn down into themselves these archetypal forces, or, if you will, have allowed these forces within them to surface—can have a spiritual and psychical union that is truly divine. It is the modern form of the sacred marriage, or "hierogamy," that appears in many ancient religions.

Most covens meet for spiritual, psychic, and social types of "work." I have known covens that wrote poetry, others that put on mystery plays or simply worked for the good of their members. I have known covens that created astral temples to Athena and Demeter, or spent most of their time in reforestation work, or put their energy into the feminist movement.

Most covens meet at "esbats." Most scholars believe Murray invented this term. These are working meetings that can occur at the full moon, or the new moon, or every weekend, or once a week, or whenever. Covens also usually meet on the "sabbats," the eight great festivals of European Paganism, the Quarter days and the Cross Quarter days. The lesser four are the solstices and the equinoxes. The greater sabbats are: *Samhain* (Halloween or November Eve), the Celtic New Year, the day when the walls between the worlds were said to be thinnest and when contact with one's ancestors took place; Imbolc, or Oimelc (February 1), the winter purification festival, the time of the beginning of spring movement; *Beltane* (May 1), the great fertility festival, the marriage of God and Goddesses; *Lughnasadh* (August 1), the festival of first fruits and, in some traditions, the time of the fight between the bull and stag god for the Lady, or the death of the Sacred King. These are the briefest of descriptions, and different Craft traditions, following different myth cycles from different parts of Europe, treat the festivals in diverse ways. But almost all traditions at least celebrate Samhain and Beltane.

These festivals renew a sense of living communion with natural cycles, with the changes of season and land. But many Wiccans, almost always an innovative group, are perfectly capable of changing the festivals and their meanings. As one priestess from a city in Ohio remarked to me, "We were sitting around trying to decide what we were going to do for the Summer Solstice [June 21]. What did the solstice mean to us here?

And we realized it didn't mean a hell of a lot. So why were we celebrating? We decided that we would try and celebrate new festivals, tied in to things that really mean something to us."

In fact, a few Witches have totally rebelled against most of the festival rituals that have come down to them. One man wrote to me:

> Most Craft rituals that I've observed are completely absurd, because they're rooted in traditions alien to the people who are performing them. Very few people involved in re-created Celtic Paganism even bother to learn Old Irish or Welsh, let alone go beyond that and really try to understand what the various symbolisms were supposed to mean. . . . I've been trying to get together a group of people to invent a Pagan ritual based on modern English and symbolism that has real meaning to a modern American.
>
> Everyone says, "That's obvious," when I point out the true modern equivalent to a sword to a modern American, even a "liberated" one, is a .38 police special—like they see on TV shows—or a military rifle, or possibly the Colt .45 of Western movies, but swords are still used in magical and Pagan rites and people think it's absurd to even suggest substituting guns.

Personally I have no desire to handle guns, and swords have a beauty and romanticism that I find acceptable, but the point is well taken; many feel that the festivals and rituals of Wicca must begin to fit changing times and needs.

The deities of most Wicca groups are two: the God, the lord of animals, lord of death and beyond, and the Goddess, the Triple Goddess in her three aspects: Maiden, Mother, and Crone. Each aspect is symbolized by a phase of the moon—the waxing crescent, the full moon, and the waning crescent. In general, there is a great divergence among the Wicca as to what these "gods" are. Are they thought forms, built up over centuries? Are they archetypes? Are they literal entities? The answer depends on whom you talk to.

The names used for the gods also differ, depending on tradition and group. Most often the names are Celtic, Greek, or Latin. Most Witches do say that the polytheistic personification of the gods is what allows them to make contact with Divine Reality; that while Divine Reality may ultimately be unknowable, personification allows one to begin to approach it.

Most Witches believe in some form of reincarnation. Many believe in the "threefold law": that whatever you do returns to you threefold. Some Witches don't believe in the threefold law, but most believe that you get back what you give out. And I must stress that I have met priests and priestesses in the Craft who are agnostic on all "beliefs," who joined the Craft simply because they found its poetry beautiful or its "path" self-actualizing.

Some covens meet in robes, some in street clothes. Some work nude—the revivalist term is "skyclad"—generally because of the freedom they feel nudity engenders or because of its leveling quality. Gardner may be responsible for much of the nudity in the Craft. Many covens in the United States follow the sensible custom of nudity in the summer and clothes in the winter.

Most covens have an entry or initiation ceremony. Sometimes it's very simple; sometimes it's complex, involving a test, an oath, and a symbolic rite of death and rebirth. The concept of initiation is certainly a rich one. A woman who had just been initiated into a coven wrote:

The push in the Magic Circle was like the slap given the newborn, welcoming it into a new life. The room was crowded with people I could not see, but whose presence made me feel I was on a witness stand.

My ankle was tied—neither bound nor free. What is this strange state of limbo that causes me to run in circles, stumbling as I do in every-day life . . . but not really circles? I felt I was racing through a long tunnel. In a sense I felt bound in a special way to living my life with a fresh consciousness, glowing and unconfined . . . a dedication of who I really am . . . a responsibility. My forehead on the altar awakened me: my mind must become the altar for the Mother, my body the living temple for the Gods.

The abrupt, almost harsh order to kneel reminds me of the kind of acceptance I must make when things in my life do not go pleasantly for me.

Blood rushing through every cell in my body felt warm and glowing. I am Blessed![16]

ʼraft Traditions

...awing Down the Moon* was first published, it was pretty easy to
...ibe Wicca traditions: There was Gardnerian, Alexandrian, Dianic,
Georgian, NROOGD, and Continental, which meant anything from
Strega (Italian) to several other European offshoots. There was something
called "Traditional Wicca," but it wasn't exactly clear what it was. At this
point, twenty-five years down the road, there are many more traditions
and many more offshoots from those traditions. But one truism is still
valid. In the same way that judging a good psychotherapist usually has
nothing to do with whether he or she was trained as a Jungian, a Freudian,
an Adlerian, a behaviorist, or whatever—that the issue is the art, the
style, and the humanity of that particular therapist—similarly, the tradition of a coven may be somewhat important, or it may be the least
important thing about the group. It's also important to note that thirty-
five years ago, when I was first looking for a group, most seekers had no
knowledge of different traditions. All of us neophytes ended up with
the group that happened to be in the neighborhood. Today it is very different. Anyone can go on the Web, look up www.witchvox.com on the
Internet and find pages and pages on different Wiccan traditions and their
history, with accurate and even scholarly information on each one. At last
glance, there were fifty-seven essays on different traditions on the Web
site. Most, but not all of them were Wiccan. A simple Web search will get
you hundreds of other articles on different Wiccan traditions. I am listing only a dozen traditions here; I included only five in the last edition.

Stewart Farrar had some fairly amusing things to say about "traditions" in his book *What Witches Do*. He wrote:

> The Hereditary witches are those, of course, who have kept the Craft
> alive in a direct family line. The theory is that those lines descend unbro-
> ken from the Old Religion itself; how true this is only the families know,
> if indeed they do know.

Turning to the "Traditional," Farrar observed wryly:

> Quite what it is that the Traditionals do (except that they apparently wear
> robes for their rites) I cannot say. They keep themselves to themselves,
> and I have never to my knowledge met one. . . .

Then he turns to the Gardnerians and Alexandrians, whose history is fairly easy to chart.

Most descriptions of traditions fall flat because they concentrate on the *forms*—the rituals, for example, which lose almost everything in description—and ignore the eternals, the nonverbal things, the experience of people. To quote Farrar again, the "detail of form" does not matter, "but the spirit and whether it works" matter greatly. In all the descriptions of traditions that follow it should be remembered that these differences are important for their richness and diversity, but most people join "the Craft" and *not* a particular tradition. Farrar, for example, joined the Craft because he found "its symbolism beautiful, its ritual satisfying, its tolerance (and indeed encouragement) of individual attitudes civilized, its deep roots nourishing, its small-group organization comradely and effective. . . ."[17] It just happened to be an Alexandrian coven he wandered into on a newspaper assignment.

Similarly, Valiente writes:

> I have danced at the Witches' Sabbat on many occasions, and found carefree enjoyment in it. I have stood under the stars at midnight and invoked the Old Gods; and I have found in such invocations of the most primeval powers, those of Life, Love and Death, an uplifting of consciousness that no orthodox religious service has ever given me.[18]

The fact that Valiente worked with Gardner at one time really seems irrelevant. Most people who join the Craft join the "tradition" that happens to be "around," that exists in their particular area. And no matter what "tradition" they enter, the stories of how and why they entered the Craft are similar. For example, New York City priest Lyr ab Govannon described his entry into the Craft:

"I entered a Protestant seminary at the age of nineteen, partly because I came from a cultural milieu in which this was a high calling and partly because I am an innately religious person. But within a very short time I began to have doubts about what I was being prepared to teach.

"Then one day, I came across *King Jesus* by Robert Graves. The book treats Jesus as a Sacred King in the old tradition. It was a startling idea to me. Midway through the book there is a chapter in which Jesus seeks out Mary the Hairdresser, a priestess of the older religion which worshipped the Goddess, whom Mary calls, 'My Lady of The First Eve,' meaning Lilith. Pow! There was a concept of the deity as feminine, not just a subsidiary Virgin Mary, but THE big one.

"A year later, Robert Graves came out with *The White Goddess,* and by then I knew what he was talking about and I agreed. From then, it was a long odyssey in search of . . . my people, I suppose . . . and believe me, I found some of them in pretty peculiar places. And we were always surprised to meet each other, because each of us thought we were somehow singular.

"I found the Goddess worshipped in a lot of places, under a lot of different names. And I sometimes found lip service being given Her when it was actually the same old patriarchal image that was being perpetuated. In Vedanta, for example, the great Sri or saint is Ramakrishna, a man who had been an intense devotee of the Divine Mother all of his life. He was drunk with Her! But his so-called followers do not pay homage to the Goddess. They worship a good old patriarchal image, Sri Ramakrishna.

"I began candle meditations and began to get flashes of pictures. I was led step by step. One time I saw a tall figure in the distance. It was a woman in a long cloak. The cloak hid everything but her face, and from that face there was a brightness so that I couldn't see her features. Often, I felt I had little choice in my direction. I fought against it, but was drawn back again.

"One day, a fellow sent me a book called *The Divine Mother.* It was like the top of my head came off. There were other worshippers. Not just one or two, but groups. I heard about a Witchcraft magazine called *The New Broom,* and then an organization called Nemeton. Suddenly everything seemed to blossom, and I moved into the mainstream of the Craft."

Carolyn Clark, a priestess from St. Louis, also described her process of entry:

"I got interested in Witchcraft when I was twelve. When I was a little kid, about nine or ten, I had the good fortune to live on the outskirts of a small town, surrounded by woods, and I used to go out in the woods and take a candle with me and find a tree stump and put the candle up, light it, bring flowers, and pour out a little honey, usually, because I didn't have any wine, to make an offering to Apollo and Diana.

"I read everything I could about Witchcraft and the paranormal. I took the School of Wicca's correspondence course, but since I was primarily interested in goddess worship, I ended up creating my own tradition.

"It was difficult. I had to find the sources. I raided the St. Louis public library to find books on Celtic mythology. I tried to track down the Tain and the Mabinogion. I picked up a little here and there. I had a few contacts and I began to put together a tradition and some rituals.

"I was turned on to the Goddess. It was the religion. I didn't care if I acquired any personal power. The Goddess just sort of flicked her finger and said, 'Hey!'"

These stories, more than any of the traditions, reveal the nature of the Craft. The people I meet rarely enter a tradition out of deliberate choice. They seek "the Craft." They get in contact, perhaps, with whatever group they run into. This group or coven gives them a plan of study, often lasting a year, sometimes more or less. Then, if they seem to mesh with the people of that group, they enter it. Usually that coven has a particular practice and tradition, but often that's the least important thing that's going on. Obviously, the tradition *can* matter. A person may respond to a particular myth cycle or a particular set of rituals, but often these are not the essentials. Often a person may enter a Wicca *in spite of* a particular tradition, like this woman who spent a number of years with a Welsh-oriented group:

"I am a Witch. A Witch is a person who uses one set of tools—gods, rituals, and objects—to do the same things other Pagans do. For me, the Craft is my way of actualizing myself, my life; I am constantly exploring why this is so. The only real answer I can give is that there is an affinity between me and the Craft. But I do not know why that affinity and not some other. Perhaps it is because my anima has been rising and in rising has met the Goddess. But there are forms of goddess worship other than the Craft, and other crafts than goddess worship.

"The Craft is home to me. Not to say I do not have problems with it, and by 'it' I mean my own particular 'tradition.' I do not like hierarchical structure and some of its means of expressing itself via dualities which may or may not be part of nature. There are aspects of my tradition that institutionalize things I do not find institutionalized in myself. These are real problems.

"But I name myself Witch. I am named Witch, and Witch I am and I like it. But both me and my craft are *always* changing. It is discovering what will endure.

"I do not believe Witches are different from other people, or that they have different powers. The Craft has helped me actualize these aspects of my being. I have allowed them in me."

Although the Craft is eclectic by nature, there are some useful distinctions that can be made about each "tradition" within it.

TRADITIONALIST WICCA

Despite Farrar's humorous remark that the only thing he knows about "traditionalist" Witches is that they wear robes (which actually isn't necessarily true), there *are* many covens in the United States that call themselves "traditionalist," but that can mean several different things. Some covens follow the myths and folk traditions of a particular country and regard those traditions as more important than the forms of the Wiccan revival. For example, a "Welsh traditionalist" coven that I knew of used the Welsh Mabinogion myth cycle as the prime source for its rituals, poetry, and the names of its deities. The "tradition" of this coven was really the heritage of literature and scholarship related to the pre-Christian beliefs of the Welsh people. Besides groups defining themselves by a particular country—Irish traditionalists, Greek traditionalists, Scots traditionalists, etc., there are hundreds of covens in this country and in Europe that consider themselves British Traditional Wicca, or Traditional Craft Wicca, or similar names. This is a complex group of traditions and coven lines, many of which have links to the Gardnerian and Alexandrian traditions, but which have important histories of their own. A few of the groups listed below fall into this category.

GARDNERIAN

As we have seen, many Wiccans use this word to describe those covens in the United States that descend in a line of "apostolic succession" from Gardner's coven on the Isle of Man. Of the Witches quoted in this book, several came to Wicca through this route, including Rosemary and Ray Buckland, who started a Gardnerian coven in the United States in 1964; Theos and Phoenix of Long Island, who took over the Buckland coven in 1972; the late Donna C. Schultz; and Athena, the priestess and scientist.

But, as we have also seen, the term *Gardnerian* can be used to describe covens that use Gardnerian rituals, many of which are publicly available. Occasionally these covens call themselves Neo-Gardnerian or Gardnerian eclectic.[19] Some of the more well-known external elements of Gardnerian Witchcraft include: the 162 (more or less) Craft Laws, now accepted by many covens; ritual nudity; a circle of nine feet; the symbolic use of the scourge to purify; a quasi-ceremonial form of casting the circle with similarities to rituals in the *Key of Solomon;* the use of the "Great Rite," either symbolically or actually; the Charge of the Goddess, written by Doreen Valiente, but derived from *Aradia;* three degrees of advancement; and the ritual known as the Drawing Down of the Moon.

C. A. Burland, the English writer and ethnographer, wrote of this tradition in *The Magical Arts:*

> [These covens] studied the subject, and mostly held their ritual dances around a magic circle in houses. They realized that the ancient rituals have to be revived, and used a magic circle with symbols of the kind shown in sixteenth-century paintings. The priestess was equipped with her two traditional knives, the black and white knife, and wore necklace and tiara. Many prayers were used, and they are again of older origin, some coming from *Aradia.* The purpose of the movement has been to bring peace of heart to its members and to help them to gain a knowledge of the powers of Nature which witches have always known as a kind mother force.[20]

Although it was back in 1939 that Gardner met the Fellowship of Crotona and was initiated into a coven, Fred Lamond, a long-time British Gardnerian and the author of *Religion Without Beliefs* (1997) and *Fifty Years of Wicca* (2004), asserts that Gardnerian Wicca really took off in 1953, when Gardner initiated Doreen Valiente and Valiente rewrote Gardner's Book of Shadows, transforming it into the version that has become authoritative today.

Most Gardnerian covens in the United States have a matrilineal system that passes leadership through successive priestesses. Each coven is autonomous. Most covens stress a balance between male and female principles. Some are quite flexible. The late priestess Donna C. Schultz, who led a Gardnerian coven in Chicago, told me that her group often wore robes, had abandoned the use of the scourge, and played down much of the sexual symbolism. Instead, they stressed more general forms of occult practice. Other covens are quite rigid and "by the book."

Many Gardnerian covens spend more time with their "family of covens"[21] than in ecumenical activities with other Neo-Pagan/Craft groups.

Many Gardnerian rituals can be found in *The Witches' Way* by Janet and Stewart Farrar. Some of the rituals have also been published in *Lady Sheba's Book of Shadows*. Three of Gardner's books are also relevant: *High Magic's Aid, Witchcraft Today,* and *The Meaning of Witchcraft.*[22]

Many different traditions and "lines" have come out of the original Gardnerian covens, including the Sheffield Line, begun by Pat Crowther, one of Gardner's initiates, although apparently she would never name it such, as well as the Whitecroft Line, begun by Eleanor Rae Bone, another initiate. Gardner's last high priestess was Monique Wilson. Wilson initiated Ray Buckland. The Long Island Gardnerians began when Ray Buckland and his wife, Rosemary, brought the Gardnerian Tradition to America.

ALEXANDRIAN

The Alexandrian tradition comes out of the coven started by Alex Sanders in England, the same coven into which "Jane" was initiated.* In the 1970s and 1980s it often seemed as if half the photos of Witchcraft rituals in the media depicted Alex and Maxine. Alex claimed he was initiated into the Craft by his grandmother in 1933. But, according to Ronald Hutton, in *The Triumph of the Moon,* Sanders was initiated into what seems to have been a Gardnerian coven, by a priestess named Medea, in 1963.[23] Alex told his story at a time when many Witches were creating fabulous tales about their origins. Many Alexandrian rituals are almost identical to Gardnerians ones, but there is more of a sense of theatrics and more emphasis on ceremonial magic.

Whatever the truth, Sanders did much to popularize the Craft. Perhaps one of his most astute acts was to initiate the English journalist

*See pp. 92.

Stewart Farrar, whose books are among the better introductory books on modern Wicca. Farrar later formed his own coven and went his own way.

Many Alexandrian covens formed in the United States. Very few maintained any connection with Sanders.

Mary Nesnick, an American who was initiated into both Gardnerian and Alexandrian traditions, combined them in 1972 and created a new tradition called Algard.

A number of vibrant traditions in the United States have combined Gardnerian and Alexandrian Wicca. Many simply call themselves British Traditional Wicca, or in Europe, Traditional Craft Wicca. Among the many traditions that have come out of the Gardnerian and Alexandrian fulcrum are the Kingstone, Greencraft, Mohsian, and Silver Crescent. Others, like the 1734 tradition, have added more shamanic and mystical elements.

1734 TRADITION

The 1734 tradition is based on the philosophy of Robert Cochrane, a British Witch whom Doreen Valiente once called "perhaps the most powerful and gifted personality to have appeared in modern witchcraft." According to an article on the tradition, by Chas Clifton, written for *The Witches' Voice,* Valiente joined Cochrane's circle after she left Gerald Gardner's coven.[24]

Cochrane became involved in the Craft in the early 1950s, and eventually formed a coven called The Clan of Tubal Cain. He was known to love poetry and riddles, and the name 1734 is apparently a riddle that involves the name of the Goddess. During the 1960s, Cochrane corresponded with Joseph Wilson, who published one of the earliest American Wiccan journals, *The Waxing Moon.* While Joseph Wilson and Cochrane never met, and Cochrane died in 1966, Wilson later went to England and met several members of Cochrane's coven. The correspondence between Wilson and Cochrane led to the 1734 tradition.

It is only recently that 1734 has been considered a tradition. It is said that no two covens in the 1734 tradition are exactly alike, and all of them are autonomous. There is no central authority, no common liturgy or Book of Shadows, although Cochrane's letters and articles have been passed around and are currently available on Web sites. Clifton writes in an article in *The Witches' Voice* that the letters between Wilson and Cochrane have been so widely circulated that many of the people who had them just thought that they were "traditional Craft."

> You cannot trace the precise movement of Cochrane's teachings into the American Craft scene, but his letters to Joe Wilson flowed in underground pathways. Never published (although they are now on the Web at Wilson's www.metista.com site), they were retyped and re-photocopied and, no doubt, at some times their authorship was obscured and they became simply "traditional." They appealed to the creators of the new American Witchcraft because they spoke in hints and in riddles rather than laying down dogma. Sometimes these riddles inspired other riddles, or they became the challenge laid down before new students. Bits of what Cochrane had written were mixed with later material by his students and from other sources to produce a stew of "traditional British Witchcraft" that influenced many North American practitioners in the 1960s and 1970s—as well as later.[25]

Joseph Wilson, who considered himself the founder of the 1734 tradition, died in 1994, but his Web site is still available to the public. He describes the 1734 tradition in this way:

> 1734 is a mystical tradition within a strong religious context rather unlike the other "Craft" or neopagan traditions you may have encountered. Its focus is on bringing about a change within the participant through work with certain elements that may be vaguely similar to the Zen Koan—but which are certainly different from that. This is sort of an accumulation of, or a creation of, a "personal power" which comes about not from what you know, but from what you are. . . . It's a means of strengthening oneself and in the process of opening oneself up in a manner that allows communication with spirit and spirits without delusion while maintaining control. In a nutshell it is the skill of understanding and communicating in the language of poetic metaphor, the true language of the spirits.[26]

Today, quite a few covens have been influenced by the 1734 tradition. Clifton says that Cochrane's letters to Joe Wilson conveyed a mystical Pagan teaching, but had little to say about ritual and coven organization, so the groups often borrowed from the generic Gardnerian Craft—such things as casting the circle, using invocations at the four quarters, and using the Drawing Down the Moon ritual. Most of the covens that trace their lineage to the 1734 tradition use dance, chant, and trance. Clifton also writes that there is a certain flavor to 1734 covens: a love of the outdoors and a more mystical and shamanic orientation. In one of the letters to Joseph Wilson, Robert Cochrane wrote:

> As you have gathered we teach by poetic inference, by thinking along lines that belong to the world of dreams and images—there is no hard and fast teaching technique, no laid down scripture or law, for wisdom comes only to those who deserve it, and your teacher is yourself seen through a mirror darkly. The answers to all things are in the Air—Inspiration, and the winds will bring you news and knowledge if you ask them properly. The Trees of the Wood will bring you power, and the Waters of the Sea will give you patience and omniscience, since the sea is a womb that contains memory of all things. . . . There is no secret in the world that cannot be discovered if the recipient is ready to listen to it, since the very Air itself carries memory and knowledge.[27]

GREENCRAFT

Greencraft, like a number of other Wiccan traditions, emerged out of the Alexandrian tradition, after it was brought to the Benelux countries—Belgium, the Netherlands, and Luxemburg. It started with a single coven, started by Hera and Arghuicha, who originally were members of an Alexandrian coven, the only one in Benelux. In 1994 it became its own tradition in Amsterdam. Now there are covens in Belgium, the Netherlands, and the United States. Two new training groups were later formed in Belgium, and two of those initiates returned to Texas. Two other members were also trained in the Tuatha de Danann tradition. These six people originated the Greencraft Tradition and the Sacred Well.

In Europe many of the strands that came out of Alexandrian and Gardnerian Wicca, including the Greencraft, Danann, and Whitecraft traditions call themselves Traditional Craft Wicca, or TCW. In the United States most of the groups coming out of the Gardnerian and

Alexandrian traditions call themselves British Traditional Wicca. According to the Web site of the Sacred Well, a Greencraft group in the United States, Greencraft defines Wicca as "an earth-based nature religion with some branches, including our own, claiming a 'Western Mystery Tradition.' According to the Sacred Well:

> Traditional Craft Wicca (TCW), as we define it, is an initiatory tradition that celebrates the Sacred Myths surrounding the Charge and Descent of the Goddess and Sacred Myths of the death and rebirth of the God. Most of what is regarded as Sacred Mythology is drawn from Celtic and Germanic sources, with an ample smattering of Classical Mediterranean, Egyptian, and Middle Eastern mythology as well as considerable ritual material.

Among the special characteristics of Greencraft covens—in addition to any Alexandrian aspects—are the use of a tree alphabet, a unique rune system developed by Michael Ragan, founder of the American Tuatha De Danann tradition, a non-Hebrew form of the Kabala and a Tree of Life based partly on R. J. Stewart's work. Greencraft draws from ceremonial magic, folk magic, and nature religions. It also uses shamanic techniques such as drumming, dancing, chanting, and the development of sensory awareness.

Members of Greencraft say their main effort has been to provide a structure for covens to cooperate and to give more than lip service to the idea of being both a nature tradition and a mystery tradition. Greencraft provides common teaching materials. There are annual Greencraft and Sacred Well conventions, and there is a foundation (Greencraft Creations) that publishes a quarterly magazine, maintains a Web site and organizes events. In order to promote the "nature" aspects of their religion, Greencraft organizes monthly "treewalks," based on a Celtic tree calendar, as an alternative to pub moots. They have also created a Greencraft Tarot based on Celtic and Germanic lore. They have several books in preparation as well.

To become a member of Greencraft, you must subscribe to the Covenant of Five Tenets. These include reverence for the God and Goddess as representations of divine reality, both immanent and transcendent; reverence and respect for the natural world and the worth of all life forms, a belief that it is the right of every individual to be their own authority in all matters of spirit and religion; and a belief in tolerance of all of humanity that leads to a refusal to convert, or seek to convert those of other beliefs and practices.

In the United States, the main organization involved in Greencraft is the Sacred Well Congregation, which has more than 1,200 members in the United States, about half of them in the U.S. military. The military connection began in 1997, when the Sacred Well Congregation agreed to sponsor a group of practicing Wiccans at Fort Hood.

GEORGIAN

George Patterson founded the Georgian Tradition in 1971. It was incorporated as the Church of Wicca of Bakersfield and later as the Georgian Church. According to a Web site devoted to traditionalist Georgians, the name of the tradition was chosen because "many British Traditional Wiccan groups were spearheaded by men that gave their names to these traditions." Georgian Wicca draws together elements of Alexandrian and Gardnerian Wicca, as well as the Pagan Way material created by Ed Fitch. Many of its practices—and its use of the Wiccan laws and initiations—are very similar to British Traditional Wicca; Georgian Wicca considers itself a close cousin to Gardnerian Wicca.

There have been a number of different stories about the late George Patterson's history. At times he said he was initiated into "a Celtic coven," although there has been other speculation that he was involved with a coven that used classical Greco-Roman and Norse deities. After George Patterson died, many Georgians became more eclectic; some explored other teachings and even rewrote the initiation rituals. There were now eclectic Georgians and even Dianic Georgians. Those that decided to remain traditionalists have now joined together into one branch. There are three lines: Silverknife, Elven, and MoonStar. The traditional Georgians have their own Web site (see Resources). Traditionalist Georgians emphasize male to female initiations in their original form as written in their Book of Shadows; they also celebrate the sabbats according to the original form. They keep the same laws (Ordains) and they do not delete or change the Book of Shadows.

NROOGD

The covens of NROOGD—The New Reformed Orthodox Order of the Golden Dawn—are described in detail in Chapter 7 (see also Resources). The tradition was created entirely out of research, poetry, inspiration, and the gathering of a small group of friends. Those Witches quoted in the book who come from NROOGD include Glenna Turner and Aidan Kelly. Kelly, one of the founders of NROOGD, has been known to say that poetry led him to the Craft, and that is as good a clue as any to the tradition.

FERI

This tradition has been called Faery, Faerie, or Feri. The poet Victor Anderson started the tradition in California. As you can see from some of his quotes in this book, Victor Anderson had a very poetic way of looking at the world; the late Alison Harlow once told me that the stories Victor told about his origins often changed. Anderson always said that his sources were Hawaiian Kahuna and African Voudoun. But according to an article by Steve Hewell in *The Witches' Voice*, at the age of twelve Anderson met a group of economic refugees from Southern Appalachia who taught him various magical practices "rooted in American folk magic," with some "elements of European, African-American and Native American traditions."[28]

Later, some of the most important people involved in the Pagan resurgence—Alison Harlow, Gwydion Pendderwen and his wife, Cynthia, Caradoc Ap Cador, and a number of others—were part of Victor Anderson's coven, and that is when the Feri tradition really took off. Later, Starhawk brought many Feri elements to the Reclaiming tradition, but gave it a more political direction. Victor Anderson and others added Gardnerian elements, and other initiates have taken it in Celtic, Native American, and countless other directions. Some of the hallmarks of the tradition are shamanic practices and sexual mysticism. Steve Hewell writes of the tradition:

> The Gods are seen as monads, having dark and light, male and female within themselves. Some of the concepts and teaching tools unique to the Feri Tradition have become widely known. . . . In particular, the Feri

concepts of the tripartite nature of the human psyche (which resembles similar ideas in the Hebrew Kabalah, as well as Hawaiian Huna of which Victor was particularly fond) and the Iron and Pearl Pentagrams have become familiar to many outside of our tradition. The Pentagrams embody the fundamental values of Feri, and represent our basic approach to magic and the nature of being human.

Solitary practice is common in Feri, there is only one initiation, and coven structure is often informal. A number of different lines of transmission of the tradition are available, and some of the current teachers are Gabriel, Francesca di Grandis, and Tony Spurlock. Hewell sums up the tradition this way:

> The path of Feri is not always easy or safe; it's not for everyone. It requires a rigorous self-honesty and a willingness to delve into our own darkness as a source of power and self-healing. It teaches us to go into all the hidden places where we have buried the parts of ourselves we fear and hate, and find there the source of beauty, love, creativity, and authenticity. It brings us face to face with our own divinity, so that the raw power of the living universe flows through every part of our being. It is an awesome and frequently challenging experience—the way to wholeness is rarely a comfortable one! Feri Witches strive to live according to what we refer to as the "Warrior Ethic," which involves balancing personal freedom and love for ourselves as manifestations of the Divine, with the need for discipline, responsibility, and respect for others.

RECLAIMING

The Reclaiming tradition began in northern California in the 1980s and now has groups throughout North America and in parts of Western Europe. The tradition has always emphasized community and collective action. Starhawk is Reclaiming's most famous member, and her books *The Spiral Dance, Dreaming the Dark,* and others, have been the springboard for countless covens. But from the very beginning, decisions in Reclaiming have been made by consensus decision making—somewhat similar to that used by the Religious Society of Friends (Quakers). There has never been one leader, although Starhawk has been one of the prime theologians. From its inception classes and workshops have been co-taught to model a different notion of power. In 1982, after a political protest—a blockade of the proposed nuclear plant at Diablo Canyon, and Reclaiming's first Spiral Dance—the community came together as the Reclaiming Collective. Soon after, the first summer intensives were started, a newsletter began, and in 1994 Reclaiming incorporated. Eventually, Reclaiming became a tradition of Witchcraft. The Reclaiming tradition is eclectic and based on personal empowerment and is structurally non-hierarchical. Starhawk was trained in Victor and Cora Anderson's Faery tradition, as well as having experienced the Dianic Wicca of Z Budapest. According to an article by M. Macha NightMare, with input from Vibra Willow, and found on Reclaiming's Web site, the Reclaiming tradition, "unlike most other Craft traditions, has espoused a connection between spirituality and political action."[29] M. Macha NightMare says the tradition can be characterized as being non-hierarchical; it has no specific pantheon, no set liturgy, except in very large public rituals, no requirement of initiations, extensive use of chanting, breath work and energy raising, and a strong emphasis on political involvement and ecological consciousness. Reclaiming proudly uses the word "Witch" and Reclaiming's understanding of feminist spirituality—a spirituality that includes men and women—is based on an analysis of power that sees all systems of oppression as interrelated and rooted in a structure of domination and control. "Power within" is contrasted with "Power over." In its Principles of Unity, printed on its Web site, Reclaiming says:

> The values of the Reclaiming tradition stem from our understanding that the earth is alive and all of life is sacred and interconnected. We see the Goddess as immanent in the earth's cycles of birth, growth, death, decay and regeneration. Our practice arises from a deep, spiritual commitment to the earth, to healing and to the linking of magic with political action.

Reclaiming has groups and communities in many parts of the United States, as well as in Germany, Spain, Canada, and the Netherlands. Reclaiming runs Witchcamps, weeklong intensives where drumming, dancing, chanting, storytelling, guided visualization, trance, and energy work take place. At least five thousand people have experienced these camps. As this book went to press in 2006 there were close to twenty annual Witchcamps in the United States and Europe.

DIANIC

The term "Dianic" describes a number of different traditions. The name comes, in part, from Margaret Murray's description of Witchcraft as "the Dianic cult." In the United States all groups that call themselves "Dianic" are linked by one thing: their emphasis on the Goddess.

Perhaps the earliest and most important stream of Dianic Wicca was created, revived, and inspired by author and activist Zsuzsanna Budapest in the early 1970s. Her first coven, the Susan B. Anthony Coven, in Los Angeles, led to many others—the Amelia Earhart Coven in New York, the Elizabeth Gould Davis Coven in Florida, and, later, scores of other groups. By the 1980s, there were many Dianic groups, some of them with no connection to Z Budapest and her teachings. Ruth Barrett, the priestess who inherited Z's ministry in 1980, and serves the Dianic Tradition in the Midwest, describes the Dianic Tradition as:

A vibrantly creative and evolving Women's Mystery tradition, inclusive of all women. Our practices include celebrating and honoring the numerous physical, emotional, and life cycle passages that women share by having been born female. Contemporary Dianic tradition recognizes the greater or lesser effects and influences of the dominant culture on every aspect of women's lives. Since 1971, the Dianic movement has inspired and provided healing rituals to counter the effects of living in patriarchy, and has worked to understand, deconstruct, and heal from the dominant culture wherein we live and practice our faith. We define patriarchy as the use of "power-over" thinking and action to oppress others, both institutionally and within the personal sphere of our lives.[30]

This stream of the Dianic Tradition is for women only. It is based on a cosmology centered on the Goddess as "She Who Is All and Whole Unto Herself." The Goddess is the web of life itself. Barrett writes that the Dianic Wheel of the Year celebrates the traditional Pagan festivals— the solstices, equinoxes, and cross-quarter holidays, but unlike other Wiccan traditions, there is no focus on the heterosexual fertility cycle of

Goddess and God. As Barrett writes in her book *Women's Rites, Women's Mysteries* (the second edition will be republished by Llewellyn in 2007):

> The Goddess is celebrated in Her triple aspect of Maiden, Mother, and Crone as a manifestation of the entire life cycle: birth, maturation, and death. The Goddess has the power to bring forth life, nurture, protect, sustain, and destroy it. This concept contains nature's entire continuum.[31]

Although there is a sense that the Goddess is a universal presence, there is also an understanding that the Goddess has been worshipped under many names and in many different cultural forms. Dianic rituals honor women's rites of passage. There's an emphasis on what Barrett calls "the five blood Mysteries," which are birth, menarche, giving birth/lactation, menopause, and death. She writes, "These Mysteries acknowledge and honor women's ability to create life, sustain life, and return our bodies to the Goddess in death. Whether or not a woman births children, all women pass through the Mother phase as they choose life paths that sustain our species or other life forms."[32]

All that is male in nature is seen as a variation of the Goddess, coming from her, birthed from the wombs of women. And women's wombs are seen as the source of creation, and the source of women's power, whether or not women have had a hysterectomy. As a result, Dianic Wiccan feminism is basically "essentialist" as opposed to a view that most of the differences between men and women are culturally produced. Most Dianics in this tradition do not accept transgender or surgically altered men as female, a controversy that has raged throughout the women's movement for years. They also tend to distrust most male goddess scholarship. Many classic works about the history of goddess worship, such as works by J. J. Bachofen, Helen Diner, Merlin Stone, E. G. Davis, Barbara Walker, and more recently Marija Gimbutas, among others, have not been accepted by mainstream academia. This has often put Dianics and other spiritual feminists at odds with the broader Pagan Studies Movement, which is described in another chapter.

In the past, Dianics have often emphasized creativity, psychic skills, feminism, and anti-patriarchal politics, and have often de-emphasized structure and formal rituals. They encourage improvisation over a scripted liturgy.

Another Dianic stream in this country began in Dallas with the Dianic Covenstead of priestess Morgan McFarland. This tradition exalts the feminine but does not exclude men from the worship. When I visited Morgan McFarland back in 1976, she was priestess of three covens, one of them exclusively female.

In this stream of the tradition, the Goddess is seen as having three aspects: Maiden-Creatrix, Great Mother, and Old Crone, who holds the door to death and rebirth. It is in her second aspect that the Goddess takes a male consort, who is as Osiris to Isis. To show this relationship, Dianics quote a phrase attributed to Bachofen: "Immortal is Isis, mortal her husband, like the earthly creation he represents." So there is a place for the God, but the female as Creatrix is primary. Dianics also see the Goddess symbolized in nature as the Triple Creatrix: as the moon, the Queen of Mysteries; as the sun, Sunna, the Queen of Stars, provider of warmth and care; and as Mother Earth, to whom all must return.

Mark Roberts, who was McFarland's partner until 1978, told me that Dianics are also pantheists, since they recognize the sacredness of all that exists. But, he said, "The Goddess is the touchstone to this planet and this life cycle." And at the time, Mark and Morgan seemed to be—of all those I interviewed—the most concerned with the ecological fate of the planet. In *The New Broom,* a former Dianic publication, Roberts wrote that there was less distinction between "mortal" and "deity" than there was between those who had lost touch with nature and those beings whose rhythms and pulse were attuned to the universe. He also wrote:

> The lifestyle of a Dianic is a composite of three values and ideals. First, an awareness of self. Second, an increasing and evergrowing kinship with Nature. And third, an open sensitivity to the pulsebeat of the cosmos. As we near the common goals of awareness, kinship, and sensitivity, we attain the level of attunement that outsiders call "magic." We are well aware that in our workings we have achieved and produced nothing supernatural: we have simply reached our level of natural capacity.
>
> In a society obsessed with artificiality, our lifestyle seems strange, "unnatural," even revolutionary. . . .
>
> And we are revolutionary: in the sense that we whirl about the axis who is the Goddess and are completing the cycle that sees her worship

returning in strength; and we are advocates of a drastic and radical change from the pell-mell, break-neck, destructive world in which we find ourselves; and in that, in a technological age where mechanical improvements take their increasing toll in human sensitivity, we train reawakening sense to a level of awareness that frees the human to once again be whole and independent and alert. In a patriarchal culture that becomes increasingly authoritarian, we find no choice but to stand as rebels against dehumanization. . . .[33]

In connection with these principles the Dianic Covenstead had a very effective series of exercises and techniques for regaining kinship and attunement with nature.

The origin of the Dianic Covenstead in Dallas goes back about forty years. Morgan McFarland, the daughter of a minister, lived part of her youth in the Orient and then moved to the American South. She was trained in a Southern Witchcraft coven. It had no name for its tradition, simply calling it Witchcraft. She adopted the term *Dianic* later. The rituals of this coven placed great emphasis on the moon, were very "Gravesian." They focused on the myths, lore, and mystery behind the thirteen lunar months and their connection with the Beth-Luis-Nion tree alphabet of ancient Britain.*

While both men and women could become initiates, those women who had experienced the rituals of all the lunar months could go through an additional five "passage" rituals, after which they could "hive" off and start their own covens. Within the tradition, it is the women who choose their priests, and they may revoke their choice at any time.

I asked Mark the obvious question: how it felt to be a priest in such a heavily matriarchal tradition. He said, "I'd rather be first mate on a ship that is solid than captain on a ship that has a rotten hull, a ship that is sinking. Patriarchy is such a ship."

---

*Much of Robert Graves's *The White Goddess* is a metaphoric investigation of this alphabet, said to be an ancient druidical alphabet. It has eighteen letters—thirteen consonants and five vowels—and each has a corresponding tree known well in European folklore. Beth is birch, Luis is rowan, Nion is ash, and so on. The consonants are often used for the thirteen lunar months. The covenstead of Morrigana used this system. So do many recent lunar calendars, such as those by Nancy Passmore, published by Luna Press (Boston).

I asked Morgan to talk about her feelings on the difference between her two covens that include men and the one that doesn't. She said, "We have found that women working together are capable of conjuring their past and reawakening their old ascendancy. They are capable of putting together many of the pieces. This does not seem to happen when men are present. Perhaps this is a societal thing. It seems that in mixed covens, no matter how 'feminist' the women are, a kind of competition begins to happen. Among the women, alone, none of this occurs, and a great reciprocity develops, unlike anything I have seen before."

Morgan McFarland has been a housewife, a lecturer on feminism and Witchcraft, the owner of a small business in plants and baskets, and a woman working up the professional ladder at a large corporation. She has two children. I spent a week with Morgan and Mark during the period they were working together. I found them to be lively, spontaneous, and wonderful people.

Their circles were primarily celebratory. As Mark wrote in *The New Broom:*

> We do perform healing and problem-solving, scrying and protective measures, but the majority of our ritual circles are for the praise and worship and contact of and with the Goddess. The protective spirit of our circles is more to shield us from the 20th century than to protect us from malicious harm. Our circles are a haven from the present that frees us to touch the past and to restore our old attunement to nature.[34]

Within the circle, all were equal, despite the "feminist" edge, and there was much room for innovation in regard to ritual, tools, clothing (or lack of it), size, and structure. In 2005, Morgan McFarland says she is watching the new generation of Dianics from the sidelines. She is no longer running a coven and describes herself as a reclusive matriarch. But there are many active groves and covens that are continuing her work.

There is a third stream of Dianic Wicca that should be mentioned— The Reformed Congregation of the Goddess, International (RCG-I). RCG-I began in 1982, when Jade River moved from Kentucky to Wisconsin and began searching for women who wanted to "serve the Goddess." In 1983, Jade and Lynnie Levy began publishing *Of a Like Mind,* which quickly became the most important networking magazine of the Women's Spirituality Movement, and remained so for years. That same year they incorporated the Re-formed Congregation of the Goddess in Wisconsin, and since then the RCG-I has grown and expanded, with more than two thousand members. There are circles and priestesses in about seven states. RCG-I has a Women's Thealogical Institute with several different training programs, as well as an ordination program for priestesses. While they do not call themselves "Dianic," it is a woman-only tradition, with exclusive emphasis on the Goddess.

MINOAN BROTHERHOOD AND SISTERHOOD

The Minoan tradition is an initiatory path of Witchcraft, based primarily on Cretan sources, with some Aegean and Ancient Near Eastern mythology. It was founded in 1977. Edmund M. "Eddie" Buczynski, the founder of the tradition, was extremely creative at writing ritual and poetry. He was trained in Gardnerian and Welsh Wicca. Later in his life he became involved in studying classical and Near Eastern archeology. He broke with the Welsh and Gardnerian traditions and went on to found the Minoan Brotherhood. It was created in part to celebrate male mysteries and to create a safe place for gay and bisexual men in the Craft. Soon after founding the Brotherhood, a group of priestesses in New York created the Minoan Sisterhood. Eddie Buczynski died of AIDS in 1989, but the tradition continues. There are Minoan Brotherhood groups in California, Michigan, Florida, Washington, Louisiana, Indiana, and Canada. The Minoan Sisterhood is active in the New York City area. There is also a meeting ground between the two sexes called the Cult of Rhea, or the Cult of the Double Axe. Like many Wiccan traditions, the Minoan tradition has three degrees of initiation. It celebrates rites at the full moon and the eight festivals of the Wheel of the Year. Although the framework of the tradition is similar to Gardnerian Wicca, the core beliefs of the Minoan tradition center on the worship of the ancient Cretan Snake Goddess—the Great Mother—and her divine son. The Minoan Brotherhood continues to be influenced by the current of queer spirituality. There is no published information on the inner workings of the tradition, and the elders say that is as is should be: "As a mystery tradition we value our privacy and secrecy to preserve the sacredness and wonder of the spiritual quest." The most important ethical law of the Minoan tradition is "Love Unto All Beings." Elders of the tradition write: "While the Wiccan Rede is neither taught nor ascribed to as an absolute that must be adhered to, many Minoan Elders see it as good advice against which to measure one's actions." In the interest of full disclosure, the first Craft group I entered, in 1971, was a Welsh Wiccan training group in New York City. Eddie Buczynski had written most of the rituals and almost all of the poetry, and much of it was extremely beautiful.

SCHOOL OF WICCA

The School of Wicca is a large U.S. correspondence Witchcraft school. It is also a legally recognized church.

It is debatable whether the School of Wicca should be included in this book about Neo-Paganism and about Wicca as a branch of Neo-Paganism. The School of Wicca does not consider itself "Pagan," and Gavin and Yvonne Frost, who head it, have always defined Witchcraft as a monotheistic religion.

Still, the School of Wicca may have created a hundred covens through its activities, and in years past, the Frosts have often been at the center of Neo-Pagan ecumenical ventures, as well as numerous disputes within the Craft—disputes over sexuality, homosexuality, monotheism versus polytheism, to mention only a few. Meanwhile, tens of thousands of students have begun their twelve-lesson Witchcraft course, although apparently only several hundred have ever finished it.

Part of the controversy that surrounded the Frosts came from Gavin Frost's wry and rather bizarre sense of humor, and his tendency to say almost anything to get a rise out of someone. Because of this, the Frosts have been much misunderstood. For a time their opposition to homosexuality in the Craft raised a great debate. Since their particular tradition stressed heterosexual sex magic, this attitude was somewhat understandable, as long as they stopped short of claiming that their methods were "the Way"; unfortunately, Gavin did not always do this.

They made another mistake. They wrote a Witchcraft book and called it *The Witch's Bible*—or, at the least, their publisher did.[35] When it appeared, many people in the Craft were outraged and labeled it a "Witchcrap book." This book, with its emphasis on an asexual monotheistic deity, described a religion very different from that practiced by most Wiccans. There were also questionable statements about sex and race. There were descriptions of the use of artificial phalli—an old magical tradition, but one not familiar to most people in Wicca. The title of the book was the worst part. Many Witches fumed at the word *The*, since the book, in their view, had nothing to do with their religion.

In person, the Frosts have always been delightful. Gavin is kind and humorous. Yvonne, who has long gray hair down to her waist, is forthright and even a bit prim. When I visited them back in 1975 they lived in southern Missouri, near a town aptly called Salem. (They have since moved to West Virginia.) At the time, they lived with their daughter in an old red schoolhouse on fourteen acres of land, and they ran a pig farm. The sense one got of their life was *solidity*. Despite my strong religious and political differences with them, I left thinking that they had truly translated the Craft into a living philosophy that placed a high value on techniques of survival and simple rural living. They had many rural-based covens connected with their school and church. This was a welcome change from the mostly urban covens I had encountered.

Gavin Frost told me that he was an iconoclast who believed in an abstract monotheistic deity. He divided "gods" into two types. On the one hand, "God" was abstract, unknowable, beyond the need for worship. But there were also "stone gods," the gods we "create" for a purpose. These gods are used as storehouses of energy. They are necessary for magic. Gavin said that people make "stone gods" or "idols" in order to have something to put energy into, so that later they can draw power out. Both kinds of deities "exist," but "stone gods" are of one's own creation. Gavin said he was not a "Pagan" because he did not worship "stone gods." "What do you mean?" I asked, as we sat around the cozy schoolhouse farm. At this point, the following conversation took place:

M.A.: You both say you are not Pagans, is that true?

Gavin: Absolutely!

Yvonne: I do not consider myself a Pagan. I do not worship any nature deity. I reach upward toward the unnameable which has no gender.

M.A.: How do you define "Pagan"?

Gavin: A Pagan is someone who worships a nature spirit.

Yvonne: Or a named, finite deity.

M.A.: Or many of them.

Yvonne: I say there is one deity, without gender.

Gavin: Okay, but if you want to make something happen, magically, you have no problem or objection to worshipping a statue of Isis, and then dumping power.

Yvonne: Oh! My mascot? *My* deity is my Volkswagen ignition key. That's what makes it happen for me. I do not reach up to it. But if I am going to work a procedure, that is the deity or mascot I use.

Gavin: And you don't have any objection to calling on Mars, let us say, if Mars seems to be appropriate for magical procedure.

Yvonne: But that is not a *reverence.*

I asked them if, had they known *The Witch's Bible* would create such a furor, they would have changed anything in the book.

"Maybe we'd change the title to *A* instead of *The,*" Gavin said.

And Yvonne added, "If there are still masculine overtones in regard to deity in the book, we might change them to asexual ones."

Gavin Frost's interest in the Craft began when he was working for an aerospace company on the Salisbury plains. He told me that there, "surrounded by monuments," it was easy to become interested in the druids. When he came to the United States, he said, he was initiated by a group in St. Louis. Gavin said his tradition was "thirty seconds old" and that "we have a bunch of traditional stuff, but it keeps changing all the time and we encourage people to experiment and change." And while the Church of Wicca—an organization connected with the School of Wicca—includes many covens, several follow their own path, which has no connection with the Frosts' tradition; they chose to affiliate themselves with the Church in order to obtain the tax-exempt status of a religious organization.

The Frosts are militantly public, and they have stated that "the conscious decision to be a Witch should be at least semi-publicly acknowledged and admitted." They believe firmly that communication between groups should be fostered and that "secrecy brings with it persecution, for fear of the unknown results in destruction and death."

Here are some of the things that distinguish the teachings of the School of Wicca from other Wiccan traditions.

1. Monotheism: the view that Witchcraft is not a Pagan nature religion.
2. No particular emphasis on the feminine.
3. A very structured concept of "the astral," called *Side,* by the F
   The *Side* has ten levels.

4. Very structured beliefs in progressive reincarnation as the primary learning tool of human beings and all "souls." They also told me that they believe that overpopulation is causing "inferior souls" to reincarnate on the earth plane.

5. Kundalini sex practices, including "introitus," a practice in which sex without orgasm is used as a form of surrender to God.

6. The use of the Egyptian ankh as a symbol of regeneration. The use of artificial phalli.

7. An antimatriarchal bias. Gavin called the theory of matriarchy "a Marxist heresy."

The beliefs of the School of Wicca are often stated as follows:

> One individual cannot define a path in another's reality.
> God/dess is not definable. In Bardic language,
>
> There is nothing truly hidden but what is not conceivable;
> There is nothing not conceivable but what is immeasurable;
> There is nothing immeasurable but God.
>
> An it harm none, do what you will
> Power is gained through knowledge.
> Reincarnation is for learning
> The Law of Attraction (good begets good, evil begets evil)
> Harmony of man with the psychic and physical worlds.[36]

Today, despite their differences, the Frosts seem to get on well with most other Witches, most of the time.

Again, these traditions are not "hard and fast." As one priestess from the Midwest wrote humorously, "Mary Nesnick began as a Gardnerian, Jesus Christ began as a Jew, I began as an Alexandrian. None of us stayed that way."[37] Most people in the Craft are coming to feel that traditions should be guides, no more, no less. "A tradition," one New York Craft priest wrote to me, "should be rich enough in associative values and nuances not to wear thin, but to lead to deeper pathways, deeper mysteries. Its images and symbols must not be trite. It should give you supportive values and relationships that aid growth with people or growth with other planes of reality. It should offer an introduction to the world of spirit, but be balanced in regard to the world of the senses and the flesh. In short, it should be stable enough to offer a pathway, a guideline, but it must not be so rigid that all spontaneity is lost."

As the Witch Diana Demdike told the British magazine *Quest:* The best thing Witches could do, she said, would be to make a huge bonfire of all their carefully copied old books of rituals and then "drink the water of knowledge fresh from its source," which was "the light of the moon, the shape of the clouds and the growing of green things."[38]

Witches and Persecution Today

Despite the constitutional amendment that gives citizens of the United States the freedom to practice their religion—"Congress shall make no law respecting an establishment of religion, or prohibiting the free exercise thereof . . ."—Witchcraft is not accepted as a valid minority religion by most people in the United States, and many of those I interviewed told me of persecution they had encountered once they were identified as Witches. There were stories of firings from jobs, of children taken away from parents and placed in the custody of others, of arrests for practicing divination. There were stories of stones thrown through windows, and several tales of people who moved away from an area after fundamentalist groups decided to take literally the biblical injunction: "Thou shall not suffer a witch to live."

Among the Witches quoted in this book, Judy Myer lost custody of her children in a divorce proceeding after her husband said she was practicing Witchcraft. Z Budapest was "set up" by a police informer and arrested for doing a tarot reading for which she charged ten dollars; the informer told the court that the reading seemed quite accurate, but Z was convicted and fined three hundred dollars. Local teenagers tried to set fire to Bran and Moria's house; they threw tomatoes through the windows, as well as stones and other objects. This happened after Moria appeared on the *Tomorrow Show* to talk about the Craft. As a result, Bran and Moria picked up and left for northern California; they told me they regarded the incident as a "sign from the Mother" that it was time to get out of Los Angeles.

Then there was the probable murder of a man by his "caring" relative who wanted to make sure his soul would be saved, and the case of Robert Williams, a psychologist who, after he mentioned the Craft in an interview in a local newspaper, was fired from his job at a Kansas reformatory and shortly after committed suicide.[39] But now, twenty-five years later, these kinds of incidents are quite rare.

Most persecution is not this blatant. It takes the more subtle form of the images of Witches portrayed in television shows and in films like *Rosemary's Baby* and *The Exorcist.*

The late Leo Martello, long an activist for civil and gay rights, organized a "Witch-in" in New York's Central Park on October 31, 1970. He had to fight, with the help of New York's Civil Liberties Union, to obtain a permit from the Parks Department. Martello then formed the Witches Anti-Defamation League, devoted to securing religious rights for Witches.[40] That organization eventually changed its name to AREN: The Alternative Religions Education Network.

Several years later Isaac Bonewits and a number of other occultists formed the AADL—the Aquarian Anti-Defamation League—an organization dedicated to fighting legal battles on behalf of Pagans and occultists. Writing in *Gnostica,* Bonewits gave details of anti-occult laws and statutes on the books in many states. For example, in Delaware pretending to be able to do magic, divination, or "deal with spirits" made one a vagrant. In Massachusetts to "pretend" fortune-telling for gain was larceny and fraud. In Michigan any form of divination was illegal, including dowsing. In many states, it's still illegal to practice astrology, palmistry, and so forth without a license.

Bonewits observed in an article called "Witchburning . . . Now and Then" that since most people don't consider Witches members of a "real" religion, they often don't get the protection the law gives to churches.[41]

The idea for AADL occurred after Bonewits and a number of other occultists were approached by some apparently sympathetic people who said they were trying to make a documentary on the occult. They turned out to be a fundamentalist group. The film, *The Occult: An Echo from Darkness,* was narrated by Hal Lindsey, the author of *Satan Is Alive and Well on Planet Earth, The Late Great Planet Earth,* and other such books. Bonewits observed:

The film is a venomous, vituperative propaganda picture. Its sole purpose is to warp and confuse well-known data of world history and comparative religions, to convince ignorant viewers that all occultism, from newspaper horoscopes and tarot cards to Witch meetings and ritual magic, to ESP laboratories and mind training systems, is a unified Satanic plot to enslave the world and destroy Christianity. Every single person in the film, except the preachers, is equated with a young girl who "confesses" that she helped burn a baby to death in a Satanic ritual.[42]

Bonewits said that the film, a full-color production costing at least a hundred thousand dollars, used misquotes and trick editing. Many Neo-Pagans, psychics, Witches, and Neo-Christians appeared in it, including Bonewits.

The AADL was formed in response to this kind of problem, but the organization died from a lack of volunteers to do the work and a lack of funds. Today, the most important groups fighting for religious freedom for Wiccans and Pagans are the Lady Liberty League, AREN, and ERAL—the Earth Religions Assistance List.

In the past, attitudes within Paganism and the Craft concerning persecution were evenly divided between two schools: "If we're respectable and quiet, we won't get persecuted—only flashy troublemakers do," and "It's time we stood up and fought for our religious rights." Today most Wiccans lead very normal lives and do not experience much discrimination. There are occasional incidents that play out in the courts and the media and there are continuing battles to give Pagans in the military and in prisons the rights that members of other religions receive. These efforts require political action and vigilance. But they are the exception and not the rule.

Essentials

A great many modern witches feel that they have brought back the ancient religion of pre-Christian times. In so far as they have retained the love of nature and followed the festivals of the turning sky they have an argument in their favor. Those were the essentials of the ancient belief.

. . . In this environment of growing threats to human existence there is a surge toward the works of life. Hence the growth of witches of the old greenwood

type, the dancers of the gods. Nakedness, sex, song and dance are their marks, and their hearts are mostly innocent and happy. The newly invented groups have a validity which springs from the emotional needs which created them. Often without any conscious planning they throw up from within themselves echoes of ancient ceremonies. . . .

Witchcraft is in its essence the worship of the powers of this world, beautiful or terrible, but all in a circle under the turning sky above which is the One.

—C. A. BURLAND[43]

Most popular talk about Witchcraft is about *trappings*. This misleads and mystifies. Our society teaches us to regard objects as the essentials. Thus we are apt to focus on ritual daggers and spells and strange herbs and all the paraphernalia of modern Wicca, thinking that these *are* the Craft.

"Why did you put a *red* cloth on the altar?" a novice asks a priest of Wicca, framing the question softly, as if a big secret is about to be revealed.

"Because I just happened to *have* a red cloth," the priest replies.

We should not make the novice's error. Rather, we should heed the words a woman recently wrote to me:

It sounds as if there are really very few beliefs that one needs to be a Witch. In fact—correct me if I'm wrong—the only thing one *really* needs, the only thing all varieties of Witches have in common, is a belief in the power of what I shall call the moon principle (for lack of a better term)— that from which springs the intuitive, the psychic, the mysterious, that which is somehow aligned with the female, the hidden, the unknown.

This is a vague concept, true, but I think necessarily so, for two reasons: (1) Our culture, being so strongly based on the antithetical principle, has few means of dealing with this side of life other than to clothe it in ambiguous shadowy terms or condemn it as evil. (2) Being so vague, it is closer to being universal than the more rigidly defined religions or philosophies; more different types of people, as you found, can associate themselves with it.

I have no trouble believing in such a principle, for there *are* things in life which cannot be explained by logic and rationality. There is the evidence of my senses, the feelings which cannot be denied. And I have no doubt at all (on a gut level) that I can grow to experience the principle at first hand.

For the time being, then, I am quite willing to do spells, perform rituals, to chant over candles at midnight, because I've come to believe that this is a way to the power. The principle comes from within us, the source of it or the channel through which it manifests itself. (I'm not sure which, yet, though I suspect it's the latter.)

But knowing that intellectually does not help us gain access to it; we don't order it to come forth with our rational minds, for it does not obey rationality. Therefore I chant, I gaze at a picture of a triune Goddess through incense-smoke as it wavers in candlelight, I turn off my rational mind for a while, and soon I feel it flowing through me like electricity, breathlessly, and I am the same and not the same as I was before. . . . Goodness, it's easy to get poetic when talking about this! I guess poetry comes from Her/It/Me too. . . . But the trick is to keep from forgetting that candles, incense, images, etc., *are* props.[44]

The Witch, as we said, is the changer—the one who bends. Wicca, at its best, is the most flexible and adaptable of religions, since it is perfectly willing to throw out dogmas and rely on these types of experience alone.

By the time you read these pages, some of the covens mentioned may have dissolved and entirely new ones may have sprouted. Don't look to find exactly what has been described here. You may not find it, or, everything may all be a little different. That is the real beauty of Wicca when it is true to itself.

6.

Interview with a Modern Witch

THE FOLLOWING INTERVIEW took place in the winter of 1976, in Oakland, California. The woman, Sharon Devlin, is an American of Irish descent. She is a member of the Craft; she is a mother; she is a weaver, a player on the Irish harp; she is an Irish civil rights activist; and she works in the field of health. She is *not* typical—if there is such a thing as a "typical Witch," which I doubt. Devlin's views would be considered very controversial by most modern Wiccans. In particular, her views on drugs, sex, and politics must be considered a minority position within the modern Craft. Still I chose this interview out of all of the others because of its peculiar richness and depth, because it is my favorite interview, and because it touches on many of the themes in this book.

Q. How did you come to be a Pagan and a Witch?

A. First of all, I am a hereditary Witch, but this does *not* mean that I have a direct lineage from mother to daughter, although [laughter] I did allege this as a neurotic teenager. What it does mean is that I am from a Witch family. My great-great-grandmother on my father's side was named Mary MacGoll. She was a fat, little, pudgy, brown-eyed woman of Scots descent (whom I am supposed to resemble). She was a local midwife and healer, basically a faith healer. I doubt she would have described herself as a Pagan. She was raised as a Presbyterian and she remained a devout Christian, but her Christianity was of the peasant variety; it was centered on the Virgin Mary. She got her power from the Tuatha De Danaan. Most people called them the Gentry or the Sidhe or the Shining Ones. And there are many stories about the fairies that are associated with her.

She fell in love with an impoverished but apparently terrifically lovable Catholic named Jenkin Devlin, who is my great-great-grandfather. She eloped with him after she became pregnant and her family disinherited her because she had married a Catholic. She was an intense clairvoyant and she foretold to her family that because they had robbed her unborn child of its inheritance, they would be childless, and that someday they would come begging her descendants to take back what they had not freely given. And this prediction was fulfilled. I was told many other stories of things that she did. She apparently was taught artificial respiration by the fairies and she revived "dead" children. She did not live long. She died during the potato famine in County Tyrone.

I was brought up as a strict Irish Catholic, but this did not have the negative connotations people generally associate with it. My family was basically working-class Irish. They were not lace curtain in any way.

Q. How did you come to enter the Craft?

A. It was an independent decision on my part because at the time I didn't believe that anyone else had the same interests. When I was a young girl I was deeply religious and I was looking desperately for an ecstatic and deep religious experience. As a result I wished to become a nun and enter a contemplative order. My parents were radically against it. They felt it would be a copout. For a young girl faced with the terrors of sex, chastity is a very comfortable way out. The convent situation is one which lends itself to safety, and I found that attractive. Of course, as I matured, this alternative became less and less attractive.

The peak of my "convent period" was when I was about fifteen. I entered a convent for a brief time—about six weeks—and then was forcibly removed by my parents. My mother went to bed and simply refused to get up unless my father removed me. My father told the Mother Superior that he didn't want my tits to dry up on me as hers had. So I was spirited from my spiritual refuge and back into the world.

Well, back in the world, I soon became aware of the narrowness of the philosophical viewpoint of orthodox Catholicism. At the same time a strange awareness began to dawn on me of something of far greater potency. Now, I had been into a thing of praying to the point of ecstasy. This is one of the more positive aspects of Catholicism. I have met a few priests and nuns who have actually achieved enlightenment this way. Most of their personal views were pretty heretical, and this was one of the tools my parents used to get me away from the convent. They located a famous artist and nun, Sister Corita, and I spent a summer working for her at Immaculate Heart College in Los Angeles. She told me that the best thing I could do for my spirituality was to *work out my own.*

During that crucial sixteenth year I started to read philosophy. I read a lot of the classics, a lot of Attic and Roman philosophy. I stumbled onto the Hermetic tradition and I found some books on alchemy. I began to talk about alchemy with a wonderful high-school chemistry teacher, and one thing led to another, and before I knew it I'd gone to Larsen's Books on Hollywood Boulevard and had bought a copy of *The Greater Key of Solomon.* I began to work spells. It was at this point—after I had worked my first spell—that it flashed on me that I was fulfilling something to do with my ancestry.

After that I went down to UCLA and sat in on a bunch of classes on the language and mythology of the Welsh and Irish Celtic peoples. I read every book on Irish mythology that I could get hold of. Before the year was out I was calling myself a Witch because I knew that was what I was.

Later my grandmother gave me a beautiful cast-iron cauldron which had been brought over from Ireland as part of the personal possessions of our family. It had belonged to my great-great-grandmother, Mary MacGoll. In her time an iron pot was an investment of several months' cash money. Irish families cooked their entire meal of buttermilk and potatoes in the pot. This was probably the biggest possession my family had. So I have my great-great-grandmother's potato pot, which may or may not have been used as her cauldron. And although I told people some "ugga bugga" about being initiated by my grandmother and being given the cauldron, the fact is, *I was* given the cauldron and I was told the story.

Q. What is your present relationship to Catholicism?

A. It's an uneasy truce. I believe that Christ was a genuine avatar of the Great Mother—a Dionysus incarnation, pretty much. His worship has been desperately perverted. They have turned him into this dreadful sort of pathetic thing instead of the sacrificial god of Inspiration. I go and eat his Body and Blood every once in a while, and I consider that to be valid. But to "confess my sins" to people who refer to themselves as his "minions" but do nothing but assassinate his character and purpose, I would find that pretty sacrilegious. I know without doubt that if I lived in a Catholic community and if it were known that I was practicing magic, I would be asked not to communicate. I just go into various churches and take advantage of the social confusion that Berkeley offers.

Q. Do you consider yourself a Pagan?

A. What I actually am is an offshoot of Paganism and early Irish Christianity. I follow beliefs which formed the basis of the Culdee Church. The Culdee Church was the only true union of Paganism and the real teachings of Christ; it was brutally stamped out by the papacy. The Culdee Church continued to believe in the ancient Celtic gods. It continued to believe in the Danu and the Dagda and it considered all the ancient heroes and heroines of Ireland to be saints. They had women clergy. They did not believe that sexual intercourse was sinful and, as a matter of fact, on all the church doors was a big portrait of the Great Mother giving birth with her clitoris exposed and her labia pulled wide and her mouth open because she is in the birth ecstasy. Those are called Sheila-Na-Gigh.

Q. Do you consider yourself a polytheist?

A. I believe that all so-called gods are thought-form emanations of human beings toward the One Consciousness of which we are a part. I believe that there are many races of sapient beings in the universe, some of which are physically greater than we are or, perhaps, have nondelineated bodies, like the Shining Ones, or who live on a different dimensional plane. All these things are within the realm of possibility. It has been our nature to call these "gods." What is a god? A god is an eternal being, and in that sense we, too, are gods. So yes, I am a polytheist. But I also believe there is a unity to the whole trip and in that sense I'm a monotheist. There is one Spirit, but a multitude of delightful forms from which to choose, or to create new ones, as you will.

Q. What does it mean to you personally to be a Witch?

A. Well, unfortunately, it means that I have set myself off from humanity to a large extent. I do not see myself as a leader and I have no desire to be a leader. I would, however, like to help initiate a change of spirit in the world. I think that it is time for humanity to stand up and take a pro-life stand on everything. To say *no* to killing, *no* to the destruction and rape of our environment, *no* to the valuing of goods above human life, *no* to the senseless divorcement from our aged parents and our little children, *no* to the force that cuts us off from our ancient past, *no* to all these things that are meant to enslave us.

I'm not saying we should return to the ox cart. That is obviously ridiculous. To a large extent I believe, along with Bucky Fuller, that if we get the right head-set, this technology that we have can be used in a really beautiful way. But we've got to get off this rape-head. And I think Witchcraft offers an ethical alternative to this. Now, Papa Crowley was a fucked-up man in many ways. But, contrary to popular belief, he led a life of intense suffering, and his life of suffering was for one purpose, and that was to say, "Do what thou wilt shall be the whole of the Law. Love is the Law, love under will." They should inscribe that on the Rock of Gibraltar. It should be hung up in flags from the top of the Empire State Building and the Golden Gate Bridge. It should be carved on the book that the Statute of Liberty is holding. . . .

Q. If you were to paraphrase Crowley's statement in a way many people could understand, what would you say?

A. It means this: So you think you are helpless. You think all this is just happening to you. Well, that's bullshit! Because you are not just a son or a daughter of God. To be a son or daughter of God means you are equal to God and you have a responsibility to the One to get it together and make your Godhood count for something, because other than that, you are just another fuckin' insect. Now that's what it means. It also means that if we were all doing what we *really* wanted to do, we would do it in perfect harmony. Why do people kill and rape each other? This is an expression of the denial of love in that person's life. Now, I have been attacked, but frankly, I believe in my heart of hearts that the one who kills is enduring greater suffering than the one who is killed and that all "evil" is an expression of ignorance, an expression of the frustration of the Law of the One. And the Law of the One, whoever She is, in all Her many forms, is that we give to each other constantly. I am not talking about giving to the negation of self, I'm talking about giving to the glory of self. If you were what you could be the best and you did what you loved to do with all your might, you would create such light and such power that it would give pizazz to everybody in your immediate area, and even to those distant, perhaps.

Q. But how does this relate to the Craft's purpose—if it has a purpose?

A. I would say the ultimate purpose is to become that. If we become those kinds of people we will create an energy source for the regeneration of the whole world. We won't have to proselytize. We won't have to sell it on the street. That is what I consider my task to be, to bust my ass to achieve my Godhood. And if I fail to do that, I have become hopelessly debauched.

Q. Could you talk about ritual? One of the things about the Craft is that we do a lot of ritual. Why ritual? What is its purpose? Why do it?

A. The purpose of ritual is to change the mind of the human being. It's a sacred drama in which you are the audience as well as the participant, and the purpose of it is to activate parts of the mind that are not activated by everyday activity. We are talking about the parts of the mind that produce the psychokinetic, telekinetic power, whatever you want to call it—the connection between the eternal power and yourself. As for *why* ritual, I think that human beings have a need for art and art is ritual. I think that when we became sapient, we became capable of artistic expression. It is simply a human need.

One of the things I am deeply involved in is that I am trying to recreate the sacred music and dances of the Culdee tradition. I have reconstructed what I believe to be a good approximation of the circle dances, since few Irish circle dances have survived.

Q. It has seemed to me that much of the modern Craft and the Neo-Pagan movement lacks real music and real dance, in comparison to indigenous Pagan religious movements.*

A. That's absolutely true. Many things are lacking in modern Paganism. For example, in all indigenous Paganism possession of the participants by the gods and goddesses occurred frequently. This is not occurring frequently among Neo-Pagans and I consider it to be a sign of ill health in the Pagan movement. I attribute this to our loss of skill in the use of music, rhythm, dance, and psychogenetic drugs. In the Irish tradition music was essential to the success of the rites. I have finally initiated a traditional Irish piper so that we would be able to have the pipes, the harp, and the drums together in our rites. Another thing that was essential to the rites in ancient times was ritual drunkenness and sex. And I find this also lacking. We have to create those ecstatic states again. We have to offer people an energy source and a theological alternative, and we can only do this by offering real experience. We have to introduce real sacraments.

*This was written in 1976. Since that time there has been an incredible growth of ritual, music, dance, and drumming within Neo-Paganism.

But here the negative aspects of Christianity—the fascist political Christianity which has become the pervading form of Christianity in the world—this form of Christianity has produced fear of ecstatic states, fear of intelligent use of hallucinogens, fear of intelligent and sensitive use of sexuality to produce ecstasy. Now those are the three elements that have really been lacking, and worse still than any of that, Christianity has produced fear of personal responsibility for spiritual development. It has produced fear of independent thinking.

Q. What is your position on the use of drugs in the Craft? Most people I have interviewed take a very strong antidrug stance. Contrary to popular report, I came across very few groups that permitted any use of drugs in ritual.

A. I think that drugs, used with intelligence (like anything else), are important. Flying ointment was used in ancient times. Our ancestors definitely used drugs. Frankly, most Pagans and Witches are stumbling around in the dark. A Diabellero would laugh at us. A Southwestern Indian would think us ridiculous. I want people to start getting off. Drugs and sex are an essential part of magical rites. Some of the heaviest power is obtained that way. Do you know that there was a period in Irish history when people were so liberated that they were able to make love in any public place, without shame.

Q. I would find that very difficult.

A. Well, it's hard for me too, but I think this is the ideal we should attain to. I'm not saying we should fuck each other in public, but at least let's do it in private. Much of Neo-Paganism lacks the same content I've described before. The raising of power is an accidental occurrence among most of us at the present time. I find that difficult for my own self-esteem. It makes it difficult to work with people. I don't like going through empty ritual with anybody, especially my closest friends. Only once have I been to a Pagan gathering that happily enough "degenerated" into a Great Rite, and that was only because the Lady chose to give it to us at that time. I personally believe that anyone who calls themselves a Witch should have the capability to deal with different types of ecstatic states. But of course, these things have to be done with intelligence.

I wanted to tell you a story that fills me with humility, about a time I almost killed myself through stupidity. I was living on a commune that was situated in the middle of an apple orchard that was shaped like a long oval dish. And a peculiar thing that used to happen was that the dogs would start to bark at one end of the dish as if something was walking around the lip of this dish, and then they would stop. They would bark all the way around, and then stop. This happened a lot. My daughter was two months old at the time and when this "presence" would go around, I would get sensations of cold in my daughter's room. So on Halloween night I went out under the moon and I put on my ritual gear and I went out to look for this entity. The dogs began to bark. It was so beautiful out and I felt really strong. I suddenly felt this presence and I felt I was looking at an old Indian man, an old Pomo Indian. I couldn't see him, it was a feeling of his presence. I asked him what he was doing and he said he was a shaman and that he had died and needed help to get to the other world. He said he had been the last, and that there was no one left when he died to help him, no one who knew how to do it. So I stuck my knife in the ground and out of my knife came a path of light—again, I saw this in my mind. Well, he started to walk up this path like someone would walk up a staircase and when he was just about out of sight he looked down at me and said, "By the way, I give to you everything that comes into your hands if you close your eyes and walk back to the house."

So when he was up there, I pulled up the knife and put it back into my sheath, closed my eyes, and walked back through the orchard toward the house, and I realized at that point that I was in a field of belladonna. When I got to the house my hands were filled with the leaves of the "devil's weed" and I put the belladonna in a little velvet bag that I had and hung it up on the wall and kept it there for a long time.

One day I decided to make a flying ointment. I was doing it in front of a student who I wanted to impress. Well, I made it about a thousand-fold stronger than I should have because I was using denatured alcohol instead of spirits of wine to extract it, which is what they did in the old days. And instead of lard I was using hydrophilic ointment. As a result I increased the potency about two hundred to three hundred percent, and I got enough under my fingernails just by mixing it to kill me. And I would have died if it hadn't been for a friend of mine who was a doctor and a magician, whom I called immediately. I learned a very hard lesson. It was my first heavy experience with death, and a lot of bullshit pride went down the toilet with the rest of the flying ointment. So that was my gift from the old Indian man.

Q. How much of the Craft is really ancient?

A. I don't think it matters. I think a lot of it is. I think the important part is, again, that we get on it and produce these ecstatic states in which real generation of energy occurs.

Q. It's always seemed to me that it is going to be difficult to write an accurate history of the Craft revival because so many people lied for so many years about their origins.

A. Well, that's true, but I'm owning up to my bullshit. I'm not an adolescent anymore. As a matter of fact, I was an adolescent with a streak of psychological difficulties that was a mile wide. But I'm perfectly willing to admit that I was not passed all of this "shit" down and that what I had was largely intense scholarship and, thank Goddess, a little bit of real inspiration.

Q. Do you think there was a universal Old Religion such as Murray describes?

A. Not necessarily. I think people have always been very diverse. You get these people together over on one side of a village and three people on the other, and before you know it, you have two magical systems because somebody on one side had a dream about goats and someone on the other side had a dream about frogs. So you end up with a goat god on one side and a frog god on the other. What difference does it make how universal it is? Universality of form, *no!* Universality of content, *yes!*

And Margaret Murray missed another point. In Ireland all of the great Witches like Biddy Early were potato diggers. They were not aristocrats. They were among the so-called ignorant. They were denied formal schooling, but they flocked to the hedgerow schoolmasters to get a classical education. They ended up as hard-drinking old peasants with dirt on the floor and no plates to eat their spuds out of, but they were honored by poor people, because they were poor people.

Let me tell you a story, an Irish national liberation story associated with Biddy Early, the greatest of all Irish Witches. Biddy Early lived from the late 1700s to just before the famine in the 1870s. She was from West Clare, and when she died she was a very old lady, well into her nineties. She was a normal woman in many respects. She had a husband and two children. Her first husband died quite young. She married again and survived her second husband by about twenty years. After Biddy Early had been widowed for the last time, she lived in a stone cabin a little way out from town. I visited her house and everything she owned has been carefully preserved by the people in the town of Feacle. The townspeople love her so much, even though she has been dead for a hundred and thirty years. I was shown her grave and I talked to a woman who swears that her son, who almost died of infantile paralysis, was saved from death by the fact that she took him while he was dying and laid him on Biddy Early's grave, and I saw him walking around, so . . .

Like most Irish Witches, she would not necessarily have called herself a Pagan, even though she always used to say that she got her powers from the fairies. She was not on friendly terms with the orthodox Catholic clergy, but the people loved her, and finally she so proved her worth that the parish priest was completely won over to her way of thinking.

She was a drunk during the latter part of her life. She had rheumatism very bad and, like most Witches, she could not heal herself, so she drank to blunt the pain. Well anyway, Biddy Early became old and weird, and her power increased. She saved cattle, healed people, helped women to get pregnant, saved babies, prognosticated, and in general, excited the admiration of everybody so that people came from all over to be with her.

There was a man in the area who was what they call a "cabin hunter," which means he got bounty from the landlords by hunting out and evicting people who were squatting on basically useless pieces of land without paying rent. In those days dispossession from your home was tantamount to death by starvation, and a cabin hunter was, without doubt, one of the most ruthless and revolting kinds of men to arise on Irish soil.

After this guy had dispossessed a few families, Biddy Early confronted him. She showed up at church one day to everybody's amazement. She walked up to the guy and grabbed him by the collar as he was going out of the church and forced him down on his knees and she said, "I'm putting you down on your knees because I want you to realize that's where you are going to be by the time I get through with you, if you do any more of this to people." Well, the guy was terrified, but he didn't pay any attention to her, which was a big mistake. He had amassed quite a decent amount of money and had a good-sized farm and a number of servants. Well, word came to Biddy that he was at it again. It was a pouring rainy night and she was at a Ceili—which is a big musical event very common among Irish people. She was sitting around and the rain was pouring down and she said, "Well, he's up and at it again." "Who?" they asked. And she said, "That cabin hunter." And she picked up a burning stick near the fire and she blew on it a little, and at that moment the granaries and home of this guy were seized with a terrific fire in the middle of the rain. Everything the guy owned was burned to the ground. Nobody was killed, but his wife and kids barely managed to escape with their clothes. He was reduced to the same level of poverty as the people he had fucked over, and he came begging forgiveness to Biddy Early and she just told him to get out of the district or she would kill him.

Q. I guess I have to ask you at this point—because many people in the Craft would raise this question—what do you think about interfering magically in that way? Many in the Craft would say that was unethical. What do you say about such an action, burning down someone's house?

A. I would ask whether it was justified under the circumstances. I would say that if a grave injustice of that sort was committed, it was permissible. I myself have never willfully attacked anyone. But one of the things about the old Witches, they protected their community from oppression to the greatest of their ability to do so. And you would admit that this person was an alien to that community. He had made himself an alien, a tyrant. He was no longer a member of that community.

Q. This brings up a related question. Many Neo-Pagans and Craft folk feel the Craft is apolitical and should remain so. But I gather you think of yourself as a political person. First of all, how would you describe your politics?

A. I would describe myself as a spiritual socialist. I grew up in an anarchist family and, frankly, I love the statement "There's no government like no government," but what I believe, undoubtedly, is that the answer is equal distribution of goods. In the one period of successful Pagan society that my people enjoyed, we enjoyed perfect socialism.

Q. What period do you mean?

A. I am talking about ancient Ireland, the period between the time that Ireland was so-called "Christianized" and the time that the Vikings interrupted the socialist economy and forced Ireland to revert back to the chieftain system in order to get enough military organization together to fight the Vikings. And then, once the chieftains found themselves in power, they started boogying with the English . . . so need I say more? There was a hundred-and-fifty-year "Golden Age." But the problem was, we forgot that everybody else in northern Europe (despite the Aryan myth) had just barely swung down from the trees . . .

Q. Let's get back to this idea of Paganism being apolitical . . .

A. It is not! Nothing could be more "political" than an idea of this kind. But this is the knotty problem: if I lived in a country where there was a Marxist takeover, I would be just as much a threat to them as I am now, despite the fact that I am a socialist. A *truly* socialist culture would be working for the same ends as I am working for as a Pagan—the elimination of all constraint. But few socialist regimes are working for these goals. And the belief in socialist ideology based on materialism is, unfortunately, hollow. It leads to many of the same abuses as capitalism because it tends to ignore the true spiritual needs of human beings which are, in many cases, as important as material ones—although, frankly, I'd be the last person to tell someone who's starving that it will be all right in the next world. I don't think there is a next world. *This* is the next world!

Q. You mean reincarnation?

A. Yes. Like I said, *this* is the next world. I think we keep coming back. We are our children, so we had better get with it and make it better.

Q. Do you think the Craft poses an alternative, a counterthrust? Are we a threat to the status quo?

A. We always have been. We are for the absolute liberation of the human spirit from all constraint. We are for the godlike beauty and development of all persons.

Q. Do you have a fantasy of what an ideal Pagan-Craft life would be like, *for you?* And what kind of society would it be?

A. I would like to be the local nurse-Witch-midwife of a good-sized Irish village, the person people consulted when they got in trouble. The society would be socialist, Gaelic, free, and Culdee.

Q. I keep coming back to this, but how do you reconcile your socialist politics with the common viewpoint on the left that the occult is a "copout"—you know, "Religion is the opiate of the people," et cetera.

A. The problem is this: Many people go into rabid politics to escape self-examination, just as many people go into heavy guru trips or straight religious trips to escape self-examination. A commitment *only* to politics is as much of a copout as anything else because it avoids the responsibility of developing the god-self along with developing the political self. I'm trying to do both. I think it's quite possible to do both.

As for religion being the opiate of the people, I'd say that opium is the religion of the people, at the present time. The real problem is that *institutional* religion is indeed an opiate and, in the form Marx saw it, religion was appallingly evil; it was satanically evil in that it crushed the free will of people and dulled their will to resist injustice. But you've got to remember that in his day and age the women and children were dragging coal carts through three-foot-high caverns in England, getting killed by the hundreds, never seeing the sun rise, working until they cast themselves down exhausted onto beds of rags, or drank themselves into insensibility, and then had to go out and "hook" to get enough money to feed their kids. Then these bastards would get up in the pulpit and refer to rich people as the "betters" of these people, these martyrs who patiently endured the most horrible insults to humanity. Sure, religion was the opiate of the people, but it was debased religion, *not* magic. Magic is not the opiate of the people.

Q. What do you think is the relationship between feminism and the Craft? What do you think of the feminist Craft, of people like Z Budapest?

A. I think that because the present rape-head is very antiwoman, the feminist Craft has a great amount of validity. And what Z and others are proposing—the idea of a purely woman's religion—has a definite place in Paganism. I think a lot of women need it in order to heal themselves of their terrible wounds. I think Z and the others are doing something important. But I do not find the feminist Craft *personally* important to me, largely because I did not go through a stage in which I was sexually subjugated. Most women have not been so fortunate. I think Z has been persecuted because she is a threat to everything straight people represent—and if you ain't a threat, you ain't worth much. But for me, the idea of a purely woman's religion is difficult. My own preference would be to draw power with males and females of equal number and equal levels of dominance.

I don't believe that there are any psychological differences between men and women. In fact, I think the big mystery of our society is that men and women are exactly alike and that this truth is being hidden under an incredible load of bullshit. I think that women are just as capable of being dominant and men are just as capable of being kind and loving. The proof of the latter is that men are dying off in droves at an early age because their emotions are being crushed. Now, I have driven bulldozers. I have shoveled shit. I have built barns. I have flattened men on their backs and fucked them until their eyeballs popped out. I have carried a knife from time to time. But also, I am incredibly tender and loving to my children. I am the biggest nurturer you ever saw in your whole life. I also cook well. What I want to see the end of is the frustration of the male father instinct, which is being diverted into violence, and the end of the frustration of the female lioness instinct, which is being diverted into bitchiness.

Of course men and women are physically different and that is really pleasurable, but I don't think their minds are that different. Men and women seem physically stronger than each other in different ways. Women have far more endurance than men. They have to, in order to endure the childbirth experience. Men are capable of brief, intense bursts of muscular output which were meant to be used in hunting down deer and whatnot.

As for religion, remember that in the ecstatic state it is very common for male gods to possess females and for female gods to possess males. As a matter of fact, the reversal of male and female roles in a body has long been considered a typical sign of the true ecstatic state.

Q. Do you believe there was a former matriarchal period?

A. Yes, at least in my culture—Ireland. Let's put it that way.

Q. Do you believe a future one would be desirable?

A. No, I do not. I do believe in a society in which all beings, male and female and neuter (if such should arise), would be valued. Some people do not ever want to define themselves sexually and I believe they should have that freedom.

Q. Do you have any thoughts on homosexuality and bisexuality in the Craft?

A. I consider bisexuality, by and large, a higher state than simply homosexuality or heterosexuality because it offers a greater number of alternatives. You should be able to love all people that you love freely. If you desire to give physical expression to that love, that should be permitted. If men choose to make love only to men, and if women choose to make love only to women, that's fine, but they should remember it is just as limiting as restricting yourself only to a member of the opposite sex.

Q. As a Witch looking at our present civilization, how would you describe it? Since Witches look to pre-Christian sources for inspiration, what of the past should we look to, and what should we reject?

A. First of all, I agree with the Tantric Buddhists that this is an age of darkness. This is an age of darkness greater than the darkness of the Middle Ages. We are seeing humanity's catastrophic hour in which we can either rise above it to greater glory than we possibly can imagine, or we can be obliterated as a species by the Great Mother.

After stating that idea of doom, I must say that I have hope. I'm just an optimist. If I weren't, I wouldn't be having any children. I do think we have progressed. I think scientific knowledge is wonderful and I think it has tremendous possiblities for increased spirituality. For one thing, it has opened to us the possibility of contact with other beings, ultimately. It has given us a far greater comprehension of the vastness of the cosmos than we ever had before. This is such an essential breakthrough.

There is no doubt in my mind that human beings as a species are growing up. The problem is we are in a sort of shaky adolescence. This is a critical point. The teenager can either commit suicide or it can accept life and go on to adulthood. The tendency to reject everything is the hallmark of evolutionary adolescence. And I think it is the duty of those of us who can see the writing on the wall to look with a mature eye on what our ancestors actually had before we progressed.

I do not believe that the past age was the Golden Age. Any time in which children are sacrificed or old people are sacrificed, or where slavery exists or where blatant sexism exists, is not a Golden Age. In ancient Ireland, for example, there are many myths that reveal a past history of both matriarchal and patriarchal abuse.

As far as those things from the primitive which should be preserved— the rites of passage, which are basically the links between ourselves and the natural cosmos which give our lives rhythm and meaning. *That* is the biggest message primitive life had to offer. It was the only thing that made it survive. Often they did not have a pot to piss in, or a window to throw it out of. If they didn't have good mysteries, they did not make it. There was tremendous discomfort and suffering that people had to face every day to survive. Primitive life is not idyllic. It is incredibly difficult, and the only thing that made it possible was that they had a spiritual technology which enabled them to survive the terrible physical hardships.

I went through a period in which I thought all technology was evil. But for those of us who have lived on farms, let me tell you, you go out and bust your ass in the hot sun for a while and you'll find out how much time you have for thinking about your life.

Q. But don't you think there is too heavy a reliance on technology in our society, and a resultant limitation of our sensory awareness, of our faculties?

A. Oh yes, but that's due to the stage of society we now live in. We live in a society where technology is used to *diminish* human faculties. That is why I say this is an age of darkness. People are turning away from their faculties generally, not because of technology, but because of the head-set of the present society, the present exploitation-oriented culture in which goods are the measure of personal achievement, not the development of faculties. In ancient Ireland, during the period I was talking about earlier, we had a tremendous burst of artistic and intellectual expression. And the reason we had it is that people's honor was defined not by how many cows they had, or goats, or boar tusks, or gold coins; their honor depended on how well they could sing, how well they could produce poetry, how well they could make things of incredible beauty. It was those things that brought status. The arts of poetry and music became important because they were detached from goods.

Q. What do you think is the relationship of Paganism and the Craft to the ecology movement?

A. Paganism is the spirituality of the ecological movement, and the people's spirituality has always been a threat to the state.

Wicca priestess Elspeth consecrates the salt. *(Photo by Govan)*

Four Wicca priestesses (clockwise from upper left): Moria, Z Budapest, Sharon Devlin, and Theos.

Oberon and Morning Glory Zell-Ravenheart with one of their unicorns.
(Photo courtesy of The Living Unicorn)

Dancing around the sacred fire in the Opening Ritual at the 2005 Pagan Spirit Gathering in Ohio. *(Photo by Selena Fox, courtesy of Circle Sanctuary)*

A Druid procession in California—the New Reformed Druids of North America.

The late Gwydion Pendderwen in ceremonial robes. *(Photo by Selena Fox)*

LEFT: Dancers performing in the Temple of the Sabaean Order in Chicago.

BELOW: A May Day celebration at the 1982 Rites of Spring Festival in Massachusetts.
(Photo by Selena Fox)

The Church of the Eternal Source stages its annual Egyptian New Year's party in Los Angeles. *(Photo by Church of the Eternal Source)*

Selena Fox and friends gather herbs at Circle Sanctuary in Wisconsin. *(Photo courtesy of the National Film Board of Canada)*

Pagans at the 2004 Parliament of the World's Religions in Barcelona, Spain. Photo taken at the Pagans at the Parliament reception sponsored by Circle Sanctuary. *(Photo courtesy of Circle Sanctuary)*

7.

Magic and Ritual

The craft of the Craft is the craft of producing altered states of consciousness, and, traditionally, always has been.

—AIDAN KELLY

Ritual is to the internal sciences what experiment is to the external sciences.

—TIMOTHY LEARY[1]

Magick is a science in which we never know what we're talking about, nor if what we are saying is true.

—THE ABBEY OF THELEMA (MAGICAL ORDER)[2]

"THE CANDLES, the incense, and the images are props," the woman wrote to me. The spells, the chants, the dances are props. These things are not *magic*. The magic is the art (or science) of using the props. But to say this implies that magic and ritual have some purpose beyond the aimless activities of the ignorant, uneducated, and superstitious. Bonewits observes that "as intellectuals, we have been raised to have a kneejerk reaction to such terms as 'magic,' 'the occult,' 'ritualism,' 'the supernatural,' etc., so that we can only think about these subjects in the ways that we are supposed to."[3]

I have found it impossible even to discuss these subjects with certain upper-middle-class intellectuals; they elicit an almost religious response. Those who uphold the secular religion of rational humanism put up more blocks to such discussion than adherents of any other ideology.

I am hoping that most readers will adopt, at least temporarily, a more open position: a position that assumes that most of what has been written about magic is nonsense and that the truth about psychic realities lies under a thick web of ignorance, passivity, and conditioning. Perhaps the best approach is to allow yourself to play with the idea of magic in the way that Robert Shea and Robert Anton Wilson in their book *Illuminatus* allowed themselves to play with the idea of Eris, the Goddess of Chaos, letting her lead them in some unexpected directions. According to Wilson, that's precisely how magic works.

> The most advanced shamanic techniques—such as Tibetan Tantra or Crowley's system in the West—work by alternating faith and skepticism until you get beyond the ordinary limits of both. With such systems, one learns how arbitrary are the reality-maps that can be coded into laryngeal grunts by hominids or visualized by a mammalian nervous system. We can't even visualize the size of the local galaxy except in special High states.[4]

We have seen that most Witches and Neo-Pagans do not link "magic" with the "supernatural." The best comment on this subject comes from Leo Martello, author of *Witchcraft: The Old Religion.* He wrote: "I make no claims as a witch to 'supernatural powers,' but I totally believe in the *super* powers that reside in the *natural.*"[5]

Bonewits calls magic "a combination of an art and a science that is designed to enable people to make effective use of their psychic talents. These techniques have been developed for centuries all over the globe."[6] While "paranormal" events are extremely difficult to chart, or to repeat under laboratory conditions, much recent research has shown that the chances these events will occur increase dramatically during altered states of consciousness—in dreams, hypnosis, drugged states, sensory deprivation, deep meditation, and highly emotional experiences. Those who do magic are those who work with techniques that alter consciousness in order to facilitate psychic activity.

In *Real Magic,* one of the most intelligent explorations of this topic, Bonewits writes that the only real difference between magic and science is that magic is an art and a science that "deals with a body of knowledge that, for one reason or another, has not yet been fully investigated or confirmed by the other arts and sciences." He adds:

The physical Universe (assuming it's there) is a huge *Web* of inter-locking energy, in which every atom and every energy wave is connected with every other one. The farthest star in the sky has *some* influence on us, even if only gravitational; the fact that this effect is too small to mea-sure with present equipment is totally irrelevant.[7]

Bonewits also points out that all the traditional definitions of magic have been well in accord with natural philosophy. The popular belief that magic comes from a source alien and outside the natural contra-dicts the opinions of all the practitioners of the art throughout history. Bonewits gives copious examples, including S. L. Magreggor Mathers, one of the founders of the Order of the Golden Dawn, who wrote that magic is "the science of the control of the secret forces of nature," and Aleister Crowley, who called it "the Art and Science of causing changes to occur in conformity with Will." In fact, almost all definitions of magic seem to use the word in connection with "will," "concentration," and "attention." The English Witch Doreen Valiente said that magic re-sides in "the power of the mind itself," and that "the mind, then, is the greatest instrument of magic."[8] And the noted scholar of religions Jacob Needleman wrote that "attention is the key to magic, both as decep-tion and as real power." Needleman observed that most people's entire lives are characterized by misdirection and suggestibility, the very traits that are manipulated so successfully by the stage magician. This passiv-ity of attention, said Needleman, may be the most important human failing. In contrast, almost all who study real magic work vigorously to strengthen their attention.[9]

Some occultists say that there is really no need to talk about any "sixth sense," that the truly awakened use of the five senses by them-selves produces what we think of as "paranormal" activity. Colin Wilson implies this in his lengthy study *The Occult*. Wilson talks about "Fac-ulty X," which is not a "sixth sense" nor an "occult" faculty, but an or-dinary potentiality of consciousness. "It is the power to grasp reality, and it unites the two halves of man's mind, conscious and subcon-scious." "Faculty X" is latent within everyone; it is the key to all poetic and mystical experience. It is "that latent power that human beings pos-sess *to reach beyond the present*."[10] Doreen Valiente states a similar idea in *Natural Magic:* "By using our five senses rightly, the inner sixth sense is

added to them."[11] A training manual put out by the Dianic Covenstead
of Morrigana in Dallas says:

> Before you begin to doubt my use of the word magic, let me describe a
> study that was done on the Aborigines of Australia. . . . It was verified
> that they really knew where a herd of game was though it grazed beyond
> the horizon; knew when a storm was approaching; and knew where wa-
> ter was—though it lay some 10 feet below the surface. These are abilities
> that our society calls "magic." . . .
>
> These talents are achieved, not by any sixth sense, but by using the
> five senses to their full capacity. The native of Australia is no more super-
> natural than your dog. Keep your dog out in the woods long enough
> without access to water. . . . Your dog will scout around a bit, then dig a
> hole. As a reward for his efforts *and* his ability to *smell,* he'll receive a pud-
> dle of water. We accept this as a natural ability in a dog but think it's im-
> possible for a human because, too often, we relate to cement and steel as
> our natural habitat. It becomes possible once we recognize our real envi-
> ronment and begin to regain our kinship with it. The Aborigines knew
> about the distant animals because they *heard* them. In the same, but more
> obvious way, Amer-Indians heard distant sound by placing an ear to the
> ground. The Aborigine knows when a storm is forming through a very
> important sense. The aware native *feels* the storm, feels the change of
> barometric pressure. That same highly developed sense of feeling can
> also . . . increase the odds for the storm to bring rain.[12]

This definition equates magic with those techniques that lead to an
awakened, attentive, attuned sense of being.* Seen in this light, the various

---

*Not all occultists agree that magic is merely another way of talking about changes in conscious-
ness. In particular, Bonewits has said that these kinds of definition muddy the water; they "pretty-
up" magic. In a letter (winter 1978) he writes:

> As science gave people more control over areas that, previously, were only controlled hap-
> hazardly by magicians and priests, priests began to redefine magic in *religious* rather than
> *engineering* terms. They began to define it as a change in consciousness. A change in con-
> sciousness is certainly *required,* but when magic is really magic it involves changing the world
> as well as the interior person doing the magic.

> Most of the people who emphasize that magic is a system of enlightenment, or a system
> for spiritual development or changing consciousness, or that it is a way of seeing things, are
> people who for one political reason or another do not *dare* to suggest that magic can be a way
> of actually changing the physical world due to the control of psychic energies. It's much safer
> politically and socially to pretty-up magic as a spiritual development system.

fads for meditative disciplines, the weekend courses in "Mind Control," "Mind Dynamics," and other brand-name growth programs are, quite simply, brief magical-training courses that attempt (with more or less success and with a greater or lesser use of unnecessary and even harmful dogmas) to reawaken imaginative faculties, to increase concentration, attention, and self-confidence, and to facilitate a student's ability to enter altered states of consciousness at will. The wide interest in these programs can be explained as part of the contemporary search for self-mastery, initiation, growth, and change. The regenerative aspects of such programs should be applauded while the dogmas that grow out of them should be opposed.

Just as Neo-Pagans and Witches define magic in a pragmatic way, the trappings surrounding Witchcraft and other magical systems can also be understood without mystification. Chants, spells, dancing around a fire, burning candles, the smoke and smell of incense, are all means to awaken the "deep mind"—to arouse high emotions, enforce concentration, and facilitate entry into an altered state. Again, Bonewits has said some of the most sensible words on this subject, observing that "mandalas," "sigils," "pentacles," and "yantras" are all pictures to stimulate the sense of sight; "mudras" or "gestures" stimulate the kinesthetic sense; "mantras" or "incantations" stimulate the sense of hearing. The use of props, costumes, and scenery can also be seen as a method of stimulating the senses. In addition, drugs, alcohol, breathing exercises, and sexual techniques can serve to alter one's state of consciousness. According to Bonewits, these techniques function in the same way for a Witch or a ceremonial magician as for a Native American shaman or a Catholic priest. To say that these methods never cause psychic and psychological changes in the people involved is as absurd as other common attitudes—that certain religions have a monopoly on these experiences and that certain religions worship "God" while others worship "demons." These techniques have existed for thousands of years and were developed by human beings for the purpose of widening their perceptions of reality and changing their relationship to the world. They can be used creatively or destructively, for the enhancement of self or the destruction of self.[13]

Often our conceptions of psychic reality and the magical techniques we might use are simply a function of the particular culture we live in. Robert Wilson humorously observes:

Modern psychology has rediscovered and empirically demonstrated the universal truth of the Buddhist axiom that phenomena *adjust themselves* to the perceiver. . . .

Take Uri Geller as a case in point. . . . Geller saw, probably, the Looney Tunes in which wizards bent metals and he saw, probably, class B Hollywood Sci-Fi in which interstellar beings had names like "Spectre." Mr. Geller can now bend metal by thinking of bending it and gets messages from interstellar beings named "Spectre." . . .

The fairy-folk are like that. They come on as Holy Virgins to the Catholics, dead relatives to the spiritualist, UFO's to the Sci-Fi fans, Men in Black to the paranoids, demons to the masochistic, divine lovers to the sensual, pure concepts to the logicians, clowns from the heavenly circus to the humorist, psychotic episodes to the psychiatrist, Higher Intelligences to the philosopher, number and paradox to the mathematician and epistemologist.

They can even become totally invisible to the skeptic. For nearly 200 years all transmissions were cut off to the university-educated portion of European-American civilization. (It is doubtful that the Hottentots, the ants, the fish or the trees have ever been cut off for even 200 seconds.)[14]

Many people mistakenly identify magic with its opposite—religious dogma, or what some have called "failed magic." The concept of "failed magic" is often expressed by both scholars and Neo-Pagans. Jane Ellen Harrison, in her monumental *Epilegomena to the Study of Greek Religion*, writes that the dancer who plays a god in a sacred rite "cannot be said to worship his god, he lives him, experiences him." Only later, when the god is *separated* from the worshipper and magic is seen to fail, is religion born, and later, doctrine and dogma.[15] Robert Wilson expresses it this way:

> Most of humanity, including the theologians of all faiths from Catholicism to Mechanistic Scientism, represent a point where magic stopped, i.e., where the results of previous research inspired no further investigation but instead solidified into dogma.[16]

Or, to echo Sharon Devlin, religion was the opiate of the people, not magic.

Another way of looking at magic and at psychic reality would be to use the image of the ceremonial magician's circle with its "demon" as a metaphor. The circle is the microcosm of the universe, a place apart from the world and protected. It is a positive environment in which the serpents of one's own psyche can reveal themselves creatively. Within the circle the psychic barriers we erect to survive in the world can be eased down and those parts of ourselves that we seldom confront in daily life can be brought to the surface—here we face Graves's azoological creatures who "come to be questioned, not to alarm." Traditional warnings against the use of magic and occultism suddenly seem similar to warnings against the use of psychedelic drugs. Certain strengths are necessary before using both—a knowledge of oneself, a correct environment—so that these new perceptions can come to us in a manner that encourages our growth rather than our harm.

While it is generally and rightly stressed that rituals in the Craft and other Neo-Pagan religions are quite different from those of ceremonial magic, some of the same ideas apply. A Witch's circle generally serves as a reservoir to hold group energy, which is then directed. No "demons" or "angels" or other thought forms from a Judeo-Christian context are used. But psychic barriers do fall, energy is "felt" and exchanged, and azoological creatures do occasionally appear.

A beautiful description of psychic reality appeared in NROOGD's journal, *The Witches' Trine*. The art of divination, one writer observed, is "a process by which the conscious and unconscious minds of a particular person . . . cooperate to draw relevant information out of chaos, in answer to a question posed." The author describes this experience as "allowing one's mind to float upon the stream of the Tao, and observe the patterns of the current and the shapes they form." He then describes psychic reality:

I am an unabashed Jungian in regarding the mind and the personality as if it were an island in a psychic sea: what we perceive of ourselves, the conscious mind and the will, is like that part of an island above water; the edges and margins, outlines and heights, are pretty clear, but vary somewhat with the tides and waves on the surrounding ocean. . . .

Lying below this area, there is a vast and swarming depth of mystery which Jung calls the "collective unconscious," and it is from this deep and awe-full sea that the powerful, compelling archetypes rise up in their magical majesty, like a great whale or sea monster broaching the surface of consciousness, sending ripples and waves of change and renewal across the becalmed surface.

It is precisely these dwellers in the psychic deeps, with their protean shape-shiftings and vast power and numinosity, which are the gods and the powers consulted in divination. Their essence is perhaps objective— we cannot see to say—but their appearance is certainly subjective, moulding and shaping the stuff of an individual's mind into shapes which have meaning for her, and which she must, in turn, try to signal other islands.[17]

If one conceives of reality in this fashion, "magic" becomes the development of techniques that allow communication with hidden portions of the self, and with hidden portions of all other islands in this "psychic sea."

Bonewits, Aidan Kelly, and Wilson each approach magic from very different perspectives. Bonewits is a magician and Druid priest, Aidan's approach has been in terms of poetry and the Craft, and Wilson seems to combine his own iconoclasm with the theories of Timothy Leary and Aleister Crowley. Despite this, they all seem to agree that Neo-Pagan magical systems are "maps" for learning about what appears to be an objective reality but often defies analysis. This reality lies within the unconscious mind, although, Aidan observes, "Actually, it's not unconscious at all; it is you and I who are unconscious of it, but it is definitely real."[18]

Once we accept the notion of reality as this kind of psychic sea, from which a minority have been able to extract certain kinds of information, at least one purpose of ritual becomes clear: it is a sequence of events that allows this type of communication to take place. I asked Aidan, when I visited him in Oakland, "Why do you think people do rituals? What is the purpose of ritual?"

"No one really knows. It's a wide open question. Most theorizing that goes on about ritual goes on in a Christian context and Christians tend to be very heady people. The theories focus on what people 'believe.' But you do not understand the religion of a culture unless you know what people *do,* and what people do is their ritual. Why do you do a ritual? You do a ritual because you need to, basically, and because it just cuts through and operates on everything besides the 'head' level. And in this culture, this heady, agnostic, Christian, scientific, materialist culture, ritual is ignored. And since ritual is a need, and since the mainstream of Western civilization is not meeting this need, a great deal of what's happening these days is, simply, people's attempts to find ways to meet this need for themselves."

Bonewits has defined ritual as "any ordered sequence of events or actions, including directed thoughts, especially one that is repeated in the 'same' manner each time, and that is designed to produce a predictable altered state of consciousness within which certain magical or religious results may be obtained."[19] The purpose of a ritual is to put you into this altered state "within which you have access to and control over your psychic talents." He has also written that magical rituals are psychodramas, "designed to facilitate the generation of psychic energy and the focused disposition of that energy, in order to accomplish a given result."[20]

> Almost every magical-religious ritual known performs the following acts: emotion is aroused, increased, built to a peak. A *target* is imaged and a goal made clear. The emotional energy is focused, aimed and fired at this goal. Then there is a follow-through; this encourages any lingering energy to flow away and provides a safe letdown.[21]

A much more complete and complex explanation of how rituals work can be found in *Real Magic* and in "Second Epistle of Isaac," published in *The Druid Chronicles* (*Evolved*).

It is important to note that when Neo-Pagans use the word *ritual*, they mean something far different from what most people mean. For the majority, rituals are dry, formalized, repetitive experiences. Similarly, myths have come to mean merely the quaint explanations of the "primitive mind."

From my own experiences of Neo-Pagan rituals, I have come to feel that they have another purpose—to end, for a time, our sense of human alienation from nature and from each other. Accepting the idea of the "psychic sea," and of human beings as isolated islands within that sea, we can say that, although we are always connected, our most common experience is one of estrangement. Ritual seems to be one method of reintegrating individuals and groups into the cosmos, and to tie in the activities of daily life with their ever present, often forgotten, significance. It allows us to feel biological connectedness with ancestors who regulated their lives and activities according to seasonal observances.

Just as ecological theory explains how we are interrelated with all other forms of life, rituals allow us to re-create that unity in an explosive, non-abstract, gut-level way. Rituals have the power to reset the terms of our universe until we find ourselves suddenly and truly "at home."

How do these principles work in practice? Many Neo-Pagan or Craft groups could serve as illustrations, but perhaps the best example is the New Reformed Orthodox Order of the Golden Dawn (NROOGD), a tradition that has always emphasized ritual, poetic intuition, and vision.

NROOGD had its beginning in 1967. In 1972 an article in the order's journal, *The Witches' Trine,* declared:

> The NROOGD (and we got that name from the Goddess) is an assemblage of natural anarchists, bootstrap witches and alienated intelligentsia. . . . By us, a major vice of Christians is that they take themselves Very Seriously; we don't. Our motto: It is all real; it is all metaphor; there is always more; all power from the Triple Goddess.[22]

NROOGD took its rather mystifying name from the original nineteenth-century Order of the Golden Dawn, but added *New Reformed Orthodox* "because we aren't the old one . . . we're trying to operate on different principles from theirs . . . we're trying to cast back to principles that are much older than theirs."[23]

NROOGD is an entirely self-created Craft tradition.* The inception of NROOGD is revealing. It began not with one person's vision,

---

*In 1976 eight covens existed in NROOGD and large public sabbats were held often. Sometimes two hundred people would attend. Each coven was autonomous. All members spoke as equals, and issues were talked through until a decision was reached that all could accept. Decisions that involved the Order as a whole were made by the Red Cord Council, which was composed of the members of NROOGD covens who had belonged for more than one year and had attained the second degree (Red Cord). The covens, however, remained autonomous, and Red Cord Council decisions were treated as advisory for any one coven. The council merely suggested guidelines—that each coven observe the basic Craft Laws and keep its requirements for initiation at least as strict as the ones generally in force in the Order. In 1976 the Red Cord Council was dissolved. NROOGD declared itself to be no longer an organization, but a "tradition."

"How can such a system work? I asked one priestess, who laughed and told me, 'It took a lot of self-control.'" Aidan Kelly added, "Being a group of friends, we would discuss things the way friends would, until we reached an agreement. Later, we realized that this is what tradition says about how a council has to work, and the information that's available from anthropology says this is how tribal councils work."

but with a *ritual experience* that happened to a group of people almost by accident. Aidan Kelly, a founder of the group, described the event in an issue of *The Witches' Trine*.[24] He calls his account "true to the spirit, fictive like all human craft, and, like anything that has ever been written, incomplete." A woman called Morgana was taking an arts class in ritual at San Francisco State College. After the professor told the class that "the only way you can learn anything important about rituals is by doing them," she decided, having read Robert Graves's *The White Goddess* many times already, to attempt a Witches' sabbat. She invited a few close friends, including Aidan Kelly and Glenna Turner. Aidan composed a ritual outline after combing through his notes on the writings of Robert Graves, Margaret Murray, T. C. Lethbridge, and Gerald Gardner. He wrote:

> Reading through them, I began to feel intrigued and challenged. All I had was fragments, hints, innuendos, a riddle, a puzzle. But I also had some ideas about what general principles might weld these fragments into a whole. . . .

The outline was turned in, the professor said, "Do it," and a large group of friends gathered to work on the ritual.

> As we sat about the room, looking at copies, Glenna asked, "I assume there must be some point to all this, but what is it?"
>
> "If I understand Gardner right," I said, "the point is to raise the energy he talks about, and everything that goes on in the ritual is directed toward that raising. . . ." "Is there *really* such energy?" "Well, I dunno," I said.

The group polished the ritual, practiced it a number of times, and performed it for the class on January 11, 1968.

> We all enjoyed ourselves immensely. However, we realized afterwards that the ritual had not worked for us: we had noticed no unusual changes in our perceptions or emotions either during it or after it. . . . We made no plans to do the ritual again. . . .

However, Aidan noted, "a subtle change came over us." And the meetings of friends that had once been for games and gossip turned into an informal occult study group. And the ritual "refused to fade into the past; we found ourselves talking about it again and again." In the summer of 1968 the group decided to do the ritual again, this time as part of a wedding, a genuine participatory celebration rather than a performance, and this time something *did* happen. "As we lay around on the grass afterward, . . . some singing, some listening, and talking about the ritual, a comment kept cropping up, in one form or another, until it finally dawned on us that we were all saying: *this time I felt something.*" As a result, the group decided to do the ritual again, with a few changes, but this time on a true sabbat, Lammas, on August 1, 1968, in a grove of redwood trees. Again the group—this time numbering over forty—experienced a change.

> As Glenna began the opening conjuration of the ritual, a silence fell over the circle. Through the castings and chargings of the circle, through the invocations of the Goddess, it grew, and as Albion and Loik and Joaquin Murietta hammered out a dancing rhythm on their drums, as we whirled in a double sunwise ring, that silence swelled into waves of unseen lightness, flooding our circle, washing about our shoulders, breaking over our heads.
>
> Afterwards we wandered about the gardens, laughing and clowning, drunk on the very air itself, babbling to each other: it worked!

"We were hooked," Aidan told me. "And the thing has been going strong ever since." In the written account he added:

> I had already hoped, of course, but that day I became sure that the Craft could be religion for us skeptical middle-class intellectuals: because it did not require us to violate our intellectual integrity, because it operated nonintellectually, striking deep chords in our emotional roots, because it could alter our state of consciousness. Thus, that day began our actual evolution toward becoming a coven.

By the end of 1969 the members of NROOGD knew that what they were doing was, in fact, their religion. They initiated each other, began to have meetings (esbats) during the full moon, and declared themselves a potential coven. Then, during the Fall Equinox, during that time when, traditionally, the Eleusinian Mysteries were held, Aidan broke the usual order of the ritual and led the group in a torchlight procession through a state park, crying the ancient words, "Kore! Evohe! Iakkhos!"

> . . . down the hillside, across the wooden bridges, down to a spring, where, as I recall, I first spoke the myth of Kore's gift, then back to the circle, where with nine priestesses, we invoked the full Ninefold Muse, whom I, as Orpheus, audaciously led in a chain dance about the fire; then all joined the chain, and we danced until all but Isis and I had dropped from exhaustion, until again that silent energy rose and lapped its waves around us filling the entire campground with a warm mistiness that was everywhere except where I was looking.

By the end of 1971, "we knew," Aidan wrote, "we had somehow been transformed, that we had indeed become Witches."

All Craft groups talk about this "raising of energy" or "raising the cone of power." But how is this done? And what does it mean in terms of *ritual?* Since the methods used by a particular group are usually considered part of the "secrets" of a tradition, and methods vary, this information is often unavailable. But one of the best published explanations I have seen comes, again, from NROOGD:

> The coven, holding hands, and alternating male and female as closely as possible, dances sunwise, at first slowly, then gradually faster, perhaps singing, perhaps chanting a spell made up for the specific purpose the energy is to be used for, perhaps with music, perhaps silently. When the Goddess is the one who has been invoked, the Priestess stands in the center of the circle, in the persona of the Goddess, holding the appropriate tool. When she feels the energy reach its peak she calls out or signals a command to drop, which all in the circle do, letting go of the energy which the Priestess then directs onward to its intended goal. . . .[25]

Aidan notes that this explanation leaves all real questions unanswered. *How* are these things done? What does the energy *feel* like? How can the priestess tell when the energy has *peaked?* How do those in the circle *let the energy go?* The answers to these questions, he writes, can be learned only by experience. It is this experience that constitutes the "real secrets" of the Craft.

Many Craft rituals—NROOGD's included—are primarily religious and mythical. The rituals touch on the mythic themes of birth, death, and regeneration and assert the unity of mortals and deities. It is these aspects that seem to link the Craft (as well as a number of other Neo-Pagan religions) to the mystery traditions. What is striking about both Neo-Paganism and the mystery traditions (from our limited information about them) is that both assume that human beings can become as gods. In some traditions (as with the Church of All Worlds concept of "Thou Art God")* the idea expressed is that we *are* the gods, only some of us (perhaps all of us) have not realized it. In other traditions the idea expressed is that we are gods in *potential*. Many Western magical traditions have thus sought a path to the divine by strengthening the self rather than by obliterating the ego. And many Neo-Pagan groups have kept to this tradition, which is one reason why most of them have been blessed by a relative absence of authoritarianism, as well as a lack of "gurus," "masters," and so forth. The entire shamanistic tradition seems to assume that humans can, as I. M. Lewis has written, "participate in the authority of the gods."[26]

Aidan writes that all rituals in the Craft, at some level, celebrate the myth and history of the Goddess. That is similar, of course, to Graves's description of the true function of poetry as religious invocation of the Goddess, or Muse. Aidan describes the beginning of NROOGD rituals, all of which start with the Meeting Dance.

The dance begins with all facing outward, alternating male and female, and holding hands. We begin dancing withershins, the direction of death and destruction, singing, "Thout, tout a tout, tout, throughout and about," which are the words the Witches of Somerset used to begin their meetings. The men dance with the left heel kept off the ground, in the hobbling gait of the bullfooted god, the lamed sacred king. The Priestess who leads the dance lets go with her left hand, and leads the dance in a slow inward spiral: Ariadne leading Theseus into the labyrinth to face the sacred bull; Arianrhod leading Gwydion into Spiral Castle, where his soul will await rebirth. When the spiral is wound tight, the Priestess turns to her right and kisses the man next to her, as the Snow-White Lady of the Briar Rose kisses the prince who sleeps in the Glass Castle, to awaken him to a

*See pp. 158ff.

new life. The Priestess leads the new spiral outward, sunwise, the direction of birth and creation, and she (and each other lady) kisses each man she comes to. The spiral thus unwinds into an inward-facing circle, dancing sunwise. In this dance, withershins is transformed into sunwise, destruction into creation, death into rebirth, and those who dance it pass symbolically through Spiral Castle: here all the traditions and myths of the Craft are pulled together into a single, moving symbol. In a very real sense, all the other rituals of the Craft are merely "explanations" of this dance.[27]*

To go through this experience with understanding is to repeat symbolically the initiatory experience each time the circle is formed and the dance is completed.

Another point where initiatory symbolism occurs in many covens is during the invocation of the "Lords [although they may as easily be Ladies] of the Watchtowers." Aidan observes that these "Lords of the Towers"—the Craft may have stolen the term from Masonry—are archetypes, both human and immortal, who serve to remind coveners that they have "risen through the spiral of life and death and rebirth," and who thus represent "the goal toward which the spiral of reincarnation strives: to become both fully human and fully divine." An invitation for these "beings" to join the coveners and aid them in their work comes near the beginning of most modern-day Craft rituals, particularly those in the Gardnerian, Alexandrian, and other British Craft traditions. These archetypes are also called "the Mighty Ones."

Most covens operating in these ways also have a ceremony of "cakes and wine," during which the ritual dagger or athame is lowered into the cup and the cakes and the wine are consecrated. Aidan writes out of his experience with NROOGD:

This is the sacred marriage, the "great rite" of fertility, in a single image. . . . But notice, then, that the sacred marriage is not just between male and female, but also between "spirit" and matter, between the heavens and earth, between the worlds of gods and men, between death and birth. What is being said by the symbols is therefore something like "Sex is a true vehicle for the spiritual evolution of humankind for death and re-

---

*Truthfully, there is no "correct" way to do the Spiral Dance. There are fast spirals, and slow ones where you gaze into each person's eyes. There are kissing spirals, and a myriad of other forms.

birth are the two halves of the cycle that drives us up the spiral to the Goddess's realm."[28]

It was Aidan Kelly who first made me aware that the phrase "Drawing Down the Moon" originates in antiquity. "The Drawing Down of the Moon" and the "Drawing Down of the Horned God" are, perhaps, the two most extraordinary parts of Craft ritual, as performed in the covens of the revival. For here, in true shamanistic tradition, the Priestess (or Priest) can become the Goddess (or God) and function as such within the circle. Aidan notes that:

> The Priestess may begin by standing in the arms-crossed position called "Skull and crossbones" which symbolizes death, then later move to the arms-spread position called the "Pentacle," which symbolizes birth. She may also dance sunwise around the circle, from the quarter corresponding to death, to that corresponding with birth, and, back again. . . . What is thus symbolized, as in the Meeting Dance, is the Goddess's gift of immortality through reincarnation.
>
> What the Priestess does internally during this process is—either purposely or "instinctively"—to alter her state of consciousness, to take on the persona of the Goddess, whom she will represent (or even, in some senses, be) for the working part of the ritual.[29]

I have seen priestesses who simply recited lines and priestesses who went through genuinely transforming experiences. I have seen a young woman, with little education or verbal expertise, come forth with inspired words of poetry during a state of deep trance. I have heard messages of wisdom and intuition from the mouths of those who, in their ordinary lives, often seem superficial and without insight.

In a diary that Aidan wrote several years ago there is an unusual entry concerning the training of a new coven—unusual, certainly, from the point of view of the common assumptions of what covens are and how they work. It reads:

> Read them some poetry, explained how tetrameter couplets or quatrains work; assigned them each 8 lines of rhymed tetrameter on horses for next study group.[30]

Elsewhere, within his *Essays toward a Metathealogy of the Goddess,* he writes that poetry, "being emotionally charged language that operates on many levels of meaning at once, can arouse the interest of the Lady and open up a channel of communication with Her, whereas ordinary prosaic speech has no such effect."[31]

This is another key to the distinction we have been making between *belief* and *ritual experience.* The prosaic and poetic ways of looking at the world are different. But within the polytheistic framework of multiple realities, both can be maintained in a single individual. Once one comprehends this, much else becomes clear. One understands why the theories of Robert Graves have remained so popular throughout Neo-Paganism, despite the many criticisms of the scholarship in *The White Goddess.* One understands that it is precisely this visionary aspect of the Craft, with its emphasis on poetry and ritual, that is responsible for the creation of a group like NROOGD. Glenna Turner, a former atheist, described to me how she once told a newcomer to her coven (to his apparent shock) that she remained quite skeptical about all gods, goddesses, and psychic reality. This, however, had nothing to do with the fundamental reasons for her being in the Craft.

"I'm in the Craft because it feels right. I'm a visionary. The Craft is a place for visionaries. I love myth, dream, visionary art. The Craft is a place where all of these things fit together—beauty, pageantry, music, dance, song, dream. It's necessary to me, somehow. It's almost like food and drink."

Aidan and Glenna are not alone in stressing the relationship of poetry and art to the Craft. Almost half of all Neo-Pagans and Craft members interviewed for this book told me, unasked, that they wrote poetry and created rituals. Many of them have had their work published, at least in the pages of Neo-Pagan journals. It is no accident that those who are most respected within the Neo-Pagan movement are the poets, bards, and writers of rituals. These include, first and foremost, the late Gwydion Pendderwen, whose extraordinary *Songs of the Old Religion* are used throughout the Neo-Pagan movement; the late Victor Anderson, the blind poet and shaman; and Ed Fitch, the creator of an enormous number of Pagan and Craft rituals used in both this country and England. But these are not all. The poems of Penny Novack (writing often under the name of Molly Bloom), Caradoc, Aidan Kelly, Morning Glory

Zell-Ravenheart, Isaac Bonewits, and now countless new and younger poets fill the pages of Neo-Pagan magazines. Some of these people were always poets, but others told me that Neo-Paganism had opened a wellspring within them and led them to write poetry for the first time since childhood.

We have been focusing on NROOGD as a way to talk about Neo-Pagan (in this case Craft) poetry, magic, and ritual. But the emphasis on ritual in Neo-Paganism has other implications. A religion with such an emphasis is bound to have a different kind of theology and organization.

During much of the 1980s and early 1990s Aidan Kelly was in the curious role of theologian (or, more correctly, thealogian) in a most nontheological religion. His writings on the Craft seem to show more clearly than others the strongly antiauthoritarian nature of the Craft, since "No one has to believe anything" and "There is no authority in the Craft outside each coven." And if this were not so, we "would never have touched it with a ten-foot broom. We value freedom above all."[32] Aidan has said that the Craft, unlike Christianity and other world religions, is totally defined in terms of ritual—of what people *do*—and not what people *believe*. The religion therefore demands a creative response from people.

"It's a religion of ritual rather than theology. The ritual is first; the myth is second. And taking an attitude that the myths of the Craft are 'true history' in the way a fundamentalist looks at the legends of Genesis really seems crazy. It's an alien head-space. This is one of the ways in which the Craft *is* a type of mystery religion, because the classical mysteries functioned similarly. The promise of the mystery religions in the classical world was that of immortality and regeneration, something like that. And in one of the associated legends, after death the soul confronts the Guardian of the Portals and is asked the question, 'Who are you?' The reply given was never, 'I believe in such and such,' but a statement like: 'I have eaten from the drum. I have drunk from the cymbal. I have tasted the things within the holy basket. I have passed within the bridal chamber.' These are statements of having passed through certain experiences. And this seems to be very much the Gestalt and tradition of the Craft as well. . . . What makes a person a Witch is having passed through certain experiences, experiences that happen down on a subconscious level and bring about a type of transmutation."

A Witch, writes Aidan, is one who is "pliable, adaptable, change-able, in short, able to learn." He notes that those who change their opinions often appear "wicked" to others:

> But anyone who believes in an orthodox truth—is like a great tree, which will be toppled and destroyed by the hurricane of change that blows through this century, where the Witch is like the reed, which bends with the wind and survives.[33]

This emphasis on ritual rather than creed makes the Craft a "shrew," not a "dinosaur." It is small, but can adapt and survive. It is not encumbered by those structures that have characterized the major religions of the last five thousand years. Aidan contends that the major religions evolved to rationalize an agriculturally based civilization, a civilization that has been breaking down for the past two hundred years. The Craft never developed in cities where complicated religious structures evolved; it operated out in the country among people who were close to the land and "who were still, in effect, living in villages like the first villages that evolved ten thousand years ago." And, ironically, considering the many pronouncements against Witchcraft as a threat to reason, the Craft is one of the few religious viewpoints totally compatible with modern science, allowing total skepticism about even its own methods, myths, and rituals. This ability to coexist with modern science, writes Aidan, is a great strength, since "for many reasons one can strongly suspect that any belief system incapable of such coexistence has no future."[34]

Noting the tendency for some persons within the Craft to regard it as merely another ancient and revealed religion, Aidan told me that, were that so, the Craft would have no chance of surviving. But, as he wrote in "Aporrheton No. 1," the Craft is "not an ancient system of knowledge or metaphysics or doctrine, but an ancient way of perceiving reality that is again becoming available."

A major reason why the Craft is reviving now is that it depends on an "open" metaphysics, the only kind that can work in this century. The explanation I have evolved of such an "open" system is this: Reality is infinite. Therefore everything you experience is, in some sense, real. But since your experiences can only be a small part of this infinity, they are merely a map of it, merely a metaphor; there is always an infinity of possible experiences still unexplored. What you know, therefore, may be true as far as it goes, but it cannot be Whole Truth, for there is always infinitely further to go. In brief: "It is all real; it is all metaphor; there is always more." Everything in the Craft, no matter how useful, no matter how pleasing, even the Great Metaphor of the Goddess, is still only a metaphor.

Knowing that all truths are merely metaphors is perhaps the greatest advantage you can have at this point in history. Thinking that you know the "Whole Truth" keeps you from learning anything more; hence you stagnate; hence you die. But knowing that every truth is merely a metaphor, merely a tool, leaves you free to learn and to grow, by setting aside old metaphors as you learn or evolve better ones.[35]

If you asked Aidan, "Is the Goddess 'real'?", he would reply that She *is* real "because human energy goes into making Her real; She exists as a 'thought form on the astral plane,' yet She can manifest physically whenever She wants to. She does not exist independently of mankind, but She is most thoroughly independent of any one person or group." And yet, he continues, "She is a metaphor because, great though she may be, She is finite, like any other human concept, whereas reality is infinite."

Why do we need such a concept? "Because the human mind seems unable to grasp an undifferentiated infinity," he continues. "By creating our own divinities we create mental steps for ourselves, up which we can mount toward realizing ourselves as divine."[36] But he cautions that any such name for this reality "is an attempt to map (part of) psychic reality that seems all too willing to accommodate itself to any map you use, and you will get nowhere in trying to understand that reality if you don't keep its plasticity firmly in mind. The reason that dogmatism about magical systems is so poisonous is that everyone seems to live in a unique psychic universe. The magical system that works for one person may be totally contradictory to the system that works for another."

The lack of dogma in the Craft, the fact that one can *worship* the Goddess without *believing* in Her, that one can accept the Goddess as "Muse" and the Craft as a form of ancient knowledge to be tested by experience—these are precisely the things that have caused the Craft to survive, to revive, and to be re-created in this century. "This is a paradox," writes Aidan, but "the Lady delights in Paradoxes."[37]

As of 2006, there are about fifteen NROOGD covens active in California, Oregon, Washington, and Michigan. Covens in the San Francisco area cooperate to host seven or eight public sabbats each year and to provide local and national leadership in the Covenant of the Goddess. As this edition goes to press, NROOGD was in the early stages of planning a fortieth anniversary ingathering for initiates and dedicants to take place in 2007 or 2008. As for Aidan Kelly, he has had a long and complex journey, and has dealt with a number of personal problems.

In 1974, Kelly received copies of some Book of Shadows materials written by Gerald Gardner. These were owned by Carl Weschcke of Llewellyn Publications, and were sent to him by Isaac Bonewits, who first recognized their importance. Kelly also visited Ripley's in Toronto in 1975. It was there where he first saw the manuscript entitled "Ye Bok of Ye Art Magical," and deduced that it was the prototype of Gardner's Book of Shadows. He wrote a manuscript, "The Rebirth of Witchcraft," for Llewellyn. Kelly says it was too scholarly for Llewellyn's market and Carl Weschcke declined to publish it. Kelly used it to satisfy some requirements in his doctoral program, which he completed in 1980.

In 1976 Aidan realized that he had a serious personal problem and began seeking ways to deal with it. At the time the Pagan movement was not a mature enough movement to have its own resources for counseling, or twelve step programs, although some of these programs exist today. Unable to see how to use Craft methods to help him, in 1978 he rejoined the Catholic Church in order to cope with his problem. Aidan's memoir, *Hippie Commie Beatnik Witches,* covers the period of his life from 1953 to 1977. In 1978 he wrote me:

Very few people have noticed that I'm primarily a poet and that I am in no way a true believer in anything, neither the Craft nor in Christianity.

For a time, Aidan believed that the Goddess movement was simply a radically dissenting type of Christian sect, and that it was not Mary who was a pale reflection of the Great Goddess, but the Goddess who was a "de-Christianized and backdated version of Mary."

But in 1988, along with a second marriage, he returned to the Craft, joining a Gardnerian coven. His book *Crafting the Art of Magick* was published in 1991, and his *Religious Holidays and Calendars* in 1993. After that marriage ended and another began, Kelly and his present wife began to work in a 1734 tradition coven. (See "Traditions" in Chapter 5). Now living in Tacoma, Washington, and married, with a number of children, Kelly has made his living teaching at various colleges and high schools, as well as working in the computer industry. He has still been beset with a number of psychological problems, although he has conquered the problems that plagued him in earlier years. And perhaps, showing that things do come full circle at times, he and his current wife, Melinda Taylor-Kelly, founded Witch Grass Coven in 2000. It is a NROOGD-based coven with 1734 influence.

Women, Feminism, and the Craft

Note to the 2006 Edition: I have very complex emotions about this chapter. The passion and power is so striking. But today it reads as an amazing piece of history, and one that seems to have taken place a very long time ago. It was written in 1975, before President Ronald Reagan entered the White House and before Bill Clinton and George W. Bush. There was an incredible optimism about changing society and ending patriarchal oppression; from the perspective of twenty-first century America, there was perhaps a certain naïveté. But the power and spontaneity that came from the second wave of feminism and led directly from the consciousness-raising group to many feminist spirituality groups and covens changed the lives of countless women. I have decided to leave the chapter pretty much as is, with a few minor corrections, and address the question of feminist spirituality today at the end.

I.D.
I am a secret agent
Of the moon
> *Ex-centric*
> *Extra-ordinary*
> *Extra-sensory*
> *Extra-terrestrial*
Celestial subversive
Con-spiritorial
Spirita Sancta
> *Holy*
>> *Holy*
>>> *Holy*
And then some
And I have friends.

—BARBARA STARRETT[1]

For rebellion is as the sin of witchcraft. . . .

—I SAMUEL, 15:23

THERE ARE FEW moments in life, for most of us, when one feels as if one has stepped into a Minoan fresco or into the life of a wall painting from an Etruscan tomb. But on a full-moon summery night, in the unlikely borough of Staten Island, I entered such a moment.

Nineteen women, including a visiting Italian feminist and a well-known writer, sat nude in a circle in a darkened room. Molded candles of yellow hung by thongs from a loft bed. The small, bright flames cast a pattern of light and shadow. The room seemed powered by the muted oranges and reds of the bed coverings, and by the sweet scent of damiana mixed with marijuana, and by the pungent incenses that permeated the air, incenses with names like Vesta and Priestess.

A bathtub was filled with cool water, scented with musk and flower petals. A flutist played soft music while the women, one by one, entered the water, bathed, and were towel-dried by the others. There was laughter and a sense of ease.

After a short ritual a goblet was filled to the brim with wine and passed sunwise around the circle. The most powerful moment was yet to come: the pouring of libations to the goddesses and heroines of old. Each woman took a sip, then dipped her fingers into the wine and sprinkled a few drops into the air and onto the floor. As she did so, she invoked a particular goddess, gave thanks, or expressed a personal or collective desire. The well-known writer asked for the inspiration of Sappho to aid her in the work on her new book. The Roman Goddess Flora was thanked for the coming of spring and summer. Laverna—Roman goddess of thieves—was invoked to help a woman gain acquittal in a court case. Laverna was invoked again by a woman who had been caught using "slugs" instead of tokens in the New York subways.[2] Demeter, Isis, Hecate, Diana—the names continued. The goblet passed to each woman three times and the requests became more and more collective. Concerns were expressed for the coven as a whole, for women in struggle everywhere, for women in prison and in mental wards, for the feminist movement. And great hopes for the future were expressed by all. The ritual ended with the music of drums and flutes.

Fruit was brought out and shared—a large bowl carved from a watermelon, filled with blueberries and pieces of honeydew and cantaloupe. There were plates filled with olives and dates. There was a foamy strawberry drink and a huge block of ice cream covered with berries, and one large spoon. It was easy to feel transported to another age, some great festival, perhaps, an ancient college of priestesses on a remote island somewhere in the Aegean. . . .

This meeting was not unique. Such rituals have been taking place in many parts of the country. Feminist covens are springing up all over the United States, some of them showing more creativity, more energy, and more spontaneity than many of the more "traditional" groups that have been in existence for years. I have had personal contact with nine of these covens, located in Texas, California, New York, Oregon, Florida, and Massachusetts. There are others in Missouri, Illinois, Pennsylvania, and, almost certainly, many other states.

The presence of the feminist movement as a force that connects with Neo-Paganism and modern Witchcraft has had many ramifications. Links have been forged between these groups and new strains have been created. Many men (and some women) in the more mainstream Craft groups are upset by the growth of feminist covens, since many feminist Witches have purposely rejected some principles, norms, and structures of the modern Craft. Moreover, a number of feminists have stated that women are Witches by right of fact that they are women, that nothing else is needed, and feminist Witch Z Budapest has at times declared the Craft to be "Wimmins Religion," a religion not open to men. In addition, feminist Witches have stated that Witchcraft is not incompatible with politics, and further that the Craft is a religion historically conceived in rebellion and can therefore be true to its nature only when it continues its ancient fight against oppression.

In most of what we still may call the "counterculture," the split between the political and the spiritual seems to be widening. In contrast, portions of the feminist movement seem to be combining political and spiritual concerns as if they were two streams of a single river. In the early '70s there were a number of feminist conferences on questions of spirituality; several attracted more than a thousand participants. On the same agenda with discussions of Witchcraft, matriarchies, and amazons and workshops on the psychic arts, such as tarot, astrology, massage, psychic healing, and meditation, were discussions and workshops on the relationship between political, economic, and spiritual concerns.[3] It became clear at these conferences that many women regarded political struggles and spiritual development as interdependent, and felt that both were needed to create a society and culture that would be meaningful to them.

Linking feminist politics with spirituality and, in particular, with Witchcraft is not a new idea; the connection, which may be very ancient, was noticed in 1968 by the founders of WITCH, a group of women who engaged in political and surrealist protest actions. In its first manifesto WITCH stated that the link between women, Witchcraft, and politics is very old:

> WITCH is an all-woman Everything. It's theater, revolution, magic, terror, joy, garlic flowers, spells. It's an awareness that witches and gypsies were the original guerrillas and resistance fighters against oppression—particularly the oppression of women—down through the ages. Witches have always been women who dared to be: groovy, courageous, aggressive, intelligent, nonconformist, explorative, curious, independent, sexually liberated, revolutionary. (This possibly explains why nine million of them have been burned.) Witches were the first Friendly Heads and Dealers, the first birth-control practitioners and abortionists, the first alchemists (turn dross into gold and you devalue the whole idea of money!) They bowed to no man, being the living remnants of the oldest culture of all—one in which men and women were equal sharers in a truly cooperative society, before the death-dealing sexual, economic, and spiritual repression of the Imperialist Phallic Society took over and began to destroy nature and human society.[4]

The organization came into existence on All Hallows Eve 1968. The original name of the group was Women's International Terrorist Conspiracy from Hell, a name that certainly ruffled the feathers of conservative members of the Craft. But actually, only the letters were fixed; the name kept changing to suit particular needs. At a demonstration against the policies of Bell Telephone the group emerged as Women Incensed at Telephone Company Harassment. This kind of change happened a number of times.

At the time WITCH was founded it was considered a fringe phenomenon by the women's movement. Today its sentiments would be accepted by a much larger number of feminists, albeit still a minority.

Up to now we have seen the Neo-Pagan revival as a movement of men and women attempting to live a way of life and uphold values that have been a minority vision in Western culture. In general, Neo-Pagans embrace the values of spontaneity, nonauthoritarianism, anarchism, pluralism, polytheism, animism, sensuality, passion, a belief in the goodness of pleasure, in religious ecstasy, and in the goodness of *this* world, as well as the possibility of many others. They have abandoned the "single vision" for a view that upholds the richness of myth and symbol, and that brings nourishment to repressed spiritual needs as well as repressed sensual needs. "Neo-Pagans," one priestess told me, "may differ in regard to tradition, concept of deity, and ritual forms. But all view the earth as the Great Mother who has been raped, pillaged, and plundered, who must once again be exalted and celebrated if we are to survive."

Most women and men who have entered Neo-Paganism have done so because the basic tenets or the actual practices of one or another Neo-Pagan group came close to feelings and beliefs they already held. It "felt like home." It provided a spiritual and religious framework for celebration, for psychic and magical exploration, and for ecological concern and love of nature.

But some women have taken a very different path to Neo-Paganism. These feminists have a history of political action. They view all human concerns as both spiritual and political, and they regard the separation between the two as a false idea born of "patriarchy," an idea unknown before classical times and one that has produced much bitter fruit—the splitting of human beings into "minds" and "bodies." In this country, as we shall see, the writings of Native Americans often make this same point: that there is a relationship between the political and the spiritual. What is the nature of this understanding? How have feminists come to it? And how has this led to an identification with Witches and Witchcraft?

The two women who edited the *New Woman's Survival Sourcebook*[5] describe what they found on a cross-country journey:

> . . . we found wherever there are feminist communities, women are exploring psychic and non-material phenomena; reinterpreting astrology; cre-

ating and celebrating feminist rituals around birth, death, menstruation; reading the Tarot; studying pre-patriarchal forms of religion; reviving and exploring esoteric goddess-centered philosophies such as Wicce. . . . When we encountered this trend on our first stops, our initial reaction was indifference bordering on uneasiness and apprehension, a frequent reaction among feminists who are intellectually oriented or who are political activists.

Susan Rennie and Kirsten Grimstad said that they began to feel that their early impressions stemmed from a conditioning that had led them to suspect and ridicule anything that could not be "scientifically validated" and that they had always associated things spiritual with reactionary politics. They soon changed their view. As they traveled, they came to feel that women were becoming sensitized to "the psychic potential inherent in human nature," that women are "the repository of powers and capabilities that have been suppressed, that have been casualties of Western *man's* drive to technological control over nature." They put forth the idea that women have an even deeper source of alienation than that which comes from the imposition of sex roles; that, in fact, patriarchy has created the erroneous idea of a split between mind and body and that women's exploration of spirituality is "in effect striving for a total integration and wholeness," an act that takes the feminist struggle into an entirely new dimension. "It amounts," they said, "to a redefinition of reality," a reality that challenges mechanistic views of science and religion as well as masculine politics.

As we listened to women (these were the long night sessions) telling about their discoveries, explorations, experiences of the spiritual, nonmaterial in their lives, our conviction grew that this trend is not reactionary, not authoritarian, not mystical, not solipsistic. The effect we observed was that this reaching out for a broader conception of our natural powers, a larger vision of wholeness, is energizing, restorative, regenerative.[6]

Morgan McFarland, feminist and Witch, told me that for years she had kept her feminist politics and her Witchcraft separate. She said that when she first "blew her cover" and told her feminist friends that she was a Witch, she did so because she wanted to share with women a perspective that was broader than political action.

"I felt they were standing on a spiritual abyss and looking for something. And also, that I was looking for strong, self-defined, balanced women who were capable of perpetuating something that is beautiful and vital to the planet. Within my own tradition it is the women who preserve the lore and the knowledge and pass it on from one to another. I have begun to see a resurgence of women returning to the Goddess, seeing themselves as Her daughters, finding Paganism on their own within a very feminist context. Feminism implies equality, self-identification, and individual strength for women. Paganism has been, for all practical purposes, antiestablishment spirituality. Feminists and Pagans are both coming from the same source without realizing it, and heading toward the same goal without realizing it, and the two are now beginning to interlace."

The journey of feminist women toward a spirituality that does not compromise political concerns took less than five years. It probably began with the consciousness-raising group, which gave women a chance to talk about their seemingly private, personal experiences and find them validated by thousands of other women. The great lesson of CR was that personal feelings were to be trusted and acted upon, and that the personal was political. The step from the CR group to the coven was not long. Both are small groups that meet regularly and are involved in deeply personal questions. Only the focus differs.

Consciousness-raising provided an opportunity for women (some of them for the first time) to talk about their lives, make decisions, and act upon them, without the presence of men. Women used such groups to explore their relations with women, men, work, motherhood and children, their own sexuality, lesbianism, their past youth, and the coming of old age. Many women began to explore their dreams and fantasies; sometimes they tentatively began individual and collective psychic experiments.

Most of the original CR groups no longer exist. Most of the women have moved on. Some became politically active. Others began to explore women's history. Still others began to research the question of matriarchy. This research has turned up legends of the amazons and the myth cycles involving ancient goddesses and heroines; it has led women to the Great Mother Goddess in all her aspects. It has also led many women into magic and psychic work. Jean Mountaingrove, a coordinator of *WomanSpirit,* talked with me about this process.

"Feminism tells us to trust ourselves. So feminists began experiencing something. We began to believe that, yes indeed, we *were* discriminated against on the job; we began to see that motherhood was not all it was advertised to be. We began to trust our own feelings, we began to believe in our own orgasms. These were the first things. Now we are beginning to have spiritual experiences and, for the first time in thousands of years, we trust it. We say, 'Oh, this is an experience of mine, and feminism tells me there must be something to this, because it's all right to trust myself!' So women began to trust what they were experiencing. For example, a woman has a dream about stones and she goes to the library to see what there is about stones. Then she finds Stonehenge. Then she gets interested in the Druids and discovers that people do ceremonies and that this is often called Witchcraft. Then this woman becomes interested in Witches, and goes to them to find out what's going on. I think that's how connections are made."

Enter one of the many feminist bookstores in this country and look at the titles of poetry and literary magazines with names like *Hecate, 13th Moon, Dykes and Gorgons, Hera, Wicce,* and *Sinister Wisdom,* and you will have an idea of the connection between Witchcraft and goddess worship and the women's movement.* Almost all these magazines identify women with the Goddess and with Witches. The Witch, after all, is an extraordinary symbol—independent, anti-establishment, strong, and proud. She is political, yet spiritual and magical. The Witch is woman as martyr; she is persecuted by the ignorant; she is the woman who lives outside society and outside society's definition of woman.

In a society that has traditionally oppressed women there are few positive images of female power. Some of the most potent of these are the Witches, the ancient healers, and the powerful women of preclassical Aegean civilizations and Celtic myth. Many women entering on an exploration of spirituality have begun to create *experiences,* through ritual and dreams, whereby they can *become* these women and act with

---

*Most of these magazines no longer exist. And sadly, many feminist bookstores have gone out of business.

that kind of power and strength, waiting to see what changes occur in their day-to-day lives. After all, if for thousands of years the image of woman has been tainted, we must either go back to when untainted images exist or create new images from within ourselves. Women are doing both. Whether the images exist in a kind of atavistic memory thousands of years old (as many women believe) or are simply powerful models that can be internalized, women are beginning to create ritual situations in which these images become real. Priestess McFarland writes:

> We are each Virgin Huntresses, we are each Great Mothers, we are Death Dealers who hold out the promise of rebirth and regeneration. We are no longer afraid to see ourselves as her daughters, nor are we afraid to refuse to be victims of this subtle Burning Time. The Wicce is Revolutionary.

The images are especially powerful for women who have made the biggest break with the society at large: the lesbian separatists, many of whom seek to remove themselves entirely from the mainstream of a society that they view as contaminated by masculine ideology. Thus, while most of the members of the Neo-Pagan movement are heterosexual or bisexual, and the feminist movement includes women with every conceivable attitude toward sexuality, the feminist Craft and the movement toward feminist spirituality seems to have a larger percentage of lesbians than either. But lesbianism today seems to be only partly a sexual orientation. It is also, perhaps primarily, a cultural and political phenomenon. For example, I have met a number of women who call themselves "lesbians," but from a purely sexual definition would be considered asexual or celibate. A large number of lesbian separatists have essentially made a political choice, often leaving husbands and families as part of a reaction against patriarchal attitudes.

Special issues of such feminist magazines as *Quest, Country Woman*, and *Plexus* have been devoted to "spirituality" and its relations to feminist politics. For example, an editorial in *Country Woman*'s special issue noted that women's experiences, both political and spiritual, have never been part of noticed events. Women political leaders have been figureheads for the most part; women religious leaders have usually been considered "minor" or "eccentric," as opposed to the male "gurus" or "messiahs." The editorial also noted that just as the private emotional experiences of women turned out to have been shared by countless numbers, "the hidden, private, unconfirmed experiences of our spiritual search" should be revealed, "in the belief that they too are shared by many women, and are significant." The editorial then observed that while many women believe that politics and spirituality are incompatible, the division between the two is artificial, a product of the patriarchal misconceptions built into the language:

> Two streams are developing in women's consciousness—a political and a spiritual stream. Since women are noticing different parts of their experiences and categorizing them in terms used by the patriarchal culture, they feel suspicious of each other.
>
> To "political" women, "spiritual" means institutions and philosophies which have immobilized practical changes and have channeled women's energies into serving others to their own detriment. To "spiritual" women, "political" means institutions and philosophies which deny the unity of people and have channeled women's creativity into destroying and fighting each other. But each stream is trying to examine deeply the human experience—on the material and on the non-material levels. Women are revolutionizing their consciousness in both directions and challenging the patriarchal ideas and institutions of religion and government by holding to their own women's experience of life.[7]

An article in *Quest* took a similar position:

> The so-called division between cultural feminism and political feminism is a debilitating result of our oppression. It comes from the patriarchal view that the spiritual and the intellectual operate in separate realms. To deny the spiritual while doing political work, or to cultivate the spiritual at the expense of another's political and economic well-being is continuing the patriarchal game.[8]

The enormous response to the "spirituality" issue of *Country Woman* gave birth to the quarterly *WomanSpirit*. It comes out of Oregon, coordinated by Ruth and Jean Mountaingrove and a changing collective of women who often move around the country, issue to issue, to give a new group of women a chance to get involved with the magazine.* *WomanSpirit* comes together in an unusually cooperative and collective manner. Nothing is "pushed," and both Jean and Ruth have said that they feel the magazine is subtly guided. Each issue carries poetry, art, and articles filled with personal experiences—a kind of consciousness-raising effort of the spirit.

Jean and Ruth have described their editorial policy as open, growing, and evolving. "We feel we are in a time of ferment. Something is happening with women's spirituality. We don't know what it is, but it's happening to us and it's happening to other people. *WomanSpirit* is trying to help facilitate this ferment. Ruth and I feel that women's culture is what we want. We want so much to live what we can glimpse. Now that we understand what our oppression has been, and have fantasized what it would be like not to be oppressed, we want to *live* like that. That is what we're looking for; we want the world to be a wonderful place for us to live in; and we don't want it in three thousand years; we want it this afternoon; tomorrow at the latest."

Most feminist Witches feel the spiritual and political can be combined. They are moving toward a position that would, in the words of Z Budapest, "fight for our sweet womon souls" as well as our bodies.[9]

Others, such as writer Sally Gearhart, have maintained the division between spiritual and political, arguing strongly against the effectiveness of most present-day political action. Gearhart has written, in the pages of *WomanSpirit,* that the three known strategies of political action—political revolution, seizing power within the system, and setting up alternative structures—have failed, and that only a fourth strategy, "re-sourcement," finding a "deeper," "prior" source as powerful as the system itself, can threaten it and lead to change. She has noted that thousands of women have separated themselves from society and the world of men to lead isolated lives with other women, and she has called upon women who choose to remain in the mainstream of society, or women who have no choice, to set up a buffer state to protect the separatist women until they can gain the strength to create a new women's culture.[10]

WomanSpirit is no longer published, although back issues are still available (see Resources).

But other women, such as Z Budapest, believe in the firm, continuing connection between spirituality and day-to-day political action. As an exile from Hungary, feminist, Witch, and leader of the Susan B. Anthony Coven in Los Angeles, Z has made her life a vivid example of this connection. We have seen how she left Hungary in 1956, but soon found her oppression as a woman in the United States equal to her oppression in Hungary. Z brought the status of Witchcraft as a religion to public attention with her trial in 1975 on the charge of violating a Los Angeles statute against fortune-telling. This law is one of the countless vague antioccult laws that exist in almost all cities and states. Ostensibly they exist to prevent "fraud," but they ban divination of all kinds, not merely divination for money. The Los Angeles law forbids the practice of "magic," clairvoyance, palmistry, and so forth. Since Z does tarot readings professionally, she was "set up" by a woman police agent who telephoned for a reading. Z was brought to trial, convicted, and fined. Many witnesses, ranging from anthropologists to Witches, came to her defense.

Z told me she regarded the trial as important to establish the right of women to define their own spirituality and to practice their own talents independent of religious and behavioral codes set up by men. Since fortune-tellers are numerous in Los Angeles, Z felt she was singled out because of her feminist politics and the visibility of her small shop, The Feminist Wicca, which is a center for women and Witchcraft. Some Neo-Pagans objected to the manner in which the case was fought; they felt it could have been won if it had been argued differently, and that losing established a dangerous precedent. There were also objections to the slogan of the trial: "Hands off Wimmin's Religion." Z replied that most fortune-tellers pay their fines quietly and go on practicing, and that her court battle had been useful in awakening the community to the links between politics, women, and religion; "winning" was irrelevant.

Z Budapest is a dynamic woman full of energy and humor. Despite the fact that her feminist and separatist politics have alienated her from much of the Neo-Pagan community, she has inspired love and respect in California Neo-Pagans who have come to know her, no matter what "official" attitudes toward politics and feminism they hold. For a while, articles and letters in the Neo-Pagan press denounced her. But many members came to her defense, including one of the most esteemed bards of the Craft: Gwydion Pendderwen. Gwydion, to the surprise of many, went further than mere support. He repeated several times his view that the feminist Craft has some of the truest representatives of the Goddess; as might be imagined, this view has not won him praise from all quarters. "I have seen women in a lot of different head-spaces," he told me in 1976, "but never, until this past year, had I seen the Goddess incarnate. I've seen the most supreme expression of Woman in these lesbian feminist Witches. Often the women are in their late thirties or forties. They have gone through an incredible load of bullshit in their lives; they have found their true selves and have risen above it. They look head and shoulders above the rest of us. The combination of feminism and Witchcraft has produced some Amazons, some true giants."

Z Budapest, with a few other women, started the Susan B. Anthony Coven on December 21, 1971. When I visited Z in 1976, the coven had twenty to forty active members and a larger group of three hundred women who joined in some activities. Related covens had been started in at least five other states. The Manifesto of the coven says in part:

> We believe that in order to fight and win a revolution that will stretch for generations into the future, we must find reliable ways to replenish our energies. We believe that without a secure grounding in womon's spiritual strength there will be no victory for us. . . . We are equally committed to political, communal and personal solutions.[11]

Z told me that "religion" was "the supreme politics." "Religion is where you can reach people in their mysteries, in the parts of their being that have been neglected, but that have been so important and painful; and you can soothe and heal, because self-images can be repaired through knowledge, but only experience can truly teach. The experience is to allow us these conditions again. Let us be priestesses again. Let us feel what that feels like, how that serves the community."

Z's vision for the future is a socialist matriarchy. Like many feminist Witches, she has a vision of a past matriarchal age, during which "the Earth was treated as Mother and wimmin were treated as Her priestesses." The manifesto accepts many of the theses proposed by Elizabeth Gould Davis in *The First Sex:* that women were once supreme and lost that supremacy when men, exiled from the matriarchies, formed into bands and overthrew the matriarchies, inventing rape and other forms of violence.

The Craft, Z wrote, is not a religion alone.

It is also a life style. In the time of the Matriarchies, the craft of wimmin was common knowledge. It was rich in information on how to live on this planet, on how to love and fight and stay healthy, and especially, on how to learn to learn. The remnant of that knowledge constitutes the body of what we call "witchcraft" today. The massive remainder of that knowledge is buried within ourselves, in our deep minds, in our genes. In order to reclaim it, we have to open ourselves to psychic experiences in the safety of feminist witch covens.[12]

Z's interest in the idea of matriarchy is not unique among women involved with goddess worship and Witchcraft.

Matriarchy

It is not surprising that spiritual feminists, in their explorations of the hidden and distorted history of women, have been attracted by the idea of a universal age of goddess worship or a universal stage of matriarchy. These women have been reexamining those philosophers, historians, anthropologists, and psychologists who have argued that women in the ancient world held a position of relative power. Sometimes that power is political, as in the Marxist theories of a prehistorical classless society (as stated, for example, by Friedrich Engels and, more recently, Evelyn Reed); sometimes it is mythic or religious or psychological, as in the theories of J. J. Bachofen, Helen Diner, C. G. Jung, Erich Neumann, Robert Graves, and Esther Harding.[13]

The idea of matriarchy has ramifications that go beyond the question of whether or not the matriarchy ever existed in reality. When a feminist reads Strabo's description of an island of women at the mouth of the Loire, or when she reads an account of an ancient college of priestesses or Sappho's academy on Lesbos, or the legends of the Amazons, a rich and possibly transforming event takes place.

It is easy to get sidetracked by details, and that is the game many scholars play. We will play it also for a while. Prehistory is a wide open field. There is little agreement on what the word *matriarchy* means, and even less on whether ancient matriarchies existed, or if they did, on how "universal" they were. It is fashionable for scholars to dismiss the idea. This seems due partly to the lack of conclusive evidence in any direction and partly to (predominantly male) scholars' fear of the idea of women in power. The question may never be answered satisfactorily. Sarah Pomeroy, in her careful study, *Goddesses, Whores, Wives, and Slaves*, observes that most questions about prehistory remain unanswered. She allows herself to wonder why archeologists have unearthed four times the number of female figurines as male statues, why Minoan wall frescoes portray many more women than men, why the lyric women poets of Sappho's time appear to have so much freedom and independence, and what meaning lies behind the strong, dominant women depicted in those Greek tragedies and myths that speak of the preclassical age. It is as foolish, she notes, to postulate male supremacy in preclassical times as it is to postulate female supremacy.[14] According to Bonewits, we may have to wait until the field of archeology and prehistory is no longer dominated by men. Most women, however, are not waiting.

Many scholars have seemed to delight in showing certain weaknesses in the arguments of some of the more popular feminist writers on the subject of matriarchy, such as Elizabeth Gould Davis in her book *The First Sex*.[15] It's fairly easy to argue that one cannot always take myths literally, as Davis often does, nor can one assume that societies that venerated goddesses necessarily gave power to women. Such "reasonable" arguments have been used, however, to avoid dealing with the central thesis of the matriarchy argument: that there have been ages and places where women held a much greater share of power than they do now and that, perhaps, women used power in a very different way from our common understanding of it.

It is therefore important to stress that, contrary to many assumptions, feminists are viewing the idea of matriarchy as a complex one, and that their creative use of the idea of matriarchy as *vision* and *ideal* would in no way be compromised if suddenly there were "definite proof" that no matriarchies ever existed. In the same way, Amazons may prove to be fictions or creations of the deep mind, or, like Troy, they may suddenly be brought to the surface as "reality" one day. In either case, the feminist movement is giving birth to *new* Amazons, a process that is bound to continue no matter what we unearth from the past. An illustration may be helpful.

In Gillo Pontecorvo's extraordinary film *The Battle of Algiers,* Algerian women confront the French by giving out an eerie yell, a high ululation that makes the flesh crawl. After the film appeared I occasionally heard the same cry in the demonstrations of the late 1960s, but never in the way I heard it later, in the 1980s in meetings of women. Amazons are coming into existence today. I have heard them and joined with them. We have howled with the bears, the wolves, and the coyotes. I have felt their strength. I have felt at moments that they could unite with the animal kingdom, or ally themselves with all that is female in the universe and wage a war for Mother Nature. These women are creating their own mythologies and their own realities. And they often will repeat the words of Monique Wittig in *Les Guérillères:*

> There was a time when you were not a slave, remember that. You walked alone, full of laughter, you bathed bare-bellied. You say you have lost all recollection of it, remember. You know how to avoid meeting a bear on the track. You know the winter fear when you hear the wolves gathering. But you can remain seated for hours in the tree-tops to await morning. You say there are no words to describe this time, you say it does not exist. But remember. Make an effort to remember. Or, failing that, invent.[16]

These spiritual feminists do not feel their future is contingent on a hypothesized past. They do not feel they need the words of scholars to affirm or deny their reality. "After all," I was told by Z Budapest, "if Goddess religion is sixty thousand years old or seven thousand, it does not matter. Certainly not for the future! Recognizing the divine Goddess within is where real religion is at."

In other words, the *idea* of matriarchy is powerful for women in itself. Two feminist anthropologists have noted that whatever matriarchy *is,* "the whole question challenges women to imagine themselves with power. It is an idea about what society would be like where women are truly free."[17]

There is no consensus on what the word *matriarchy* means, for either feminists or scholars. Literally, of course, it means government by mothers, or more broadly, government and power in the hands of women.

But that is not the way the word is most often used. Engels and others in the Marxist tradition use the word to describe an egalitarian preclass society where women and men share equally in production and power. A few Marxists do not call this egalitarian society a matriarchy, but most in the tradition do.

Other writers have used the word *matriarchy* to mean an age of universal goddess worship, irrespective of questions of political power and control. A number of feminists note that few definitions of the word, despite its literal meaning, include any concept of power, and they suggest that centuries of oppression have made it impossible for women to conceive of themselves with such power. They observe that there has been very little feminist utopian literature. (The exceptions are the science fiction of Joanna Russ,[18] Monique Wittig's *Les Guérillères,* and some of the fiction published in the feminist small presses.)

Elizabeth Gould Davis and Helen Diner do see matriarchy as a society in which women have power; and they conceive of *female* power as qualitatively different from *male* power. This has led many feminists to define *matriarchal* as a different kind of power, as a realm where female things are valued and where power is exerted in non-possessive, non-controlling, and organic ways that are harmonious with nature.

Echoing that kind of idea, the late Alison Harlow, the feminist Witch from California, told me that for her the word *patriarchal* had come to mean *manipulative* and *domineering.* She used *matriarchal* to describe a world view that values feelings of connectedness and intuition, that seeks nonauthoritarian and nondestructive power relationships and attitudes toward the earth. This is far different from the idea of matriarchy as simply rule by women.

In addition to feminists, a number of Neo-Pagans have been exploring the question of matriarchy, and ending up with similar views about power. Morning Glory and Oberon Zell-Ravenheart, of the Church of All Worlds, told me they disliked that term "or any 'archy'" and preferred to use the word *matristic.* The Zell-Ravenhearts call themselves *matristic anarchists* and, noting the views of G. Rattray Taylor in *Sex in History,*[19] say that they consider matristic societies (generally matrifocal and matrilineal) to be characterized by spontaneity, sensuality, anti-authoritarianism; embracing, in other words, many of the values Neo-Pagans share today.

There are a number of ways to approach the question of ancient matriarchies. Many have their roots in the historical theories of J. J. Bachofen and Friedrich Engels. Both men wrote in the nineteenth century, and although they had very different perspectives, both set forth the idea of a universal matriarchy in terms of historical laws and universal stages of evolution. The idea of a universal stage of matriarchy was, in fact, widely accepted until the twentieth century; it is now, like Murray's theory of the witch cult, out of favor.

Engels and the Marxists who followed him based their views on the theory of historical materialism. According to Marxist theory, a primitive egalitarianism prevailed before class society; women and men shared equally in production and power. Feminist writers such as Evelyn Reed continue to base their views on an evolutionary perspective and to define matriarchy as this kind of egalitarian society. Reed, it should be emphasized, has many original ideas in her book *Woman's Evolution,* including a novel speculation on the origin of the incest taboo as women's control of cannibalism.

J. J. Bachofen also sought universal laws of history, although he based these on religious organization, myth, and symbol rather than on materialism. In his *Myth, Religion, and Mother Right* (1861), he wrote that matriarchal societies were characterized by universal freedom, equality, hospitality, freedom from strife, and a general aversion to all restrictions. His works were attractive to poets, artists, and psychologists. Some of the feminists who come out of the Bachofen tradition, such as Davis and Diner, have dropped all reference to evolutionary theory, but accept the primacy of myth and symbolic forms. Davis has a cyclic and cataclysmic theory of history, influenced greatly by Immanuel Velikovsky. Patriarchy is seen as a degeneration, morally and even technologically.

Interestingly, it is non-Marxists such as Davis and Diner who are able to envision a dominance matriarchy with women in power, although that power is exercised in a very different fashion. Some feminist anthropologists have also noted contradictions in Davis's work; for example, she says that the rule of the matriarchies was totally benevolent, but that one reason for their downfall was the revolt of men who had been cast out. One feminist, knowledgeable in both Marxist theory and current feminist thought, told me that she was sympathetic to the argument that wars exist because of masculine aggression, but she noted, "I'm sus-picious of it. I've read enough Marxist theory to feel that such a view may be a reactionary way of looking at things."

Since theories of stages of evolution in history are hard to "prove," most leading anthropologists and archeologists outside the Marxist tra-dition refuse to concern themselves with them. Many feminists, like-wise, tend to drop the arguments for a universal stage of matriarchy and instead simply state that goddess worship was widespread in many an-cient societies, and that archeological evidence continues to mount, with the unearthing of ancient societies such as Catal Huyuk and Mersin. Matriarchy may not have been *universal,* and present matrilin-eal societies may be oppressive to women, but there *is* plenty of evidence of ancient societies where women held greater power than in many so-cieties today. For example, Jean Markale's studies of Celtic societies show that the power of women was reflected not only in myth and legend but in legal codes pertaining to marriage, divorce, property ownership, and the right to rule.[20]

Many women are also looking at the idea of matriarchy from points of view other than those of political theory, history, archeology, and ethnography. They are reexamining those writers, poets, and psycholo-gists who have talked for years about *feminine symbols, feminine realms,* the *anima,* and so forth. The theories of C. G. Jung, Esther Harding, and Erich Neumann are being reexamined, as well as those of poets who have claimed to get all their inspiration from the Great Goddess— Robert Graves and Robert Bly, for example. Neumann, in *The Great Mother,* asserts that matriarchy was not a historical state but a psycho-logical reality with a great power that is alive and generally repressed in human beings today. Writers like Neumann and Graves, in the words of Adrienne Rich, have seemingly rejected "masculinism itself" and have "begun to identify the denial of 'the feminine' in civilization with the roots of inhumanity and self-destructiveness and to call for a renewal of 'the feminine principle.'"

The recurrence of strong, powerful women in myth, legends, and dreams continues, and Rich observes:

Whether such an age, even if less than golden, ever existed anywhere, or whether we all carry in our earliest imprintings the memory of, or the longing for, an individual past relationship to a female body, larger and stronger than our own, and to female warmth, nurture, and tenderness, there is a new concern for the *possibilities* inherent in beneficient female power, as a mode which is absent from the society at large, and which, even in the private sphere, women have exercised under terrible constraints in patriarchy.[21]

Philip Zabriskie, a Jungian, has also noted the power and *presence* of the ancient archetypes of goddesses and ancient women, and has stated that they can be evoked in one's present psychic life.[22] It is obvious that even the Greco-Roman classical goddesses who were known in a patriarchal context are much richer images of the feminine than we have today, although it is equally true that such images can be used to repress as well as to liberate women.

As we have seen, women are looking at the matriarchy from a complex point of view. They differ as to the existence of past matriarchies, and even as to what a matriarchy means in terms of power. Some, such as Davis, see childbearing as the source of women's ancient power, the innate difference that creates a kind of moral superiority stemming from closeness to nature and life. Other feminists, starting with Simone de Beauvoir and continuing through Shulamith Firestone, see in childbearing the root of women's oppression.

Feminists also differ on the question of matriarchy as a "Golden Age," a view expressed forcefully in Davis's *The First Sex*. Some see matriarchy as, above all, an *idea* about women in freedom. They often picture the ancient matriarchies as societies governed by the kind of loose, supportive, anarchic, and truly unique principles that many of today's feminist groups are organized around, principles developed from the tradition of consciousness-raising. But others see the matriarchy rather as a place that *was* better for women, but had problems and difficulties of its own. Alison Harlow, for example, told me that she once had a vision, a small glimpse of the matriarchy.

"I was standing with my mother, father, and sister as a long procession passed by. A priestess was being carried along. She pointed at me with a long wand. I was chosen. Suddenly I was taken away from everything I knew. Now, maybe I loved it, but the lack of freedom scares me. A theocracy is only good if the priestess is always right. Now perhaps they were more intuitive than us, but . . ."

The matriarchy, according to Alison, was a period of thousands of years when women functioned strongly in the world.

"I do not consider there was ever a matriarchy that was a utopia. I do not consider it the ultimate answer to all our problems. I do think there were values from the ancient matriarchal cultures that we would do well to readopt into our present lives. I've spent a long time trying to come to grips with what it would mean to live in a goddess-centered theocracy, where people belonged to the Goddess, where cities belonged to the Goddess, where you are born to serve Her will. Concepts of human freedom as we understand them are not very compatible with any sort of theocracy and I am very committed to individual freedom."

If feminists have diverse views on the matriarchies of the past, they also are of several minds on the goals for the future. A woman in the coven of Ursa Maior told me, "Right now I am pushing for women's power in any way I can, but I don't know whether my ultimate aim is a society where all human beings are equal, regardless of the bodies they were born into, or whether I would rather see a society where women had institutional authority."

In any event, most women who have explored the question do see a return to some form of matriarchal values, however that may be expressed, as a prerequisite to the survival of the planet. We might note that Robert Graves wrote in 1948:

> I foresee no change for the better until everything gets far worse. Only after a period of complete religious and political disorganization can the suppressed desire of the Western races, which is for some practical form of Goddess worship . . . find satisfaction at last. . . . But the longer the hour is postponed, and therefore the more exhausted by man's irreligious improvidence the natural resources of the soil and sea become, the less merciful will her five-fold mask be. . . .[23]

The idea of a matriarchy in the past, the possibility of matriarchy in the future, the matriarchal images in myths and in the psyche, perhaps in memories both collective and individual—these have led spiritual feminists to search for matriarchal lore. The road is not merely through study and research. It involves the creation of rituals, psychic experiments, elements of play, daydreams, and dreams. These experiences, women feel, will create the matriarchy, or re-create it.

Ritual

In Chapter 7 we looked at the idea that ritual may be seen as a way human beings have found to end, at least for some few moments, their experience of alienation from nature and from one another.

To reiterate, theorists of politics, religion, and nature have often viewed the universe in a strangely similar way. Many have noted the interconnectedness of everything in the universe and also the fact that most people do not perceive these connections. Spiritual philosophers have often called this lack of perception "estrangement" or "lack of attunement"; materialists have often called it "alienation" or, in some cases, "false consciousness." Perhaps theory, analysis, and the changing of society can end our experience of alienation on the conscious level. Ritual and magical practice aim to end it on the unconscious level of the deep mind.

By ritual, of course, we do not mean the continuation of those dry, formalized, repetitive experiences that most of us have suffered through; these may once have produced powerful experiences, but in most cases they have been taken over by some form of "the state" for purposes not conducive to human liberation. We are talking about the rituals that people create to get in touch with those powerful parts of themselves that cannot be experienced on a verbal level. These are parts of our being that have often been scorned and suppressed. Rituals are also created to acknowledge on this deeper level the movements of the seasons and the natural world, and to celebrate life and its processes.

Many strong priestesses in the Craft have talked about the primacy and importance of ritual.

Sharon Devlin: "Ritual is a sacred drama in which you are both audience and participant. The purpose of it is to activate those parts of the mind that are not activated by everyday activity, the psychokinetic and telekinetic abilities, the connection between the eternal power and ourselves. . . . We need to re-create ecstatic states where generation of energy occurs."

Z Budapest: "The purpose of ritual is to wake up the old mind in us, to put it to work. The old ones inside us, the collective consciousness, the many lives, the divine eternal parts, the senses and parts of the brain that have been ignored. Those parts do not speak English. They do not care about television. But they do understand candlelight and colors. They do understand nature."

Alison Harlow: "It is a consciousness-altering technique, the best there is. Through ritual one can alter one's state of consciousness so that one can become perceptive to nonmaterial life forms, whatever you choose to call them, and through this perception one can practice subjective sciences."

In what additional ways do feminists think about ritual? Jean Mountaingrove began by telling me that, since dreams seem to speak from our unconscious mind to our conscious mind, perhaps ritual is the way our conscious mind speaks to our unconscious mind. She and Ruth would occasionally share water from a stream, she said, to symbolize the sharing of the waters of life. She added, "If I want my unconscious mind to understand that I love Ruth and that she is my partner, then we engage in a ritual together and the connection is very deep. All the words we say to each other may not do that. Ritual makes the connection on another level."

Jean observed that ritual has a particular and radical relevance for feminists. "Since our culture—the one we share with men—is so contaminated, often when a group of women get together we only have words to use, and these words are all conditioned. Often we can argue and use words to divide. But our actions have not been so limited by men's definitions. So we need to find actions that have clearness about them, that do not have hierarchical connotations . . . because some of our symbolic behavior has also been contaminated. If I pat someone on the head, it may mean that I am bigger and better than she is; it may be condescending . . . but if we can find ways, like washing each other's hands, actions that we do mutually and that have not been contaminated, we can use such actions as a kind of vocabulary that cuts underneath all the divisiveness and unites us."

Women are creating this new language. They are developing psychic skills in workshops with names such as "Womancraft" and "Womanshare"; they are reinterpreting events related to women in a new light and using these insights to create new ritual forms. For example, a number of women are using "Moon Huts" for retreats during menstruation. In doing this, they are re-creating an experience common to women in ancient times and in many tribal societies today. These women are convinced that, contrary to popular scholarly assumption, such retreats were not forced on women because of "uncleanliness" but were introduced by women themselves to celebrate their mysteries and to have a time of collective interchange. It has also been theorized that before artificial light and modern forms of contraception all the women of a tribe often menstruated at the same time.

Some women have begun to work with their dreams. In one instance, twelve women spent a weekend in the wilderness together. They slept in a circle with their heads together, facing inward, their bodies like spokes of a wheel. They wove "dream nets" from wool and fibers and sewed "dream pillows" filled with mugwort and psyllium seeds. A woman who experienced this weekend told about her dream:

> I am with a mass of chanting women under the deck of an old ship which we are rowing across the sea. All the women are looking for their city. We have come to this land and see a man standing on the shore. He asks, "Why have you come here?" We say, "We came here to find our city." He says, "Go back. Your city is not here." We pay no attention to him but start through this forest right at the edge of the water and walk down an inward-turning spiral road which leads us down to a city in its center. At the bottom is an old woman. We say, "We have come to find our city." She says, "This is an old city. This is not your city. Your city is not here. You have to look further." The women then disperse to look for our city.

WomanSpirit commented:

> Margaret's dream tells me that we will not find our culture in the men's world, but neither will we find it in our ancient woman culture. It is still to be found.[24]

One example of a simple and powerful ritual is described in an early issue of *WomanSpirit:* an attempt to come to terms with the concept of Eve. Feminists and Neo-Pagans naturally feel that the story of Adam and Eve, as commonly interpreted, has probably done more to debase and subjugate women than any other such tale in Western history. In addition, the story has been used to inculcate demeaning attitudes toward mind, body, sensuality, and the pursuit of knowledge. *Woman-Spirit* suggests that only by turning over biblical tradition and regarding Eve positively, as the bringer of knowledge and consciousness, can we end permanently the split between mind and body and the hatred of both that was foisted upon us by Christianity and much of the classical and Judiac traditions from which Christianity sprang. In an article titled "Eve and Us" a woman leading a class in theology speaks of coming to acknowledge Eve. She presents a counterthesis: Eve was "the original creator of civilization." The Fall was really "the dawn of the awakening of the human consciousness." The class notes that it is Adam who is passive. Eve is persuaded logically and rationally to become "as the gods." "Eve and the serpent were right," said the leader of the discussion. She opened up "a whole new world of consciousness. Every advance in literature, science, the arts can be traced mythically back to this event and in this light it is indeed Eve who is the original creator of civilization . . . and we women have the right and the responsibility to claim her as our own."

At this point in the class a spontaneous ritual occurred. Unlike many rituals in the Craft, which are learned carefully, this came from an immediate need to affirm women's being. A woman produced an apple and "the apple was ceremoniously passed around the circle and each woman took a bite, symbolizing her acceptance of and willingness to claim Eve as her own and recognize our mutual oneness with her."[25]

Women have also begun to create lunar rituals. The association of women with the moon is, of course, an ancient association.

> Last night [one woman writes] we hung out of the east windows and howled at the moon, incredible orb gliding up over the eastern hills . . . and made up a song to her. During the night I fell into a dream that enabled me to undersee the belly of death, as the giver of life. . . .[26]

Another wrote of a celebration of the New Moon in June 1974:

Women seemed to be coming up the hill for hours. I hear voices and flutes in the distance. . . . We sit in a large circle in front of the cabin. We join hands and follow each other down to the meadow, down into the darkness. We tell stories of darkness. Ruth tells the myth of Persephone being abducted by the lord of the dark underworld. . . . We begin a free word and sound association from the word "darkness." This is very moving. Words and sounds come fast and flowing and die down again. There are images of fear as well as power and strength expressed, a lot of images of calm, warmth and rest. A large candle is lit. . . . [Billie] has made ten small bags with drawstrings, each from a different material. Each has a black bead attached to the drawstrings, signifying the dark moon. She gives them to us to keep. We are very pleased as the bags are passed around the circle. . . . We find seeds inside the bags. Seeds, the small beginning, the New Moon. . . . We stand for a farewell reading of Robin Morgan's 'Monster,' ending with us all shouting, 'I am a monster!'[27]

Confronting the "Goddess"

It is not surprising that women involved with these rituals and perceptions should begin to confront the idea of a feminine deity. They have found the Goddess, or have been led to the Goddess, and the idea of "Goddess" is fraught with problems and potentialities for feminists.

No matter how diverse Neo-Pagans' ideas about deities, almost all of them have some kind of "Thou Art God/dess" concept, even though a few whom I have met would say that such a concept as articulated by the Church of All Worlds contains a bit of hubris. Nevertheless, most would agree that the goal of Neo-Paganism is, in part, to become what we potentially are, to become "as the gods," or, if we *are* God/dess, to recognize it, to make our God/dess-hood count for something. This is a far different notion from the common conception of deity in Western thought as something "exclusive," "above," "apart," and "outside." Oberon Zell-Ravenheart has said that in Neo-Paganism deity is *immanent,* not *transcendent.* Others have said that it is *both* immanent and transcendent.

But whatever "deity" is for Neo-Pagans, there is no getting around the fact that the popular conception of deity is *male.* And this is so, despite the countless esoteric Christian and Jewish teachings that say otherwise. The elderly Neo-Pagan author W. Holman Keith, whose little-noticed book *Divinity as the Eternal Feminine* came out in 1960, noted:

> In spite of all that Christians say to the contrary, they conceive of deity as male. They will protest that they do not believe in anthropomorphism, that God is spirit, etc. But these protestations do not completely dispose of the above contention.[28]

Mary Daly has written extensively on the idea that all the major religions today function to legitimate patriarchy and that since "God is male, then the male is God," and that "God the father" legitimates all earthly Godfathers, including Vito Corleone, Pope Paul, and Richard Nixon.[29] Since this image called "God" is the image beyond ourselves, greater than ourselves, it becomes the image of power and authority, even for most of those who profess atheism. It functions as a powerful oppressive image, whether or not we believe in "him." And this remains true whether "man" created "God" in "his" own image or the other way around. As many occultists would say: There is a continuing relationship between the human mind and its creations, and those creations affect all other human minds.

Western women have been excluded from the deity quest for thousands of years, since the end of Goddess worship in the West. The small exception is the veneration paid by Catholics to the Virgin Mary, a pale remnant of the Great Goddess. So, if one purpose of deity is to give us an image we can *become,* it is obvious that women have been left out of the quest, or at least have been forced to strive for an oppressive and unobtainable masculine image. Mary Daly has proposed to answer this problem with the idea of "God as a verb," but many women find this too abstract and prefer to look to the ancient goddesses.

A female deity conceived of as all-powerful and all-encompassing can create contradictions and other problems in an anarchistic feminist community that emphasizes the value of self. But the attractiveness of the Goddess to women was inevitable. She touched a deep chord. Just listen to the Goddess songs that have come out of the women's community, ranging from Cassie Culver's humorous "Good Old Dora" to Alex Dobkin's extraordinary hymn to the Goddess and the Goddess within all women, "Her Precious Love."[30]

Many women have had powerful experiences with deity as feminine. "It never occurred to me to create my own religion," wrote one woman, "or more importantly, that god was female. Discovering that femaleness gave me a tremendous sense of relief. I felt her blessing touch me for the first time. I felt a great weight drop from me. I could actually feel my last prejudices against my own female mind and body falling away."[31]

Jean Mountaingrove, who spent twenty years as a practicing Quaker, told me of her first experience of deity as feminine.

"There was this Quaker meeting at Pendle Hill, a Quaker retreat center outside of Philadelphia. We used to have meetings every morning and lots of weighty Quakers came to these meetings. And I sat in the back row, morning after morning, listening to all these messages coming through about 'the fatherhood of God' and 'the brotherhood of Man' and 'he' and 'him.' And one morning, after about thirty minutes, that feeling inside of me that I have always learned to trust as guidance just swelled and swelled until I was shaking, a feeling that I should say something. And I felt if I didn't say it, I would be betraying something I had learned to trust. All I said was, 'Mother. Sister. Daughter.' And it fell like a rock through this still pool of fatherhood and brotherhood. But then, everyone in the stillness could reflect on what that might mean. I had declared myself. I had declared myself as being—what shall I say?—on the fringe. My feminism was considered 'in poor taste.' But several women came up to me afterwards and hugged me, and that meant a lot."

Jean told me that years later, at a commune in Oregon, she began getting impressions from a special grove of trees. "I had a scientific background which makes fun of this sort of thing," she said. "I thought it was pretty kooky. But Ruth had a background in Jungian psychology and had read *The White Goddess,* so she watched all of this happening with a lot of understanding which I myself did not have. I was drawn to the tallest tree in the grove and I would come to it and just cry; and it was tears of joy and relief; and I would feel that I was whole and perfect; my own judgment of myself was that I was very inadequate, but the spirit of the tree, which I called Mother, seemed to think I was all right."

Some of the women I met had an easy and long-term relationship with the Goddess. One woman told me that she would go hunting with her father and brother as a child, and would call upon Diana as mistress of the hunt. This recalled my own invocations to Artemis and Athena when I was twelve.

Other women had a problem with the idea of "Goddess." "It's amazing," one wrote, "how much the basis of my life now has to do with the things I was raised not to believe in and to some extent still don't . . . that goddess business makes me very antsy too. I would like to know more about how spirituality ties in (or doesn't tie in) with what I call 'real life'—going to work, having relationships, getting sick, doing or not doing politics."[32]

In another example the editors of *WomanSpirit* described the results of a discussion among a group of women:

> Many of us had a real difficulty with the concept of a goddess. Who was this goddess and why was she created? We felt she represented different forms of energy and light to different people. Even though we had trouble with the words, we felt that the force of the goddess was inevitable, she was flowing through us all by whatever name, she was the feeling of the presence of life. Goddess was a new name for our spiritual journey, the experience of life.[33]

The obvious criticism is that the idea of a single Goddess, conceived of as transcendent and apart, creates as many problems as the male "God." Trading "Daddy" for "Mommy" is not a liberation. A woman takes up this question.

> I have been thinking for days and weeks about Goddess. The word, the concept, the idea, the projection, the experience. For many months I have been experimenting with the word, using it freely, reverently, longingly. That is my strongest experience in regard to it, one of longing—oh that there were a Goddess to pray to, to trust in, to believe in. But I do not believe in a Goddess.
>
> Not a Goddess who exists as a being or person. Yes, the goddess who is each of us, the one within. . . . She is the inner strength, the light, the conscious woman who knows her own perfection, her own perfect harmony with the cosmos. . . .
>
> This common existence of all things is holiness to me. . . . I understand that the word "Goddess" is used to express this unity reality in a

symbolic way. So too is "God" used. There is no one called "Goddess" to seek outside of ourselves or to enter into us. There is only in each our own center of unity energy which is connected to all. . . .

But I do not believe that changing the sex of that concept does away with its problems. Not at all. To say Goddess instead of God still continues the separation of power, the division between person and the power "out there!" . . .[34]

I doubt this dilemma exists as forcibly for women in the Craft, perhaps because some of them have never considered these ideas. But, more importantly, as priestesses, they are taught that within the circle they *are* the Goddess incarnate. And they have been taught to draw that power into themselves through the ritual of Drawing Down the Moon. Women who have come to the Goddess outside the channels of Neo-Paganism and the Craft are beginning to find rituals and concepts that allow for the same idea. They are finding the Goddess within themselves and within all women. And, as might be expected, those feminists who have found joy in ritual, and who have discovered that the concept of "Goddess" feels right inside, are often drawn into the Craft.

"Feminist Covens" and "Traditional Covens"

Today the Craft has been adopted as "the religion" of a large portion of the feminist spiritual community. In a few cases feminists have joined with other women (and very occasionally with some men) in the more "traditional" Craft. In other cases feminists have formed their own covens. The word *traditional* is used here as a convenient way to distinguish between feminist Witches and those who have come to the Craft and Neo-Paganism by routes previously described. To understand the differences between "feminist" and "traditional" Witches, it is instructive to look again at the leaflets put out in 1968 by the feminist group WITCH.

Almost all the qualities that distinguish feminist Witches from members of the "traditional" Craft appear in the leaflets. One assumption of WITCH was that any group of women can form their own coven and declare themselves Witches by simply making the decision to do so and enforcing it magically.

If you are a woman and dare to look within yourself, you are a Witch. You make your own rules. You are free and beautiful. You can be invisible or evident in how you choose to make your witch-self known. You can form your own Coven of sister Witches (thirteen is a cozy number for a group) and do your own actions. . . .

Your power comes from your own self as a woman, and it is activated by working in concert with your sisters. . . .

You are a Witch by saying aloud, "I am a Witch" three times, and *thinking about that.* You are a Witch by being female, untamed, angry, joyous, and immortal.

It is obvious that these ideas easily come into conflict with notions of formal training, priesthoods, and hierarchical structures. The second assumption of WITCH was that Witchcraft is inseparable from politics.

Witchcraft was the pagan religion of all of Europe for centuries prior to the rise of Christianity, and the religion of the peasantry for hundreds of years after Catholicism prevailed among the ruling classes of Western society. The witchcraft purges were the political suppression of an alternative culture, and of a social and economic structure. . . .

Even as the religion of witchcraft became suppressed, women fought hard to retain their former freedom. . . .

Thus, the witch was chosen as a revolutionary image for women because they did fight hard and in their fight they refused to accept the level of struggle which society deemed acceptable for their sex.

The third assumption that WITCH made in its leaflets was that it was necessary to create new rituals, "festivals of life, instead of death." These three assumptions have continued as the wellsprings of feminist Witchcraft, but they—particularly the first two—have often been at odds with the assumptions of the mainstream Craft.[35]

We end up with a kind of paradox. Thousands of women have suddenly found the Craft. They have come to it, as most people do, not by conversion but by a kind of homecoming. As the woman told me at the lecture, "I always knew I had a religion, I just never knew it had a name." But often these same women find a Craft somewhat different from the one we've been talking about. They have defined it differently to meet their own needs. And, having found the Craft through inspiration, poetry, reading, dreams, feminist politics, and discussion, they are often ready to throw all the "traditions" and structures and initiations to the winds. The "traditional" Craft has frequently reacted with shock and horror, but then been forced to change from within. The impact of feminism on the Craft in the United States has been enormous. The impact of the mainstream Craft on feminism is harder to see. But each has been affected by the other.

Neo-Paganism in general and the Craft in particular have been good for women. Women have strong positions in almost all the Neo-Pagan religions discussed in this book, not only Witchcraft. This chapter concentrates on Witchcraft because most feminists do not seem to be interested in other Neo-Pagan religions. Witchcraft is one of the few "new age" religions where women can participate on an equal footing with men. Outside of Neo-Paganism in general, and Witchcraft in particular, the "Aquarian Age" new religions have not been particularly comfortable with the idea of women as strong, independent, powerful, self-identified persons. One has only to peruse the pages of "new age" journals such as *East West Journal* or the Buddhist *Maitreya* to conclude that most of the new spiritual organizations are still in the dark ages when it comes to women. Neo-Paganism, from its inception, has been less authoritarian, less dogmatic, less institutionalized, less filled with father figures, and less tied to institutions and ideas dominated by males. The religious concepts and historical premises behind Neo-Paganism and Witchcraft give women a role equal or superior to that of men. It is important to state these things before qualifying them. For while all these things are true, they are not always or completely true. It is important to find out how the role of women is defined in the Craft; how the "traditional" Craft is perceived by feminists; and how these feminists are perceived by the "traditional" Craft.

The question of attitudes toward women in the Craft, and in much of Neo-Paganism, is complex. For example, Robert Graves, whose book *The White Goddess* has had an enormous influence on women, the Witchcraft revival, and the creation of groups such as Feraferia, has often been viewed as a sexist. But *The White Goddess* is one of the few books by a male author that is easily found in most feminist bookstores. Published in 1948, it contains extraordinary passages about the Great

Goddess, and Graves has often said that the return of Goddess worship is the only salvation for Western civilization. He writes:

> The age of religious revelation seems to be over, and social security is so intricately bound up with marriage and the family . . . that the White Goddess in her orgiastic character seems to have no chance of staging a come-back, until women themselves grow weary of decadent patriarchalism, and turn Bassarids again.[36]

Despite this, Betty and Theodore Roszak in their book *Masculine, Feminine* place Graves among notably sexist authors such as Nietzsche and Freud. They accuse Graves of placing women on a pedestal, one of the oldest tricks in the fight against women's rights. They contend that Graves, while appearing to support freedom for women, actually views them as outside the real world and maintains a position not far removed from orthodoxy. In "Real Women," the selection chosen by the Roszaks, Graves writes, "A real woman's main concern is her beauty, which she cultivates for her own pleasure—not to ensnare men." The real woman, he says, "is no feminist; feminism, like all 'isms,' implies an intellectual approach to a subject, and reality can only be understood by transcending the intellect." He says further, "Man's biological function is to do; woman's is to be," and that "womanhood remains incomplete without a child."[37] Most feminists would find these statements highly objectionable.

To take a less-known example: Pagan theologian W. Holman Keith wrote in 1960 that the fundamental religious error of our time has been "to substitute force as the divine and ruling principle in place of beauty and love, to make destruction, in which the prowess of the male excels, more important in life than the creativity of the female."[38] Keith seeks a Neo-Pagan revival in which nature will be seen as divinely feminine, in which the divine Mother is worshipped again as the Goddess of love and beauty. Keith has also written, in articles for the Neo-Pagan press, that feminist liberation has to do with carnal sex and that "only the fair sex can ennoble eroticism." He has said that "Beauty and graciousness are the ideal attributes of the woman; manly strength of the man,"[39] and that therefore men must acknowledge the leadership of women in the movement of the human spirit.

While Keith, like Graves, is an ardent supporter of the matriarchy, while he supports the right of women to be lesbians, most feminists would argue that his vision has no place for the old woman, the hag, the crone, the woman who is "ugly" according to classical standards, the intellectual woman, the woman who desires to be celibate or who is simply uninterested in sex. Feminist Witches would argue that Keith's position denies certain aspects of the Triple Goddess—most particularly the Goddess of the waning moon, the dark moon, the Crone—that such a position condemns women to be maidens, mothers, and creatures of sensual play. They would say that archetypes are fine until they become stereotypes, whereupon they become repressive and destructive. One Neo-Pagan priestess put it this way:

> Those who insist upon seeing the Goddess as a stereotype as opposed to an archetype have lots of "Tradition" on their side. For instance, I'll bet you can't think of a single mythic Goddess whose attributes include being a musician, poet, painter, sculptor, or any other example of what we would call a fine artist. The exception being Isis/Hathor who is sometimes shown with a sistrum. The Goddess appears as a Muse but never as an artist. So much for Pagan "Tradition" . . . I will not be bound to the albatross of patristic Paganism, no matter how bloody traditional it is. Traditions are merely roots and roots are only one part of the whole tree.[40]

It's no wonder that the pages of Neo-Pagan journals reflect a diverse spectrum of positions on women. Despite what some psychologists say, no one really has the slightest idea what a woman (or, for that matter, what a man) is. We do know that whatever a woman is, it is hidden under thousands of years of oppression. We will need at least a century of living in a society devoid of prescribed role divisions to begin to answer that question. Since everyone is operating in the dark, the two prevalent views among feminists, and the views of others, are all simply opinions, or perhaps intuitions.

The opinion of many women today is that there are no important differences between men and women, with the exception of anatomy; all the rest is simply conditioning. In most societies that we *know* about, child raising and domestic chores are done by women, but there are a few societies in which this is not true; anthropology has shown us societies where women exhibit those characteristics we tend to think of as "male": concern and involvement in warfare, politics, and so forth. And there are societies where men exhibit characteristics we tend to label "female." The advantage of this view is that it produces a great amount of freedom from role stereotyping. It leaves us free to become what we want to become. Devlin, for example, once told me that she had been raped by a woman, one of the most horrible experiences of her life. To repeat her words, "I think, that the great mystery of our society is that men and women are exactly alike and this truth is hidden from us under an incredible load of bullshit."

Another view, accepted by many feminists, is that there is, in fact, a specifically female nature. Freud, we know, said that biology is destiny. And while most feminists would oppose his interpretations, not all of them oppose his idea. Feminist writer Sally Gearhart has repeatedly said that women *are* receptive; they are nurturers; they are the source of life, the symbol of creativity; they are more intuitive and more magical than men. "We are *not only* those things," she writes, "but neither is it accurate to say 'we are also aggressors, penetrators, attackers, etc.'"[41] The advantage of this view is that it gives a convincing explanation for the present rape of the earth, the abuses of technology, and the desperate need to return to a world centered on woman and the idea of a Goddess. A world ruled by women would be a better world, the argument goes; end male dominance, and human beings will live again in harmony with nature.

Women have been discussing these issues seriously. When men like Graves or Keith begin to define the "real woman," real women get angry. Then when male writers of less stature begin to echo these arguments in articles defining what a woman "is," and what her "proper" role in religion and magic should be, the anger increases. Until quite recently Neo-Pagan journals were filled with self-congratulatory articles by men on how women in the Craft have no need of "women's lib." Here is an example from *Waxing Moon*, in which the author first talks about the important position women have in the Craft. He then observes:

> This is not to say that female witches are domineering, mannish creatures . . . nothing could be further from the truth.

Likewise they are not Women's-Lib types. Most Witches view the Lib as a "masculinizing" outfit reminiscent of the "Anti-Sex League" in Orwell's *1984*. There are advantages which society must grant to women, as their right, but not at the cost of throwing away a woman's deepest strengths and most splendid powers.[42]

As Alison Harlow once remarked to me, "Until several years ago most Craft people had bought the media image of the feminists. For these people, the popular stereotype of the radical feminist and lesbian is more frightening than the traditional stereotype of the Witch is to people outside the Craft."

Thus, for a period of time, a number of letters and articles appeared in the Neo-Pagan press denouncing feminist Witches as "sexists" and "bigots," and expressing a general fear of any alliance between feminism and the Craft. A subtle reaction against a total emphasis on the Goddess began. Several articles called for more emphasis on male gods and on the male principle, a return to balance between male and female. Some of these were written by women. Also, a number of women and men expressed concern over the oppression of men, "tangled in the shadow of Yahweh's crippling image."[43]

In return, some feminists called the Neo-Pagan movement "contaminated." One woman wrote to *Earth Religion News* that the newspaper was simply "an extension of the patriarchy"[44] and made a mockery of the Goddess. Z was more reflective. "*Green Egg* was just polluted with men's fears," she said, "but then it cleaned itself up." Among all these articles and letters, one truly serious criticism of feminist Witchcraft has emerged, albeit often under a pile of chauvinistic garbage: the fear that exclusive goddess worship can lead to a transcendent monotheism, whereas the diverse, polytheistic outlook of Neo-Paganism is the main reason for its freedom, flexibility, and lack of dogma. "Mother Hertha," writes Morning Glory Zell-Ravenheart, "spare us from Jahveh in drag!"[45]

In all fairness, several Neo-Pagan men have taken strong public stands supporting the liberation of women—notably Leo Martello, Gwydion Pendderwen, and Isaac Bonewits. Bonewits, in his short but brilliant editorship of *Gnostica,* refused any manuscripts of a racist or sexist nature. In one editorial he noted the tendency of Neo-Pagan articles to imply that any woman not interested in homemaking, religious activities, and raising children "is somehow a psychic cripple; that she is an incomplete and inferior image of the Goddess." This notion, Bonewits said, was not so far from the Nazi conception of women: *Kirche, Küche und Kinder* (church, kitchen, and children). He wrote that Neo-Pagan men have a tendency to praise women "for the very qualities that many women consider sexist traps designed to prevent them from their full development as human beings," an attitude reflecting the dominant Christian schizophrenia that treats women as either Virgin Mothers or whores. "The priestess of Artemis," he wrote,

> or Morragu, or Kali is not going to be a simpering idiot or a Kirche-Küche-Kinder sort of woman. She is more likely to be a strong, domineering, combative intellectual. If you find that frightening, go ahead, admit it. But don't accuse her of being "unfeminine" or of trying to castrate every man she meets. . . . Similarly, a priest of Apollo, or Oberon, or Balder is quite likely to be gentle, intuitive, receptive, and very creative. This you may find frightening too. But again, it is more honest to admit your fear than to call him "unnatural," "a queer," "unmasculine," etc.

"Why," he asked an unnamed author whose manuscript he rejected, "do you forget the Norse and Mongol women, who picked up their swords and fought beside their men? Why do you forget the many societies of Pagans in which the men did the cooking, weaving, and art while the women plowed the fields and handled the trading?" Bonewits concluded that these articles continue to appear because millions of men are struggling with the question of liberation, and because it is easier to *sound* liberated than to go through the difficult psychological changes necessary to *become* liberated from sexual stereotypes.[46]

Leo Martello, author, graphologist, and Witch, has defended the feminist movement from the beginning, as he has defended all civil rights movements. Martello once wrote that in medieval times "the only liberated woman was the witch."

> All others were programmed into roles of wife, mother, mistress or nun. The witch was totally independent. She slept with whom she damn pleased. She was a threat to the establishment and to the church. . . . Of

all the religions, especially Western, witchcraft is the only one that didn't discriminate against women.

Martello went further; he struck to the root of the problem in a number of articles by noting that women *within* the Craft are still oppressed and unfree. He pointed out that many women came to the Craft because it offered them a sense of self-esteem, and their self-esteem had been "badly bruised by the male chauvinism-sexism predominating in our society." These women then overcompensated for their sense of personal inadequacy or inferiority by becoming big fish in a small pond (the coven). They might be forced to play housewife-mother-mistress in their daily lives, but they held great influence over a coven of five to thirteen people. Instead of becoming feminists, they perceived feminism as a threat to their status in the coven.[47]

This is a common problem. Many priestesses I have met lead lives that are not fulfilled in regard to work and other endeavors outside the Craft. Often they remain meek and silent, allowing husbands, who are often less intelligent, to hold forth. But magically, when the candles are lit and the circle is cast, these women become, for a short while, priestesses worthy of the legends of old. Two Witches, Margo and Lee, write about this problem in *The New Broom*.

> When a Witch steps into the consecrated Circle, she steps beyond time. Within that circle, the High Priestess assumes Woman's rightful role as a leader with power equal to and sometimes greater than man's. The woman of Wicca, like the women of the matriarchies of old, are proud, free, confident, and fulfilled . . . within the Circle.

The two women note that it is chiefly men who speak for the Craft; men write most of the books about the Craft, found the Witchcraft museums, and give their names to the traditions, such as Gardnerian and Alexandrian. "The truth is that today no Wicca woman speaks with authority to the public outside her Circle."[48] This is not completely true. The most notable exception is, of course, Sybil Leek. But all you have to do is leaf through the pages of this book to see how true it is most of the time.

One might almost say that the Craft at times acts as a "safety valve" for the establishment, providing an outlet for oppressed women but stopping short of true liberation. If so, the Craft in these cases becomes a conservative force, making real change even more difficult.

I. M. Lewis, in his study of ecstatic religions, makes a related point: that the cult of Dionysus and other cults that produced ecstatic states were often forces for real change, centers of defiance and rebellion. He observes, however, that women's possession cults in Africa often existed in those societies where women lacked more direct means for getting their aims. These women would use the cults as a method of protest against men, but were always contained by mechanisms clearly designed to stop true insubordination.[49]

The Craft is a religion using ecstatic states that has been a force for change. It has put women in touch with powerful energies within themselves and it has given them a self-image that equates women with the divine. But in our society it operates within the same kinds of constraints that Lewis is talking about. And so it is no wonder that many fear the coming together of feminism and the Craft. Together, they might be a truly revolutionary force.

At any rate, a few women within the Craft who also consider themselves feminists have explored these questions. They have written articles in *Nemeton* and *The New Broom,* the two Neo-Pagan magazines that included a regular, specifically feminist column.

Margo and Lee, in their *New Broom* article, note that many in the Craft have been disturbed by the appearance of feminist Witches outside the "traditional" Craft, as well as the emergence of all-women covens.

A Feminist calls herself Witch and claims, "Witchcraft is totally ours." The Craft rustles uncomfortably. She has never been initiated into a Coven. She knows little of Coven Law and myth, but proudly states, "I worship the Mother, I am a follower of the Old Religion, I work for the restoration of matriarchy under the Goddess." Wicca squirms. *Witch* is our name, our identity, our life. How, we demand, can these political women drain our identity of its deepest emotional and religious significance? Do they have any right to our name?

Yes, say the writers.

Feminist "witches" are seeking their own heritage as women. They are reaching back, beyond five thousand years of patriarchy. Independent of *any* help from the Craft, they have found the Goddess. They have found Her in the past; they have witnessed Her rape in the man-ravaged earth; they have found Her within themselves.

What the feminist Witches hold is a new, yet ancient, essence of pure worship. They hold the future.

And they come, as the North Wind: with the chill of change, and the freshness of rebirth.[50]

Another article suggests that women in the Craft, instead of criticizing feminism, should come to terms with the idea that they continue to be oppressed in this society.

Despite the criticisms, we feel that Wicca women must admit to one thing: as women, we are surrounded in day-to-day contact with the Outside World, so to speak, by open and accepted chauvinism in our male-run, male-dominated, man-made society. The temporal power and spiritual sway of its majority are male-oriented. No matter how early or late in this, our present life, we came into Witchcraft, no matter what position we hold within it, no matter how self-assured, self-identified, self-confident we are as Witches, we are none of us isolated from the contemporary state of everything. The twentieth century woman is the end product of two thousand years of suppression and oppression. The Craft, too, has suffered drastically in this same time. The deliberate erasure of truth and history, both about women and about Wicca, seems to go hand in hand. It helps little, in our opinion, that Witchcraft is being more open and openly tolerated if women are no closer to their proper, egalitarian position as people than they are at this moment.

The writers note that many in the women's movement are "feeling a flash of recognition, a call from a distant past," and are reexamining their religious as well as their political beliefs. "Somehow to us, the touching of Feminists and Witches happens at numerous important points . . . these two groups are entwined closely and irrevocably."[51]

Alison Harlow expressed much the same point of view when she wrote in *Nemeton* that the Craft and the feminist movement were "two tributaries flowing to form a single river"[52]—the Old Religion providing the psychic interaction and the women's movement the political context, both seeking to transform the society and provide a more open life for all.

It must be emphasized, however, that positive reactions to feminism have not been prevalent in the Craft; Alison Harlow worked with a coven composed mostly of women, although she was far from being a separatist; *The New Broom* spoke for the Dianic tradition of the Craft, a tradition that conceives of the Goddess almost monotheistically. Other articles expressed opposition to any feminist direction in the Craft as a whole, and stated that such a direction lacks balance.

But those women who accepted feminism as an integral part of the Craft began to compare the feminist Craft with the Craft into which they were born, brought, or trained. Some began experimenting with all-women covens, and by the mid-1980s all-women covens were accepted as a valid form by some of the larger Craft organizations, such as the Covenant of the Goddess in California. (There have also been some experiments with all-male covens.)

In the past, the idea of an all-woman coven was considered impossible by much of the Craft. The traditional Craft is solidly based on the idea of male-female polarity, which is basic to most Craft magical working and ritual symbology. The Craft Laws within the revivalist traditions state that Witchcraft must be taught from male to female and female to male, and books and articles on Pagan and Craft magic often say that the use of male-female polarity is absolutely necessary to produce psychic energy, that it's "more natural," "better," "stronger," and the like. The new feminist covens don't work with such polarities.

For example, a coven of eight Dianic women, many of whom had worked previously in mixed groups, told *The New Broom* in an interview that they had decided to work with women because they felt "free enough as women together to totally know our strengths and weaknesses and to trust each other and ourselves because of this knowledge." In response to the argument that they were going against "the natural current," they said, "If the natural current isn't within each person, just where is it?"[53] History and legend, the article noted, give many examples of all-women mystery religions and colleges of priestesses.

Some feminists have also challenged the idea that energy works male-to-female. Deborah Bender, writing in *The Witches Trine* about her coven, Ursa Maior, said that the "male principle" had not been found to have any usefulness in their work.

> The original study group, "Woman, Goddesses, and Homemade Religion," out of which Ursa Maior developed, was offered through a feminist free university. The people who came to our first meeting were women who would have greeted the statement, "You can't do it without a man," with extreme scepticism. Most members of the study group had previously participated in various woman-directed and -operated enterprises (bookstore, health clinic, theater group, newspaper, living-group) and expected working in the exclusive company of women to be a source of strength and creativity, not weakness. This has proven to be the case. . . .
>
> Our rituals are the expressions of the energies of seven very different personalities, energies which are different every time we begin a ritual and continue to change during it as we respond to the ritual and to each other. If a polarity exists, it is not twofold, but sevenfold.
>
> We take as a working hypothesis that there is such a thing as specifically female energy. However, we do not have some model in our heads of what that energy is like, which we then attempt to achieve. Rather, we try to set up circumstances such that each of us feels encouraged and accepted however she chooses to express herself. Whatever good energy is released in such a situation is female energy as far as we are concerned. The ideas any of us might already hold about female energy are likely to be distorted by the repressions and lies we have been subjected to in our upbringings in a patriarchal society. Only by growth and experimentation can we find out our true powers. To impose male and female polarities upon ourselves would not only be irrelevant to our work, it would interfere with our ability to notice the kinds of exchange of energy that are taking place between us.[54]

Another difference between strictly feminist and mainstream covens is evident in their use of symbols. The Craft in general has a fairly fixed set of symbols, stemming from Western magical traditions. The God is represented by the Sun; the Goddess is the Moon in her three aspects and phases. The Horned God is more often pictured as lord of animals, lord of the hunt, lord of death. The Goddess is the lady of the wild plants and growing things, as well as the giver of rebirth. Symbols and elements that most of Western occultism has long associated with the "male," such as air and fire, sword and wand, are similarly associated in the Craft. Likewise, the "female" is most often associated with water, earth, cup, and pentacle.

These polar opposites have much less application for feminist covens. Typically "female" symbols are often still used: the moon, the cup, the cowrie, the turtle, the egg, etc. But feminists celebrate sun goddesses such as Sunna and Lucina. They look at all goddess myths worldwide, and often take the attitude that it is merely certain cultures that have determined what is "masculine" and what is "feminine." The moon, after all, is a masculine word in the German, Celtic, and Japanese languages, and there are a number of myths with moon gods and sun goddesses. In other words, feminists reject most of the polarizing concepts common to Western occult circles: male-female, active-passive, light-dark, and so forth.

In an article called "I Dream in Female: The Metaphors of Evolution," Barbara Starrett, a feminist poet, writes that "male" structures are dependent on such pairs of opposites. She notes that women have long been associated with the "unknown, the irrational, the 'bad' half of the good/evil binary." Men, in contrast, are always linked with "the logical, clear, luminous, systematic half of that same binary." Starrett says that women should embrace *both* sets of symbols. They must see the traditional feminine symbols equated with the dark, the unconscious, the receptive, and so on as positive, but, she adds, "We need not relinquish their opposites. We will, in embracing the female symbols, incorporate within them the meanings of the male symbols, nullifying the binaries."

When women replace the symbol of the father with that of the Mother, we, too, are committing a political act. The image of the Mother does not lose its old connotations of earth, intuition, nature, the body, the emotions, the unconscious, etc. But it also lays claim to many of the connotations previously attributed to the father symbol: beauty, light, goodness, authority, activity, etc. . . . . What is significant here is that the duality, no matter which opposite is preferred, gives us only two choices. We may choose the reasoning, observing, dominating ego; or we may choose the annihilation of the personality. But if we learn to think beyond that binary, beyond the given choices, we can honor, equally, the conscious and the unconscious mind.[55]

Women in feminist covens seem to agree with Starrett, and so their rituals differ greatly from those in the "traditional" Craft.

Deborah Bender described the kind of ritual that might take place at a meeting of Ursa Maior. First the women might do a breathing exercise to achieve an interconnectedness within the group, "to make the 'circle' a present reality instead of an abstraction." Bender then described one case where the group worked to help one of its members, a woman who was upset and had been threatened with losing her job. The purpose was to replenish the energies of the woman and give her new strength. After all the women breathed and chanted together, a woman began to chant the woman's name, let us say "C": they chanted, "C strong woman, C strong woman." Other women joined in, adding new verses created spontaneously: "Like a redwood, strong; like a she-bear, strong; mountain-strong, strong woman." Bender said, "We spent a good half hour singing and praising C, calling out images of strength and sending her energy through our clasped hands." The woman in question said she felt much more self-confident, and she kept her job.[56]

It's important to stress that feminist covens, like most of the Witch covens we have been talking about, are diverse, autonomous, and difficult to generalize about. Since most successful covens are places where personal growth is a major concern and no dogma prevails, they are constantly changing. This situation of great flux has been noted by a member of academics who have judged, rightly, that the Neo-Pagan scene is even more fluid than the general situation pertaining to "cults." Since they believe in the great value of stability, they judge such fluidity to be a weakness. Only if a religion becomes institutionalized, is it judged "successful." But Neo-Pagans and Witches often regard fluidity as a strength, since the more institutionalized groups are less able to put primary emphasis on the personal growth of their members.

Occasionally, a feminist Witch coven will come together because of the energy and leadership of one particularly dynamic woman. Such was the case with the Susan B. Anthony Coven and Z Budapest. But most feminist covens do not have, and in some cases do not want, a strong, leading priestess. These covens have certain advantages and certain weaknesses. Many feminists have had strong experiences in collective decision-making beginning in their consciousness-raising groups and continuing in other feminist organizations. It is therefore not surprising that most women who come to the Craft from the feminist movement favor a nonhierarchical, informal structure. In general, they are suspicious of rules and formalized rituals—at least at first. Bender stated it this way:

> We take a questioning, even sceptical attitude toward all traditions, formulas, the ways of talking about the Goddess, covens, magic, and Witches. We have two final criteria for using anything: Does it feel right? Does it make sense to me? If one member feels uncomfortable with something we are doing or saying, we drop it and look for another way that feels right to all of us.

Feminist Witches seem to prefer the loose types of decision-making that have evolved in other radical feminist groups. This includes rotation of responsibility and leadership. In Ursa Maior, for example, leadership was based on initiative and knowledge rather than degree or length of experience. And any commitments, any bonds or oaths, were purely voluntary.

Bender gave me a series of characteristics that seem to distinguish many feminist covens:

1. They have no men.
2. They do not work from a handed-down Book of Shadows. Bender said she personally believed that such books were a nineteenth-century innovation, adding, "The medieval and premedieval traditions must surely have been oral. Ursa Maior adapts freely from published books of shadow and from the poetry and ritual of tribal peoples." The main source for rituals, however, is the women themselves. If a good ritual is created by the coven, or a song or dance or new mode of organization, it might well be published in a feminist magazine or newspaper.
3. While feminist covens generally adhere to the basic Craft Laws pertaining to ethics, money, and self-defense, they often disregard

those pertaining to coven structure and regulations. Bender said, "Since we regard our circle as an institution with roots in time preceding the persecutions and the adoption of the secret-cell coven structure, we do not regard ourselves as bound by those laws regarding initiation and coven governance."

4. Feminist covens often attempt to recover matriarchal ideas and institutions through means of research, art, play, psychic exploration, and daydreams. These covens, in contrast to heterogeneous ones, are attuned to women's experiences, bodies, and needs.

5. Feminist covens, unlike most mixed covens I know of, actually serve a viable community: the feminist community. Bender told me that Ursa Maior devoted about 10 percent of its time to work within the community, and that this was one of the reasons for the coven's existence.[57]

In 1976 Ursa Maior was a small, intensive, active group of women who worked well together. Their experimentation and spontaneity apparently led to great creativity and growth. This has not been the case with all such groups. In some covens, where the group has not solidified or where the group is too large, the distrust of structure and formal ritual can lead to none at all, and an unwillingness to take responsibility for making things happen. As one woman wrote to me, "These covens and groves seem to melt like spring snow." In contrast, the mixed covens that exist in more "traditionalist" Wicca have a large body of formal ritual and practice, rules, chants, psychic exercises, and oral teachings, but often lack the energy and spontaneity of some of the feminist groups.

In the winter of 1977 the members of Ursa Maior dissolved their coven by mutual consent. Two of the members wanted to explore more deeply the "traditional" Craft. The others wanted to continue to involve themselves in feminist spirituality and holistic healing. In 1978 one former member wrote to me:

At present, I am putting my energy into learning more of the hierarchically structured, semi-secret side of the Craft (Dianic when possible, but this is difficult when there are not trained Dianic priestesses in the neighborhood). I am working to some extent with men. I do not see this as canceling out what I was doing before. I am trying always to find solutions to certain weaknesses in the feminist Craft. Also, I have always wanted to learn the Craft in its fullness and not just a few parts of it. Perhaps after some years I will be able to find a synthesis.

Meanwhile Deborah Bender and another feminist Witch began the *Women's Coven Newsletter,*[58] "to provide some kind of accessible institution outside of the small groups that appear and disappear," as well as "to help build a large body of formal ritual and practice, rules, chants, psychic exercises and oral teachings, that seem to be one of the strengths of the mixed covens."

The Streams Converge

On a Friday night in Boston, April 23, 1976, some one thousand women sat down on the benches and pews of the old Arlington Street Church. The benches filled up and the women spilled over onto the floor and into the aisles, and became silent as the flute music of Kay Gardner created a sense of peace. The lights were dimmed and Morgan McFarland, Dianic High Priestess, came to the front, wearing a long white robe, accompanied by four members of her women's coven, the same coven that we have seen mentioned in *The New Broom.* The occasion was a ritual: "Declaring and Affirming Our Birth," to mark the beginning of a three-day women's spirituality conference, with the unusual name "Through the Looking Glass: A Gynergenetic Experience." The conference was attended by over thirteen hundred women, and besides an address by feminist theologian Mary Daly, the conference was most noteworthy for the large number of Witch priestesses who attended from as far away as Texas and California.

This relationship between feminist spirituality and the Craft is complex. Perhaps, if we had to choose one instant to catch all the qualities, problems, strains, and enormous potentialities in that uneasy relationship, this ritual would be such a prism. There are Morgan and the women in the coven standing in the church, looking a bit apart, somewhat too elegantly dressed, too stereotypically "feminine." I remembered how much more at ease they were working a ritual in a Dallas living room, where none of us wore anything except a string of beads.

But here they are, standing in front of the altar of a church, holding candles, while a thousand women watch and wait. Morgan steps out in front and speaks.

"In the infinite moment before all Time began, the Goddess arose from Chaos and gave birth to Herself . . . before anything else had been born . . . not even Herself. And when She had separated the Skies from the Waters and had danced upon them, the Goddess in Her ecstasy created everything that is. Her movements made the wind, and the Element Air was born and did breathe."

A candle is lit in the East. Morgan speaks.

"And the Goddess named Herself: Arianrhod—Cardea—Astarte. And sparks were struck from Her dancing feet so that She shone forth as the Sun, and the stars were caught in Her hair, and comets raced about Her, and Element Fire was born."

A candle is lit in the South.

"And the Goddess named Herself: Sunna—Vesta—Pele. About her feet swirled the waters in tidal wave and river and streaming tide, and Element Water did flow."

A candle is lit in the West.

"And She named Herself: Binah—Mari Morgaine—Lakshmi. And She sought to rest Her feet from their dance, and She brought forth the Earth so that the shores were Her footstool, the fertile lands Her womb, the mountains Her full breasts, and Her streaming hair the growing things."

A candle is lit in the North.

"And the Goddess named Herself: Cerridwen—Demeter—the Corn Mother. She saw that which was and is and will be, born of Her sacred dance and cosmic delight and infinite joy. She laughed: and the Goddess created Woman in her own image . . . to be the Priestess of the Great Mother. The Goddess spoke to Her daughters, saying, 'I am the Moon to light your path and to speak to your rhythms. I am the Sun who gives you warmth in which to stretch and grow. I am the Wind to blow at your call and the sparkling Air that offers joy. I give to all my priestesses three aspects that are Mine: I am Artemis, the Maiden of the Animals, the Virgin of the Hunt. I am Isis, the Great Mother. I am Ngame, the Ancient One who winds the shroud. And I shall be called a million names. Call unto me, daughters, and know that I am Nemesis.'"

Later, the cauldron is filled with fire and the chanting begins, at first very softly: "The Goddess is alive, magic is afoot, the Goddess is alive, magic is afoot." Then it becomes louder and louder until it turns into shouts and cries and primeval sounds. Morgan speaks for the last time.

"We are Virgins, Mothers, Old Ones—All. We offer our created energy: to the Spirit of Women Past, to the Spirit of Women yet to come, to womanspirit present and growing. Behold, we move forward together."

At the end of the ritual the women in the church begin to dance and chant, their voices rise and rise and rise until they shake the roof.

Later, a few women said they didn't want priestesses standing apart on pedestals and altars; they did not want to see energy sent "upward"; they wanted it aimed "at the oppressor." Despite this, acknowledging this, the uneasy, explosive, potentially powerful alliance between feminism and the Craft was apparent for all to feel, during this conference where many women said they felt, for the first time, that a new "women's culture" was a reality.

Morgan and her priestesses stand at the crossroads. This Dianic coven was perhaps the most feminist of the "traditional" groups. But that night in Boston many women found it too formalized and structured. These women were determined to set their own terms and start from scratch.

Alison Harlow also stands at the crossroads. She told me that her greatest mission is to be a bridge between feminism and the Craft. Still, she has doubts. She wondered out loud what, if anything, feminists want or need from the "traditional" Craft. She talked candidly about the intolerance she has felt from some separatists toward her bisexuality and the personal enjoyment she gets from associating with Neo-Pagan men. We both wondered if separatism was the ultimate answer for these women, or whether it was but a necessary time of healing and renewal. We both felt that one thing the Craft did have to offer feminists, outside of its knowledge of ritual and lore, was the polytheistic perspective and its view toward diversity and flexibility. And I expressed to her my own feeling that some of the feminist groups had a startling lack of curiosity about other forms of working outside their own.

What can the two Crafts give each other? Perhaps the most important thing that the feminist Craft can give the "mainstream" Craft is the understanding that Witchcraft is a religion and a practice rooted firmly in rebellion. Feminists see the Craft as a people's survival tool; as a source of affirmative power and strength; as a way of living and working creatively with vital energies; as an empirical *folk wisdom,* but one that is *never far removed* from daily life and from human needs, human problems and "mundane" concerns. "Paganism," Z once told me, while remembering her youth in Hungary, "fits the common people like bread." Many feminist Witches see the Craft as a kind of village woman's wisdom, the knowledge of village midwives and healers. This notion of folk wisdom is often denied by more "traditional" groups, who still tend at times to be impressed by ideas of royalty and by titles such as "Lady so-and-so," and by "bloodlines" and lineages. These groups also fall victim to the illusion that they can exist and practice comfortably within our society by simply pulling the blinds and dancing in secret in darkened rooms. "Mainstream" Craft members often split their lives in two; they have two sets of friends, two sets of interests. This kind of split life leads easily to the notion that something called "politics" is separate from something called "spiritual life."

The feminist Craft is brashly political and spiritual at once. Many feminist Witches would argue that the split life ultimately leads to self-imprisonment, to being cut off at the roots, to alienation. These women might argue that to live such a life is to perpetuate an ultimately sterile fantasy, as opposed to making a real attempt to create an integrated life.

The feminist Craft can build a good case for this argument because it has so much vitality and spontaneity. In addition, its suspicion of hierarchy and structure is good medicine for the rest of the Craft. But its "politics" have upset many of the "mainstream," who have accused the feminists of "using the Goddess for their own ends." The feminists say the reverse: "The Goddess is using the feminist movement to bring Craft principles to a wider variety of women than could have been possible otherwise."

The "mainstream" Craft can offer the feminist Craft the openmindedness characteristic of polytheists. Feminist groups often have a tendency toward dogmatism, substituting "Big Mama" for "Big Daddy." The problem of Goddess monotheism will have to be resolved if the feminist Craft is not to become just another One True Right and Only Way. The feminist Craft groups often dismiss the "mainstream" groups as "hopelessly contaminated by patriarchy," but the groups, having been around longer, have a rich knowledge about how rituals work and how the coven structure can function. Their healthy distrust of hierarchy often leads feminist groups to abandon all structure, and this has resulted in the dissolution of many groups. Likewise, the fear of ritual as too "formalized" has at times led to stagnation. Ironically, many women within the "mainstream" have visited feminist covens and groves, have gained new knowledge based on new experiences, and then have made significant changes in their original groups or formed new groups altogether. This has not often happened the other way around. Lastly, the Neo-Pagan movement as a whole is rich in humor and ease. These are qualities the feminist Craft often lacks.

One difference between the two Crafts can be seen in the lives of two women who shall remain nameless. The first is the priestess of a Gardnerian coven in the West. During working hours she is a top scientist with a major corporation. No one at her job has any idea of her religious affiliation. Despite her prestige and success, and her integration into "normal" society, she remains afraid that her job would be imperiled if her religious activities become known. The second woman is better known. She was once a political fugitive wanted by the FBI. She made a growing commitment to feminism, and during the period when she turned herself in and was brought to trial she was initiated into a Dianic tradition from the Southwest.

It can be said that, generally, most members of the "mainstream" Craft function outwardly as "ordinary" members of society, while at least some members of the feminist Craft live on the edge of society; that the feminist Craft serves, at least in part, as a source of renewal for women who are among the dispossessed and the oppressed—a function of the Craft that may be most "traditional."

> And thou shalt be the first of witches known;
> And thou shalt be the first of all i' the world;
> And thou shalt teach the art of poisoning,
> Of poisoning those who are the great lords of all;
> Yea, thou shalt make them die in their palaces;
> And thou shalt bind the oppressor's soul [with power] . . .
> And ye shall all be freed from slavery,
> And so ye shall be free in everything;

And as the sign that ye are truly free,
Ye shall be naked in your rites, both men
And women also: this shall last until
The last of your oppressors shall be dead. . . .[59]
—*Aradia, or the Gospel of the Witches* (1899)

Feminism and Paganism in the Twenty-First Century

In 2005, when I read the passage about creating new Amazons—about howling with the bears and the wolves and the coyotes and uniting with all that is female and waging a war for mother nature—I have to admit, I cringed. As I said at the outset, it was written before Reagan, Bush, and a host of other changes in the United States and the world. At the time, it truly seemed that women were creating a revolution. Today, despite incredible gains, much of that revolution seems stalled. Where *are* those Amazons? What happened to that revolution? On the one hand, women's spirituality is all over the place: books, workshops, rituals, and music. Some of this has nothing to do with Paganism or Wicca. As Patricia Monaghan, the author of more than twenty books—quite a number of them on the Goddess—observed to me:

> Women's spirituality is quite large and includes women in drum circles, indigenous women, lots of nuns, Christian women who honor Sophia or Mary, Jungian psychologists, literature professors—lots of people who do not ritualize the Sacred Feminine but who object to strictly patriarchal constructions of spirituality. Ninety percent of these people, I would estimate, would hesitate to define themselves as Pagan; some would flee from the term. Even fewer, I think, would call themselves Wiccan.[60]

Women's spirituality has made huge inroads in Judaism and Christianity. A few examples: The May'an Seder, a feminist Passover observance for women has attracted more than a thousand women in New York City each year. Cakes for the Queen of Heaven and its follow-up, Rise Up and Call Her Name, are two Goddess spirituality study courses that were created by and for women within the Unitarian Universalist Church. The "Cakes" curriculum is now almost twenty-five years old; it has been used in hundreds of churches and religious education courses, and it has influenced thousands of women. It has also brought profound changes to Unitarian Universalist congregations, in some cases totally altering the liturgy.

The idea of the Goddess has entered mainstream literature and there have been countless non-sexist reinterpretations of various myths (*Mists of Avalon,* for the Arthurian legend, for example.) Feminist spirituality also led to the publishing of non-sexist reinterpretations of tarot, Kabala, and the I-Ching. Turning to Wicca, Starhawk's book *The Spiral Dance,* not to mention the score of annual Witchcamps created by Reclaiming, have led to the creation of hundreds of covens, many of them women's covens, not to mention an enormous amount of political activism, much of it with a feminist tinge.

Tensions between feminist groups and "traditional" Craft groups seem less evident today. By the middle of the 1980s, women's circles and men's circles were happening routinely at Pagan festivals. Dianic Witches came to mixed Pagan festivals, and women from the traditional Craft experienced all-women rituals. For many years there seemed to be increased contact between feminist women and Neo-Pagan men, although there are still many within British Traditional Wicca who do not believe that feminist Witches should be called Wiccans. Within the mixed Wiccan traditions, and at Pagan festivals there was a dramatic decrease in sexism. Although some would argue that it depends on your perspective, and the pendulum simply swings back and forth. Todd Allen of Wysteria, the nature sanctuary, recently told me that he feels the biggest change within Paganism over the last fifteen years is the incorporation of men and families into the movement. He remembers that the emphasis on the Goddess was so strong and intense that: "If you were a guy you had to lay low, there were a lot of areas you were not allowed to go."

But what seems noticeable, at least within Paganism and Wicca, is that the energy seems very different today. Jean Mountaingrove, one of the founders of the magazine *WomanSpirit,* who is much quoted in this chapter, and who turned eighty in 2005, says, when she thinks back to the time that chapter was written, much of women's spirituality was a challenge—a pushing of boundaries: Z Budapest getting arrested, Mary Daly challenging academia. Today, there are "many teachers, books on

rituals and stores filled with items about goddesses and tools for ceremonies," she says. And living as she does, in Oregon, women's spirituality seems a "given" in her community, with frequent seasonal rituals
and socializing. Women's spirituality doesn't seem to be "a controversial
topic," she says, "nor does it seem to be as central to one's being as it was
in the 1970s and 1980s." She adds:

> In this time of "bread and circuses"—TV, fast food, multiple jobs, mas-
> sive advertising to consumers (not citizens)—our active commitment to
> the growth of spiritual experiences and information is not happening.[61]

She and others note that a new generation of women has little knowledge of the second wave of feminist foremothers. In fact, the history of
feminism is foreign to them.

Morgan McFarland—now the matriarch of the McFarland Dianics—
looks back and says, "We were optimistic and naive and serious and exuberant. When you came to Dallas in 1976, it seemed as though there
were only a handful of us, and certainly very few feminists among us.
What controversy we stirred! Now I go to places like WitchVox and am
constantly amazed at how widespread Neo-Paganism has become."

> There was a freshness about everything in 1979, an enthusiasm, a certain
> and sure belief that we could open doors and minds and create change,
> that isn't there anymore. This next generation of Neo-Pagan women are
> frankly confused by any discussion of feminism and Craft: they either be-
> lieve that all the barriers are gone or they have no idea what feminism
> even means, much less in relation to spirituality. They seem to be con-
> fused by the idea that we grandparents protested, agitated or took our
> livelihoods in our hands when we came out of the broom closet.
>
> Somewhere along the line, my generation birthed a bunch of conser-
> vatives, and *that* I do not understand at all! In the process, we also birthed
> a group of Neo-Pagan folk who seem to lack spontaneity. I've recently
> spent weeks trying to persuade one of the most gifted McFarland Dianics
> that doing sharings within her Circle as an extension of Moon Ritual ex-
> pands the meaning of the ritual. The reason she was hesitant to do them?
> She might do the sharing "wrong." But there is no wrong way to share!
> After all, it isn't how the mystery is presented so much as how it's re-
> ceived. So what does it mean if a whole new generation out there doesn't

know about sharings or feminism or what it took to have one's face all over the *Dallas Morning News?*

We always felt that we could take the traditional and present it in non-traditional ways. We felt free to invent. I think that's what feminism contributed to the Craft. It didn't seem to matter whether we were Dallas Dianics or Z's women, for example. We invented something new each time we cast a circle. I felt that Z was too excluding, and I'm certain she felt I was too lenient when it came to having men in some of my covens. But we were tolerant of each other and willing to share the term "Dianic" and quite happy to share rituals. I'm quite often amazed at the rigidity of some McFarlands when it comes to sticking to the written word. I wonder if Z is amazed at the direction of her Circle's circles. Although I have a feeling they may be the last bastions of revolutionary Craft![62]

And they may well be. As Z watches the nine priestesses that she has ordained, including her first spiritual daughter, singer and musician Ruth Barrett, who is continuing Z's ministry in Wisconsin, Z says that most of her priestesses *are* ardent feminists. Those nine women have, in turn, created a new generation of Dianic priestesses—about twenty-five of them. And they are a much more diverse group than years back, including African American, Hawaiian, and Filipino women. With the exception of one group, all remain women-only. As Z put it to me:

There was never any payoff letting men into women's circles. Except men's fluttering egos. My most fervent objection is: women must learn to OWN something in this universe alone. If not even Dianics are women only, what is left?[63]

Z notes the many women's studies courses available in colleges; she ticks off a couple of colleges that have women's spirituality curriculums, and she notes the large number of Goddess sites on the Internet; she sees women's spirituality reaching an ever wider audience.

But besides Z, and her daughters, and annual events like the Michigan Womyn's Music Festival, it doesn't seem as if there is much energy behind separatism. Feminist writer Sally Gearhart, the author of *Wanderground,* who once argued that women should set up a buffer state so separatist women could gain the strength to establish a new society, now believes that much of cultural feminism has been assimilated. She says that "much of what is happening in the environmental movement, in the Goddess movement, in Queer Theory, and in New Age metaphysics is actually good old cultural feminism in new (and even higher) drag."

> What you find on the web seems to me to be proof that the dominant culture is now infected with feminist theories and practices. With the exception of cultural feminism's requirement of a separatist stance for women, the consciousness rising to meet the escalated violence of patriarchy is teeming with the ideas, values, practices, structures, and personnel of the (cultural) feminism of the 1970s.[64]

Gearhart argues that many groups have come to believe that the earth (with its biosphere) is, "ultimately, the Mother of us all, constituting the (evolutionary) Source from which all of life springs and to which it ultimately returns." She notes that many values our society thinks of as "female"—compassion and cooperation, the valuing of emotions and inclusiveness—have been embraced by these groups, and the men in these organizations are often "praised and respected for their courageous embrace of these too-long dormant social values." Gearhart says she believes the rise of fundamentalism is the last ditch gasp of a dying ideology. "The future," she says, "is and will continue to be female, whether or not it is so labeled."

> I truly feel that these changes, so rampant globally and in such stark contrast to the violence we are so tempted to be absorbed by, are the best fruits of all our earlier labors in the ranks of feminism's First and Second Waves. The world, in short, is awash with the best of what feminism has meant to so many of us.[65]

But even if the culture has absorbed many of these ideas, it does seem fair to say that there is less energy and vibrancy around them at the moment, at least in Paganism. After a decade where separate men and women's rituals took place at well-known festivals, it is no longer so common to find them. That may simply mean that separatist groups, which do still exist, are not spending much time connecting with the Neo-Pagan movement. But in talking to women who spent years in all-women groups, I have been struck by the fact that many are no longer working in them.

It's important to stress that the separatist current in women's spirituality was essential—and may still be essential for some women today. For many women it was the only safe harbor—a place where they could become strong and vibrant in a culture where women were silent and invisible.

Willow LaMonte, the editor of *Goddessing,* an international news journal that looks at the Goddess spirituality movement around the world, says there *has* been a loss of vibrancy and energy—of juice, if you will. She ticks off several factors. First, the loss of grassroots woman's organizations: bookstores, restaurants, radio shows, and local newsletters. Think back! There were hundreds of women's bookstores in the early 1980s. Many of them are gone. Lesbians led many of these efforts, but they provided space for all kinds of women. Women's radio shows on public radio—most of those are also gone now. LaMonte does not believe the Internet is a substitute for a grassroots newsletter, any more than Amazon.com is a substitute for a community bookstore. The Internet does not create real community, she says, and there is an access and class problem: there are still many people without easy access to computers. What about prisoners, for example? The loss of grassroots organizations means the loss of political consciousness.

LaMonte also believes that there has been an increasing "vapidness and vagueness" in the movement, and a shifting away from language that confronts the issue of power. She attributes this partly to so many groups stepping away from the use of the word "Goddess" and embracing more Jungian, and ultimately disempowering, descriptions like "Divine Feminine."

The woman's spirituality movement does have vibrant women leaders. Leadership styles vary. The Covenant of the Goddess and Reclaiming both have based their leadership style on consensus. Many of the mixed Wiccan groups tend to be more hierarchical. British Traditionalist Wicca sees itself as a mystery religion: A seeker slowly gains knowledge by studying with a coven leader and rising through several levels. In contrast, as we saw, many early feminist Craft groups were quite anarchistic; they did not like the leadership style of the traditional Craft, and their own flaws went in the opposite direction: disorganization. But today, many of the feminist covens have inherited their style from power-ful and charismatic women priestesses—such as Z Budapest and Morgan McFarland, and some current women leaders are following in that tra-dition. This is an oversimplification; there are many priestesses who share power well, who allow different women and their skills to flourish. But in doing the research for this edition, I was struck by the irony of com-ing across many Heathen kindreds that worship Northern European gods (that some feminists might consider extremely "macho"), yet have truly egalitarian organizations, while I came across a few feminist groups with charismatic leaders and more hierarchy.

Here are some other issues to think about when you compare femi-nist spirituality then and now. There have always been tensions between feminist scholars and mainstream scholars, over issues like matriarchy and the role of women in ancient societies. But mainstream scholars now include Pagan studies scholars, as the growing Pagan studies movement comes of age (see Chapter 13). The majority of Pagan scholars no longer accept Margaret Murray's theory of the witch cult, and they have come to accept that the persecution, torture, and killing of people ac-cused of witchcraft in Europe involved a relatively small number of peo-ple: forty to fifty thousand over about a hundred and fifty years, not a holocaust of nine million, as many Witches and other women alleged for years.[66]

Many feminist writers still look at the witchcraft persecutions as clear proof of patriarchal oppression—the stamping out of midwives and healers, and the oppression of the poor and outcast. These theories are in dozens of books, many beautifully written with powerful prose. And what makes it so difficult is that they are part of the most important founding and empowering myths of Wicca, Paganism, and the entire Earth religions revival. Take Barbara Ehrenreich and Dierdre English's groundbreaking work, *Witches, Midwives, and Nurses,* which argued that the persecutions were used to destroy the power of midwives and healers and bolster the emerging male medical profession, or Starhawk's exquisitely beautiful essay in the appendix of *Dreaming the Dark: Magic, Sex, and Politics,* "The Burning Times," which argues that perse-cuting Witches was a way to destroy community power and the com-mon lands. Over the last fifteen years, most Pagan scholars have come to believe there is little hard evidence for these theories. Sometimes reading the current scholarship makes one feel like the title of that old Firesign Theatre album: *Everything You Know Is Wrong*. For example, Jenny Gibbons, in an article in *The Pomegranate*, "Recent Developments in the Study of the Great European Witch Hunt," argues there were about fifty thousand deaths; the greatest number of deaths occurred during the Reformation, in places where both the church and the state were weak; and most deaths were decided by non-religious courts (in fact your best chance of getting off was going before a church court). Few of those killed were Pagans in any sense a modern Pagan might recognize. (See Chapter 4 for more on this issue.)

In contrast, a number of feminist writers and academics now argue that although nine million is clearly a mythical number, the current low numbers put forth by scholars have their own problems. For example, Max Dashu argues that records in many communities were not kept; others were destroyed, and, in a response to Gibbons, she writes:

> My own count would have to include those who were drowned, branded, beaten, fined, imprisoned, scored, exiled, shunned, expropriated, and deprived of their livelihoods. This much is certain: no one knows how many were killed.[67]

Looking at this controversy, some of those involved in feminist spirituality say why should we be so different than every other religion? Patricia Monaghan, the author of many books about women and goddesses, observes that she has heard the following argument in some feminist circles:

> Why are we the ONLY religion in the world that has to be based on historical truth? So is there any real evidence for the Virgin Birth? The scholar in me winces; I sort of want to say, yes, we should be based on actual verifiable truth, and not the kind of lies that made my Catholic childhood miserable. But that's holding Paganism to a higher standard than any religion ever before.[68]

When I asked Z Budapest about the scholarship issue, she said: "Is this really an important point to settle? I don't essentially care. Nine million, or fifty thousand. Bad is bad." But since this notion of a holocaust of nine million has found its way into Pagan popular songs and into the film *The Burning Times,* often shown on PBS during fund-raising week, accuracy—not wildly inflated numbers—seems important. After all, for many, *The Burning Times* film is the only face of Paganism and Wicca that is seen by much of the public.

But historical accuracy is not the only issue. Sabina Magliocco, in her wonderful book *Witching Culture,* notes that these myths have helped create the oppositional culture that remains so very important to Paganism. She writes:

> While the sacred narratives of the Burning Times and the Paleolithic Origins of Matriarchy are not literally true, like all myths they have a kernel of metaphorical truth: experiences and ways of knowing that belonged to a pre-Enlightenment, interconnected view of the universe have been banished from modern Western Consciousness. In conjuring an oppositional culture, contemporary Pagans seek to reclaim that worldview.[69]

It is this alternative, ecological paradigm that made many of us embrace the modern Pagan and goddess movements. It's important to retain the oppositional culture, even as we correct mistaken notions and numbers.

Looking back on this chapter, it's important to say one more word about matriarchy. An important feminist scholar, who was barely mentioned in previous editions of this book, does give important weight to the idea of ancient goddess cultures: the late Marija Gimbutas. Gimbutas was a serious archeologist, with an extensive knowledge of the languages and cultures of Greece, the Balkans, and Eastern Europe. She argued in her books, *The Language of the Goddess* and *The Civilization of the Goddess,* that what she called "Old Europe" had once been settled by peaceful, women-centered cultures who venerated the Goddess. She further argued that these civilizations were matrilinear and egalitarian until the coming of the Indo-Europeans. Many archeologists have contested her theories, but as Hutton writes in *The Triumph of the Moon,* none of her theories have been disproved, and they "may well never be. The controversy has centered upon the issue that the evidence is susceptible of alternative interpretations."[70]

As I come to the end of this chapter, I have also been mulling over a critique that I've occasionally heard from some scholars: that the women's spirituality movement is not really a religion, as much as a human potential movement. Since both religion and therapeutic ideas consider deep questions of being, of consciousness, and the meaning of life, it seems reasonable to assume the lines between religion and therapy will occasionally blur. I noted near the beginning of this chapter that the consciousness-raising group gave women the lesson that personal feelings could be trusted and acted upon, and that the "personal was political." As someone who spent a number of years in a CR group during the 1970s, the experience was more life-changing than any therapy or education. It was also an incredible catalyst for political change, as women realized their issues were not simply personal and could be explored, challenged, and transformed through political action. Having said that, women's spirituality is not therapy. Many years ago I remember seeing a leaflet that advertised a goddess circle led by a therapist who was charging group therapy rates for her rituals; at the time it seemed shocking— it still does. But women's spirituality has given countless women a sense of health and empowerment, and this process clearly continues for a new generation of women. Patricia Monaghan says that doing slide shows on goddesses in small towns has given her great insight about what the idea of the Goddess means for women.

> I find that women, especially, though some men too, are literally dreaming Her back to life. I cannot tell you how many times I've had a woman come up to me in some small town in Indiana or Nebraska or somewhere, and say that she was at the lecture because she had a dream in which a female figure identified herself as a goddess. (Hmm, I can't think of a single man telling me that.) So there seems to be some conduit to the collective unconscious, or the spirit, or whatever you want to call it, that is seeking to rectify the balance in these out-of-whack times.[71]

But looking back, years later, I do see a downside to the notion that one can always trust one's personal experiences: the possibility of self-delusion. Assuming that one's personal experience is "truth" can foster confusion between material reality and the psychic reality of dreams and daydreams. That confusion ripped through certain parts of the women's movement and the lesbian community in the 1980s, leading some to maintain false stories of ritual abuse. It might be noted that

Jenny Gibbons, in her article on the Witch persecutions, observes that the Pagan community would have been more resistant to those claims, and would have seen how similar they were to the old false accusations of witchcraft, had they had a more realistic and historically accurate view of the scope of the witch persecutions in Europe.[72]

Today, a new generation of women is redefining feminist spirituality. Many of them have no real knowledge of the past, but they are also not overwhelmed with the same forms of oppression that burdened feminists in the 1970s. They may come up with different ideas and different forms of organization as a result. Many women have rejected the essentialist thinking that informed much of early spiritual feminism; they simply believe in equal rights for all; they believe that, as Lisa Jervis writes in an essay in *LiP* magazine: "The actual workings of power will not change with more chromosomal diversity among the powerful."[73] They have less hope than we had that a world of women will be more nurturing, more peaceful, and more cooperative. Their view may produce better politics, in the end, but it was not an idea we could easily hear when we felt our oppression so deeply that it was impossible to act from a non-oppressed place. One wonders what kind of feminist spirituality a new generation will create; what would feminist spirituality look like if it did not originate, in part, as a response to oppression?

The ancient goddesses are incredible models; whether or not you believe they are *real*, or archetypes, or simply images to emulate, they can be used to explore notions of power and possibility in the world as well as inform an exploration of ancient cultures and their gifts. In past editions of *Drawing Down the Moon*, I said that the women's spirituality movement had yet to define itself as either a monotheistic Goddess movement or a polytheistic movement with many goddesses, more similar to the rest of Neo-Paganism. The claim that there is one universal Mother Goddess worshipped widely throughout the ancient world is a kind of monotheism that only differs in gender from the religions most modern Pagans have rejected. It may also be a kind of universalism at odds with Pagan concepts of diversity and bioregionalism. The greatest strength of the Pagan perspective is that it looks to many goddesses and gods, not one.

III. Other Neo-Pagans

Religions from the Past—
The Pagan Reconstructionists

OUTSIDE OF THE VARIOUS Witchcraft traditions, the most prevalent forms of Neo-Paganism are groups that attempt to re-create ancient European pre-Christian religions.

Church of Aphrodite

In the United States the first reconstructionist Neo-Pagan organization was the Long Island Church of Aphrodite, established in West Hempstead, Long Island, on May 6, 1938.

Gleb Botkin, founder and priest of the church, was the son of the court physician to the last Russian Tsar. After Botkin came to the United States he wrote several novels about Russia before and during the Revolution. Some of them, such as *The Real Romanovs,* concern the last days of the royal family; others depict the lives of students, priests, and more ordinary folk. But the theme of goddess worship drifts through many of them. The titles themselves are revealing—*The Woman Who Rose Again* (about Anastasia); *Immortal Woman; The God Who Didn't Laugh;* and *Her Wanton Majesty.*[1]

All the novels, dating from 1929 to 1937, involve women who inspire men to worship them, and men who are tempted and allured by the "divine feminine." In two of the novels the Pagan religious ideal is stated directly: the protagonist becomes a worshipper of Aphrodite. *Immortal Woman* (1933) is the story of Nikolai Dirin, the son of a Russian priest, who flees to America shortly after the Russian Revolution and becomes a world-famous conductor. His musical ability is inspired by a vision of Aphrodite and by the remembrance of a real woman, a playmate from his youth. His dreams and daydreams lead him to reject his Russian Orthodox upbringing and to adopt the Aphrodisian religion:

> The more he studied, the more convinced he became that his Goddess was no myth, that millions upon millions of human beings had worshipped her for thousands of years and that many continued to worship her in the present.[2]

Another novel, *The God Who Didn't Laugh,* is the most autobiographical of Botkin's works. It is the story of a Russian man who studies to be a monk, but is visited early in life by a vision of Aphrodite and, again, by actual women who seem to embody that vision. At one point, the protagonist imagines a world of Greek temples of white marble where naked worshippers sing hymns, burn incense, and fall asleep on the grass after laying wreaths of roses at Aphrodite's feet.

While training for the priesthood, he is repeatedly instructed that women are the "Vessels of the Devil" and that he must reject all his experiences with them as dirty, repulsive, and sinful.[3] Just before his ordination he realizes that his feelings toward women were the purest and most sacred he had ever experienced. He begins to find Christ at fault for thinking of women with disgust. At the end of the book he leaves the monastery with ambivalent feelings.

Gleb Botkin converted his vision into reality when he established the Long Island Church of Aphrodite in 1938. He had only about fifty followers. He created three different liturgies and he held worship services four times a week, before an altar with a replica of the Venus de Medici. Behind the statue was a purple tapestry. There was incense of frankincense and myrrh. Nine candles were placed on the altar, as well as the symbol of the church, the planetary sign for Venus.

In 1939 Botkin told a reporter for the *New York World-Telegram* that the purpose of the Aphrodisian religion was "to seek and develop Love, Beauty and Harmony and to suppress ugliness and discord." The principle of Christianity, he said, was to suppress desire in order to develop the spirit; but the religion of Aphrodite sought to develop the spirit through antithetical principles. Botkin conceived of nature as good. He considered hate, selfishness, and jealousy "unnatural." While in theory he idealized sex as a "divine function," in practice he was conservative and concerned lest the church "attract neurotics and those emotionally unstable."[4]

Botkin envisioned the Aphrodisian religion as a formal structure, complete with church, clergy, and liturgy. Unlike most Neo-Pagans today, he believed in monotheism and creed and dogma. *Belief* was considered necessary for salvation; one had to come into a "correct relationship" with the Goddess. During the services worshippers chanted their creed before the altar:

> Blessed thou art, O beautiful goddess; and our love for Thee is like the sky which has no bounds; like eternity which has no ending; like thy beauty itself that no words could describe. For we love Thee with every atom of our souls and bodies, O Aphrodite: holiest, sweetest, loveliest, most blessed, most glorious, most beautiful Goddess of Beauty.[5]

Botkin died in 1969, and none of his five children carried on the faith.[6] But one man who did was W. Holman Keith, a former Baptist minister who attended services at Botkin's church in the early 1940s and became a convert. He wrote *Divinity as the Eternal Feminine* (1960), and has continued to write articles for Neo-Pagan publications. Keith is considered to be one of the true elders of the Neo-Pagan movement, but his views, like those of elders in many religions, are not very similar to the views of younger Neo-Pagans. Keith died in 1995.

Keith described Botkin as a man who seemed to dislike both communism and democracy and to be for "some kind of Theocratic rule through the Aphrodisian religion." In an article in *Green Egg* he observed that many of Botkin's views would not coincide with those of most Neo-Pagans today.

> Freedom of conscience took second place for him to a rightly informed conscience from childhood on. . . . He did not believe in natural immortality . . . but in conditional immortality. The soul must come into the right relationship with the Goddess if it is to escape extinction. . . . Rev. Botkin was a monotheist in his doctrine of Deity. . . . Rev. Botkin was not cooperative with other Pagan sects. He believed that he had the Goddess truth in his teaching in all its purity.[7]

In many of these beliefs, Keith wrote, Botkin was more in line with the ancient mystery traditions than most Neo-Pagans would admit. Keith finally left Botkin's church in a dispute over its dogmatism and today is an elder in the Neo-Pagan group Feraferia.

Feraferia: The Beautiful Jewel That Lies in Its Box

"How do you like New Crete?"

I blushed and said slowly: "Why ask me, Mother?"

"Mothers often ask their children questions to which they already know the answers."

"Oh, well—it isn't really beyond criticism. Though the bread's good and the butter's good, there doesn't seem to be any salt in either."

—ROBERT GRAVES, *Watch the North Wind Rise*[8]

In 1949 Robert Graves created a fictional utopia called New Crete in a book titled *Watch the North Wind Rise*. New Crete, he wrote, came into existence during a period filled with wars and revolutions, culminating in a nuclear war. An Israeli philosopher, concerned with the survival of humanity, recommended the creation of anthropological enclaves, each of which would represent a stage in the development of civilization.[9] Each enclave was to be sealed off from the world for generations, communicating only with an anthropological council that studied the reports from these societies to determine which of them were viable and where civilization ultimately went wrong.

The enclaves devoted to the Bronze Age and early Iron Age became so successful that they were resettled on Crete. A new society evolved and, with it, a new religion devoted to the Mother Goddess, Mari, a religion similar to pre-Christian European Paganism, complete with agricultural festivals and mysteries. The new society on Crete was seen as "the seedbed of a Golden Age."[10]

But the society of New Crete was not perfect. Although much different from the bureaucracy to which we are accustomed, it was no less authoritarian. Nothing outside the dictates of poetry could be manufactured; nothing purely utilitarian. Rigid patterns of custom ruled the country's five classes. The protagonist, an Englishman from the 1940s, is sent for by the Goddess to shake the society up a bit, to put a little salt in the bread and butter, as the above quote suggests, and bring about the winds of change and freedom.

Graves was writing fiction, of course, but the idea of a Goddess religion emerging after a cataclysm is not uniquely his. Many Neo-Pagans told me they envisage a similar outcome, and several spoke to me of the Hopi prophesies of a Great Purification. Many of them seemed to feel that only a great catastrophe could bring about the seeds of change from which a new society could be created. "Look at the freak weather phenomena all around us," was a comment I heard frequently. "Mother Nature is beginning to take things into her own hands." Certainly the utopian vision that is central to a number of Neo-Pagan religions makes sense only in a world far different from the present one. And there is at least one group that could fit Graves's description of a new Goddess religion awaiting the blessed cataclysm. That religion is Feraferia, founded by Frederick Adams.

What Fred Adams has in mind is having this magnificent reconstruction of a very ancient Goddess religion, which is a finished product—polished and sitting encapsulated on an upper shelf.

After the cataclysm, who is going to have faith in Christianity? So we simply pull it down from the shelf and say, "Look, Feraferia! We've gone through Hell; so let us celebrate the return of the Kore, the Maiden Goddess from Hell!"

—ED FITCH, Gardnerian priest

Of the many groups I have encountered, Feraferia is one of the most difficult to describe. Feraferia—the name is derived from Latin words meaning "wilderness festival"[11]—is the most intricately formed of the Neo-Pagan religions in the United States. As the quote by Fitch implies, it is a jewel, an artistic creation, the private vision of one man, which sits like a beautiful crystal on a shelf, highly admired but mostly from afar. It is never contaminated by offshoots, or schisms, or changes, or even by many followers who might spread it too thin. As the sound of its name implies, it is a religion of both wildness and delicateness. Considered by its small following to be the aristocrat of Neo-Paganism, it has all the advantages and disadvantages that the word "aristocrat" implies.

Frederick Adams is a kind and gentle man who has spent most of his creative energies as an artist, astrologer, and researcher into archeology and geocosmic lore (such as ley-lines and henge construction). When I met Adams, he lived in Los Angeles with his partner, Svetlana Butyrin, in a small house covered with his artwork. When I visited them, I was welcomed with a short ritual in English and Greek. I was given a drink that tasted of cinnamon and mint, and a dish of fresh raspberries. The house radiated peace and beauty, and there was a frailty about Adams as he sat barefooted in a blue robe; I came away with the feeling that he had been buffeted by a harsh world that would not accept his sensitivity.

They were evicted from their former dwelling place several years before, after neighbors told their landlord about strange religious activities. Robert Ellwood described this home:

> A visitor to Frederick Adams' home is made immediately aware that this is no ordinary suburban house. The front porch is full of signs and symbols from out of the past—wreaths, crossed sticks, painted stones. In the backyard trees have been planted and given names. There is a henge— a circle of forked sticks oriented to the pole star and the rising sun. The group has a larger henge in the mountains to the north. Within the house are shrines to sun and moon, and a shrine room whose floor is a large wheel on which the passing days and seasons and motions of the planets are marked with stones. Here, the important news is not what comes in the paper, but what nature is doing.[12]

Fred Adams described Feraferia in *Earth Religion News:*

> Feraferia is a Paradisal Fellowship for the loving celebration of Wilderness Mysteries with Faerie style, courtly elegance, refinement & grace. The Great Work of Feraferia is the lyrical unification of Ecology, Artistry, Mythology and Liturgy. In such Love-Play-Work many Women & Men achieve reunion with Great Nature, each other, and their own Souls, before and after the Transition we call "Death." . . . Wilderness is the Supreme Value of Religion and Life! Feraferia offers, perhaps for the first time in known history, a Poetic Liturgy and Altruistic Theurgy of Holy Wilderness.[13]

Much of Feraferian philosophy is connected to a body of utopian thought. It did not spring full blown from the head of Zeus, or even

Fred Adams. Adams was the artist, but the vision shows the influence of many sources: the utopian novels of William Morris (*News from Nowhere*), Robert Graves (*Watch the North Wind Rise*), William Hudson (*A Crystal Age*), and several others[14]; writers on nature and wilderness, particularly John Muir and Henry David Thoreau; the archetypal psychologists (C. G. Jung, Erich Neumann, J. J. Bachofen, Karl Kerényi); surrealist artists and philosophers; naturalist and nudist movements; *The White Goddess;* and perhaps most of all, the work of Henry Bailey Stevens, whose *The Recovery of Culture* provided Adams with the philosophical basis for the paradisal vision of Feraferia.

Stated simply, the basic idea in *The Recovery of Culture* is that human beings have forgotten their primate origins and that this primate past, far from being a time of violence, was, in fact, the paradise of which all the myths speak. Stevens, a horticulturist, argues that the ancestors of human beings lived peacefully in trees for millions of years. It was no accident, he says, that the legends speak of Buddha's gaining enlightenment under a tree. Eden, Avalon, the Garden of Hesperides, all these visions of paradise hark bark to a time before the last ice age, a peaceful time before the beginning of animal husbandry, the eating of meat, and blood sacrifice. This paradise was no myth, but a real period of peace and plenty. The myth of the Fall was simply the story of the end of that era. The story of Cain and Abel was the story of the cropper versus the herdsman, of human beings steeling themselves to the necessity of throat cutting.

According to Stevens, grazing animals had caused the infertility of the soil, creating deserts out of gardens. "Only through gardens," he wrote, "can the neolithic civilization be understood." He added:

> Green plants form a marvelous partnership with animal life . . . they purify the air for us, giving us the vital oxygen and themselves using the carbon dioxide which we throw off. Thus there is literally a magic circle between the plants and men. This relationship has reached its most intimate form in the food-bearing trees, which fed the primate family throughout its physical evolution and became the principal inspiration of its culture.[15]

For Stevens, history began at the point where matters turned wrong. And all the great reformers in history were, in effect, attempting to turn civilization back on course. Pythagoras, Tolstoy, Wagner, Shelley, and Shaw all attempted to return humankind to a vegetarian, frugivorous existence. The end of that existence was the fundamental factor responsible for the wrong turning of civilization, the fundamental cause of wars, famines, and other catastrophes.

Stevens advocated that we "take up again our membership in the primate family," since a properly developed plant-human ratio could make of the world "a new and more marvelous Garden of Eden."[16] He hinted that one mechanism to bring all this about could be a new world religion. Frederick Adams clearly designed Feraferia to be this religion.

Adams's first direct experience of the Goddess came in 1956, while he was doing graduate work at Los Angeles State College. Before that he had explored the work of Robert Graves and C. G. Jung. He had immersed himself in occultism and ceremonial magic, and had long had a love for ancient Greece and the myths of the gods and goddesses. He also loved wilderness and had begun to draw and paint feminine religious figures.

On a spring day, during a period when he was rereading Robert Graves and studying anthropology and the works of Mircea Eliade, Adams was walking across the college campus, he told me, when "It flashed upon me! The feminine aspect of deity, the femininity of divinity. I realized at that moment that the divine feminine is the most important, most valid, most world-shaking truth that we can possibly realize. It came out of the blue, and I just started walking crazily in circles, thinking, *'That's it, that's it, She is It.'*"

After that, Adams began a series of notebooks on a new theology. Their theme was that the Goddess was the only spiritual force and Jungian archetype capable of reuniting humanity's instincts with the biosphere, nature, and the cosmos. It had to be done through the feminine modality. This did not mean the masculine would be excluded, but the balance could be restored only *through* the feminine.

A year later, in 1957, Adams and some friends formed the group Hesperides, which preceded Feraferia. Adams wrote a pamphlet, *Hesperian Life and the Maiden Way,* which has been revised several times. Here is how the 1970 edition describes Feraferian philosophy.

> There is a way of life for Man which allows him to remain Man and yet also be an integral part of Nature. This way of life was abandoned not

yesterday, not even in the space of many hundreds of years. It was disrupted and given up thousands of years ago. . . .

But the Way once existed in the world. It had hardly survived infancy when the urban-hierarchical-militaristic culminations of the different Neolithic phases of human History abruptly ended its career. However, the Way survives and smolders, imaginally, in the collective depths of the Human Psyche. If one taps these depths, dredges up the lost images of the Way, and takes them seriously, she or he is usually stigmatized as a hopeless romantic, or even worse.

Adams argued that the vision of Hesperian life still existed, to a limited degree, in various reform movements—nudist, naturalist, vegetarian, utopian, and so on. But these movements always failed because they functioned separately, and also because they lacked a "strong religious center."

The elements needed to create the Hesperian life included organic gardening, with emphasis on tree crops; promotion of forestation and reverence for the Tree as the Guardian of Life; a diet of fruit, nuts, berries, and leafy vegetables; reverence for all animal, vegetable, and mineral life; no more use of animals as chattel and pets; the promotion of regionalism with small villages and palaces, as opposed to cities; outdoor living, preferably in warm climates where only a minimum of clothing is necessary; a reverence for health and natural medicine; the end of all divisions between "mind work" and "body work"; the end of rigid scheduling and regimentation, of arbitrary coercion, codified laws, and penalization; the elimination of artificial conditions that generate competitiveness, insensitivity, and indifference; the elimination of hierarchy, authoritarianism, and inequality of work; the implementation of safeguards against overpopulation and overorganization; the maximization of "free creative play and erotic development"; and finally, the elimination of "all purely utilitarian, instrumental, automotive devices and activities as loveless and disruptive of the *living* Cosmos."[17]

Adams was clear in his disdain for most modern technology, as well as in his belief that apocalypse could be avoided only by willing an end to industrialism. "The only task remaining," he wrote, "for our overestimated, painfully inflated engineering, is to clear the Earth of its own debris and trappings, systematically and gradually over the next several hundred years. Otherwise the clearing of the Earth must be violent, for a clearing there will be."

Fred Adams and Lady Svetlana described to me their vision of the future. It is far removed from the world of today, and far removed from their own life in Los Angeles. They envision a planet that would support a human population of ten to twenty million, living off horticulture, similar to the paradise pictured by Stevens. It would be "an egalitarian aristocracy, based on arborial culture," since tree crops, they argued, produce more food per acre with less work than corn or wheat or livestock. This new aristocracy would be most feasible in a warm and fruitful climate, like Java or California. Lady Svetlana told me, "We think communities should have no more than a thousand people, all self-sufficient, since trees, when you get them going, are not hard to take care of. You could sing and dance as you picked the fruit and nuts. It's totally nonviolent." Fred Adams said that, in his fantasy of the future, nation-states would erode into temple-palace estates. These would exist amidst garden groves that would graduate into wilderness. Each temple would be connected with every other by ley-lines,* like the ancient sites of Britain. Vast tracts of land would be returned to their wild state. The population would be lowered drastically, either by sensible human measures or by the actions of the Goddess which, he told me, had already begun in earthquake activity and weather phenomena. "She will strike back," he said. "She is not going to let the whole biosphere be torn apart by nuclear maniacs."

The vision of Feraferia is of a Paganized world, but one that is far from primitive. Adams told me that it was his firm belief that if relatively small numbers of people lived in climates that were suitable and did not engage in destructive practices such as "animal husbandry and

---

*The theory that important ancient British sites are aligned, that they are linked by prehistoric trackways (ley-lines), was formulated by Alfred Watkins in his book *The Old Straight Track* (London, Methuen and Co., 1925). More recently, the theory has become well known through the works of John Michell. In *The View Over Atlantis* (London: Sago Press, 1969), a book that has enjoyed the same kind of fame among occultists as Louis Pauwels' and Jacques Bergier's *Morning of the Magicians,* Michell argues that the entire planet is marked with traces of prehistoric engineering, and that the straight tracks, or ley-lines, of Britain are one such form. A British magazine, *The Ley Hunter,* has been devoted to the study of leys, megaliths, folklore and cosmology. Janet and Colin Bord's *Mysterious Britain* (London: Garnstone Press, 1963, pp. 175–206) also takes up the question of leys.

warfare," a high culture would be conceived, exemplifying the best of ancient cultures such as Crete.

I asked Adams and Lady Svetlana for their views on the future of cities. They hoped that permanent cities would cease to exist, replaced by large cultural and sacramental centers where people would come together for seasonal festivals and cultural events. "Why then," I asked them, "does Neo-Paganism grow up in cities?" I had noticed that the Neo-Pagan movement, like the ecology movement, is mostly an urban phenomenon.

"I'll tell you why," Adams replied. "Most people who live on the farm are always fighting nature. They don't have the aesthetic distance to see other possibilities of relating to nature. Who, after all, started writing sensual literature during the early decades of this century? Who talked about freeing the sensual nature? D. H. Lawrence, an Englishman, a man from a country where people were more uptight and less sensual than anywhere else. Sometimes reversals have to come from their complete opposite; the yin gives rise to the yang, and the yang gives rise to the yin. I've known many people from the farm who can't sense Thoreau's love of wilderness; they can't sympathize with it because they are struggling with nature due to what we feel is a false agricultural approach."

And Lady Svetlana added, "We call this false approach the corn-cattle-battle syndrome."

Living in Los Angeles, a city far removed from the Feraferian vision, the life and actions of Frederick Adams exemplify the contradictions that sometimes afflict a Neo-Pagan. He is a man who functions best as Pagan priest, magician, teacher, and artist in a world that has no use for these vocations. Gentle, peaceful, almost an innocent, Adams made his living for many years as a caseworker for the Los Angeles County Welfare Department. He told me that the problem of living a split life, of trying to do meaningful nonalienating work, had been with him constantly since 1957. "All my life I have sensitized myself to be a visionary artist in a magic circle," he said. "I used to spend all my time thinking about the Goddess and the Gods. Then I had to go into the freeway world." Adams told me that he had often been subjected to harassment on the job because of his unorthodox religious beliefs. At the time, it was still his goal to find work that was not psychically damaging, and to leave Los Angeles. Neither goal seemed to be around the corner.

* * *

Adams often writes poetically, sometimes in language that few can understand. Much of it presumes a knowledge of esotericism and occultism. Occasionally, it falls into a social-science jargon.[18] A woman once wrote to him, "You need to get some of this stuff down to grade school level . . . or don't you intend for the common people ever to understand it?" The answer to that question is complicated. Fred Adams clearly believes that the philosophy and theology of Feraferia are all of one piece and cannot be separated or watered down. Still, he did publish a piece called "Feraferia for Beginners" in an issue of *Earth Religion News*. He wrote that the religion celebrated "the processes of Nature as a whole" and worshipped them as "a family of Gods issuing from a cluster of Goddesses."

> Feraferia is a mystery religion in the most ancient sense because it teaches that Life in Nature cannot be reduced to logical formulae and that it is really wrong to try to do so.
>
> The Divinities of Feraferia may appear as mighty spirits that people can feel surging through them, uniting them with Earth and Sky; or as radiantly beautiful bodies, as in myths and dreams; or as those mighty intelligences that dwell in the different forces of Nature.
>
> The main sources from which the Queendom of the Gods has reached Feraferia are associated with ancient Britain, Greece, and Minoan Crete, although all wholesome Pagan Ways, such as the American Indians, ancient Egyptian and Eastern ones, have influence . . .
>
> From Temples of the Earth Mother and Soul Daughter, like Eleusis, a wonderfully refined sense of Mystery has flowed secretly through the centuries from ancient Greece to us. And from the excavation of places like the Palace of Minos, on the island of Crete, the beautiful Earth devotions of the peaceful Minoans can now inspire and educate us. In our time of ecological crisis, we really need these original root-systems of Nature Religion.[19]

After it appeared, a number of people wrote to Adams that they were more confused than ever. Adams laughed when he told me this and said, "After that I gave up. I told myself, 'You have a convoluted, schizoid mind and you just have to accept it.'" We should bear this in mind as we approach his writings.

According to Feraferian thealogy, the center of the universe, of all universes perhaps, is the Arretos Koura, an ancient Greek phrase for the ineffable bride, the Nameless Maiden. The Arretos Koura spins a cosmic dance from which all things come into existence, each of them unique and particular. The Nameless Maiden is not the "One" from which all things leave and return; she is, rather, the "transcendent unique," the creatrix of all uniqueness. All the entities she creates interrelate with her, but never lose their individual essence. Thus, she represents polytheistic wholeness as opposed to monotheistic unity. An analogy to this might be a symphony, where each note is differentiated, but the whole is something beyond a "unity."

Under the Arretos Koura are what Adams has called "the Goddess-given Gods." These are the archetypal beings—Mother, Father, Son, Daughter. Feraferia is unlike many other Neo-Pagan revivals in emphasizing the Young Maiden rather than the Mother Goddess. Feraferia deemphasizes the paternal and maternal aspects of life, which imply relationships based on a notion of authority. Lady Svetlana said, "We don't want to think that authoritarianism is the primal thing in the universe."

The Korê—the Maiden Goddess—is at the center of Feraferia's paradisal vision. In Adams's view only a new religion that worships the Maiden Goddess—beauty, creativity, and desire—and that "draws strength from all the mysteries of Immanent Nature and the flesh," can bring the vision into reality. It is she "who is the ultimate image of delicacy and nonviolence, of playfulness and sensitivity and childlikeness. From such an archetype a society might develop in which no matriarchs or patriarchs would exist, and people would not develop hard and fast hierarchies."

Adams stated this idea in an essay called "The Korê."

To inform the dawning Eco-Psychic Age of Aquarius, wherein celebration will determine subsistence, a long repressed image of divinity is re-emerging: The Merry Maiden, Madimi, Rima, Alice in Wonderland, Princess Ozma, Julia, Lolita, Candy, Zazie of the Métro, Brigitte, Barbarella, and Wendy—a grotesque and incongruous assembly at first sight—are all early harbingers of the Heavenly Nymphet. She alone may negotiate free interaction between the other three anthropomorphic divinities of the Holy Family. These are the Great Mother, Who dominated the Old and New Stone Ages; the Great Father, Who initiated the Early Patriarchal Era; and the Son, who crystalized the megalopolitan mentality of the Late Patriarchal Era. It is the Dainty Daughter of the Silver Crescent who will transmute the saturate works of Father and Son to wholeness in the Maternal Ground of Existence, without sacrificing the valid achievements of masculine articulation. And She accomplishes this without a crippling imposition of parental or heroic authority images. How delightful to behold her tease and tickle Father and Son into respectable natural, Life-affirming Pagan Gods again.[20]

Adams argued that the central problem of our time is how to reconcile "the primal parents," the Mother and Father, the yin and the yang. The dominance of the Father excludes the Mother, but, said Adams, the Mother principle includes the Father, and must take precedence.

The emphasis on the feminine yin meant freedom for both yin and yang in their fusion. "In Yin," he wrote, "Yin and Yang find full scope for the expansion of Life between them. This means Yin, in some transcendent-immanent way, is TAO."

Within the Holy Family of four, it is the Daughter who brings about their harmony.

The Mother is Source and Center. The Son is creative separation, opening and outgoing. The Father is full outwardness, withdrawal and particularization. The Daughter or Holy Maiden is Creative Return, configuration, form. But the Daughter as Nameless Bride of ancient Eleusis is also the Mysterious Wholeness of the Four which consists in their dynamic separateness. We are initiating the Age of the Daughter, the Korê Age. (Korê is another name for Persephone, the Goddess of Spring and the Dead, Daughter of Demeter—the Great Mother, in the Eleusinian Mysteries.) The Korê Age will bring about the re-synthesis of the Maternal Whole of the Sacred Family.

It is only through the Maiden, Adams argued, that the balance can be restored in a way that will elevate freedom, playfulness, sensuality, and the imagination. The flaw of Christianity—and of most of the Eastern religions—is that they sought to create a balance through the Father principle, and were forced to do so through asceticism and the images of a pure, castrated male. Such an image, he wrote, would only continue the "Age of Analysis." In contrast, the Maiden Way would provide the necessary spiritual cohesion to begin a shift in history that would end "the prisons of hierarchy and the garbage heaps of industrialism." And this "Great Shift" or "Great Return" to the feminine could be seen by anyone who carefully examined the news of the day, or took a look at recent films, or novels, or essays, or poetry, but all "with an inner eye sharpened by the depth psychology of C. G. Jung."

In *Hesperian Life and the Maiden Way* Adams wrote that all previous attempts at revolution were trying to return to some contemporary aspect of the Goddess, but failed because they could not rid themselves of "mechanization, hierarchy, exploitation of animals, [and] sex repression." He argued that such an impulse had inspired Marx to talk about the "withering away of the state"; it was present on banners depicting the Virgin of Guadalupe during the Mexican Revolution. But the Maiden Goddess was never acknowledged as the guiding spirit of these reforms. Neither liberal education, nor totalitarian propaganda, nor the education of an elite vanguard, nor the victory of science and technology could ever bring this revolution about. "Only a great Religious Revolution, springing from the very broadest collective base of the Human Soul, can spread rapidly enough and thrust deeply enough without cataclysmic consequences to win the whole Human Race back to its Root Sense of the Organic Feminine Balance, and its natural destiny of Hesperian Life."[21]

> All life on Earth participates in
> the dance of Moon and Sun.
> And we, engendered in the oceans,
> feel in our blood the pull of
> our Moon upon the tides.
> We are sunlight transformed by
> trees into fruit and plasm, and we
> are so intimately of the Earth that
> our collective dream is paradise.
> Thus we are moved to celebrate
> the ceaseless play of the seasons
> and to ensoul ourselves,
> landscape and heaven.[22]
>
> —*Frederick Adams*

Frederick Adams has lived in the wilderness, and Feraferia has participated in reforestation work, regarding wilderness as "the supreme value of religion and life."[23] Feraferia has stressed its spiritual link with ecology, stating that the lyrical unification of ecology and religion is its prime task. Adams has written that "The only way to reunite Mankind is to reunite Mankind with Nature. Mankind will become humane toward Man only when he becomes humane toward all nature."[24]

Feraferia's first article of faith has been a belief that from wildness springs love, wonder, and joy, and that, as the famous quotation from Thoreau goes: "In wildness is the preservation of the world." Adams has written that the primary cause of alienation and most psychological disorders is the severing of humanity from wilderness. Poetry, ritual, dance, and song unite the inner and the outer: they link "visionary nature within and ecological nature without," microcosm and macrocosm. Adams emphasizes techniques that lead to a feeling of connectedness to the natural world. These include not only ritual techniques for producing ecstasy but techniques to reconnect one to the living cosmos— knowledge of wilderness, ecology, astronomy, astrology, and henge construction. Since all nature is sacred space, the planet and sky are Feraferia's temple. Adams has devoted many articles to building temples in nature, orienting them to the four directions and the positions of the stars and planets. "Land-Feeling," wrote Adams, "is absolutely essential to the Spiritual Reclamation of Man to Nature in Her hour of crisis," and building a henge or "topocosmic mandala" promotes a feeling of "Land-Sky-Love."[25]

Feraferian rituals are oriented toward the play of the seasons and the transformations of the Maiden Goddess and her lover and son as the year progresses. Adams writes:

> Our Earth, a very great Goddess in artistic communion with The Cosmic Korê, displays the magnificent pageant of the seasons. . . .
> The year is a continual courtship between Moon and Sun. On May Day . . . Moon and Sun become engaged. At this time flowers are in full bloom. On the first day of Summer, They are married: fruits are forming. In the middle of Summer, Lammas, The Goddess and God are on Their Honeymoon: fruits are ripening.

On the first days of Autumn, Moon Goddess and Sun God come home: the fruits are dropping, crops being ingathered. At the middle of Autumn, Hallowe'en, the Divine Lovers prepare for the long Winter sleep of all Nature: leaves and seeds are settling to soil.

On the first day of Winter, Yule, the Goddess suddenly reawakens. She finds The God has mysteriously departed, but She is pregnant with The God of the coming year, really the same God, the Lord Sun Himself. . . . Yule is when the Sun starts North again, thus promising that Spring will follow the long cold rest period of Winter.

At the middle of the Winter, Candlemas, The Goddess emerges from Her Royal Bedroom, The Great Earth-Sphere, and prepares to give birth to The Sun God again as an infant: enscaled buds stand out on bare branches.

Then, on the first day of Spring, Ostara, She does give birth to the baby Sun: fragile buds emerge from their scales in the dewy Sunrise of the year. The Goddess bathes in Her magic fountain and becomes a girl again. She and The God grow up together, very rapidly. Once more They become engaged on May Day, when buds are opening into flowers.[26]

Feraferia lays great emphasis on sensuality and eroticism, but by these words Adams does not mean genital sex. Rather, Feraferia stresses the idea that human beings should open themselves up to their own sensual nature, to the landscape, the earth, and sky, as well as to all other beings. Feraferia, like a number of Neo-Pagan groups, talks about sensuality as a sacrament, as the "feast of the Goddess and the Goddess-given Gods."

Feraferia distrusts modern technology much more than does any other Neo-Pagan group. Adams and Lady Svetlana feel that most mechanization has disrupted the flow of human life so that humanity is no longer in tune with the pulse of nature's own rhythms: solar, lunar, and the circadian rhythms of our bodies. Adams told me that he hopes for a new science—a small, highly refined technology embodying solar energy, laser technology, and a combination of forms—some of it old, known to the megalithic stone builders, and some of it new. In one flight of imagination Adams told me of his fantasy of priests and priestesses creating orgone energy in great ley-line temple centers through the use of highly developed sex magic.

Some Neo-Pagans have called the Feraferian vision unrealistic, as well as too blatantly antitechnological. Others have criticized its vision of nature as "unnatural" because it accepts only the calm, refined, elegant, peaceful, and romantic aspects of nature. These Pagans believe that nature has a dark side, that the destruction caused by storms, the killing of one species by another, are part of nature's laws and necessary for life. Adams told me, "Evolution is now maintained on this planet by predation and competition. There may be other principles for regulating evolution on other planets that are not as cruel as those on earth."

Feminist Neo-Pagans have criticized Feraferia for emphasizing a glamorous, seductive, playful goddess. And both Fred and Svetlana have said that women should not make themselves less glamorous; rather, men should make themselves more childish, more delicate. Svetlana said, "Wilderness is highly decorative. We should emulate her beauty."

But the main criticism by Neo-Pagans is that Feraferia is primarily an artistic creation rather than a functioning religion. In practice, it has had few followers. Feraferia emerged out of Hesperides during the 1960s; it was incorporated in 1967 and reached its height in the early seventies. Even then, it had an active group of only about fifty people (occasionally more appeared for big festivals), of whom only twenty or thirty were initiates. Feraferia has been very selective in accepting initiates.

In 1971 Robert Ellwood wrote about Feraferia:

Serious members are typically people who have been involved in pacifist, ecological and utopian movements. They seem in Feraferia to find a religious expression adequate to what has long been their real spiritual concern. . . . Adams's exercise of the leadership role has illustrated the problems inherent in this vocation. The vision is preeminently his, and he has himself done most of the writing, created most of the art and devised most of the rites. In some ways he approaches religious genius, and undoubtedly without his labors the movement would not exist. . . . It is essentially a circle around a charismatic leader and has no real structure otherwise. It is not clear whether at this point it has any potential to survive him as a sociological entity. Yet there are those who feel that his personality stifles the creativity of others in the evolution of Feraferia, albeit he is a mild and winsome person whom all love and revere. Some feel his vision is so personal and intricate it does not communicate as easily as it should. Some have been through Feraferia and left to establish their own henges and forms of neopaganism, though no off-shoots have yet attained real structure.[27]

At least one person told me he left Feraferia when Adams began to insist on *belief* in its thealogy. One couple, the Stanwicks, left to form an autonomous Feraferian group called Dancers of the Sacred Circle. Even though the circle around Adams was small, he continued to develop his artistry and vision. He and Lady Svetlana continually stressed the need to keep the vision pure. They were openly elitist. Lady Svetlana said, "We want to keep it small because it is so precious, like a diamond; you can't just throw gems to the wind. Everything is worked out in so much detail that if any detail is changed ideologically, it would be very upsetting." And of course, Feraferia *is* like a necklace of precious stones, intricately worked out: the religion is very detailed, complete with rituals, calendar, thealogy, and vision. Adams has said that he doesn't think the vision will even begin to be realized until after his lifetime. He says that Feraferia's aim should first be to find a territory, a sanctuary, where the Hesperian vision can be actualized. Then the training of priestesses should begin.

Feraferia's purpose, according to Adams, is to save the earth and return humanity to a state of harmony with nature; to begin a transformation that will end with the dawning of a new culture throughout the galaxy, focused on the Korê. In Ellwood's words, its purpose is clearly "to recover an ecstatic vision of wholeness and unity which utterly respects the reality of the particular. It brings together not only man and nature, but man and each seasonal and geographic particular of nature, and also man and each style of his own consciousness—masculine and feminine, analytic and dream, vision and fantasy."[28] But, says Adams, the vision must be freely accepted; never imposed. "If we impose it, we'll abort the attempt. We will become monsters and lose our historic mission to save the planet from disaster and to convince the Goddess to let us reenter Her Queendom."

By the late 1980s Fred and Svetlana were not very active. They separated for a period, and later got back together again. Although Fred Adams was doing occasional rituals and leading discussions, and Svetlana Butyrin held public services for a while, Feraferia's activities in the 1980s and 1990s were pretty minimal. But a new generation is becoming receptive to Feraferia's vision.

Fred Adams remains the prime elder and visionary. In 2005, Fred Adams sat down with Harold Moss, priest of the Church of the Eternal Source, and talked about the origins of his vision. Moss has been video-taping a number of Pagan elders to make sure that their insights will not disappear. Asked what he would tell young people today, Adams said he would tell them to "get some acres, and set up a paradisial sanctuary." "You could have started a witch coven," said Moss, but Fred Adams said that seemed "too narrow." He loved Gerald Gardner's books, he said, but years before he knew anything about Wicca, he had wanted to create some institution that would emphasize a paradisial way of life, filled with orchards and gardens, a life with no violence or conflict—one that would emphasize a clothing-optional lifestyle, vege-tarianism, and sensuality:

> I was thinking and imagining a paradisal sanctuary long before I ever heard of witchcraft—a place where I and my friends would live in peace and harmony and have a beautiful sensual life, and the spiritual and the sensual were not separated.

In creating the name for Feraferia, he had sought the right word that would combine a sense of faery with service to nature. The word *Feraferia* seemed to have that right combination—joining a notion of faery with ideas of celebration and wilderness.

When he met Svetlana they had talked about founding a new religion based "squarely on the bliss between lovers." It would have to emphasize the importance of the feminine and give ecology prominence. It would have to have new concepts of love that were sensitive and creative.

Today, halfway through the first decade of the twenty-first century, the Internet has revived Feraferia. Until recently it would have been al-most impossible to get a hold of Feraferia's rituals, essays, and artwork. In 1999, an artist living in Amsterdam came across Feraferia at a Euro-pean Wiccan conference in Germany and got into correspondence with Fred Adams. Peter Tromp (Phaedrus) has his own Wiccan group, and has combined Feraferia with Wicca in his own work. He is now one of the two contact people for Feraferia worldwide (see Resources). Phae-drus offered to put Feraferia on the Web and to produce official versions of Feraferia's core rituals. *The Nine Yearly Festivals of Feraferia* were produced in Dutch and English. Phaedrus says, "By way of the Internet, we now have the possibility to save Feraferia's heritage from getting lost." Phaedrus believes that with contact points in Europe and the United States, Feraferia is ready to regain its place in the Pagan community. He writes:

I do think the message is still important to make people in this modern world aware of the unity that exists between them and the natural landscape. We must not only preserve the heritage of those who came before us, but also actively use it to get maximum impact. Religion should be a way of living with poetry, art and magic, instead of blindly copying and following rules and traditions which in the end will suffocate every inspiration and energy we so desperately need to personally rediscover our connection and oneness with our fragile planet.

In my opinion, to be alive and fertile, every tradition has to be reinvented again and again by every new generation. Feraferia is and will always be Fred and Svetlana's creation, which we will continue and elaborate— inspired by their example. After some years of silence, we now can use modern ways of communication to reach out. Instead of the artificial indoor traditions of too many Pagan movements, Feraferia is ready to guide and help people to regain their lost connections with nature in her wild aspect.

The Sabaean Religious Order: Rite as Art

One night, during a Midsummer Solstice festival held in a city park, a friend of mine observed the Neo-Pagan phenomenon for the first time. Afterward my friend remarked, "It was lovely. Sweet. Almost Edwardian."

Those words grated upon me, because I agreed. I have always felt that a Pagan celebration should be powerful, energizing, ecstatic—never merely "sweet." Seasonal festivals should suspend the dictates of convention and dissolve, however temporarily, the bonds of time and space. I remember being mesmerized many years ago by a Zuni corn festival in Colorado which lasted from morning until night. My attention never wandered from the dancers for that period of many hours. I have only rarely achieved such rapt attention during the rites of Neo-Pagans and Witches.

That this should be so is not surprising. It is the dilemma of modern life, a dilemma that arose with the destruction of the Pagan-folk-peasant traditions of Western Europe. The rise of Neo-Paganism in the United States must be understood as, in part, a search by uprooted Westerners for their own roots and origins, for a vibrant, rich culture equal to the cultures of tribal peoples and the great ancient civilizations. The Neo-Pagan movement is tied in ambiance if not in fact to those movements that seek to retain, preserve, and strengthen traditional cultures in Europe—the pan-Celtic movement, for example. It is no coincidence that some of the non-Gardnerian Witchcraft groups label themselves "Irish Traditionalist" or "Welsh Traditionalist."

Many Neo-Pagans are drawn to Native American traditions, to Voudoun and Santeria: Pagan traditions involving whole cultures, communities, and even countries. People who are drawn to Neo-Paganism usually do not have a vital, indigenous tradition and are seeking to recover their roots, to rediscover folk tales, stories, songs, and dances that have largely vanished in the last hundred years.

Neo-Paganism in the United States is primarily a white phenomenon because it is mostly a revival of Western European Paganism. Many blacks and Latinos who are engaged in the same process—searching for roots—are drawn to Voudoun, Santeria, and Candomblé, all of which combine African religious and magical practices with elements of Roman Catholicism. (In Haiti the religion of the French colonialists and slavemasters mixed with the religions of the Dahomeans, Ibos, and Magos to produce Voudoun. Elsewhere in Latin America the Yoruba religion mixed with the religion of the Spanish and Portuguese colonialists, creating Santeria and—in Brazil—Candomblé).

These traditions are often more vital than the groups we have been discussing, simply because they took form within whole cultures and communities. But most white North Americans lack a culture that is still tied to the earth and its seasons. The Neo-Pagans are attempting to rebuild a whole new culture from a pile of old and new fragments. When they are honest with themselves, they admit their impoverishment; for even if their groves and covens succeed, it will take generations to create successful traditions.

At present, some of the most powerful rituals in the United States take place in the theater, in modern dance performances, sporting events, and rock concerts.

In the 1970s and 1980s, powerful Neo-Pagan rituals were rare. This should not be surprising, since the Neo-Pagan priesthood was in its infancy, picking up small pieces and discovering things often by chance.

Devlin, the Witch from California, once remarked to me, "Unfortunately, the raising of power is an accidental occurrence among us most of the time. In ancient Ireland the music of pipes and drums and harps was essential to the success of the rites. And so, I must say, was ritual drunkenness and ritual sex. I do not respect many 'public' Witches because I find among them a lack of ecstatic experience which I think marks these people as having incomplete traditions. And I hope that, in time, these incomplete forms will give way to complete forms."

During my travels around the United States I attended many rituals, ranging from the full-moon ceremonies of small Witch covens and visits to private and personal shrines, to large, public, seasonal festivals attended by hundreds. Some were totally captivating. Often the simplest were the most powerful. But frequently, I felt that something was missing.

One of the most important exceptions to this was a wedding ritual in Chicago at the Temple of the Moon of the Sabaean Religious Order, a religious order inspired by ancient Basque, Yoruba, Sumerian and Babylonian sources. Like Feraferia, the Sabaean Religious Order comes out of the vision of a single man, Frederic M. de Arechaga, who is called Odun, but his vision is far different from Frederick Adams's.

When I went to Chicago in the fall of 1975 I found so many rumors circulating about the Sabaean Religious Order that it was impossible to sort them out. Everything I had read about the order was confusing, almost as if Odun had sought to surround it with mystery. My first encounter was symbolic.

I had just arrived in Chicago and went to visit an old friend, the former editor of an underground newspaper—now defunct—and a veteran of many unusual experiences. This man had no particular interest in "the occult," and I thought he would not easily succumb to fear of the unknown. But as we were walking on the North Side in Chicago, my friend began to cross the street in order to avoid passing a small magic shop. On the sidewalk in front of the shop were various magical symbols drawn into the concrete. I asked him why we were making this detour. He said that the owner of the shop was very strange, and was said to have put broken glass on his roof to prevent children from climbing. He described him as "weird and unpleasant." He waited on the other side of the street while I entered El-Sabarum, the occult supply store of the Sabaean Religious Order and one of the five or six places in Chicago I was determined to visit.

In the next few days several occultists also warned me to be wary of Odun. I was told he practiced negative magic and performed animal sacrifices. I could find nothing to substantiate the first charge; the second was true—all animal food consumed in the temple had to be killed ritually. But since I was not a vegetarian, I felt I could hardly complain of this practice, any more than I might complain of the kosher laws of the Jews.

My own meeting with Odun (pronounced Ordun) was cloaked in mystery. There was a series of phone calls in which it was never clear whether Odun was in or out. I was kept waiting in a back room of the temple building, filled with statues and paintings. While I waited, a young woman in purple stockings practiced operatic arias on a piano. An hour later Odun arrived with six or seven members of the order, all carrying large grocery bags filled with food—a preparation for a wedding. Odun was dressed casually in jeans, a shirt, and sweater, but all were white, as might be required of an initiate into Santeria, which in fact he was.

Finally our interview began. I felt somewhat at a loss, having much less to go on here than with any of the other groups I'd met—a few articles, some confusing pages by Hans Holzer, and a bagful of rumors, some of them perhaps true, others perhaps the product of jealousy. My confusion had been aided and abetted by Odun's evident love of weaving a bit of mystery around him. I came away with a wealth of impressions, a sense of great creativity and variety, but also the feeling that the group was hard to pin down, that I was missing certain signals.

Odun has described Sabaeanism as a philosophy of action that states that human beings should live in the present, identifying with those principles that are unchanging even in the face of death. One such principle would be the pursuit of knowledge, since knowledge, he observed to me, is the one thing we are not born with, but which we take with us when we go. Sabaeanism, he has said, is a system of thought that can be applied to all aspects of life.

According to an article in the order's occasional publication, *Iris,* Sabaeanism is "a unique philosophy" that "extends back in time 6000 years or more, and as a living undogmatic principle is evasive when put into impersonal written words." Sabaeanism was originally part of an effort "to preserve an antediluvian philosophy by means of deliberate hieroglyphics superimposed on the illusion of star groups in the heavens."[29] According to Berosus, a Babylonian historian, the last antediluvian kings were ordered to write down all history and deposit their writings at Sippar, the city of the sun god, Utu. This was to be no earthly city, since man-made and natural disasters would destroy such writings. So the city of the Sun God was really the heavens, and the history was recorded in the stars. Thus, astronomy evolved as the most important feature of Sabaeanism, along with astrology, temple building, and the study of the relation of place, time, and celebration to the planets and stars. "Sabaeanism" means worship of stars or star lore. But the Sabaean Religious Order has been involved in a large number of activities that have nothing to do with astrology and astronomy. Odun told me that Sabaeanism came to Egypt at the time of Menes (1st dynasty), and later emissaries brought it westward. He told me that during the seventeenth century, during the slave trade, it was brought to the New World and that is why the tradition has deep ties with Santeria.

Odun's background in the arts seems to be the key to the order's richness and mystery. He has been a choreographer and a designer. He told me he worked with the Lyric Opera of Chicago and designed jazz pianist Ahmad Jamal's nightclub, the Alhambra. I once watched him work with a dancer during a wedding rehearsal in the temple. He ran and leapt and directed her until she moved gracefully to the music of the small temple orchestra. From the little I saw, Sabaean rituals are the most complex and beautifully organized of any Neo-Pagan group I visited. The use of music and dance was truly inspiring. The order has mounted mystery plays; they have synthesized art, dance, song, and ritual to a height I have not seen elsewhere. In addition, there are classes in herbalism, magic, and astrology. The priesthood seems small, with certainly less than a dozen members, but I noticed that many Chicago

Neo-Pagans came to work with Odun for a period of time. Most of the Pagans I met in Chicago had dealt with the order—some favorably, some not favorably—and many had been influenced by Odun.

Frederic de Arechaga came to the United States from Spain. He changed his name to Odun Arechaga after his initiation into the mysteries of the god Obatala. He told me that he inherited the Sabaean tradition from his mother, but, whatever its origins, it bears the stamp of his own artistry. The order consists of the small supply store, El-Sabarum, which opens in the late afternoon and seems to cater to members more than the general public. El-Sabarum also runs a mail-order service and an occasional newsletter. Behind the shop is the temple, some space for classes, and living quarters for the priesthood. The temple was completely designed and built by members of the order and is the focus for religious gatherings small and large.

Sabaean theology describes God or the Gods as *Am'n,* a word that is said to mean the hidden, numberless point. Unlike the word *God,* the word *Am'n* can be singular or plural; it suggests neither maleness nor femaleness. The Am'n are seen as a Source, but hidden like the wind, which can be felt but not seen. An article in *Iris* observed that the Am'n "cleanse the imagery of deity to its original premise of self-metamorphosis; man's ultimate responsibility to himself."[30]

The Am'n are seen as total knowledge; they are "indifferent, amoral and pure source." They are "above being adored." They "do not exist for the morbid preoccupation of a fanatic. But rather as avenues that can develop the individual to an awareness of himself and the universe that hitherto has remained unearthed."

For the sake of convenience, the Am'n can be divided. Odun told me that the order represents the Am'n symbolically as five different goddesses. "Poetically we use the term *goddess.* After all, the female is a formidable symbol for creation. We always know who the mother is, and even the mother does not have to know who the father is. Still, the idea of creation must not be misunderstood. We are not feminists. The entire universe is *not* based on the feminine precept. The incident of sex or gender which comes about in an incarnation is only a necessity or need of evolution. Divinity is sexless. The most ancient descriptions of gods are androgynous. But it is very hard for people to concentrate on the abstract. That is the whole purpose of mythology, to familiarize yourself with certain mysteries in an unmysterious way through storytelling."

The order also divides the Am'n to represent various races, seasons, philosophies, and theologies. The Red Goddess represents Autumn and the peoples native to this continent. The White Goddess represents winter and Caucasians. The Black Goddess represents the spring and blacks. The Yellow Goddess represents the summer and Asians. And the Blue Goddess represents leap year, the day between the years, and the races and peoples beyond earth.

The Am'n are also used to represent five aspects of philosophy— logic, aesthetics, ethics, politics, and metaphysics—and five aspects of theology—atheism, pantheism, polytheism, monotheism, and heno-theism. The Sabaean Religious Order adheres to henotheism as the most inclusive. A henotheist is a person who worships one god *without excluding the existence of others.* "A henotheist," Odun said, "is a person who relates to deity in a personal way. For a time, one might be attuned to Venus; at another time, to Saturn." An article in *Iris* explained further;

> As a henotheist, a Sabaean can relate to an individual imagery that particularly reflects himself. . . . However he never forgets that there is another imagery he can [use] if it comes to pass that he changes and no longer can identify with the image he so fondly admired.[31]

Odun described henotheism as the "ultimate wheel of the five-pointed star which would begin with atheism, go through pantheism, polytheism, monotheism, and finally end up with henotheism before beginning all over again." These five theisms, he observed, relate to all of human knowledge, to the five aspects of philosophy.

"Atheism seems to relate to logic (the idea that this is this and that is that). At the point when a person realizes that there is a form and a move-ment to things, this brings about a sense of aesthetics and leads a person to pantheism (the feeling of a tree, or a flower, of the wind). When a person comes to the realization that these feelings, these 'spirits,' have a kind of personality, this leads to polytheism, and the sensing of these di-verse points of view and individualities leads a person to a sense of ethics. At this point, people often begin to manipulate reality and to move in one direction or another. Thus they come to politics and monotheism.

At the point when a person realizes there is something beyond all this, they develop a sense of metaphysics and become henotheists."

Odun said that one could be an atheist and still be a Sabaean, although, later, an atheist woman told me that she had left the order because she felt that her views were too far removed from the general conceptions of the priesthood.

Odun calls the Sabaean Religious Order a kind of finishing school and says that learning about the ancient philosophies and mystery traditions is equivalent to learning to be civilized. "We do not believe in teachers," he told me. "The purpose of a priesthood is to be a catalyst, to sustain a strength for people who come to it so they can be vitalized." Most people, he said, are unable to read the ancient books properly and to open themselves to the ancient myths. But despite his stress on ancient knowledge, Odun points out that the order is not anachronistic. There is no purpose to living in the past or attempting to mimic ancient times; most religions failed precisely because they did not take into account the metamorphosis of people, nations, mind. "The object of life," he told me, "is to know yourself, to learn, to become, to grow; it's the becoming divine, the principle of the mystery of deification. *Sabaeanism* is simply a term given to our people. But they are people who follow their own heads. They are not hung up on a book or on a prophet. They are not idolators of books. They know there are many different paths within Sabaeanism."

The feeling one gets in visiting the order is of a constant stream of diverse activities. Odun told me that the one thing that was not allowed was wasting time. "We are constantly busy. We build. We teach. We do research. We write mystery plays. We choreograph. We teach dancers. We *are* a source."

My visit to the Sabaean Religious Order culminated in a magnificent wedding ceremony, or "eclipse," as the Sabaeans call it—literally, the movement of one planet in front of another. The length of an eclipse is decided by divination. If a couple decides to join for a period of years, it is called a solar eclipse; if for a period of months, a lunar eclipse.

The ceremony I attended in the late fall of 1975 was the solar eclipse of a priestess in the Sabaean Order. She was marrying a man who had no connection with the religion. It was, ritually speaking, the most beautiful wedding I have ever seen, surpassing a magnificent traditional country wedding I once attended in England.

The eclipse took place in early evening in the Temple of the Moon behind the small occult supply store run by the order. A door in the shop opened into a large high-ceilinged room lined with two rows of tall gray columns, each topped with a statue of a white elephant. The columns were ringed with wreaths of ferns and daisies. A brownish-gold curtain cut the inner portion of the temple in half.

Before entering the temple, we took off our shoes. Inside, on one side of the curtain, the bride sat on a golden chair covered with a soft animal skin. Her head was covered by a light yellow silk veil that fell loosely in folds like an Arab burnoose. A wreath of ferns and gardenias held it in place. Her dress, which she had made herself, was translucent light yellow with long silk tassels. She was barefooted and held in her hand a single white gardenia. All the women sat beside her—friends, mother, and the groom's mother. On the other side of the curtain, seated on a silver chair, sat the groom with all the men around him. According to Sabaean lore, the woman is symbolized by the sun, and the man by the moon. In this it differs from most Neo-Pagan traditions.

After a while, Odun Arechaga appeared, dressed in white satin priest's garb and a large white cap. He held a long white feather in one hand, and in the other a beautiful sistrum, an ancient musical instrument. Odun spoke of the Am'n. He then told a story. It was a pre-Hellenic myth that forms much of the basis for the Orphic mysteries, often called the Pelasgian creation myth. It went something like this:

"In the beginning the goddess Eurynome, mother of all things, arose naked from chaos, not finding a place upon which to stand. Moving through space she grabbed hold of the north wind and, catching that gust that moved behind her as she turned, she rubbed both winds between her hands to create the great cosmic serpent Ophion.

"No sooner had life breathed into his nostrils and he saw those divine limbs than did he lust to couple with her. But the action of time was slower for him than Eurynome. Whilst he still saw the divine naked matrix she in fact had metamorphosed into a dove and had laid a large silver egg that shone with divine eminence.

"Ophion, desiring to satisfy his lust, wrapped himself around this egg seven times. But so tightly did he coil that the egg split in two!

"Out tumbled a heaven of a thousand suns and moons without number. Planets and comets, nebulae and galaxies of stars!

"Ophion, stupefied and proud, boasted to the very plenum of his creation. He gorged himself on the self-adulation of genetrix and claimed the sole authorship in creation. He looked down upon Eurynome as a mere functionary of his great work.

"Instead, Eurynome bruised his head with her heel, and kicked out his teeth for this presumption. She split his sex as male and female and placed him on the many thousand worlds he created so that in time he can justify and merit that position he once had.

"Since then it seems that all male seeks female so as to regain a fragment of his other half, and somewhat nostalgically we are awed with the expanse of the night heaven, looking out there knowing not where we have come."[32]

The meaning of marriage is the reuniting of these two halves. To achieve this unification, both partners must die symbolically, they must abandon their individualities and become one. This death and rebirth, then, was the ritual we would witness. And we would do more than witness it, for Odun said that there could be no "observers" present but only those who were willing to participate fully in the rite. Those who did not wish to participate were asked to leave. No one left.

Odun began to shake the sistrum and to move in and out beneath the columns. He gave one candle to the bride and one to the groom. He told them to stand if they still wished to be united. The mothers of the pair stood with the bride, the fathers stood with the groom. The room was darkened. The temple orchestra played dark Middle Eastern themes intensely and rhythmically. There was a predominance of bells and drums. Suddenly, Odun pulled down the silken dividing curtain. It fell on top of the pair, covering them. Odun wrapped the curtain around them. He led them around the pillars in a slow dance, then down a flight of stairs and into a ceremonial chamber. There, out of sight, the couple did various rituals which we did not see. Meanwhile we danced circle dances.

Then the temple priests strewed barley and rice in patterns across the temple floor. While the music continued, the pair, still bundled together, was led up the stairs and through and around the pillars. They were taken into another chamber for divinations, and finally, into a third room where a bed waited, covered by elaborate spreads. They were left alone to consummate the marriage while, outside, the women danced together to send energy to the bride and the men danced together to send energy to the groom. Then we waited while a temple dancer, the one I had seen work with Odun several days before, danced for us with graceful, sensual movements. After a time, the couple opened the door and emerged. All the women danced with the groom and all the men with the bride.

Then the feast began, and what a feast it was! The bride and groom sat at either end of a long table covered with a cloth. Young priests, dressed in white, brought forth a large cauldron that stood on a tripod. With great ceremony they threw spinach and romaine lettuce into the cauldron from large straw baskets. To the sound of cymbals and drums, lemons were ceremoniously squeezed, eggs were shelled and tossed into the mixture, along with anchovies and salt. The priests poured vinegar and oil from large carafes. Finally, one of the young priests rolled up his long sleeves, thrust his arms deep into the cauldron, and tossed the enormous salad. Odun took a lettuce leaf and gave it to the bride, who approved it. Then all the guests dug in with their hands.

That was merely the beginning. It was followed by a procession of courses—vegetables, fish, beef, and fowl—from shrimp in sauces, deviled eggs, and stuffed clams to plates of stuffed grape leaves, sweet fried plantains, pita bread with various dips, tomatoes and peppers, and platters of pigeons, oysters, chickens, and geese. Each set of dishes had been prepared by the priests; they appeared with the flourish of cymbals and drums, and each course was washed down with a strong, foamy punch. In the midst of the banquet came the ritual meal of the bride and groom, and in contrast to our feast, it was simple. Two fish were broiled and served with parsley. Dessert included carrot cakes, wedding cakes and puddings, honeycombs dripping in honey, rows of papayas, persimmons, pomegranates, figs, and dates.

During the feast I came across a bowl of enormous goose eggs. I picked one up and gazed at it, to remind myself later that this had been a feast out of a fantasy. Finally, I could contain myself no longer. I walked up to Odun and said, "This is the most amazing feast I have ever seen, barring the banquet scene in Fellini's *Satyricon*."

Odun gave me a wry smile and said with a touch of affected humorous contempt, "Remember *Satyricon* was *merely* a movie."

The Sabaean Religious Order moved to New Orleans in 2000. At the time of this latest edition, Odun had suffered a terrible stroke from which he still has not recovered. Bill Koeppen, a Sabaean who has been with Odun for many years, says, "There is a void in all our lives without his presence and all of us pray to the Am'n for his well-being." As a result of Hurricane Katrina the staff of the Sabaean Religious Order made the decision to move to Denver, Colorado. Sabaeanism will continue. The priesthood intends to complete the books Odun was working on and publish them in his name. It plans to reopen the temple and storefront again.

The Church of the Eternal Source

Feraferia and the Sabaean Religious Order each sprang from the vision of one person. The power of these two groups reflects the energy, charisma, and talent of their founders.

The Church of the Eternal Source (CES), a federation of Egyptian cults, stands in contrast—devoid of charismatic leadership. Instead, it centers on the power, artistry, and beauty of a culture—ancient Egypt. Involvement in CES depends on a direct personal, intellectual, and emotional encounter with the force of Egypt, with its gods, with the beauty of its art. Most members usually had such an encounter at an early age, perhaps in a library or a museum, or through a book or a film. Since relatively few people in our culture have had such a fortunate experience, the Church of the Eternal Source is very small.

Many of the founders and priesthood of CES have similar stories: early identification with ancient and classical cultures—Greek, Roman, Egyptian—and an early religious bent. The late Donald Harrison, for example, one of the founders of the Church of the Eternal Source, was a commercial artist whose home was decorated with exquisite hand-carved replicas of Egyptian works of art. Harrison began carving statues of gods and models of temples as a child. Later, he converted to Catholicism and entered a Benedictine monastery. Then he rebelled, declared Christianity "anti-life," and left the monastery a confirmed Pagan, determined to reestablish the ancient religions. Influenced by Gore Vidal's novel *Julian,* in 1967 he founded the *Julian Review,* one of the earliest Neo-Pagan journals. Believing that the ancient Egyptian religion was

too esoteric for most people, he joined Michael Kinghorn in founding the Delphic Fellowship, a group devoted to Greek Paganism. In the
meantime, he began a six-year-project to create a full-size replica of
the throne chair of Tehutimes III, hand-carved in two thousand pieces
of ivory and rare woods. Finally, when the Church of the Eternal Source
was established in 1970, after much study, Harrison declared himself a priest of the Egyptian god Thoth and began to reestablish the
Thoth cult.

Jim Kemble had planned a career as an Episcopalian priest, but later
became enamored of the classical religions of Greece and Rome. In high
school he performed secret ceremonies to the old gods. He would walk
to the beach in California and drop wine and bread into the sea, invok-
ing Zeus, Poseidon, Bacchus, and Pluto. After 1970 he came upon CES,
and the gods he had worshipped merged into the figure of Osiris. He
began to study Egyptian history and religion and became a priest of
Osiris, reviving the Osiris cult.

Elaine Amiro, a priestess of Neith, was fascinated as a child by native American and Egyptian cultures. She was attracted to the desert and
at various times kept many strange animals, including iguanas, bobcats,
monkeys, ocelots, and alligators. She taught Navajo children in New
Mexico and studied the Navajo religion although, she told me, "as an
Anglo, I was barred from learning much of the rites."

After returning to her home in Massachusetts, Amiro said, she discovered the Goddess at the end of a period when her life had "just
seemed to fall apart." One day she was looking in an encyclopedia at the
names of Egyptian gods and goddesses. "One name caught my attention," she wrote me, "and I kept coming back to it. I had never heard of
the Goddess Neith before. I wondered why I was so attracted."

Neith, writes Amiro, was the great lady who was mother and daughter to Ra, the sun god, who "brought forth herself in primeval time,
never having been created." She was the "first to give birth to anything,
when nothing else had been born, not even herself."

Amiro found that her name matched Neith's numerologically, and
several strange experiences convinced her that Neith was her spiritual
guide. She wrote that after this discovery her creative energies seemed
set free. She began to paint, to write poetry, even to carve statues. "Life
has never meant more to me than when I rediscovered ancient Egypt

and the Goddess. All my talents began to surface. I was amazed at the number of things I could do and do rather well." She began doing healings. Amiro, the mother of three children, worked as an elementary school teacher. She told me that she made Egypt and other ancient cultures come alive for children.

Later she found out about the Church of the Eternal Source and established the cult of Neith at her home in West Wareham, Massachusetts. "I finally discovered who I was and what my job on earth was—to be a servant and priestess of Neith." Only after this, she said, did she really begin to live.

Harold Moss was one of those most instrumental in founding the church. One could say that CES began in fun, as a series of Egyptian costume parties originating with a group of students known as the Chesley Donovan Science Fantasy Foundation (CD). The group was formed in 1953, when Harold Moss was in high school in California. A CES pamphlet described the Chesley Donovan Foundation as "an elitist science fiction club and atheist organization." Its members "quoted Thomas Paine and Willy Ley and Robert Heinlein, read horror comics, wore military helmets with meat cleavers implanted in them to social functions and school, and used 'normal,' 'average,' and 'Christian' as swear words."33

Harold Moss is a warm and compassionate man who, when I first met him, worked as an engineer in the daytime and by night lived in a house whose walls were covered with shelves of classical records. We spent a long evening talking, listening to Bach cantatas, and looking at pictures of the California desert. Harold told me that he had long been fascinated by the sophisticated cultures of the ancient Egyptians, Greeks, and Romans.

"Just precisely how I became aware of Egypt is pretty clear to me. I did a lot of reading as a child and I loved to go to the movies. I was aware of the Arabian Nights stories, and movies such as *The Thief of Baghdad*, and even the old *Cleopatra*—as corny as it was. Roman epics fascinated me.

"I remember I particularly liked the idea that ancient people wore few clothes. I thought clothes were stupid and ridiculous and even as a child I kept trying to take them off. The Hebrews always seemed to wear too many clothes, whereas the Romans and the Egyptians ran around naked, and this made a lot of sense to me as a child.

"But mainly, I was captivated by the sense of beauty of the Egyptians. I find I am using this phrase a lot these days. I was utterly captivated by this magnificently developed sense of beauty. I felt there was no possibility that anything could be wrong with a people who could manifest such beauty."

In 1954, after seeing the film *The Egyptian,* Moss went to the library and read James Breasted's *History of Egypt.* The child of Theosophists, Moss was brought up as a free thinker, and it was natural for him at the time to identify with Akhenaten and the religion of Aten, finding it to be a kind of Pagan rationalism. "I was under the spell of Breasted," Moss said, "with all his highly fictionalized accounts of Akhenaten as the lonely progressive in a world of hidebound people who were worshipping blindly, through habit. Akhenaten was the one who dared to think, to do something different, to be unusual. So, of course, he was the proper hero for an eighteen-year-old."[34]

Members of the Chesley Donovan Foundation adopted Akhenaten as their hero and began to wear ankhs. Moss pursued his interest in Egypt with his friends, who may not have taken it as seriously as he did. As the years progressed, he came to realize that he was captivated by *all* of the Egyptian religion, not just Akhenaten. By 1967 he had rebelled against Akhenaten's monotheism, declared himself a polytheist, and immersed himself in the classic cult of Horus, the god of light.

Moss and a number of friends had started a tradition of Egyptian summer costume parties in 1964. Eventually, they were scheduled to coincide with the ancient Egyptian New Year's celebration in mid-July. By 1970 Moss had come into contact with other Pagans, including Feraferia's Fred Adams and various Wiccan groups. He met Don Harrison and Sara Cunningham, a priestess of Wicca, and together they founded the Church of the Eternal Source officially on August 30, 1970. It was incorporated the next January. Sara Cunningham later left CES and returned to Wicca.

The Church of the Eternal Source considers itself to be the *refounded* religion of ancient Egypt, authentic in spirit, scholarly, and intense. An early CES leaflet proclaims:

The Church of the Eternal Source is the refounded church of Ancient Egypt. We worship the original gods of mankind in their original names in the original manner as closely as possible. This religion produced in Ancient Egypt a golden age of peace, happiness, tranquility, and accomplishment unmatched since. . . .

Nothing stands still. . . . Our work is to establish a constantly evolving synthesis of ancient and modern knowledge under the direct guidance and in direct contact with the Eternal Gods. . . .

How can we reconcile a polytheistic faith to the "modern" ideas on religion? It is true that the central religious experience is unity with the universe. . . . But the distinctness of the Gods is a fact of our revelation. Like the facets of a precious jewel, each of them should be approached separately. . . . The human spirit is beautiful only when it is free. The diversity of the Gods commands a deep commitment to human diversity.[35]

But what does it mean to be authentically Egyptian today? CES understands that the answer to that question is complicated, and that it can easily be misunderstood by those who think of ancient Egypt simply in terms of pyramids, burial customs, bureaucracies, and powerful pharaohs.

The priesthood of CES sees Egypt as the first truly religious culture and to them "Egyptian" means remaining true to the spirit of the ancient religion, a spirit exemplified by three things: ecumenicism, polytheism, and the mythopoetic view.

CES encourages its students to continue any religious practice they have found meaningful in the past. "We think our general viewpoint is more meaningful, more powerful and more satisfying, but whatever of value you have found we will urge you to keep. . . . Our purpose—the purpose of true religion—is to help you become *more;* not to tell you a lot of things you have to give up, nor to insult you, nor try to terrorize you."[36]

What, then, is this more meaningful, more general viewpoint? First of all, it holds that the Egyptian gods are not "Egyptian" in any national sense of the word. CES has no ties with the present-day Arab world. It views Egypt today as a place that has been devastated and violated by unbelievers and infidels. The sanctuaries have been desecrated; the shrines are in ruins. The Egyptian gods are seen as eternal forces, and all modern religions are simply aspects of the Egyptian view narrowly focused. For example, modern Judaism may be seen as a cult of Ra, Christianity as a cult of Amen-Ra-Harakhte with a touch of Isis thrown in, Buddhism as a cult of Amen. "This," wrote Moss to a Protestant clergyman, "makes perfect sense, explains why men disagree, and gives us the ultimate answer to ecumenicism—freedom."[37]

The priests of the Church of the Eternal Source have often said that there is more of the truly Egyptian in Nepal, or in a Hopi pueblo, than in late Egyptian texts, which are tainted by foreign elements. CES encourages dressing in the Egyptian manner, learning hieroglyphics, using Egyptian dates and names, but at the same time it upholds the view that "the Egyptian culture we imitate was ancestral to the present culture of all Western nations," and that therefore understanding of and respect for all religious practices are beneficial.[38]

I asked Harold Moss how he looked at the gods. "I'm a Jungian introspectionist," he said. "The Egyptian gods and goddesses represent constructs—personifications. . . . Do the gods exist? Yes. The conceptualization of polytheistic divinities is a useful way of explaining the kind of contact we *do* have with the transpersonal and transinfinite forces of life. These forces are beyond human conception, but we can establish a path of communication so that these forces react to us, to people, *as though there were gods*." "Still," Moss added, "the gods are real."[39]

CES is adamantly polytheist. "Polytheism," a CES pamphlet states, "accepts a concept of Divinity based on the plurality of the Gods in human perception." What a Christian might call God, a priest of CES might call "the gods"; but both stand for the totality of divinity.

> There is surely a single source of Divinity, but this abstraction when translated into human institutions often results in the worship of the Ego, or in an enantidromia, a dualistic split, with "God" in an exalted position placed in opposition to Man and everything human. A polytheistic concept, on the other hand, can embrace the religious experiences of Monotheism and Pantheism also: we view Divinity as a balance of distinct divine vectors.[40]

In this very Jungian view, the parts of a human being are infinite. Likewise the parts of "the gods." When they are brought into harmony, health results; sickness comes when they are in disarray. In this scheme the goal of life would be to bring one's own individuality into balance with these forces, into harmony with *Ma'at,* a word the ancient Egyptians used to describe the preexisting original order of the universe.

Unlike many of the "new" religions, CES does not print its own religious books. There is an occasional pamphlet and one can still get back issues of the magazine *Khepera.* But generally CES relies on the basic texts of scholarship on Egypt and the best translations of ancient texts.

If CES has one basic recommended introduction to the study of Egypt, it is Dr. Henri Frankfort's *Ancient Egyptian Religion.* Frankfort stresses that to understand Egypt we have to begin to understand the mythopoetic outlook, a totally different way of perceiving reality, and dispense with our evolutionary bias. Whereas most Westerners are used to the idea of revelations from a single God transmitting one central truth, the ancients "admitted side by side certain *limited* insights, which were held to be *simultaneously* valid, each in its own proper context." There was no single truth, no central dogma, no single coherent theory to explain reality, no one holy book. Frankfort wrote that this habit of thought, which is so unlike our own, "agrees with the basic experience of polytheism." The universe is alive with multiple forces. The question of their "unity" does not arise. There are many gods and they are immanent in nature.[41]

In addition, Frankfort writes that many of our assumptions about Egypt are incorrect. For example, it is wrong to say that Egyptian religion evolved from more primitive forms, or that modern religions evolved from Egyptian forms that were more primitive. Nor was the worship of animals and animal gods a transitional phase toward the worship of human forces. Frankfort argues that the Egyptians viewed the universe "as a rhythmic movement within an unchanging whole" and believed that only the changeless participated in divinity. Since animals, unlike humans, have no history, and since the lives of animals change little in comparison with those of humans, animals shared more in divinity, in the eternal, than did humans.

Like Frankfort, the members of CES have a view of Egypt that is very different from the popular conception, which, they are quick to point out, has been distorted by Egypt's conquerors. For example, we commonly think that in Egypt all religious power was invested in a priesthood, and that priests always functioned as intermediaries between a worshipper and the divine. But Harold Moss contends that this is a mistaken view; Egyptians had personal shrines and worshipped individually. One tenet of CES is that people should contact the gods daily. The priests are used for exceptional circumstances. Moss told me, "It's controversial whether the Egyptians were really that sacerdotal. I think they were less so than Catholics today. The religion was political, but not in the sense of a state arm to oppress. The priesthood functioned to advise in all major undertakings. It oversaw rituals for fertility, for the rising and setting of the sun. The religion had the same ethical base as the Hopi religion—the great national festivals were for the purpose of securing the bounty of nature."

Moss also told me that CES did not follow Egyptian burial customs and practices; his own travels to Egypt convinced him that those customs were conditioned by the environment of the Nile Valley and had continued to be practiced there long after the religion had faded. Most members of CES favor cremation and the return of their ashes to the earth. "The real question," Harold said, "is what of the ancient Egyptian religion is truly for all the world and not simply for the Nile Valley? What parts of this religion fit in with the life of the United States?" He concluded that these questions must be solved by practice, not dogma. "We're trying to avoid the mistake of the Christians. They started out with a whole lot of writings which they then spent the rest of their existence defending and trying to live up to."

In practice, the Church of the Eternal Source is a federation of independent cults, each led by a priest or priestess who maintains services for a particular deity—such as Horus, Ptah, Sekhmet, Hathor, and Anubis—supervises initiatory procedures of that cult, and corresponds or meets personally with those students who express interest. Each cult is autonomous. Rituals are held separately. Most students reach CES through correspondence with one of its priests or initiates, who advise a course of study. Books and later rituals are suggested. If at a certain point a student makes a commitment to a particular deity, the study program is tailored in that direction.

As of 2006, the church has about six functioning priests and priestesses, three major shrines, three fully dedicated temple rooms, and substantial congregations in California, Oregon, and Idaho. The church also conducts correspondence with students in the United States, Britain, Canada, and Africa. The Egyptian New Year's party continues, and has developed into an ecumenical Pan-Pagan gathering for many Neo-Pagans in California.

Religious practice in CES is centered on the personal shrine, which is created by each individual and may or may not be devoted to a particular deity. In addition to study of Egypt and worship at the shrine, members of CES are encouraged to learn psychic and divinatory arts ("Divination reminds us on a day-to-day basis that the macrocosm and the microcosm—the universe and man—are interrelated in function"), to produce works of art with Egyptian symbolism, to explore the wilderness and nature, and to involve themselves in community actions.

A church pamphlet, "Our Modern Practice of the Ancient Egyptian Religion," states:

> Tell us what you want, what you seek, and we will provide the maximum assistance possible. Our purpose is to aid each person to become her or his own Priestess or Priest, to aid each person in the attainment and fulfillment of her or his own vision and Goddess or God experiences.

The pamphlet says that the church provides information and instruction about "things Egyptian" and various occult techniques, but all from the following general standpoint: The church does not manipulate or coerce its members. "Power" is understood to mean a sense of wholeness that comes from living in harmony with the flow of the universe (Ma'at). The church does not believe that power shared is power lost, but rather that knowledge is increased as it is shared. There are no secrets. CES does not claim to teach "Ultimate Truth," which, according to the pamphlet, "is endlessly discovered for and by one's self, throughout one's existence and incarnations."[42] Moss reiterated this point by observing, "When a person assumes that his or her revelation is the only true one, it only says that this person has had very few religious revelations and hasn't realized how many there are." The pamphlet goes further:

> We enjoy different peoples' being different and do not teach sameness, conformity, or a rigidly bound system, but rather encourage diversity and "varieties of religious experience."

We seek to help to open one to learning more and to heal the damage done by various religious and political systems that seek to degrade and use people. . . .

Harold Moss once observed that the Church of the Eternal Source faced one great hindrance as a religious organization—it lacked charismatic individuals. Its appeal has always been to intellectuals who enjoy scholarly pursuits. "My own approach to religion is intellectual," Moss told me, "and since I am writing most of the introductory letters to people, as secretary of the church, this is a stumbling block. The only people the church has gathered are those who have been captivated by this force which reaches through Egyptian art across the centuries and which seduces people. Then a person has to be driven to want to understand what sort of intellectual force produced such a culture.

"Our smallness is a source of disappointment to some of us. The number of people who are interested in ancient Egyptian religion is rather limited. But we have made a beginning." Moss became reflective and began to talk about why he has not lost his fascination with ancient Egypt. "I have always been wrapped up with the idea of permanence and commitment. And Egypt was a very conservative society, where obligations were often life-long, and where permanence and commitment were stressed. In our society, we often collide with one another like molecules in a gas; we interact briefly to form submolecular species and then go our separate ways. This is all part of the unfolding of the universal life force to understand itself, and I understand this intellectually, but it bothers me. Perhaps Egypt becomes, for me, a kind of utopia, where things never change."[43]

If the Church of the Eternal Source remains small, its importance for Neo-Paganism is disproportionately great, for it emphasizes more clearly than any other Neo-Pagan group a commitment to diversity, multiplicity, and freedom. Writing to *Green Egg* several years ago, Moss summed up the essence of CES:

Many people I think are disappointed in us because we are not the most mysterious of the mysteries. They think Egypt was like that, from the testimony of her conquerors. But Egypt was actually one of the most uncomplicated places that ever was, and religion was no exception. . . .

The power of Egypt was closeness to the Earth. Her religious symbols were all of the Earth. Her religious acts were all celebrations of the cycles of the Earth. That is what I/we mean when we say: "We are all Egyptians." The true living "Egyptians" are the American Indians. . . .

Many today seek the true Gods, the Egyptian wisdom, in dark rooms, arcane studies, ferocious secrecy. If they reach their goal they will find themselves standing in the sun under a clear blue sky, on the banks of a river—5000 years ago—singing and dancing for joy, heart brimming with love, mind afire with certainty of the harmony between the Gods and Man, of the brotherhood and sisterhood of all life.[44]

In a recent series of films on Pagan elders, Harold Moss said, in November 2005, that, "Polytheistic religions, in general, command a reverence for diversity. Human diversity is a sacrament. That is the important thing we have to teach." In 2005, Harold Moss told me he now lives on a farm and does work as a music critic and audio producer. The Reverend Donald Harrison died in 2004. The Church of the Eternal Source has several new priests and priestesses. There are also several new Web sites (see Resources).

Heathenism

When *Drawing Down the Moon* appeared in 1979, one of its most glaring oversights was the omission of Heathenism. While I had received many publications relating to Odinism—*The Runestone, The Raven Banner*, and others—I found myself in a quandary. Some of the information I received was from groups genuinely seeking a Norse Pagan path, but there were other groups clearly using Odinist symbols and mythologies as a front for right-wing and even Nazi activities. I even had a neighbor, around the corner from me in New York City, who was a leading member of a Nazi political party and who was communicating his religious ideas in the forum of the *Green Egg*. His cramped apartment on Ninety-third Street was crammed with books—one wall was filled with Nazi regalia and literature; the other wall was filled with books on the occult, with particular emphasis on Norse and German (and Vedic) mythology.

In addition, the common notion within much of the Pagan movement at that time was that Norse Paganism was filled with such people.

And since the Heathen community was generally more conservative in its values and ideas *anyway,* stressing concepts like family, courage, and warrior virtues, it was easy to become confused. In the end I just gave up, deciding it was a can of worms I just didn't want to open.

But Pagans interested in Norse mythology wouldn't go away. There were serious seekers, flourishing organizations, and good scholarship. There are even places where indigenous Heathenism continues. For example, public Pagan worship was outlawed in Iceland over nine hundred years ago, but the ancient restrictions were repealed in 1874. In 1972, Nordic Paganism was officially recognized as a legitimate and legal religion, and Icelandic Pagan groups exist today.

The problem of being confused with Nazism is one that almost all Heathens have had to confront. As Alice Karlsdóttir, who used to edit *Boreas,* a journal of Northern European Paganism, said to me, "You will always find fringe people attracted to Paganism. Just as Witches have to contend with the occasional news report of weirdos torturing animals and calling themselves Witches, we in Norse Paganism have our own fringe types. There's been a general assumption that the Norse religion is connected with the Nazis because the Nazis used Norse symbols. And Neo-Nazis sometimes get attracted to Odinism, because the trappings are the same." And Prudence Priest, the editor of *Yggdrasil,* wrote me, "How are we ever to reclaim the swastika—symbol of both Thor's hammer and the wheel of the sun (and dating back thousands of years before Hitler's perversion of it)." Karlsdóttir told me of putting on a Norse ritual at a large Pagan festival and finding that many who came to it were wary that it "would be negative," an impression that was only dispelled by the ritual itself.

As with Pagans from all cultures, people attracted to Scandinavian and Germanic forms of Paganism often come to it as part of a search for their own ancestral roots. Alice Karlsdóttir told me, "My family is Scandinavian, and as I was growing up, my mother read me the Norse myths, and they remained my favorite ones." After attending an extremely conservative Christian college in Texas, Karlsdóttir decided she was not a Christian. She studied different religions, became interested in the occult, and, through a poetry teacher, began learning about Paganism. "The minute I realized Paganism was the religion for me, and that it was OK, and not weird, I *immediately* went back to the Norse gods, which had been in the back of my head all this time. There was never a question. I just knew. I thought, 'I can really believe in these guys again!' Perhaps it was the way I was raised, or perhaps I just had these images in my head."

When I revised *Drawing Down the Moon* in 1986, the largest and most successful organization promoting Norse Paganism in the United States was the Ásatrú Free Assembly (AFA), which was started by Stephen McNallen in 1971. It later changed its name to the Ásatrú Folk Assembly. "I had wandered out of high school in rural Texas," McNallen told me, "and had shaken off Catholicism because it conflicted with my basic instincts. I sampled many religions, read about Wicca, looked into Crowley, but none of it clicked. Then I ran across a novel about the Vikings. In retrospect, it wasn't a great novel, but the Vikings, in contrast with the monks, were real; they were alive. They had all the intensity and courage. It was clicking into something I already believed, but it was still awhile until I became aware that you can choose your gods."

McNallen said that many of the main Odinist groups (the Odinist Fellowship, the Odinist Committee in England, Ásatrúarfolks in Iceland, and the AFA) started within a very few months of each other, with no knowledge of each other's existence. Perhaps it was "a wind blowing through the World Tree," he said. The AFA published *The Runestone,* a quarterly journal, as well as assorted books and tapes on the religion, mythology, rituals, and values of Ásatrú. Every year the AFA holds an annual three-day festival called the Althing. Held in a rural setting, there are rituals, fellowship, music, and feasting. The AFA also created a system of guilds to encourage fellowship and the sharing of skills: the artists' guild; the brewing guild; the warrior guild; the computer/shamanism guild; the writers' guild; the sewing guild; even the aerospace technology guild.

Many people involved in Northern European Paganism use the word Asatru to describe themselves. Ásatrú means "belief in the gods" in Old Norse, or, more correctly, loyalty to the Aesir—one of the two races or groups of gods in Norse mythology. The other group is the Vanir. The Aesir consists of gods many people will find familiar: Odin, who is often seen as the high god, a kind of All Father principle; his wife, Frigga; his son Thor; Tyr; Balder; and many others. The Aesir, in Scandinavian myths are a race of sky gods. They are generally the more aggressive and outgoing, the movers and shakers. The Vanir consist of the gods of the earth, of agriculture, fertility, and death. The most well known are Frey and Freya, and there are some people involved in Norse Paganism who have concentrated on the Vanir. The Vanir also include Nerthus and Njord. The myths tell of a time way in the past when the Aesir and the Vanir warred. Later, the two pantheons merged. Most people involved in Heathenism are very polytheistic, preferring to honor all the gods, Aesir and Vanir.

On one level the gods are examples and models—inspirations, self-aware personifications of the forces of nature. On another level, McNallen says, "they are a numinous logic-defying reality, something apprehended only by means of symbols, something that speaks to us on deeper levels where words are inadequate. Studying the Gods, we can all add richness and power to our religious lives by tapping this ancient, non-verbal wisdom."

In a pamphlet titled "What is Ásatrú," McNallen describes the spiritual beliefs of Asatru as:

> We believe in an underlying all-pervading divine energy or essence which is generally hidden from us because it surpasses our direct understanding. We further believe that this spiritual reality is interdependent with us—that we affect it, and it affects us.
>
> We believe that this underlying divinity expresses itself in the forms of the Gods and Goddesses. Stories about these deities are like a sort of code, the mysterious "language" through which the divine reality speaks to us.[45]

The gods are honored in daily rituals, and there are seasonal celebrations on the solstices and equinoxes and other ancient festival days. Some have told me that rituals are often sparser than those in Wicca. There are some groups that do circle rituals, using different symbols for the elements—perhaps a sickle or cakes for North, a spear or rune wand for East, a sword for South, a horn for the West. Many groups do not find the circle form of ritual appropriate. Some groups celebrate six of the eight traditional Pagan sabbats, having a six-spoked wheel of the year, rather than the eight of many Pagan traditions.

When I revised *Drawing Down the Moon* in 1986, most people involved with Heathenism would carefully distinguish themselves from other forms of Neo-Paganism, and only a few of them interacted with the larger Pagan community, went to festivals, or engaged in ecumenical activities. Part of this was because they did not see themselves in any way as part of a universal movement; in fact most Heathens do not believe in universal religions. Stephen McNallen has written that the various branches of humanity have different ways of looking at the world and that this is natural. McNallen wrote to me:

> We're not eclectic. You won't find tarot or astrology or I Ching incorporated into Ásatrú—not because they're not valid or powerful, but because they aren't *ours*. This isn't to say of course that an Odinist can't utilize these systems as an individual, but they're not a part of Asatru.
>
> A second difference is that we are so intimately involved with the idea of ancestry as to be almost a "Norse Shinto."

This is where it got complicated and problematic. Many of the Heathens I spoke with in the 1980s and much of the literature I read put a heavy emphasis not only on ancestry but on a belief in the primacy of genetics, as well as a belief that certain aspects of the soul are transmitted down the family line, that reincarnation comes within race, tribe, and family. In looking at the Jungian idea of archetypes, several articles in *The Runestone* observed that Jung's original idea was that these archetypes were not culturally transmitted but inherited genetically. Today, Heathen thought on these issues is much more diverse, but at that time, one member of the AFA told me, "We are not racists, but we are racially aware. I look at my children's red hair and freckles and think how many generations it took for them to get that way. I want them to be the same color as me." To which I refrained from replying, "Suppose it was just a random mutation?" A woman in AFA told me that she had never had a black person apply to be in her group, but she would wonder why they weren't interested in "their own religious roots." This was completely at odds with, for example, Isaac Bonewits's Druid group. "Most of the black people in the group have more Celtic blood than I do," he observed. Speaking personally, if religious impulses and archetypes are transmitted genetically, I would never have been influenced by Athena and Artemis, and this book would never have been written. As David James, also a member of the AFA, once observed to me, "It's rather funny, there are a whole bunch of Jews in the Celtic groups and a whole bunch of us Celts in the Norse groups."

Despite observations like these, members of the AFA told me that duty to one's ancestors and kin is a holy duty that comes first. Blood *is* thicker than water. "This way of looking at things is contrary to the dogma of this day," McNallen observed, but he contended, "We know in our hearts . . . Ancestry is better than schemes which would deny these truths and propose a formless, alienated and unnatural universalism."[46]

In talking about Ásatrú as a very ancestral religion, with bonds that are genetic, "even paragenetic," McNallen conceded that "it can easily be misinterpreted." "How do you prevent misinterpretations?" I asked. Partly by explaining over and over again, he said. "We used to get people who thought we were out to save the white race. But we are not for putting anyone down. We are simply for the spirituality of our own people. This is a real religion. It is not a front for any political group." McNallen says that while a lot of Heathens in the past were attracted for political and cultural reasons, a real religious development had been taking place with interest in magic, ritual, and runes.

But while the AFA stressed the religious aspects of Norse Paganism and downplayed the political, when I was originally writing about Heathenism, some Odinist organizations had a different view. The Odinist Fellowship, for example, devoted much of its journal, *The Odinist,* to political and philosophical articles on subjects ranging from attacks on liberalism to a defense of the original goals of apartheid. Instead of avoiding these political discussions, the Odinist Fellowship met them head on. It was frankly racist, although they would have probably preferred the term "racialist." One article had these words: "The most distinguishable feature of Odinism is that for the first time a religion has declared itself founded upon the concept of race, with its correlation to culture and civilization. Without race there is nothing; therefore our first duty is a study of race and the significance of Aryan people to world history."[47] As you will see, this kind of language is in no way typical of most Heathen groups today.

There do remain differences between Neo-Pagans and Heathens in regard to beliefs about ancestry, politics, and race; there are also some differences in values. A leaflet describing the values of the AFA lists them as follows:

Strength is better than weakness
Courage is better than cowardice
Joy is better than guilt
Honor is better than dishonor
Freedom is better than slavery
Kinship is better than alienation
Realism is better than dogmatism
Vigor is better than lethargy
Ancestry is better than universalism.

At the time I wrote this chapter, Heathenism did attract people who were more politically conservative than the majority of Neo-Pagans. They were uncomfortable with feminism, anarchism, and diversity in sexuality and life style. Of course, there were also conservatives in the general Neo-Pagan community. But all in all, there was less vegetarianism and more alcohol as opposed to other mind-altering methods. There was a stress on martial arts and on warrior values. (The Vikings are seen as freedom fighters, not robbers.) The AFA has, in the past, advertised in *Soldier of Fortune*. McNallen disagreed with my label "conservatism," saying that modern society didn't have much to conserve. "We are seeing the decline of the West," he said, "we are living in the ruins." Still, as Ariel Bentley, a woman in the AFA, put it to me, "I'm no longer a bleeding heart liberal," and Alice Karlsdóttir said, "There's stress on independence, courage, on not being pacifistic. The idea that life is a struggle and that's fun, so go out and *do* it. It's definitely not a meditative religion." I asked her if she agreed with those ideas, and she said: "If someone came for me in an alley, I'd rather wipe 'em out, than rehabilitate them. In the '60s it was uncool to have those thoughts and I repressed them. But I realized I was lying to myself."

As for Heathen gatherings, Ariel Bentley described workshops, presentations by the guilds, rituals, feasting, songs around the campfire, and a sumbel—a Germanic ritual in which a drinking horn filled with mead is passed around and each person toasts, recites a poem or song. It is a place where the psychic storehouse of a group can be brought into the present. "There were songs, stories, prayers, bragging and boasting." "Bragging and boasting?" I queried. "Yes," she said. "Bragi is the god of poetry. All my life," she said, "I was trained not to blow my own horn.

But in Ásatrú, it is considered fine, a way of linking oneself to one's ancestors."

Like most Neo-Pagans, most Heathens do not believe in sin and regard guilt as a destructive rather than useful concept. In an article called "Joy is better than Guilt," McNallen writes that guilt is a tool for forging a brave new world, filled with docile, interchangeable units. In Ásatrú, the gods inspire one to a different view.

> Odin, pragmatically breaking the rules to safeguard the worlds of gods and men; Thor, indulging his appetites without shame or fear; Frey and Freya, reveling in healthy sexuality; these are powerful, liberating models casting off the chains of restraint. By invoking them into our lives we can experience the joy of existence in a world where strength, ambition, competence, and pleasures are not fettered with alien, life-denying bonds.[48]

While Heathens tend to be more conservative than most Neo-Pagans, their religion puts them at odds with the mainstream conservative culture. Stephen McNallen has written that the religion of Ásatrú is under assault by Christian fundamentalists. "After a period of religious tolerance that has lulled us for several decades—a tolerance that has protected both the best and worst in American behavior—it is apparent that we are entering a time when we of Ásatrú are going to meet greater and greater resistance from the powers that rule this country." McNallen notes that there is some irony in this situation, because "Many of the values championed by those who would oppress us are values with which we can readily identify, such as a strengthened family, less bureaucratic intervention in the life of the individual, and the rest. Unfortunately," he adds, "it was the followers of the pale Galilean who coopted the movement back to traditional values more in keeping with those of our Folk—and we, who follow the gods that hallowed those values, stand to be crushed, if the new inquisitors have their way."[49]

Another distinction between much of Neo-Paganism and Heathenism is the relative position of male and female gods. In fact, some Pagans simply dismiss Norse Paganism as "patriarchal." "People ask me, 'How can you be a woman in Ásatrú?'" Alice Karlsdóttir told me. "It is true that there are more patriarchal aspects, after all, the head god is Odin.

But I would call it 'balanced,' with a certain leaning toward male gods. It is true more men have been attracted to it than women, but that seems to be changing. And while some people in Ásatrú have traditional role models in mind, I have not found men to be hostile to me as a woman. I have only had encouragement, and I am not a traditional woman. I'm independent, I'm unmarried, I'm an actress. Remember that in ancient Norse culture, women had much more freedom than in Greece or Rome. Women could own property, divorce their husbands and take back their dowry. It's true the most visible gods are Odin and Thor, and they have warrior values. They are very macho gods—so they appeal to men and more men join the group and people say it's a male religion. But I'm hoping more women will become visible."

Heathen women also reminded me that the Norse goddesses are powerful figures. Freya, for example, may be a goddess of love and procreation, but she is also a warrior, a goddess of passion and change. Stephen McNallen wrote in *The Runestone:*

> Lest we fall into the snare of thinking of the Lady of the Vanir in the somewhat predictable female roles of sex goddess or promoter of the perpetual pregnancy, we must remember her fiercer side. . . . When we recall that she chooses half the battle-slain, when we reflect on her links to the valkyries, when we consider her many parallels with Odin, we are led to conclude that Freya's martial abilities must be formidable. . . . Her message is simple: women too, can be strong, assertive, and full of fight. As Frey tells men that they can be lovers AND fighters, Freya says the same thing to women.[50]

Alice Karlsdóttir and Maddy McNallen, Stephen's wife, both told me there is beginning to be a determined effort to foster the role of the goddesses in Norse Paganism, to "redress the balance."

A beautiful description of Northern European Paganism appears in the journal *Yggdrasil,* put out by the American Vineland Association. It describes Heathenism as a religion with a deeply felt spiritual link to the land, the forests, the seas, our ancestors, our successors, and to the celebration of life experience. Its principles are honesty, honor, the value of one's word, keeping a healthy environment, placing principle above gain, and leading a worthy life.

Heathenism in the Twenty-first Century

There seems to be an amazing flowering of Heathenry today. Heathen groups now include a whole range of Northern European Pagan traditions. Volkhvy, a member of Minnesota Heathens, said, "Heathenry has grown in diversity."

> While the main mythic/cultural focus is still Aesir/Scandinavian & Germanic, new Heathen groups have formed around the Vanir gods and goddesses, the Anglo-Saxon, Sami, Baltic and Slavic peoples and cultures. Today, Heathens are anyone who follows one of the Northern European folkways. Basically, anything north of a line formed by the Rhine and Danube rivers—the cultures that were not subsumed by the Romans.

Heathen groups are also more diverse philosophically—they differ depending on whether they consider themselves to be folkish, universalist, or tribalist. Those who are folkish tend to believe that your genetic heritage gives you easier access to the deities. Heather Demarest of the Eldhrinir Kindred says many folkish people are not racist—they do not believe they are superior, but simply believe that "all people should follow the gods and goddesses of their blood ancestors, with none being 'better' than the other. They do tend to believe that only those descended from Northern Europeans should follow Ásatrú." Some Heathens are tribalists. Demarest believes that the majority of Ásatrú falls into this category:

> They honor the ways and practices of the Germanic peoples, holding to the lore and sagas for inspiration while allowing personal gnosis to guide them when it is reasonable and possibly circumstantially supported by cultural/historical evidence. They feel the religion can be practiced by anyone, regardless of bloodline or race. So, in tribalism, there tends to be a balance or middle ground between complete cultural reconstructionism and personal revelation, as well as an openness to all those who feel called by the God/desses.

Then there are universalists, who use practices of other traditions as well as Heathen practices in worship. They might focus more on the shared culture of a geographic area or historical era, such as Scandinavian, Germanic, or Viking. Volkhvy puts it this way:

> Universalists recognize that there really is no such thing as a "pure" culture; each culture has influenced and has been influenced by its neighbors. Given the tendency for expansion and interbreeding, almost all cultures contain members whose ancestors were not originally members of that culture. So for universalists, it's not necessary that your ancestors were Heathen, just that you have a deep attraction for one of the Northern Traditions.

Other Heathens say that the term folkish has taken on many different meanings to different people. As Ben Waggoner of the Troth puts it:

> Some "folkish" types say that Heathenry can only be practiced by those of northern European descent. Others say that it comes most naturally to those of European descent, but that non-Europeans are capable of being Heathen if they choose. Still others seem to use "folkish" to mean "religiously conservative and anti-eclectic" without necessarily implying anything about people's race; others use "folkish" to mean "restricted to a tribe of people" without necessarily defining that "tribe" in ethnic terms. There are also a lot of "folkuniversalists" out there, who would recognize one's ancestry and ethnic origins as valid and good reasons for being drawn to Heathenry, but not necessarily discount other reasons.

Behind the debate over folkish, says Waggoner, lies something deeper. "A lot of Heathens are Heathens because they're looking for something more integral," he says, "something that offers a complete world view, something that breaks away from what scholars of postmodernism call 'pastiche.' Most feel that Heathenry is not and should never be 'just another option' in the marketplace that anyone can try out one day and abandon the next."[51]

Many Heathen organizations are called "kindreds" and most are non-hierarchical. There are many different rituals, but among the most common are Blot and Sumbel. Blot, in its simplest form, is an offering to the gods. For example, mead might be consecrated, a libation poured and the drink shared. Sumbel is a ritualized toasting ceremony where stories are shared and sometimes oaths are given. It can take many different forms.

Heather Demarest says not only is Heathenism much more diverse, but the biggest change is the amount of information available through publishing and the Internet.

> I think a lot of people started out in other paths because they didn't really know about us, or the religion. Once the information got out there, many people embraced it. Also, people are becoming more willing to share the information. This sharing and expanding of knowledge is helping Ásatrú to evolve quicker and form a relatively cohesive practice that is more "newbie" friendly and less overtly challenging. We are also gaining information from shamanic journeying to help fill in some gaps of knowledge where written sources are lacking. This helps tremendously too as we get to know our deities better and realize that they seem far less concerned with infighting than humans are and that helps us to get a broader perspective and accept each other more.

One of the most exciting developments in the last decade or so has been research into shamanic practices within Northern European Heathenism, in particular the use and development of a particular form of trance-working known as seidh or, sometimes, oracular seidh.

Skill in various forms of divination was a specialty of the goddesss Freya, who taught it to the Aesir. The god Odin also practiced it.[52] Seidh was used to describe many different shamanic practices, from calling up storms to prophesy. There is a description of seidh in Erik the Red's Saga. But the modern reconstruction of seidh really began when writer Diana Paxson began exploring shamanism. As Paxson tells it, she had been practicing neo-shamanism based on Michael Harner's teachings for several years, and finally had a chance to take his workshop in 1987.

> At the workshop, "On the journey to the upper world" I rather unexpectedly encountered Odin, who became my teacher. After immersing myself in Norse culture by a year's study of the runes, I began to analyze everything I could find about seidh in the lore, especially, the account in

the Saga of Erik the Red, and the poems in which Odin talks to the Völva in the Eddas. As I have reconstructed it, we begin by purifying the space and honoring the dwarves who uphold the earth and Freyja, Odin, Hella, the Norns and the ancestors. We then journey to Hella's kingdom, where the seer or seeress goes into deeper trance in order to answer questions.

Paxson's group, Seidhjallr, first presented the oracular ritual publicly in 1990. She has also taught many seidh workshops in other parts of the country and in Europe. After working with seidh for a year, the group, Hrafnar, began performing it in various settings, including Pagan festivals like PantheaCon.

In oracular seidh, as practiced by Hrafnar, there is often first purification with water and sacred herbs. There may be honoring of directions and of local nature spirits. Gods may be invoked. There is a transition into the world of Norse myth. There is drumming, sometimes other kinds of music, relaxation exercises, and journeying. There is a trance-inducing chant that is sung after the journey, which allows the seidh-workers to go to a deeper level of trance. Paxson writes that in seidh "as performed by Hrafnar, singing is used to change consciousness and raise energy, the journey to the Underworld serves to bring everyone to the source of knowledge, and the formulaic questioning keeps the visionary state under control."

A number of other Heathens have developed other approaches to seidh, some based on Paxson's work and others independently. There are actually many different forms of divination used among Heathens. Some Heathens talk about "spae," which many describe as a more passive form of divination than seidh.

Jennifer Culver is the founder of Widsith, a seidh group in Dallas, Texas. Her group has a different approach than Hrafnar, and is involved, for example, in many other kinds of rites that enhance luck, communicate "with the wights of the land and tap into various parts of the Heathen soul for reasons such as building strength and enhancing will." She differentiates between spae and seidh this way:

If wyrd (seen by some as fate, a dynamic of the past shaping the present and what is becoming) is seen as a web, spae work is viewing the strands of the querent asking questions and where and how they intersect. Nothing is done with the strands, the seer is merely "seeing" information and relaying what is seen, be it an object, person, rune, or abstract form. I put seeing in quotes, because some people hear things or feel things as well. Seidh workers historically were working within a much more active context. These folk performed rituals involving weather working, removing the luck from a person, sending a nightmare, influencing battle, creating a fog, or singing on a rooftop so that the people who came out would fall down and die. Widsith's approach to seidh is to acknowledge that if negatives exist, the positives exist as well. We create rituals, for example, that enhance (not remove) the luck of a person.

There are many Heathens who don't do seidh at all or are even skeptical of it. For example, Stephen McNallen of the Ásatrú Folk Assembly said seidh was not really part of the AFA.

Today, oracular seidh is a limited but accepted part of Heathen tradition. Paxson says that there are active seidh-workers in California, Wisconsin, Kentucky, Texas, New England, and Washington state. Groups are also being created in Florida and North Carolina. The performance of seidh at Pagan festivals has brought one form of contemporary Heathenry into a much larger setting.

Volkhvy says that this is just one aspect of how Heathenry has become more visible to the public. Groups such as the Troth have given public lectures. There is also generally much more of a Heathen presence at conferences and Pagan gatherings—both in the United States and in Europe—compared to when I last updated *Drawing Down the Moon*. Ben Waggoner, a member of the Troth, says Heathens have given presentations and put on rituals at Pagan gatherings such as Starwood, PantheaCon, and also at local Pagan Pride Day events. "Although small family oriented Blots and Sumbels are still the prevalent form of group ritual," says Volkhvy, "Heathen networking is increasing—in large part because the Internet allows isolated individuals and small kindreds to find each other."

Volkhvy says that he has also seen a change in the attitudes of Heathens toward non-Heathen Pagans. "While they still disparage the 'fluffy bunnies,' many are beginning to recognize that there are a core of groups in Wicca and Neo-Paganism that are just as serious about researching and understanding *their* traditions, as *we* are about our Heathen traditions. I see more of the attitude that 'what you're doing is not for me, but I can still respect you as a person of honor and integrity.' This has spread to encompass non-European religions and cultures." There is also more receptivity to alternate lifestyles and to gay and transgendered participants, something which did not seem common fifteen years ago.

On the other hand, Ben Waggoner says there is a debate within Heathenism: "What, exactly, should the relationship be between Heathenry and the wider Neo-Pagan community?" He says that from a Heathen perspective, "Wicca, or Wicca inspired Neo-Paganism, is the proverbial 800-pound gorilla." Heathens often feel stifled by the assumption that they are simply a part of Neo-Paganism. And Waggoner says many Heathens are "baffled, if not offended, by a lot of what they see in the Neo-Pagan community."

In an article, "The Pentagram and the Hammer," written back in 1994 by Devyn Gillette and Lewis Stead, but considered by many to be "on the money" still today, the writers say that Wicca and Ásatrú have a few things in common: a respect and reverence for the earth (Nerthus to the Ásatrúar, Gaia to the Wiccan), but Nerthus plays a less dominant role in Ásatrú than the Earth Mother plays in Wicca and Paganism. Both rely on a romanticized past—and both have a belief in and use of magic. But Gillette and Stead argue that all similarities end there. They argue that Wicca—while nominally polytheistic—is more pantheistic, seeing the divine in everything, harmonious and in balance. In contrast, Ásatrú is more polytheistic, seeing the gods as separate and distinct and sometimes in conflict. They write, "The overall theological message in Wicca is essentially one of keeping attuned to natural cycles, while the overall message in Ásatrú involves continual vigilance and struggle for the same spiritual development." So, they write, many Heathens do not like it when Pagans use Norse gods as archetypes, since they regard them as distinct entities whose minds and wills are separate from their own. Gillette and Stead also argue that Wicca tends to see itself as a mystery religion, with as much attention devoted to magical practice as religious devotion. The opposite is true of Ásatrú, which they describe as a votive religion, based on veneration of the gods. Magic is distinctly secondary. In addition, there is no belief in Ásatrú of a direct lineage to ancient times. We have seen that most claims of such a lineage in Wicca are questionable, and today many Wiccans understand that, but Gillette and Stead argue that Heathens have been up front about this from the beginning—that Ásatrú is the re-creation of a religion that did exist in history, but has been "re-created through modern research."[53]

Today, Heathens are forging ties with many other traditions: Native American tribes and Hellenic, Celtic, and Kemetic (Ancient Egyptian) Reconstructionists. Volkhvy writes:

> We're all working towards rebuilding modern expressions of our ancestral tribal folkways and have much that we can share. We're finding we can work together as an alliance without endangering our individual group identities.

Northern European Pagan groups are also struggling to establish the right to hold ceremonies in prisons, and many prisons have Heathen groups that meet for Blot. One prisoner has been writing to me for years from a federal prison in the Midwest. At one point he sent me a photograph of a ritual—eighteen Heathens at the prison holding Blot in a tiny grove—three trees—right next to the Native American sweat lodge.

There is no question that Heathenism is one of most important and creative parts of contemporary Paganism today.

A Final Note on the History of Pagan Reconstructionism

Many of the organizations described in this chapter were influential in creating a Neo-Pagan consciousness. Feraferia and the Church of the Eternal Source, along with the Church of All Worlds and the Reformed Druids set the terms of much of the early debate and led the discussions that developed in Neo-Pagan journals. The leaders of these organizations developed key concepts and theories that are now common within Paganism as a whole. Although there is a tendency for many people to assume that Neo-Paganism and Wicca are synonymous, with the exception of unusual Wiccan groups like NROOGD and Nemeton, many of the most interesting ideas in contemporary Paganism came from these Pagan reconstructionists, as well as from the creators of futuristic religions like the Church of All Worlds.

10.

A Religion from the Future—
The Church of All Worlds

Someday, people may speak of the last two thousand years as "The Christian Interlude."

—TOM WILLIAMS, priest, Church of All Worlds

MY FIRST MEETING with the Church of All Worlds took place on a cold day in late October 1975 in a small house in a predominantly black suburb of St. Louis. Eight or nine people sat around a long low table that was covered with large stacks of freshly printed pages. The house was decorated simply—beds and sofas covered with Indian print spreads, cushions on the floor, posters on the wall.

In a large enclosure of hand-carved wood and glass, four reptiles (rock pythons and boa constrictors) reposed quietly. A yellow flag lay draped over the top of the cage. "Don't tread on me," it stated, with its coiled serpent below. On a shelf, toy dinosaurs stood amid a collection of fossils, seashells, rocks, and bones.

The sound of friendly chatter mingled with the rustling of pages, the steady firing of a staple gun, and the occasional crunching of popcorn, which was being passed around in a large bowl. On the inside of the doors of the house, only a few feet from shelves littered with books and records, a sign read, "Did you remember to dress?"

The sign was quite appropriate. Only one person in the room was wearing any clothes, a fact that didn't seem particularly noticeable after a few minutes. The house was very warm, and undressing seemed to be one way to be comfortable. But everyone—dressed or undressed—was engaged in the business of the day, which was sorting, collating, stapling, and mailing the seventy-fourth issue of *Green Egg*. This peculiar journal had become one of the most important sources of information on Neo-Paganism, and until recently it played a key role in facilitating communication among Neo-Pagan groups.

The *Green Egg* Mailing Party was an eight-times-yearly event of the Church of All Worlds. This particular party lasted for two days, with people wandering in and out for a few hours here and there.

Now, describing a religion founded by a prophet or under the leadership of a central charismatic figure is easy. The words of the founder and the praises of the followers are the story. But since most Neo-Pagan religions—certainly the most interesting ones—are leaderless groups with multiple voices, even contradictory positions, it is difficult to describe them without leading readers down an easy path where they can all too quickly slip on their own assumptions. By starting out with a description of a nude gathering, even a businesslike one, I may already have led you in a wrong direction.

Almost every time (and there is one notable exception to this) an outsider has attempted to write up the Church of All Worlds (CAW), he or she has misunderstood and misrepresented it, probably because CAW refuses to fit into any easy set of boxes. Mircea Eliade refers to CAW briefly in his essay "The Occult and the Modern World":

> A rather unusual sect, even judged by the standards of the contemporary understanding of the occult, is the Church of All Worlds, founded in 1961, by two students at Westminster College in Missouri, after reading *Stranger in a Strange Land*, by the noted science fiction writer Robert A. Heinlein. The members greet each other with the phrase "Thou art God."[1]

Hans Holzer, a popular writer on the occult, implied that there was an unfortunate amount of controversy and bickering in *Green Egg*, and he disparaged the group for basing its vision "on the work of a prolific and popular science fiction writer" and "not on any ancient tradition."[2] A Neo-Pagan group that takes its myths from the past seems obvious. One that looks to the future is something else again. But Holzer's criticism is simply not valid. In fact, science fiction and fantasy probably come closer than any other literature to systematically exploring the central concerns of Neo-Pagans and Witches. Such writers of science fiction and fantasy are bound less than any others by the political, sexual, and racial mores of their society. In recent years some science fiction writers (notably women—Ursula K. Le Guin, Joanna Russ, Pamela Sargent, Vonda McIntyre)[3] have even gotten beyond the traditional sexism of the genre to look anew at men and women. Science fiction has been the literature of the visionary; it has been able to challenge preconceived notions about almost everything, while at the same time attending to fundamental questions of the age. No wonder, then, that not only do many Pagans and Witches read science fiction, but some of them write it. In my travels I came across four well-known science fiction and fantasy writers who were members of Neo-Pagan groups. Of the four, only one—Robert Anton Wilson—was public. The remaining three did not wish to have their identities disclosed.

There has always been a relationship between science fiction and the occult, but it has often baffled serious scholars. Mircea Eliade writes: "The literature of *fantasy* and the fantastic, especially in science fiction, is much in demand, but we still do not know its intimate relationship with the different occult traditions."[4] Neo-Pagans often mentioned science fiction. "Science fiction/fantasy readers tend to think of things in terms of the galaxy as a whole," one wrote to me, "rather than think in a local or national sense." Another said, "Readers are usually more acutely aware of the problems of ecology, utopia (and dystopia), and changes brought about by technological advancement."

"Science fiction," Isaac Bonewits told me, "is the one element in my life most responsible for my not being a racist or a cultural bigot," and Aidan Kelly said, "Science fiction is the major literature of the most intelligent people in this country at this point. The only authors who are coping with the complexity of modern reality are those who are changing the way people perceive reality, and these are authors who are tied in with science fiction."

Science fiction might even be called a form of divination. Certainly history offers many examples (H. G. Wells, Jules Verne) where such divination was accurate. Robert Scholes in his essays on science fiction, *Structural Fabulation,* writes: "To live well in the present, to live decently and humanely, *we must see into the future,*" and he observes that good science fiction allows us to leap from worlds we know to quite different worlds and thereby illuminate our situation. This is done through the techniques of defamiliarization and estrangement. Using such techniques, we are able to see the universe anew. Scholes, from the halls of academia, utters pure Neo-Pagan sentiments:

> We are now so aware of the way that our lives are part of a patterned universe that we are free to speculate as never before. Where anything may be true—sometime, someplace—there can be no heresy. And where the patterns of the cosmos itself guide our thoughts so powerfully, so beautifully, we have nothing to fear but our own lack of courage. There are fields of force around us that even our finest instruments of thought and perception are only beginning to detect. The job of fiction is to play in these fields. . . .[5]

The Church of All Worlds has called science fiction "the new mythology of our age" and an appropriate religious literature. Tom Williams, a former editor of *Green Egg* and a priest of the church, wrote that science fiction could evoke a new age by generating new metaphors and an infinite array of new possibilities. Reality is "a construct," a product of unspoken beliefs and assumptions that seem unalterable simply because they are never questioned. "It is from the oppression of overwhelming consensual reality constructs that the mythology of science fiction/fantasy so frees us. It does this in two ways: one, the most obvious, by offering us alternate reality constructs, and two, by revealing to us the *way* in which realities are made." The true function of myth, he said, is not simply to explain the world in some simple form that a "primitive" can understand, but like art, music, and poetry, to *create* the world. Williams argued that both Neo-Paganism and speculative fiction were based on the expansion of human consciousness and both arose at the same time. Today, he wrote, we have a rare privilege—to choose consciously the myths we wish to live by and to know "that the world which is evoked is dependent on the mythic structure of a people and can literally be anything from the oil and bombers and pollution of the Pentagon and Kremlin to the Magic Wood of Galadriel."[6]

The Church of All Worlds has been called everything from a "subculture science-fiction Grok-flock"[7] to a "bunch of crazy hippie freaks." But the real origins of CAW lead back to a small group of friends who, along with untold numbers of middle-class high-school and college students in the late 1950s and early 1960s, became infatuated with the romantic, heroic, compelling right-wing ideas of Ayn Rand. It is a sign of the peculiarity of North American consciousness that thousands of young students, at one time or another, have become possessed by her novels—*Atlas Shrugged, The Fountainhead,* and *Anthem.*

Jerome Tucille, in his witty, tongue-in-cheek tour of the libertarian right, *It Usually Begins with Ayn Rand,* could not have been more precise in his choice of title. He noted that Rand's works were particularly appealing "to those in the process of escaping a regimented religious background." Despite the author's rigid philosophy of Objectivism, in her fiction she stirred a libertarian impulse and *Atlas Shrugged* became a "New Marxism of the Right."

> If Marxism, with its promise of a proletarian utopia, was tailor-made to the aspirations of the working-class crusader, Objectivism and its ethic of self-sufficiency and achievement was intoxicating to the sons and daughters of the middle class, graduating from college at the end of the Eisenhower era.[8]

It was easy to be swept up by the intense struggles of Rand's artists and creators, who stood larger than life, battling government and bureaucracy. The late Karl Hess, the former speechwriter for Barry Goldwater who later became an anarchist on the left, once observed to me, "At a time when no one made arguments, when intelligence was undervalued, when smart kids were looked down on, Ayn Rand seemed to say to them, 'You're important.' She seemed to have a philosophical system with a rigorous structure at a time when no one wanted to talk sensibly at all. She scratched that peculiarly American strain—ironically, the same strain scratched by Emma Goldman. She was appealing, even if her philosophy was better expressed by others, such as Max Stirner, and her writing style seemed to come straight from Jack London."

The novels of Rand were seeds that sprouted and bore many strange fruits, most of which must have horrified her. CAW is certainly such an example. It is a religion, and Rand has consistently been intensely atheist. It has long considered ecology the supreme religious activity and study, and the harmony of human beings in the biosphere the goal of highest priority. Ayn Rand, on the other hand, has praised pollution as a sign of human progress. Her heroines have wept with joy at billboards and saluted smokestacks, regarding them as a sign of the human struggle against nature. She called people concerned about ecology "antilife" and "antimind," and condemned Native Americans as "savages." She even called smoking cigarettes a moral duty that aids the capitalist system.[9]

The ironies of life are many, I thought, after speaking to Karl Hess, a renegade from Rand as well as from Goldwater. He was building, by hand, a solar-heated house in West Virginia. I wondered about the founders of CAW, some of whom voted for Goldwater in 1964, the same year I was arrested on the steps of Berkeley's Sproul Hall. CAW can only be understood within a broad libertarian framework, but one that is hard to define within our traditional political notions of "left" and "right."

CAW began in 1961 when a young group of high-school friends, including Lance Christie, later a priest of CAW, began discussing the novels of Ayn Rand. Six months later, now college students, they began to explore the self-actualization concepts of Abraham Maslow. In the beginning, as Christie described these discussions, they were "dialogue/fantasies over the ills of the world," and, much as in the plot of *Atlas Shrugged*, these friends fantasized "a withdrawal of creative, unenculturated people to a remote place to await Armageddon." Christie wrote, "After Babylon had fallen again, we saw ourselves as coming forth to rebuild the world along rational lines."[10]

After Christie entered Westminster College in Fulton, Missouri, he began ESP experiments with a new acquaintance, Tim Zell, who later played a key role in the formation of CAW.*

Maslow's attraction stemmed from his theories about the characteristics of those he called "self-actualizers"—people who perceived reality more clearly than others. They accepted themselves without unnecessary guilt or shame, and tolerated—even gravitated toward—the new, the ambiguous, and the unknown. They were spontaneous and natural, with a sense of humor that was neither hostile nor sick. They tended to be independent and at ease in solitude; they were ethical; they had social feeling; they had a wide perspective, a sense of wonder, and a sense of the mysterious. But Maslow's "self-actualizers" were, he found, alienated from

*Tim Zell later took the name Otter Zell, and today is known as Oberon Zell-Ravenheart.

ordinary convention. They felt detached from the values of the culture. Maslow referred to such persons as "aliens in a foreign land,"[11] a phrase that struck a deep chord in Christie, Zell, and their friends.

Combining Maslow with Rand (some might think it a most unlikely combination), Christie envisioned an educational institution that would produce "Ayn Rand heroes, alias Maslonian self-actualizers."[12] In Rand's capitalist utopia of *Atlas Shrugged,* brilliant industrialists, creative artists, and pirates against the poor waited until the dross of civilization killed themselves off, or, more correctly, became so weakened that a takeover was possible. But at Westminster College, with the introduction of Maslow, Rand's right-wing utopia got turned on its head: change the system, educate for intelligence, and Randian heroes and heroines can be the norm.

In the next year the group read Robert Heinlein's *Stranger in a Strange Land.* Christie later wrote that reading the novel, he was "seized with an ecstatic sense of recognition. It is as if I had found in completed form the ideas which I was trying to jell on my own."[13]

The novel tells of Valentine Michael Smith, who was born of Earth-parents on Mars and raised there by aliens. When he returns to Earth as an alien, Smith looks at the planet with amazement. For example, he wonders if the grass minds being walked on since, after all, "these live." In general, he expresses the philosophy of someone in tune with the universe.[14]

Only one writer, Robert Ellwood, Jr., has written well about the subtleties of the Church of All Worlds. His book, *Religious and Spiritual Groups in Modern America,* devotes a chapter, "The Edenic Bower," to modern revivalist Neo-Pagan groups. He is, incidentally, Eliade's one source. Ellwood writes of Heinlein's novel:

> The principal purpose of a Martian's life is to "grok," to intuit the "fullness" of something completely from within.
>
> When Smith was brought to Earth, he seemed at first out of place. He did not understand elementary things, yet the deep things of character and Earth's wisdom he could accurately intuit in a moment. He moves about the Earth at once guileless and wise. . . .
>
> Eventually Smith created a religion, the "Church of All Worlds," for his companions. It took the form of paradisical communities called

"Nests," in which the best of both planets was brought together. In the Nests they could learn Martian, and be initiated into the lore and psychic skill of the planet. They also joyfully practiced sexual love within the family of the Nest.

Ellwood wrote that *Stranger in a Strange Land* was one of the bibles of the youth of the sixties, for in a real sense they felt they were Martians on Earth. . . .

Childlike and mystical, lovers of beauty and harmony and magic, impatient of materialistic values and moral codes, they too seemed not to fit, almost to have dropped from another world. Many, like Smith's friends, were seeking with eager desperation an alternative life style, other modes of relationship between man and nature, and different ways of understanding the relationship of consciousness and cosmos.[15]

In *Stranger in a Strange Land* the most profound ceremony is waterbrotherhood, the sharing of water, during which each person "groks" the other's godhood and an empathic bond is formed between them. In April 1962 Zell and Christie shared water together, and during the next fall the concept of a waterbrotherhood, called Atl, emerged among this group of friends now living in Fulton, Missouri.

In a sense, the waterbrotherhoods seemed to create Maslow's self-actualizers, and the statement "Thou art God," used in Heinlein's novel, expressed what Christie and his friends had sensed in the works of Ayn Rand. They began to criticize Rand's philosophy at the many points where it conflicted with Maslow, and decided that intelligence was more important than doctrine.

The name *Atl* was said to come from an Aztec word for water that also had the esoteric meaning of "home of our ancestors." The closeness of Atl to words like *Atlas, Atlantic,* and *Atlantis* was also noted. Water was seen as an appropriate symbol of life, since the first organisms came into existence in water and water is essential to life. Atl had its own emblem, the *tiki,* based on the Caribbean water god Ruba-tiki. One Atlan called the tiki "a not-for-sale sign" to hang on one's life. Atl soon had a logbook, an inside journal called *The Atlan Annals,* and a student paper called *Atlan Torch.*

But Atl was never a formal, rigid organization. Lance Christie said the relationship of Atlans to one another was like "the ties between siblings" in a large family. They were "a group of friends around the country who shared a desire to explore human potential and social structure and to give each other emotional support"—an extended family in a world of nuclear families. "When the chips are down," wrote Lance, "the family defends and shelters its own," but there are, he added, "no 'parents' in Atl. One's own judgment maintains in their place." Atl was conceived to have no leaders and no followers. Besides being a family, it was also a dream, and Zell wrote: "We do not 'belong' to it. . . . *Atl* belongs to us, the dreamers."[16]

The small group of Atlans, never greater than a hundred, saw themselves as the promoters of alternatives that would lead to the creation of human beings with godlike potentialities. Atlans attempted to infiltrate Mensa. They concerned themselves with educational experiments, studying the Montessori system and the works of A. S. Neill. They had a strange fascination with IQ and personality tests. Just when these tests began to be adversely scrutinized by radical critics, the Atlans were using them experimentally in their search for new Atlans. Still, tests were not primary; Atlans became Atlans by the same process we have seen in regard to Pagans generally, a process of coming home, an intuition.

Atlans were, above all, survivalists. They encouraged their "members" to learn such diverse skills as "speedreading, memory training, karate, yoga, autosuggestion, set theory, logic, survival training and telepathy."[17] Atlans saw themselves as brighter, more active, more creative, more in need of stimulation and interaction, and more able to make their own rules than other people. They often considered themselves outcasts, a "leper colony," dangerous because they were uncompromising and refused to fit into the general "sociological matrix."

Politically, they were hard to define. One Atlan described himself as a "left-wing-type democrat"; another said he favored "dictatorship without oppression"; a third said she hated "the NAACP, ban-the-bombers, farm subsidies, and social 'sciences.'" Zell wrote that his dislikes included the military, missionaries, isms, labels, commercials, atomic annihilation, and "original sin." His greatest wish for the world was for the "full and controlled use of all the powers of ESP and PK for the entire human race."[18]

Atl was not revolutionary in the ordinary sense of the word; it did not proselytize, and one Atlan wrote that "the happiness of this group can be assured without harming the rest of the world." Still, Atl's reading list was filled with visionaries of diverse and contradictory stripes: Neill, Maslow, Fromm, Leary, Huxley, Heinlein, Rand, *The Realist.* Some Atlans, like Zell and Christie, had visionary goals. They had short-term aims like establishing a press, a school, a nudist colony, a coffee house. In the long term their goals were, as Lance wrote, "to work toward a world along the lines seen in those books, a world where the children of Man may walk the hills like Gods."

Others disagreed and felt Atl should have no real purpose "except to maintain communication" between friends. As Lance observed:

Atl is not a unitary movement with a rigid dogma and a narrow, specific Cause. It is a vast, heterogeneous assemblage of ornery, cantankerous, intelligent, independent, unenculturated human beings who have an indefinable something that sets them apart and binds them together. Expecting all Atlans to agree at any given time on anything is a classic example of wild-eyed optimism.[19]

The Church of All Worlds grew out of Atl in 1967. It was conceived, according to Christie, as a "living laboratory" to work out problems in communal living, philosophy, and communication. As in Heinlein's novel, the Church had a structure of nine circles, each named for a different planet. The Church was "Tim Zell's baby,"[20] Christie wrote at one point, and much of what came to pass was the evolution of Zell's own vision, with which not all Atlans sympathized. Nor was sympathy considered obligatory.

From the beginning, Zell's description of Atl was "a society dedicated to the maximal actualization of human potential and the realization of ultimate individual freedom and personal responsibility." Within a few years the Church of All Worlds would only slightly rephrase that to proclaim that CAW was, in fact, a Neo-Pagan religion "dedicated to the celebration of Life, the maximal actualization of Human potential, and the realization of ultimate individual freedom and personal responsibility in harmonious eco-psychic relationship with the total Biosphere of Holy Mother Earth."[21]

The real story of CAW is how contact with the ecology movement and other groups and research into the history of ancient and "primitive" peoples (the worship of the Mother Goddess, etc.) transformed into a Neo-Pagan religion an organization originally based on the visions of a science fiction writer, a psychologist, and a right-wing philosopher who hated with a passion all forms of reverence for nature and all forms of religion. And the transformation revolved around the word *Pagan.*

In 1967 Tim Zell was using "Pagan" to describe the idea of CAW. In 1968 Paganism, as expressed in *Green Egg* (then a single-page newsletter), was a "life affirming religion without supernatural elements, such as were the Dionysians, the Epicureans, the Stoics, the Druids, the Transcendentalists, the Existentialists."[22]

How, we might ask, did this word *Pagan* come to include newly emerging nature religions? Until the late 1960s the word had been used to designate either an ancient or indigenous tribal religion or an irreligious, immoral approach to life.*

The change may have been due largely to Kerry Thornley, a man who appears in the next chapter in a most amusing role. Thornley, under the unlikely name of Omar Ravenhurst, helped found a complex of delightfully bizarre and surrealist Neo-Pagan groups—among them the Erisians, the Discordian Society, the POEE, the Erisian Liberation Front—all devoted to the Greek goddess of chaos and strife, the Lady Eris. In 1966 Thornley, calling himself "Young Omar," wrote an article for a communitarian group called Kerista. He noted that B. Z. Goldberg, in his book *The Sacred Fire,* had observed that one function of primitive religions had been to provide refuge and relief; to lift temporarily the taboos of the society. Goldberg, according to Omar, wrote: "What was forbidden at large in the bush not only was permitted, but in fact, became a duty in the temple of the gods."[23]

Taking off from Goldberg, Omar said that since the Jewish and Christian traditions were not credible in this age of science, they should be abandoned. He wrote:

*Ronald Hutton, in his monumental work, *The Triumph of the Moon* (1999), devotes many pages to the word "pagan" and its use by nineteenth-century English and European romantic writers and poets. Hutton says the first use of the word "Neo-Pagan" was in 1891 by W. F. Barry, a Christian critic who disparaged Neo-Paganism as a corrupting creed, concerned with "a great unceasing festival of flowers and lights and easy sensuous love."

Let us forget them. Instead, let us look at the jobs of the far less intellectual, but far more constructively functional religions of old. These were the "pagan" religions—the religions that survive to this day in England and the United States as "witchcraft."

Pagan religions "both stabilized and overthrew the social structure." Modern psychotherapy, sensory awareness workshops, and existential games were attempting to do the same thing and had, most likely, been reintroduced into society for a similar purpose. To Omar, science provided confirmation of Paganism as "an institutionalized cultural countertrend" and paved the way for the return of Paganism as a legitimate social force.

As for Kerista, that group espoused spontaneity, community, eroticism, and liberty. Omar wrote that the aims of Kerista and Paganism, in general, were strongly opposed to dogma and creed:

> Kerista is a religion and the mood of Kerista is one of holiness. Do not, however, look for a profusion of rituals, dogmas, doctrines and scriptures. Kerista is too sacred for that. It is more akin to the religions of the East and, also, the so-called pagan religions of the pre-Christian West. Its fount of being is the religious experience and that action or word or thought which is not infused with ecstasy is not Kerista. And Kerista, like those religions of olden times, is life-affirming.[24]

Kerista disappeared and Young Omar became involved with the vagaries and intricacies of the Lady Eris, but he was perhaps the first person, at least in the United States, to use the word *Pagan* to describe past and present nature religions. Some have actually alleged that the entire Neo-Pagan movement is an Erisian Plot (see next chapter and Robert Wilson and Robert Shea's *Illuminatus*). At this time the word *Pagan* was also being used by Witchcraft covens in the United Kingdom and the United States. It found its way into the publications of the Witchcraft Research Association in 1964 and 1965. But most Witches were using the term to describe the ancient religions of the British Isles and Continental Europe and their own religious practice as Witches, not the Neo-Pagan phenomenon outside the Craft revival.[25] It took a catalyst to create a sense of collectivity around the word *Pagan*, and in the United States the Church of All Worlds and its *Green Egg* filled this role. It was Tim (Oberon) Zell who picked up the term from Young Omar's article.

For this reason alone the Church of All Worlds deserves a large place in this story. CAW was not the first Neo-Pagan group in the United States. As we have seen, Gleb Botkin's Long Island Church of Aphrodite may well have been the first, and Feraferia was probably the first group to espouse polytheism openly. But CAW helped a large number of distinct groups to realize they shared a common purpose, and this gave the phenomenon new significance. Until then, each group had existed on its own, coming into contact with others only at rare events like the Renaissance fairs in California or science fiction conventions. CAW and Zell, by using terms like *Pagan* and *Neo-Pagan* in referring to the emerging collectivity of new earth religions, linked these groups, and *Green Egg* created a communication network among them.

The Church of All Worlds was formally chartered in March 1968. It rented a building for meetings and began publishing *Green Egg*. At this time it came into contact with Feraferia and a number of Witchcraft covens, and began to involve itself in the growing environmental movement. In the earliest issues of *Green Egg* Paganism was seen as encompassing transcendental meditation and liberal Unitarianism. But contact with these groups changed CAW's conception of Paganism.

At first, CAW was most inspired by Feraferia's vision. In 1969 CAW was using Feraferia's calendar and its greeting "Evoe Korê!" hailing the Divine Maiden. It was Feraferia's Fred Adams who coined the term *eco-psychic* to explain Neo-Paganism's religious ecology. Zell wrote that Feraferia had developed virtually all aspects of a Pagan religion—myths, rites, ceremonies, celebrations, and a eco-psychic vision of truly gigantic proportions—whereas the Church of All Worlds had concentrated more on ethics, psychology, sociology, human development, and morality. An alliance seemed to Zell most natural.

Green Egg became more serious in tone, as befitted the newsletter of a church with a mission. CAW began to look seriously at the question of rite, ritual, and myth. Fred Adams wrote:

It is the Neo-Pagans' Destiny to supply the *"Cult-Culture-Cultivation"* foundations for the now rising, yet psychically rootless Conservation Action Movement(s). Not only must we re-implant the *Soil of Holy Earth.* We must also re-implant the Human Soul & Body! Thus reforestation as Celebration for one thing—Pagan celebration. . . . The gap between work and play must be closed.

These two Turtle-Back movements must be joined: 1) Panerotic Freedom and 2) Wilderness Conservation.[26]

CAW and Feraferia jointly founded the Council of Themis, a Neo-Pagan ecumenical alliance. They invited all groups working for "the realization of the eco-psychic potential" of human beings and nature to join. The council was short-lived, dissolving after a dispute involving questions of philosophy, organization, and leadership.

Tom Williams, a priest of CAW, described to me the slow transformation of the church. He had joined in 1968, after stumbling across a sign advertising a meeting that read: "You may be a Pagan and not know it." Having considered himself a "Pagan" (as opposed to "Christian") for many years, and having a deep love for Greek mythology, Williams was interested. "I found out that there were other people who called themselves Pagans, but it took a while, because CAW did not accent its connection with earth religions in the beginning. Since the church came out of a conglomeration of Heinlein and Rand, it had to evolve."

Williams remembered that CAW's original attitude toward occultists was uniformly negative; Williams even remembered pulling a few harmless practical jokes on local occultists and ceremonial magicians in the area. "In the beginning," he said, "one might have been *justified* in calling CAW a science-fiction Grok-flock, but things began to change. We began to work with the Coalition for the Environment in the community. We began to meet people who were into Witchcraft, the modern Craft. At first I did not understand what the Craft was all about. I had more or less lumped it together with spiritualism and ceremonial magic. But then, gradually, we began to realize that there was *something here,* involving a connection with the ancient and modern earth religions. I think exposure to these things awakened something within us that apparently had been there for quite some time without us knowing it. I think it was a process of discovery. We had always felt we were the outcasts, the dispossessed. Of course, we had some of this feeling in the beginning, as the title *Stranger in a Strange Land* implies. But when we recognized that our emotional feeling lay with the planet; that there was a real distinction between the path of things and the path of the heart, these feelings went further than they had in the beginning."

In 1970 Williams wrote that the church was placing a greater emphasis on ecology and on the idea of a reverent identification with nature. "We are basically life-affirming and nature oriented as opposed to the anti-life, spirit oriented, anti-nature religions of the Judeo-Christian tradition. . . . Hence the only word for us is Pagans—the lovers of trees, the mad dancers in moonlit groves, the reverers of our beloved Earth for the mere fact of her immediate intoxicating existence."

The idea of linking a number of Neo-Pagan groups was not merely "to flee the smokestacks, stifling gases and filth that man has surrounded himself with in his 'pursuit of happiness,'" but to build in a positive way, "to create the dream of eco-psychic-land-sky-love-body-Wilderrealm," a time when all would "walk the Green Hills of Earth [a reference to another Heinlein novel] as Gods in the paradisal garden of Great Nature!"[27]

Another CAW priest, the late John McClimans, of the Chicago nest, also talked to me about the church's growth and evolution. He said, "When CAW was started, we used the word *Pagan* to mean non-Christian, even anti-Christian." But as the group spread out and came into contact with other groups, that changed. "The next thing I knew, I was a *real* Pagan instead of an anti-Christian type of Pagan. . . . There was a change of attitude, a change of value. I remember I felt it inside my head. I suddenly felt we were in the midst of the creation of something entirely new, something that offered us a way out of all the shit around us."

These transformations ended CAW's relationship with Atl. Many Atlans had no wish to involve themselves with the church, objecting to CAW's relationship with the occult—tenuous though it was—as well as CAW's unconventional tendencies. While the church was never officially interested in conversion, some Atlans objected to what they felt was its missionary zeal. Zell's hair and beard got longer. Occasionally, he would carry his lovely pet boa constrictor, Histah, around his shoulders when speaking in public. In 1972 Zell, Histah, and Julie, the woman he lived with, took the part of Cerridwen and Cernnunos and won a prize at the Costume Ball of the World Science Fiction Convention in Los

Angeles. Two years later Zell and his present partner, Morning Glory, won another prize at the World Science Fiction Convention in Washington (Discon) for their portrayal of two characters in Philip José Farmer's novel *Flesh*. Both Morning Glory and Zell had their pet serpents with them and they both looked quite dazzling. It was episodes such as these that led a number of Atlans to dissociate themselves from the church on the grounds that they did not want to be involved in a "public spectacle." As McClimans observed, "Most of the people in Atl were confirmed agnostics. They had no use for anyone who could even conceive of a theistic universe." He remembered once trying to explain Neo-Pagan philosophy to a former Atlan who had a Ph.D. degree in philosophy. McClimans said his friend didn't want to hear about it. "If it wasn't Kant, if it hadn't made the big time, it was worthless. My friend only wondered how I could be so stupid."

I asked if Atl still existed. "Yes," he said, "in a small way." McClimans told me that in the last two years he had been accepted by total strangers in another state simply because he possessed an Atl tiki. Some members of the original Atlan group left Missouri and settled elsewhere. They purposely chose a state with low population density, one that might prove fertile ground for innovative political and social changes. There are still Atlan nests, but they do not wish to be publicly known. Apparently, the goals remain the same.

As for the Church of All Worlds, during the next few years it began to evolve its own philosophy, which is quite distinct from the philosophies of Feraferia and other Neo-Pagan groups. Zell began writing about the planet Earth as deity, as a single living organism, and this became the Church of All World's central myth. Since 1971, the myth has been revised constantly and has become a unique eco-religious perception.

In the first article, "Theagenesis:* The Birth of the Goddess,"[28] Zell wrote that all religions should be considered subjectively "true," as should all opinions. Personal reality was necessarily subjective, so a belief was "true" by definition. He observed:

*Originally Theogenesis but changed in later printings for obvious reasons.

A Voudou death-curse is as real to its victim, and as effective, as being "saved" is to a Christian fundamentalist, or the kosher laws are to an Orthodox Jew. A flat Earth, with the stars and planets revolving around it, was as real to the medieval mind as our present globe and solar system are to us. Hysteric paralysis and blindness are as real to the sufferer as their organic counterparts. The snakes and bugs of alcoholic and narcotic deliria are real to the addict, and so is the fearful world of the paranoiac. From the standpoint of human consciousness, there is no other reality than that which we experience, and whatever we experience is therefore reality—therefore "true."

Only when we compare our subjective experiences with the experiences of others and come to a consensus of reality, Zell wrote, do we arrive at a more objective truth, although even the consensus of a community is often subjective. While all religions are subjectively "true," their objective truth depends on how much they themselves depend on blind faith, dogma, tradition, and authority. A religion that could accommodate itself to new discoveries and changes, hold dogma and creed to a minimum, and encourage curiosity and questioning would stand a good chance of holding up under objective scrutiny. With this idea as background, Zell described the ancient Pagan religions:

The Paleo-Pagans, diversified though they were, held among them certain common viewpoints. Among these were: veneration of an Earth-Mother Goddess; animism and pantheism; identification with a sacred region; seasonal celebration; love, respect, awe and veneration for Nature and Her mysteries; sensuality and sexuality in worship; magic and myth; and the sense of Man being a microcosm corresponding to the macrocosm of all Nature. These insights, however, were largely intuitive, as science had not yet progressed to the point of being able to provide objective validation for what must have seemed, to outsiders, to be mere superstition.

These attitudes, Zell wrote, take on entirely new implications in the twentieth century. He took the reader on a long tour through biology, cell division, reproduction, and evolutionary theory. The central idea of this tour was that all life had seemingly developed from a single cell that divided and subdivided, passing its cellular material on and on. All life was interconnected, part of a single living organism.

"Literally," wrote Zell, "we are *all* 'One.' The blue whale and the redwood tree are *not* the largest living organisms on Earth; the entire planetary biosphere is." This organism Zell called "Terrebia" (later changed to Gaea). He began to make analogies between her and other living organisms. Like all organisms, Terrebia, or Gaea, was composed of many organs; she had her own forms of specialization. Each animal and plant was "the equivalent of a single cell in the vast body of Terrebia." And "each biome, such as pine forest, coral reef, desert, prairies, marsh, etc., complete with *all* its plants and animals," was the equivalent of an organ. And, just as in a human being each organ contributes to the total coherence of the being, similarly, in Gaea, you cannot "kill all the bison in North America, import rabbits to Australia, cut or burn off whole forests" without disrupting the integrity of the whole. To anyone viewing the earth as a living being, ecological principles became obvious.

Unlike the views of many evolutionists, Zell's was not open-ended but progressive. At first, he saw humans as the nervous system of the planet, among the last to evolve and the most complex. Human beings were the stewards of the planetary ecology of Gaea. But Zell soon changed this view. He concluded that all sentient life functions collectively as the nervous system of the planet, and that the primary "brain" function may well belong to the cetacea, and not to human beings. Zell saw modern humans as a cancer on the planet, cells multiplying out of control. At one point he even postulated nuclear war as a kind of ghastly radiation treatment that he hoped could be avoided.

The ultimate potential of Gaea was the telepathic unity of consciousness between all parts of the nervous system, between all human beings, and, ultimately, between all living creatures. Evolution to such a point would be similar to Pierre Teilhard de Chardin's emerging planetary consciousness, "the Omega Point," although without Teilhard's Christian trappings. The evolutionary goal was a total telepathic union, a destiny like that described by Arthur C. Clarke in *Childhood's End,* but without the loss of individual consciousness and sense of self. When the Omega Point or *Apotheasis* was reached, the planetary organism Gaea would truly awaken.

In this context, Zell redefined divinity and deity as the fulfillment of potential, as "the highest level of aware consciousness accessible to each living being, manifesting itself in the self-actualization of that being." Thus, the cell was God to its components; the tissue was God to the cells, and so on. And a human being manifested a wholly new level of awareness, organization, and "emergent wholeness." Of this level of organization, Zell wrote, "We find it appropriate to express recognition of this Unity in the phrase: Thou art God."[29] And since all beings were connected biologically, all eco-systems expressed a new level of awareness. Mother Earth herself could be seen as God. Zell wrote:

> Indeed, even though yet unawakened, the embryonic slumbering subconscious mind of Terrebia is experienced intuitively by us all, and has been referred to instinctively by us as Mother Earth, Mother Nature (The Goddess, The Lady.)[30]

God became Goddess, as had so intuitively been understood for centuries. In a later article Zell noted:

> Countless mystics, poets, shamans and children the world over have through all ages had their lives uplifted and transformed by the appearance or vision of She whom they have named Isis, Ceres, Rhea, Dana Gaea, Oestra, and in the Christian lands, Mother Mary. She whom we know as the All-Mother; The White Goddess; The Great Goddess; Mother Nature, Mother Earth. She is a real living Being, and like all living Beings, She too has a Soul-Essence which we can perceive, although "translated" into images familiar to our limited imaginations. . . .
>
> And just as every cell in our own bodies contains the essence of the Whole in the genetic code imprinted within the intricacies of the double helix DNA molecule, and as indeed each cell in my own body is Tim Zell, so does every living plant and creature share in the essence of the Whole of Mother Earth. To each we can rightly say, "Thou Art Goddess."[31]

The publication of "Theagenesis" was followed by a number of other articles. In "Biotheology" Zell wrote that, since we are all Goddess, deity should be conceived of as "immanent," not transcendent; deity is within. He wrote:

We see that the Humanists are right; God is Mankind. Also correct are the Pantheists in their recognition that God is all Nature. Even the Christians touch upon the truth when they realize that God is "revealed in the forests, the glens, the meadows. . . ." The "religious experience" of mystics, which seems to show them "the naked face of God," is actually an experience of coming into complete attunement with this highest level of aware consciousness. . . .

Such an experience could be brought about by fasting, religious or sexual ecstasy, or hallucinogens. In all cases, "the experience itself appears to be identical, an experience of total beingness, of ecstatic revelation." To anyone having such an experience, Zell wrote, the phrase, "Thou art God" becomes obvious. Heinlein's idea of "groking" was "a kind of total empathic understanding in which identity of subject and object merge into One." Thus, "to grok something," wrote Zell, "would be to relate to it with one's full potential." This, he said, was something that happened naturally with plants and animals. Only human beings seemed not to know who they were and to act accordingly, and this human failing was perhaps at the root of all human suffering. It is why, he wrote, there is so little species awareness, life awareness, and environmental awareness among human beings today.

This awareness *was* known to many ancient celebrants, the Pagans, the "naked dancers of moonlit groves" who were put to death by monotheists. "Monotheism," wrote Zell, "is a synonym for genocide," and yet, the new Pagans emerged in "the midst of the most monolithic, monotheistic state ever erected," rejecting transcendent deities and finding deity where it was all along, within each person.[32] The cosmic purpose of Neo-Paganism was to facilitate that increased awareness—to work for it by supporting all ecologically oriented movements, establishing alternative communities, demonstrating alternate possibilities for survival on the planet, and ultimately, awakening Gaea, the Goddess, the planetary mind.

Zell's articles had a strong influence on the development of the Church of All Worlds. Lance Christie wrote of them:

You've begun the creation of a myth, and a most livable one at that. It is a myth which defines a role for man and answers a lot of mystic questions.

It seems to fit very well within the total tradition of man's symbols and myths, expressing in clearer and expanded form a theme as old as consciousness can remember.

Christie viewed the myth as a beginning, adding, "I still think we need to explore Jung et al. to get the whole concept within a full psychological/anthropological perspective. . . . Be that as it may, the world view you are creating is compatible with objective consciousness and science in a way no other religious myth is. . . ."[33]

Several years after the articles were written, *Newsweek* magazine, as well as a number of less popular journals, mentioned the work of British scientist James Lovelock, who had posited the "Gaia hypothesis": the living matter on earth, air, oceans, and land was all part of a system that Lovelock called after the Earth-Mother Goddess, Gaia. He said that this entire system seemed to "exhibit the behavior of a single organism—even a living creature," and argued that the biosphere was able to exert control over the temperature of the earth's surface and the composition of the atmosphere. *Newsweek* stated that the "Gaia hypothesis" was, in the main, "an elaboration of general ecological notions of close relationships between living things and their environment," but that Lovelock had carried this idea further, saying, "in man, Gaia has the equivalent of a central nervous system. We disturb and eliminate at our peril. Let us make peace with Gaia on her terms and return to peaceful coexistence with our fellow creatures."[34] Zell entered into a short correspondence with Lovelock, comparing their world views.

The concept of Gaea was never, officially, a dogma of CAW. There were, and still are, no dogmas. But the effect of "Theagenesis; The Gaea Hypothesis" on CAW's history and on the thoughts and goals of church priests, priestesses, and members was extraordinary. All the CAW members I interviewed felt that the goals of Neo-Paganism were enormous, involving a total transformation of Western society. In contrast, only half the other Neo-Pagans I interviewed thought in such sweeping terms.

Tom Williams once told me that CAW's goal was to change the world. "After all," he said, laughing, "why be petty?" Another time he said that one goal of Neo-Paganism was to learn to see ourselves "as a total entity—rational and irrational at once, within a total environment, and with a total identification with all life."

Carolyn Clark, a priestess in CAW, told me, "If there *is* an ultimate goal or purpose, it has to be the purpose of achieving Chardin's Omega Point, the union of consciousness with all living things." And Zell, as might be expected, said the ultimate goal was "totally and completely to transform human consciousness and planetary consciousness." When I asked if he had anything less ambitious in mind, he smiled and said, "Anything less is not quite enough."

"It is a choice between Apocalypse or Apotheasis," Morning Glory said to me. "The purpose of Neo-Paganism is to put us back on the track; we took a wrong turning somewhere around thirty-five hundred years ago. But our purpose is not to compromise, to rework, to integrate ourselves back into the culture, but rather to be a viable alternative to it. Now that it is a challenge that many of us are not going to be up to. I myself have nightmares about it. Still, that is the challenge. That is where it lies, because there is no way to reform the system."

"For me," John McClimans told me, "the idea of theagenesis is *it!* But I don't want CAW to be enclosed by it. As long as we truly stay open for others to come in and show us other ways, the theagenesis idea is sure to be modified, or someone will show us something that seems better entirely."

While many members of CAW see their church as "a total, holistic, cultural alternative to the entire fabric of Western Civilization,"[35] the Gaea hypothesis remains hypothesis. The Church of All Worlds has only one real dogma—its belief that it has no beliefs.

Most people find the idea of a religion without creeds difficult. Many within the Church of All Worlds have thought about a new definition of religion. They confronted the problem from the very beginning, particularly when describing Neo-Paganism to people who they felt were their kind of people, but who were hostile to the idea of all religions. As Zell explained, "Most of the people who think in ways similar to us, have been turned off by conventional religions. This is the greatest problem we have. Ten years ago, if someone had presented me with Neo-Paganism and put it in terms of a 'new religion,' I would have had nothing to do with it. And yet here I am. We had to get a new definition of religion. Because everywhere else religion is defined in Judeo-Christian terms; it means belief in a supreme being, heaven, hell, and so forth. And none of us believe in any of that, yet we consider ourselves deeply religious. We slowly came to understand that religion is a form of relinking, of increasing consciousness and communication. Worship is a form of communication, of communion. And communication can only be between equals. It can't be abasement, a bowing down before something greater. When I make love with a woman, when I sleep under the trees, when I compost my garbage, all these things can be acts of worship."

With this different understanding of religion, the Church of All Worlds began to formulate a concept of its relationship to Neo-Paganism and to the Pagan religions of the past. CAW members saw themselves as a family, a kind of tribe. The ancient Pagan religions were seen as tribal religions, based on custom and tradition rather than on dogma and belief, grounded in what one *did* rather than in what one *believed*. Zell made a distinction between what he called philosophical religions (taught by prophets and formulated into creeds) and natural religions (the evolving, indigenous folk or Pagan religions of particular peoples). The former, he wrote, were artificially constructed; the latter emerged out of the processes of life and nature, and continued to evolve organically.

> Philosophical religions are like buildings: an architect (prophet) gets an inspiration (revelation) and lays down his vision in blueprints (prophecy; scriptures). Then contractors, carpenters, masons, etc. (disciples and followers) build the building more or less according to his specifications. It is *made* of non-living materials, and does not *grow* naturally; it is assembled. When it is finished, it cannot grow further, and begins to deteriorate, until it is eventually so outmoded and rundown it is demolished to make way for new buildings. A world of philosophical religions is like unto a city, with all the problems (hunger, war, hatreds, crime, pollution, disease) of a big city, and for much the same reason: unnaturalness.

> A Pagan religion, on the other hand, is like a tree: it emerges alive from the Earth, grows, changes (both cyclically in seasons, and continually in upward and outward growth), bears flowers, fruit, shares its life with other living beings. It is not made, or designed according to any blueprint other than genetic. And when, after many thousands of years, perhaps (for many trees are potentially immortal, never dying of old age), it should come to the end of its time, it does not pass from the world entirely, for its own progeny have, in the interval, begun to spring up all

around, again from the Earth, and again, similar yet each unique. A world of Pagan religions is like a forest.

Included in natural religions would be animism, totemism, pantheism, much of Witchcraft, all indigenous religions of Africa, Australia, and America and the old religions of the Celts, the Gauls, the Norse, and the fairy faith in Ireland. Zell wrote:

> The old Pagan religions were never "created." . . . What little we can trace indicates a descent from Paleolithic and Neolithic fertility cults, hence the common symbols of the Earth Mother Goddess and the Horned God, representing, respectively, the vegetable and animal life of the Earth. We find them therefore unanimous in their veneration of Nature and their sensual celebration of life, birth and death as expressed seasonally in aspects of sexuality.
>
> All the Great Festivals of Paganism, wherever they may be found, correspond in common with the Solstices, Equinoxes, and other natural annual cycles of life (animal mating seasons, planting, harvest). Most of these remain with us today in more or less disguised form as the so-called "Christian" holidays of Christmas (Yule), Easter (Ostara), May Day (Beltane), Thanksgiving (Harvest Home), Halloween (Samhain) and even Groundhog's Day (Oimelc). In addition to these six, there are two others, Midsummer and Lugnasadh, comprising a total of eight Festivals (or Sabbats as they are known, under different names, in Witchcraft).[36]

Another CAW member who sought to describe the nature of Neo-Paganism was Lewis Shieber, who divided religions into two categories—those that functioned from a base of "Tribal/Tradition" and those that functioned from a base of "Dogma/Belief." The latter, said Shieber, were, more often than not, based on a "universal" idea. Such religions were often large, evangelistic, and based on a powerful but closed system. The religions based on "Tribal/Tradition" were usually small ones, functioning out of a local "cultural matrix." In such religions *participation* in tribal actions was emphasized; it was never that important to *believe* in the myths and legends of the tribe. In Judaism, for example, Shieber noted that one could disbelieve in God, as long as you followed the tradition. "All primitive Pagan religions have this [Tribal/Tradition] base,"

Shieber wrote, adding, "Thus many sometimes contradictory beliefs may be held by individuals without harm to the religion as long as the *identification with the Tribe and tribal practices is strong.*"

Tribal/Tradition religions stressed social and personal interaction. The governments in these societies were often "basically anarchistic," tribal order being maintained by "conventions and discussion leading to consensus." The Church of All Worlds fell into the Tribal/Tradition category. While "there are some practices and ideas which have been associated with CAW," he wrote, "all these associated things are unofficial and not even accorded the name of tradition."

CAW's antipathy toward dogma is typical of many but by no means all Neo-Pagan groups. Feraferia, for example, has, as we have seen, definite beliefs and creeds, and even with CAW there was a temptation to "require belief in the poetic and useful vision of Tim Zell's 'Theagenesis' theory." Shieber concluded that CAW as "tribal religion" could never claim universality, and therefore would always be small. "We must assume," he said, "that we are a guest people in a possibly unfriendly nation and act accordingly."[37]

Many people in CAW talked about the strange position of being a priest or priestess in a church that stressed lack of dogma. John McClimans told me that those who remained in CAW were usually people who didn't want someone in the middle—between themselves and the discovery of their own God/Goddess within. "You're the Goddess. I'm the Goddess. When a person becomes aware of that idea; when they begin to conceive that this might even be a tentative possibility, they're hooked. They don't need someone else to tell them how to touch "god" or "goddess." They may need someone to give them the impetus to put their hand on the pulse; but once they've felt it, they don't want you there anymore. Once their hand is there, they are going to say, 'Get away, so I can feel it without you interfering!'"

Besides a tribal/tradition base and lack of dogma, most members of CAW felt that all the new Pagan religions, from Feraferia and CAW to the Witchcraft covens, held certain other values in common. To describe this common thread, Zell used Fred Adams's term, "eco-psychic." As we have seen, it was Feraferia that first put forth the idea of a life of religious ecology and Fred Adams worked out elaborate rituals to complement such a life. An early statement from the Council of Themis put the idea this way:

> Everything we encounter in the Biosphere is a part of Nature, and ecology reveals the pattern of this is-ness, the natural relationships among all these things and the organic unity of all of them as a Biospheric Whole. . . .
>
> Of all man's secular studies, ecology comes closest to bringing him to the threshold of religious relationship to his world. Ecology not only confirms the wonders of form and function that other secular studies have revealed, but it brings these into organic union with each other as one dynamic, living Whole; and it points out the conditions for the well-being of both this overall Unity and the parts that comprise it.
>
> An intensive realization of these conditions, and of one's own immediate role in their sustainment and development, brings one to the threshold of religious awe.[38]

The Church of All Worlds, like Feraferia, saw Neo-Paganism as a response to a planet in crisis. And if science fiction provided the myths and vision for CAW, ecology was the supreme religious study. A Pagan religion meant a life of harmony with the earth, not a set of rituals. The ritual was nothing less than a truly integrated life.

Carolyn Clark put it this way: "It has to become second nature. So that when you take the garbage out to your compost heap, there's this moment of awareness and attunement between yourself and the collective unconscious of the Earth; so that as you throw it on the heap, you think, 'Say there, Mom, I'm feeding you.'" But unlike Feraferia, CAW's support of ecology was coupled with support for sophisticated technologies, as long as they were based on an understanding and respect for eco-systems. As might be imagined, CAW also consistently supported space exploration.

In keeping with Arthur C. Clarke's famous remark that any highly developed technology is indistinguishable from magic, I often heard church members quote a remark made by Tom Williams: "You gotta admit, any magic that can erase an entire city from the face of the Earth in a single instant, well—that plenty big Ju-Ju, B'wana!"[39] Similarly, Zell observed to me, "Magic is the science you don't understand, the science you don't take for granted. Science and magic are both approaches to understanding the universe. If you have a theory to explain something, it gets called science. If people don't understand something, or lack a theory to explain it, they label it 'magic.'" In general, members of CAW saw Neo-Paganism as a religious philosophy that combined intuitive *and* rational modes of thought.

Lance Christie wrote in *Green Egg* that the problem with modern technology was not the inventions themselves but a "mechanical world picture," a mechanistic view of the universe. He noted that against this picture many people such as Mumford and Dubos had opposed an "organic world picture." CAW, according to Christie, was uniquely able to combine "a scientific skepticism and rationality with an acceptance of that which is non-analytic and non-rational in human experience."[40]

Since most members of CAW have been visionaries, anarchists, and religious ecologists, they have naturally gravitated to "alternative" forms of energy—solar, wind, and so forth. But they have always supported scientific inquiry in order to broaden and enrich our ways of thinking, not to obliterate them. Scientific inquiry has never been seen as contradictory to psychic development or magic. The ancient Pagan peoples were seen as sources of skills that could be learned to advantage by modern Neo-Pagans. CAW has always had its eye on ancient dolmens, as well as civilizations light years away. The Church, Ellwood noted, had become "a lively meeting of an old Pagan world view, the provocative images of some modern novels and biophilosophic reflection, and a group of vigorous, socially experimental young adults."[41] CAW has had a history of attempted communes, group marriages, Heinleinian sex experimentation, and even vows of poverty, all in an atmosphere where the only sin is hypocrisy (sin is an act against God, and Thou art God) and the only crime is "that which infringes against another."[42]

Most CAW members did not see themselves as "political"; many defined themselves as "apolitical" or even "antipolitical." Zell has been known to assert that all "real" revolutions are concerned with changes of consciousness rather than shifts of power.

The Church of All Worlds was set up with a nine-circle structure. One advanced through the levels by progressive involvement and participation, as well as study and getting through CAW's long reading list, as interesting and filled with contradictions as any I have ever come across. For example, to move from the fourth to the fifth circle, a person had to read seven books listed in the basic bibliography, including one on perception, one on Native American religion, and one from a section called "Homo Novus." In addition, the person had to begin some form of psychic training (anything from Arica to Akido would suffice) and write a long paper comparing three different religions, one of which should be Neo-Paganism. The process of advancement was conceived of as continuous and never-ending. No one, not even Tim Zell, had ever made it to the ninth circle.

Groups within the church were called "nests"—another practice taken from *Stranger in a Strange Land*. Each nest was autonomous. Most decisions were arrived at by consensus. I visited meetings of two of the St. Louis nests in the fall of 1975. At each one there were twelve to fifteen people. The Dog Star Nest met in the nude. The meeting I attended concentrated on shamanism. I participated in a beautiful Native American ritual, followed by CAW's very simple ritual of watersharing, the clearest reminder of CAW's Heinleinian origins. A goblet of water was passed from one to another. All shared this cup and said appropriate phrases to one another: "May you never thirst," "Drink deeply," "Thou art God," "Thou art Goddess."

The other nest, led by Don Wildgrube, met clothed and was experimenting with sensitivity awareness techniques. Most CAW members were in their late twenties and early thirties. But there were members in their late teens, and at least one member in his sixties. Members included psychologists, engineers, bus drivers, salesmen, and students. Most were white, middle-class, and college educated. And, unlike many Neo-Pagans, the vast majority came from Protestant backgrounds.

One scholar of Neo-Paganism, the Reverend J. Gordon Melton, a Methodist minister from Chicago who had been studying new Pagan religions for many years, said that the majority of Neo-Pagans are ex-Catholics, followed by ex-Jews. The abundance of ritual in Neo-Pagan groups may appeal to Catholics and Jews, whose religions included much ritual. Protestants, however, have little experience with ritual, according to Melton, and do not seek it. He has described CAW as the Neo-Pagan group with the most ex-Protestants, the least ritual, and the greatest tendency to proselytize, even to the point of having religious tracts. His perception of this one group seems accurate, but in my own experience in the Neo-Pagan movement, there are equal numbers of ex-Catholics and Protestants, with a smaller number of Jews. I also found many who had been deprived of any religious ritual as children.

It was clear that one of the most important reasons for CAW's existence was a response to a need, a lack, a longing. The bond that united past and future visions within the church was a yearning for a real culture. "A common thread in Neo-Paganism," said priestess Carolyn Clark, "is nostalgia, a yearning to get back to a time when people seemed more in control of their own lives, and societies, while complex, had a definite cultural pattern, not this weird shifting kaleidoscope that's called American culture."

Morning Glory Zell expressed it this way: "We're orphans, we're bastard mongrel children in a beautiful land that isn't really ours. We're grafted and transplanted, saddled with a tremendous guilt for everything from strip mines and city dumps to the death of the people who lived here before. One of the reasons for CAW's success is that everyone identifies with being a Stranger in a Strange Land. The only people who have a real tradition here are the Native American people. There is much to identify with them. But it is not our tradition. We were never chanted the chants and rocked in the cradle and told the working rhythms and rhymes. Most of us were raised in concrete and steel, totally removed from the seasons around us. Some of us smiled when the air would get a certain taste from burning leaf smoke and we felt that stirring inside of us. But nobody else noticed it; they walked on past. Some of us are attuned to the same rhythms as indigenous people, but we have no traditions. We live in an impoverished culture. We have to create our culture from scratch."

By 1978 much had changed in the Church of All Worlds. There were CAW nests in Chicago, St. Louis, Atlanta, and Milwaukee. There were other nests in Indiana and Illinois. New priests and priestesses had been ordained. But CAW's role as catalyst for the Neo-Pagan movement receded after the *Green Egg* stopped publication in 1976. The journal was revived in 1988. It remained a vibrant publication until 2001.

How important *Green Egg* was to the Neo-Pagan community is a matter of controversy. There are some who welcomed its death with a sigh of relief. But others, including myself, believed that it was a key to the movement's vitality.

In each issue fully a third of its pages were devoted to letters from various types of Pagans, Neo-Pagans, Witches, occultists, ecology activists, anarchists, and libertarians—among others. The writers of letters ranged from Neo-Nazi James Madole, head of the National Renaissance Party, to advocates of Timothy Leary's theories of space migration and life extension.

Unlike most mainstream intellectual magazines, where issues become narrowly defined by a more or less reigning ideology, *Green Egg*, both in its Forum and in its articles, had maintained a hands-off, free-for-all policy. Debates raged on the merits of Velikovsky's theories, the place of technology, the teachings of Aleister Crowley, the evidence for ancient matriarchies, and hundreds of other issues, with emphasis on ecology, ethics, tribalism, magic, science fiction, and the relationship of human beings to the planet. *Green Egg* served to create the sense that hundreds of diverse and even contradictory groups were part of an eclectic movement with certain common goals.

It is popular today to talk about "synergy"—a combination that has a greater effect than the simple addition of its components—and that perhaps best describes the effect of *Green Egg*. It connected all the evolving and emerging goddess and nature religions into one phenomenon: the Neo-Pagan movement.

But the goals of many of these groups were diverse, even contradictory. To those with a conservative lifestyle, CAW seemed to be a bunch of crazy anarchists. The *Green Egg*'s hands-off policy created controversy. Increased contact between groups led at times to an increase in internal bickering. When *Green Egg* first ceased publication at the end of 1976, a number of Neo-Pagans and Witches told me they were glad because now there would be more tranquillity in the movement. And perhaps there was. Many groups began "sticking with their own" and with those others they felt close to. They simply ignored the rest of the movement.

Tom Williams and the Zells left for the West Coast. Those who stayed in St. Louis, at least the majority, remained loyal to their CAW nests and friends. Many felt that *Green Egg* had never served the CAW community as well as it had the Neo-Pagan community as a whole. No other Pagan publication has ever filled quite the same role. Today, perhaps the *Witches' Voice* on the Internet (witchvox.com) comes the closest.

Meanwhile, Tim (Oberon) and Morning Glory Zell converted a school bus into a home for themselves, their two snakes, a possum, a tarantula, and a rat colony—food for their snakes and spider. They spent a year in Oregon writing, lecturing, and teaching. They formed a coven called Ithil Duath. Morning Glory was quoted in a local Oregon newspaper as saying, "We realize that we don't have 'The Way.' After all, that's been done. . . . We want to restore the role of the shaman (or witch) in our culture. . . . We really must return the Goddess to the earth if we are to keep a balance and avoid ecological apocalypse. . . ."[43] Tom Williams moved to Palo Alto. Don Wildgrube founded several covens and became a Wiccan priest.

In 1977 Oberon and Morning Glory moved to northern California. In the spring of 1978 they wrote to me: "We are living in a pioneer community comprising twelve square miles of Sacred Wilderness somewhere in the mountains of Ecotopia." They lived in their converted school bus with Tanith, a six-foot-long Boa, Ananta, an eleven-foot-long Burmese python, and two tarantulas—Charlotte and Kallisti. They conducted seminars in the local community and they began to earn some money by making ceramic figures. They described their life as simple, with almost no expenses other than food and fuel.

They continued to share their dream, a longing to expand possibility and potential, or as Oberon once told me, the desire "to eat the fruit of both trees, to recover the sense of the Home."

Recent Notes

The Zells' saga has taken amazing twists and turns since *Drawing Down the Moon* was first published; their journey has included creating and patenting a process for creating unicorns—the unicorns that were exhibited at the Ringling Brothers Barnum & Bailey Circus were their creation—a search for mermaids which took them to the South Seas; and the opening of a school of magic, The Grey School of Wizardry.

In the late 1970s, the Zells came across the work of W. Franklin Dove. Beginning in 1935, Dove, a biologist at the University of Maine, wrote several articles in scientific journals describing various attempts to create single horned animals and documenting his own efforts. It is not generally known that during the first week of a horned animal's life, the horn buds are only attached to the skin; they have not yet attached themselves to the skull. Dove observed that all unicorns have been developed by a surgical procedure (a very minor one—since it only involves the layers of the skin) in which the horn buds are moved to a central position.

The Zells began looking at the ancient pictures of unicorns; they noticed that the earliest depictions were more goatlike than horselike. They theorized that unicorns may well have been produced, an ancient process once known and lost, and they speculated that ancient herders might well have found a one-horned creature useful in protecting their flocks. They also believed that creating a unicorn would be a powerful magical symbol that would say to millions: "If a unicorn exists, why then anything is possible. I can even change my own life."

The Zells created a number of unicorns from various breeds of white goats. For several years, Otter and Morning Glory made the rounds of renaissance and medieval fairs with several of their adorable creatures. Children were photographed with the unicorns, and the animals were treated more lovingly than 99 percent of male goats on this planet. In the winter the unicorns roamed on Coeden Brith, the same magical land in Mendocino where Nemeton was founded, adjacent to Annwfn, where Gwydion lived until his death, and where Forever Forests still makes its home. To see the unicorns wandering around seemed miraculous, even if in humorous moments one might find oneself calling them "unigoats." But on a magic morning on the land, they did seem to have wandered in from faerie.

Attitudes among Pagans differed. Most people took the unicorns Lancelot and Bedevere, and the five or six other creatures who appeared, to their hearts. And the Zells continued barely to eke out a living despite unicorn postcards, the Living Unicorn Calendar, and various public appearances.

A few Pagans were disturbed by the unicorns. Does making a unicorn "real" destroy the power and romance of the myth, some asked? Is it appropriate for members of a Pagan religion to alter surgically an animal—even if the operation only involves cutting flaps in the skin and moving the horns toward the center?

In 1984, the Zells signed an agreement with Ringling Brothers Barnum and Bailey Circus. The circus bought four of the unicorns. Under the terms of their contract Otter and Morning Glory were not allowed to talk to the press for three years. The Zells received $150,000, although by the time lawyers, agents, trainers, and debts were paid, less than a third of the money was left.

Once the circus had the animals they proceeded to shroud them in mystery. They never admitted there was more than one but claimed the unicorn had mysteriously "appeared" in Texas. They showed the unicorn with pomp, glitz, and ceremony but refused to tell its true history. At a New York press conference, when a reporter pointed to evidence of the Zells' existence, the question was ignored. Almost none of the many news accounts, fueled by protests by the ASPCA, ever got the story right.

In April 1985, Alison Harlow came to New York and we decided we would go to the circus and see an old animal friend. As glittering human butterflies swung from high wires, the unicorn Lancelot appeared on a movable cart, a woman in a pink gown standing by his side. He was followed in the procession by eager children who rode in white carts. His hair had been oiled. It had been kept long—making him seem more goatlike than usual. I don't know the reason, but I would surmise that they wanted to hide his genitalia. As the procession advanced, Alison started giggling and whispered to me, "To think, that's the same little fellow that once pissed on me," and we all broke up. But one row down, a five-year-old boy told his mother, "It really *is* a unicorn—it *is!*" So, perhaps, the Zells' magic was working.

The Zells started a new organization called the Ecosophical Research Association. ERA, they said, would study and explore the territory of the archetype, the basis of legends and the boundaries between the sacred and the secular. One prime area of research would be cryptozoology—the identification of unknown animals such as the Loch Ness Monster, Unicorns, Bigfoot, and Mermaids.

Taking some of the money from their first cryptozoological adventure, and convincing other backers to put in the rest, they planned an expedition to New Ireland in Papua, New Guinea, to look into stories of possible mermaid sightings. They chartered a boat and assembled a group of fourteen adventurers to look for the mysterious "ri." "You doubt?" wrote Otter in a Pagan journal, "O ye of little faith . . . remember the lesson of the Unicorn."

But when they arrived in New Guinea, they quickly found out that the indigenous word for mermaid, *ri*, was the same word as that used for the aquatic creature called the dugong. The mermaid was a dugong.

After 1985, the Zells, along with Anodea Judith and others, undertook the resurrection of the Church of All Worlds. The Church expanded and established new nests, as well as an international presence in Australia, Canada, England, Germany, Japan, Israel, France, Greece, South Africa, and New Zealand. *Green Egg* returned in 1988, edited by Diane Darling, and soon it again became a leading Pagan journal. The Zells traveled widely to Pagan festivals and re-created several ceremonies based on the ancient Greek Elusinian Mysteries and the Panathenaia.

But as the century neared its end, CAW and *Green Egg* became embroiled in convulsive internal conflicts and power struggles. Diane departed, and Oberon Zell-Ravenheart was ousted from control of *Green Egg*. Four years later, the magazine folded. Zell was excommunicated from the church he'd founded; he was formally impeached, and the board of directors was shifted to Ohio.

Then, in 2004, following the resignation of nearly all the long-term clergy, the Ohio board dissolved itself. In 2005, Oberon regained control of what he has called "the ashes of CAW," transferring its legal corporate status back to California, and becoming the new president. He is now working to help resurrect the organization yet again, "the 3rd Phoenix rebirth," as he calls it.

And as this rebirth comes about, some of the old Atlans are joining it. Atl does still exist. It was incorporated twenty-five years ago into the Association of the Tree of Life. Lance Christie says that both CAW and Atl were always joined in their effort to substitute a holistic ecological paradigm for "the reductionist paradigm which underlies the industrial growth culture." If CAW used ritual and spectacle, says Christie, Atl members were science nerds and computer types. Their goal was to look at "the renewable techniques of energy production, agriculture, hydrologic management," and so forth. CAW was designed to bring into consciousness certain eco-spiritual values; Atl was designed to do the engineering that would permit people to engage in "right livelihood" within an ecological paradigm should they seek to do so.

Christie says he stayed on the sidelines during the first and second incarnations of CAW, and he says both he and Oberon "wandered into a few blind alleys." But both of them, he believes, have not wavered from their commitment to right action and they have both been committed to an understanding of the ecological paradigm. Christie hopes to be involved in the third generation of CAW, which he hopes will take stands on public issues and their ethical dimensions. He also hopes that Atl can help create the communities that will allow a renewal paradigm to come into being.

Meanwhile, Oberon and Morning Glory have been involved in a host of other activities. Together with several other friends and partners, they started the Ravenheart Family, which some have called the "first family of polyamory" (a term that Morning Glory coined). They also continued their "Mythic Images" business, which produces and markets a line of Pagan statues and art. One statue comes directly out of Oberon's 1970 "TheaGenesis" vision: a statue called "The Millennial Gaia."

In 2003, Oberon began a new and ambitious effort: The Grey School of Wizardry, an online school of magic with courses on subjects ranging from healing and wortcunning, to divination and nature studies. Oberon has written a course book for the school, *Grimoire for the Apprentice Wizard,* which he describes as both a handbook (something like the *Boy Scouts Handbook*) and a textbook. As one teacher at the school told me, "We're sort of the real Hogwarts." Who knows where the next adventure will take Oberon and Morning Glory.

11.

Religions of Paradox and Play

"LARGE PARTS of the Neo-Pagan movement started out as jokes, you know," Robert Anton Wilson, author, Witch, and a former editor of *Playboy,* told me one day. "Some of the founders of NROOGD will tell you their order started as a joke; others will deny it. There is a group that worships Mithra in Chicago which started out as a joke. The people in many of these groups began to find that they were getting something out of what they were doing and gradually they became more serious."

There have always been spoofs on religion. But religions that combine humor, play, and seriousness are a rare species. A rather special quality of Neo-Pagan groups is that many of them have a humorous history. As we have seen, the Church of the Eternal Source, a serious attempt to revive the ancient Egyptian religion, began as a series of yearly Egyptian costume parties. The Reformed Druids of North America began as a humorous protest movement against a regulation at Carleton College requiring attendance at chapel. The Elf Queen's Daughters, a network of "elves" located mostly in the Far West, sent out each week three pages of quite beautiful poetic prose, most of it composed by automatic writing. "Most of it's nonsense," they told me. "We don't take it too seriously." In Minneapolis a group calling itself the First Arachnid Church began to publish hilarious leaflets calling for the worship of the Great Spider and the True Web.[1] It was pure satire and a great parody of fundamentalist Christian leaflets. But it was also pure Neo-Paganism. And, most preposterous of all, there is the worship of Eris, goddess of chaos and confusion, popularized in the science fiction trilogy *Illuminatus.*[2]

Since we live in a culture that makes a great distinction between "seriousness" and "play," how does one confront the idea of "serious" religious groups that are simultaneously playful, humorous, and even (at times) put-ons? How *seriously* can we take them?

The relationship between ritual and play has long been noticed. Harvey Cox, in *Feast of Fools,* develops a theory of play, asserting, like others before him, that our society has lost or mutilated the gift of true festivity, playful fantasy, and celebration. In 1970, when an interviewer asked Cox about the "rise of the occult," he replied that astrology, Zen, and the use of drugs were "forms of play, of testing new perceptions of reality without being committed to their validity in advance or ever." When the interviewer observed that sociologist Marcello Truzzi had called the occult "trivial" because people were not serious about it, Cox replied, "That's exactly the reason it's *important.* People are playing with new perceptions."[3]

The classic study on play was written in 1944 by Johan Huizinga. "Human civilization," he says, "has added no essential feature to the general idea of play." Both animals and humans play, and play is irrational, defying logical interpretations. Yet the "great archetypal activities of human society are all permeated with play from the start." Further:

> You can deny, if you like, nearly all abstractions: justice, beauty, truth, goodness, mind, God. You can deny seriousness, but not play. . . . Play only becomes possible, thinkable and understandable when an influx of *mind* breaks down the absolute determination of the cosmos.

Huizinga writes that play and ritual are really the same thing and that all sacred rites, mysteries, sacrifices, and so forth are performed in the spirit of play, that poetry is a play function, and that all these things may well be serious since "the contrast between play and seriousness proves to be neither conclusive nor fixed . . . for some play can be very serious indeed." In addition, "The outlaw, the revolutionary, the cabalist or member of a secret society, indeed heretics of all kinds are of a highly associative if not sociable disposition, and a certain element of play is prominent in all their doings."[4]

In the light of these words we can look at two Neo-Pagan groups that have combined seriousness with play: the Reformed Druids of North America and the worshippers of Eris. These two groups, while differing in almost every way conceivable, illustrate the idea that once you embark on a journey of change in perception, even when you start this journey as "play," you can end up in waters far different from those you may have originally intended to enter.

The Reformed Druids of North America (RDNA) began in 1963 at Carleton College as a humorous protest movement directed against the school's requirement that all students attend a certain number of religious services. Since "attending the services of one's own religion"[5] was one way to fulfill this requirement, a group of students formed the RDNA to test it. The group was never intended to be a true alternative religion, for the students were Christians, Jews, agnostics, and so forth and seemed content with those religions.

In 1964 the regulation was abolished but, much to the surprise—and it is said, horror—of the original founders, the RDNA continued to hold services and spread its organization far beyond the college campus. One of the founders, David Fisher, who wrote many of the original rituals, is now an Episcopal priest and teacher of theology at a Christian college in the South, having apparently washed his hands of the RDNA. Many of the original founders considered Reformed Druidism not so much a *religion* as a philosophy compatible with any religious view, a method of inquiry. They certainly never considered it "Neo-Pagan."

The original basic tenets of Reformed Druidism were:

1. The object of the search for religious truth, which is a universal and a never-ending search, may be found through the Earth-Mother; which is Nature; but this is one way, one way among many.
2. And great is the importance, which is of a spiritual importance of Nature, which is the Earth-Mother; for it is one of the objects of Creation, and with it do people live, yea, even as they do struggle through life are they come face-to-face with it.

These tenets were often shortened to read

1. Nature is good!
2. Nature is good![6]

The original founders seemed to hold the fundamental idea that one should scrutinize religion from "a state of rebellion," neither embracing traditional faiths nor rejecting them. They intended RDNA to avoid all dogma and orthodoxy, while affirming that life was both spiritual (Be'al) and material (the Earth-Mother) and that human beings needed to come to a state of "awareness" through unity with both spirit and nature. The founders also seemed to distrust ritual and magic, sharing the prejudices and assumptions of most of the population.

RDNA has always had a sense of humor. The *Early Chronicles* of the Druids, as well as many later writings, are written in a mock biblical style. Here, for example, is a description of how the regulations at Carleton were abolished:

1. Now it came to pass that in those last days a decree went out from the authorities;
2. and they did declare to be abolished the regulations which had been placed upon the worship of those at Carleton.
3. And behold, a great rejoicing did go up from all the land for the wonders which had come to pass.
4. And all the earth did burst forth into song in the hour of salvation.
5. And in the time of exaltation, the fulfillment of their hopes, the Druids did sing the praises of the Earth-Mother.[7]

Similarly, the original "Order of Worship" has many similarities to a Protestant religious service, complete with invocations and benedictions. Reformed Druids are not required to use these rituals and—as is true of so many Neo-Pagan groups—participants have created new rituals to take their place. I did attend a RDNA ritual in Stanford, California, that sounded not much different from a number of liberal Christian services I have attended, despite its being held in a lovely grove of oaks. But when I described this ritual to another leader of a Reformed Druid grove, he merely laughed and remarked, "It all depends on who's doing the ritual. A service by Robert Larson [Arch-Druid of an Irish clan in San Francisco and a former Christian Scientist] often sounds like Christian Science. My services are influenced by my own training in Roman Catholicism. Besides, most religious ceremonies follow the same kinds of patterns. It is natural to find similarities." The Reformed Druid movement is extremely eclectic, to say the least.

The festivals of the Reformed Druids are the eight Pagan sabbats we have come across before: Samhain, the Winter Solstice, Oimelc (February 1), the Spring Equinox, Beltane, Midsummer, Lughnasadh (August 1), and the Fall Equinox. The rituals are held (if possible) outdoors, in a grove of oaks or on a beach or hill. The officiating Druids often wear robes—white is traditional, but other colors are acceptable. During the ritual, which can include readings, chants, and festival celebrations, the waters-of-life are passed around and shared to symbolize the link between all things and nature. (During the ritual I attended in Stanford, California, the waters-of-life was good Irish whiskey. Whiskey in Gaelic means "waters of life.") All worship is directed toward nature and various aspects of nature retain the names of the Celtic and Gaulish gods and goddesses:

> Dalon Ap Landu, Lord of the Groves
> Grannos, God of Healing Springs
> Braciaca, God of Malt and Brewing
> Belenos, God of the Sun
> Sirona, Goddess of Rivers
> Taranis, God of Thunder and Lightning
> Llyr, God of the Sea
> Danu, Goddess of Fertility

The "paganizing" of the Reform Druids came as a great surprise to many, and some of the originators regard it as a regression. But from its inception there has been much in RDNA that is Neo-Pagan in nature. The "Order of Worship" includes hymns to the Earth-Mother, to Be'al, and to Dalon Ap Landu, lord of the groves, as well as ancient Welsh and Irish poems. This is fertile ground for anyone with a love of nature, an interest in Celtic lore and myth, and a love of poetry, music, and beauty.

Once the initial protest was over, the most important aspect of Reformed Druidism had to be that it put people in touch with a storehouse of history, myth, and lore. Isaac Bonewits, who was Arch-Druid of the Mother Grove of the NRDNA in Berkeley (see below) and certainly an avowed Neo-Pagan, told me, "Over the years it grew and mutated, much to the horror of the original founders, into a genuine Neo-Pagan religion. There were actually people who were worshipping the Earth-Mother and the old gods and goddesses, who were getting off on it and finding it a complete replacement for their traditional religion." Bonewits, Larson, and one or two others played a large role in this change in direction.

As of 2006, the Reformed Druids of North America have about fifty groves and proto-groves in the United States, Canada, and Europe. Besides members of groves, there are about three thousand solitary RDNA members. The grove at Carleton has existed on and off to this day as a philosophic path open to members of many different religions. Over the years there have also been a number of offshoots, Norse Druids in San Diego, Zen Druids in Olympia, Wiccan Druids in Minneapolis, Irish Druids (with services in Gaelic) in San Francisco, Hassidic Druids in St. Louis, and various Eclectic Druids in Oakland, Berkeley, and Los Angeles. These groups come and go. For example, the Hassidic Druids formed in 1976; the group was made up primarily of former Jews who wished to keep certain aspects of Hebrew and Yiddish culture, but wanted to avoid what they considered a patriarchal theology. They added Yiddish and Hebrew scriptures to the Gaulish and Celtic ones. They had a set of additional scriptures called the Mishmash and the Te-Mara, which, in Reformed Druid tradition, satirized, in a good-natured way, the scriptures—this time the Talmud. Most of it was both humorous and somewhat profound. I could not locate the group in 2005, and I assume it no longer exists.[8]

Some Druid groups are Pagan; some are not. Isaac Bonewits often publicly stated that Reformed Druidism could only survive if it recognized its own nature, which was that of a Neo-Pagan religion.[9]

Since the RDNA was not Neo-Pagan, per se, Bonewits started the New Reformed Druids of North America (NRDNA), which was avowedly Pagan. He described his grove as:

... an Eclectic Reconstructionist Neo-Pagan Priestcraft, based primarily upon Gaulish and Celtic sources, but open to ideas, deities and rituals from many other Neo-Pagan belief systems. We worship the Earth-Mother as the feminine personification of Manifestation, Be'al as the masculine personification of Essence, and numerous Gods and Goddesses as personifications of various aspects of our experience. We offer no dogma or final answers, but only continual questions. Our goal is increased harmony within ourselves, and all of Nature.[10]

Over the last fifteen years, contemporary Druidism has undergone a stunning renewal. In 1985, when the last serious revision of *Drawing Down the Moon* took place, most of the Reformed Druid groups were moribund. There was a Druid group in Seattle, and a lively group in Berkeley, California—the Live Oak Grove, which published *A Druid Missal-any*. Then, after a long absence from the Pagan scene, Isaac Bonewits started Ár nDraíocht Féin (Our own Druidism), as well as a new journal, *The Druid's Progress*. At the time, Bonewits told me, "It started out as a simple network for a few dozen people who wanted to coordinate research on the old religions of Europe. Then more and more people wanted rituals and clergy training. Now it's a collective act of creation. With the help of 200 people we're creating a new religion."

Bonewits said that he came to realize that the Reformed Druids was not an appropriate vehicle, at least not for him. "Most people in the RDNA were Zen anarchists," Bonewits said. "They had a philosophical approach, applicable to any religion. Most of the RDNA were not Pagans. They resented me and felt I was infiltrating their group."

In *The Druid's Progress,* Bonewits laid out his vision of Ár nDraíocht Féin. It would be an attempt to reconstruct, using the best scholarship available, what the Paleopagan Druids actually did, and then try to apply such knowledge to creating a Neo-Pagan religion appropriate for the modern world. It would use the scholarship of authors like George Dumézil, Stuart Piggot, Anne Ross, and Mircea Eliade. It would create rituals and liturgy and would set up a complex training program to achieve excellence. It would "keep nonsense, silliness and romanticism down to a dull roar," he told me. "After all, the Druids had some unpleasant customs which I have no intention of perpetuating. They were headhunters, for example. But it is important to know where you are coming from if you are going to claim you are connected to certain ancestors or traditions. If you say you are a 'Druid' you ought to know what kind of people they were and what kinds of thoughts they had. Then you can pick and choose what parts make sense in modern America."

Bonewits' vision of Druidism was not entirely Celtic or even Pan-Celtic, but Pan-European. It included all the branches of the Indo-

European culture and language tree—Celtic, Germanic, Slavic, Baltic, even pre-classical, archaic Greek, and Roman. While most people are aware that fragments of Druidism seem to have survived in parts of Wales and Ireland, some of them surviving in disguise through the institutions of the Celtic Church and among bards and poets, research done by Russian and Eastern European folklorists, anthropologists, and musicologists, writes Bonewits, "indicates that Paleopagan traditions may have survived in small villages, hidden in the woods and swamps, even into the current century! Some of these villages still had people dressing up in long white robes and going out to sacred groves to do ceremonies, as recently as World War One!"[11] Much of this research had been published in Soviet academic literature and had never been translated. Much of it is coming to light today. Bonewits believes that this material, combined with Vedic and Old Irish sources, will provide many of the missing links in reconstructing Paleopagan European Druidism.

One of the most important aspects of Ár nDraíocht Féin was its training system, which was based on a series of levels or circles, somewhat like the organization of the old Church of All Worlds. You can move forward and (if you lose knowledge or skills) backward! Since the Indo-European clergy were supposed to be the intelligentsia of their culture—the poets, the musicians, the historians, and the astronomers, the training for each level included drama, music, psychic arts, physical and biological and social sciences, counseling, communications, and health skills. Languages were also emphasized.

Bonewits has always been extremely opinionated and often difficult, even egotistical, but he remains one of the most interesting Pagans around. In talking about Druidism, he says flatly that there is no indication that the Druids used stone altars. They did not build Stonehenge, the megalithic circles and lines of northwestern Europe, the Pyramids, or have anything to do with the mythical continents of Atlantis or Mu. What's more, he will not accept what he considers to be the questionable scholarship of Louis Spence, Margaret Murray, Robert Graves, H. P. Blavatsky, and others.

While the local druid groves would have lots of autonomy, Bonewits made no apologies for the fact that this group would have a structured hierarchy and that Bonewits would be the Arch-Druid. He told me, "I'm being extremely out front about running it as a benevolent dictatorship. I get a lot of feedback, but I make the final decision. These are the rules of this game. You can criticize them, but the rules of the game are the rules of the game. If you don't want to play by them, you should probably start your own Druid group, and I hope you succeed. Some people will think that makes me autocratic," he laughed, "and they're probably right."

Reaction to this approach in Pagan periodicals ranged from attacks: "Bonewits has come out with *his* plea in the wilderness. 'Support me and I'll be your Guru.' Give me a break Isaac" (*Pegasus Express*) to great praise: "This is actually a good approach for a young organization whose founder wishes it to proliferate and generally be successful" (*Panegyria*). Appearing at major Pagan festivals, Isaac had a rousing response. Clustering around him on an evening, you might find an intense discussion, or three Celtic harpists playing for each other and exchanging information. His training program got many people talking.

By 2006, Ár nDraíocht Féin was thriving, and many other Druid groups had come into existence, often going in a slightly different direction from either ADF or RDNA. These groups included the Henge of Keltria—which goes in a more Celtic direction than Ár nDraíocht Féin, the Order of the White Oak, and many other organizations (at least a dozen are listed in the Resource guide). As for the Reformed Druids of North America, they are still going strong. And they illustrate something important: When one combines a process of inquiry with content of beauty and antiquity, when, even as a lark, one opens the flow of archetypal images contained in the history and legends of people long neglected by this culture, many who confront these images are going to take to them and begin a journey unimagined by those who started the process.

If a number of Neo-Pagan groups began in a spirit of play and, while remaining true to that spirit, grew more serious, there is one Neo-Pagan phenomenon that will never become too serious: the Erisian movement and groups connected with it that have been engaging in absurdist and surrealist activities for many years.

In a way, it's ridiculous even to talk seriously about the Erisians, a group, or collection of groups, that has called itself a "Non-prophet Irreligious Disorganization" that is "dedicated to an advanced understanding of the paraphysical manifestations of Everyday Chaos,"[12] and at other times has stated, "The Erisian revelation is not a complicated put-on disguised as a new religion, but a new religion disguised as a complicated put-on."[13]

The Discordian Society was founded (if one can call it that) in 1957 (or 1958—even this primary confusion has never been cleared up) by Greg Hill (Malaclypse the Younger) and Kerry Thornley (Omar Ravenhurst). After the initial "Erisian Revelation" (see below), Malaclypse the Younger went on to start an Erisian Neo-Pagan Paradox Cult called the Paratheoanametamystikhood of Eris Esoteric (POEE), and in 1970 POEE published the *Principia Discordia, or How I found Goddess and What I Did To Her When I Found Her*. The first edition—there have been five—was five photocopies; the second was quickly offset in New Orleans, and the third was printed in Tampa. By now, at least several thousand have been distributed. Omar Ravenhurst went on to form his own Erisian organization, the Erisian Liberation Front (ELF). *The Principia* puts the story of the beginning of the Erisian movement this way:

THE BIRTH OF THE ERISIAN MOVEMENT

The Earth quakes and the Heavens rattle; the beasts of nature flock together and the nations of men flock apart; volcanoes usher up heat while elsewhere water becomes ice and melts; and then on other days it just rains.

Indeed do many things come to pass.

HBT; The Book of Predictions, Chap. 19

The Revelation

Just prior to the decade of the 1960s, when Sputnik was alone and new, and about the time that Ken Kesey took his first acid trip as a medical volunteer; before underground newspapers, Viet Nam, and talk of a second American Revolution; in the comparative quiet of the late 1950s, just before the idea of RENAISSANCE became relevant . . .

Two young Californians, known later as Omar Ravenhurst and Malaclypse the Younger, were indulging in their habit of sipping coffee at an all-night bowling alley and generally solving the world's problems. This particular evening they were complaining to each other of the personal confusion they felt in their respective lives. "Solve the problem of discord," said one, "and all other problems will vanish."

"Indeed," said the other, "chaos and strife are the roots of all confusion."

FIRST I MUST SPRINKLE YOU
WITH FAIRY DUST

Suddenly the place became devoid of light. Then an utter silence enveloped them, and a great stillness was felt. Then came a blinding flash of intense light, as though their very psyches had gone nova. Then vision returned.

The two were dazed and neither moved nor spoke for several minutes. They looked around and saw that the bowlers were frozen like statues in a variety of comic positions, and that a bowling ball was steadfastly anchored to the floor only inches from the pins that it had been sent to scatter. The two looked at each other, totally unable to account for the phenomenon. The condition was one of suspension, and one noticed that the clock had stopped.

There walked into the room a chimpanzee, shaggy and grey about the muzzle, yet upright to his full five feet, and poised with natural majesty. He carried a scroll and walked to the young men.

"Gentlemen," he said, "why does Pickering's Moon go about in reverse orbit? Gentlemen, there are nipples on your chest; do you give milk? And what, pray tell, Gentlemen, is to be done about Heisenberg's Law?" He paused. "SOMEBODY HAD TO PUT ALL OF THIS CONFUSION HERE!"

And with that he revealed his scroll. It was a diagram, like a yin-yang with a pentagon on one side and an apple on the other. And then he exploded and the two lost consciousness.

Eris—Goddess of Chaos, Discord & Confusion

They awoke to the sound of pins clattering, and found the bowlers engaged in their game and the waitress busy making coffee. It was apparent that their experience had been private.

They discussed their strange encounter and reconstructed from memory the chimpanzee's diagram. Over the next five days they searched libraries to find the significance of it, but were disappointed to uncover only references to Taoism, the Korean flag, and Technocracy. It was not until they traced the Greek writing on the apple that they discovered the ancient Goddess known to the Greeks as ERIS and to the Romans as DISCORDIA. This was on the fifth night, and when they slept that night each had a vivid dream of a splendid woman whose eyes were as soft as feather and as deep as eternity itself, and whose body was the spectacular dance of atoms and universes. Pyrotechnics of pure energy formed her flowing hair, and rainbows manifested and dissolved as she spoke in a warm and gentle voice:

"I have come to tell you that you are free. Many years ago, My consciousness left Man, that he might develop himself. I return to find this development approaching completion, but hindered by fear and by misunderstanding.

"You have built for yourselves psychic suits of armor, and clad in them, your vision is restricted, your movements are clumsy and painful, your skin is bruised, and your spirit is broiled in the sun.

"I am chaos. I am the substance from which your artists and scientists build rhythms. I am the spirit with which your children and clowns laugh in happy anarchy. I am chaos. I am alive, and I tell you that you are free."

During the next months they studied philosophies and theologies, and learned that ERIS or DISCORDIA was primarily feared by the ancients as being disruptive. Indeed, the very concept of chaos was still considered equivalent to strife and treated as a negative. "No wonder things are all screwed up," they concluded. "They have got it all backwards." They found that the principle of disorder was every much as significant as the principle of order.

With this in mind, they studied the strange yin-yang. During a meditation one afternoon, a voice came to them:

"It is called THE SACRED CHAO. I appoint you Keepers of It. Therein you will find anything you like. Speak of me as DISCORD, to show contrast to the pentagon. Tell constricted Mankind that there are no rules, unless they choose to invent rules. Keep close the words of Syadasti: 'TIS AN ILL WIND THAT BLOWS NO MINDS. And remember that there is no tyranny in the State of Confusion. For further information, consult your pineal gland."

"What is this?" mumbled one to the other, "A religion based on the Goddess of Confusion? It is utter madness!" . . . And amid squeals of mirth and with tears on their cheeks, each appointed the other to be high priest of his own madness, and together they declared themselves to be a society of Discordia for whatever that may turn out to be.[14]

The *Principia* was composed from articles and ideas that Greg Hill (Mal) collected during communications with co-conspirators. In 1969 Mal started the Joshua Norton Cabal. (Emperor Joshua Norton lived in the late 1800s in San Francisco. He declared himself emperor of the world and issued his own money, and, proving that one *can* often create one's own reality, much of San Francisco humored him—accepted his money in bars and so forth. It is said that thousands came to his funeral.) Other Erisian cabals formed. At one point there were rumored to be more than twenty, although some may have had a membership of only one. Since radical decentralization is a Discordian principle, it is impossible to know how many Discordians there were and are, or what they are doing. Most of these cabals engaged in various nonviolent, absurdist, revolutionary, magical, and surrealist endeavors. A number of these "actions" were done under the name of the supposed "Bavarian Illuminati," a rather mysterious organization founded by Adam Weishaupt in 1776. The Erisian "Illuminati" have mostly been the inspiration of someone known as Thomas Gnostic. Similar actions were initiated by ELF. Omar Ravenhurst, for example, invented a Do-It-Yourself Conspiracy Kit, complete with assortments of stationery bearing dubious letterheads. Robert Anton Wilson, a leading Discordian (sometimes known as Mordecai the Foul), described one such action.

> Omar would send a letter to the Christian Anti-Communist Crusade on Bavarian Illuminati stationery, saying, "We're amused you've discovered that we've taken over the Rock Music business. But you're still so naive. We took over the business in the 1800s. Beethoven was our first convert."

A number of these Discordian actions found their way into the underground press in the late sixties and early seventies. They were not, Wilson told me, "hoaxes," for "a hoax suggests something that's done out of adolescent perversity. I regard them rather as educational projects. We are teaching people that there are alternate realities."

Discordianism is an anarchist's paradise. One of its mottoes is "We Discordians Shall Stick Apart." And all you have to do to become a member of the Discordian Society is (1) decide it exists and (2) include yourself in it. Greg Hill has described himself as a "Transcendental Atheist" who has always been interested in absurdist religion and, discovering that the ancient Greeks had a goddess of confusion, decided it was the funniest thing he had ever heard. But POEE is a priesthood of sorts, and you can become a priest by (as you might expect) declaring yourself one. POEE has thousands of wallet-sized "Pope Cards."

Wilson (Mordecai) has described himself as a "Transcendental Agnostic," although, he added whimsically, "There are many me's." He once told an interviewer from a science fiction magazine:

> I'm an initiated witch, an ordained minister in four churches (or cults) and have various other "credentials" to impress the gullible. My philosophy remains Transcendental Agnosticism. There are realities and intelligences greater than conditioned normal consciousness recognizes, but it is premature to dogmatize about them at this primitive stage of our evolution. We've hardly begun to crawl off the surface of the cradle-planet.[15]

THE BEARER OF THIS CARD
IS A GENUINE AND AUTHORIZED
⮕ 𝔓𝔬𝔭𝔢 ⮕
So *please* Treat Him Right
GOOD FOREVER
Genuine and authorized by The HOUSE of APOSTLES of ERIS

Every man, woman and child on this Earth is a genuine and authorized Pope. Reproduce and distribute these cards freely P O.E.E. Head Temple, San Francisco

Wilson, along with another Erisian named Robert Shea, coauthored *Illuminatus*, a three-volume science fiction/occult/conspiracy novel that takes place in an Erisian framework. Its success in both science fiction and occult circles may prove to be the springboard for more Erisian activity, although the opposite could just as easily occur. In fact, one Erisian magazine in New Jersey published a notice dissolving the local Erisian cabal. The reason: "Since the beans were spilled in the proverbial manner (see *Illuminatus*) it is necessary to retreat to a more esoteric position."[16] Meanwhile, Malaclypse has given notice that the Eris in the *Principia* and the Eris in *Illuminatus* are *not* the same Eris.

Whichever Eris you choose, she always seems to take the form of paradox, and an Erisian notice printed in *Green Egg* said that the Erisian path generally appealed to those who have "an affinity toward taoism, anarchy and clowning; who can feel comfortable in a Neo-Pagan context; and who probably have a tendency toward iconoclasm."[17]

And Discordianism plans to stay humorous. Wilson says, "Much of the Pagan movement started out as jokes, and gradually, as people found out they were getting something out of it, they became serious. Discordianism has a built-in check against getting too serious. The sacred scriptures are so absurd—as soon as you consult the scriptures again, you start laughing. Discordian theology is similar to Crowleyanity. You take any of these ideas far enough and they reveal the absurdity of all ideas. They show that ideas are only tools and that no idea should be sacrosanct. Thus, Discordianism is a necessary balance. It's a fail-safe system. It remains a joke and provides perspective. It's a satire on human intelligence and is based on the idea that whatever your map of reality, it's ninety percent your own creation. People should accept this and be proud of their own artistry. Discordianism can't get dogmatic. The whole language would have to change for people to lose track that it was all a joke to begin with. It would take a thousand years."

The Erisian position on humor has always been clear, and to prove it, here is another section from the sacred scriptures, the *Principia*.[18]

THE DISCORDIAN SOCIETY
Joshua Norton Cabal
San Francisco

THERE IS NO ENEMY
ANYWHERE.

GREYFACE

In the year 1166 B.C., a malcontented hunchbrain by the name of Grey-face, got it into his head that the universe was as humorless as he, and he began to teach that play was sinful because it contradicted the ways of Se-rious Order. "Look at all the order about you," he said. And from that, he deluded honest men to believe that reality was a straightjacket affair and not the happy romance as men had known it.

It is not presently understood why men were so gullible at that par-ticular time, for absolutely no one thought to observe all the *disorder* around them and conclude just the opposite. But anyway, Greyface and his followers took the game of playing at life more seriously than they took life itself and were known even to destroy other living beings whose ways of life differed from their own.

The unfortunate result of this is that mankind has since been suffer-ing from a psychological and spiritual imbalance. Imbalance causes frus-tration, and frustration causes fear. And fear makes a bad trip. Man has been on a bad trip for a long time now.

It is called THE CURSE OF GREYFACE.

The Curse of Greyface and The Introduction of Negativism

To choose order over disorder, or disorder over order, is to accept a trip composed of both the creative and the destructive. But to choose the cre-ative over the destructive is an all-creative trip composed of both order and disorder. To accomplish this, one need only accept creative disorder along with, and equal to, creative order, and also be willing to reject de-structive order as an undesirable equal to destructive disorder.

The Curse of Greyface included the division of life into order/disorder as the essential positive/negative polarity, instead of building a game foundation with creative/destructive as the essential positive/negative. He has thereby caused man to endure the destructive aspects of order and has prevented man from effectively participating in the creative uses of disorder. Civilization reflects this unfortunate division.

POEE proclaims that the other division is preferable, and we work toward the proposition that creative disorder, like creative order, is possible and desirable; and that destructive order, like destructive disorder, is unnecessary and undesirable.

Seek the Sacred Chao—therein you will find the foolishness of all ORDER/DISORDER. They are the same!

Principia Discordia or How I found Goddess and what I did to Her when I found Her

And yet Erisianism should not be treated frivolously. Greg Hill told me his experiences with Eris had been quite profound. Although it started as an atheistic joke, his perceptions began to change.

"Eris is an authentic goddess. Furthermore, she is an old one. In the beginning I saw myself as a cosmic clown. I characterized myself as Malaclypse the Younger. But if you do this type of thing well enough, it starts to work. In due time the polarities between atheism and theism became absurd. The engagement was transcendent. And when you transcend one, you have to transcend the other. I started out with the idea that all gods are an illusion. By the end I had learned that it's *up to you* to decide whether gods exist, and if you take a goddess of confusion seriously, it will send you through as profound and valid a metaphysical trip as taking a god like Yahweh seriously. The trips will be different, but they will both be transcendental. Eris is a valid goddess in so far as gods are valid; and gods are valid when we choose them to be. The Christian tradition has become so totally alienated from reality in the Western world that people have had to start inventing their own damn gods. Some people are doing it seriously and it is validly working. The Neo-Pagan phenomenon is an example. Another path would be transcendental atheism: using atheism as a spiritual path. The phenomenon of Eris is a hybrid between the two. She is an absurdist deity who shows that nonsense is as valid as sense, since Eris is as preposterous a deity as ever invented. Yet, if you pursue her, it can be a valid spiritual experience that can carry you to the point where you no longer relate to things in terms of deities and nondeities."

For Wilson also, Discordianism is a perceptual game, a means of expanding one's perception of reality. The Discordian position, he has written, "demands, then, continuous motion. To stop at any one meta-phor and establish it as dogma is to put the mind in chains." He adds, "Although Discordians move about the country and the world con-stantly, in many guises, there is always one major Discordian ashram in the San Francisco Bay Area 'on the site of the beautiful future San An-dreas Canyon.' The only way to remain sane is to *know* that the ground below you is pure Void."[19]

I asked Malaclypse, "What's Omar Ravenhurst doing these days?" He said, "Ravenhurst has recently been in a state of extreme discord. We were talking about Eris and confusion and he said, 'You know, if I had realized that all of this was going to come *true,* I would have chosen Venus.'"

The Erisian Movement Today

Discordians and Erisians still make their presence known at Pagan gath-erings and in the pages of newsletters. And there are many Erisian sites on the Web (see Resources). Dennis Moskowitz (Brother Max Flax Bee-blewax), who was part of the Five-College Discordian Society of Saint Rufus a number of years ago, writes that what's most noticeable now is the influence of Eris in the culture at large. "Most Pagans and magicians seem to be familiar with Discordianism," he says. Moskowitz notes that Eris was one of the main characters—albeit a villain—in a recent Sin-bad animated movie, and Discordian references can be found in Grant Morrison's 1994–2000 comic series, *The Invisibles.* There is a role-playing game created by designer John Wick called *Discordia!* It is free to the public. There were some Discordian protests of the movie *Troy* because it told the story of the Trojan War without mentioning any gods, and therefore denied the role of the Goddess Eris in starting the war. Moskowitz observes that Discordianism "will always be a movement that begins with high school and college students who discover it, per-haps take it too seriously, mellow out as they get older," but then, every so often, Erisian elements will wind up in their future artistic work.

Another Discordian, who calls herself Elfwreck, notes that Eris is a recurring villain in the Cartoon Network show *The Grim Adventures of Billy and Mandy.* She also says there is an annual Discordian convention called *KallistiCon a Discordian (un) Convention,* usually in California. And at PantheaCon, an annual Pagan convention in northern California, there is usually a Discordian ritual attended by a couple hundred people. There are also occasional pilgrimages to Emperor Norton's gravesite. A member of the Avatar Jones Memorial Cabal (AJMC) is in the process of starting an Erisian church, the Fifth Trinity Church. Elfwreck said the Discordian/Erisian movement was as strong as it ever was, "which is to say, there are tiny clots here and there with delusions of grandeur, and the illusion of a much larger web connecting all the dots." Elfwreck says that the fact that public Paganism has developed a tolerance for Discordians "rather shocks me," and she says it may well show the superficiality of much of Paganism.

Some Pagans argue that since Erisianism is mostly playful nonsense, people leave it once they get into Paganism more seriously. An entry on a Pagan scholars list read "The jokes get tiresome . . . perhaps the movement has lost steam." The writer adds that any real reading of Greek writers like Hesiod shows Eris to be the mother of all harm—and not a goddess to emulate.

But others would argue that the Pagan community is one of the only spiritual communities that is exploring humor, joy, abandonment, even silliness and outrageousness as valid parts of spiritual experience. Oz, a Craft priestess from New Mexico, wrote these words to me, just days before the 1986 edition of *Drawing Down the Moon* went to press.

The Pagan movement is exploring social change in a way that I don't see it done anywhere else. We are living with nudity, sexual freedom, license for experimentation, freedom of thought and a loose, fun joy that is unique. I don't see other "magickal" people developing a culture of boisterous joy. To find it in expression, silliness, outrageousness, pushing the limits—to find that in this there is spirit. If you think about the dual meaning of the word "spirit" for a moment, I think you have it. I now get much of my intellectual and even spiritual stimulation from people who are not Witches or Pagans, but when I want to be around people with whom I am comfortable living my life the way I like to live it, who are being exceedingly open about everything from soup to nuts, who won't think you're crazy if you express a silly desire and act on it, I hang out with Pagans.

There are now many places where you can find alternatives to patriarchal Christian culture, places that are open to the mystical and the feminine. What exists in Paganism is the exposure to others that aren't afraid to dream a different dream and try to live it. We're not following anybody. We are like explorers on a new planet in some ways. And we say as Discordians say, "Don't make plans."

Now, almost twenty years later, the Pagan movement has matured and some of these aspects are a bit more muted. And as Paganism becomes a more mainstream movement, many Pagan festivals are family friendly and are downplaying alternative forms of sexuality and other more edgy ideas. The Erisians still have that flavor of outrageousness of twenty-five years ago, and it would be sad to lose all of that as Paganism comes of age.

12.

Radical Faeries and the Growth of Men's Spirituality

STARTING IN THE LATE 1970s, alongside the enormous and continuing growth of women's spirituality, there sprung up, in almost parallel fashion, a small spiritual movement among men. This movement was connected with the feminist critique of patriarchal notions of religion and authority, and with the attempt of both gay and straight men to create a new definition of maleness.

Many men within Neo-Paganism have asked the question "What is our role to be?" This question is not being asked very much within the British-based traditions of Wicca. In fact, some men within the dualistic traditions of the Craft, where the Goddess and the God are given equal, if polarized, roles, simply feel that the pendulum has swung too far and that the male aspects, the "God" aspects of the Craft, have been neglected.

Starting in the 1980s, many Pagan groups began adding "male" or "god" verses to "female" or "goddess" chants. And a number of Pagan festivals added men's rituals. Several articles in Pagan publications argued that it was time to look at the pain that many men were feeling about their own roles. In the Yule, 1983 issue of *Brothers of the Earth Newsletter,* the editor, Gary Lingen, wrote that he hears "the pain of Brothers who are aimlessly searching for alternatives and whose confused and oppressed natures need yet to be challenged and healed."[1]

Lingen wrote that men must accept responsibility for their own transformation, and they must connect with each other to achieve that goal. Brothers of the Earth was created to be a network—a separate place for men and boys to celebrate and empower themselves, a place to examine and celebrate the cycles of life and the passages of men's lives.

In the past, ideas about men's roles have been examined deeply by intellectuals like Jean Paul Sartre and Simone de Beauvoir, but these ideas seldom filter down to the culture at large. For years, the man who was speaking most publicly about these questions was the poet Robert Bly. Bly has lectured across the country on the subject of men. Articles sharing his views with readers have found their way into magazines like *New Age*. Bly argued that over the last thirty years, many men came to acknowledge their feminine side; often they became more nurturing and gentle. But often these men seemed incomplete; they lacked energy.

In his lectures, Bly often used a fairy tale sometimes called "Iron John." In this story, there is a kingdom far away where men are constantly disappearing in a forest, and no one knows why. Finally a stranger comes to the kingdom and sets out to find the answer. He finds a strange hairy Wildman, and he pulls him up from a deep pool. The man is put in a cage. For Bly, this hairy man represents the deep and dark part of man's psyche, a part of their natures with which they must reconnect if they are to be whole. Getting in touch with the feminine gives men one key to their nature, but, says Bly, the Wildman holds the other key.

In a second part of the story, a child loses a golden ball and it rolls into the cage of the Wildman. To get the ball, the child takes the key to the cage from under his mother's pillow and lets the Wildman out of the cage. For Bly, the golden ball is the unity of our natures, a unity that we usually only experience as children. Bly suggests that, for men, the golden ball lies within the deep, dark, primal field of the Wildman; that men, to become whole, must go deep into this place of the true masculine. To do this, men must confront the ancient mythologies, must in some way move against the forces of Western civilization, must leave the force field of the mother and the force field of collective male society and, as the initiate, confront the Wildman alone. In this way, said Bly, men can regain their true fierce energy, but it will not be a strength based on chauvinistic concepts of domination and control.[2]

There have been many different perspectives in the search for new male roles, but in an article in the April/May 1986 *Utne Reader*, writer Shepard Bliss wrote that two viewpoints were emerging as dominant: the feminist and the mythopoetic. The feminist approach (led by organizations like the National Organization of Changing Men) emphasized the problems of sexism and patriarchy. The mythopoetic tradition, led by Robert Bly, argued against certain aspects of the feminist critique. Our society may be sexist and even male dominated, said Bly, but patriarchy means "the rule of the fathers," and our society is characterized by an absence of fathers.[3]

The Pagan community has taken a very different approach than that of Bly. It was gay men within Paganism who led a fearless examination of male roles, in the same way that lesbian women forced women in the Pagan movement to examine their own situation. Just as women in the mixed branches of Paganism were forced to confront an energetic movement of women's religion and were changed by it, in the 1980s and beyond, many men (and women) were affected by their encounter with the "radical faeries."

From lingerie "tea dances" to explosive encounter sessions between gay and heterosexual men, the radical faeries have brought changes to the Pagan community.

The Radical Faeries

The movement of radical faeries began around 1978. Its official beginning can be traced to a 1979 gathering, a Spiritual Conference for Radical Fairies that was held at a desert sanctuary near Tucson, Arizona. A couple of months earlier, Arthur Evans—whose book *Witchcraft and the Gay Counterculture* argued that gay men needed to look at the connections between gay spirituality and the old Pagan nature religions—held a faerie circle in a redwood forest. This led to a conference, "A Call to Gay Brothers," in Arizona. As one writer wrote in *RFD*—a journal that has consistently detailed the growth of faery spirituality—"the conference was issued as a 'call' in the Sufi sense." Those who were ready to hear the call would come.[4]

The gathering, and the subsequent growth of radical faery spirituality, came out of a deep spiritual need. As one man told me, "We all wanted something that we didn't have and we desperately wanted it, but we didn't know what it was." Jody, a man who has been involved with shamanic forms of Witchcraft for a number of years, told me that before meeting with the radical faeries, his experiences in gay culture had left him frustrated, angry, and disillusioned. "When I first 'came out,'

I experienced this rush—'I can finally love, I can finally have sex, I can finally express myself.' But in many ways the gay culture did not serve my needs. I felt that, in many ways, it was an oppressive parody of straight culture. It takes place primarily in bars, where music is loud and people are not encouraged to talk, or form bonds or care for each other. It imitates the worst of heterosexual culture. I found I had to become a different person to get laid, and I didn't like that at all. I became ashamed and I wondered, 'Is this the best we have to offer?'"

Jody went to the second faerie gathering, held in the mountains of Colorado. "When I arrived," he told me, "I knew I was home. This is my culture. These are people who don't become someone else in order to make love. They live their sexuality in a way that is very connected to the earth."

At the first faerie gathering in Arizona, the rituals were often completely spontaneous and unplanned. At one point, a man said that one of his urges was to go out into the desert with buckets of water and cover himself with wet sand. In the end, forty men went with him on a Sunday morning. "What started out to be a lighthearted romp," writes one, "turned into a serious tribal affair. Something about the nudity and the primitiveness of the chanting and the ambiance of the gathering triggered a primal urge in them all and the chanting became more real." A bystander, taken by the spirit of the gathering, took off his clothes and started down the bank.

> Immediately there was a sense of initiation. They held him on their shoulders—a completely white body amid the mud people. They lowered him into the ooze and covered him over. They held him up high again and began to chant. After they put him down another spontaneous dance broke out. It was truly watching a tribal ritual. Even the photographs I've seen since are uncanny—like right out of *National Geographic*. The men in the photos aren't accountants or teachers or movie cameramen or lawyers or students or radical leftists or physicians or clerks or postal workers. They're members of the same tribe. It did not escape anyone how leveling the mud was. They were all the same and they got an electric sense of unity and power from it.[5]

Another man, describing the curious onlookers, wrote, "I saw tourists with Nikons standing on a bluff above us, stealing our visions to sell and felt maybe how aborigines feel when they find their faces in *National Geographic*."[6] A third participant observed, "Joyously caked with mud and with several dozen of my brothers—singing, dancing, shouting— I evoked a sensation of timelessness that I sometimes feel during especially satisfying love making, that I am in touch with something thousands and thousands of years old. This skeptical Marxist-Buddhist-Unitarian has become a true believer in the Fairy Spirit."[7]

There was one large, structured ritual—the Great Faery Circle. It began with a torchlight procession, parading through the Arizona desert, to the sound of flutes. "The moon grows full; we dance in its light,"[8] wrote one. Another said, "In the twilight the gathering . . . was extraordinary. There was no self-consciousness, everyone seemed to anticipate doing a great work and they began clapping and chanting as the musicians began to play. . . . As soon as they got away from the compound and into the desert under the moon, they became quiet, and as soon as they entered the wash with its scraggy trees and low mesquite bushes, power seemed to enter them."

A small wire cage was brought out. "There were things we had come with—thoughts, ideas, anxieties, fears, anything which chained or shackled us—we would not be taking back to our other world with us. These were whispered, spoken, screamed into the cage and never let out again. As the cage began to make its way around the circle, spontaneous chants began. . . . A low hum began but quickly moved into more agitated, coarser, emotion-filled cries. Hisses and isolated screams—and then came the most frightening of all—the animal noises. From seemingly nowhere, howls, barks, growling, roars, began softly and grew to a terrifying proportion. . . . It died as quickly as it had started and was replaced by a soft keening. I have never experienced so many people in harmony, nor had so much gooseflesh.

"When the cage had been around the circle, the leader took it to the center, and held it up, over his head. Slowly he walked around the fire so everyone could see what they were throwing away and then, with a great shout, he flung the cage and everything it contained far into the desert darkness."[9]

"In the beginning," Peter Soderberg, a radical faerie from Iowa told me, "we had no answers, we cried a lot, and laughed a lot, and sometimes we were cruel to each other. Living in a culture that has this idea that the physical and the spiritual are split, we didn't even have a vocabulary for speaking about what we needed. When we say 'spiritual' in our society, it usually doesn't encompass my flesh, the food I eat, the art I make, and the pleasure I get from my friends. But what I came to understand quickly was that being around faeries was the first safe place for me." And Don, another faerie man added, "We wanted a family, not a club, not an organization." Peter chimed in, "a place that we could be really honest with each other in this really direct way that scares people."

One important impulse behind the notion of radical faeries was the idea that there had to be something beyond assimilation. Just as radical feminists wanted to go beyond women attaining equal rights in a man's world, toward a notion that feminism implied a totally different reality, a different language, a different attitude toward power and authority, this group of gay men saw their own movement as implying a totally different view of the world, with different goals and different spiritual values than the "straight" world. Harry Hays is said to have once put it something like this: "People who are trying to be accepted by the 'straight' world pander to the straights, saying, 'We're really just the same as you, the only thing we do different is what we do in bed.' No," says Hays, "the only thing we do the *same* is in bed."

In an article in *RFD* called "A Sprinkling of Radical Faerie Dust," Don Kilhefner wrote that the dilemma facing gay men is "our assimilation into the mainstream versus our enspiritment as a people. . . . There is a reality to being Gay that is radically *different* from being Straight. . . . It is real. We can feel it in our hearts and in our guts."[10] But where does one find role models for such a person? One article in *RFD* suggested:

> We gays cast our nets out into the mythic sea, searching for our own lost archetypes, our spiritual role models . . . those symbols of the human psyche which we may claim as emblematic of our particular way of being.[11]

Gay men began looking at the role of the shaman, the berdache, and the bardajo. Writing in *RFD*, J. Michael Clark described the magical and spiritual role of the "berdache" in certain tribal cultures. Berdache was a term, first popularized among French explorers, which came to mean a person of one sex who assumes the role and status of the opposite sex. This person was socially accepted in these cultures and often was considered to have an enhanced spirituality. Similarly, other writers in *RFD* and elsewhere noted the role of homosexuality, cross-dressing, role changing, and androgyny in shamanic cultures and the fact that it is often easier for someone who is not tied down to specific gender roles to walk between the worlds.[12]

"We are the equivalent of Shamans in modern culture," said Peter Soderberg, during an interview at the 1985 Pagan Spirit Gathering. "Many gay men want to be middle-class Americans. They want to be respected as human beings and they want their sexuality to be ignored. But radical faeries are willing to live on the edge. We feel there is a power in our sexuality. You know there is a power there because our culture is so afraid of us. And there is a lot of queer energy in the men and women most cultures consider magical. It's practically a requirement for certain kinds of medicine and magic. The Pagan movement doesn't give credit to this, or even know about it, but then, there's a lot of heterosexism in modern Neo-Pagan culture."

Similar ideas were expressed to me by Jody, as we sat in a forest in the Berkshires at the 1985 COG Grand Council. "Look," he told me, "if most of the traditions of Wicca have been destroyed, gay spirituality has been totally eradicated. After all, think of the origin of the word 'faggot,' we were burned along with the Witches. Our magic was destroyed. It was not preserved like indoor ceremonial magic was preserved."

Jody quoted from *Visionary Love* by Mitch Walker;[13] he said that a door can be opened when you have psychic knowledge of male and female united within yourself. You then form a oneness that is a gate which connects you with the sexuality of nature creation. Jody believes that the elements of play and shape-changing so necessary for magic come more easily when you are one body instead of two, when the idea of gender doesn't come between you and the various parts you might play. "It is simply easier," he told me, "to blend with a nature spirit, or the spirit of a plant or animal, if you are not concerned with a gender-specific role."

Many radical faeries were preoccupied with questions of process and form. Just as feminist women had been struggling with questions about authority, forms of leadership, decision making, language, and control, these gay men seemed to spend much of their time struggling with the same kinds of questions. "Process *is* content," Peter told me. As a person who has always felt content was more important than form, I was dismayed. But in Peter's view, society's violence begins at the place where creativity and self-expression is controlled. "In our system of male dominance," he told me, "there is an unexpressed contract that says: 'It is safer to control energy than it is to experience energy.' In our society men are the 'control' referents, and women the 'experience' referents." On the most superficial level this would mean: "Women are feeling people. Women must be controlled." But on a subtler level Peter believes that this system exists within every human being. We tend to control our experiences, instead of participating in them and acting from them.

In contrast, faerie reality says, "It is more enjoyable to experience energy than to control energy," that the need for violence will disappear as creativity and real self-expression increase. Faerie gatherings, at their best, would be places where experimentation with new social forms could take place. They would not be a place for set rituals or workshops given by "leaders." One man wrote: "Spirituality has to be discovered . . . by each individual. Even the Native American cultures with a highly spiritual worldview did not 'teach' it. Instead, the young of the tribe, as part of their initiation, went on a vision quest to seek their own personal experience with the spirit realm."[14]

When they would come to conferences about men, or participate in Pagan festivals, radical faeries would often promote what might be called Discordian or Erisian energy (see Chapter 11). They would be the public anarchists. As the main, formal ritual was about to begin at a Pagan gathering in the 1980s, a group of faery men stood at the entrance to the circle, calling out, "Attention! No spontaneity! We're the spontaneity police!" In general, they have been uncomfortable with formal workshops, with discussions by "leaders," with models that are top-down or front-to-back. They have not wanted "elders," or parental authority figures. Above all, they have wanted to elevate the transformative power of play.

At the Pagan Spirit Gathering, Peter told me, "If you want to come to the faery camp, bring lots of clothes, bring lots of toys. If you bring things that are fun, you will find out what the process is about. It's the flip side of our culture. It seems nonsensical but it makes perfect sense." "Patriarchy, in a nutshell," said Don, "is about taking control. It permeates everything in our culture, including Paganism." If the problem is control, faeries see spontaneity and play as the antidotes. "There's lots of laughter and gossip among the faeries," said Don. "We love to share and we hate secrets."

The first Pagan gathering where there was a significant presence of gay men was the Pan-Pagan Festival in 1980. The presence of feminist women like Z Budapest combined with the men created explosive divisions and change. One afternoon at the gathering, Z Budapest led a circle of some sixty women. For many women at the campsite in Indiana, it was their first experience in an all-woman ritual. Z had enlisted the aid of a group of men, many of them gay, to protect the perimeter of the circle, since the camp was adjacent to a public camping area, and many at the ritual went skyclad (or nude).

The ritual began with a procession past a lake. Women holding branches of flowers walked through the camp singing. Many Pagans heard for the first time the words that would soon become one of the best-known festival chants:

We all come from the Goddess, and to her we shall return, like a drop of rain, flowing to the ocean.

The women gathered in a circle, chanted, danced, and wove webs of brightly colored yarn to symbolize their connection with each other. Unbeknownst to the women in the circle, one of the organizers of the festival was so angered and upset by the all-woman skyclad ritual that he tried to break through the circle of men guarding the rite, in order to pull his wife and child out. The controversy was one of several—all of them confrontations over politics or life style—that led to the breakup of the ecumenical council that had put on this gathering for four years. Three separate factions put on festivals the next summer.

Since 1981, at the Pagan Spirit Gathering, and at many other festivals—from Georgia to Ontario, from Massachusetts to New Mexico—there have been workshops and rituals for men. There have been faerie circles, but there have also been rituals and workshops where men of different sexual persuasions have come together, sometimes explosively, often joyously, and frequently with some unease.

One new development at festivals was the "tea dance." When it first appeared at a festival put on by the Athanor Fellowship, it seemed strangely out of place—disco music, alcoholic beverages, and dressing up in lingerie and crazy clothes. It seemed more suited to the gay community on Fire Island, not a wooded setting filled with Witches, vegetarians, and ecology buffs who rarely drank anything stronger than wine. The Athanor Fellowship—a group with few gays in it—found the dance so successful that it began to take it around from gathering to gathering until an enormous number of Pagans had let down their hair, dressed in costume, put on wigs and makeup, and had simply let loose.

"I remember someone saying the other night," Jody reflected, "that when he first entered the Pagan community, you could not even touch another man. And there were regular polarity checks in circles—you know, boy, girl, boy, girl. There's been a wonderful loosening and blossoming in the last few years, but there is also much resistance.

"I remember one meeting of men, at a gathering, where I decided I would come in a dress. I was asked to give 'the gay perspective.' I talked about the evils of competitive aggression, how it alienates men from each other. When I was finished, one man rose to speak. 'I love women and I get along with other men,' he said, 'but I'm a *man*, understand?' and I said, 'Look buddy, *I* am a man. A *strong* man. A man who knows how to get what he wants, and I don't have to stomp on others to get it. And nobody backs me down.'"

But thinking over his experiences in the 1980s, Jody observed, "I do think we have a place here, a voice here and I think it's the voice of the faery spirit coming through these men." And writing after a week-long festival in 1982, another man observed, "This is difficult and delicate work we are doing. There are many changes that we need to make, much violence we need to transform and lots of old hurts we need to face. It is a sturdy, easily-found playfulness we are headed toward. . . . But this journey being taken by men of all persuasions (plus a few that we haven't managed to persuade yet) is just beginning."[15]

Think about the tea dance, Jody said at the end of our interview. "All those men and women in crazy lingerie, dancing weirdly and loving it! Five years ago, it would never have happened. It's wonderful! Think of all the new ideas they may now have, now that they have found a way to get beyond their locked perceptions of role and place."

Radical Faerie and Gay Pagan Spirituality Today

Since this section was written around 1985, the gay spirituality movement, or what many now call the GLBT spirituality movement, has grown and diversified. There are scores of unique groups, radical faeries being only one element in the mix. At the time this chapter was written, however, the only groups providing a place for gay Pagan spirituality were the radical faeries, The Minoan Brotherhood, an initiatory mystery tradition of Witchcraft that serves gay and bisexual men (see Wicca Traditions, Chapter 5), and for women, Dianic Wicca, The Minoan Sisterhood, and various eclectic lesbian women's spirituality groups. The early history of both the women's and men's spirituality movements has been chronicled in two journals—*WomanSpirit,* which began in 1974, and *RFD Magazine,* which began a couple of years later (see Resources).

There were always gay men and women in other Wiccan and Pagan groups. But back in the 1970s, many gay Pagans found themselves in a strange position. Some gay men were initiated Gardnerian, and they had women working partners in covens that emphasized the belief in male-female sexual polarity. Many of them functioned very well, and many continue to do so. But as Michael Lloyd (Garan du), a founding member of the Green Faerie Grove, a worship group for queer Pagan men in Columbus, Ohio, observed, there was something ironic in gay people escaping the intolerance of their childhood religions and "entering a path that preached 'all acts of love and pleasure are my rituals,' only to be confronted with denunciations that some acts of love were still considered to be perversions." Lloyd is also a High Priest in the Minoan Brotherhood and is currently working on a biography of that tradition's founder, Eddie Buczynski.

Another long-time observer of the Gay Pagan scene is Sparky T. Rabbit (Peter Soderberg), who has written some of the most beautiful Pagan chants that have been used in rituals and festivals across the country. He notes that gay men and women who came into Paganism in the 1970s and 1980s had to "squeeze their way into local communities where there was no room for them until they made room for themselves." They entered straight Pagan groups, were tolerated and eventually accepted, but Sparky adds: "only as long as they towed the line and didn't get too uppity." Remember, he notes, many queer people can pass as part of the mainstream:

> So we learn to use the safety net of camouflaging ourselves pretty often, even from each other. Some queer people do that by sublimating their sexuality and focusing on heterosexual people. The internalized message is: "I must pay more attention to those who have power over me than to myself, in order to survive," a message which becomes "They are important, I'm not." The way that shows up in the Craft and other Pagan religions is in the fact that queer people are still for the most part invisible in religious ceremonies.
>
> I've been to multitudes of rituals planned by straight people that celebrated the God and Goddess as the Great Hetero Couple Whose Loving Creates the Universe. And I've been to lots of rituals planned by queer people that did the same thing. I've even been to a few rituals planned by queer Pagans that celebrated Gay Gods and Lesbian Goddesses. But how often has *any* of us ever been to a Pagan ritual planned by *straight* people which focused on the powers of queer gods and the gifts of queer people?

Sparky notes that Pagan women often tell a compelling story of how they felt inferior in the religions of their families, and how important it was to find a religion that celebrated women with powerful goddess images. Seeing oneself reflected in one's own religion was a great attraction, says Sparky, "and a big part of the healing we all need to do in order to create powerful, living communities of Pagan faith."

> We hear voices that say, "Being tolerated is fine. At least they don't want to kill me here." And, "Focusing on lesbians and gay men in religious ceremonies is part of a radical agenda." And "Hey, I *like* those people and I don't oppress them. So there's nothing to talk about." And "I really don't want that kind of attention." And, "*Gay* Gods? That's ridiculous!" These voices are both internal and external, and they come from both queer and straight Pagans. They are the vestiges of our collective homophobia, a skin it is time to shed. It doesn't help us, and we don't need it anymore.

But others note that there has been a fair amount of change within the Pagan community. Michael Lloyd says that many queer Gardnerians, Alexandrians, Heathens, Druids, and Santeros can be found, "and where existing organizations or ideas do not offer exactly the right blend of life-affirming philosophy and mythos to assuage one's soul, then people are free to forge one that does."

Another change he has noticed is the growing acceptability of solitary practice. It's easier and more acceptable to strike out on one's own today. Pagan solitaries and groups are found in the smallest communities, and the number of books, Web sites, and magazines addressing the specific needs of the GLBT subculture and queer spirituality continues to grow. He writes:

> *The Witches' Voice* alone has 66 entries for GLBT Pagan groups, and this is just the tip of the iceberg. And although lineaged traditions continue to play an important role in the Pagan community, we have moved, forever, from the time when they held the center stage. We are in the era of pop-influenced Paganism; a time characterized by fluid and rapid growth and a multiplicity and diversity of ideas. There are arguably more solitary practitioners than members of formal groups at this point in time. No one holds the keys to the kingdom; or, rather, everyone does.

There are of course negative and positive sides to the growth of what he calls "pop-influenced Paganism," but Lloyd says it has been more positive than negative for the gay community. Lloyd divides contemporary queer spirituality into a number of categories:

- Dianic Wicca (covered extensively in Chapter 8 of this book and in the section on Wiccan traditions in Chapter 5). Most covens are open to women of all orientations, although many have a strong lesbian presence—and many trace their origins to Z Budapest and the feminist covens of the 1970s. Others trace their origins to Starhawk, Reclaiming, or Morgan McFarland.
- The Minoan Brotherhood (see the section on Craft traditions in Chapter 5). This is the tradition of Witchcraft based on Cretan sources started by Eddie Buczynski as a safe haven for gay and bisexual men. There are now groups throughout the United States and Canada. There is also a Minoan Sisterhood.
- The Radical Faerie movement continues to grow, characterized by spontaneity and anti-authoritarianism. Michael Lloyd describes it as

"having a pro-humanist, pro-environment, pro-sex vision of the world that contrasts sharply with the mainstream Western religious traditions." He adds that while some groups include straight men and women, and even children, "gender bending is a hallmark of the radical faerie movement."

- Feri Tradition (see the section on Wicca traditions in Chapter 5 and quotes by Victor Anderson). Blind poet and shaman Victor Anderson, author of *Thorns of the Blood Rose,* his wife, Cora Anderson, Gwydion Pendderwen, and several others founded the Feri Tradition. It began in the San Francisco Bay Area, and it is certainly not a "gay" tradition, but Michael Lloyd (Garan du) insists that "its emphasis on the movement of energies that are at once sensual and sexual, ecstatic and mystical, creative and eclectic, invocatory and trance-possessory, and its respect for the wisdom of Nature and a love of beauty," have made the tradition more open to gay, bisexual, and transgendered people.
- Two-Spirit. This "modern phase," writes Garan du, refers to the seers, visionaries, and peacekeepers of many Native American tribes before the arrival of the European explorers. Often they dressed in women's clothing and were what we now call "gay." Garan du says many gays are learning to reconnect with their gifts, and that a new "Two-Spirit" tradition is rising.

There are now also other groups within the Pagan movement that are open to gay and transgendered individuals—certain Heathen, Wiccan, Druid, Yoruba, and shamanic groups.

When asked what gifts queer Paganism brings the larger Pagan movement, Sparky T. Rabbit says that queer Pagans can help others get beyond the assumption that "masculine" equals "male" and "feminine" equals "female." He says many people see these as unchanging, universal absolutes:

> Our culture is absolutely obsessed with this concept of gender. We are so preoccupied with it that we even assign gender to human characteristics. So courage, boldness and strength become masculine—and therefore male, while gentleness, nurturing and empathy are labeled feminine—and therefore female.

Many, if not most, Wiccans and Witches have gone a step further by using the mythic image of the God and the Goddess to *spiritualize* masculinity and femininity into the very heart of their traditions. So, ironically, a religion that is often viewed by its adherents as being a radical alternative to mainstream society can actually reinforce the damaging gender stereotypes our culture presents to us.

Queer people, says Sparky, are called "unmasculine" and "unfeminine" because they do not fit into the rigid categories of the dominant cultures' story:

But the secret we know is that *all* humans, regardless of their gender or sexuality, have the potential to express *all* of the characteristics which society labels masculine and feminine. The fact is that femininity and masculinity are not universal absolutes, but rather social constructs which can and do change from culture to culture. Courage does not have a penis, and compassion does not have a vulva. Yet we talk about "men getting in touch with their feminine side," as if men were explorers hacking their way through dense jungle in search of the Lost Gold of the Incas. We know it's there but it's *really hard* to find. As if tenderness were a foreign substance that has to be injected into men from the outside in order to take. The danger in talking about human characteristics or emotions as if they had gender is that we make it very tough for people to possess those qualities which have been assigned to another group. I know I am not a woman, and if I hear gentleness spoken of constantly as if it belongs only to women, then I will find it difficult to be a genuinely gentle man.

Michael Lloyd said he believes that queer spirituality brings a sense of mystery, of "otherness" to humankind. The old gods are far from dead, he says:

If you go to a gay club on a Saturday night, you will feel Dionysus throbbing in the sweaty, heated air around you on the dance floor. We know that the gods continue to live in us, because we feel them on a personal, visceral level even when we don't understand the "why" of it. Ecstatic faiths almost never arise from the upper strata of society where all the marrow has been sucked out of life in the process of screwing over the little guy while morally posturing with the Joneses. Ecstatic faiths manifest themselves amongst the little guys who are getting crapped on. The speakers-in-tongues, the shakers, and the gay clubbers all give those in power today the heebie jeebies, just as the Galli and the Bacchantes gave the Roman establishment the willies at the turn of another millennium. We have more in common with a gibbering, shaking Pentacostal than we do with any moralizing, self-righteous Baptist with a broomstick firmly lodged in his posterior.

Lloyd says that queer spirituality brings to the greater Pagan movement a sensibility that speaks to the gut and provides a vision of a different way of doing things:

Shake it up and shake it out, be hermetic, be mercurial, react, reject, rebel, look outside the bone box, look up the Goddess' skirt, be more than they'll let you be, breathe the free air, fight the good fight, seize the day, brave the elements, bust a nut, and live! All magick is an act of rebellion against the status quo.

He says queer Pagans also offer experience as healers, nurturers, artists, and musicians, perhaps because they are often able to see things from both a male and female point of view. Just as in some tribal societies, transgender people were able to walk between the worlds of the men's and women's houses, so he believes they may play a similar function in modern society.

In his *Resource Guide for Queer Pagans,* Lloyd argues that there were many ancient Pagan cultures where gay and transgender people thrived and where homoerotic activities were part of the priesthood, including the Assinu priests and priestesses of Inanna and Ishtar in Mesopotamia, the Galli priests and amazon priestesses of Cybele in Asia Minor, and the seidh priests of Freyja in Northern Europe.

Sparky T. Rabbit puts forth another idea. He says that oppression is the normal condition of many queer people. Their own "woundedness" often takes them through a shamanic initiation "that can take a heavy toll, resulting in depression, addictions, extreme feelings of unworthiness and other forms of self-destructive behavior." He argues that many of the people who formed the early gay spirituality groups were in various forms of recovery and became extremely sensitive to patterns of abuse and dysfunction in the society at large. In addition to practicing an ecstatic, erotic, queer kind of Witchcraft, "we worked at creating communities that valued clear communication and emotional honesty, and groups that nipped abusive, manipulative behavior in the bud and taught folks to take care of themselves." Indigenous societies have often acknowledged certain gifts of queer spirituality, but he believes that these gifts need to be acknowledged and celebrated in the larger Pagan community if that community is to share in them.

"So what does the greater Pagan community offer GLBT Pagans?" I asked. Garan du answered with the words: breathing room. Sanctuary. A place to belong. Community. Acceptance. And a way to connect with all kinds of people, gay, bi, straight, celibate, transgender, in a way that is hard to do in the greater society, even today.

Sparky T. Rabbit says the straight community can give its gay brothers and sisters the gift of celebration.

IV. The Material Plane

IV The Material Plane

13.

Living on the Earth

When I wrote this chapter in the late 1970s, the two quotes at the beginning were, I think, pretty accurate. They no longer fit as well: Many more Pagans think seriously about environmental issues, and many more are active politically or in their communities. I have cut this chapter down significantly, leaving a good part of that early history and including some new thoughts about changes in Pagan attitudes toward politics and ecology in this century. The section on Pagan Festivals and their impact on creating community has been greatly expanded.

The circle is a nice defensive mechanism to get away from the twentieth century and you need an escape point in this day and age. But we must also respond to the rest of our life on the outside. If we are not an alternative, we are not living our religion. It is as pure and simple as that. We are not a transcendental religion. We are not trying to transcend nature. Our religion is reality.

—MARK ROBERTS, Dianic priest

Most Neo-Pagans and Crafters have never done any serious thinking about the implications of their belief system. Most of them—like most Americans—are extremely shallow about religion. Take some of the basic issues that are tearing apart American Christianity—abortion, euthanasia, the morality of war— most Pagans have not thought through on a logical basis what their belief systems really mean in making practical decisions in day-to-day life.

—ISAAC BONEWITS, occultist and writer

MANY NEO-PAGANS will tell you that their religion is a "way of life." There is no separation between the spiritual and the earthly; there is no retreat from the world of matter. A British Witch once observed to me brightly, "Your head in the clouds, your feet on the ground, *that's* the proper place for an occultist."

Neo-Pagans do not live in ashrams. Most live in city apartments and suburban homes. A smaller but growing portion live on farms and in rural areas. While there has been a growing movement to buy land and create Pagan nature sanctuaries, this is still, by and large, a movement of people who live very much within the modern world. The temple of a Wiccan priestess is most likely either her home, a secluded backyard, or a neighboring park. Unlike those who enter highly organized and highly financed religious groups, Neo-Pagans do not, as a rule, live in a sympathetic religious community. They do not live apart. They do not live in a Neo-Pagan world. They often have quite "ordinary" jobs, raise ordinary families, and live very normal lives.

What then does it mean to call oneself a Pagan, or Neo-Pagan, or Witch in our society? What does this "way of life" look like? How different is it? Does it make a difference? To us? To others? To the world? If the primary bond between Pagans is one of imagination, does this bond make any difference in the "real" world? Does it affect the daily living of Pagan folk?

Furthermore, how do Pagans face the struggles of working and living in the United States? What do their lives look and feel like? Are they wealthy? Are they poor? Do they find contradictions between their spiritual values and their material realities, between their professional lives and their religious lives? Are they forced to split their personalities and lead double lives? If so, does it bother them?

For example, what do these participants in newly created or newly revived religions of nature think of modern civilization, modern technology? Are they antiscience, as so many scholars assume? Have they forsaken the cities and run off to the land? What are their views on ecology? How do they answer the standard accusation that occultism is an escape from reality, a cop-out from the vital issues of the day? Are they concerned with politics? Or do they believe that politics is a waste of time? Are they concerned with the transformation of society as well as the transformation of the self?

All these seemed to be proper questions to ask a modern Pagan living on the Mother's Earth. And strange it was back in 1976 to find that most of these questions had never been asked or answered, despite the many books on modern Witches and the sprinkling of books and essays on Neo-Paganism. Most books had focused on the "beliefs" of Pagans, on stories and anecdotes of psychic experiences, on descriptions of initiation rites and seasonal festivals, and on the history of the worship of ancient deities. But none had asked how comfortable these Pagans were with the world around them.

In seeking answers to some of these questions, I typed up a questionnaire with more than seventy questions. The questionnaire was published in *Green Egg*[1] and became the basis for the interviews I conducted around the country. Several Pagan groups used the questionnaire as a basis for discussion topics. All told, I received about one hundred replies.

In 1985 I passed out another much shorter questionnaire. It was published in *Panegyria* and four hundred copies were passed out at three Pagan festivals. One hundred ninety-five were returned.

Coming to Terms with One's Own Biases

I came to Neo-Paganism out of a search for a celebratory, ecological nature religion that would appease my hunger for the beauty of ancient myths and visions without strangling my mind with dogmas or cutting off the continuing flow of many doubts. In a family of agnostics, atheists, and Marxist humanists I was a secret childhood worshipper of the Greek gods and goddesses. But later I was heavily influenced by the politics of the sixties and early seventies. I was jailed and convicted in Berkeley, teargassed in Chicago, and nearly killed in Mississippi. Still later, as a journalist, I witnessed political trials and covered political demonstrations, and I twice visited Cuba and East Germany. I have come to understand that all things are interconnected. I reject *nothing* in this past, neither the jails nor the goddesses, neither the moonlit rituals nor the political activism and analysis.

My views have changed during the last thirty years. It would be fair to say that I now tend toward a "longer," more "cosmic" view of the world, and that my politics are more decentralist, if no less radical. Still, I did not come to Neo-Paganism out of a *rejection* of or escape from the political. Instead, Paganism seemed to me a philosophy that could heal the breach between the spiritual and the material. If ecology studied the interrelatedness of all living things and their environment, Neo-Paganism seemed to be a religion that would celebrate those interrelationships, that would heal into synthesis all oppositions: primitive and civilized, science and magic, male and female, spirit and matter.

Given this position, I was drawn to those writers who perceived a split in humanity's consciousness and sought to heal it. For example, I was drawn to the works of anthropolgist Stanley Diamond, especially his book *In Search of the Primitive* (1974).

Diamond argues not only that the spread of modern civilization has conquered and imperialized primitive peoples, but that it is "ultimately man's self, his species being, which is imperialized." Civilized humanity, by losing touch with the primitive, the primary, lost and subordinated what was essentially human within itself. The central question, Diamond writes, is, "What part of our humanity have we lost and how and why we have lost it and how and in what form we may regain it." It is clear that primitive societies had their disadvantages, but it is also clear that many of them allowed for more participation in community life and that many primitive religions were more in tune with human existence. "The sickness of civilization," Diamond observes, consists in "its failure to incorporate (and only then to move beyond the limits of) the primitive."[2]

Hundreds of other writers have discussed the split between mind and body, that split which historian E. R. Dodds called the most far-reaching and perhaps the most questionable of all the gifts we received from classical culture.[3] Lynn White placed the blame on Christianity. Theodore Roszak wrote eloquently on the perils of objectifying nature to the exclusion of ecstasy, and B. Z. Goldberg described that ecstasy in *The Sacred Fire.* Neo-Paganism, it seemed, was a philosophy that could join ancient and modern values. As Pagan writer Allen Greenfield observed to me, "The future must be built from the best material of past and present, and on the grave of those elements in both which were/are adverse to human life and living." Neo-Paganism seemed also to be a religion and way of life that allowed one to regain kinship with nature without sacrificing one's individuality or independence.

These influences, among many, led me to certain assumptions. NeoPagans, it seemed to me, had turned to new and old nature religions for nourishment and inspiration at a time when the degradation of nature and the artificiality of the environment were among the supreme facts of life, particularly in urban and suburban areas, where most Neo-Pagans—and most people in the United States—lived.

Since Pagans often looked to the past for *sources* of inspiration, I assumed that they, like myself, would have an ambivalent and troubled attitude toward modern civilization and would distrust linear concepts of progress. I assumed that the majority would be fervent ecologists, that most (given the prominence of female deities) would be sympathetic to feminism and would favor decentralized and regional forms of governance. I also assumed that Neo-Pagans, critical of the society around them, would find their lives filled with contradictions that they would be trying to resolve. They would see Neo-Paganism as an alternative to much of the status quo, and even a vehicle for ultimate transformation. And finally, I assumed that the excesses of Neo-Pagans would be my own: a tendency to ludditism and to romanticizing the past.

Many of these assumptions turned out to be false, but they were natural ones to make—not only because of the philosophical influences that informed my own journey but because such views have often been central to the political movements of indigenous peoples. A journal like *Akwesasne Notes,* for example, the newspaper of the Mohawk Nation at Akwesasne in upstate New York, had always taken such a critical perspective.

Akwesasne Notes: A Voice for Natural People

Orginally *Akwesasne Notes* was a newspaper that reported on the ferment in Native American communities. Starting in 1969, with the occupation of Alcatraz by a group of Native Americans, it chronicled the development of the American Indian movement. It reported on the situation at reservations throughout North America. It described with unparalleled excellence and accuracy the occupations, arrests, trials, shootings—all facets of Native American political struggles in North America. In addition, it combined religious traditionalism and political radicalism in a unique way.

Eventually, as one editor told an interviewer, "we began to realize that it was not going to be sufficient to remove an oppressor off our backs. We had to discover something positive. We had to recreate a destroyed way of life."[4] Soon *Notes* came to embrace a viewpoint more universal than Native American traditionalism. The newspaper advertised itself as a voice for all "Natural" as well as Native people, the voice of people who were trying to live lives in tune with the natural world and the "Laws of the Creation." Many of its articles pointed out that people in North America—natives and non-natives alike—were caught up in complicated social processes that they did not understand, processes that were destroying them physically and spiritually. The newspaper took the position that Western culture was impoverished, artificial, and diseased—"a cancer." Western culture offered visible ease and convenience, but at a price that was indirect and invisible, except to those who had purified themselves by returning to a less artificial way of life. The flushing of a toilet was visible and direct; the lowering of water tables and pollution of waters was often invisible and indirect.

Many articles in *Notes* stressed a central theme: the pervasive penetration of artificiality into daily life, coupled with the loss of diversity and freedom. As one *Notes* editor remarked, after traveling around the country with the Native American group White Roots of Peace,

> We find the same things in New York and California. We find the same things in Northern Canada and Southern Florida. Everything has become standardized. Why should people on the Pacific Ocean be listening to the same music and the same commentators as people on the Atlantic? . . .
>
> Now, if people want to put all their eggs in one basket, that is their business. But when you recall that there were hundreds of native nations . . . , native languages, native systems of government, you will realize what a rich diversity there was of human culture. And of course, in nature, where there is diversity, there is the greatest richness of life and where there is conformity, such as the planting of one crop that can be wiped out by one weevil or one fire or one fungus, that is not a way for life, but something that ultimately brings death.[5]

The task at hand was to define and begin to free oneself from consumer culture. The newspaper saw itself "at war with the most destructive forces ever assembled in the history of mankind," but in "a unique position to raise the most critical questions," to voice concerns about survival that were generally unspoken.[6]

Notes did not romanticize the situation of Native Americans, as many whites tend to do. It often pictured the ancient traditions as fragmented, much like those of modern Witches. Most "Indians" were as much the victims of Western culture as most whites. But Native American traditions were seen to contain many answers to the problem of how to live a human life on the North American continent. Most important, the conditions and problems were universal problems of survival, of "being human-human beings," that other political movements had failed to address.

"Natural people" had to struggle to regain those "real ways, not in words or ceremonies, but in reality."[7]

How did one "regain those real ways"? Many articles conceded that it was almost impossible, the job of a lifetime, since most people's lives were enmeshed in a web of contradictions that clouded true perception. To take one example, an article describes the plight of a Native American farmer whose cattle are dying of chemical poisoning from the nearby Reynolds aluminum plant. Once his cattle begin to sicken, the farmer is forced to find outside work. Where can he find it? Why, at the Reynolds plant, of course, the company that is destroying his way of life. His understanding becomes clouded when he becomes thankful to get the job. "How can you fight something that you work for?" The article adds, "The monster gives you no choice. It pokes you in the eye at the same time that it fills your wallet and it destroys your garden and cattle at the same time that it offers you jobs."[8]

Another writer describes the progress of his family and neighbors during a rent strike in a large Eastern city. After a long struggle that takes up most of their energies, they win a difficult court case and possibly will soon own the building themselves. Is this a victory? The writer begins to notice the knotweed that threatens the foundations of their building. Eventually these houses will decay. His family has stopped planting lettuce in the front-yard garden because the lead from passing automobile exhausts will coat the lettuce and build up in the body of their child. What does it really mean, he asks, to fight for an artificial reality? He continues:

The folks I live with have already abandoned the more gross forms of greed and consumerism. But we have been schooled from birth to think that ownership and control are the only alternatives to weakness and failure, and those lessons remain deeply etched in our minds. What frightens us about winning this house from the landlord is that our inner desire to possess could keep us from recognizing when the time has finally come to desert it.

The writer notes that he has begun to change his perception. While he remains a political activist, he no longer feels that the overall struggle is simply between warring classes. He now believes that the issue is survival (everyone drinks the water), he admits his fear and ignorance of "the natural world to which we must head for survival," and he asks himself, Will I become so caught up in the survival struggles of the artificial world that I forget what the real issues are?[9] The idea that one must constantly strive to attain clarity on these issues was a constant theme in *Akwesasne Notes*. Rarihokwats, editor of the paper until 1977, told an interviewer:

A person in this culture may be very sympathetic and outwardly moral. They would never consciously hurt a human being. They may feel very bad about native people. Yet, just by the flick of a switch that turns on their air conditioner, they may cause native people in James Bay or Black Mesa to be moved off their land in order to produce the power that is turned on. . . .[10]

Although it should be clear to readers of this book that modern Witches are creating their traditions from fragments, using past sources for inspiration but mixing them with modern creativity, many whites tend to assume that most Native Americans, in contrast, possess *complete* traditions. *Notes* showed Native Americans in a similar struggle to revive natural religions that have been suppressed over centuries. The position of many Native Americans did not seem so far removed from that of modern-day European descendants of the ancient Celts, although it can be argued that more of the ancient traditions survived on the American continent, since the arrival of Christianity here was a more recent event.

Several articles in *Notes* underscored the idea that there was a non-exploitative European heritage, embodied, one article noted, in "the old tribal/peasant heritage of Europe (still not absolutely corrupted, even today),"[11] Many Neo-Pagans were searching in that "old tribal/peasant heritage" for their cultural roots. In this they were much like Native Americans who newly adopted traditionalist values. After all, as Leo Martello remarked on many occasions, "If you go far enough back, all of our pre-Judeo-Christian or Muslim ancestors were Pagans."

It is striking how many of the *religious* values expressed in *Akwesasne Notes* were similar to the ideas of many Neo-Pagans. For example, in an article called "The Non-Progressive Great Spirit" a writer observed:

> Our entire existence is of reverence. Our rituals renew the sacred harmony within us. Our every act—eating, sleeping, breathing, making love—is a ceremony reaffirming our dependence on Mother Earth and our kinship with her every child. Unlike Christians, who dichotomize the spiritual and the physical, put religion in its compartment, and call the physical world evil and a mere preparation for a world to come, we recognize the "spiritual" and the "physical" as one—without Westerners' dichotomies between God and humankind, God and nature, nature and humankind, we are close and intimate and warm with Mother Earth and the Great Spirit. Unlike Christian belief, which claims that our species is both inherently evil and the divinely ordained ruler of Earth, we know that, being of our sacred Mother Earth, we are sacred.[12]

This statement is close to words I heard over and over again from Neo-Pagans.

But on matters that were *not* connected with religious values, most Neo-Pagans had fundamental differences with most of the positions taken in *Akwesasne Notes*. Many articles in *Notes* rejected much of Western technology, viewing it as "extractive" and therefore exploitative and disharmonious.[13] Neo-Pagans, in contrast, often expressed positive feelings toward modern technology, and almost everyone I talked to had astonishingly positive attitudes toward science, the scientific method, and Western modes of thinking.

Working and Living in the World

Susan Roberts, in her book *Witches U.S.A.,* stated that Witches "are mostly middle-class Americans who, on the surface, live quietly and unobtrusively in the mainstream of American life." But, she said, privately they are nonconformists. They defy categorizing and "can never be measured with any degree of accuracy." Publicly, "most witches . . . appear to the world to be conventional men and women. They fit themselves into society as comfortably as they can." Roberts said that all Witches do share one trait—they have never lost the simple wonder and curiosity of small children. She also concluded that most Witches were not religious rebels; that is, they did not come to the Craft out of a rejection of a previous religious upbringing.[14]

In my interviews with all types of Neo-Pagans, including Witches, two statements of Roberts rang completely true: they defy categorizing, and they maintain a childlike wonder at the world. I found many religious rebels, and many who had made peace with their religious past. I found former Catholics who still took communion and others who had harsh words for all organized religion. I found every conceivable lifestyle, occupation, and financial position, and I found remarkably diverse political viewpoints.

But when asked, Neo-Pagans were adamant in insisting that they were "different" although often the differences were subtle and hard to express. "What *are* the common traits of Pagans?" I asked. The answers I received included, again, that sense of childlike wonder, acceptance of life and death, attunement to the rhythms of nature, sense of humor, lack of guilt-ridden feelings about oneself and about the body and sexuality, genuine honesty, and unwillingness or inability to play social games.

"We tend to include people who seem to be in touch with the essence of life," Alta Kelly told me as she lounged on a sofa in her house in Oakland. "Witches may be frivolous in some ways. They certainly have their problems in day-to-day living, but they have a quality of eternalness about them. They feel comfortable with living and dying, and that's something I find lacking in folks who are non-Craft."

Others told me that being a Pagan was simply a more comfortable, freer, friendlier way to be. "I can cope with loneliness and solitude, whereas most of my neighbors must surround themselves with noise," said one woman who lived in a small town. "And psychic phenomena no longer seem supernatural," she added. Feminist Witch Z Budapest told me, "Trees talk to me. My plants are telling me right now that they could use some more water. I am surrounded by my ancestors and by spirit friends. The sky kisses me. I can talk to stones, and sometimes clouds part if I ask them to."

This feeling that Pagans have a friendly relationship to the universe, that they feel a vital contact with natural forces, came home to me most forcefully when I received a letter from a friend who had visited Z's little shop in Los Angeles, The Feminist Wicca. This friend was not a Pagan. In the summer of 1977 she had walked into the shop several times out of curiosity. She wrote:

It's my reaction to that place, those people, that's got me confused. On the one hand, the teachings seem a trifle silly and the rituals seem like just words, meaningless in themselves. My rational mind argues this way for hours. But then I feel a current when I am there, a force that surrounds us. It's alive, it pulsates, it ebbs and flows like the waxing and waning of the moon. . . . I don't know what it is, and I don't know how to use it. It's like being near an electric current, very near, so near you can hear it humming and crackling, but not being able to tap into it.

I know it must be a wonderful thing to be able to use it, or open oneself to it completely, for just being aware of it makes me feel wild and excited and very much alive, more alive than at any other time in my life.

And then I remembered, at various times in my life, having this same sensation—of being on the verge of something tremendous, but never quite knowing what it was, where it was coming from, or what to do with it. Stuck without a vocabulary to describe it, as it were, it slipped away from me again and again until I thought it a thing of childhood, which I'd put behind me forever. Quite a pleasant surprise to find that not only is it still alive in me, but that others feel it too! To know that there are people who, though they speak of it in terms my rational mind rebels at, have felt it flow like me.

Others expressed it more simply. The late Alison Harlow, a computer consultant, said, "I think we're a lot more fun. We use ourselves better. We're clear in how we want to live. We play fewer games determined by other people. We are free to choose our roles and find ways to live in accordance with our feelings." She thought a minute, laughed, and added, "Paganism says I am alive and therefore I am good and the Goddess rejoices in my joy. The more I celebrate life, the happier She is, the happier I am." Still others said that becoming Pagan had allowed their imaginations to flower. A successful scientist told me, "A few weeks after I had entered the Craft, I was driving home, looking at the mountains. I said to a friend, 'Those mountains are alive. You can almost see the Indians marching through them.' My friend said, 'Wow, two months ago you would never have said a thing like that to me.'"

When *Drawing Down the Moon* came out in 1979, most Neo-Pagans were white and from middle-class backgrounds. That is still true today, but there is an enormous range of professions and lifestyles.

In the 1970s there was a great division between those who had an integrated identity and were fairly public about their beliefs while on the job and those who led separate lives, with two different sets of associates. While some found unpleasant discrepancies between their working life and their Pagan/Craft identity, others felt no sense of contradiction, and in a few cases accepted and even enjoyed the double life. What is different today is there are many more public Pagans.

Twenty-five years ago a striking number of Neo-Pagans worked in scientific and technical fields, and all felt there was absolutely no conflict between their scientific work and their belief in, or use of, magic. A doctor of physical chemistry, working at a major corporation in a high position, told me, "Science is the study of natural phenomena. Witchcraft is learning to live in this world on a natural basis. There is a lot in common. It's all one world. The energies we study in science are the same energies we work with in Witchcraft."

This chemist was the priestess of one of the most active Gardnerian covens in the United States. She is a good example of someone whose work life and religious life were totally distinct. As she described it, her life was equally divided between the two occupations. She enjoyed her professional life; she enjoyed her Craft life. "I have found no way to integrate the two, at this stage of the game," she said at one point. "I absolutely refuse to mix them," she said at another. But another priestess, referring to this woman, put it more bluntly: "Despite her Ph.D. and successful position, she lives in mortal terror that her employers will discover that she's a Witch."

I asked this scientist how her two sets of associates differed. She replied, "The Craft is a way of life. It's a way of being yourself, of feeling comfortable. You don't have to fight natural tendencies. People in the Craft appreciate you for what you are. They don't put guidelines and restrictions on you. I am constantly struck by how open and honest people in the Craft are about who they are and what they feel about things. Whereas in my mundane life as a scientist, showing your individuality is not really accepted."

Alison Harlow was, in contrast, open and public about her beliefs. I asked her if she found any contradictions between her work and her religious life.

"No," she said. "I am a systems analyst which, on one level, seems contradictory. But I feel that the work that I do is basically intellectual work. It does not put a drain on my resources of empathy, sensitivity, and magical perception. I have all of that available to me when I go about, in a sense, my "real" life of relating to people as a Witch and a priestess." She added that science and magic were simply "subjective" and "objective" sciences, and that different sets of tools were needed for each.

Ed Fitch, who has written some of the most beautiful Pagan rituals ever published—the Pagan Way rituals—composed most of them on a bus that took him to work at a military base. "Didn't you find *that* a contradiction?" I asked him.

"Not at all," he replied. He told me that in his experience some of the best Neo-Pagans were, by profession, either technocrats or in the military. And today, in the twenty-first century, there are Pagan organizations that cater specifically to people in the military.

On the other hand, the late Craft bard and priest Gwydion Pendderwen spent many years working for the Internal Revenue Service and the Department of Health, Education and Welfare. Finding such work troublesome and filled with contradictions, he finally left those jobs to live a rural life in Mendocino County. He once said to me, "You get up in the morning, go to work for eight hours a day, turning off your psyche. The hardest part for most Witches and Pagans is that they have to lead two separate lives. They are doubly victims because they have the desire to be free, but most of them do not have enough trust in themselves, or in the gods, if you will, to get out."

Aidan Kelly, of NROOGD, observed to me that the question of contradictions was often skirted by Pagans, and understandably so. "A lot of jobs in this society are life-denying. And anyone who has a strong sense of ethics is going to be faced with difficult personal problems about working in a great many jobs in this society. It's unfair to be too idealistic about this. What people generally do is compartmentalize. They set up a mental wall and refuse to look at the problem because it hurts and seems unsoluble."

Others in the movement have been less charitable. New York Witch Leo Martello, now deceased, publicly stated that any Pagan who worked for the government or the military was hypocritical. "There were no Witches in Watergate," he once wrote to me, years ago.

One issue that is often debated by Pagans is whether making money in the "magic racket" is ultimately corrupting. A machinist in St. Paul, Minnesota wrote this:

Like a lot of old-fashioned Anarchists and Communists, I'm a skilled worker who relates almost entirely to the work I do rather than to the employer I work for, and always refuse promotions that would force me to relate to the power structure.* If a significant number of my co-workers are political leftists, I'll work with them openly on various political projects, like radicalizing an existing union local, or founding one from scratch. If not, I keep my mouth shut on the job. (Not really a difficult thing to do, since my job requires me to bend over a machine at least three-quarters of the time anyway.)

I was originally trained in the biological sciences and worked in the field for a few years, but couldn't take the frustration of being forced into being an active participant in the "Rape of Nature," knowing the whole time that improvements, when they came, wouldn't come from within the field but would be entirely political. (Also, that no significant improvements will come until ecological and economic necessity forces them, probably not in my lifetime.)

So I work at reasonably well-paid working-class jobs, the sort of thing where no one questions my background much when I apply for work (either you have the skill or you don't, and if they suspect you're faking your background, they just assume you're coming off a messy divorce or a stretch in the penitentiary for some barroom brawl, like practically everyone else).

I received a lot of criticism for this from my friends, but I still think my method of making a living is what's best for me. Sure, I could make my living through "the magic racket" if I wanted to, but I saw what that

*In several interviews I was told that the person had refused a promotion for similar reasons.

did to my aunt and uncle, and I don't think it's a good idea. The same goes for trying to make a living as a professional writer—most of the writers I know don't make much money at it, work much harder than I do, and worse yet, end up compromising themselves. If you make your living by either magic or the arts, you have to go out of your way to relate to and please "straight people." The longer you do this, the harder it is to keep these conscious compromises from influencing your thinking and the development of your personality. I prefer to keep my life compartmentalized doing work that can't very easily contaminate my personality because it's essentially neutral and without meaning, either positive or negative.

But today, many more Pagans and Wiccans are making their living as clergy.

Urban or Rural?

Most Neo-Pagans live in urban areas and most, but not all, plan to stay there. "Why does Paganism grow up in cities?" I asked. "Because most *people* live in cities," was the most common reply. "Because strange ideas grow up in cities," was another. "Because books are printed there," was a third. Many of the people I questioned believed that new ideas enter through cities. Publisher Carl Weschcke put it this way: "Most covens are urban covens. As long as we're talking about a *live* religious phenomenon, it's going to occur primarily in urban areas, just because that's where people are and that's where the need is. We will not all leave the city and go back to the land. The cities will either have a healthy future or we will have to condemn ninety percent of the population to extinction."

It is clear that Weschcke differed greatly with the Feraferian vision of ten to twenty million people living in a horticultural paradise. Not all Pagans agreed with Weschcke, but his was the majority view. Today, there are more rural Pagans, but it is still a minority.

One common thread was the idea that the disadvantages of city living produced a reverence toward nature (the same idea was expressed by Fred Adams in an earlier chapter). Alison Harlow told me, "Urban Pagans feel most uprooted, most alienated from nature. Those in the country are living quietly. They don't need to talk about it. They don't know we're around. Maybe they don't need us." Another priestess, Bobby Kennedy, from Ohio, expressed a similar idea. "City dwellers," she told me, "are so isolated from nature that they need to venerate it more because it's so far away from them. Most religions, as far as I'm concerned, answer a need for something that's missing."

"Is it contradictory to celebrate a harvest festival in the city?" I asked her.

"No," she said. "We are still eating the harvest. November is the only time pomegranates come around. That's something to celebrate!"

Attitudes Toward Technology and Science

In contrast to the views expressed in *Akwesasne Notes,* and contrary to my own expectations and the assumptions of various scholars, the majority of Neo-Pagans are optimistic about the uses of science and modern technology. Furthermore, while they may take inspiration from the past, they do not want to return to it. Many, in fact, do not view the past positively at all. They were quite adamant on this point. Perhaps they reacted strongly because I expressed forcefully my own ambivalences and my surprise at their seeming complacency. My own Pagan journey had been highly colored by the writings of Theodore Roszak and Stanley Diamond and by the vast ecological literature of the early seventies. To me every "advance" seemed to have a heavy price.

Among those who felt differently was Leo Martello, who wrote from New York: "A Pagan life as currently and loosely defined is *not* a return to the mud hovel." And Lady Cybele of Madison told me, "I'm all for technology, as long as it doesn't destroy the earth in the process. I'm very happy with technological advances. I'm very happy to climb in my car and drive two hundred miles to see Pagan friends." She began to laugh and added, "It's a bummer flying my broom in the winter. Besides, modern conveniences have eliminated a lot of drudgery. Modern technology has freed up time so people can develop philosophical pursuits."

Gwydion Pendderwen, the Craft bard, said, "There is a tendency among some Pagans to want to be back in, let us say, sixth-century Wales instead of wanting a *transformed* world. Going back to sixth-century Wales is a fantasy that is dear to me. It's part of the archetypal dream. But that is all it is. Nobody really wants to go back into the past, except a bunch of space cookies. It is not modern technology that is desensitizing. It is the misuse of it that is. I would not throw out my tape recorder for a bunch of lutes. I can use both to make music."

The bluntest statement of all came from the late Herman Slater, who used to own the Magickal Childe, a New York occult shop. He wrote to me:

> The good old days were not so good. We have lost nothing. We have just taken the names of old religions and applied modern forms and ideals that would not stand up to the original barbaric worship we claim to emulate.
>
> I look to the past for some of the simplicities of life, but to the future for the realization of my ideals. I don't feel we have lost anything except the primitive trappings of the old ways.

A few people were concerned about the idea that modern technology costs a heavy price in desensitization. "We are dulled by technological overload," wrote Pagan writer Allen Greenfield, who observed that technology had "many gifts" but that our "high-energy culture was dehumanizing and alienating."

Priestess Morgan McFarland of Dallas reflected, "Our civilization has tricked us into accepting as normal or natural things that are not. We only have flashes of insight and we are no longer producing real individuals, but cookie-cutter stereotypes."

McFarland spoke also of her fear that television was destroying the "secret kingdom" of children's street games and play rituals, "the only place where *real* ritual still exists," and she told me she often felt that it was almost impossible to attain a clear perspective. "I know that I am so involved in a lifestyle filled with modern technological conveniences that I do not really know what I need and what I could do without, what Pagans really need, and what we could do without." Then, as we talked into the early hours of the morning, this priestess of three flourishing Dallas covens, a woman who struck me as one of the most perceptive coven leaders I had encountered during my travels, told me how deeply aware she was of contradictions in her own life. "The Craft is a way of life," she said softly, "but that does not mean that we live it, that I live it. It is something I strive toward."

The late Bonnie Sherlock expressed similar feelings. She was a bright, lovely, lonely woman in her forties who lived in the small town of Lander, Wyoming. Along with a small group of friends, Sherlock had published *The Medicine Wheel,* a small, sensitive Neo-Pagan journal that had never gone out to more than a hundred people. She had also presided as priestess in a coven that combined Celtic and Native American traditions. They called themselves the Delphians. A diabetic, dependent on extensive medication, she died in the fall of 1976. Her witty letters to *Green Egg* ceased, along with *The Medicine Wheel.*

Less than a year before she died we sat in her tiny, cozy house and talked. She talked about the initiation she had received, years before, into a Native American tradition. Despite her diabetes, she had gone on a three-day fast and vision quest that landed her in the hospital and nearly in the grave. Recalling the experience, she said it had been worth it. She would do it again in a minute. "I'm not in tune, always, with the life I would like to lead," she told me, pointing to her medications. She said that there was no history of diabetes in her family and called her illness "a disease of civilization," aided in its course by commercial foods, sugars, and additives. "The Craft is a way of life. It is a religion that celebrates life and love of nature. But there are times when I am not living it, when I step in and out of it."

She told me of her fantasies. They were simple. She said that she would like to be a caretaker of gardens, of temples with gardens where flowers bloomed and waters constantly flowed. It was February. The Wyoming desert lay under snow.

Despite the deep division in opinion about modern technology, almost everyone talked of the need for a return to the "primal," the unconscious, the "primitive"—but a "primitive" *within,* not a "primitive" that one *went back to.* Tony Andruzzi, a Witch of Sicilian origin and former stage magician, told me, "A Pagan is a believer in the primitive," but for him this meant a return not to the world of the primitive but to the roots of things. This did not necessarily conflict with a technologically advanced society, he said. Sitting in a room decorated with red and black velvet, Andruzzi said, "A Pagan is a believer in the values of self-survival, in literally sitting down in the swamp, knee deep in mud, and becoming a part of it, letting it become a part of one; of becoming earth, of becoming stars, of becoming a piece of something that encompasses beyond understanding a part of the spectrum of all we know.

"We have subjugated that. We have to shear away, we have to tear out the rock wall, the crypt of our social, psychological being. We need to get back to a more elemental way of being, of living with our environment. We must protect that flame from all wind or threat. We must allow the growth of that diamond chip of god within us.

"We have to get back to a more elemental way of *being,* not feeling, of *being.* I mean a living with our elements, a living with our environment instead of being superior to it."

Turning to the question of "scientific" versus "magical" thinking, almost everyone I questioned felt that there was no conflict between the two; and most would have agreed with Robert Anton Wilson's humorous saying: "Advertising, Magic and Behaviorism all say the same thing—invoke often!" But two of the most important Pagan theorists made a careful distinction between scientific research done by scientists and what they called "the religion of science" or "Scientism" or "Scientolatry."

"There is no fight between 'science' and 'magic,'" Aidan Kelly said. "But there is a fight between two different kinds of religions, one of which often falsely claims to be science." He went on:

"I remember that I first thought about this over a year ago, when the American Humanist Association came out with their manifesto against astrology. The real clue was this—the newspapers reported the manifesto as if it were a pronouncement by the American Academy of Science on the discovery of a new planet, as if this were the scientific opinion of scientists speaking as scientists. But in fact, the manifesto was the dogmatic *opinion* of members of the American Humanist Association, speaking as members of a secular religion, the major religion among intellectuals in America today.

"This religion of scientolatry is usually referred to as science. But it is not. The first two dogmas of this religion are, first, that it is not a religion at all, but a purely rational philosophy. The second dogma is that all other religions are purely superstition. And intellectuals who do not subscribe to this religion are discriminated against.

"Unfortunately, the rebellion against the spiritual poverty of sciento-latry, often ends up becoming a mistrust of science itself and a mistrust of any kind of technological development. This is a confusion. There is a great deal of wistful archaicism going on in this society, going back to the way it used to be. That is a fantasy. Science is a method, a technique. And technology is very useful. The problem is not with the tools, but with this idolatrous attitude toward science, this secular religion that denies all other aspects of being human."[15]

Another who expressed this view was Isaac Bonewits, who described himself as a "materialist" as well as an occultist, adding, "I just have a somewhat looser definition of matter than most people." Bonewits told me that he preferred to take a "practical approach" in analyzing psychic phenomena. "Reality is consensual," he said. "People define what reality is. In my personal definition of it, I include the fact that you can come up with a moderately logical explanation for everything that happens, provided that you are not hung up on using only Western logic."

What about Aidan's distinction between "science" and "scientolatry," I asked. Bonewits concurred: "Scientism is the worship of nineteenth-century science. It is also the unthinking acceptance of any statement made by any man wearing a white lab coat. That's scientism, and it's a very strong religion in America, mostly among mediocre scientists. You'll find very few topnotch ones who are scientistic in thinking. It's the second-level ones who are terrified of the occult."

This distinction was stressed over and over by Neo-Pagans. They ex-pressed anger *not* at "science" but at the "religion of science."

Despite most Pagans' positive attitudes toward science and technol-ogy, real differences have surfaced from time to time, occasionally lead-ing to open conflict between Neo-Pagan groups.

One example was an early dispute that came to be known as the Council of Themis War of 1972, perhaps the worst conflict to take place within the Neo-Pagan community. It was made worse by inaccurate reporting in several Witchcraft books.[16]

Ostensibly, the issues in the dispute were twofold. The Council of Themis was an ecumenical meeting of some twenty Neo-Pagan groups that wanted to issue statements of common purpose. The dispute revolved, on the one hand, around the drug and sexual practices in Berkeley's Psy-chedelic Venus Church and the attitudes toward animal sacrifice in an-

other group, the Hellenic Order; and, on the other hand, around uni-
lateral actions taken by two members of the Council to expel these two
groups without discussion and without the consent of all member
groups. But underlying these issues were philosophical differences on
the question of sexuality, drugs, authoritarianism, and technology.

During this dispute there was an interesting exchange of letters between Feraferia's leading lady, Svetlana Butyrin, and CAW priestess Carolyn Clark. Svetlana observed:

> I have my doubts about incorporating technology into any Pagan system;
> of course, Feraferia totally rejects modern technology and the scientific ex-
> perimental method. The only allowable science is strictly observational—
> not manipulative.

To this Carolyn Clark replied:

> . . . . even when Australopithecus picked up a stick and used it to kill
> food, he was using technology. I believe our argument is over *degree*. To
> what extent can we go with our technology and still retain eco-psychic
> equilibrium? . . . I doubt it is possible/probable to survive on Mother
> Earth without manipulating Her. Manipulation She doesn't seem to
> mind. She is, in fact, responding favorably to my manipulation of our
> back yard into an organic garden. Hurting Her is something else again.[17]

In retrospect I see that I should not have been so surprised that many
Pagans favored technology, since most of those I talked to were highly
imaginative, were avid readers of science fiction, and tended to put their
ideals and fantasies in as many future settings as past ones. My own
views began to change and adapt. I had a more receptive attitude
toward technology, science, and cities after conducting these interviews.

Ecology

As a person who had entered the Craft in part because it was "an ecological religion," when I began my research in the 1970s, I assumed that
an ecological concern would be one of the two or three unifying bonds
among all Neo-Pagans, one of the unarguable points. I confess I tended

to the position that anyone who did not feel this way either was not a "real Pagan" or was a person who had not begun to make connections between belief and daily life.

Verbally, most of those I interviewed agreed that "a reverence for the earth and nature" was a common bond between Pagans. Leo Martello wrote, "Neo-Paganism is a pre-Judeo-Christian religion of nature worshippers: spiritual ecologists." Morgan McFarland said, "A Pagan world view is one that says the Earth is the Great Mother and has been raped, pillaged, and plundered and must once again be celebrated if we are to survive. Paganism means a return to those values which see an ecologically balanced situation so that life continues and the Great Mother is venerated again. If nature disappears, all my spiritual efforts go up in smoke. Both ecology and Paganism seek a restoration of the balance of nature. If you're not into ecology, you really can't be into Paganism." Morgan's partner, at the time, Mark Roberts, was even more emphatic. "Ecology should not be an arguable point within the Craft," he said. "If our goal is seeking kinship with nature and the nature we are seeking kinship with is being poisoned, then we must become religious militants. We should be the chaplains of the ecology movement, at the least, if not in the front ranks of the fight."

Almost everyone spoke somewhat in this vein. The Ph.D. chemist told me that if there was a goal of the movement it was "the salvage of the earth." Carl Weschcke, the publisher, stated it clearly: "A Witch can't think of nature as something to be conquered. . . . Paganism is a response to the planet as a whole . . . the planet is in crisis and we must get back in tune with the natural world. We must live within nature." Finally, I asked Bonewits if there were certain positions that most Neo-Pagans and Crafters would "have to come to." "Yes," he said, "I think one would wind up being very concerned about environmental and ecological matters," although, he added wryly, "Most Neo-Pagans are too loose and liberal to be fanatic about *anything,* including their own survival!"

This comment may have been the truest of all, for despite this widespread verbal agreement there was a deep split between Pagans whose commitment to ecological principles was strong and practical, and those whose commitment was limited to a religious vision. The former often felt the latter were not living up to their commitments. The latter generally felt that no extreme measures were needed. The real difference was political—between those who believed that a complete change in lifestyle or economy or consciousness was needed, and those who felt such a change was unnecessary or undesirable or something that would evolve by itself, given time.

Quite a few spoke against any kind of militant action to save the environment. "The principles of the Craft," said one priest from the Midwest, "are more universal than environmental. The same planting, growing, ripening, harvesting, storage, and quiet period that nature goes through we go through in our own lives, even in the city. They may not be as apparent, but these same cycles are here in almost everything we do."

This coven priest then expressed to me opinions I have heard over the years from many people in the United States. "I am pulling a little ways away from ecology. The environment is constantly changing. The minute you plant a seed in the ground, you have altered the environment. It's really not a matter of man trying to rape the earth. We simply do not yet know the results of our actions and reactions. Yes, the Craft is involved in ecology, but I do not think it is a major Craft problem."

Roberta Ann Kennedy, the Craft priestess from Ohio, told me, "I see people in the Craft talking about ecology, but not living it. I believe there's a problem, but until it gets a lot worse nobody's going to do anything about it." She added, "I'm judging from my own behavior," and told me that she enjoyed her comforts and would find it hard to change her way of living. Theos, the Gardnerian priestess from Long Island, told me that she could not "recall any persons seeking membership in my coven via the ecology route."

Most of the strong statements supporting ecological militancy came from Neo-Pagans involved in groups other than Witchcraft—groups like the Church of All Worlds and Feraferia. The most militant statements came from Penny Novack, for many years a leader of Philadelphia's Pagan Way. Penny told me she found a great difference between those she labeled "Pagans" or "celebrants" and those she labeled "occultists." "Many occultists can't really plug in to the earth," she maintained. She felt the movement should involve itself heavily in ecological activities and had failed to do so because most people "did not make connections" and remained on a "pretty fantasy trip."

The world, she observed in a letter to *Earth Religion News,* needed less Witchcraft training circles and more celebrant nature worshippers. She concluded:

> Our Mother is in trouble, folks. Although the Earth and Moon will doubtless survive, the living flesh of our world biosis is endangered by mankind, by that devouring cancer which is humanity. It is up to those of us who are aware of this to turn from petty ego-trips. . . . We must join the ecologists and philosophers of the holistic universe and our native American Indian brothers and sisters in their desperate attempts to change the consciousness of all people no matter what "religion" they profess.[18]

Penny and her husband began to call themselves Judeo-Pagan Taoists. She said she was disillusioned; she felt there was little chance for a Neo-Paganism that would unite with the ecology movement. She had converted to Judaism, the religion of her husband, because, she said, she believed in tribal religions. She felt a hunger for a tribe. She had hoped the Neo-Pagan movement would provide it, but so far it had not.

So I asked Penny, "How, then, *do* you get people to relate to nature?"

And she replied, "I would trick them into going into the wilderness with me. And maybe we'd get lost. And maybe we would get cold. And perhaps we would have to trap and find herbs and learn basic things, like how you bury your shit. And by the time they got back, they would be so pissed at me they would never go anywhere with me again. But they would know the earth!"

As we sat around at the Novacks' house, relaxing, Penny pulled out a stack of *Akwesasne Notes* and pointed out articles to me. I opened one of them. It read:

> Ecology is not continuing the exploitation of the earth in a "clean way," it is the development of non-exploitative relationships with the creation. . . . Ecology will never take place without a massive reordering of the social and economic structure of the United States.[19]

The Novacks took a position that assumed the necessity of political and economic *and* religious transformation, but this was not typical of the Pagans I had encountered.

As we have seen, the Church of All Worlds and Feraferia consistently took a militant position on ecology, although they differed on the question of technology and on ultimate vision. The Church of All Worlds published many articles on the *religious* nature of all ecological activities, and articles in *Green Egg* often talked about "the murder of the planet" or "Terracide." According to one article, CAW was seeking to end the destructive course of events by engaging in various activities, by seeking to live close to nature, and by emphasizing the values of decentralism and small-village life.[20]

A number of Pagans held up to me other models of ecological sanity. Among these were the works of Murray Bookchin, the anarchist writer whose book *Our Synthetic Environment* had appeared in 1962, well before the ecology craze. Bookchin advocated a decentralized society composed of moderate-sized cities and involving a highly developed system of what we call alternate technologies—solar, wind, etc. This future would neither be a return to the past nor a "suburban accommodation to the present."[21]

Another book that Pagans thrust into my hands was Ernest Callenbach's *Ectopia,* a utopian novel that takes place in the Pacific Northwest in 1999, after northern California, Oregon, and Washington have seceded from the United States and have established an ecological stable-state system. The new society is democratic, decentralist, filled with separatist and communitarian values. New technologies (like biodegradable plastics) exist alongside certain delightful primitivisms, and a Pagan religion of tree worship is subtly alluded to but never detailed.[22]

These two works reflected some of the ideas that I came across many times in my interviews. But few of those I spoke to considered any of these models seriously. Most continued to subscribe, consciously or unconsciously, to the majority American view in these matters. The nature paradise was vision—no less, no more.

A number of scholars and writers have looked at the relationship of ecology to modern Paganism since the publication of *Drawing Down the Moon.* Regina Smith Oboler wrote a paper, "Nature Religion as a Cultural System?" which was published in an issue of *The Pomegranate.*[23] Oboler went to three large Pagan Gatherings in 2002 and 2003, as well as several smaller events. She conducted interviews, taped group discussions, and distributed a questionnaire. She wanted to analyze whether those who described their religion as a "nature religion" were more committed to environmental politics than others. Many *talked* about a link between a Pagan identity and ecological concerns. In fact, 93.5 percent of her respondents said they were sympathetic to "environmentalist political movements," and 72 percent said they were strongly sympathetic.

Oboler compared her Pagan respondents to people who were asked the same questions in a Gallup Poll, and found that, in many cases, the responses of Pagans were not so different; the main difference was a higher percentage that belonged to environmental organizations and voted or worked for candidates based on their environmental record. But looking deeper, Oboler decided many had come to these environmentalist positions *before* they became Pagans, although many saw their ecological ideals "flowing naturally from Pagan spirituality." But whether or not Paganism attracts people who are already environmentalists, it's clear from just observing recent Pagan Pride events and the growing number of Pagan nature sanctuaries that there are more Wiccans and Pagans today who believe that ecology is important to a Pagan world view than there were in the 1970s, although no one has calculated how many more. Judy Harrow, in an essay titled "If You Love Her Why Not Serve Her," which will be published in a collection: *Paganism and Ecology* in the spring of 2007,[24] interviewed six Pagans who are seriously involved in environmental issues: a geologist working on environmental restoration, an organic farmer, an environmental attorney, a custodian of an urban green space, a gardener, and a biologist/nature writer. Although their stories are anecdotal, Harrow said it was easy to find six people who had a serious ecological commitment that translated into their daily lives. When *Drawing Down the Moon* was first published, I could not have easily found six people within the community. In the 1970s many Pagans *talked* about a relationship to nature, and nature was important in ritual; but now, in the first decade of the twenty-first century, quite a few Pagans are involved in preservation efforts, permaculture, organic gardening, and ecology activism. And a number of Pagan festivals have moved from anonymous rented campsites to Pagan-owned nature sanctuaries; a couple of them are even off the grid. How large a difference this makes is not yet clear, but it is a marked change.

Politics

Differences between Pagans in regard to ecology really come down to differences in regard to "politics," although that word may seem to many Neo-Pagans a bad choice, since so many of them described themselves as "apolitical," while espousing very political views. Ed Fitch observed to me, "You find in Paganism the strangest mixture of people. You find revolutionaries and radicals. You find former army intelligence types, maybe even active CIA types. This is because they are all action-oriented. They crave something new. They crave dignity and adventure. They want to know what's just over the next physical or intellectual or emotional hill. All these people work together, thoroughly enjoy each other's company, and ignore each other's politics."

This statement holds true not only for Neo-Paganism but for other movements and groups that are bonded primarily by imagination. It holds true for science-fiction fans and for members of the Society for Creative Anachronism—the medievalist society. Among such groups *nothing* is taken for granted, politically or philosophically. Nothing is "given," and nothing is assumed as common ground. You are as likely to meet up with a monarchist as with a Marxist. The views expressed in various Pagan journals, most particularly *Green Egg,* were especially free-ranging and diverse. At the same time, they were seldom analytical or theoretical (since there was no common theory). An issue of *Green Egg* might have a long essay on the theories of Velikovsky, an article on tribal communes, a long essay on DNA, a reprint from an organization dedicated to saving the whales, an article from *Akwesasne Notes.* There was less common ground assumed in *Green Egg* than in any other publication I had ever seen.

In the 1970s, when I asked one hundred Pagans to list their political positions, the assortment was astonishing. There were old-style conservatives and liberals, a scattering of Democrats and Republicans, twenty different styles of anarchists (ranging from Ayn Randists to leftist revolutionaries), many libertarians, a couple of Marxists, and one Fascist. Despite this range, the majority were not very self-critical and many defined "politics" in a very narrow way.

"Politics" means something very different in the mainstream of American society from what it means on the fringes. The questions I asked—Are you political? do you think there is a political aspect to Paganism?—were, I saw later, badly framed. Many of those who said they were apolitical were, by another definition, highly political.

For most of America, "politics" means such things as voting, political campaigns, the actions of Congress, lobbying. Those Pagans who defined politics in this fashion—and many did—generally told me that Neo-Paganism was totally removed from politics and should remain so. The comments of Theos were typical: "I think that most of the people in my coven are not very active participants in any political movement. I suppose that they vote, but I don't find that the topic ever comes up in conversations we have. I myself owe no allegiance to any one political philosophy or party, at times abstaining from the whole scene when it turns me off."

On the other hand, most feminists, most militant ecologists, and most people who had gone through the sixties understood "politics" to be something akin to "the decisions that affect our daily lives." These people often said that Neo-Paganism was intensely political.

Most Neo-Pagans felt that their religion presented an alternative world view, but some of them said that this had nothing to do with "politics," while others felt that "politics" and "world view" were synonymous and that a change in world view implied a change in politics. Others felt there was a great distinction between "political" and "spiritual" transformation. Still others felt the two were inseparable. Again, these differences had little to do with the tradition one belonged to. Even in the Church of All Worlds, all of whose members described themselves as some sort of anarchist and believed that Neo-Paganism had a transformative mission, there were great differences in how that mission was described. And most felt it was "not political."

To give another example, many felt strongly about ecological problems. Those who felt that such problems were the result of ignorance or apathy would often tell me that ecology was of great concern to Pagans, and then say, "Paganism is apolitical." But those who felt that ecological problems were due to "the patriarchal rape-head" or "the profit motive" would often describe Paganism as very political.

If there was any clear division, it was between two groups: those who saw Neo-Paganism as a vehicle for the transformation of society through a heightened ecological or feminist consciousness, for example, as well as an avenue for personal growth; and those who merely saw the latter. Those who saw Paganism as a transformative vehicle generally tended toward the extremes, both left and right; they might be "rational anarchists" or "spiritual socialists" or, in Paul Goodman's words, "neolithic conservatives." Those who saw Neo-Paganism as simply a vehicle for individual development tended to be "moderates."

In general, one could not escape the conclusion that Neo-Paganism and the Craft are adaptable to almost any stance on politics. The differences were often extreme, but the Pagans got along well together.

Here are some examples of the range in replies of the many Pagans who disavowed all political connections:

"I don't consider myself political. I look at politics like I look at children playing with a revolver. I just hope they don't hurt themselves."

—TONY ANDRUZZI, Chicago magician and Witch

"A proper Witch response would be: The government doesn't recognize us, well that's fine, since we don't recognize the government."

—AIDAN KELLY, in a letter to *Green Egg*

"Paganism is not a threat. It can only offer, persuade, beckon, entice, enchant."

—TONY KELLY, a Pagan living in Wales

"The Craft is adaptable to every society it has been in."

—LADY CYBELE

"Politics has absolutely *nothing* to do with what's going on. It's a red herring. Any true revolution is a religious and cultural revolution, a revolution of values. The political situation is really irrelevant."

—OBERON ZELL-RAVENHEART, CAW

Of those who felt that Paganism was political, all were residents of the San Francisco Bay Area, or ardent feminists, or ecology activists, or activists on behalf of gay or civil rights. Taken together, they were perhaps one-fourth of the people I interviewed.

Caradoc, a Pagan who lived in a small house in Berkeley, had this to say:

"If one is working within the Craft as anything that is recognizable to me, one is working with a set of values which are totally at odds with the values of this society. This society has replaced the old state religions with a state-supported reality construct. If the Craft is so little different that it doesn't come up with different attitudes, viewpoints, and answers than this culture, then what good is it?

"Craft values say you are basically good. The world is holy. Your body is holy. It isn't a piece of dirt. Evil arises not from some 'force' of evil, but from a misconstrual of that which is good. The only way the Craft can be apolitical is if Craft people do not in their own lives challenge the basic assumptions of the American value system, and, in my own view, if they don't do that, they're not Witches no matter who initiated them."

Others who saw Paganism as intensely "political" came from an intellectual universe where it was assumed that all things are interconnected, that *everything* is "political." The strongest statement came from Devlin, the hereditary Witch of Irish descent, a mother, musician, and weaver. It appears in an earlier chapter.

Another person who, while not using the world "political," expressed ideas similar to Devlin's was Gwydion Pendderwen, who told me, "The Craft is a spiritual movement, a psychic development movement, and a movement based on the absolute worth of the individual as opposed to corporate principles. The principles of the Craft don't seem to allow for accommodation with the establishment. In a way, we're trying to have the same rights blacks have asked for: asking that 'Witch' like 'nigger' stop being a pejorative term."

And I must not forget the one reply to my questionnaire that stated it most simply: "Life celebration is always a threat to those bent on destruction."

These replies show that the politics of Pagans were not dependent on their "tradition," but on the community and universe to which they belonged, on their lifestyles, and the history of their interactions with the world. A Gardnerian priestess in the Bay Area might have far less in common with her counterpart in New Jersey than she would with a feminist Witch in Los Angeles. The differences within their traditions were far less important than the differences created by their lives in the world.

Politics and Ecology

By the late 1980s, many of the attitudes described in the previous pages of this chapter had changed.

In particular, there was more political activism among Pagans and a lot more concern with ecology issues than there was when *Drawing Down the Moon* was first published.

Before delving into an area as sensitive as this, it is essential to say, once again, that Pagans are a diverse, individualistic lot. There are Pagans who go camping in RV's with bags of Fritos and there are Pagans who seem to eat nothing but nuts and sprouts. Likewise, there are Pagans who voted for Ronald Reagan and George W. Bush, as well as Pagans who have put their bodies in front of military trucks. While most of the political activities of Pagans have been about peace and ecology issues, it's absolutely essential to say over and over again that the groups and individuals described below do not reflect the Pagan movement as a whole. Some people—myself included—may even wish they did, but they only represent a segment. In a 1984 editorial in *Red Garters,* the official newsletter of the New Wiccan Church, an organization of English Traditional Witches, Allyn Wolfe wrote:

A quick survey of current Pagan periodicals gives the impression that Witches are: politically liberal, or libertarian; "feminist"; anti-hierarchical; "save-the-whales"; and tolerant of homosexuality. The truth is that right-wing, nuke-the-whales, bomb-the-ruskies-back-to-the-stone-age Witches don't subscribe to such commie-faggot, nouveau-witch, anarchist bird-cage-liner. The following are just a few of the things that Witches DON'T agree on: Abortion and Birth Control; Animal Rights; Astrology; Environmentalism; Foreign Policy; Nuclear Armament; Nuclear Energy; Premarital Sex; Politics; President Reagan; Recreational Drug Use; and Vegetarianism. Believe it or not, some of the oldest branches of Wicca do not worship a Goddess! Of course you are free to argue that your fellow Witch SHOULD hold certain views, but it is ridiculous to assert that they DO hold such views. Witches are as diverse in their views as are Christians.[25]

Some Pagans were very upset with this editorial, which was published in at least four different magazines in 1985. Ann Forfreedom called it "bigoted" and "hate-filled." In her view, being anti-feminist, anti-gay, anti-ecology, and politically right-wing was simply not compatible with a Pagan or Wiccan perspective. One group of political Pagans, the Thomas Morton Alliance, even circulated a petition that said they took great exception to Wolfe's views, saying, "It is the very root of Paganism to respect *all* Her living beings," and that there could be no room for racists, sexists, nationalists, or nuclear proponents among those who were "truly Pagan." But I think Wolfe was not, himself, espousing the values above—at least not all of them—but was giving an essentially accurate picture of the true political diversity within Neo-Paganism.

With that caveat in mind, in the 1980s there was a growth of political activity, *most* of it in support of alternative, feminist, ecological, "green," or peace objectives. In 1974, at a Gnosticon festival in Minneapolis, Carl Weschcke, the head of Llewellyn Publications, led an audience in a meditation for peace and healing of the Earth. It was perhaps the most political Pagan event I had seen that year. By the 1980s this had changed. There were quite a few Pagan periodicals with a political emphasis, among them, *Pagans for Peace Newsletter, The Pipes of P.A.N. (Pagans Against Nukes), Faeire Fire, Heretics Journal Forum,* and *Reclaiming.*

Goddess rituals have taken place in the midst of demonstrations at military bases and nuclear plants. Goddess symbols were placed, rituals danced, and webs woven at Greenham Common, at the Seneca Encampment for a Future of Peace and Justice, and at similar encampments around the world. Goddess affinity groups were arrested blocking the Lawrence Livermore Laboratories again and again. Starhawk, whose books *The Spiral Dance* and *Dreaming the Dark* have perhaps reached more women and men than any other books written by a Pagan, was arrested more than twenty times. In *Dreaming the Dark* Starhawk merges the insights of coven work with lessons learned from anarchist anti-nuclear affinity groups. In addition, Starhawk and other leaders of Reclaiming have taught these ritual and leadership techniques all over the United States and Europe. Moreover, Starhawk is not the only well-known Pagan to involve herself in political action, and face arrest. Several months before his death, Gwydion Pendderwen wrote me these words in a letter, after his own arrest at Livermore:

> I spent three days in jail as a result of the blockade of Lawrence Livermore Lab. It was a very empowering experience, in which I learned that my personal power and greatest potential in healing and reaching people is in music. The brothers, on the way to arraignment, began singing, "We won't wait any longer," which I had sung in jail. They prevailed upon me to lead a chorus and sing it as my statement in court. It's in the record, with a men's chorus of 25.

In 1985, when I asked Pagans to name the most important issues, the top categories were ecology, peace issues, and religious fundamentalism. In the 1970s there wasn't much concern with peace and ecology issues. In the 1980s and 1990s, many Pagans turned their attention to issues of religious freedom. In the fall of 1985, Pagans mobilized to defeat several congressional attempts to deny them religious validity. These attempts came about after ABC aired a television special about Satanism and cult killings. The *20/20* program did not mention the word "witchcraft" even once, but several congressional leaders used this program as a springboard to take actions against Wicca as well as Satanism. Senator Jesse Helms attempted to attach a rider (Amendment 705) to the Treasury, Postal Service, and General Government Appropriations Bill for 1986. A version of this bill, with the amendment, passed the Senate. After an extensive letter-writing campaign, probably the most concerted political effort ever attempted by Pagans, a House-Senate conference committee killed the amendment.

This was the first time fundamentalists had launched an attack on the legitimacy of Wiccan organizations. The Secretary of the Treasury at the time, James Baker III, wrote in a letter to Helms, "Several organizations have been recognized as tax-exempt that espouse a system of beliefs, rituals, and practices, derived in part from pre-Christian Celtic and Welsh traditions, which they label as 'witchcraft.' We have no evidence that any of the organizations have either engaged in or promoted any illegal activity."[26] There are plenty of laws on the books to deal with crimes—and murderers should be prosecuted. But we should remember that some of the worst cult abuses—Children of God, Jim Jones, Sun Myung Moon—have been the excesses of people who considered themselves Christians, not Witches.

The Helms amendment actually tried to set out definitions of "Witchcraft" and "Satanism," and one of the definitions of "Witchcraft" was simply "the practice of sorcery." Since sorcery is defined by many as "the practice of magic," a law that would deny legitimate religious status to groups that practice sorcery could include most traditional, tribal religions as well as Voudoun and Santeria. Are healing groups practicing sorcery? Even Christian ones? It's a real black hole and it quickly makes you realize the wisdom of this country's founders when they took these kinds of issues out of the hands of the state.

Pagans were also worried for more practical reasons. The tax-exempt status given to religious groups has allowed lower postage rates so Pagan periodicals can flourish (most of them, however, are already operating at a loss). Legal recognition has also allowed a Wiccan or Pagan priest or priestess to perform legal marriages and be accepted as pastoral counselors in many states. These laws also make it easier to establish nature sanctuaries.

Sanctuaries, Legal Recognition, and Institutionalization

One very significant trend in the last twenty-five years is the growth of legally recognized Pagan religious groups—groups that have all the tax-exempt privileges and other rights of religious organizations. One has only to look at the resource section of this book under "groups" to see how true this is. Whether we are talking about COG or Circle or the Aquarian Tabernacle Church, we are often talking about groups that have made a decision to be incorporated as tax-exempt religious bodies. While the vast majority of Pagan organizations are tiny, with extremely low budgets, tax-exempt status eases the fight to obtain legal Pagan marriages, allows reduced postal rates, and makes it easier to establish nature sanctuaries.

The movement to establish Pagan/Craft sanctuaries comes out of several needs: the desire to have land where rituals can take place in privacy, the desire to have access to wilderness settings, and the desire to protect wild areas. Circle Sanctuary, Wysteria, Lothlorien, Annwfn, Camelot of the Wood, and Diana's Grove are but a few of the names of Pagan nature sanctuaries.

Most Pagan and Wiccan groups still meet in living rooms or in public parks, and in most covens you still bring food or wine, rather than give a donation. But the number of correspondence courses, Wiccan businesses, attempts to buy land, and attempts to set up a temple or seminary have increased exponentially. While much of this seems positive—the victory of Pagans to attain the rights given to all bona fide religious groups in this country—a few things seem worrisome.

One of the things that has distinguished Neo-Paganism from the many religious cults has been the strict separation of the religion from profit. In fact, one of the things that attracts many people to Neo-Paganism is that it is not primarily a religion of temples or paid clergy. "Money seldom passes from hand to hand," I wrote in one of the first paragraphs of this book. But by the late 1980s there was a raging debate within Paganism on the "money issue" and at this point there are many Pagan groups that are businesses as well as religious organizations.

In many traditions of Wicca, teaching the Craft for money has always been strictly forbidden—a violation of Craft Law. There have always been exceptions to this, from Maxine Sanders' ritual groups in England to the many correspondence courses on Witchcraft that are advertised. But these were never considered the norm, and many people looked at them askance. But now, the number of people teaching and charging for workshops on ritual and magic has increased tenfold. There is a funny saying in the Pagan movement: "The difference between Pagan and 'new age' is one decimal point." In other words, a two-day workshop in meditation by a "new age" practitioner might cost $500, while the same course given by a Pagan might cost $50. While Pagan workshops still cost only a fraction of similar "new age" seminars, there's no telling what could happen if, Goddess forbid, Paganism became really popular.

While the "Craft Laws"—writings which some argue are probably only sixty years old—forbid the taking of money, other more indigenous Pagan religions charge large fees for initiations: Santeria and

Voudoun, for example. There are beginning to be priests and priestesses within Neo-Paganism who firmly believe that a clergy should be supported, that if Paganism ever wants to develop a truly skilled clergy, there will have to be people who work at their religion all day and who do not spend most of their hours programming computers, waiting on tables, or selling books. Z Budapest asks for a tithe from women to support her work. Isaac Bonewits also believes that a clergy can function only if there is community support and funding. Often the division on this issue comes between those who work in the Craft full time and therefore need some means of livelihood and those, like myself, who work at other paying jobs in the "real world."

The greatest challenge in the next years will be defining how to walk the very fine and problematic line between the beneficial and negative aspects of institutionalization. The question comes down to: Can you support yourself through the Craft without being corrupted? The history of religions in this society doesn't offer too many good examples. The growing institutionalization of Paganism is, at this point, a fact, and there are many blessings that come with it. But it is important to remember many people come to Paganism precisely because it is fundamentally anarchistic and uninstitutionalized and because most celebrations are free of charge—just as they would be if they were happening within your own family, or tribe.

Meanwhile, many Neo-Pagans are not thinking deeply about these issues. They are fighting the more practical battles to achieve legitimacy, without exploring what that might mean farther down the road.

Twenty-First Century Paganism

Although the resource guide for *Drawing Down the Moon* was last revised in 1996–97, there has not been a serious revision of the body of the book for twenty years. During this time the Pagan movement has exploded in the United States, around the world, and on the Internet. It is still impossible to give "real" figures for the size of the Pagan and Wiccan movements in the United States. This is partly because Neo-Paganism is a decentralized movement or subculture, and there is no overarching authority that would collect such data. In addition, the U.S. census does not ask for a person's religion as, for example, the Canadian census does, so there are no government figures to work with.

There have been many attempts to estimate the size of the movement by looking at Pagan journal subscriptions, festival attendance, and census attempts by a number of Pagan groups; there have also been various estimates by scholars and writers. Danny and Lin Jorgensen and Scott Russell estimated that there were 200,000 Neo-Pagans in 1999. Helen Berger and Sarah Pike gave similar estimates in 1999 and 2001. The Covenant of the Goddess (COG) conducted an Internet poll and received more than 32,000 responses. Assuming a return of 4 percent, the Covenant of the Goddess estimated there were 768,400 Neo-Pagans.

Some people argue (see, for example, *The Encyclopedia of Modern Witchcraft and Neo-Paganism,* edited by Shelley Rabinovich and James Lewis, 2002) that the differences in those numbers can be explained by a new phenomenon: "Internet Pagans": people who have no affiliation with a specific group or coven, but have become Pagans online and associate by means of chat rooms and Internet networking organizations. James Lewis, writing an appendix in that encyclopedia, says that at the time (March 2002) there were five thousand Pagan Web sites. Having spent much too much time on the Internet during the months before this book went to press, in the winter of 2005, I can say only that there are now so many Pagan sites that there is no easy way to analyze them. Lewis has a chart in his appendix listing the Web hits and unique visitors at *The Witches' Voice* (see Resources) between 1997 and 2001. The increase has been steady and steep. In 2001, there were almost four million unique visitors, leading Lewis to believe the COG figures may even be conservative, and that most Neo-Pagans today are solitaries. If you go to the Web site www.adherents.com, which gives figures for thousands of religious groups, Paganism is listed as the nineteenth largest religion, with one million adherents worldwide. Whatever the truth of the numbers, the movement is growing larger.

Between 1982 and 1999, Larry Cornett published an *International Calendar of Pagan Events.* Between 1982 and 1996, Cornett kept precise charts of the number of Neo-Pagan festivals in the United States, and he entered them on a spreadsheet. For example, he listed 23 Neo-Pagan events lasting more than two days in 1983; and 347 such events in

1995, with a steady upward trend, a doubling about every 4.5 years. There are not only more festivals; many of the gatherings are larger. Pagan Spirit Gathering had about five hundred people attending some of its festivals in the early 1980s. When I last attended in 2005, there were almost one thousand people registered. A similar situation holds for a number of other festivals.

Why do numbers matter? Because it gives a partial answer to the question whether or not the Neo-Pagan religious movement should be taken seriously by the world. In my own view, Paganism is important because of its ideas, but if we are talking about a religion that has more members in the United States than Unitarian Universalists, Quakers, or Baha'is, that's something worth noting and studying.

Before we look at some of the other changes that are taking place in Paganism, Wicca, Heathenism, and Goddess Spirituality, I want to go back to the past for a moment.

In 1985, about six years after *Drawing Down the Moon* was published, I conducted a survey at three festivals, and published the questionnaire in one Pagan journal. Four hundred fifty questionnaires were distributed and one hundred ninety-five were returned. This was not the kind of extensive questionnaire I had used at the beginning of my research; it was mainly designed to get Pagans and Wiccans to answer a series of questions about changes in the movement that were taking place, and to weigh in on several controversies then raging. You can read the entire survey in the last two editions of *Drawing Down the Moon,* but I want to summarize the findings here as a sort of baseline before going on to what has changed over the last two decades.

Among the findings: The religious background of Pagans and Wiccans pretty much mirrored that of most Americans, with about 23 percent Catholic, 48 percent Protestant, 9 percent Jewish (somewhat bigger than the American average), 14 percent non-religious, and the rest a mix of other categories. The 1985 survey also asked what had brought them into the religion. The top categories—in order—were feminism, occultism and magic, reading interesting books, an interest in science fiction or fantasy, a feeling for nature, the Society for Creative Anachronism (SCA), the result of a religious or philosophical search, an interest in psychology, and an interest in mythology.

The survey asked about occupation. In my first survey in the 1970s, the top professions were housewife, farmer, salesperson, nurse, writer, student, and psychologist. In 1985, the top professions were, in order: (1) some kind of computer programmer, systems analyst, or software developer; (2) student; (3) secretary or clerical; (4) psychotherapist or counselor; (5) teacher or professor; (6) writer; (7) housewife.

Because of the huge number of computer professionals in contemporary Paganism at that time (16 percent of the respondents), the survey asked what relationship if any exists between a Pagan or Wiccan philosophy and an interest in computers. And because the answers were so fascinating, I am putting this part in the new edition in full.

1. Computers are like magic.

"Symbolic thinking and patterning are essential to magical thinking. Like magic, computers work in unseen ways to accomplish tasks." "Like magic, computers require a procedural and logical mind, yet sometimes defy logic." "A computer is like a sigil." "Computers often seem to be living entities." "Computers are elementals in disguise." "They are the new magic of our culture." "Pagans are beginning to view the products of the human mind as sacred; what else could possibly be sacred to a largely urban people?" "Coupled with modems, computers are the oracles of the future." "Magic is metaphorical, like programming." And my favorite: "If you learn the obscure and arcane magic words, you can force a powerful entity, whom many people fear to do your bidding."

2. Paganism is a pragmatic and practical religion.

"Scientific, sensible, reasonable people are drawn to computers; it makes sense that they would be drawn to a scientific, reasonable, sensible religion." "Witches believe if it works use it. They are pragmatic, not dinosaurs. Save the old, use the new. Computers are practical." "Logical people will not tolerate an illogical religion like Christianity, but will accept a prelogical or alogical faith."

3. Computers are simply where the jobs are these days. A number of people noted that many people who delayed their careers because of sixties activism or countercultural activities, found that when they

did decide to go to work, computers were one of the few possibilities.

"Computers were developed so people like us could earn a living," says Bonewits. "It's just a job." "Computers are the easiest way for an educated person to make a living."

4. Computers are simply the best way to communicate; they are practical tools.

"They are the networks for the new age." "They give us more time to grow, study, be creative." "They help us put out newsletters, which are Paganism's main way of communicating." "A tool for decentralization and dissemination of information."

5. Paganism provides a balance to people who are heavily involved in linear forms of reality and vice versa.

"It's a balance of left and right brain." "Computers are getting away from the earth, and Paganism is getting down to it." "Computer folk want a religion that allows them to get 'hands on' with their souls and 'debug' themselves by their own efforts. No packaged software for these 'self-programmers.' Paganism offers a spirituality that uses instrumentalities (ritual) under the control of the self." "People who work with computers are often removed from nature in their work; they turn to Paganism as a reaction to the sterility of their world." "After working with the mind and the intellect, one needs a religion of the senses, the emotions, the world."

6. Oddball people are attracted to both.

"Both attract slightly unenculturated, solitary, creative thinkers." "Both types like mental games." "It takes us less time to adapt to new ideas." "Both types distrust authority." "Both types are on the leading edge." "Pagans are playful by nature, and the computer is the most endlessly fascinating toy ever invented." "Computer people and Pagans often lack social skills and have had painful experiences with family relationships leading them to seek alternatives to 'normal' society."

There were a few people who disagreed with any attempt to find a relationship. They wrote things like: "A truly Pagan world would not have computers, but if we are oppressed by them, we have the right to fight back with them." Others said, "Neo-Pagans tend to be faddish, so are computers." "Don't be ridiculous; most Pagans are therapists or gardeners." "Educated, intelligent people have computers—they also have cars." "The only correlation is intelligence."

The 1985 survey also asked Pagans if they were public about their identity as Pagans or Witches. There was a pretty even split. Of those who responded, fifty-nine said they were public, fifty-eight were in between: "I am public, except at work," for example. Thirty-nine said they were very secretive. In the early seventies more Witches and Pagans were secretive, often by necessity. Some, like Carl Weschcke, were entirely open about their religious views. Others, like Bran and Moria, found their house stoned, or like Z, their psychic consultations considered illegal. The Frosts, of the School of Wicca, were militantly public. At one point, they lived in a small town in Salem, Missouri, and yet they sold pigs in the name of the School of Wicca. "The people who really get in trouble are the people who are semisecret; that's how rumors start. Be public," they said. "The government will defend your right to the bitter end, because that's the way we're set up in the U.S. But if you're private and secret then people will come around and burn down your barn in the middle of the night. And then who will defend you." Many more Witches are public today than ever before.

The survey asked about drug use. The majority said it was an individual choice, but most believed it was inappropriate and unnecessary. A minority talked about the importance of "sacred substances" when used properly.

The survey asked people to define "Pagan" and "Witch." All but seven considered themselves Pagans. Several people simply defined Paganism as any religion outside Judaism, Christianity, and Islam. Several others defined a Pagan as anyone who worships the old gods of any culture, but most expressed the notion that Paganism involves multiple deities and a concept that the earth is sacred. Several said Pagans based their religion on the laws of nature rather than the teachings of a "divinely" inspired individual or group. Others said that modern Neo-Paganism embodied a respect for the earth and nature's laws and a conception of deity as immanent. Many emphasized the sentience and aliveness in all nature, the importance of attunement to the earth and to lunar, solar, and seasonal cycles, as well as the need for human communities to, once again, have the experience of ecstatic celebration, rites of passage, and Mystery traditions. Others mentioned the idea of the earth as a living organism, as Gaia, and still others mentioned qualities such as life-affirming, fun-loving, non-dogmatic, flexible, pragmatic, and ecstatic.

In *Drawing Down the Moon,* I used the term Neo-Pagan to describe the broad revival, re-creation and new creation of earth religions in the United States. In the intervening years I have seen many slightly different spellings of this term: *neopagan, neo-Pagan,* and *contemporary Pagan,* a term I first heard about twenty years ago from members of the Covenant of Unitarian Universalist Pagans. I am going to stick with Neo-Pagan and Pagan because it is easier to be consistent, although I can see some arguments for neo-Pagan.

Two-thirds of those who answered the survey considered themselves Witches. Some felt the word would never be reclaimed and should even be abandoned. Others felt it was essential. We saw in an earlier part of the book that the word *witch* is a difficult word, with negative connotations not only among Christians, but also among anthropologists and most tribal peoples. Are modern Witches called *Witches* because Margaret Murray said so? Or, are they called *Witches* because those who persecuted them called them that? Or are there deep, important, archetypal reasons for modern Witches to use this word, with its notions of power, wisdom, healing, independence, and female strength? Those that defended the use of the word brought up the Inquisition and other persecutions. "The word carries a part of our past," one person said. "It would be dangerous to forget it and leave it behind." Others said that the very thing that made the word uncomfortable gave the word its importance. "The words of comfort are usually not the words of power." Or this: "For years I fought against the term *witch,*" wrote a graduate student in religious studies. "I wanted the juice without the term. Now I think Starhawk is right— the 'juice' goes with the term."

Some people liked the word because of its association with mavericks, outcasts, and the unconventional. Others liked the word because of its association with ancient healers in touch with hidden forces in nature. One woman wrote, "I like the word . . . It's on the edge." Many women said the word had simply claimed them and that there was no other word that brought together the concepts of women, solitary wisdom, isolation, healing, and power. "It feels right to say 'Witch,' right from the souls of my feet!" "It emphasizes my woman self, wild, free, and strong." "It is essential to what I am," said yet another.

Of those who expressed reservations over the term, the basic argument, expressed in many ways, was that there were so many stereotypes surrounding the word that it usually took several hours, an afternoon discussion, perhaps, to dispel them. It certainly wasn't something you could achieve in a twenty-five second sound bite. "I call myself 'Witch' in private," wrote one person, "but to do so in public invites confusion." Others said it simply didn't communicate the reality of the Pagan experience to most of the public. Haragano, an elder in the New Wiccan Church, told me, "I don't see myself as an apologist, spending my life reclaiming the word. I live my religion. Within the New Wiccan Church we identify ourselves to each other as Witches, but to the general public we are elders in our church." Laurie Cabot, often called the "official Witch of Salem," held a very different point of view. She and other Salem Witches have often said, "You can walk the streets of Salem in a black robe and pentagram and feel totally safe. That's because for years we have been on the frontlines every day as public Witches."

There is another problem. For most people, the word *Witch* means someone with magical powers—and not the kind of "power from within" that people like Starhawk are talking about. There is also the dilemma that not even everybody in the Craft means the same thing by the term *Witch*. For some, it's a specific initiatory religion, for others, like Marion Weinstein, for example, it's something they knew in their bones from the time they were a child. For still others it is something that happened to them the magical moment someone looked them in the eye and said, "Thou Art Goddess, baby . . . This is it!" There is also a controversy over whether the word *Witch* means something different than the word *Wiccan*. Some British traditionalist Witches make the claim that Wiccan only can refer to their traditions. Some writers, including M. Macha NightMare, have adopted the term "Witchen, for the beliefs of Witches as opposed to the beliefs of Wiccans." I will continue to use both terms interchangeably.

Many of those uncomfortable with the word *Witch* are more comfortable with terms such as *Pagan, Wiccan, shaman, nature religionist, earth-centered, nature spirituality,* and a bunch of other terms. But it is hard to get around the sense of the witch in its Jungian, archetypal sense; there are so many people who feel the word's connection with the hidden, primal forces of nature that often the arguments against using the word are tactical, and the arguments for using the word are spiritual, even if one can argue they are historically problematic. The arguments against the word are never quite able to counter the deep feelings expressed by those who consider the word a part of their essence. A woman named Oreithyia wrote me this letter after a discussion on the topic at a Pagan festival:

I am not a Pagan; I am a Witch. And for many, many of us, Uncle Gerald and Aunt Doreen have nothing at all to do with how or why we are Witches. Over the last ten years there have been women who have cast the circle, howled at the moon, danced the Spiral, invoked the Goddess in her myriad forms; women who have gathered together in groups of three or three hundred to celebrate the turn of the seasons; to pour handfuls of rich, brown earth over a map of nuclear waste dumps, missile silos, and power plants.

Women who have sat together, pained and fierce, calling the wind, asking Her aid, sweeping up, in great gentle swirls the dirt and degradation and fear clinging to the woman in that circle's center, the woman who, three days before, had been attacked on the mid-afternoon country roadside as she jogged along . . . the women sang the wind's song to add to their strength. It was a howl of pain, a howl of mourning. It moved and grew. It became a song of fury, an Amazon battle call, the sound of the sacred axe swung round and round to turn the tide . . . Together they called to the woman who was its center, together they forged the fury and the love that coursed through the pain, transforming what had been rendered numb back into wholeness and self-respect. What had been broken had begun to heal. The power for the healing rested where it belonged, in the person of she who must be healed.

Then Oreithyia described the rest of the ritual. The women asked that what he did would return to him threefold. "We ask for nothing beyond what is just," they said. "Only let him understand, at some time, in some way, that his actions cannot be disconnected from their results."

The ritual went on a while longer. There was tea for the woman in the center, and soft, strong arms to hold her, more than one breast to rest against. More than one set of hands to rub her back, massage her shoulders, catch her tears, and see her safely to sleep.

None of these women have ever considered what they did as arising from anything beyond the wisdom they find in their own woman's soul. They, we, have found our roots in the Great Mother Tree, looking back through our own women's heritage. We look to the Amazons of Scythia and Dahamey, we look to the names we find buried in forest and desert and ocean; names found in the ashes. Sometimes they are the names of Goddesses; sometimes they become names of Goddesses. Sometimes, the names are our own. We look, most important of all, into each other's lives. We ask ". . . what does the world look like when I sing the Goddess in my heart . . . ?" and then act, whenever we can, from that place. And it is from that place we define ourselves as Witches. Pagan is a word that some of our kin, for a variety of excellent reasons, have chosen to use. It is not the word we choose. For many of us, the word "Witch" speaks less about how we do what we do, and more about the fire inside.

The argument over language is still with us today. But looking back over that letter, twenty years later, I would argue that the word *Pagan* is as important, perhaps even more important in some ways, than the word *Witch*. The words *Pagan* and *Neo-Pagan* allow us to see modern earth religions, in all their diversity, as one growing movement—with certain values and ideas about the world. It's those values and ideas that *Drawing Down the Moon* has always emphasized.

Pagan Studies

One of the biggest changes since the last serious revision of *Drawing Down the Moon* in 1986 is the emergence of Pagan studies as a serious academic discipline. Ronald Hutton, a historian at the University of Bristol in England, and the author of a groundbreaking book on modern Paganism and Witchcraft, *Triumph of the Moon,* says "Pagan studies are now a recognized part of academic research in both the U.S. and the U.K." And, it should be added, Canada as well. In the United States, there are three journals that get much of the credit for the emergence of Pagan studies: *Iron Mountain: A Journal of Magical Religion* published many of the first scholarly articles by Pagans. Begun in 1984, the journal was published by Chas Clifton and featured articles by Aidan Kelly and Doreen Valiente and many graduate students in religion and anthropology. *Iron Mountain* lasted only two years and was absorbed into *Gnosis: A Journal of the Western Inner Traditions,* a beautifully produced journal that lasted until 2000. *Gnosis* seriously examined transformational paths in the Western religious traditions, from Jungian psychology to philosophy and comparative religion. Clifton continued to write many articles, and in 1997, Fritz Muntean started *The Pomegranate: The International Journal of Pagan Studies.* Currently edited by Chas Clifton, who teaches at Colorado State University, it is the first peer-reviewed scholarly journal devoted to Pagan studies.

How do you define Pagan studies? Fritz Muntean, now editor emeritus and reviews editor at *The Pomegranate,* defines Pagan studies as being about "modern (capital *P*) Paganism as opposed to Classical studies which would deal with historical (small *p*) paganism." He says it would be a subcategory of the study of New Religious Movements, and would include sociology of religion, the study of texts, and the study of the evolution of myth.

Clifton says in the 1980s many of the scholars who studied Paganism were outsiders who tended to be patronizing. He cites Tanya Lurhmann's *Persuasions of the Witch's Craft,* and articles by George Kirkpatrick at San Diego State University.

But Fritz Muntean notes that by the mid 1990s, many scholars of religion were attracted to studying Paganism and thought such a study important. He observed that: "Scholars of religion are interested in the study of New Religious Movements for the same reason physicists study the Big Bang. Everybody knows that whatever their own religion might now be, at one point in time it too was a New Religious Movement, and whatever scholars can learn about religions that are starting up now can, or may, be useful in understanding the processes by which the other, older religions began." Muntean says there was another reason for scholarly interest in Neo-Paganism—very few religions survive the death of their founder. But Wicca and Paganism are thriving, many decades after Gerald Gardner's death. This is also true for Mormonism, for example, and Christian Science.

Discussions of Pagan religions have always taken place at the American Academy of Religion's (AAR) annual meeting, during panels on New Religious Movements, on Religion and the Environment, on Women and Religion, and in other religious disciplines. But, starting in 1995, various researchers interested in Pagan studies began to have unofficial meetings prior to the AAR's annual convention. The next year, Clifton agreed to set up the Nature Religion (Natrel) listserve, which, he says, has been hugely important in creating an international community of scholars over the past decade. Non-official meetings before the official AAR annual convention continued for a number of years. And in 2001, there was an entire day of unofficial programming devoted to Paganism.

In 1997, the small group of scholars decided to apply to be a formal AAR program unit—a "consultation," the lowest of several grades, which lasts for three years and then is reviewed to see if it is making a worthwhile contribution. The proposal was rejected, and non-official meetings continued. That changed in 2005. The Consultation on Contemporary Pagan Studies was held at the 2005 AAR convention. The field is beginning to take off.

Pagans have also been more active in interfaith efforts, which has helped Pagans and Pagan scholars gain more respect. Selena Fox, of Circle Sanctuary, says, "Paganism has been getting positive press not only in the United States, but internationally. Part of this shift has come from Pagan participation in international interfaith conferences, including the Parliament of the World's Religions." This has led, she says, to Paganism increasingly being understood and depicted as a world religion. Muntean notes that one of the things that eased his own way into academia was that he started back to school the year after the Parliament of the World's Religions took place in Chicago. Almost all the faculty in his department had attended, and they were apparently delighted to find a genuine representative of modern Paganism among their students. From that time on, he says, Pagan speakers were welcome at many seemingly unlikely venues, including Catholic colleges and seminaries.

Besides entering academia, another significant and related development is that many Pagans have entered ministerial programs and seminaries. While it is hard to know how many have entered such programs, over the years many women, in particular, who were interested in women's spirituality entered theological institutes, including Harvard Divinity School, the Graduate Theological Union in Berkeley, and various Unitarian Universalist seminaries, like Star King in California. While some of these programs were more ministerial than academic, it is clearly another form of seeking and obtaining official credentials.

There has also been a growth in Pagan seminaries, and although they vary in quality and very few are yet accredited, that too is changing. One seminary, Cherry Hill, in Massachusetts, has begun serious professional training programs for Pagan ministers—creating courses in, for example, pastoral counseling and prison ministry.

But returning to purely academic as opposed to professional courses of training, Fritz Muntean says that many of the grassroots writers who began sending their essays to *The Pomegranate* are now working their way through graduate school. And *The Pomegranate* now has an academic publisher and is a fully peer-reviewed journal. All the writers and all the reviewers are working academics. Muntean believes the Pagans in the academy (and not everyone in Pagan studies is a practicing Pagan) are doing quite well, if you look at how young most of them still are, and the number of books being published.

British historian Ronald Hutton paints a less rosy picture of Pagan studies in England. Most departments ignore the field and Pagan studies have had little influence on disciplines like history, archeology, and literary criticism. "In Britain," he writes, academics that study Paganism are "few and found mainly in the least prestigious and well-funded institutions, and in fixed-term temporary posts." He says Pagan studies "have not managed to establish a presence as more than a marginal, and expendable, aspect of theology and religious studies." He says things are even worse in Australia.

Chas Clifton says there are no teaching jobs in Pagan studies, and that it's worse in the United States than in the United Kingdom. To begin with, he says, Christianity, Judaism, and Islam dominate the teaching of religion, followed by the study of Asian religions. Then there is the problem that no one knows how many Pagans there really are, and the U.S. census doesn't ask for religious information. The Canadian and Australian census do collect that kind of information. Thirdly, although courses in Paganism are popular at colleges, there is no perception that teaching these courses is necessary. Fourth, he argues that scholars who are writing about Paganism often made their mark in another field: Ron Hutton specialized in seventeenth-century history, for example. "We have the journal, we have conferences, we are gradually developing quite a number of books—even an introductory Pagan studies textbook," Clifton says, "but there is not yet a larger feeling that the subject matter is vitally important. 9/11 did wonders for Islamic studies," he adds wryly, "but I would not want some Witches to fly an airplane into an office building, so I suppose that we will just have to be patient and keep chipping away." But Muntean argues that many of these problems are simply due to the newness of the field, the youth of many of the scholars involved, and the problems in the United States of creating an educated citizenry.

Shamanism

When the second edition of *Drawing Down the Moon* was published in 1986, there was a new section on Shamanism. There had begun to be serious exploration of techniques of ecstasy, and some groups were even calling themselves Shamanic Wicca or Wiccan Shamanism. EarthSpirit, Circle, and other groups were using the word to describe some of their practices. Over the years, some people within Paganism had studied with Michael Harner, who created the term "core shamanism" to explain the techniques of journeying to other worlds that could be seen across many cultures.

The word *shaman* is one of those words, like *witch,* that means something different to everybody. The term itself comes from a word used by the Tungus people of Eastern Siberia. But as Michael Harner once put it, the word can be defined as a method to open a door and enter a different reality. A shaman is someone who enters an altered state of consciousness and goes on a journey in order to gather knowledge from a different reality. The knowledge depends on a deep connection with nature—with the spirits of plants and animals. The methods used to enter this altered state depend on the culture. Some cultures use drugs; more cultures use drumming and ecstatic dancing. What many Wicca traditions call the eightfold paths of power—chanting, dancing, trance, wine, and sexuality among others—is another way of talking about methods to enter altered states. As you will see in the section "Pagan Festivals Today," drumming, dancing and, in one case, exhaustion, are the main methods modern Pagans are using to access ecstatic states.

Since the second edition of *Drawing Down the Moon,* Chas Clifton has written a very useful book that explores the connections between Witchcraft and Shamanism, *Witchcraft Today: Witchcraft and Shamanism,*[27] and he notes that Mircea Eliade, in his noted book *Shamanism: Archaic Techniques of Ecstasy,* used the word "ecstasy" in its original Greek sense: to be driven out of one's senses, and he concluded that the ecstatic experience was a fundamental part of the human condition. Writes Clifton:

> Surveying many past and present cultures, Eliade assembled a definition of shamanism that is still appropriate. First of all, it is not a religion, but a technique. Shamans are not the same as priests; they may coexist with priests or even fulfill priestly functions as well as shamanic ones. A shaman is more a mystic than a priest or minister.
>
> Nor are shamans strictly medicine men/women, magicians, or healers. A shaman is not "possessed" and is not a medium or trance-channeler, a shaman may appear unconscious when working, but upon returning, the shaman can tell where he or she has gone. The shaman is not the instrument of the spirits. Traditional Shamans cure people through their trances, accompany the souls of the dead to the Otherworld and communicate with the gods.[28]

In our society, the most common encounter with ecstasy for millions of Americans today comes at rock concerts. In the 1960s, many encountered the psychedelic movement. In the 1970s and 1980s, some people encountered ecstatic experiences through Rainbow gatherings or ceremonies at the largely white Bear Tribe. Which brings up one of the problems that Clifton and others have noted. Shamans were tied into their communities, and one continuing question is: What community are modern shamans serving? In some cases, in the Pagan community, it is fairly clear. There are Pagans that are blending European Pagan symbolism—the wheel of the year, the elements, the deities with animism and ecstatic techniques. Many years ago, in an article in *Circle Network News,* Selena Fox wrote about her own path that—at the time—she called Wiccan Shamanism, but now calls Circle Craft.

I am a traveler between the world of Daily Life and the Otherworld, which is the land of Dreams, visions, and spirits. I journey into the Otherworld for a reason—to bring back healing and knowledge to apply to Daily Life, helping others, myself and the Planet. I see the Divine in all things. My friends and allies include not only humans but also plants, animals, rocks, winds, waters, fire, stars, and other life forms. I commune with the Source some people call "God" as both Mother goddess and Father god, for both aspects are necessary for the Unity.

The main focus of my Shamanic work is healing. I was called to this path as a young child in Dreams and Out-of-Body experiences, but I didn't begin my work until my adult years when I started Healing myself. To do this, I journeyed alone into the Pit of my shadow Self and came face-to-face with my problems and hang-ups; with my doubts, fears, disillusionments, rejections, angers, and hurts; with all my false self-images. Words cannot begin to express the misery, the utter despair, the powerlessness I felt during this time. Yet coming apart was essential; it enabled me to break through the barriers which I had formed and let others form in my psyche that had kept me from being one with my true Self. In the deepest Darkness, I felt the Light on my own Inner Self beginning to shine through. I focused on that Light and slowly emerged from the Pit, stronger and more integrated than ever before, and with the power to heal others as well as myself.[29]

Many have debunked Carlos Castaneda's "Don Juan" novels, which popularized shamanism for millions of people. And many have observed that throughout the New Age movement, there have been scores of people claiming to be shamans with no training, and certainly no community. Others have cried that all of this is cultural exploitation of native peoples. More than twenty years ago, Brandy Williams, in an article in the *Georgian Newsletter,* a journal of the Georgian Wiccan tradition, wrote that too many Pagans were going off to the mountains for a weekend and then making portentous statements about their visions:

> We are not Native. We do not resemble Natives. We are not any of us prepared to be shamans. How could we be? Modern Americans, Neo-Pagans among them, lack the supporting context in which shamanism functions. We have not lived in a single place for many generations. We are removed from the web of interaction with the natural world; the rhythms of our daily movements do not relate us to the earth and sky, weather, seasonal changes, sources of our food. Our language does not structure the natural world into sacred space, either in vocabulary or in categories of thought. Our grandparents did not know one another, and did not transmit to us a body of oral tradition in that language which reinforced those concepts of the sacred and prepared us for shamanic experience. Our art forms do not express those concepts or depict those experiences. We do not have shamanic role models.[30]

A few Pagans have gone even further and suggested that anyone not from a genuine tribal culture does not have the training or background. But one of the problems with this argument is that many indigenous cultures are not intact. Michael Harner has given workshops to people from tribal cultures that felt many of their own traditions and teachings had been lost and that they would gain knowledge from recent scholarship.

Moreover, as Eliade noted, shamanism is a worldwide phenomenon. Michael Harner has noted that many of the methods used by shamans are remarkably similar worldwide, whether they are used by indigenous peoples of Australia, Lapland, the Amazon Jungle, or Eastern Europe. Harner argues that the reason that cultures thousands of miles apart with different kinship structures, religious ideas, and ecological requirements developed strikingly similar shamanic techniques is that over thousands of years, through empirical trial and error, these techniques worked from culture to culture, as a means of healing, of finding lost children, of finding animals and sources of food.

Here's a mundane example. As a descendant partly of Russian Jews, experiencing a sweat lodge ceremony was a deep and extraordinary experience, but it was not entirely foreign. Going to Russian steam baths, experiencing the traditional *platzkas*—being beaten with oak leaf branches as you experience the hot steam and then are doused with ice cold water, is clearly part of the same continuum. There are plenty of ways for modern Pagans to use shamanic techniques without "stealing" the traditions of indigenous people.

While Wiccans and Pagans who are exploring shamanic paths must respect and learn from the traditions of others, and avoid the pitfalls of Western arrogance, this worldwide search is really a quest for our own lost traditions, traditions which were, way back, from all we can tell, not so very different from some of the practices of traditional cultures today. And even more important, as the Pagan community slowly evolves into a real, multigenerational community, there is more of a real basis for shamanic work.

Contacts Between Pagans and Other Spiritual Groups

Pagans have been eagerly embracing interfaith work. The Pagan presence at the Parliament of the World's Religions has increased with each international meeting, and Pagans have been involved with many other interfaith efforts. Pagans and Witches are working to be taken seriously as a world religion. They are also making connections with animist and other traditional polytheistic groups around the world.

Pagans have also connected with various Christian and Jewish denominations. There has been an important connection between Pagans and the Unitarian Universalist Association, which remains one of the only "mainstream" religious organizations where women involved with Goddess religion can enter the organized ministry. Wiccan priestesses have enrolled in Unitarian seminaries, and a number of them have graduated with ministerial credentials. Beacon Press, a publishing company that is coonnected with the UUA, has put out many women's spirituality books, including those by Starhawk and Mary Daly.

In an essay written in 1985, four months before he was to be elected president of the UUA, William F. Shultz, who later went on to head Amnesty International, wrote that there had been "a religious revolution" in the Unitarian Universalist Association, that, "to put it in symbolic terms, Ashtar, the Goddess, had been issued invitation where formerly only Lord Jehovah dared to tread." Schultz said that the Women and Religion resolutions passed by the UUA General Assemblies in 1977, 1979, and 1980 "must first be appreciated THEALOGICALLY." He said the resolutions laid the basis for a new kind of Unitarian Universalism and there were at least five implications: that religion is to be experienced, as opposed to being understood in terms of right and wrong beliefs; that the religious experience is personal and found in ordinary experience; that personal religious experience can be shared in community; that creation is a whole; that human beings are not rulers or even "stewards" of nature, but co-creators with all living things; and that from this kind of spirituality flows a commitment to peace and justice. Among the most interesting suggestions made by William Schultz was the creation of a new hymnal that would reflect feminist spirituality through words, songs, and liturgies.[31]

Since 1985 the UUA has said that its traditions are drawn from many sources. And in 1995, after a fight of several years, the UUA embraced the Pagan nature traditions by adopting a sixth source to draw from: "Spiritual teachings of Earth-centered traditions which celebrate the sacred circle of life and instruct us to live in harmony with the rhythms of nature." Although many congregations had gone through a virtual revolution in their liturgies over the last twenty-five years, much of it inspired by the feminist spirituality curriculum, Cakes for the Queen of Heaven, which went like wildfire through congregation after congregation, as well as the presence of the Covenant of Unitarian Universalist Pagans (CUUPS) in many UUA churches, the decision to approve the sixth source meant that Unitarian Universalism officially became a welcoming home for Pagans. And although there are many, many Pagans who have no use for an official base within the Unitarian Universalist Association, it has been extremely important for Pagans in many communities to have the option of an accepted place in the "mainstream" for worship and community.

One side effect of this is that although there are many CUUPS chapters active throughout the United States, there has been somewhat less energy in that organization, possibly because it is no longer so deeply needed.

Pagan Festivals—The Search for a Culture

The 1986 edition of *Drawing Down the Moon* emphasized the growth of Pagan festivals and said that these gatherings had helped create a national Pagan culture. It's important to describe this history before talking about Pagan festivals today.

When *Drawing Down the Moon* was published on Samhain 1979, the principal mode of communication was through newsletters. Finding Pagans was not easy. It took determination and luck. There was a feeling, often communicated by covens and groves, that this hard and long search was part of the growth process. When you were ready, your teacher or group would materialize. The upside of this was that when you did find a group, even if it wasn't quite the right group, you still were committed. The downside was that people were often alone and completely isolated in their search for years. And if the group they entered was inappropriate, unacceptably hierarchical, or the leaders were simply on a power trip, there was often no recourse.

I think my own search was not untypical. I came across an English Pagan journal, *The Waxing Moon,* and eventually corresponded with an English coven. But, turning to my own community, I was reduced to looking through ads in the *Village Voice.* I entered an occult shop, only to find out that it was a front for La Vey's Church of Satan. I finally saw an ad for a lecture series on Witchcraft at a Brooklyn church and visited yet another occult store, finally happening upon a Pagan study group that was linked to a Welsh tradition coven. At the time I began I did not know there were a dozen excellent Pagan newsletters. In fact, a member of this coven, hinting great mystery, told me that the newsletter *Green Egg* was an "insiders' journal" available only to advanced students. I had no idea that the United States was filled with active and creative Pagan groups.

It is still not easy to find an appropriate group, but today it is much easier to enter the Pagan community, to attend rituals and workshops, and to encounter an extraordinary number of different Pagan traditions. Some people do this without ever belonging to a coven, grove, or kindred. Their route to the Pagan community is through festivals or the Internet. As one person told me, "There are people who have searched for years. I went to a festival and met ten people who are my friends five years later. It took me four years to get invited to a ritual. At my first festival I saw four rituals in five days."

Festivals completely changed the face of the Pagan movement. It is the one most enormous and striking change that occurred between the time *Drawing Down the Moon* was published in 1979 and its second edition in 1986. Festivals created a national Pagan community, a body of nationally shared chants, dances, stories, and ritual techniques. They even led to the creation of a different type of ritual process—one that permits a large group to experience ecstatic states and a powerful sense of religious communion. And while perhaps less than 10 percent of the Pagan community went to festivals then or goes now, the importance of the information brought back to the many hundreds of small groups all over the United States, Canada, and beyond far outweighed the number of people who actually attended one or more major festivals in a given year.

There had been large gatherings before the late 1970s, but except in California almost all were indoors and at hotels. Often they were sponsored by a large organization like Llewellyn, the publishing company, which for many years put on Gnosticon and several smaller conferences. These events, which took place in Minnesota, were geared to a diverse mix of people—occultists, astrologers, magicians, Pagans, and Wiccans. Carl Weschcke, the head of Llewellyn, had always had a personal interest in the Craft, but his publishing company made its bread and butter on occultism and "new age" subjects. Most of those who attended these gatherings were more Christian than Pagan, but many Pagans—Oberon and Morning Glory Zell, Isaac Bonewits, Alison Harlow, for example—met with each other at Llewellyn events.

One of the most beautiful rituals I ever attended, the handfasting of Oberon (then Tim) and Morning Glory Zell, took place at such a festival in Minneapolis in the spring of 1974. I also remember an amazing experience at a Fall gathering, when twenty Pagans simply decided to go skinny dipping in the hotel pool sometime well after midnight; I remember it as an ecstatic event. The pool was empty. There were no hotel employees around. A sudden decision, pulling off our clothes, jumping in. The water so cool and fresh. It seemed right out of the Garden of Eden when Oberon and Morning Glory let their two pet snakes—a python and a boa constrictor—out of their cage to enjoy the pool with us. Very few people saw us, except for a tourist from India, who immediately joined us in the pool, accepting it as a natural part of American culture. (Although I think he was greatly disappointed when an orgy did not follow.) I do not think the Hyatt House Lodge was amused, however, for Llewellyn's next festival took place elsewhere. Carl Weschcke was probably not pleased either; it seemed too much of a hippie vision for his sensibilities. Its hard to know if such an event would happen today.

Another organization with a history of indoor gatherings was the Church and School of Wicca. For many years, starting in the late 1970s, they held an annual Samhain Seminar, with workshops, rituals, and guest speakers. The gatherings were primarily for the students of their correspondence school.

In California, the mid-seventies were filled with gatherings. The Pagan organization Nemeton was founded in 1972, and a year later an overnight Summer Solstice gathering was held on the land at Coeden Brith. About 150 people attended, including many in the NROOGD tradition. In the desert near Los Angeles, overnight ritual gatherings were held since 1970, starting with a small group and growing to hundreds. In the Bay area, NROOGD pioneered large public and semi-public seasonal celebrations and each fall, starting in 1968, NROOGD would present its re-creation of the Eleusinian Mysteries. For the fortunate hundred or so who attended, one could relive the Goddess Persephone's abduction and descent into the underworld as personal initiation: one could stumble into the dark cave, groping and struggling to find the way, one could eat of the pomegranate seed. NROOGD no longer holds this annual event. Other groups have held ceremonies based on the Eleusinian Mysteries, including the Zell-Ravenhearts and the Aquarian Tabernacle Church.

But all of these gatherings did not in themselves lead to the Pagan festival phenomenon. The indoor festivals were too much like ordinary conventions to create a real community feeling, and many of the outdoor festivals were geared to one group, or tradition, or school and so did little to create a broad ecumenism.

Outside of California, one of the first organizations to think about an outdoor camping festival was the Midwest Pagan Council. The Midwest Pagan Council was originally organized in 1976 among groups in the Chicago area. Most of these groups came from the same English-based Wiccan tradition, but many of them had gone their own way and there was some friction between the groups. "Our goal was uncertain," Ginny Brubaker, an organizer of many Midwest festivals, told me. "But we felt there were tensions between us and we should at least be talking to each other."

Originally, the idea may have been to celebrate one of the two summer sabbats together—Lammas or the Summer Solstice. Christa Heiden, a Pagan priestess and long-time leader in CUUPS, remembers suggesting that there be instead a special festival that would not interfere with individual coven celebrations—a Pan-Pagan festival that would celebrate unity in diversity. Ginny Brubaker remembers Dick Clark, another council member saying, "Why don't we all go camping?" So, she said, "we put some notices in a few publications and used a few of our mailing lists and lo and behold, 80 people showed up.

"In retrospect, we weren't very organized. Our campsite wasn't reserved, and we ended up with chicken for 300 people. We decided that if we ever did it again, we would do it right, and in 1978 we had 150 people."

Even at the very first Pan-Pagan festival in 1977, many things were in place. The program included lectures, workshops, a main ecumenical ritual, a mystery play, and lots of music. For a while the numbers seemed to double each year. In 1980, almost six hundred people attended Pan-Pagan 1980; up to that point it was the largest Neo-Pagan and Wiccan outdoor camping festival ever held in the United States. It was sponsored by the Midwest Pagan Council and the Covenant of the Goddess.

Other groups began organizing around the same time. The Georgian tradition started annual gatherings in Bakersfield, California. In 1978, southern Pagans in the Church of Y Tylwyth Teg organized a festival at a private retreat in the mountains of Georgia. It was called the Gathering of the Tribes. By 1979, there were beginning to be ecumenical festivals in many parts of the country, but no one really thought these gatherings would change the face of the Pagan community.

Reaction to the festivals was explosive. In 1985, there were at least fifty annual regional or national gatherings with a Pagan or Wiccan focus. In 1995 there were almost 350. Groups like the Covenant of the Goddess even published a booklet giving details on how to organize a successful festival. Why did festivals catch on? Probably most critical

was the fact that outdoor festivals established a sacred time and space—
a place apart from the mundane world, where Pagans could be themselves and meet other people who, although from a variety of traditions,
shared many of the same values. Many festival organizers have told me
that the most frequent feedback they receive is the comment "I never
knew there were other people who believed what I believe, let alone several hundred at one place. I never knew that I could come totally out of
the closet and be what I am openly." This feeling of being at home
among one's true family for the first time was probably the fundamental reason that festivals spread throughout the country. As one organizer
told me, "It's a trip to the land of faery, where for a couple of days you
can exist without worrying about the 'real' world. It seems absolutely
logical that people would come to a festival and see all this and say,
'Let's go home and make one ourselves.'"

Some things are more possible in a small group, other things in a
larger one. The small coven has an intimacy that no large tribal village
will ever share. But large gatherings have their own special energy. Certain things can happen at festivals. I remember at Pan-Pagan 1980, wit-
nessing for the first time, although people told me it had occurred the
year before, the beginning of spontaneous group ritual processes: the
leaping over bonfires, the rising and falling of ecstatic chanting and
dancing, lasting until the early morning hours. For those of us whose
previous ritual experience had been running around a small circle while
Carmina Burana played on the living room stereo, this was heady stuff.

"I remember," Ginny Brubaker told me, "I was working in a Wiccan group where you weren't even supposed to talk to people in other
groups. Going to festivals changed everything. The kind of gurudom
that tries to censor sources of information is totally destroyed by this
kind of event. You ain't going to keep 'em down on whatever your farm
is after they've seen all the possibilities. Even if you snicker at 80 percent
of the workshops and rituals, there's going to be that other 20 percent
that makes you say, 'I wonder why we don't do that.'"

Within a few years, a body of chants, songs, and techniques for
working large group rituals was known to thousands of people from
coast to coast. This knowledge has affected the conduct of small groups.
"Our coven changed," Ginny Brubaker told me. "We started using
more songs and chants in ritual. We had only done a few before and

they were very boring. Suddenly we had all this music." Since the Erisians and Discordians were making their presence known at festivals (see Chapter 11), there was a lot more humor. "Meetings became more fun, there was more playfulness. And our group got exposed to new psychic techniques like the Bach Flower remedies. Our ritual style loosened up. Our ritual garb changed."

Festival organizers had to learn new methods. When ten people are chanting in your living room and you want a moment of silence, it's very easy to make that suggestion known; when there's a group of two hundred dancing in the open air, you suddenly understand the usefulness of drums. Organizers became skilled at facilitating large rituals and at running large community meetings, adapting techniques from tribal gatherings. As years went by, the festivals developed a feeling of their own. At first people would bring a simple sign or draw a pentagram on their tent. Now the campsites often have the flavor of a country fair, with poles and banners and hand-designed flags. There was also an explosion of crafts and music, now that there was a large audience with which to share these things. At the first festivals, only the local occult bookstore sold its wares. Within a few years there were scores of jewelers, robe makers, sellers of incense, T-shirts, herbs, Pagan buttons and bumper stickers, and beautiful arts and crafts. Tapes of original music, and later CDs, proliferated. Festival concerts and variety shows got better and better.

Many people were really not prepared for the results of Pagan ecumenism and community building. At Pan-Pagan '80, groups confronted each other that had never conceived the possibility of working or being together. Sometimes there were political fireworks. For example, at the time of Pan-Pagan '80, the movement of Radical Faeries was just beginning. Several gay men came to the gathering to share their perspective. There were several gay workshops at a festival that only two years before had been unwilling to even mention a gay workshop in its brochure.

Many of the people in the Midwest Pagan Council were uncomfortable with the large and growing feminist segment of the Craft and many firmly believed that there should never be separate male and female events at a public festival. Yet at Pan-Pagan '80, Z Budapest led more than sixty women in a skyclad ritual. Many of these women came from more conservative traditions that stressed the duality of deity and the polarity of male and female energy. Many of these women were for-ever changed by their experience. Z Budapest changed as well. She had not only used men to guard the perimeter of the circle (the first time men had ever had a role in her rituals), but, as she observed later, she had spoken to more men in that weekend than she had in her entire life. In the years following, more feminist and Dianic Witches came to large ecumenical Pagan gatherings and women from the British traditions have made appearances at all-women events. During the 1980s and 1990s there was a flowering of women's and men's separate mysteries.

Some people could not accept these kinds of changes in the Pagan community. Deep differences in philosophy, politics, attitudes toward sexuality and lifestyle, even differences in class, surfaced as the festival ended and a number of groups left the Midwest Pagan Council. The next year, three different Midwest festivals occurred, one put on by the Circle, another by those remaining in the Midwest Pagan Council, and a third by a group called Epiphanes. The Pan-Pagan Festival continues today and there are many large gatherings. The Pagan Spirit Gathering, orga-nized by Circle and held in Wisconsin during the week of the Summer Solstice, has close to one thousand people. Starwood, Heartland, and PantheaCon are as big or bigger.

After the Pagan Spirit Gathering of 1980 and 1982, Circle pub-lished a booklet of reflections, essays, and poems written by some of the hundreds who had participated. Many of the things that were written could well be said about most current festivals; the booklets provide a window into the special festival realm.

The organizers spoke of creating a magical village, a special place where songs, dreams, meditations, rituals, food, ideas, work, fun, and future visions would be shared. And many who came did indeed speak of living those few days in a dream. "Each one passed through a portal, and was transformed," wrote a woman from Milwaukee. "Each one gave their quest a name, and in the fires, nightly searched. Like the grasses we were nourished there. Like the trees, learning the wind's dance, we sought our earth-bound fruition, rooted and reaching, drink-ing in the sweet rain."[32]

Another woman wrote: "To go out walking and not have the fear of ravenous glances, cat-calls, come-ons, and other unasked for responses. To feel the sun, wind, fire, and water on my naked body without feeling vulnerable to physical or psychological attack. To be able to chant and sing loudly with the power of my lungs. To dance and move with the strength of all the muscles in my body. To feel that I can be whoever I am with total acceptance and unselfconsciousness—and to have that feel as natural as breathing."[33]

A man from Chicago wrote these words: "It was twilight and there was a gentleness in the air. As I heard the distant sounds of flutes and drums, I felt a thrill of recognition, as if something I had felt fleetingly in rare moments of my life, something beautiful beyond words to describe, something I had sought for, was beckoning to me. . . . I felt the music flow throughout my body and felt grounded in the earth. . . . But it was not the music, but some feeling or energy behind it, a communion of consciousness that infused it. It was the same feeling I've had whenever I've felt closest to a vision of spiritual and social wholeness."[34]

These festivals, like many others, have certain guidelines. All participants are expected to put in work shifts at childcare, firewood gathering, gatekeeping, health care, and security. Many of the rituals are cooperatively planned. "Who could have imagined," wrote Dierdre Arthen of EarthSpirit, "that a group of 250 strangers camping together for a long weekend in the wilderness of Wisconsin could have formed a community with such a strong sense of group identity. It seemed like such an ideal. You think, 'People can't come together for such a short period and really become a unit.' What happened over that weekend was magick. From the moment we arrived, we were drawn into the feeling of it."[35]

Many people wrote about how difficult it was to return to their ordinary life. "it felt hard to adjust . . . upon my return home. I still felt so open and free. The festival has the effect of opening the doors inside me that I keep closed most of the time."[36] "I carry that Magick Village home with me in my heart," wrote another. "With the Cree Indians I sing, 'There is only beauty behind me. Only beauty is before me.' Carrying this vision of beauty in my heart changes my life. There is a new depth of my being; a new primal dimension of spirit which allows me to shake off the sophistication of the twentieth century American and to hark back."[37]

In the 1985 questionnaire, I asked Neo-Pagans about their thoughts on the impact of festivals on the community. It's only fair to say that the 195 people who answered the questionnaire are a biased sample. Most of the questionnaires were handed out at large festivals. Perhaps only 10 percent of the community goes to festivals, but over 85 percent of those who responded to the questions had been to at least one large gathering. Still, there were a number of criticisms. Some people said the festivals were elitist and that many people with nine-to-five jobs found it impossible to go. If you have a family or must travel great distances, the expenses can be high. Time is another precious commodity. Most people with regular jobs can't take five days off to commune in the woods.

One person argued that festivals give people a false sense of security and acceptance. Another said that festivals foster a certain commercialism, a concern with pretty robes and jewelry. "They focus on the socially extroverted," one complained. "There's too much lust in the dust," said another. "It's hard for the elderly and the disabled to go camping," said a third. And today some festivals are taking place in hotels and retreat centers as the Pagan population ages.

But twenty years ago the most serious critique of the festival phenomenon was that it was changing the basic structure of Pagan and Craft groups. "The coven is losing its magic," a priestess wrote to me. Covens and groves are no longer as central as the festivals and large networking organizations. Since people could enter the Pagan community through festivals and never feel the need to commit themselves to a group, festivals tended to break down the authority of coven leaders. Some of this was good, but there was a price. "At one time covens were given time and the required space to develop their own identity. They had time to seed. But now, with organized groups waiting for members, a temporarily dissatisfied student never takes the time to sort things out. They just split. The easy availability of networking prevents a student from staying and working things out." In addition, this priestess wrote, "There is a tendency to replace one hierarchy with another. The new celebrities are the authors, the musicians and the leaders of large networking organizations."

"You know," Ginny Brubaker said to me thoughtfully, "in the long run, the festival movement will be held responsible for destroying the uniqueness of traditions. Nobody is as isolated or as 'pure' as they were ten years ago. Everybody is stealing from everybody else. That's real good for the survival of our religion as a *whole,* but in another ten years no one's going to know what a Gardnerian was." Others disagreed with that prediction. The British traditions are flourishing, they said, and staying very much intact.

Most of the people who answered the questionnaire said that festivals were important because they exposed participants to new ideas, challenged assumptions, ended isolation and loneliness, reduced divisiveness among traditions and groups, renewed people's energy, provided stunning proof that unity can be achieved amid diversity, and beyond all, proved that an alternative culture was possible—even if it lasted for only a weekend or a week. As one respondent wrote: "It is absolutely crucial for our identity that we can be a part of something larger than a coven. Festivals disempower the idea, just lurking below the surface of our consciousness, that we and our goals and our visions are somehow deviant."

Haragano, a traditional Wiccan priestess, put it this way:

Pagan festivals are the meeting of the tribes. You come from different parts of the country, from different trainings, and traditions. You may have read some of the same books. You meet people from all spiritual backgrounds and all levels of spiritual growth. You see the whole spectrum of our belief and practice in a few days. Gardnerians and Dianics, Druids and Faeries, all acting like neighbors.

Everyone's finding out how much of their own beliefs they are really comfortable with. You start to discard things because they encumber your own reaching out to someone who is spiritually valuable. Perhaps you are homophobic, and suddenly the person who is making the most sense at a meeting, whose ideas pierce your heart, turns out to be gay. Or perhaps you arrive with a fear, and there are a whole bunch of workshops that strip away that fear and after dancing and worshipping you go away from the festival, having your personal demon exorcised.

These large groups come together for such a short period of time, but that's when the gods dance. We meet the Goddess and the God in everyone and in ourselves.

Pagan Festivals Today and the Future of Paganism

The number of Pagan festivals keeps growing, and the number of people who attend festivals seems to be growing as well. As I noted in an earlier chapter, festivals that had five hundred or six hundred people in the 1980s now often draw one thousand attendees. These facts alone have changed the impact of these gatherings on the movement as a whole.

At the early festivals there were few drums. Mark Rudden, whom I met at Pagan Spirit Gathering in 2005, told me he went to his first Pagan festival in 1988. At the time, he says, he remembers seeing a few frame drums—that was it. A few years later, doumbeks began to make their appearance at festivals; then, a couple of years later, some people brought Native American drums to gatherings. Then, suddenly, African djembes began to dominate, as they do today. Now, many festivals have all night bonfires and drumming circles, in many cases led by very experienced drummers.

Morwen and Jimmy Two Feathers have been facilitating drumming circles at Rites of Spring for about fifteen years. When the drumming started, says Morwen, it was a small group of people; it was even a bit exclusive. So, in 1989, she and her husband went to Dierdre and Andras Arthen, the leaders of EarthSpirit, and said, "let's have a weekend gathering where we can explore drumming, so that we can create something we can bring back to the larger community." For six years the Two Feathers led a magic drum workshop circle, exploring how drumming and fire circles could be used to raise magical energy and build community spirit. "Anyone could join and feel welcome."

> And people would begin to have ecstatic experiences and wonder what that was about, and we would say, "go to Rites of Spring and check it out," and so the Drumming circles became a gateway. When we started there were really no other drum and dance events taking place in New England. Now there are drumming events every weekend.

Many people have powerful, ecstatic experiences at these drumming circles. Some people dance all night; others drop in and out. Food and water are shared communally. Occasionally alcohol is passed around, like you might see in certain Voudoun ceremonies. Energy rises and falls throughout the night and early morning. In some of these events there is a level of spiritual connection and shamanic practice that would have been inconceivable twenty years ago.

There are some Pagans who come to festivals for the drumming circles alone, and some people see this as a downside. And since some of the festivals are now very large events, attracting nine hundred to twelve hundred people, some people can decide to connect with one part of a festival. You can come to a gathering and never attend a community ritual or meeting or workshop. Conversely, there are people who participate in the community rituals and never hike over to the bonfire circle.

David Doersch has been leading rituals at Pagan Spirit Gathering for about fifteen years. He says there is more diversity now, but it has come at a price—what he calls the secularization of the Pagan Movement.

If you came to this festival 18 years ago, there were six major rituals a week and no concerts. Every night there was a major ritual brought in from a different group from around the country. It was a wonderful study in eclectic Paganism. The Druids would do one ritual; the Covenant of the Goddess would present another; The Church of All Worlds would do a third, and so on. Most of people who came to the gathering would come to the rituals and many would stay for ecstatic dancing that would sometimes last throughout the night. Now the bonfire circle is in a different place from the main rituals, so ritual and ecstatic dancing have become separate events. As I look around, I can almost see and feel the various chakras over this valley where the gathering takes place—there is the crown, there is the root. People camp in one section or another. The people on this end all participate in the rituals, and the people at that end all participate in the bonfires. There is crossover of course, but there is a split. Some people have no idea of the community life here; they don't go to morning meetings—they come strictly for the bonfire. That is why they are here.

Orion Foxwood, an Elder in several Craft traditions and the author of *The Faery Teachings,* says he looks back at the gatherings he used to attend—those with fifty to one hundred people—with some sadness. The gatherings were a real sanctuary at that time, he says, "and the home feeling was stronger and tighter. Perhaps we were tighter because there was so much less. Perhaps now that there are so many gatherings, they are taken for granted, people don't realize how precious they were, and the struggles people went through to create them." Some argue that large festivals have less community feeling.

But Shell Skau, who has worked for Circle for many years, says that although she honors the concerns of Doersch and Foxwood, it's somewhat natural that as the movement grows and festivals get bigger that you won't have the same intimate level of community. "Some people can't handle large rituals of three hundred or five hundred people," she says. "They are just not up for that. So people pick and choose, and there is so much more choice, and isn't that phenomenal."

We may simply be seeing the price that comes with the growth of a movement. Here's another example. Songs and chants are no longer so universal. In the 1980s the festival phenomenon led to the creation of a national Pagan culture through the dissemination of chants and songs. A new chant would become popular and catch on like wildfire. A song or chant might originate on the East or West Coast, or in the Midwest, but within a year it would be all over the country. Now there are so many chants, singing groups, bands, and Pagan CDs that it is impossible for two or three chants to achieve that kind of universality. On the one hand, this represents a real flowering of art and music within Paganism and Wicca. MotherTongue, a wonderful singing group connected with EarthSpirit, is about to release a CD of its own chants. "Today," says Andras Corban Arthen, one of the members of the group, "many people at gatherings don't know our songs, and their music is often new to us." His wife, Dierdre, adds, "perhaps the number of songs was smaller then, but we all shared everything. Now there are so many Pagans creating music, art and dance, there is a much broader spectrum to choose from."

Another argument I heard at recent festivals is that community rituals have gotten much more theatrical. "It does pull people in," a man called Cygnus told me, at the 2005 Pagan Spirit Gathering, "but once you get their attention with the theatrics, then it detracts from the point of the ritual, because people see the glitz, and they don't see the spiritual work that is behind it. We are a very surface society," he adds. "We don't look behind the surface." David Doersch agrees. "There is a whole segment of the community that is here to be entertained, to watch events rather than to participate in them."

Tony Taylor, a Druid with the Henge of Keltria, puts forth a slightly different view, a bioregional notion of Paganism: Rituals look different in different parts of the country. In California, there is much more showmanship and theatrics. "When we did a ritual there," he says, "people were astounded that we asked them to participate. They had never seen that before." In New England, in contrast, participation was incredibly important. "That's really all there was." The Midwest was very inclusive; everyone had their own way of doing things. In a way, he said, "New England seems more Gardnerian, the Midwest seems more like Circle, and California more like the Zells and Starhawk."

That may be a gross oversimplification, but festivals are growing and changing. Take the phenomenon of "fire spinning," something totally unknown when I wrote about festivals in 1986. Now many festivals have fire spinners, fire breathers, flame swallowers, and other fire magicians as a regular part of rituals. And many teen Pagans have participated and learned the skills.

Besides drumming and fire spinning, there have also been some new shamanic rituals and practices. Oracular seidh and other forms of trance journeying have been demonstrated and taught at some Pagan festivals (see Chapter 9). One new ritual that has taken place at Pagan Spirit Gathering over the last six or seven years is known as The Spirit Hunt. David Doersch, who had been working in a warrior tradition, says he started The Hunt because he felt the gathering needed more male, or "yang," energy.

The Spirit Hunt is a shamanic rite that uses exhaustion as the main tool to enter an ecstatic trance state. There are three main groups in the ritual: the Hunters, who have some large issue in their life that they need to deal with (go out and hunt and kill and remove this obstacle from their life, or in some cases, they need to absorb its essence and pull it into themselves). The Hunters spend days fasting; they create a talisman, a spear that they will use in the ritual, and they decorate it. Then there are the Villagers, who are the support group. They fashion necklaces for the Hunters, provide them with food and drink at the end, and they link the Hunters back to the community. The third group is the drummers, who do very fast and loud shamanic drumming.

The ritual takes place in a special consecrated area. Doersch has written this about the hunt:

The ritual is based on the notion that each of us has within us things that we would like to extirpate from our lives, or things we perceive that we lack and wish to gain. The ritual is a profoundly personal experience, and therefore no words are spoken during the bulk of it. Only some quiet words of closure honoring the participants at the end are included. No one ever asks a Hunter what he or she Hunted or why. It is taken for granted that the work they do is sacred and should be respected.

The Hunters fast the day of the hunt, they spend time making their talisman or weapon, they mark out an area fifteen feet in diameter, which is the hunt area. When the drums begin, the Hunters run and dance and leap and do whatever they need to do to get themselves into an exhausted place, always pursuing the thing they are hunting. And when they hit that exhaustion, says Doersch,

> They then go into the far side where the magic is and they fight their personal demons. We have a hay bale—that is our effigy kill. I take one hunter at a time, and they stalk the hay bale, and they give it every ounce of their energy. And at the moment when they have reached the state they need to be in, the head of our guardians throws a bowl of red saltwater over them and says, "taste the blood of your kill," and he splashes the "blood" in their face, and they don't know it is coming, and they usually have this massive catharsis. People burst into tears. After that, the villagers come out to take care of them. They are given water, and oranges and restorative drinks like Gatorade. This last festival, we had 17 Hunters; the whole group was about 45–50 people, including the villagers and the drummers. The ritual culminates when the final hunter has come in and done his or her kill.
>
> In this last festival I remember the second to last person so well. It was a woman and she had killed the hell out of that bale of hay. She was clearly working with some intense issues, and when I went up to her, she was clearly ready. You could see it in her eyes. I found her, because each person stands by a tiki torch, and she had clearly just reached the place inside, and she was ready for her kill. It is hard to describe.

The first year the Hunt came to Pagan Spirit Gathering, there was some negative response. People apparently didn't know what to make of it. "After all," Doersch said, "this is a pretty pacifistic group," but by the next year people had calmed down. "Some people say this is the main reason they come to Pagan Spirit Gathering." Doersch describes the Hunt as "a life-changing ritual, ritual as therapy or ritual as cusp and sacred doorway."

At the same time that some festivals have experimented with these deep shamanic rituals, many gatherings have gone in the opposite direction; they have become more and more family friendly. At many festivals, both things are happening at once. There is often day care; there are special programs for children and special areas for teens. At a recent Pagan Spirit Gathering, I visited a teen discussion group that had at least twenty participants. Laura Wildman-Hanlon is a Gardnerian priestess and the author of several books on Wicca and Paganism. She is also the mother of three young children. At a recent Rites of Spring festival she was working at the day care area. "If we can retain the children," she says simply, "then we can become a religion that will alter the world; if we don't, we will go the way of the Shakers; we will be a fad and disappear."

Morwen Two Feathers said that she once thought of the Pagan Movement as something connected to "youthful exploration, adventure, and fun," but as years went by, she started thinking about transmitting her values to a new generation.

It became more about looking at the culture in which we were raising our children. What kind of world did we want them to inherit? And when you looked around, the world—as it was—it was not something we felt great about passing on to our kids. The difference between now and fifteen years ago is that now it seems more than a movement; it feels like it has its roots down deep enough that it really is a "subculture," and one with staying power. A place where the kids, when they become teens, won't immediately split. They want to be here, and take responsibility for being in the community.

Laura Wildman-Hanlon has begun conducting interviews for a study of second generation Pagans. She says that most of the teens she has interviewed say they enjoy the community, the values, the love of the planet, the connection to people, and that they plan to pass these values on to their children. On the other hand, she says, many of them say they did not receive much religious education, and they often resent it. "Sometimes they were invited into circles and were expected to understand what was going on by osmosis. Often there was little instruction or discussion at home." Wildman-Hanlon said she often heard things like "I wish that at Yule, or Imbolc, my family would get together and explain things, just like the parents of my friends who celebrate Christmas do." Of course, not all Christian families impart that kind of information either.

Wildman-Hanlon says that Pagans now have so many children (according to one census within the Pagan community, more than 40 percent of Pagans have children) that the community needs to create a sense of stability for them, and it needs to alter rituals to include them. Wildman-Hanlon says she has seen the growth of two very different types of Pagan communities. One—the festival Pagan community—is very eclectic, and open to children. Then you have what she calls the "adult section": the Mystery religions and the Wiccan, shamanic, Druid, and family traditions, which most children do not participate in, "since they are not usually considered old enough to understand the mysteries."

David Doersch says he worries a bit that as Pagans have "matured" and gatherings have become more receptive to families, the festivals have been "tamed down." Yes, he admits, there is more maturity and less freakyness. Many people seem psychologically healthier. When I tell him that I actually heard the term "high functioning Pagans," at a recent festival, referring to the fact that there are now many people in the community who lead successful lives in the mundane world, he said all that is true, and yet he worries.

Take this Pagan Spirit Gathering (2005). Ten or fifteen years ago it was not unusual to find a workshop on sex rites or some other esoteric and less publicly acceptable topic. That stuff has all gone away; it is all peace, light, and harmony now, and "what will the mainstream think?" When I began there were something like three books on the market, and you had to really search for the gems—as if you were on a treasure hunt. But if you really wanted it, you found it. Now people go into Barnes & Noble and there are shelves of books—most of them crap. I guess the bottom line is that I worry about us losing the fire at the core of it all. If we lose that fire, that sense of rebellion at the root, then we are facing the protestantizing, or the secularization of Wicca. I don't want to be offensive, but we have got to have the fire.

Another person who has been observing the "maturing" of Paganism is Kirk White, the president and dean of Cherry Hill Seminary, a New England institution that trains Pagans in the skills of ministry. "There is greater public awareness of Paganism, now," he says. "That is the good side; on the other hand, you get people who no longer hold the distinct values that make us Pagan." White says that originally many people came to Paganism as part of a rebellion against the establishment, but subsequent generations "don't carry those ideas with them. They are asking: How do we become part of the power structure? How do we gain institutional recognition?" On the other hand, some of this, he believes, is simply the aging of the population.

> When the movement started, many people were in their twenties, and as they got to marrying age, many of the rituals were about marriage. Now we are talking about funeral rites. Originally, most Pagan festivals were rustic camping affairs, now many of the gatherings on the West Coast are in conference centers because people are getting older and they don't want to sit on the grass anymore.

Ellen Evert Hopman, cofounder of the Order of the White Oak, a Druid order, says that not only is the movement a lot bigger, "there is a real attempt," she says, "to become a mature religion," and to take up issues that other religions have always emphasized, but until now, Pagans have not:

> When people came to America without a penny in their pockets, the first thing they would do is build a church or temple. It was a priority. Then they would build charities, social supports, and old age homes. We have to begin thinking along those lines. Let's face it, old age is a reality, my knees are going.

At recent festivals there have been workshops that have discussed Pagan funeral rites, nursing homes, and assisted living situations, all subjects that would never have been broached ten or twenty years ago.

Hopman says one of her students is a Druid who is presently on active duty in Iraq. She and many others have been working to get Pagan symbols like the Pentacle and Awen, the Druid symbol with three lines, recognized as official religious symbols that can be used on the tombstones of Pagan veterans. There has recently been a serious effort by groups such as Circle and the Aquarian Tabernacle Church as well as the families of several soldiers who have died in Iraq and Afghanistan to have these symbols recognized. Letters have been cordial, but so far nothing has changed. But most attempts to get Paganism recognized happen under the radar; they do not reach the news media. For example, after a seven-year battle, Selena Fox of Circle won the right for Wiccan prisoners at all seven Wisconsin prisons to wear the Pentacle as a religious symbol. It can be worn under clothes or out in the open during ceremonies.

Pagans and Wiccans have become chaplains in prisons and have helped people in the military. There is one Wiccan tradition (Greencraft) that includes many military people, perhaps most of its members. Other Pagans are beginning to form serious charities. This movement is just beginning, but there is already a homeless shelter run by Pagans, as well as a program for learning disabled kids. There are Pagan AA groups, and there are now several charitable organizations that have raised money during recent disasters like Hurricane Katrina. Many Pagan festivals and Pagan Pride events now have a charitable component, with food and money collected as a regular part of the event. Pagans participate in local highway beautification efforts. These efforts are still in their infancy, and some Pagans ask, "Where is our equivalent of Lutheran social services? The Unitarian Universalists have their Owl program for youth sexuality; where's ours?"

Shell Skau finds this "maturing of the Pagan movement" all to the good. As someone who has been involved with Circle for about seven years, and with Paganism for about ten, she tends to lump people into two categories: what she calls, with a bit of a laugh, "fluff bunny Pagans, you know—the people called bright-moon-cloud-feather-joy and so forth." But then, she says, there is this "other group that is really trying to connect the real world to our spiritual world." This second group, she says, is joining the PTA, trying to get on the city council, doing chaplain work in hospitals and prisons, and being involved in the community:

It is important to say I am Pagan and religious freedom is important to me, but you don't have to wear it on your sleeve. It's not, "I am Pagan and my name is Shell; it's my name is Shell and I have this big huge life, and being Pagan is a big part of that life." The people who are in this second category are the movers and shakers, fighting the good fight, making the differences that are necessary.

But Andras Corban Arthen of EarthSpirit says while there may be plenty of good reasons to mainstream Paganism, he personally believes it would be better to "paganize" mainstream society. "Look," he says. "In indigenous cultures there is no word for religion. Religions don't exist as separate from everyday life. If you have a religion, but you don't have a real culture, you are left with American culture—a culture that, let's face it, destroyed Paganism." Andras notes the tension between being a countercultural movement and being part of the mainstream. He says the mainstream culture is one that has separated us from the natural world, and the separation is so pervasive that "we have gotten used to thinking it is normal." He believes it's more important to create "our own culture to support our religion and spiritual beliefs," and Pagan festivals become a laboratory to do that:

When we are in an intentional community, when we are in nature, we learn that everything affects everything else. Even in the hunting of one species by another, there is cooperation. We are one of the only spiritual groups in the world that can honestly say that our original founders are still alive in the world because the people who taught our spiritual ancestors going back as far as we know, those teachers were not human beings—they were mountains, they were forests, they were lakes and springs; they were the land and they were the animals. And as long as they are still there, we still have that—as long as we develop a culture that will listen to them, and not support the separation that we find in our everyday life. We live in a competitive society, but the festivals are an ideal place to confront these issues, to put forward another model, where we can learn cooperation and interdependence.

And there have been developments in these directions. Many more Pagan festivals have permanent sites at nature sanctuaries, like Wysteria, Four Quarters Farm, or Lothlorien. Larry Cornett notes that there are many more seasonal camps where people come not for just a weekend or week but for a whole summer, or for all their weekends during warm weather. Some of these campsites become an ongoing Pagan community. Some of these are off the grid.

As I said earlier, the festival phenomenon changed many aspects of Paganism—it brought community to the fore and lessened the power of the coven. But Dierdre Arthen of EarthSpirit says there are now new developments. There is a movement away from the predominance of the coven to a local community structure.

> There are still small working groups, of course, but there are also lots of groups that get together once a month, perhaps on the full moon, that are community groups or drumming groups, or chanting groups, that are not based on the same coven structure that was the basis of Paganism when you were first writing.

In other words, it used to be that Wicca was once the doorway to a larger Pagan community; now it may be the reverse. Now the larger Pagan community is often the doorway, and then people sometimes go from that community to smaller, more intense working groups; for example, a coven working with a specific Mystery tradition, or a Druid grove or Heathen kindred. And while many of the most selective, initiatory traditions have gotten stronger, the coven is often no longer a person's first doorway into Paganism. For example, when I started out, I joined a Pagan-way group and an outer-court training coven that happened to be near me. It was a Welsh tradition. At the time there were no festivals to go to, nor an Internet to search. If there had been, I might have gone in a different direction. I might have eventually found a group practicing a revival of ancient Greek Paganism—since that was the mythology I resonated with as a child. Today, many people come into Paganism and Wicca through reading, through the Internet, through festivals, and then later make a choice to go deeper into a particular grove, kindred, or coven.

Here's another big difference from twenty or thirty years ago. It used to be common to say that Wicca and much of Paganism was a religion without a laity. In most initiatory Wiccan traditions, you become a priestess or priest and Witch after a year and a day of training. In most traditions after three years of training you can lead your own group. It is in many ways a religion of equals, at least in potential. But now, with the emergence of larger community groups, you suddenly have people who are acting as full-time Pagan clergy, ministering to a larger community. People like Andras and Dierdre Arthen of EarthSpirit, or Selena Fox and Dennis Carpenter of Circle, or Starhawk, are, in fact, operating as clergy in a way that is much more typical of other religions but was seldom true of the Craft. And there are now Pagans who do not want to be priests and priestesses and who are in fact a kind of congregation. Whether or not this is positive or negative, it is a fact.

This also means that some of the people coming into Paganism are being trained by larger community organizations, as opposed to covens. Jerrie Hildebrand has been working some twenty years in the Pagan movement. She has worked for Circle, for CUUPS, for EarthSpirit, and several other larger organizations. She notes that *her* Pagan upbringing, so to speak, was never coven based. She served on the boards of trustees of large organizations. But she sees these trends as positive. She told me, "People used to talk about community, but it wasn't really community— it was five or six people sitting around talking, or doing worship." Now, she says, "there is a trend away from the individual, toward more communitarian aspects. In some ways, we are finally getting to the real idea of tribalism."

> We have always said we were tribal and our roots were pre-Christian. We talked the talk, but we didn't walk the walk. And now, we are doing both. The larger organizations are really communities of smaller tribes; there is much more diversity as well.

A number of people told me, "Let us think of ourselves as a clan of tribes rather than being a unified Pagan nation."

Orion Foxwood doesn't talk about "tribalism"; he talks about "culture." "Twenty years ago we didn't think of ourselves as a culture," he said. "We were Pagans and Druids who did our thing, and we felt a sense of camaraderie because we were all oppressed and scared to be public and we could be weird together. Now there is an actual Pagan culture emerging and there are generations of children and parents who have grown up together, going to certain gatherings." Foxwood goes further:

> Before, there was more of a distinction between different types of Pagans. The Gardnerians were over there and the Druids over here, and Native American and Voudoun people were over there. Now I am noticing that much of that is fading away; there is more of a sense that we are all Earth Religionists. And that bodes well for us; that is healthy. When I think about Gerald Gardner and Alex Sanders—they brought Wicca together, but I bet they never knew that they were going to start a world movement— that they were actually opening the door to the entire Earth Religions movement.

Among those who expressed happiness at the growing maturity of the movement, a number of people said they were worried that the deeply ingrained anti-authoritarianism and distrust of hierarchy among so many Pagans had led to a basic distrust of teachers in general, and therefore a lack of respect for elders. Andras asks:

> How do we take care of our elders? I see people getting burned out, who step down and leave active involvement. I know many people who have passed on, and most Pagans have no idea who they were. I don't think we have begun to address those issues. I also think we have to get back to the question you posed at the end of the last edition of your book: Is this movement something that has legs; that will survive? That will go on for generations, or is it something that people do for a stage of their lives and then drop it. That is the crucial question for us to be asking.

Jerrie Hildebrand says she's spent much of her energy working in interfaith areas—fighting for Pagan religious freedoms. She echoes what I heard from many: There are now more Pagans than UUs or Quakers, and yet those groups "are seen as mainstream religions and we are not. We are still considered the odd ones, the ones whose liberties are toyed with, who fight custody battles and town prayer suits." Given the growth of the Pagan movement, the problem is no longer being a minority religion. She says it's about being unorganized. "Part of the problem," Hildebrand says, "is this illusion that we are anarchistic." "Well," I say to her, "I confess that's partly how I got here; I wanted an anarchistic religion with few dogmas." She counters: "But now our very survival hinges on being a real community, being organized—only that way will we secure our freedoms." "What kind of an organizational structure do you see?" I asked. "All I am saying," she said, "is we have strong organizations that have been doing the work, EarthSpirit, COG, Circle, Lady Liberty League. We don't have to reinvent the wheel, we just have to support those who have been doing the work and have put structures in place."

Orion Foxwood says there are several signs that the Nature Religions movement is gaining depth—and one of those signs is a concern for one's ancestors. "We have ancestors, we have elders, and we are beginning to have roots," he says. One thing he has noticed is that people are now looking to their own ancestral and cultural roots; there is much less appropriation of other cultures:

> Sometimes I think the whole movement has been in Wicca 101, almost as if the spirits or the gods said, "Let's ease the culture into it." For example, there is now much more direct contact with the spirit world. And Paganism is becoming more and more like traditional Witchcraft. For example, last night, everyone is around the fire, and going to these ecstatic places, and calling to the spirit world. And people are being fed, and watching the food and alcohol going around the circle, it was almost like white Voudoun, and you notice that more and more Voudoun and Native American folk are beginning to come to these gatherings, and they are saying, "These folks are beginning to do something." I was talking to a Wampanog who was here at the festival, and he said, "You don't know it, but you are defining your tribal tradition for the generations to come. Fifty years from now what you are doing will be traditions."

Foxwood tells his students to get exposed to other cultures—to Voudoun or Native American traditions, *not for the content,* he says; that would be cultural appropriation, but for the *taste*—how does a tradition feel when it is practiced within a culture. Bring that taste into your own magical work, he says:

> Real spiritual work is not fluff bunny stuff, it often means changing how you think, changing how you live, how you eat. And one of our real chal-

lenges is to acknowledge we have elders and listen to them. Real tribal cultures look at us, and I will tell you what one tribal elder, a Voudoun priest once told me. He said, "I am not interested in the white boys Pagan movement. Until they value their elders there must not be anything important there, so why should I waste my time." But I am beginning to notice that elders *are* being acknowledged, and it bodes well—because when you care for the roots, you care for the tree.

But at the same time that there is this growing sense of rootedness and maturity within Paganism, the movement is exploding on the Internet, bringing about a whole new set of concerns.

If you want a quick way to experience Wicca or Paganism on the Internet, there is a little program known as Stumble.com. You pick a topic out of some five hundred categories, you click, and it randomly takes you to one of the favored sites in the category. You could choose cars or wine, but you can also choose Paganism or Wicca. I chose Wicca and wandered to some forty or fifty different sites during a couple of hours. No site repeated during this process, and I only recognized one of the sites from ever seeing it before.

I noted previously that in 2002, James Lewis, in an appendix to *The Encyclopedia of Modern Witchcraft and Neo-Paganism,* said there were more than five thousand Pagan sites on the internet, and that the explosion of Paganism on the net had created a large group of "Internet Pagans," people who came to Paganism through the Internet, joined chat groups, and maintained their solitary status. In other words, they didn't join covens or other Pagan groups except in cyberspace. This, he said, was changing the nature of Paganism.

There have always been solitary Pagans. You don't need the Internet for that. In the last twenty years many books have been published, both in England and the United States, that cater to the solitary Witch or Pagan, from Scott Cunningham's *Wicca for the Solitary Practitioner,* to Marion Green's *A Witch Alone.* But the Internet has made the growth of solitary Pagans a much larger phenomenon.

Some aspects of Paganism and the Internet are very exciting— increased networking, scholarship, and an end to isolation for many. There has also been the development of new ritual forms—in cyberspace. You might think that strange, or even impossible, but one of the cyber rituals I attended was deeply moving, and there *seemed to be* a sense of community that went beyond time and space.

But Andras Corban Arthen of EarthSpirit says he has mixed feelings about the Internet. "A lot of people on the net," he says, "are not connected with other Pagans except through virtual interactions; that can't help but create more superficiality." At the very same time that all these people are encountering Paganism on the Internet, he says, there are people involved with the Pagan community that have been around for thirty and forty years. They have raised families—there are third generation Pagans:

> So, on the one hand there is a new sense of Pagans becoming multigenerational, and creating serious roots and stability, at the same time that a whole new influx of Pagans are entering the movement through the Internet. So there is a new deepening and a new superficiality at the same time.

Andras's wife, Dierdre Arthen, a priestess of EarthSpirit added:

> It is tempting to connect through the Internet, but to never sit down and hold hands, and touch the spirit of another—to never see the body language. As people connect to lists, they think that is where they *live,* but they don't really live there. There are so many Pagans who have never been to a gathering; they have never seen a real teacher teach; they have never sat down with an elder in the community to listen to what they have learned in thirty or forty years. There are people coming into the community who have never seen a fifty-year-old or sixty-year-old Witch. And it is sharing that kind of knowledge that will help us deepen as a community.

On Winter Solstice 2005, Selena Fox of Circle put out her wish list for Paganism in the twenty-first century. Here are a few of them:

- Paganism growing as a World Religion—increased awareness by Pagans that they are part of a multifaceted global community; increased awareness of Paganism in the world and in the field of religious studies; increased contact between traditional animists and contemporary Pagans.

- Pagan studies—increased numbers of courses and departments at institutions of higher learning. More understanding and respect for Pagan world views. Attention to this in health care and counseling situations.

- Pagan chaplains—More full-time, part-time, and volunteer Pagan chaplains working in hospitals, birthing centers, hospices, the military, prisons, emergency services, and other institutions. An increase in training programs within Paganism that train people for this kind of work.

- Pagans in politics—Pagans as elected representatives, Pagans in both major parties in the United States as well as in a variety of political parties in countries around the world; Pagans being able to run for office without their religion being a liability.

- Increased numbers of Pagans who are in the world as authors, musicians, scientists, or sports figures, or are in business, industry, and other fields, and the development of business and professional networks for Pagan professionals.

- Landed Pagan churches and institutions—development of multigenerational Pagan church communities that sustain these land projects; development of libraries, retreat centers, seminaries, and schools, with physical locations.

- Pagan green cemeteries

- Winter Solstice—celebrations grow in prominence as a part of Yuletide celebrations. Solstice is mentioned alongside Christmas, Hanukah, and Kwanza.

And just so we might end with some imaginative thoughts for the future, Selena also puts in:

- Paganism in space—development of new Pagan traditions as humankind lives off planet; shift from referring to Paganism as Earth religion to Nature religion in order to be more inclusive; adaptation of Pagan practices to living in space stations, lunar outposts, spaceships, space settlements; increase in the use of sacred sphere casting instead of circle casting; new forms of seasonal and sabbat celebrations developed that work with different lunar and solar cycles.

Thinking back over the last fifteen to twenty-five years, there has been so much change in contemporary Paganism that—by the end of the century—almost anything is possible!

Epilogue

Guard the Mysteries; constantly reveal them.
> —From a poem by the late Lew Welsh, now a popular Craft saying

It is primarily the attraction of a personal *initiation that explains the craze for the occult.*

> —MIRCEA ELIADE[1]

THE EMINENT ARCHEOLOGIST George Mylonas, director of the excavations of Mycenae, involved himself deeply in the final excavations of Eleusis, which was the site of the Eleusinian Mysteries for two thousand years. During that time multitudes of women and men from all over the world of the ancient Greeks participated in the rites of Eleusis and, if we can believe the poets, playwrights, and philosophers, drew great strength from them. Pindar wrote: "Blessed is he who hath seen these things before he goeth beneath the hollow earth; for he understandeth the end of mortal life, and the beginning (of a new life) given of God."[2] Cicero, Sophocles, and Aristotle likewise extolled the Mysteries. Greek and Roman political figures such as Pericles, Hadrian, Marcus Aurelius, and Julian considered their experiences there moving and joyful. And some of the most profound passages in the plays of Aeschylus were considered so close to the essence of the Mysteries that the playwright came under the scrutiny of Athenian law until it was proved that he had never been initiated, and therefore could not have revealed the Mysteries in his works.

Mylonas, being a scholar of the twentieth century, was forced to study merely their remains. He concludes *Eleusis and the Eleusinean Mysteries* with sorrow and longing. He laments:

For years, since my early youth, I have tried to find out what the facts were. Hope against hope was spent against the lack of monumental evidence; the belief that inscriptions would be found on which the Hierophants had recorded their ritual and its meaning has faded completely; the discovery of a subterranean room filled with the archives of the cult, which dominated my being in my days of youth, is proved an unattainable dream since neither subterranean rooms nor archives for the cult exist at Eleusis; the last Hierophant carried with him to the grave the secrets which had been transmitted orally for untold generations, from the one high priest to the next. A thick, unpenetrable veil indeed still covers securely the rites of Demeter and protects them from the curious eyes of modern students. How many nights and days have been spent over books, inscriptions, and works of art by eminent scholars in their effort to lift the veil! How many wild and ingenious theories have been advanced in superhuman effort to explain the Mysteries! How many nights I have spent standing on the steps of the Telesterion, flooded with the magic silver light of a Mediterranean moon, hoping to catch the mood of the initiates, hoping that the human soul might get a glimpse of what the rational mind could not investigate! All in vain—the ancient world has kept its secret well and the Mysteries of Eleusis remain unrevealed.[3]

Eleusis has puzzled scholars for centuries. Much has been discovered about the preparatory and public celebrations, the preliminary processions and purifications, the Demeter-Korê myth cycle, and the nature of certain processions and lesser rites. Karl Kerényi, C. G. Jung, M. F. Nilsson, W. K. C. Guthrie, Mylonas, and other scholars have created a large storehouse of intuitions and speculations. Many scholars would now agree with Kerényi that a profound religious experience must have occurred, repeated year after year, a psychic reality that succeeded again and again.[4]

The vision of Mylonas standing, empty in spirit, in the moonlit ruins of Eleusis stayed with me through all my explorations of Neo-Paganism and the Craft. This is not surprising, since the Craft (and a number of other Neo-Pagan religions as well) has always claimed to be a Mystery religion, although exactly what that means is not always clear even to the participants.

At one level, I think, all Mystery traditions involve processes of growth and regeneration, confrontations with birth, death, the source of life, and the relationship of human beings to the cosmos. In connection with these ideas a number of Neo-Pagans and Witches have foresworn the words "Pagan" and "Witch," saying that they regard their religion as "the revival of the Mystery tradition." A New York coven writes that rituals are really the reenactment of "cosmic drama," allowing the participant to enter "into the drama of life itself, of joining with the gods in an achievement of universal advantage, so that growth (which is the true magic) is achieved."[5]

If, with Aidan Kelly, we define the Craft as "the European heritage of Goddess worship,"[6] the connections with the Mysteries of Demeter and Korê become clearer. Above and beyond the murky area of historical and geographical connections, the philosophical connections are real. What little we know of the Mysteries seems to indicate that these rites emphasized (as the Craft, at its best, does today) *experience* as opposed to *dogma,* and *metaphor* and *myth* as opposed to *doctrine.* Both the Mysteries and the Craft emphasize initiatory *processes* that lead to a widening of perceptions. Neither emphasizes theology, belief, or the written word. In both, participants expect to lead normal lives *in* the world, as well as attain spiritual enrichment.

How can one explain the plight of George Mylonas? Aidan notes that the Athenians distinguished between lesser and greater Mysteries.

The Great Mysteries of Eleusis were, in large part, archetypical of the Mystery religions. According to Karl Kerényi, when Athens annexed Eleusis about 600 B.C.E. and made its Mysteries the state religion of Attica, the Athenians passed a law to protect the secrecy of the Mysteries. This law, however, distinguished two types of secrets, the "Lower" and the "Higher." The "Lower secrets" were those that could be told to another person by word, gesture, or whatever; these were called *ta aporrheta,* "the forbidden," and the law applied only to them—hence their name. Why didn't the law apply to the "Higher secrets"? The latter were called *ta arrheta,* "the ineffable," and it was recognized in the law itself that these secrets could not be communicated except by the Mysteries themselves; hence they needed no protection by a mere law.[7]

It is the *process* and the *experience,* not the secrets, that are the mystery of the Mysteries. Even were a secret chamber found in the depths of Eleusis, or had the basic rituals been inscribed, the Mysteries would defy discovery. This explains why, for over two thousand years, even during times of Christian domination, there were no revelations by converts, no statements from ex-initiates.

Mysteries, observe two Neo-Pagan writers, are "stages of growth in consciousness of the sacred universe, not secrets":

> A mystery can't be told or even easily shown someone, while a secret can be told to just about anyone and they can tell it to somebody else. And it will be the same secret. And yet there seem to be an amazing number of people who seem to believe the two terms to be synonymous. . . .
>
> The truly frustrating thing about the mysteries is that they cannot be taught, they must be experienced. In fact, telling most people the surface-seeming substance or "secrets" can blind them to the depth of the real mysteries, the great sea of the untellable, the unsayable. . . . As with a zen monk, the teacher must "trick" the neophyte into awakening. . . .
>
> If it were as easy as telling to introduce someone to the mysteries, then those who have perceived them would simply *tell,* and all people would become wise and awake. . . . But when people try to *tell,* the things that are said are either understandable but not true or true but not understandable. They are image-illusion, they are empty baskets.[8]

Mylonas is, then, a potent symbol. We are all searching among the ruins. He is all of us who have admitted our spiritual impoverishment, hoping that objects, words, and inscriptions will give us clues to things that can be learned only through experience. What Mylonas (and most of us) have been denied is the experience of being "tricked" into this initiatory process. We are forced to rely merely on our intellectual tools, which will not allow us to enter certain hidden chambers. The secret that Neo-Paganism seems to have begun to learn over the past thirty-five years is this: If the methods for creating such experiences have been lost, the way to find them again is to create them again.

Appendix 1: Scholars, Writers, Journalists, and the Occult

When *Drawing Down the Moon* was first published, the way Witches and other magical practitioners were depicted in the media and in academia was, to put it mildly, abysmal. By 1986 and the second edition, journalists had written a few sensitive articles on Paganism and Wicca, but most newspapers, wire services, and television shows were still only interested in a few kinds of stories—sensational descriptions of Witches' gatherings, stories involving criminal charges, clashes between Witches and Christians, and, of course, something cute and usually silly for their Halloween feature. I admit to participating in a few of these latter, after my book came out, including going on the *Today Show* (where the first question I was asked was "Do you have psychic power?" My response was "probably just about as much as you do.") Looking back to the kind of interviews I was subjected to when this book first came out in 1979–80, they included questions like "Why do you have black hair?" (I was born that way) and "is that scar on your leg from a ritual?" (No. I cut myself shaving.) Between 1980 and 1985, I pulled out approximately fifty newspaper, magazine, and wire service stories collected by *Nexus*, and noted that there were only five basic stories: the perverted individual who was killing animals and calling themselves a Witch; a custody battle between a couple, usually one of them a Witch and the other a Christian; a Wiccan gathering that was picketed by fundamentalists; a bill that would take away tax-exempt status from Wiccan religious groups; a trial of someone for murder who was supposedly a Witch.

Now, twenty-five years later, much has changed both in the United States and in Europe. Witches appear in the media at other times than Halloween. Selena Fox says that media depictions have definitely improved as "contemporary Paganism has grown in numbers and scope." Historian Ronald Hutton notes that press coverage in the British mass media is much better than it was: "Pagans are generally no longer newsworthy in themselves, and are most frequently treated with respect and understanding when they are discussed. The occasional uninformed attack is confined to the more crudely populist newspapers, and is now rare enough to be surprising." Paganism still figures in some of the fights over religion in the public square, and Pagan religious freedom organizations like the *Lady Liberty League, The Alternative Religions Education Network* (AREN), and the *Earth Religions Assistance List* (ERAL) still have plenty of work to do, but here's a story that Larry Cornett, a Pagan who has been active in many religious battles told me:

> Recently there was a case in Ohio, where someone tried to use Wicca to get custody of a child, and the judge called a recess, went on the Internet, did a quick Google search, came back and said, "this is obviously a religion, you can't use this as a basis for taking custody away."

It is still almost impossible to explain Wicca or Neo-Paganism in the several minutes allowed on most television shows, but in 2005, for example, excellent articles appeared in both *The San Francisco Chronicle* and *The New York Times.*

Things have also improved markedly in regard to scholarship, and there is even a burgeoning Pagan studies movement (see Chapter 13). *Drawing Down the Moon* is also no longer the only serious treatment of modern Pagans and Witches. Ronald Hutton's monumental *The Triumph of the Moon* and newer serious works like Sabina Magliocco's *Witching Culture* have transformed the landscape. But much of the history depicted in this chapter deserves to be remembered because many of the blunders made by reporters and researchers studying occult and magical groups are still common.

All statements are true in some sense, false in some sense, meaningless in some sense, true and false in some sense, true and meaningless in some sense, false and meaningless in some sense, and true and false and meaningless in some sense.

—PRINCIPIA DISCORDIA[1]

To account for the current resurgence of occultism in the popular culture of America by means of any monistic psychological or sociological theory is to oversimplify the reality of the many movements.

—MARCELLO TRUZZI[2]

THERE IS AN OLD psychiatric saying: People who are in Freudian analysis have Freudian dreams, people in Jungian analysis have Jungian dreams, and people in Adlerian therapy have Adlerian dreams. Our experience of the world often reflects the influences under which we find ourselves. The categories we use to define an experience often determine it.

When we look at what the media might call "the occult explosion"— of which the revival of Witchcraft and Paganism is certainly a part— this perception rings particularly true. This "explosion" or "resurgence" is a confusing and ambiguous subject, and almost everyone has a superficial explanation that usually conforms to his or her previous experience and beliefs. Stereotypical notions are rampant about most subjects that become fads for a time, and occultism, magic, Paganism, and Witchcraft are no exception.

A psychologist might attribute this resurgence to the need of certain neurotics to regress to a beatific infant stage. A professional humanist might bemoan the "rise of the irrational" and "the trend toward anti-intellectualism." A Christian fundamentalist might be troubled by the "reawakening of the demonic," and a Marxist writer might be distressed by the attempt of a wealthy leisured class to dissipate the forces of dissent by promoting ideas that mystify the "real" issues and lead to decadence and narcissism. There is an "occult explosion" nightmare to fit every ideology. And on the other side, occultists share an equal number of paradisal dreams and fantasies about the importance and ultimate benefits of their efforts.

Distortions that circulate about occult groups are generally of two types. The first and more easily dismissible is what might be called the "Exorcist-Rosemary's Baby" view that was once put forth by much of the press and is still put forward by fundamentalist Christian groups. Although books, articles, and scholarly studies have shown this view to be pure fiction (with the exception of an occasional sick individual), the feeling persists that those who practice Witchcraft or occultism are engaged in something fearful, pernicious, illegal, and immoral. This image has a long history. It is nourished by the media because it sells. But more important, this image encourages a fear of the unknown that blunts most people's curiosity and adventurousness.

These negative feelings are widely shared, even by well-educated people. I have told hundreds of people about my travels around the United States to various Witchcraft covens and Neo-Pagan groups, and the first response was usually "Weren't you afraid? Wasn't it dangerous?" This assumption was so common, and stood at such odds with the facts of my travels, that it seemed to be a clue to a general misperception. The facts were simple. I met with representatives of over a hundred groups. The majority were previously strangers. My only negative experience came when a coven of Witches walked out on me after a political disagreement. Such an event could have happened anywhere, and was certainly no more likely to occur among Witches than anyone else.

Another attitude circulates primarily among intellectuals and must be looked at seriously. This is the view that occult groups are trivial, escapist, anti-intellectual, antipolitical, narcissistic, amoral, and decadent. These charges do not come from the sensationalist press. They appear in the works of highly regarded writers and scholars, in *The New York Review of Books, Commentary, Partisan Review.* Many of the ideas in these articles filter down into ordinary "educated" conversation, becoming the basis for the rigid, defensive, and hostile reactions that many people exhibit when they talk about the occult.

Of course, there is another group of writers who have consistently praised the occult revival, viewing it as a seedbed of innovation. There are also critiques by anthropologists, sociologists, historians, and psychologists that contain few stereotypes. These writings reveal the occult world to be complex, with many themes and many layers, a world richer and far different from that portrayed in the press, in most books, in the dinner-table conversation of certain intellectuals and, for that matter, in the simple-minded postures of certain occult writers.

This chapter serves two main functions: it summarizes some of the standard arguments surrounding the revival of occult and magical groups, and it makes accessible a number of lesser known articles and less rigid ideas and perceptions.

One thing should be made clear at the start. There is no consensus on why there has been a resurgence of Witchcraft and occultism, and some people even doubt whether such a resurgence exists. There are any number of fascinating theories and speculations, many of which contradict each other. For example, in 1971 there appeared a rather unexceptional popular study of new religious sects by Egon Larsen. The book *Strange Sects and Cults,* takes a pseudo-psychological approach and describes the rise of these sects as "a subconscious protest against the faculty of thinking. . . ." Larsen argues that these new sects are peopled by a "simple kind of soul." Such people's "personalities never mature"; they remain frightened and bewildered by rigorous mental activity.[3] Several years earlier Richard Cavendish had observed the exact opposite in *The Black Arts,*[4] a study of occult and mystical practices. Cavendish wrote that people who enter mystical groups are generally seeking to take the Apple from the Serpent; they want to eat of the tree of knowledge and become "as gods." He claimed that the typical magician or mystic, far from being a simple person, is attempting to become "the complete man." Such persons, he wrote, throw themselves into all kinds of experiences, both good and evil. They tend to regard all experience as potentially rewarding.

Here are some more examples. The Reverend J. Gordon Melton, whose Institute for the Study of American Religion has amassed perhaps the largest existing collection of modern Craft and Neo-Pagan publications, has written that control and manipulation are absolutely essential to the magical world view.[5] An opposing view has been expressed many times by Mircea Eliade, Theodore Roszak, and others who believe the occult revival regards the universe as *personal,* alive, numinous, mysterious, and beyond manipulation.

The anthropologist Marvin Harris has argued that occult ideas have been used as a weapon of survival by the wealthy classes to stifle the rational growth of protest and dissent. In contrast to this view, Eliade and Edward Tiryakian have argued that many artists and writers have used the occult as a weapon to fight against the bourgeoisie.

In 1977 the scientist Carl Sagan told a symposium at the Massachusetts Institute of Technology that part of the blame for the rise of occultism and irrationality rested on an educational system that had failed to show students the mysteries and wonders of science. Meanwhile, sociologist Marcello Truzzi was writing in a series of articles that the rise of the occult was, paradoxically, a *vindication* of the scientific world view and that most occultists had not rejected science at all, but were furthering the process of secularization by making once-feared aspects of life (the occult, the paranormal) easily comprehensible and benign.

In looking at a wide variety of theoretical viewpoints in the next few pages, we might do well to heed the words of one editor of a Neo-Pagan journal who wrote to me bluntly: "I don't think Pagans share *any* beliefs! And no Witches think alike!" We should also remember Susan Roberts, the journalist who was forced to throw up her hands and exclaim, "Witches defy categorizing," but then went on to say that Witches did not like to wear hats and shoes, that Witches were nonconformists, that Witches were conventional on the surface, that Witches were clean, that Witches were not "hippies," and that Witches didn't go to psychiatrists. There are, of course, Witches who like hats and shoes, who go to therapists, who are "hippies" (whatever *that* means), and there are probably even some who lead superficially unconventional lives but are conformist way down deep.[6]

Theories that attempt to explain the growth of new magical and religious groups fall into several categories:

1. Theories that see this growth as evidence of regression, escape, or retreat.

2. Theories that see this growth as a positive reaction to, or rebellion against, the limitations of Western thought or the excesses of modern technology, that generally view occult* ideas as energizing and innovative.

3. Theories that do not easily fit either of these categories.

---

*The word *occult* and the phrase *occult resurgence* are being used broadly. Technically, the word *occult* first appeared in 1545 (Oxford English Dictionary) and it meant that which is hidden or is beyond the range of ordinary apprehension and understanding. Later, the word began to be used as an umbrella description to cover such studies as astrology, alchemy, and magic. A recent (and much quoted) sociological definition of the occult was formulated by Edward A. Tiryakian, in his essay "Toward the Sociology of Esoteric Culture." He wrote:

> By "occult," I understand intentional practices, techniques, or procedures which (a) draw upon hidden or concealed forces in nature or the cosmos that cannot be measured or recognized by the instruments of modern science, and (b) which have as their desired or intended consequences empirical results, such as either obtaining knowledge of the empirical course of events or altering them from what they would have been without this intervention. . . .[7]

Regressions and Retreats:
Psychological and Political Approaches

Some writers who have attempted to analyze the growth of the occult talk in terms of a *retreat* or a *regression* and portray the sect member or occultist as a neurotic individual whose actions can best be explained in psychoanalytical terms. At the most simple level, the psychological approach can be seen in writers like Larsen, who view the various groups as simple souls, devoid of the possibility of growth and maturity. I knew a well-known New York psychiatrist who would mutter "Schizophrenics!" whenever the subject of religious sects came up in conversation. Andrew Greeley and William McCready have described a similar reaction:

> The conditioned reflex of many social scientists when someone raises the subject of mystical ecstasy or confronts them with a person who has had such an experience is to fall back on psychoanalytic interpretations. The ecstatic is some sort of disturbed person who is working out a personality problem acquired in childhood. That settles the issue in most instances. They "know" that the ecstatic episode is in fact some sort of psychotic interlude.[8]

Despite the prevalence of these kinds of analyses, a number of psychological interpretations deserve serious consideration. In 1966 Raymond Prince and Charles Savage wrote that mystical states represented a regression to an earlier stage of adaptation, that the feeling of unity is a re-experience of unity felt by the infant nursing at the mother's breast.

Many of the articles discussed in this chapter are directed specifically at various recent phenomena, including the growth of the occult, Witchcraft, "the consciousness movement," new therapies, and new religious sects. Very few are directed specifically at Witches, and Neo-Pagans have generally been ignored by scholars. It could be argued, for example, that Cavendish's comments on those who enter magical groups apply to magicians generally, but do not apply to members of those religious sects discussed by Larsen, and that the members of those sects *are* bewildered and immature, unlike most magicians. I tend to doubt it, but a plausible case could be made. It could also be argued that revivalist Witches and Neo-Pagans differ in so many ways from the subjects of these articles that these critiques, both positive and negative, just don't apply.

This may be a good argument for a scholarly journal, but most people, and this includes most intelligent nonspecialists, lump all these phenomena together. And many of the writers do the same thing. The article that speaks of the "growth of the irrational" is often talking about many kinds of groups. For these reasons the term *occult resurgence* is used here broadly.

This analysis formed the basis for many criticisms of the youth movement of the 1960s.[9] But Prince's view of mystical experience is not so negative as the idea of "regression" implies. In "Cocoon Work: An Interpretation of the Concern of Contemporary Youth with the Mystical" (1974), Prince wrote that the increase in people seeking mystical experience could best be explained as a self-imposed rite of passage, a "cocoon work," in which contemporary young Americans were creating a place and time for their own metamorphosis in a society that lacked a clear and acceptable image of the adult.

Prince observed that psychologists had offered two main interpretations of mystical states. The first (outlined in the earlier Prince and Savage paper) said that mystical states were a regression in which the ego descended to the earliest level of experience where the universe is simple and trustworthy. The second hypothesis was that mystical states are a form of deautomatization: the mystic restores to a state of new awareness and sensitivity those actions that have been ignored and have become automatic.

In turning to the growth of new religious groups, Prince gave the movement a name—"Neotranscendentalism." Many of the characteristics he attributed to it would apply well to some Neo-Pagans: lack of dogma, exaltation of the body as a temple, interest in new types of social and economic relationships, and cooperative forms of living. Prince saw this movement as a *rite de passage* in a society that had no rituals for the passage from childhood to adulthood. People became engaged in this cocoon work and then, after a time, took up their normal responsibilities in society.[10] (A less charitable description would be that most young rebels eventually sell out.)

One trouble in applying these arguments to Neo-Pagans is that, unlike the sixties youth culture that Prince describes, most adherents of Neo-Paganism are adults whose lives—with the exception of their religious practices—are fully integrated into the mainstream of society.

But why should the occult be seen as a regression at all? Part of this tendency comes from a fairly longstanding anthropological thesis, originally put forth by A. L. Kroeber and George Devereux, that spiritualists and shamans were village psychotics who were given a unique role in primitive societies.[11] This idea has been attacked by scholars in a variety of fields—Claude Lévi-Strauss, Mircea Eliade, and Jerome Frank, among many others—but it continues in a watered-down form on the popular level. Hence the widespread notion that occultists and mystics are simply "mentally ill."

Dr. E. Fuller Torrey wrote that this "sickness" myth had its origins in the colonialism of the eighteenth and nineteenth centuries, and in the reductionist ideas applied to primitive societies. He argued that many well-known anthropologists were themselves in psychoanalysis at the time they formulated their theories, or at least were profoundly affected by psychoanalytic theory. They were, observed Torrey, ill disposed to see their own analysts as "analogous to those strange people in other cultures who are chanting and shaking a rattle." But in point of fact, wrote Torrey, spiritualists and shamans "do the same thing as psychiatrists and psychologists do, using the same techniques, and getting about the same results."[12]

Why not, instead, view the shaman as Eliade does when he writes that the shaman's imitation of animal cries "betokens the desire to recover friendship with the animals and thus enter into the primordial Paradise?"[13] Is the desire for such a paradise a regression? Greeley and McCready disagreed:

> We humans are inextricably caught up in the physical, chemical, and biological processes of the universe. We swim in an ocean of air, held by gravity to the planet earth and sustained in life by oxygen, carbon, and nitrogen cycles. We are indeed distinct from everything else, but only up to a point; and those psychiatrists who seem to think that an experience of profound awareness of how much one is involved in the natural processes is a regression to childhood have apparently come to think of themselves as archangels who live quite independently of the life processes of the universe.[14]

The assertion that the growth of mysticism and occultism is a *retreat* is primarily a political argument, made most forcefully by Marxist theorists and other progressives. Briefly stated, the critique goes something like this: Occultism, new religions, interest in magic, and so forth are tendencies that promote superstition and downgrade scientific and intellectual ideas. Worse, these ideas devalue the material struggles in the real world and aid reactionary forces by promoting confusion and a false picture of reality. The occult is a powerful weapon of mystification.

Many writers have presented such arguments. The late Marvin Harris, an anthropologist, wrote a fascinating book, *Cows, Pigs, Wars and Witches: The Riddles of Culture,* published in 1974. Harris used the last chapter, "The Return of the Witch," to launch a strong attack on all the most publicized proponents of the counterculture at that time, in particular Theodore Roszak, Charles Reich, and Carlos Castaneda.

Harris wrote that the "modern witch fad blunts and befuddles the forces of dissent."

> Like the rest of the counter-culture it postpones the development of a rational set of political commitments. And that is why it is so popular among the more affluent segments of our population. That is why the witch has returned.

Harris waxed eloquent in his fury against those members of the counterculture who attempted to levitate the Pentagon by magic during the antiwar demonstrations in Washington some thirty years ago. He seems to have taken them literally; he certainly did not understand their sense of humor and understanding of metaphor. He argued that their disdain for rationality and objectivity was dangerously "stripping an entire generation" of intellectual tools. In this he sounded much like Larsen. He accused supporters of the counterculture of ethnocentric thinking and amoral relativism.

> I contend that it is quite impossible to subvert objective knowledge without subverting the basis of moral judgements. If we cannot know with reasonable certainty who did what, when, and where, we can scarcely hope to render a moral account of ourselves. Not being able to distinguish between criminal and victim, rich and poor, exploiter and exploited, we must either advocate the total suspension of moral judgements, or adopt the inquisitorial position and hold people responsible for what they do in each other's dreams.

But Harris's main argument was that occultism and mystical thinking promoted the idea that one can change the course of history by changing consciousness rather than by changing the material conditions that, he believed, create consciousness. To Harris these movements were dangerous because "they prevent people from understanding the causes of their social existence."[15] Such doctrines were very useful to inequitable social systems.

Another writer who made a similar argument was Edwin Schur, in his book *The Awareness Trap: Self-Absorption Instead of Social Change*. Schur charged that the "awareness movement" (another catch-all phrase that included New Age groups as well as most of the groups we are talking about) addressed the problems of the affluent, the white middle class, and diverted the poor from advancing their real collective interests.[16]

But the most serious critique of this type joined a psychological and a political perspective. It came from the late Christopher Lasch, who wrote several articles on the "new narcissism" in America for *The New York Review of Books* and *Partisan Review*. Lasch argued that a "retreat to purely personal satisfactions," one of the main themes of the seventies, was reflected in everything from occultism to jogging, from the new therapies to the revival of fundamentalist Christianity. According to Lasch, these new movements, unlike the millenarian movements of the waning Middle Ages which were concerned with social justice, all included a wish to forget the past, to live only for the moment. They went no further than a search for instant gratification and a kind of survivalism.

The picture Lasch painted of the present culture was one in which people veered "between unthinking political commitments and a cult of the self, between a wholesale rejection of politics and a rejection of personal life as a bourgeois self-indulgence." While Schur characterized the members of these movements as complacent, Lasch showed them as self-preoccupied and desperate.

Lasch argued that every age has its own forms of mental illness, which simply mirror, in exaggerated form, the basic characteristics of that age. In Freud's time the dominant mental illness was hysteria and obsessional neurosis. These, wrote Lasch, "carried to extremes the personality traits associated with the capitalist order at an earlier stage in its development—acquisitiveness, fanatical devotion to work, and a fierce repression of sexuality." In our age, by contrast, the dominant illnesses have been schizophrenia and "borderline" personality disorders. These, he wrote, seemed to signify a societal change from inner-direction to narcissism. According to Lasch, narcissism and its traits—pansexuality, hypochondria, corruptibility, shallowness, the inability to mourn—

were simply the best way of coping with a warlike social environment where friendships and family life were hard to sustain, where relationships were shallow, where there was no sense of historical continuity, and where consumption and glamour were emphasized.[17]

Occultists as Rebels and Innovators

The counterthrusts to these types of arguments came from a number of sources. Some writers, such as Roszak, saw the occult resurgence as, in part, a protest against a sterile technocratic ethic. Industrial society had produced its opposite: a yearning for the sacred, the communal, the spontaneous. Others, such as Edward Tiryakian and Mircea Eliade, saw the occult as providing, both historically and in the present, fresh images for many artistic and political movements. Esoteric culture, wrote Tiryakian, "with its fantastic wealth of imagery and symbolism, is multivalent in terms of the political expressions that can be derived from it."[18] He observed that all kinds of groups from the Sinn Fein to the Nazis made extensive use of occult images. These ideas did not belong to reactionaries any more than they belong to progressives.

Both Tiryakian and Eliade mentioned symbolist poets and surrealist writers like André Breton, Louis Aragon, and Paul Eluard, all of whom were committed to radical politics as well as to occultism.[19] The entire surrealist movement seemed to speak directly against the arguments that occultism and magic were antipolitical per se. Breton and the surrealists spoke out strongly against what they considered to be the three prime evils: realism, industrial rationalism, and the bourgeois social order.*

Another writer who compared the growth of mysticism, particularly among young people, with the surrealist and Dadaist movements was Nathan Adler. He wrote that in both cases dreams, hallucinations, and

---

*While visiting Neo-Pagans in Chicago, I was led to the studio of Robert Green, a surrealist painter who uses magical rituals to renew his creative energies. Green made a distinction between *religion,* "which relies on belief," and *magic,* "which is a process to renew the subconscious." He told me that both magic and surrealist art seek to "liquefy the mind," to liberate the mind from imprisoning dogmas. He said that the problem with the rational mode was that it imposed unacceptable limits. The purpose of surrealism was "liberation period. Liberation of the mind, but also, of all human existence." Green told me that surrealists have always maintained a critical analysis of society. They have always been "political." Magic and occultism in no way contradict this, he said, so long as they are kept free of dogma and fixed beliefs.

chance were used as "an antidote to the increasing sterility of industrial and mercantile life."[20] He made a careful distinction between the surrealist movement and the group he was writing about—the youth culture of the early seventies—believing the latter was anti-intellectual. In my own experiences with Witches and Pagans I have come across very little anti-intellectualism.

Tiryakian wrote that the occult, now, as in the past, seems to function as a "seedbed," a source of change and innovation, that ultimately affects the arts, the sciences, and politics. He noted that while it was customary to regard the occult as marginal, atavistic, an odd deviation from the modernization process, another way of viewing esoteric traditions was to see them as the source for new paradigms, catalysts for modernization that appear in both the "build-ups" and the "breakdowns" of history—in the Renaissance, for example, or during the waning of the Roman Empire.[21]

As for Harris's charge that the growth of the occult leads to befuddlement, retreat, and reaction, Roszak countered with these words: "It is not transcendent experience that should be rejected but its invidious employment and attendant obfuscation of consciousness." The real evil, he wrote, lies in "setting transcendence *against* the earth, the body, the city of man, *for the sake of protecting* criminal privilege."[22] Good magic, he maintained, is rather like good art. Bad magic and bad art simply mystify; good magic and good art lay open the mysteries for all.

Still another positive view saw the occult resurgence as a healthy refusal to be content with the finite. Harriet Whitehead, as we saw, wrote that this refusal was the result of a conviction that there are gaps and deficiencies in the Western mode of comprehending reality. The search and exploration of the occult was an attempt to get at the order that lies at the bottom of things, to discover the "really real."[23]

Is occultism a retreat from the world? It must be said that few occultists, Pagans, and Witches spend much time debating this question (or, for that matter, reading these articles). But this debate did take place in the women's movement. As we have seen, a number of women disposed of the entire notion of a split between spiritual and material reality by simply saying that it was a mistaken notion born of patriarchal thinking. They saw ritual and magic as a connecting force, like art and poetry. If there was a necessity for art, why not for ritual? Artists were merely a bit more respectable these days than magicians and creators of rituals.

Other Theories of More Than Passing Interest

Some of the most interesting thoughts on contemporary occult movements have come from historian Mircea Eliade, whose more than twenty published works range from mythography to investigations of shamanism and Witchcraft. In 1976 the University of Chicago Press published a collection of Eliade's essays under the title *Occultism, Witchcraft, and Cultural Fashions,* one of the sanest books on these topics to appear in years. Three essays bear directly on the themes of this book. Two are considered here; a third was discussed in Chapter 4.

In "Cultural Fashion and History of Religion" Eliade investigated the extraordinary popularity in France of the magazine *Planète,* and of the philosophy of Pierre Teilhard de Chardin. The arguments in this essay can easily be applied to most recent occult groups. *Planète* was started by Louis Pauwels and Jacques Bergier, two authors who became famous in 1961 with the publication of *Morning of the Magicians,*[24] a book that combined politics, occultism, science fact, and science fiction. It raised quite a furor in France and became the basis for much excited discussion in the United States, particularly within the counterculture. *Planète* was founded with money earned by the book. The magazine also contained a mixture of magic, science, politics, and speculation.

Eliade argued that in France, after the Algerian War, there was a "profound malaise among the intellectuals." They had become tired of living in the "gloomy, tedious," historical moment, but Sartre and other existentialist writers had taught French intellectuals that this was the only responsible thing to do. *Planète* presented a total contrast, offering a new, "optimistic and holistic outlook" in which the universe was mysterious and exciting, and in which occultism and science combined to create infinite possibilities. The world was no longer doomed to be absurd; human beings were no longer condemned to be estranged and useless. One was no longer committed to constant analysis of one's own existential situation; instead, one was committed to the infinite process of evolution.

Eliade argued that the philosophy of Teilhard de Chardin became popular in France for similar reasons. Teilhard looked at the world from a cosmic viewpoint in which human history was a small part of an infinite progressive evolution.* Eliade wrote that Teilhard's universe was "real, alive, meaningful, creative, sacred." Teilhard, despite his Christian symbolism, was really a pantheist who ignored sin and evil and who viewed human and planetary evolution as progressive, optimistic, and infinite. Eliade wrote:

> One cannot even go back to a romantic or bucolic approach to nature. But the nostalgia for a lost mystical solidarity with nature still haunts Western man. And Teilhard has laid open for him an unhoped-for perspective, where nature is charged with religious values even while retaining its completely "objective" reality.[25]

How did Eliade sum up the ideas of those people who read *Planète* with eagerness and found themselves interested in the ideas of Teilhard? These people rejected existentialism, were indifferent to history, exalted physical nature, and held ultimately *positive* feelings toward science and technology. What is more, their antihistoricism was not really a rejection of history but "a protest against the pessimism and nihilism of some recent historicists," coupled with a "nostalgia for what might be called a macro-history—a planetary and, later, a cosmic history."

Eliade echoed Lasch, but from the other side. The indifference to history produced an ultimate optimism as opposed to the survivalism born of desperation depicted by Lasch.

Eliade's essay "The Occult and the Modern World" focused more specifically on the history of occultism and its current popularity. After discussing the nineteenth-century occultist Eliphas Levi, who was largely responsible for the vogue of occultism in France, Eliade wrote that the generation of French occultists that followed Levi wanted to regain humanity's spiritual perfection as it was "before the fall." This occult movement "did not attract the attention of competent historians of ideas of the times but did fascinate a great number of important writers, from

*For a look at how one Neo-Pagan group, the Church of All Worlds, has adapted, modified, and expanded on the ideas of Teilhard, see Chapter 10.

Baudelaire, Verlaine, and Rimbaud to André Breton and some of the postsurrealist authors, such as René Daumal."

The use of occult themes by these writers took one of two paths. Those who wrote before the second half of the nineteenth century, writers such as Balzac, Schiller, and Goethe, all "reflected a hope in a personal or collective *renovatio*—a mystical restoration of man's original dignity and powers." The second and later path, taken by such writers as Rimbaud, Baudelaire, and Breton, was the use of occult themes as "a powerful weapon in their rebellion against the bourgeois establishment and its ideology." Implicit in this rebellion was a rejection of Judeo-Christian values and the social and aesthetic sensibilities of the day.

> In the occult traditions these artists were looking for pre-Judeo-Christian and pre-Classical (pre-Greek) elements, i.e., Egyptian, Persian, Indian, or Chinese creative methods and spiritual values. They sought their aesthetic ideals in the most archaic arts, in the "primordial" revelation of beauty. . . .
>
> To conclude, from Baudelaire to André Breton, involvement with the occult represented for the French literary and artistic avant-garde one of the most efficient criticisms and rejections of the religious and cultural values of the West—efficient because it was considered to be based on historical facts.

Eliade felt that the current occult scene was distinguished from the past occult resurgence in certain important ways. The present occult explosion was "anticipated" by a new wave of scholarship and understandings made principally *not* by writers and artists, as in the previous era, but by historians of ideas. These contributions included the decoding of esoteric manuscripts found in the Dead Sea caves, new monographs on Jewish Gnosticism, new studies of Chinese, Indian, and Western alchemy, new investigations of the Hermetic traditions, and new research into shamanism and Witchcraft. This contemporary scholarship, according to Eliade, "disclosed the consistent religious meaning and cultural function of a great number of occult practices, beliefs, and theories, recorded in many civilizations, European and non-European alike, and *at all levels of culture*."

He argued that new studies had changed the thinking of scholars on many questions, including the origins of Western European Witchcraft. A hundred years ago, most historians believed that European Witchcraft was the invention of the Inquisition. The covens, the reports of orgies, and all the other accusations were seen as either imaginary inventions or declarations obtained from the accused during torture. Then came Margaret Murray, who argued that Witchcraft was a pre-Christian fertility religion. Today, Murray's theories have been pretty much discredited, but Eliade argued that her assumption that "there existed a pre-Christian fertility cult and that specific survivals of this pagan cult were stigmatized during the Middle Ages as witchcraft" was correct—and had been borne out by more recent investigations of Indo-Tibetan and Romanian materials.

Eliade also wrote that the occult resurgence continued both of the older themes, the rebellion against Western religious values and the search for renewal. But, he contended, the most important aspect for all groups from astrologists to Satanists was the hope for an individual and collective *renovatio,* or renewal. "It is primarily the attraction of a *personal* initiation that explains the craze for the occult," he wrote. And all these groups implied, "consciously or unconsciously, what I would call an optimistic evaluation of the human mode of being."[26]

One of the most important early books to chart the rise of new religious movements in the United States was the 1974 Princeton University study *Religious Movements in Contemporary America.* Among the most unusual articles in this large volume is anthropologist Edward Moody's study of Satanism, "Magical Therapy: An Anthropological Investigation of Contemporary Satanism."* Moody spent two years as a participant-observer at the Church of the Trapezoid, a branch of Anton LaVey's Church of Satan. Moody set out to answer the question, "Why do people become Satanists?" After two years he concluded that Satanists find that something they call "magic" works for them, that they accomplish

---

Drawing Down the Moon does not include a study of Satanism because it is not primarily a Neo-Pagan phenomenon. Satanists (Bonewits's "Neogothic Witches") take their myths from Judeo-Christianity. Most worship Satan as a symbolic figure of rebellion against Christianity. Moody's article is relevant here because it answers a broader question: Why are occult and magical groups so appealing?

many of the goals they set out to achieve. But *how* this magic works proved to be very complex.

From the start, Moody found himself beset by difficulties. He could not find any "traditional sociological pigeonhole" into which the Satanist could be placed. He found members who were "successful" in life and those who were "failures." He found rich members and poor ones, representatives of all classes and political persuasions. The only characteristic common to all the members he observed was a behavioral trait that placed them outside the cultural "norm." Many of them displayed a lack of knowledge of the "rules of the social game" and often felt unable to "make the system respond."

Moody observed that magic training for the new Satanist recruit was a combination of many practical skills designed to build up the ego and lessen feelings of guilt and anxiety. The techniques and rituals were a combination of psychodrama, tips on social manners, advice on how to make oneself more attractive, and techniques to strengthen confidence.

Moody observed a sample subject, "Billy G.," over a period of many months. He watched this young man change from a person whose level of anxiety was so great that he could not even speak to a member of the opposite sex into a more "normal" young man who could interact with men and women, both inside and outside the church. Billy G. slowly worked through various rituals, many of which were composed of behaviorist techniques to lessen anxiety.

In one example Moody gave a new twist to that fact of contemporary Satanism most played up by the press: the nude woman who acts as the altar. In the beginning Billy G. finds this setting so disturbing that he stands at the back of the room. In succeeding weeks he moves closer. Finally, Billy G., the son of fundamentalist missionaries, is able to stand next to this woman, to talk to her, to hand her a goblet or in some way participate in the ritual without feeling ill at ease. He is given encouragement; he is told that his sexual feelings are natural and not to be denied, as his previous education had taught him. Eventually, he is able to meet women and to go out with them. He becomes socially successful. The magic works.

Ironically, Moody showed that the Church of Satan, certainly one of the less "acceptable" occult groups, actually functioned as a normalizing force, a socializing force within the larger society. It functioned much like therapy and it apparently succeeded. Moody commented on Billy G.:

> If he attributes this new-found power and success to magic rather than to the insights of sociology, anthropology, or psychology, it is because such an interpretation is more in accordance with his world view and the categories of understanding which he uses to give structure and meaning to his world.
>
> In fact, it is sometimes difficult to argue against his interpretation. If psychology explains personal interactions in terms of hypothesized "forces" at work, forces which are known and measured only through the perception of their effects, then how is that different, the Satanist asks, from magic? Satanists say, with some justification, "When magic becomes scientific fact we refer to it as medicine or astronomy." (La Vey, 1969).

Moody ended his paper by encouraging the growth of the Church of the Trapezoid and arguing that such institutions socialized individuals for whom traditional therapy had failed and, paradoxically, served to bring people closer to cultural norms. Why is there a growth of magical groups today, Moody asked. He concluded that it was "an attempt by various people to regain a sense of control over their environment and their lives." It is important to note what Moody did not say. He did not employ the standard cliché that people become occultists to gain power over others, although, of course, some may join for that reason. He did not say that such people want to retreat from the world. Instead, he said that they join these groups in order to gain a sense of self-mastery, to be in control of their own lives *in the world*. Moody concluded:

> This seems to be a time when many of the gods of the Western world, like the old traditional gods of the urbanizing African, are being challenged. God is dead, but that means not just the Judeo-Christian god but also the gods of progress, science and technology. We put our faith in "him," but now the god of progress is discovered to be a two-faced Janus about to extract a terrible price for our progress and comfort; the god of science has failed us and has not created the paradise we were led to expect, free from disease and ignorance and death. Instead he threatens us

with destruction with either the apocalypse of atomic conflagration or a slow death by chemical pollution. The god of technology reveals his "true" face and our streams die, our lakes atrophy, and the very air is turned into a subtle poison. . . . In such time the people look to new gods or try to refurbish the old ones. . . .

Now that external sources of truth, the experts and scientists, have failed us, many people have begun to look within themselves for their source of wisdom and security. Some have begun to reassert the necessity of finding personal solutions. In a certain sense witchcraft* is a product of these needs. If the world of the Satanist is a criterion, the Satanist is training himself to be assertive and powerful *as an individual.* Although he draws a sense of security from his association with powerful forces, he is finding inner sources of strength. He is casting off the need for powerful gods to protect and care for him, insisting that he is strong enough to care for himself. He commands the gods and does not beseech them. He is turning from an ethereal and other-worldly orientation to a somewhat more realistic assessment and concern with the mundane and real world.[27]

Moody's point that the occult functions as a rationalizing force is made in another article, "Urban Witches," in which he argued that much that is called magic is actually a learning process of social behavior and interpersonal games. Magic, he wrote, allows its practitioners to cope better "with the everyday problems of life, with the here and now."[28]

Sociologist Marcello Truzzi took a similar position. In 1972, in an article "The Occult Revival as Popular Culture," Truzzi wrote that the revival of occultism involved a broad spectrum of individuals, many of whom were "not the simple identity-seeking variety that some have portrayed them to be." Truzzi argued that occultists tend to be playful with ideas that were once greatly feared and that therefore the rise of occultism is evidence of a victory over the supernatural. He wrote: "What we are seeing is largely a demystification-process of what were once fearful and threatening cultural elements."[29]

---

*Moody does not distinguish between Witchcraft and Satanism, a flaw in this otherwise excellent essay.

In another paper, "Toward a Sociology of the Occult: Notes on Modern Witchcraft," Truzzi wrote that Witchcraft groups have, in general, very little supernaturalism. He found most occultism to be naturalistic and pragmatic, "a kind of deviant science." He noted that most occultists seek scientific validation of their claims and regard themselves as scientific in a philosophical sense, working within an "ultimate purview of scientific understanding," Truzzi observed:

> In this sense, it would appear that there has been a kind of secularization of magic in adaptation to the modern scientific and naturalistic world view. Thus, what were once described in the occult literature as supernatural psychic forces are now examples of extra-sensory perception of a kind basically examinable and potentially understandable in the psychologist's laboratory.[30]

Taken collectively, these articles present a wealth of diverse viewpoints. These writers give the lie to the simple stereotypes about "the occult" that many people accept unconsciously—that it is irrational, escapist, retreatist, and so forth. These articles show that whatever is going on here is, and has always been, much more complicated than most people generally allow.

Appendix II: Rituals

Space limitations prevent me from reprinting many of the beautiful and varied rituals and poems that modern Pagans have written. I include five here. They may give you some small idea of this literature.

Woman-Charms: A Litany*

by Morgan McFarland

I AM THE WHITE DOE WHO SEVEN TIMES FLEES.
  I am pure and fleet, for I know that capture is Death to my Soul.
I AM A GREY FLOOD UPON WHICH THE BOAT IS TOSSED.
  I ebb, and I flood, and my water is uneasy.
I AM A VIOLENT WIND THAT STIRS THE DEPTHS.
  I rise up in anger from my uneasy slumber.
I AM A SUN-SPIKE RIPPING THROUGH THE CLOUDS.
  I shall give forth the pure ray of reality.
I AM A BIRD OF PREY WHO PROTECTS HER BROOD.
  I am cunning and canny and give shelter to my children.
I BRING FORTH TERROR AS THE NIGHT-CROW.
  I guard the boundaries and seek the enemy from his corners.
I AM DENSE SMOKE AND HEAVY FIRE.
  I cloud the reason of Man and elevate she who would brave my flame.
I AM THE FIRE-FORGED SWORD WHOSE BLADE IS BLOOD-TEMPERED.
  I am the Amazon who never wounds, but destroys the usurper, row upon row.

*Part of an unpublished manuscript of rites for women.

I AM WISER THAN THE CIRCLING SALMON WITHIN THE HOLY POOL.

I am the hazel nut that feeds the Wicce and spells the lore in her ear.

I AM THE VARIECOLOURED SNAKE WHO CROWNS THE HILL OF INSPIRATION.

I inflict the deadly sting upon the heavy-footed and uninspired.

I AM THE THICKET THAT WILL HIDE NEITHER THE BOAR NOR THE ROEBUCK.

I am the Daughter who wields the spear of the Sacred Name.

I AM A TIDE MORE VIOLENT THAN ITS WAVES SPEAK.

I am the terror in the shingle's rattle against the crumbling cliffs.

I AM THE SEA WAVES WHOSE CREST IS BRILLIANT FOAM.

I shall not be stopped, and I shall ceaselessly eat away the enemy shore.

WHO KNOWS THE SECRETS OF THE UNHEWN DOLMEN?

I, who am Woman: for its stones are my living, and its portal, my heart.

I, who am Woman: for I am the structure that opens to give Life passage.

I, who am Woman: for I am also the door that takes Life into Death.

I AM PRIESTESS AND WOMAN.

I am my Mother's Daughter.

Litany of the Earth-Mother*

O Earth-Mother, Thou of uncounted names and faces, Thou of the many-faceted Nature in and above All, Nature Incarnate, Love and Life fulfilled; look favorably upon this place, grace us with Your Presence, inspire and infuse us with Your powers; by all the names by which You have been known, O Earth-Mother:

COME UNTO US.

Thou Whom the Druids call Danu—

COME UNTO US.

Thou Who art Erde of the Germans—

COME UNTO US.

Thou Whom the Slavs call Ziva—

Thou Who art Nerthus of the Vanir—

---

*From the Hasidic Druids of North America (HDNA); published in *The Druid Chronicles (Evolved)*, ed. Isaac Bonewits (Berkeley: Drunemeton Press, 1976).

Thou Whom the Poles call Marzyana—
Thou Who art Frigga of the Aesir—
Thou Whom the Romans call Terra—
Thou Who art Diana to the Etruscans—
Thou Whom the Persians call Kybele—
Thou Who art Iphimedeia, Mighty Queen of the Greeks—
Thou Whom the Egyptians call Nuit, Star Mother—
Thou Who art Ninmah of Sumeria—
Thou Whom the Hittites call Kubala—
Thou Who art Mami-Aruru of Babalon—
Thou Whom the Caanites call Arsai—
Thou Who art Our Lady of Biblos in far Phonicia—
Thou Whom the children of Crete call Mountain Mother—
Thou Who art Yemanja of the Umbanda—
Thou Whom the Dahomeans call Erzulie—
Thou Who art Shakti and Parvati of India—
Thou Whom the Tibeteans call Green Tara—
Thou Who art Kwanyin of China—
Thou Whom the Nipponese call Izanami—
Thou Who art Sedna and Nerivik of the Eskimos—
Thou Whom the Pawnee call Uti-Hiata—
Thou Who art Cornmother of the Plains—
Thou Whom the Navaho call Estanatlehi—
Thou Who art Ometeotl and Guadalupe in Mexico—
Thou Whom the Islanders call Hina-alu-oka-moana—
Thou Who art the Great Mother, the Star Goddess, the All Creating
    One—
Mother of All, we call upon You—
Terra Mater, Mater Sotier, Earth-Mother—
COME UNTO US!

Self Blessing*

This ritual should be performed during the new moon, but it is not limited to that phase. Need, not season, determines the performance. There

*This was written by Ed Fitch in the late 1960s, and designated to be an introductory ritual for
those who are searching and investigating the Pagan path.

is real power in the Self Blessing; it should not be used other than in time of need and should not be done promiscuously.

The purpose of the ritual is to bring the individual into closer contact with the Godhead. It can also be used as a minor dedication, when a person who desires dedication has no one who can dedicate him. This self blessing ritual may also be used as a minor exorcism, to banish any evil influences which may have formed around the person. It may be performed by any person upon himself, and at his desire.

Perform the ritual in a quiet place, free from distractions, and nude. You will need the following:

1. Salt, about one quarter teaspoon.
2. Wine, about an ounce.
3. Water, about one-half ounce.
4. Candle, votive or other.

The result of the ritual is a feeling of peace and calm. It is desirable that the participant bask in the afterglow so that he may meditate and understand that he has called the attention of the Godhead to himself, asking to grow closer to the Godhead in both goals and in wisdom.

When you are ready to begin, sprinkle the salt on the floor and stand on it, lighting the candle. Let the warmth of the candle be absorbed into the body. Mix the water into the wine, meditating upon your reasons for performing the self blessing.

Read the following aloud:

BLESS ME, MOTHER FOR I AM YOUR CHILD.
Dip the fingers of the right hand into the mixed water and wine and anoint the eyes,
BLESSED BE MY EYES THAT I MAY SEE YOUR PATH.
Anoint the nose,
BLESSED BE MY NOSE, THAT I MAY BREATHE YOUR ESSENCE.
Anoint the mouth,
BLESSED BE MY MOUTH THAT I MAY SPEAK OF YOU.
Anoint the breast,
BLESSED BE MY BREAST, THAT I MAY BE FAITHFUL IN MY WORK.
Anoint the loins,

BLESSED BE MY LOINS, WHICH BRING FORTH THE LIFE OF MEN AND
WOMEN AS YOU HAVE BROUGHT FORTH ALL CREATION.

Anoint the feet,

BLESSED BE MY FEET, THAT I MAY WALK IN YOUR WAYS.

Remain . . . and meditate for a while.

Pagan Ritual for General Use*

A circle should be marked on the floor, surrounding those who will participate in the ceremony. An altar is to be set up at the center of the circle. At the center of the altar shall be placed an image of the Goddess, and an incense burner placed in front of it. Behind the image should be a wand fashioned from a willow branch. Candles should be set upon the altar . . . a total of five, since one is to be set at each quarter and one will remain on the altar during the rite.

When all the people are prepared they shall assemble within the circle. The woman acting as priestess shall direct the man who acts as priest to light the candles and incense. She shall then say:

The presence of the noble Goddess extends everywhere.
Throughout the many strange, magical,
And beautiful worlds.
To all places of wilderness, enchantment, and freedom.

She then places a candle at the north and pauses to look outwards, saying:

The Lady is awesome.
The Powers of death bow before Her.

The person closest to the east takes a candle from the altar and places it at that quarter, saying:

Our Goddess is a Lady of Joy.
The winds are Her servants.

---

*Another introductory ritual by Ed Fitch.

The person closest to the south takes a candle from the altar and places it at that quarter, saying:

Our Goddess is a Goddess of Love.
At Her blessings and desire
The sun brings forth life anew.

The person closest to the west takes a candle from the altar and places it at that quarter, saying:

The seas are the domains of our Serene Lady.
The mysteries of the depths are Hers alone.

The priest now takes the wand, and starting at the north, draws it along the entire circle clockwise back to the north point, saying:

The circle is sealed, and all herein
Are totally and completely apart
From the outside world,
That we may glorify the Lady whom we adore.
Blessed Be!

All repeat: Blessed Be!

The priest now holds the wand out in salute towards the north for a moment and then hands it to the priestess, who also holds it out in salute. She motions to the group to repeat the following lines after her:

As above, so below . . .
As the universe, so the soul.
As without, so within.
Blessed and gracious one,
On this day do we consecrate to you
Our bodies,
Our minds,
And our spirits.
Blessed Be!

Now is the time for discussion and teaching. Wine and light refreshments may be served. When the meeting has ended, all will stand and silently meditate for a moment. The priestess will then take the wand and tap each candle to put it out, starting at the north and going clockwise about the circle, while saying:

> Our rite draws to its end.
> O lovely and gracious Goddess,
> Be with each of us as we depart.
> The circle is broken!

Beltane Ritual May 1*

I

Spiral-circle dance.

II

First priestess: (*Casts circle.*) The heaviness of winter has ended. Let us rejoice in the budding Earth and the beauty of the Maiden now ascendant. (*Lights altar candles and incense.*) We light the Beltane fires and celebrate the fertile warmth and light of our Lord and the renewed and renewing powers of light, energy, and love that are our Lady of May.

III

Second priestess: We celebrate the fragrant spring air, the soft May breezes that refresh the Earth and Her children.

Frist priestess: We celebrate the gentle fire of the sun in spring, whose caressing warmth awakens the Earth and Her children.

Third priestess: We celebrate the cool, damp spring rains, those sparkling showers that give sustenance to the Earth and Her children.

Four priestess: We celebrate the Earth. In the full bloom of Her maidenhood, She gives life to all of Her children.

---

*This ritual took place on Beltane, 1978, in Central Park in New York City. The four priestesses were members of a group called Manhattan Pagan Way. They wrote the ritual. About thirty-five people attended. This exemplifies the kind of spring ritual a group of city Pagans might attempt.

IV

Third priestess: O source of joy and love, O Goddess of all beginnings, come and join us, for this is the season of new growth. O Lady of May, refresh our senses, make us whole, replenish the earth.

Second priestess: At the equinox, I awakened. Then I had the power to melt the winter. But now I am in the fullness of my maidenhood, and I am wild with joy!

See how the buds burst into bloom. See how all of my animal creatures are drawn together in love and pleasure. Feel how my beauty tempts you all to forget your daily chores and celebrate with me.

Drink in this season fully, for my maidenhood is fleeting, and it will seem to you as if it were only an instant, and then it will be gone. The heavy heat of the summer will be on you, and I will be the Great Mother once again.

V

First priestess: (*Displays wine.*) We celebrate the dizzying sweetness of the spring that now blossoms around us. Bless this, our offering of May Wine, and as we taste its fullness, teach us to sow your seeds in love and joy.

Fourth priestess: (*Displays bread and sprouts.*) We celebrate the cycle of life renewed. From seed to bud to flower to fruit to seed. A perfect circle. These are the beads of Her necklace! (*People in center share, then take wine, bread and sprouts around circle.*)

VI

Third priestess: Now, as the warm spring renews the Earth and our lives, let's remember how our predecessors celebrated Beltane. The hearth fire of each home would be extinguished. Then the whole community would gather for a festival. As the celebration ended, each householder would take home some coals from the communal bonfire, to rekindle the hearth at home.

First priestess: Hearth fire is not forest fire. The dangerous is made domestic by skill and experience.

Hearth fire cooked their food and warmed their homes. It stood for safety and comfort. It still represents the warmth of the heart—the friendship and caring that come from the center of the person.

Hearth fire is simple, familiar, unspectacular. It is the polar opposite of fireworks. Safety, comfort, friendship. Love "to the level of every day's most quiet need, by sun and candle light."

Fourth priestess: The winter strained us. The day was bleak and gray. The cold was painful. We wrapped our bodies and pulled in our senses. We got through.

Now, in the softness and beauty of spring, we shed the layers of clothing from our bodies and open our senses again. Together, today, we pool the warmth of our joy in the spring. We will take a portion of our shared warmth home with us, to renew our everyday lives.

VII

Cauldron dance to "The Lady's Branle" or "She will bring the buds of spring," music traditional, words by Hope, published in Songs for the Old Religion.

VIII

Second priestess: We thank you for the flourishing of new life and for the feast of spring that is the freshness of your presence. Blessed be!

The circle is ended. Merry meet, merry part.

Appendix III: Resources

THIS IS THE THIRD EDITION of this resource guide. It's no exaggeration to say that the number of Pagan groups, festivals, and Web sites has exploded—there are so many groups and gatherings that this is just a sampling, and some of the smaller groves, covens, and kindreds are not listed. The only category that has not expanded is publications, and that is probably because the Web has taken over many of the functions of the publications. Many of the newsletters and magazines listed in the 1997 edition are now defunct. Some now exist online and no longer in paper form. Most of the festivals listed in the previous edition still exist, and many new ones have been created. There are now more than 350 Pagan gatherings. Some groups are now defunct; many others are thirty years old. Please always send a self-addressed, stamped envelope (SASE) with your inquiry if you are using the mail. If e-mail addresses are available, it's the fastest way to go.

What's different today is the Internet. If you are looking for some organization or festival or newsletter and you find that the letter comes back because the address is wrong, search the Web; in my experience, more than half the time it will be there.

If you come across this book after the year 2010, these listings will be more than four years old. One thing you might consider doing to obtain more information is to contact Circle for their *Guide to Pagan Groups* (see page 519). Every few years, Circle publishes an indispensable guide to Pagan groups, centers, networks, magazines, Web sites, suppliers, and artists. Circle's guide is more comprehensive than this one, listing several hundred small groups not mentioned here, as well as individual artists and stores. This resource guide is an eclectic list, and it contains most of the larger organizations and most important journals, festivals and Web sites. But if you are looking for a group near your city or town, your best bet may be Circle's guide. Circle's address is P.O. Box 9, Barneveld, WI 53507. Although I do keep a public mailing address (Margot Adler, P.O. Box 20182, Cathedral Station, New York, NY 10025-1518), I have two jobs and a family, not counting any Pagan activities, so I will not have the time to keep this list current. Again, the Web is a great place to search for Pagan publications, festivals, and groups.

CURRENT NEWSLETTERS, MAGAZINES, AND JOURNALS

The Accord. A quarterly journal for Wiccans, Pagans, and others on a magickal/spiritual path that focuses on Pagan spirituality and topics of interest to the Pagan community. It is published near the Solstices and Equinoxes by the Council of Magickal Arts, Inc. CMA is a Texas-based association of practitioners of the religions of the magickal arts. It has over 1,800 members and is open to people of all traditions who are interested in celebrating nature, spirit, and community. Each issue of *Accord* focuses on a particular theme. Also includes reviews, columns, advice, humor, religious liberties issues, calendar, and magickal lore. Subscriptions: free with membership to CMA (see page 522); also sold in occult, Wicca, and metaphysical stores. Address: Accord Office, P.O. Box 66100, Houston, TX 77266. E-mail: accord@magickal-arts.org. Web site: www.magickal-arts.org

AFA Update. An online journal published twice monthly by the Ásatrú Folk Assembly (see page 512). Includes short articles, reviews, commentary, and links of interest. Free of charge. Address: Ásatrú Folk Assembly, P.O. Box 445, Nevada City, CA 95959. Subscribe by e-mail: AFA-Bearclaw-subscribe@yahoogroups.com.

Always in Season: Living in Sync with the Cycles. A quarterly publication from Mama Donna's Tea Garden & Healing Haven (see page 544). It offers "information, ideas, and inspiration steeped in scientific, artistic, anthropological, psychological, mythological, mystical, and religious reference from cultures around the planet and over time to aid and augment our personal practice of ceremony and celebration. Subscriptions: $28/year. Columns include "Essence of the Season," "Ask Your Mama," and "Ritual Ragout." Address: Mama Donna's Tea Garden & Healing Haven, P.O. Box 380403, Exotic Brooklyn, NY 11238-0403. Phone: 718-857-1343. E-mail: cityshaman@aol.com. Web site: www.DonnaHenes.net

Awakened Woman (AWe). An online magazine published continuously since 1999 dedicated to women's inspiration, healing, and empowerment—through the Goddess. AWe features a unique blend of politics and spirituality, with news of the women's movement, articles about women's circles, spiritual journeys, and profiles of remarkable women. *Awakened Woman* also publishes a free monthly e-newsletter available by subscription. The magazine partners with the non-profit Women for a Better World, working to foster the global women's movement by finding "bases of agreement within our diversity," and hopes women will visit the Web site and become members of Women for a Better World. Publisher/editor Stephanie Hiller. Address: Awakened Woman Publications, P.O. Box 1113, Occidental, CA 95465. Phone: 707-874-1744. E-mail: editor@awakenedwoman.com. Web site: www.awakenedwoman.com

The Beltane Papers: A Journal of Women's Mysteries. An eclectic feminist/ Goddess/Pagan publication produced for over twenty years by volunteers. This unique and beautifully produced magazine has excellent women's art and writing. It is filled with complex articles on folklore, mythology, the history of religion, ritual, festivals, as well as goddess and herb lore, recipes, personal experiences, dreams, poetry, humor, and an extensive review section. Editor: Marione Thompson-Helland. Published three times yearly. 64 pages. Subscriptions: $16/year, sample issue $5; Canada $21/year, sample issue $7; elsewhere $28/year, sample issue $8.50 (all in U.S. funds). Address: TBP, P.O. Box 29694, Bellingham, WA 98228-1694. E-mail: womensmysteries@yahoo.com.

Web site: http://thebeltanepapers.net

The Blessed Bee: A Newsletter for Pagan Families. A publication specifically for Pagans with kids. Includes Crafts, rituals, homeschooling ideas, stories, poems, book reviews, and advice. Published quarterly. 32 pages. Editor in Chief: Anne Newkirk Niven. Available by subscription only. Subscriptions: $13/year; Canada and elsewhere $19/year (U.S. funds). Address: P.O. Box 641, Point Arena, CA 95468. Phone: 888-724-3966. Call or e-mail for a sample issue: sample@blessedbee.com.

Web site: www.blessedbee.com

The Cauldron. A journal featuring serious articles on Paganism, Witchcraft, Wicca, Folklore, and Earth Mysteries. Also includes book reviews and small ads. Published quarterly since 1976. Editor: Mike Howard. 44 pages. Subscriptions: $40/year, sample issue $7 (cash only); U.K. £14/year, sample issue £2.50. No checks or money orders can be accepted in foreign currency. Address: BM Cauldron, London WCIN 3XX, U.K.

Web site: www.the-cauldron.fsnet.co.uk

Circle Guide to Pagan Groups. The most comprehensive guide to Pagan groups around, and an indispensable tool for finding out what groups are in your local area. Lists hundreds of small covens and groves, as well as churches, networks, centers, periodicals, stores, and gatherings. Includes Wiccan, Shamanic, Druidic, Pagan, Goddess, Animistic, and other Nature Spirituality contacts. Senior Editor: Selena Fox. Updated every couple of years. 80+ pages; spiral bound. $18/year U.S., Canada, and Mexico; $24/year airmail elsewhere. U.S. funds only. Address: Circle Guide to Pagan Groups, Circle, P.O. Box 9, Barneveld, WI 53507. Phone: 608-924-2216. E-mail: circle@circlesanctuary.org.

Web site: www.circlesanctuary.org/network

Circle Magazine. A quarterly magazine published by Circle and the Voice of Circle Network. This is one of the oldest and most well known Pagan journals. The articles are about Nature religions, Shamanism, Goddess studies, Animism, Wicca, Magic, and related topics. The Readers' Forum section explores a different theme in each issue. Also includes regular features, including celebrating the seasons, Pagan religious freedom issues, Gods and Goddesses, herbcraft, animal spirits, ritualcraft, Pagan family activities, and Nature religions around the world. Each issue is filled with articles, news, rituals, invocations, poetry, photographs, artwork, meditations, festival announcements, news, contacts, and more. Managing Editor: Juliana van Clausen. Published quarterly. 72 pages. Subscriptions: $19/year bulk rate U.S.; $25/year first-class U.S.; $30/year airmail to Canada and Mexico; $46/year airmail to Europe; $48/year airmail elsewhere; sample issue $5 anywhere. U.S funds only. Address: Circle Magazine, P.O. Box 9, Barneveld, WI 53507. Phone: 608-924-2216. E-mail: editor@ circlesanctuary.org. Web site: www.circlesanctuary.org/circle

Communities Magazine. A quarterly national publicaton about cooperative living, organized neighborhoods, and all types of intentional communities, including ecovillages and cohousing communities. Contains articles, columns, and opinion pieces on all aspects of cooperative and community living, including process and communication skills. 76 pages. Editor: Diana Leafe Christian. Subscriptions: $20/year, sample issue $6. Address: Communities, 1025 Camp Elliott Road, Black Mountain, NC 28711. Phone: 828-669-9702. E-mail (subscriptions): store@ic.org; E-mail (editorial) communities@ic.org.

Covenant of the Goddess Newsletter. The Covenant of the Goddess is a cross-traditional federation of more than one hundred covens (see page 524). The *Newsletter* includes articles, announcements, and resources of interest to Witches, as well as COG news and business. Published eight times a year on the sabbats; 30–40 pages. Subscriptions: free to member covens and solitaries; $30/year donation for others. Address: COG Newsletter, P.O. Box 1226, Berkeley, CA 94701. Web site: www.cog.org

Cup of Wonder. No longer publishing, but back issues available. An annual journal focused on Reconstructionist Pagan religions, African Diasporic practices, as well as Heathen and Magickal life and thought. Approximately 180 pages. Back issues are $2.50–$10.00, depending on the issue. The publishing company, VireoNyx Publications, is planning more books and articles under the Cup of Wonder imprint. Web site: www.vireonyxpub.org

Earth First! Journal. This radical environmental journal is not specifically Pagan (although published on the Old European Nature holidays), but it is a newspaper devoted to radical and deep ecology. Includes articles on the preservation of wilderness and biological diversity, critiques of the environmental movement, news about radical environmental groups, essays on deep ecology, discussions on tactics, and book and music reviews. Subscriptions: $25/year; $40/year first class. Write for foreign rates. Address: EF! Journal, P.O. Box 3023, Tucson, AZ 85705. Phone: 520-620-9600. E-mail: collective@earthfirstjournal.org. Web site: www.earthfirstjournal.org

Enchante: The Journal for the Urbane Pagan. This journal, one of the best and wittiest Pagan magazines, is no longer publishing in paper form, although back issues are available. Includes articles, reviews, poetry, humor, stories, and letters. *Enchante* has a site on the Web and John Yohalem, its creator, says it may well rise again as an e-zine. Back issues vary in price. Address: Enchante, 30 Charlton Street, #6F, New York, NY 10014. E-mail: johnyohalem@ herodotus.com.

Web site: www.herodotus.com

Faces of the Goddess. Published since 1992, the purpose of the magazine is to provide a source of information and inspiration and a forum of exploration on Goddess spirituality, mysticism, mythology, feminine psychology, and empowerment techniques. "It's a magazine for both women and men to celebrate the Goddess in themselves and in their lives." Each issue has a different theme for writers, artists, and readers to explore. Editor: Sharon/Siannan Niman. Subscription: $12/year (U.S. and Canada); $18/year (overseas; U.S. funds only); sample issue $5. Checks must be made out to Sharon Niman. Address: P.O. Box 486, Crows Landing, CA 95313. E-mail: latigrepress@the vision.net.

Fifth Estate. An anarchist magazine published in Detroit and now rural Tennessee since 1965. It prints some of the best critiques of technology and modern society. The magazine is a cooperative, non-profit project, and the people who produce it describe themselves as "a group of friends who do so neither to secure wages nor as an investment in the newspaper industry, but to encourage resistance and rebellion to this society." It includes serious articles—both historical and on the present scene—letters, reviews, and reports from battlefields and movements all over the world. Published quarterly. 56 pages. Subscriptions: $10/year; $20/year international; $25/year institutions. Free to prisoners and soldiers. Subscription address: Fifth Estate, P.O. Box 201016, Ferndale, MI 48220. Editorial address: Fifth Estate, Box 6, Liberty, TN 37095.

Web site: www.fifthestate.org

Goddess Alive! A twice-yearly publication on Goddess research and celebration, published in Cornwall. Covers Goddess news, research, and reviews in Britain, the United States, and internationally. Subscriptions: $20/(U.S. dollar bills only please) or £8/year or by Pay Pal. Address: Goddess Alive! Whitewaves, Boscaswell Village, Pendeen, Penzance, Cornwall TR 19 7EP, U.K. E-mail: editor@goddessalive.co.uk.

Web site: www.goddessalive.com

Goddessing. An international biannual Goddess-oriented news journal of "Goddess expression, scholarship, arts, events, and delight!" Includes interviews, in-depth research, serious articles, humor, poetry, extensive reviews, letters, and networking, lists of events all over the world, tours and pilgrimages, photographs and artwork, and reports of festivals and gatherings. Editor: Willow La

Monte. 40 pages. Subscriptions: $30–35 (depending on income)/5 issues (2½ years) sent first-class mail within the U.S., sample $5; free to Pagan prisoners. Overseas: $35–45/5 issues (check must be in U.S. dollars, or cash). Make checks payable to "Goddessing." Address: Goddessing, P.O. Box 269, Valrico, FL 33595. Phone/fax: 813-643-7285.

Web site: www.goddessmandala.com

The Hermit's Lantern. A monthly newsletter with articles on herbal medicine, gardening, tarot, astrology, gemstones, and more. 16 pages. Subscriptions: $25/year. Address: The Hermit's Lantern, P.O. Box 0691, Kirkland, WA 98083.

Idunna. The quarterly journal of the Troth (see page 568), an organization dedicated to exploring, practicing, and promoting the pre-Christian religion of the Germanic peoples. Each issue explores a theme of interest to the organization and its members. Content includes scholarly and personal essays, poetry, news of Heathen activities, artwork, and book and music reviews. Subscription is free with membership in the Troth; non-members may subscribe for $20/year (U.S.) or $24/year (international). Address: The Troth, P.O. Box 1369, Oldsmar, FL 34677. E-mail: troth-contact@thetroth.org.

Web site: www.thetroth.org/publications/idunna.html

If . . . Journal. Formerly *PagaNet News,* a Pagan-specific newsprint publication, *If . . . Journal* is a publication of spiritual exploration for the thinking seeker of alternative spirituality. Published by PagaNet, Inc. (see page 555), *If . . .* is produced in a tabloid-sized newsprint format eight times a year for the seasonal quarters and cross-quarters. Features include articles on alternative spiritual and religious practices, Shamanic exploration and journeying, quantum physics, sustainable living, science and spirit, health and wellness, astrological overviews, as well as poetry, artwork, opinion polls, event and networking listings, and reviews of events, books, and music. Available free of charge at targeted distribution sites around the country as well as in Europe; however, *If . . .* relies strictly on subscriptions and advertisers to stay in print. Subscriptions are available in either print or digital formats for $21/year; $36/2 years. Sample copies and back issues of *If . . .* and/or *PagaNet News* are available for $5 each. Address: If . . . Journal, P.O. Box 61007, Virginia Beach, VA 23466. Phone 757-539-4523. E-mail: if@ifjournal.org.

Web site: www.ifjournal.org

The Lunar Calendar. Nancy Passmore and Luna Press have published this beautiful moon calendar dedicated "to the Goddess in Her Many Guises" for more than thirty years. The calendar teaches the tree-alphabet as inspired by Robert Graves's *The White Goddess.* It shows the phases of the moon and provides astronomical and astrological data. Includes artwork from more than twenty artists, as well as poems, moon data, and an excellent bibliography. 32 pages. 11 x 8½; opens up to 11 x 17. $23, plus $6 shipping and handling. Address:

Luna Press, P.O. Box 15511, Kenmore Station, Boston, MA 02215-0009. Phone: 617-427-9846. E-mail: THELUNAPRESS@aol.com.

Web site: www.thelunapress.com

MAMAROOTS Forum: Connecting in Her AfraGoddess Spirit!!! A Spiritual SistahWeb and Triune Forum publication dedicated to Afrakan-Matristik Spirituality, Mythology, Herstory, Culture, and Politics, and is "a positive network where Our practicing Sistahs of MAMAROOTS community may dialogue (NOMMA . . . the power of wimmin weaving the WORD) and build stronger Sistah-bonds, spiritually and culturally." It explores and shares issues and wisdoms which "affirmatively inspire Our Sistahs who are actively seeking to learn, practice, and share their Awakened Self-Awareness of Our Sacred Principles of Afrakan Spiritual Harmony." *MAMAROOTS Forum* welcomes donations and submissions: articles, reviews, images, short stories, rituals, correspondence, networking, and other resources produced by and for and in honor of wimmin of Afrikan heritage. Subscriptions: $7/year. Address: MAMAROOTS FORUM, P.O. Box 21066, Long Beach, CA 90804. Phone: 562-961-0900. E-mail: MAMAROOTS@aol.com or SistahMIND@yahoo.com.

Web sites: www.MAMAROOTSweb.com; forums.delphiforums.com/SistahMIND

MatriFocus Cross-Quarterly. Founded in 2001, a scholarly and sophisticated online journal and seasonal e-zine containing serious articles, essays, book reviews, artwork, and photography. "The journal is for Goddess Women and others interested in Goddess Lore and Scholarship, Goddess religions (ancient and contemporary), Feminist Spirituality, Women's Mysteries, Neopaganism, Paganism, Earth-based Religions, Witchcraft, Dianic Wicca and other Wiccan Traditions, the Priestess Path, Goddess Art, Natural Healing, Mythology, Female Shamanism, Consciousness, Community, Cosmology, and Women's Creativity, Culture and Health." MatriFocus is also a non-profit organization. Subscriptions are free; donations are welcome. E-mail: matrifocus@yahoo.com.

Web site: www.matrifocus.com

Metaformia: A Journal of Menstruation and Culture. A new multiple-genre, multidisciplinary, cross-cultural publication, sponsored by New College of California's Women's Spirituality M.A. Program. The journal is edited by cultural theorist and poet Judy Grahn, author of *Blood, Bread, and Roses,* and co-director of the program. Deborah Grenn, founder of the Lilith Institute and core faculty in the Women's Spirituality Program, serves as assistant editor. The journal, *Metaformia,* emerged from metaformic theory, which posits that women's menstrual rituals created much of what we know as culture. Grahn identifies metaforms as acts, objects, or embodied ideas that make a connection between menstruation and a mental or spiritual principle. Articles range in approach from academic to personal. Issues to include articles on the Sacred

Feminine, thealogy, the powers of Black Madonnas, war, modern menarchal initiation rites, metaformic analyses of race, class, and caste, violence and peace, the roles of women, men, and transgendered people in evolution, money, religion, anthropology, sexuality, and more. The creators of the journal hope to formulate new social thought and movement, and plan a blog as well. Published twice a year online by New College of California. Contacts: Judy Grahn: jgrahn@serpentina.com or Deborah Grenn: deborah@lilithinstitute.com.

Web site: www.metaformia.com

Meyn Mamvro. A Cornish Pagan-oriented Earth Mysteries magazine that focuses on ancient stones and sacred sites in Cornwall. Includes articles on Cornwall's holy wells, Witchcraft in Cornwall, sacred sites, book and video reviews, rituals and practice. *Meyn Mamvro* also produces a range of publications, including *Pagan Cornwall: Land of the Goddess, Fentynyow Kernow: In Search of Cornwall's Holy Wells,* and *Megalithic Mysteries of Cornwall.* Editor: Cheryl Straffon. Subscriptions: $20/year U.S. (dollar bills only) or £6.50 sterling. Address: Meyn Mamvro, 51 Carn bosavern, St. Just, Penzance, Cornwall TR 19 7QX, U.K. E-mail: cheryl.straffon@meynmamvro.freeserve.co.uk.

Web site: www.meynmamvro.co.uk

The Mystic's Wheel of the Year . . . a multifaith calendar reflecting eco-egalitarian spirituality. Published since 1996 by Page Two, Inc., this is a wall calendar for rediscovering Goddess and understanding God in Nature-based non-patriarchal ways. It features holy days from indigenous spiritualities worldwide: European (Celtic, Norse, and Greek), Middle Eastern (Sumerian and Canaanite-Hebrew), African (Egyptian and Santeria), and American (Iroquois, Zuni and Navajo); from Kabbalistic Judaism, Mystic Christianity, and Sufi-Islam; and from Hinduism, Zoroastrianism, Taoism, Shintoism, and Buddhism (Tantra and Zen). It explores environmentalist, feminist, human rights, and peace movement themes. It also includes astronomical data, meditations, and photos of sacred icons from various traditions. 32 pages. 11 x 11 closed; 11 x 22 open. $12 each, plus $2 postage. Discounts for 5+ calendars. Address: Page Two, Inc. P.O. Box 1209, Beltsville, MD 20704. Phone: 800-821-6604. E-mail: info@WheeloftheYear.com.

Web site: www.WheeloftheYear.com

new Witch: not your mother's broomstick. A magazine for Pagans 18–34 and "anyone else hip enough to read it." Cutting-edge topics include Queer Paganism, Pagan rock 'n' roll, Pagan crafts, and solitary magic, and includes advice columnists. Published quarterly. 80 pages. Editor in Chief: Anne Newkirk Niven. Subscriptions: $18/year U.S.; $24/year elsewhere (U.S. funds). Address: newWitch, P.O. Box 641, Point Arena, CA 95468. Phone: 888-724-3966. Call or e-mail for sample issue: sample@newwitch.com.

Web site: www.newwitch.com

Northword Journal. An Eclectic Pagan group and publication that is interactive with Circle and other groups throughout the world. Especially involved with Science Fiction Fantasy and futuristic Paganism. A member of Northward Enterprises since 1992. For more information, contact the publisher: Jeff Redmond, 1335 Beechwood NE, Grand Rapids, MI 49505-3830. E-mail: redmondjeff@hotmail.com.

Web site: www.erdabooks.net

The Oakleaf. A quarterly publication of the Church of Spiral Oak (see page 519), *The Oak Leaf* welcomes contributions of written pieces and artwork that reflect topics of interest to Pagans. Content includes articles, essays, poetry, humor, reviews, current events, puzzles, recipes, and more. *The Acorn* is a center pull-out childrens' mini-magazine, with articles, crafts, artwork, and poetry for and/or by Pagan youth. Sample issues, submission guidelines, and contact information may be found at the church Web site. Current issues are available at COSO events and at the business establishments of advertisers. Subscriptions are available with a donation of $10.00 per year, and past issues are available upon request. Address: The Church of Spiral Oak, P.O. Box 13681, Akron, OH 44334-3681. E-mail: clergy@spiraloak.com.

Web site: www.spiraloak.com

Oak Leaves. The journal published by Ár nDraíocht Féin: A Druid Fellowship (ADF) (see page 512). Issues include articles, essays, songs, and rituals on Druidry and Neo-Paganism. Published four times a year. 40–60 pages. Back issues are available. Subscriptions: $20/year for members, $25/year for nonmembers. Address: ADF, P.O. Box 17874, Tucson, AZ 85731-7874, or online at: www.adf.org.

Odin LIVES! A radio program that broadcasts every Thursday night at 8:00 P.M. Eastern Time from the studios of WBCQ in Kennebunkport, Maine, on a frequency of 7.415 MHz. *Odin LIVES!* features the best in Northern European folk music by various artists. The program also features extensive readings from (and interviews with) authors, musicians, and practitioners of the Old Ways of the Northern European Folk. The program regularly invites submissions from its listeners as a means of fostering the growth of the Heathen community. The *Odin LIVES!* Web site maintains links to many other Heathen organizations. Downloads of archived programs are available for purchase, with all proceeds supporting the radio show or its sponsors. Chris' Larsen, Executive Producer of *Odin LIVES!*, produces Nordic folk concerts in his home state of Ohio and is Musical Coordinator for Valhallapalooza, a folk festival celebrating Nordic music, culture, and Heathen spirituality. Address: Odin LIVES!, 2625 CR 12, Bellefontaine, OH 43311. E-mail: info@odinlives.org.

Web site: www.odinlives.org

Pagan Dawn. A quarterly magazine published by the Pagan Federation (formerly *The Wiccan*, founded in 1968). Annual subscription rates: £12.00/ year U.K.; £15.00/year elsewhere (accepts pounds sterling only). Also comes free with membership in the Pagan Federation (see page 553). Contains in-depth articles, book and music reviews, news comments, and a reader's forum. Address: Pagan Dawn, BM Box 7097, London WC1N 3XX, U.K. E-mail: pd@paganfed.org.

Web site: www.paganfed.org

Pagan Times. Published by the Pagan Alliance, Inc., a Pagan networking and information organization in Australia (see page 552). Published four times a year at the solstices and equinoxes, it includes reviews and articles, information about public gatherings, teachers, groups, other Pagan publications, and anything of interest to the Pagan community. There is a contacts section for solitary practitioners. Subscriptions: AU$8.00 per issue (inc. GST) or AU$30 (inc. GST) for a year's subscription (AU$44 for overseas subscribers). Check or money order made payable to Pagan Times. Address: Pagan Times, P.O. Box 26, North Hobart, TAS 7002, Australia. E-mail: TasPAlliance@hotmail.com.

Panegyria. A Pagan/Wiccan-oriented journal and newsletter published by the Aquarian Tabernacle Church (see page 511). Includes articles, letters, news reports, legal reports, contacts, reviews, announcements, and debates. Published approximately eight times a year. Subscriptions: $22/year first class to U.S., Canada, and Mexico; $36/year overseas via air mail. Sample copies sent free on receipt of three ounces postage or three international reply coupons. Address: Aquarian Tabernacle Church, P.O. Box 409, Index, WA 98256. Phone: 360-793-1945. E-mail: atc@AquaTabCh.org.

Web site: www.AquaTabCh.org

PanGaia: A Pagan Journal for Thinking People. An 80-page quarterly magazine that explores Pagan and Gaian Earth-based spirituality at home and around the world. Articles on issues ranging from "Pagans and the Land," "Sacred Crafts," and "The new Druidism." Editor in Chief: Anne Newkirk Niven. Subscriptions: $18/year U.S.; $24/elsewhere (U.S. funds). Address: PanGaia, P.O. Box 641, Point Arena, CA 95468. Phone: 888-724-3966. Call or e-mail for a sample issue: sample@pangaia.com.

Web site: www.pangaia.com

The Pomegranate: The International Journal of Pagan Studies. The only academic peer-reviewed journal of Pagan studies. It provides a forum for papers, essays, and symposia on both ancient and contemporary Pagan religious practices. *The Pomegranate* also publishes timely reviews of scholarly books, and the editors seek both new interpretations and re-examinations of those traditions marked both by an emphasis on nature as a source of sacred value (e.g., Wicca, modern Goddess religions) as well as those emphasizing continuity with a polytheistic past (e.g., Ásatrú or other forms of "reconstructionist" Paganism).

The editors also seek papers on the interplay between Pagan religious traditions, popular culture, literature, psychology, and the arts. Editor: Chas Clifton. Subscriptions: institutional price: £80/$125; individual price: £40/$65; Student and AAR/SBL/BASR price: £32/$52. Address: Journals Department, Subscription Customer Services Manager, Turpin Distribution Services, Stratton Business Park, Biggleswade, Bedfordshire SG18 8QB, U.K. Phone: 44(0) 1767 604 951. E-mail: subscriptions@turpin-distribution.com.

Web site: www.equinoxpub.com/journals/prices.asp?jref=51

Quest. In print since 1970 and dedicated to the magical heritage of the West, *Quest* contains articles on magic, Witchcraft, divination, ritual, the Mystery traditions, and all aspects of modern, practical Western occultism. Includes articles, reviews, and letters. Editor: Marian Green. Published quarterly. Subscriptions: £8.00/year U.K.; $20/year U.S. (air mail); sample issue $5 (air mail). Cash only unless payments are in Sterling. Address: BMC-SCL QUEST, London WCIN 3XX, U.K.

Reclaiming Quarterly Magazine. Formerly *Reclaiming Newsletter, Reclaiming's* mission is to combine Earth-based spirituality with direct political, social, and ecological action. *Reclaiming Quarterly* is dedicated to the meeting ground of these two goals—Magical Activism. RQ.org brings Reclaiming-style magic to the Web. Includes information on the latest grassroots activism, how to build a labyrinth, what's going on at the various Witchcamps, and more. RQ.org also sells Reclaiming music and chant CDs. *Reclaiming Quarterly* is produced by a volunteer cell based in San Francisco, with correspondents in over twenty communities across North America and Europe. Subscribe online or via mail. Address: *Reclaiming Quarterly,* P.O. Box 14404, San Francisco, CA 94114. Phone: 415-255-7623. E-mail: quarterly@reclaiming.org

Web site: www.reclaimingquarterly.org.

RFD Magazine. A reader-written journal of queer country living and alternative lifestyles. For over twenty-eight years, RFD has explored community, diverse sexuality, caring for the environment, Radical Faerie consciousness, and Nature-centered spirituality. It provides an extensive resource listing of Radical Faeries and faerie groups/communities throughout the world. Includes reviews, community forums, poetry, and pictures. Subscriptions: $25–75/year, sliding scale. Address: RFD Magazine, P.O. Box 68, Liberty, TN 37095. E-mail: mail@rfdmag.org.

Web site: www.rfdmag.org

Sage Woman: A beautifully produced quartely magazine that celebrates "the Goddess in Every Woman." Each issue is centered around a particular theme. Includes artwork, serious feature articles, Goddess lore, ritual, practical magic, astrology, herbs, poetry, and reviews of books and recordings. Editor in Chief: Anne Newkirk Niven. Subscriptions: $21/year U.S.; $27/year elsewhere (U.S.

funds). Address: SageWoman, P.O. Box 641, Point Arena, CA 95468. Phone: 888-724-3966. Call or e-mail for a sample issue: sample@sagewoman.com.

Web site: www.sagewoman.com

Societe. A journal of Technicians of the Sacred (see page 566), the International Religious and Magical Order of Societe, La Couleuvre Noire, and Order Templi Orientis Antiqua. It is dedicated to the preservation and practice of Voudoun and other Neo-African religious systems and their magic, art, and culture. Published periodically. Averages 100 pages. Address: Technicians of the Sacred, 1317 N. San Fernando Boulevard, Suite 310, Burbank, CA 91504. E-mail: cwillis664@aol.com.

Web site: www.techniciansofthesacred.com

Spirited Women. A newsletter published four times a year by SisterSpirit (see page 564), an eclectic women's spirituality group in Portland, Oregon. Includes articles, book reviews, and announcements. 15–20 pages. Subscriptions: $15/year. Address: Spirited Women, SisterSpirit, P.O. Box 9246, Portland, OR 97207.

Survival. A Wiccan magazine published by the Church of Wicca. Includes articles by Gavin and Yvonne Frost and by many students of the School of Wicca. "The oldest continually published Wiccan magazine." Published six times a year. Subscriptions: $24/year (except for active students, who get it for free). Address: Survival, P.O. Box 297-DM, Hinton, WV 25951-0297.

Web site: www.wicca.org

Tapestry. Tapestry is the quarterly newsletter of TAWN, the Tucson Area Wiccan-Pagan Network (see page 569). Features a calendar of local events, summaries of TAWN, and individual members' activities, rituals, reviews, and other articles of Neo-Pagan interest. Subscriptions: $15/year, $5 sample issue. Address: Tapestry, c/o TAWN, P.O. Box 482, Tucson, AZ, 85702-0482. E-mail: Board@TAWN.org

Web site: www.TAWN.org

Touchwood. Originally a paper magazine, now online, *Touchwood* is published by a hereditary Pagan tradition (Clan Cornovii). It provides information about "our tradition and that of other clans, covens, groups, and Nemeds. We provide a forum for all Druids, Heathens, Pagans, Witches, and Wizards." Includes articles, news, book and music reviews, rituals, sacred sites, and letters. A correspondence course is also available. And it's free. E-mail: jeremy_crawford2003@yahoo.co.uk or webmaster@touchwood-magazine.co.uk.

Web site: www.touchwood-magazine.co.uk/

The Unicorn. A Wiccan newsletter published at every sabbat, with news, reviews, poetry, artwork, letters, and a fun sabbat reading. Published continuously since 1976, and therefore one of the oldest Wiccan publications in North America. Edited by Paul Beyerl and published by the Rowan Tree. Subscriptions: $13/year. Address: The Unicorn, P.O. Box 0691, Kirkland, WA 98083.

Web site: www.therowantreechurch.org

Waxing & Waning. An online publication that showcases creative Pagan short stories and poetry. All genres are welcome, and "we're always looking for submissions." Novel excerpts and book reviews are also featured. E-mail: editor@ waxwanemag.com.

Web site: www.waxwanemag.com

Weavings. An online newsletter published eight times a year, in time for each of the Wiccan sabbats in electronic format (PDF). Published by IPAN, the Iowa Pagan Access Network (see page 540). Subscriptions are free and the current issue is always available on the IPAN Web site homepage. Includes articles, poetry, magic, and ritual, family page, events, artwork, and reviews. Address: IPAN, P.O. Box 861, Iowa City, IA 52244-0861. E-mail: ipan@ipan.org.

Web site: www.ipan.org

White Crane Journal. Founded in 1989 as a quarterly forum for exploring and enhancing gay men's spirituality. The *Lambda Book Report* has described *White Crane* as "a literate, intelligent, and, at the same time, provocative and ground-breaking scholarly quarterly of gay culture." Committed to the certainty that gay consciousness plays a special and important role in the evolution of life on Earth, *White Crane* exists to explore the variety of the manifestations of the spiritual search among contemporary gay men. Address: White Crane Journal, 172 Fifth Avenue #69, Brooklyn, NY 11217. E-mail: Bo@WhiteCrane Journal.com.

Web site: www.whitecranejournal.com

The Wiccan/Pagan Times. This online Pagan periodical has been in existence since 1999. TWPT was founded by the husband and wife team of Imajicka and Boudica (Michael and Margaret Foster), who work together to provide insightful interviews and book reviews for their readership. Their focus is not just the better-known authors, but also the up and coming contributors to the Pagan community. The site highlights the artwork of community artists and provides rituals, book spotlights, events, and store listings. The site is updated regularly and is free to the reading public.

Web site: www.twpt.com

Wiccan Rede. An English/Dutch Craft magazine published in the Netherlands by Gardnerian Witches, in print since 1979. Includes in-depth interviews, serious articles, and philosophical and controversial viewpoints on both the initiatory Wiccan traditions and solo/eclectic Witchcraft. Editors: Merlin and Morgana. Quarterly. 80 pages. Size A5. Address: Wiccan Rede, P.O. Box 473, 3705 AL, Zeist, the Netherlands.

Web site: www.silvercircle.org/wiccanrede.htm

The Wise Woman. A national journal that focuses on feminist issues, Goddess lore, feminist spirituality, and feminist Witchcraft. Includes articles on women's history, news, analysis, reviews, photos, poetry, interviews, original research on women in history, witch-hunts, and women today. Cartoons and Goddess graphics by Bulbul. The magazine began in 1980 and has been published by Ann Forfreedom, who writes many of the articles. The periodical in its entirety is on microfilm at: UMI, University Microfilms, Inc., 300 North Zeeb Road, Ann Arbor, MI 48106-1336. *Wise Woman* is turning from a magazine into a book publishing company, but back issues are available. Sample copy, $4. Address: The Wise Woman, 2441 Cordova Street, Oakland, CA 94602. E-mail: forfreedom3@earthlink.net.

Witch Eye: A Zine of Feri Uprising. This is a small paper zine full of art, articles, spells, and lore inspired by the F(a)eri(e) tradition of Witchcraft, meaning various permutations of the tradition passed down by Victor and Cora Anderson and popularized by the works of such people as Starhawk and Gwydion Pendderwen. While much of the focus is rooted in the Feri tradition, the magazine also offers many items of interest to any Pagan or Witch. Founded in 1999 and published roughly two or three times a year. Editor: Storm Faerywolf. 52 pages; full color covers. Current issues are $8 each; available back issues are $10 (check Web site for availability). CA residents add 7.25% sales tax. Make checks payable to "Faerywolf" and send to: Witch Eye, c/o Faerywolf, P.O. Box 3736, Antioch, CA 94531. Or order online.

Web site: www.feritradition.org/witcheye

The Witches' Almanac. "The complete annual guide to lunar harmony." An occult treasury of magical lore, myths, legends, folk tales, herbal secrets, animal advice, spells, sacred rituals, and many a curious tale of good and evil. Authoritative and entertaining. Astrological information by Dikki-Jo Mullen shows at a glance the phases of the moon, aspects of planets and their influence on each sign. Also includes Wiccan holidays and monthly weather forecasts by region. Published since 1971. Despite the sad passing of editor Elizabeth Pepper in 2005, the present editor, Theitic, and staff plan to continue publication without interruption. *The Witches' Almanac* has also published eleven other titles and has plans for several more. The *Almanac* is available in most bookstores from early February and year round, at $8.95.

Web site: www.TheWitchesAlmanac.com

The Witches' Voice (AKA Witchvox). Open to all Earth Spirit paths, Witchvox is a not for profit organization and extraordinary online source of information that delivers a "no advertising" home for Pagans of the world to "share their muse and their magick." A free community resource, *The Witches' Voice* is an educational network providing information services and resources for and about Pagans, Heathens, Witches, and Wiccans. Founded by Wren Walker, Peg Aloi, and Fritz Jung in December 1996. Offers the largest collection of Pagan content and networking resources on the Web. Articles, essays, columns, and more. A great place to go to research Wiccan traditions and to find current news. Winner of the 2003 Webby Award for Best Spirituality Site on the Internet, Witchvox serves over 3.8 million page requests to over 800,000 unique visitors per month.

Web site: www.witchvox.com

WomenSpirit. This was the first feminist spirituality periodical, which began in 1974, and although it is no longer publishing, back issues are available at the original cost of $3 each. Send a SASE to WomenSpirit, 2000 King Mountain Trail, Sunny Valley, Oregon 97497. E-mail: jmtgrove@hotmail.com. The journal is also available on microfilm through University Microfilm International (UMI).

Yggdrasil. One of the oldest, continuously published (since 1984) Pagan publications in the world. A small journal focusing on Heathen religion, mythology, runes, culture, and ethos. Yggdrasil is the world ash tree of Norse mythology, whose roots and branches hold the universe together. The journal stresses Northern European Traditional (N.E.T.) religion and culture. Includes articles on history, mythology, rituals, reviews, and runes. Editrix: Prudence Priest. Published quarterly. 16 pages. Subscriptions: $10/year U.S.; $13/year elsewhere. $3 sample issue. (U.S. funds only). Make checks payable to "Freya's Folk." Address: Freya's Folk, PMB 165, 537 Jones Street, San Francisco, CA 94102-2007.

Web site: www.freyasfolk.org

GROUPS

In the event that you are new to all of this and have justifiable worries about contacting strange groups, here are a few words of advice. While Pagan groups are not cults (they do not try to "convert" you, or brainwash you, or take over your life), any person open enough to be on a spiritual quest is in a somewhat vulnerable position. There are also many people—no matter what their religion—who talk a good line but have not worked out their own emotional problems. The leader of one Wiccan group that I praised to the skies in the first edition of this book (fortunately the group has since dissolved) ended up on a guru trip and even expected sexual favors from some of the members of his group. Hopefully that is a rare exception. But there are probably lots of groups here that I disagree with politically or philosophically.

In *Real Magic*, Isaac Bonewits published what he called his "Cult Danger Evaluation Frame," which was revised in 2001 and again in 2004. He lists eighteen things to look at when you are thinking about a specific group. You can give each item a score from one to ten. As a general rule, he says, the higher the numerical score of a given group, the more likely it is to be dangerous. He notes that while many of the scales in the frame are subjective, the evaluation frame is founded on modern ideas of humanistic psychology concerning the nature of mental health and personal growth, as well as being based on Bonewits's own experience. No matter what kind of group you are exploring, from Scientology to the local Pagan grove, it's worth considering the eighteen issues mentioned below before you make your plunge.

THE ADVANCED BONEWITS' CULT DANGER EVALUATION FRAME

by P. E. I. Bonewits

1 2 3 4 5 6 7 8 9 10
low   high

1. INTERNAL CONTROL: Amount of internal political and social power exercised by leader(s) over members; lack of clearly defined organizational rights for members. 1_____

2. EXTERNAL CONTROL: Amount of external political and social influence desired or obtained; emphasis on directing members' external poltical and social behavior. 2_____

3. WISDOM / KNOWLEDGE CLAIMED by leader(s); amount of infallibility declared or implied about decisions or docrinal / scriptural interpretations; number and degree of unverified and / or unverifiable credentials claimed. 3_____

4. WISDOM / KNOWLEDGE CREDITED to leader(s) by members; amount of trust in decisions made by leader(s); amount of hostility by members toward internal or external critics and / or toward verification efforts. 4_____

5. DOGMA: Rigidity of reality concepts taught; amount of doctrinal inflexibility or "fundamentalism"; hostility toward relativism and situationalism. 5_____

6. RECRUITING: Emphasis put on attracting new members; amount of proselytizing; requirement for all members to bring in new ones. 6_____

7. FRONT GROUPS: Number of subsidiary groups using different names from that of main group, especially when connections are hidden. 7_____

8. WEALTH, amount of money and / or property desired or obtained; emphasis on members' donations. 8_____

9. SEXUAL MANIPULATION of members by leader(s) of
   non-tantric groups; amount of control exercised over sexuality
   of members in terms of sexual orientation, behavior,
   and / or choice of partners.   9_____

10. SEXUAL FAVORITISM: Advancement or preferential
    treatment dependent upon sexual activity with the leader(s)
    of non-tantric groups.   10_____

11. CENSORSHIP: Amount of control over members' access
    to outside opinions of group, its doctrines, or leader(s). 11_____

12. ISOLATION: Amount of effort to keep members from
    communicating with non-members, including family;
    friends, and lovers.   12_____

13. DROPOUT CONTROL: Intensity of efforts directed
    at preventing or returning dropouts.   13_____

14. VIOLENCE: Amount of approval when used by or for
    the group, its doctrines, or its leader(s).   14_____

15. PARANOIA: Amount of fear concerning real or
    imagined enemies; exaggeration of perceived power of
    opponents; prevalence of conspiracy theories.   15_____

16. GRIMNESS: Amount of disapproval concerning jokes
    about the group, its doctrines, or leader(s).   16_____

17. SURRENDER OF WILL: Amount of emphasis on
    members not having to be responsible for personal
    decisions; degree of individual disempowerment
    created by the group, its doctrines, or its leader(s).   17_____

18. HYPOCRISY: Amount of approval for actions which the
    group officially considers immoral or unethical when done
    by or for the group, its doctrines, or leader(s); willingness
    to violate the group's declared principles for political,
    psychological, social, economic, military, or other gain. 18_____

Quite frankly, if you find that any group here has anything but a reasonably low score according to this evaluation frame, it shouldn't be in this book.
Some groups will have a lot of structure, formal training, and a fair amount of
hierarchy. A few groups may even have charismatic leaders. Others will be leaderless, anarchistic, and make their decisions by consensus. Some groups charge

fees for workshops; many covens, groves, and kindreds do not charge fees for teaching. But none of these organizations should *ever* censor your information, control your life, decide on your friends, insist on sexual favors, demand exorbitant amounts of money, or try to prevent you from leaving. Thankfully, most Pagan groups believe that you are the master/mistress of your fate and that the only real initiation (and power and knowledge) comes from within. Since most Pagan groups are anti-authoritarian, abuses are less common, although they are still possible. With these caveats, here are the listings.

Aerious. Aerious means "of Earth and Sky." It is a non-profit educational organization founded in 1991, with the intention of remembering heaven on earth through metaphysics, permaculture, wholistic healing of mind, body, and spirit, and awareness of nature. It emphasizes hands-on experience and individual empowerment. It holds classes and gatherings at YewWood Forest Retreat Center, a nature sanctuary in the Oregon Coast Range, off the grid and "home to spotted Owls, spawning salmon and nature spirits." Hosts the Earth and Sky Summer Creation Festival and other gatherings. Apprenticeships in permaculture and live-in situations available. Address: Aerious, c/o Mark McNutt, 93640 Deadwood Creek Road, Deadwood, OR 97430. Phone: 541-964-5341. Web site: www.aerious.org

The Albion Conclave. A Druid organization that has been running since 1992. "We provide a highly respected distance learning course supporting Druids practicing within a solitary framework seeking to reconnect with their Pagan ancestors; see www.druidnetwork.org for more details." The Albion Conclave launched the Mistletoe Foundation in 2003 with the support of the Druid Network as a medium to introduce the great mistletoe harvesting ritual back into the Druidic calendar. By providing a sacred space of mutual understanding and building bridges within the diversity of modern Druidry, the Albion Conclave seeks to support Druidry in its evolution as it slowly matures, questing to transform itself once again into an enlightened spiritual tradition. "The Albion Conclave also enjoys good relations with the An Ceile De, perhaps the only authentic branch of Druidry still in existence with 2000 years of unbroken practice behind it. The Albion Conclave encourages devotion to the spiritual path as a means to raise the human consciousness working within the native Druidic traditions of Britain." Address: The Albion Conclave, 39 Dalby Road, Anstey, Leicestershire, LE7 &DL, U.K. E-mail: stefan.seniuk@ntlworld.com.

Alexandrian Wicca Incorporated. Established in 2004 as an autonomous organization concerned primarily with the preservation and perpetuation of Alexandrian-based Wicca Craft within Australia and beyond. The organization does not claim to be the official representative body of all or any specific Alexandrian Wiccan lineage; however, it hopes to network its membership across the diversity of lineages—encouraging unity, respect, tolerance of differences, and recognition of a common heritage. Address: Alexandrian Wicca Incorporated, P.O. Box 653, Ulladulla 2539, N.S.W. Australia. Phone: 61 (02) 4455 3006. E-mail: alexandrianwiccans@yahoo.com.au. E-group: groups.yahoo.com/ group/Alexandrian_Wicca_Incorporated.

Web site: www.geocities.com/alexandrianwiccans

The Alternative Religions Educational Network (AREN). AREN grew out of WADL, the Witches' Anti-Discrimination League, one of the oldest Pagan religious anti-discrimination organizations in the country. AREN has also incorporated WARD (Witches Against Religious Discrimination). Since its inception in 2000, AREN has become one of the leading Pagan religious organizations helping people with religious discrimination problems, as well as educating legal personnel and others settling these problems. Direct financial help is not possible, but they will try to help you find an attorney, know the right questions to ask, aid in the investigation, and help the attorney develop the case. In many cases, just being able to provide education and help with investigation is all that is necessary to bring a discrimination case to a successful conclusion. A newsletter, ACTION, is published eight times a year for members. Individual membership: $15/year U.S.; $30/year elsewhere. Address: AREN, P.O. Box 1655, Richmond, KY 40475-1655. E-mail: aren@aren.org.

Web site: www.aren.org

The American Vinland Association. A non-profit association founded in 1995 for Northern European Tradition (the N.E.T.) members in Canada and the United States. The AVA exists to promote the re-establishment and practice of the Old Religions of Northern and Central Heathen Europe. Includes Ásatrú, Vanatru, Romuva, Finnish, Baltic, and indigenous Siberian traditions. The association seeks to help support, encourage, network, and credential Heathenfolk of these traditions. "The AVA does not discriminate. Any Ásatrú individual or group who supports this position can join." Group and individual members: $20/year (U.S. funds only). Address: The American Vinland Association, Inc., PMB 2154, 537 Jones Street, San Francisco, CA 94102-2007.

Web site: www.freyasfolk.org

The Ancient Keltic Church. An organization dedicated to the rediscovery and revival of the Pagan Mystery religion of the ancient Celtic people. It was founded in 1976 as the Roebuck coven, which studied the work and writings of Robert Cochrane as well as other British traditionalists. In 1982, the Roebuck became associated with the Clan of Tubal Cain, Cochrane's original group, and was finally incorporated as the Ancient Keltic Church in 1989. It has since hived off five daughter groups, each with its own unique version of the Roebuck tradition. The Roebuck tradition is described as having a complex theology and a strict code of ethics. The church holds public seasonal rituals corresponding to the Celtic Fire Festivals and open full moon rituals that anyone may attend. There are also training programs and an apprenticeship program for those interested in the priesthood. Address: The Ancient Keltic Church, P.O. Box 663, Tujunga, CA 91043-0663. E-mail: akcroebuck@aol.com. Web site: www.ancientkelticchurch.org

Ancient Order of Druids in America (AODA). Founded in 1912 as the American branch of the Ancient and Archaeological Order of Druids, AODA is a Druid church of nature spirituality, rooted in the Druid Revival of the eighteenth and nineteenth centuries. It offers an opportunity for modern people to experience the teachings and practices of traditional Druidry in today's world. AODA understands Druidry as a path of nature spirituality and inner transformation founded on personal experience rather than dogmatic belief. "It is a church in the original sense of that word, a community of people following a spiritual path together. It welcomes men and women of all national origins, cultural and linguistic backgrounds, and affiliations with other Druidic and spiritual traditions. Ecological awareness and commitment to an earth-honoring lifestyle, celebration of the cycles of nature through seasonal ritual, and personal development through meditation and other spiritual exercises form the core of its work, and involvement in the arts, healing practices, and traditional esoteric studies are among its applications and expressions." Address: AODA, P.O. Box 1181, Ashland, OR 97520: E-mail: info@aoda.org. Web site: www.aoda.org

Ancient Riders. Founded in 2005, Ancient Riders is a fellowship of Pagans who are also motorcycle enthusiasts. Membership is free. Regionally, members have begun organizing for rides and Pagan Bike-blessing events, as well as meeting up at secular motorcycling rallies. Links to the associated list-serve, as well as specifics for membership, are online at www.ancientriders.org.

Ancient Ways. Ancient Ways is a store, a library, a center, a Web site, and a festival. Glenn Turner has run Ancient Ways since 1988, and the center and library feature Wicca, spells, Crowley, feminist spirituality, Afro-American spirituality, tarot, magic, astrology, and psychic development. Ancient Ways runs PantheaCon (see page 575) and the Ancient Ways Festival (see page 581). Address: Ancient Ways, 4075 Telegraph Avenue, Oakland, CA 94609. Phone: 510-653-3244. Web site: www.ancientways.com

Annwfn/Forever Forests. Founded by Gwydion Pendderwen in 1977, Forever Forests on the land of Annwfn became the ecological branch of the Church of All Worlds. Friends of Annwfn sponsors tree plantings of cedar, pine, douglas fir, and redwood on logged-over land. Over twenty-seven years, more than 160,000 trees have been planted. There are also fruit trees, roses, and herbs. Over the years Annwfn has been the site of many seasonal rituals, handfastings, funerals, as well as other ceremonies, music, and entertainment. Gwydion's home, The Shaggy Mushroom, is now a temple on the land. The basic mission continues to be reconnecting people with the Mother through tree plantings, land stewardship, and restoration. Mailing address: Friends of Annwfn, P.O. Box 48, Calpella, CA 95418. Phone: 707-468-4661.

Web site: www.annwfn.org

Appalachian Pagan Alliance (APA). The APA is a large multitradition Pagan group based in the magical Mountains of Appalachia. Founded in 1998, the APA has grown into a large group of people from various Pagan paths, including members of covens and solitary practitioners. The APA has a massive Web site of resources for its members and other seekers, including an online monthly newsletter. The APA also has a children's group, the Witchlings Circle, which has Pagan kids' WebPages: coloring pages, children's spells, and activities. The APA hosts various local gatherings, including the Annual APA May Day Celebration, Yule Gatherings, several Ladies' Night Out events a year, and Vacation Witchcraft School for the Witchlings Circle group. The APA also hosts its online chat group at yahoogroups, which is used as a daily fellowshipping meeting. APA's leading Priestess: Ginger Strivelli. Address: APA, P.O. Box 450, Weaverville, NC 28787. E-mail: EmpressGinger@charter.net.

Web site: www.angelfire.com/nb/appalachianpagan

The Aquarian Tabernacle Church (ATC). The Aquarian Tabernacle Church is a legal, tax-exempt religious organization, founded in 1979 by Pierre C. "Pete Pathfinder" Davis. The ATC is a new tradition, although it is descended from English Traditional Wicca. An open-membership Pagan church with both local and worldwide membership of both independent congregations and solitaries, ATC also serves as the mother church for many autonomous ATC-affiliated congregations throughout the United States, Canada, Australia, South Africa, and Ireland. The Church has a Retreat House, a circle of standing stones (The MoonStone Circle), the Center for Non-Traditional Religion, and Pathfinder Press. ATC publishes a journal, *Panegyria* (see page 500) as well as Hecate's Horn, a members-only newsletter. The Church sponsors full moon and new moon rituals at the church, as well as several festivals held at larger retreat facilities. These include the Spring Mysteries Festival (see page 580) and Hekatee's Sickle Festival (see page 588). ATC has also created the Woolston-Steen Theological Seminary, which has ministerial degree programs (www.wiccan seminary.edu) and has also created SpiralScouts International, an alternative to mainstream scouting youth programs, with more than 120 groups worldwide in 2005 (www.SpiralScouts.org). Address: Aquarian Tabernacle Church, 48631 River Park Drive, P.O Box 409, Index, WA 98256. Phone: 360-793-1945. E-mail: atc@AquaTabCh.org.

Web site: www.AquaTabCh.org

Ardantane. An independent non-profit educational organization established to serve the Pagan faith and community and individual Pagan practitioners. A Pagan learning center and seminary on twenty-five acres in the Jemez Mountains of New Mexico, Ardantane offers certificate programs of study in the areas of Pagan Leadership, Magickal Arts, Witchcraft, Healing Arts, and Shamanic Studies. Schools being developed include Environmental Sustainability and Bardic Arts. Ardantane fosters excellence in teaching, using a national pool of skilled and well-informed teachers who are committed to their own continual growth. Educational programs are of varying length and formats—from half-day to weekend programs. Some programs are offered in cities around the United States, by arrangement. An annual calendar of courses and more information are available on the Web site. Address: Ardantane, P.O. Box 307, Jemez Springs, NM 87025. Phone: 505-469-7777. E-mail: Registrar@ardantane.org. Web site: www.ardantane.org

Ár nDraíocht Féin: A Druid Fellowship (ADF). An international fellowship devoted to creating a public tradition of Neopagan Druidry. The name is Gaelic for "Our Own Druidism." Founded in 1983, ADF is an outgrowth of the Reformed Druids of North America, an anachronistic movement begun by college students in the mid-1960s, and describes itself as the largest Neo-Pagan Druid organization in the English-speaking world. In developing an independent tradition of Druidism, ADF has been doing research about the ancient Celts and other Indo-European peoples, designing rituals, and developing artistic skills. It sees itself as a group of "polytheistic nature worshippers, attempting to revive the best aspects of the Paleopagan (original) faiths of our predecessors within a modern, scientific, artistic, ecological, and wholistic context, taking a nondogmatic, pluralistic approach." The group was started by Isaac Bonewits and has a magazine, *Oak Leaves* (see page 499), which is published four times a year. There are more than 1,100 members of ADF located in nine countries, and about fifty-five congregations (groves) throughout the United States, United Kingdom, and Canada. Ár nDraíocht Féin has regional solstice and equinox gatherings, and publishes songbooks, pamphlets, and other works. A form for membership and/or subscription to Oak Leaves can be obtained online or by sending a request to ADF, P.O. Box 17874, Tucson, AZ 85731-7874. Web site: www.adf.org

The Ásatrú Alliance (AA). Founded in 1988 to more efficiently promote the religion of Ásatrú on a national and regional scale. Today, many of the followers of the Norse Gods and Goddesses have banded together in groups that are known as kindreds. The Ásatrú Alliance provides kindreds with a means to work together to promote common ideals and goals. The Ásatrú Alliance hosts the National AlThing every year, where kindreds work together to provide for the continued growth of Ásatrú in Vinland. The Ásatrú Alliance also publishes a quarterly magazine known as *Vor Tru,* now in its thirtieth year of publication. Its publishing arm, World Tree Publications, established in 1986, provides a wealth of information about the religion of Ásatrú. Address: The Ásatrú Alliance, P.O. Box 961, Payson, AZ 85547. E-mail: valgard@asatru.org.

Web site: www.asatru.org

Ásatrú Folk Assembly (AFA). Formed in 1994 "to honor the spiritual Way of the Germanic peoples (to include the Scandinavians, the Anglo-Saxons, and the Germanic tribes on the Continent)." Although Norse names are used for the Gods, the actual breadth of practice and interest reaches well beyond the Viking Age. The ancestors are given honor second only to the Gods and Goddesses. While the AFA honors the ways of its ancient forebears, the AFA believes in living in the present century. AFA gatherings do not feature the historic garb and weaponry favored by some groups. The AFA seeks to present Ásatrú to a mainstream audience and is family friendly. "Social interests include the preservation of our traditional freedoms (which originate largely in the pre-Christian Germanic cultures), the protection of the environment, and issues pertaining to the survival of traditional peoples and cultures, including those of Europe." The AFA also holds gatherings and encourages local activity around the country. Address: Ásatrú Folk Assembly, P.O. Box 445, Nevada City, CA 95959. E-mail info@runestone.org.

Web site: http://runestone.org

The Assembly of the Sacred Wheel. A legally recognized Wiccan nonprofit religious organization based in the Mid-Atlantic region. Keepers of the Holly Chalice, the founding coven of the Assembly, began in February 1984. The Assembly was incorporated in the state of Delaware in 1993. The Elders of the Assembly are Helena Domenic and Ivo Dominguez, Jr. The Assembly sponsors open educational events and rituals as a tradition and as individual covens. As of 2006 there were six covens in the Delaware, New Jersey, and Pennsylvania area. Larger events include the annual Spring Magick and Autumn Magick festivals, as well as the periodic Between the Worlds conference. The Assembly also sponsors the New Alexandrian Library project (see page 546). The Assembly practices a syncretic form of Wicca and draws inspiration from Astrology, Kabala, the Western Magical Tradition, and the folk religions of Europe. Religiously, the Assembly is dedicated to the health of Mother Earth, and to all of her children. "We recognize that every human carries the divine spark of God and Goddess, a gift that carries the obligation to make manifest this divine heritage. Divinity itself, source of the Universe, is a single and incomprehensible force that emanates as the God and the Goddess. Divinity is immanent, inherent in all that exists and transcendent, supporting all that exists—whole, distinct, incorruptible, and outside of time." The structure of the Assembly was designed to encourage the formation of a magical community that is close-knit and yet gives individual covens room for growth and experimentation. Address: Assembly of the Sacred Wheel, 14914 Deer Forest Road, Georgetown, DE 19947. Phone: 302-855-9422. E-mail: sacredwheel@sacredwheel.org.

Web site: www.sacredwheel.org

Association for Consciousness Exploration. An Ohio-based organization that provides services in the fields of magic, mind-sciences, alternative life-styles, comparative religion/spirituality, holistic healing, and related subjects. Founded in 1983 in the Cleveland area, ACE has provided educational, recreational, multicultural, and spiritual programs to Northeast Ohio and the public at large. ACE is best known for sponsoring the Starwood Festival (see page 585) and the WinterStar Symposium (see page 576). ACE maintains the Starwood Center, a storefront headquarters in Cleveland, complete with mind-science equipment, seminar space, and a bookstore, and shares space with a complete recording studio, Audio Kreme (run by Regis Sedlock), providing the center with terrific audio-visual facilities. ACE holds and hosts events in the community, including drumming circles, meetings, and ceremonies by Stone Creed Grove (the local ADF group), concerts, classes, and parties. ACE also produces a line of books, tapes, and CDs for sale, featuring music, lectures, and guided meditation by many past Starwood and WinterStar presenters, and the ACE/ Llewellyn Collection. Mailing address: ACE, 1643 Lee Road #9, Cleveland Hts., OH 44118. E-mail: ace@rosencomet.com.

Web site: www.rosencomet.com

Australian Pagan Information Center. Established in 1983 to provide an authoritative reference point on all aspects of Paganism, including belief structures (Witchcraft and magic) and the phenomena and practices (such as herbalism and altered states). The Center publishes the journal *Panthology,* a digest of the best articles from around the world. The Center also has an extensive library of texts and notes and video and audio recordings, and also acts as a contact point for Pagans and even for the press and the police. Address: Australian Information Center, P.O. Box 54, Castlemaine, Vic., Australia. E-mail: pclempson@hotmail.com.

Bay Area Pagan Assemblies (BAPA). A non-profit organization dedicated to providing services to the Pagan community of the greater San Francisco Bay Area (including Santa Cruz). BAPA's mission is to serve the Pagan community as an information resource and to facilitate the practice of Pagan spirituality. Address: BAPA, P.O. Box 4159, Mountain View, CA 94040.

Web site: www.bapa.net

The Black Earth Institute. Articulates and forges connections between the arts and the sacred, whether defined as divinity, ancestors, or the earth. Fellows, appointed every two years, have significant publication records in poetry and/or fiction; Scholar/Advisors are appointed for varying periods to support

Fellows' work. Public programming includes readings, conferences, and publications. The Institute is located in Black Earth, Wisconsin. Address: Brigit Rest, 4520 Blue Mounds Trail, Black Earth, WI 53515. E-mail: black_earth_arts@yahoo.com.

Web site: www.blackearthinstitute.org

The Black Witch-Hat Society. A social club–style network, co-founded by Lady Isadora and Lykaina, for Witches who enjoy having fun with "the image." It includes an e-group and local chapters with in-person activities. "Just imagine what spectacular subversion we may be brewing: rune-casting, spell-chanting hordes of wonderful Witches streaming stalwartly down Mystic Main Street, U.S.A., our trusty gnarled old besoms in hand, our tall pointy black hats and cacklesque cones of power aimed strategically at both Inner and Outer Stratospheres! Party on, noble Pentagram People!" Address: The Black Witch-Hat Society, P.O. Box 41246, Des Moines, IA 50311. E-mail: broomstick_bluestocking@yahoo.com.

Web site: www.ladyisadora.com/witchhat.html

Blood Eagle Kindred. Based in Southeastern New England, the kindred is known for assisting the production of the radio show *Odin LIVES!* (see page 499) and *Zeitgeist* magazine (official publication of the Irminen-Gesellschaft); brewing exquisite mead and beer; advocating for the religious rights of incarcerated Heathens; publishing essays on Germanic socioethnobotany; practicing spiritual midwifery at birth and death passages; hosting Pub Moots in Southeastern New England; and for taking numerous cross-country road trips together to AlThings and Moots. Blood Eagle Kindred is a member kindred of the Ásatrú Alliance, and some kindred members also belong to the Irminen-Gesellschaft and the Ásatrú Folk Assembly. Blood Eagle Kindred produces Valhallapalooza (see page 590), a folk festival celebrating Nordic music, culture, and Heathen spirituality. Address: Blood Eagle Kindred, P.O. Box 15084, Riverside, RI 02915. E-mail: info@bloodeaglekindred.org.

Web site: www.bloodeaglekindred.org

Branching. Founded in 1995, Branching is an international group that networks by mail. It publishes a newsletter, *Folio,* three times a year, which seeks to instruct newcomers on Paganism, current and ancient Wicca, Magick, ritual, and healing. Articles are written by members. Occasionally a member directory/pen pal list is issued for networking purposes. Since its founding, *Folio* has evolved into a forum for Wiccans and Pagans behind bars. The newsletter/membership fee is $4 a year, or $6 for foreign members. This fee is waived for prisoners and other indigent persons. Contact: Aradia. Address: Branching, P.O. Box 3155, East Hampton, NY 11937-0397. E-mail: crafters22001@yahoo.com.

Caer na Donia y Llew (House of Goddess and God). The Caer began as a small Cymri (Welsh, Celtic) family tradition and morphed into a large Pagan ecclesiastical corporation in 2001. Now a non-profit religious organization, members include old-line Pagans, eclectic Neo-Pagans, Ásatrú, Wiccans, Native Americans, and Druids. "We ask that members take a vow such as the Wiccan Rede or aspire to the Nine Virtues, and contribute to society by working, attending school, or caring for children. Our rituals and gatherings are very family oriented. Legally ordained clergy are available to facilitate weddings, baby blessings, hospital visits, funerals, and other rites of passage. We hold ceremonies for the Celtic holidays and Wiccan sabbats. We also celebrate American holidays such as July 4th and Thanksgiving." Members help to support the Paganstock Music Festival (see page 579) in June in southwest Michigan, the Midwest Pagan Council's Pan Pagan Festival in August (see page 584), and Pagan Pride events. The Caer sponsors several kids' field trips, service projects, and classes. They also have a group for young adults, ages 11–22: MEH (Magickally Enchanted Heathens). Address: Caer na Donia y Llew, 52188 30th Avenue, Bangor, MI 49013. E-mail: aldagffhaine@btc-ci.com.

Web site: www.cndyl.org.

California Utlandr Alliance. The CUA exists to provide Heathens a common base for networking at a local, grass-roots level among California steadings, kindreds, hearths, Hofs, etc. Any Californian group or individual may join. Current dues are 3 self-addressed stamped envelopes sent to: Freya's Folk, PMB 165, 537 Jones Street, San Francisco, CA 94102-2007. "We do NOT keep nor give out a mailing list." E-mail: prudence@freyasfolk.org.

Camp Sister Spirit Folk School. A project of SisterSpirit, Incorporated, a non-profit, tax exempt, charitable organization whose mission is to "eradicate hatred and differences through education and interaction with our neighbors." Camp Sister Spirit is located on 120 acres of sacred ground in the pine belt of Mississippi. "We host a variety of cultural events, including the Gathering of Eclectic Views, Gulf Coast SisterCamp, and the Driven by the Wind Festival. CSS has ten cabins, camping sites, meeting and conference space, nature trails, and more. Address: CSSFS, 444 Eastside Drive, Ovett, MS 39464. Phone: 601-344-1411. E-mail: CSSFolkschool@aol.com.

Web site: www.campsisterspirit.com

The Celtic Witan Church. Founded in 1984 and legally incorporated in 1992, "We gather for the study and practice of Goddess-oriented, nature-based religion of the ancient Celtic people. This is a fertility religion concerned with all aspects of prosperity, emotional and spiritual growth, abundance, creativity and healing." The church honors the Celtic deities with full moon rituals and sabbat festivals. There are many open rituals and hands-on training programs— from initiate to legal clergy. Associated congregations are: MoonDance Coven of Albuquerque, New Mexico, Moon Shadow Coven of El Paso, Texas, and

Key to the Moon Coven of Canoga Park, California. All groups can be reached through the Celtic Witan Church. Address: The Celtic Witan Church, P.O. Box 8, Canoga Park, CA 91305.

The Chameleon Club. A group of individuals involved in the exploration of inner frontiers and the celebration of the diversity of the human experience in all realms, be they magical, scientific, or spiritual. Founded in 1978, "their motto is 'Change!,' their spirit is undaunted, their energy is phenomenal, and their number is far from legion." They include magicians of many paths, teachers from many reality perspectives, and joyous entertainers. They have created ACE, the Association for Consciousness Exploration, the Starwood Festival, and the WinterStar Symposium, and run them all; and they perform as the musical ensemble Chameleon. They see themselves as an extended family or tribe in the style of the Pranksters. Mailing address: ACE, 1643 Lee Road #9, Cleveland Hts., OH 44118. E-mail: ace@rosencomet.com.

Web site: www.rosencomet.com

Cherry Hill Seminary. A low-residency, professional Pagan ministry training program offering training in Public Ministry and Pagan Pastoral Counseling. The Seminary also offers academic enhancement courses through its Cultural Studies department that are open to all students. Most courses are done online and include required readings, regular postings to a designated class discussion list, and weekly chatroom class discussions. Courses are designed to be at a graduate level of academic rigor. The Cherry Hill Seminary does not teach the practice of Paganism; it teaches Pagans how to be leaders and ministers. Address: Cherry Hill Seminary, 307 Christian Hill Road, Bethel, VT 05032. Phone: 802-234-6420. E-mail: dean@cherryhillseminary.org.

Web site: www.cherryhillseminary.org

Chesapeake Pagan Community. A group of people on diverse spiritual and religious paths within the Pagan and Pantheist family of religions. A non-profit religious corporation, "Our mission is to organize community events, workshops, and rituals open to the public in the D.C. and Baltimore area. Business meetings and events are usually open to all seekers on an ethical path." Address: Chesapeake Pagan Community, P.O. Box 25242, Baltimore, MD 21229.

Web site: www.chesapeakepagans.org

Church and School of Wicca. Founded by Gavin and Yvonne Frost, the Church and School of Wicca offers correspondence courses in Witchcraft, Astrology, Tantric Yoga, Astral Travel, and many other subjects. It also offers first-degree initiations to those who qualify. Active membership in the student body includes *Survival,* the school's bimonthly newsletter. Address: Wicca, P.O. Box 297-DM, Hinton, WV 25951-0297.

Web site: www.wicca.org

Church of All Worlds. (See Chapter 10.) Founded in 1962, and incorporated in 1968, CAW is one of the oldest legally incorporated Neo-Pagan organizations in America. Taking much of its early inspiration from Robert A. Heinlein's 1961 science fiction novel, *Stranger in a Strange Land,* CAW developed its mission into evolving "a network of information, mythology and experience to awaken the divine within and to provide a context and stimulus for reawakening Gaia and reuniting Her children through tribal community dedicated to responsible stewardship and the evolution of consciousness." The Church of All Worlds is dedicated to "healing the separation between mind and body, men and women, civilization and Nature, Heaven and Earth." In 2005, after a difficult period that encompassed the demise of its flagship magazine, *Green Egg,* the CAW embarked on a new "Phoenix Phase" of reconceptualization and reorganization. Address: Church of All Worlds, P.O. Box 758, Cotati, CA 95931. E-mail: Oberon@mcn.org.

Web site: www.caw.org

Church of the Eternal Source. "The Church of the Eternal Source is the refounded church of Ancient Egypt. We worship the original gods of mankind in their original names in the original manner as closely as possible. Our work is to establish a constantly evolving synthesis of ancient and modern knowledge under the direct guidance and in direct contact with the Eternal Gods." The Church is a polytheistic federation of Egyptian cults founded in 1970 and includes basic instruction materials and current activity information on its Web sites. It published fifteen issues of a magazine, *Khepera,* which may return on the Web. Back issues are available. The church has congregations in three states and has consecrated four Egyptian temples. Address: Church of the Eternal Source, P.O. Box 2778, Mission Viejo, CA 92690-0778. Idaho congregation address: P.O. Box 124, Notus, ID 63565-0124. Phone: 208-455-5664. E-mail: Horemas@aol.com.

Web site: www.CESwebhq.org

The Church of Iron Oak. An ATC English Traditional Wiccan/Pagan church located in the Cocoa/Palm Bay Florida area. The Church has a number of covens and groves. Iron Oak teaches classes in Wicca both in the Melbourne/Palm Bay area, and a second class in the Cocoa/Cape Canaveral area. It also conducts many workshops, including the Athame Maker's Workshop, a full weekend workshop to assist Wiccan visitors in making their own athame by metal forging or casting. Iron Oak ministers actively participate in the Defense Equal Opportunity Management Institute and local college classes to teach what Wicca is about. The Church of Iron Oak is a part of the Aquarian Tabernacle Church (see page 511). It originated the biannual Florida Pagan Gathering, now operated as an independent organization with more than five hundred attendees. Iron Oak continues to practice its religion in the open, having prevailed against efforts to prevent its worship. Address: Church of Iron Oak, P.O.

Box 060672, Palm Bay, FL 32906-0672. Phone: 321-722-0291. E-mail: CIO@ironoak.org.

Web site: www.ironoak.org

Church of the Sacred Earth: A Union of Pagan Congregations. A legal, tax-exempt church and organization of Pagans of diverse beliefs including but not limited to Wiccan, Greek Reconstructionist, Druidic, Icelandic Reconstructionist, and various forms of eclectic Paganism. All groups worship Nature and try to learn how to live more harmoniously with Her cycles and seasons. Each congregation is autonomous in its beliefs and actions. Most members are in New England and the Northeast, with others scattered around the country. Address: Church of the Sacred Earth, 307 Christian Hill Road, Bethel, VT 05032. Phone: 802-234-9670. E-mail: laurelin@sover.net.

Web site: http://cose.numachi.com

The Church of Spiral Oak (COSO). A public Pagan church based in Akron, Ohio, COSO provides a place of celebration and learning, a community, and a connecting point for like-minded individuals who identify themselves as walking a Pagan spiritual path. Founded in 1996, the church meets monthly for ritual and social time and also gathers to celebrate sabbats. State-licensed Clergy provide all manner of pastoral services, including legal/spiritual handfasting, baby welcoming, house blessing and pastoral counseling. Classes are offered periodically, and the church facilitates community involvement through volunteer work, the Akron Area Interfaith Council, Pagan Pride Day, and the annual Crop Walk. Address: The Church of the Spiral Oak, P.O. Box 13681, Akron, OH 44334-3681. Phone: 330-224-5871. E-mail: clergy@spiraloak.com.

Web site: www.spiraloak.com

Church of the Spiral Tree (CST). A non-profit, volunteer-staffed, ecumenical Pagan church based out of Georgia and Alabama, designed to foster and celebrate a sense of community and family among Pagans, both locally and in other regions of the country and the world. CST celebrates the unique Pagan family: parents, children, elders, and extended family. It is an ecumenical church in that it encompasses all traditions, and is non-exclusive. It welcomes all who revere the Earth Mother and who respect themselves and others, regardless of which tradition one is affiliated with. CST was incorporated in August 1997 by Linda Kerr (now retired). CST offers sabbat rituals, networking, several festivals, a newsletter, a library, and a Pagan prisoner outreach program. The Sacred Grove Academy also provides resources for Pagan homeschooling families. Address: Spiral Tree, P.O. Box 8396, Columbus, GA 31908. Phone: 706-570-1017. E-mail: cst@spiraltree.org.

Web site: www.spiraltree.org

Circle. Circle, also known as Circle Sanctuary, is a Shamanic Wiccan church and a non-profit Nature Spirituality resource center located on a two hundred acre nature preserve in southwestern Wisconsin. Founded in 1974, Circle continues to be one of the most important Pagan networking organizations in America. Volunteers and staff work together with many activities, such as networking, publishing, education, and environmental preservation. Circle presents sabbat festivals, Moon rituals, and training programs throughout the year. Circle promotes the creation and sharing of Pagan rituals, music, and other art forms. Circle priestesses and priests in the United States and elsewhere are involved in public education, interfaith networking, chaplaincy services, and spiritual healing and counseling, plus weddings, funerals, and other rites of passage. Circle publishes *CIRCLE* magazine (quarterly journal), the *Circle Guide to Pagan Groups* (networking directory), and *Circle Times* (e-bulletin), plus recordings and books. Circle sponsors and coordinates the Lady Liberty League to fight for religious freedom and respect for Pagans. They also sponsor the Pagan Academic Network, which facilitates communication between scholars who are involved in Pagan teaching and research. Circle sponsors classes, along with many festivals, the most important being Pagan Spirit Gathering, a one-week festival at the time of the Summer Solstice (see page 584). Circle also holds many other annual events, including festivals for Imbolc, Spring Equinox, Beltane, Green Spirit Gathering (Lugnasadh), Fall Equinox, Samhain, and Yule. Circle maintains shrines, other ritual sites, a cemetery, and library/archives on its land. Executive Director and High Priestess: Selena Fox. Address: Circle, P.O. Box 9, Barneveld, WI 53507, Phone: 608-924-2216. E-mail: circle@circlesanctuary.org.

Web site: www.circlesanctuary.org

Circle Cemetery. Operated by Circle, this is "America's first national Pagan cemetery," located in part of the oak forest at Circle Sanctuary Nature Preserve in southwestern Wisconsin. Cremains of Pagans of a variety of paths and from around the United States have been placed there since the cemetery was consecrated in 1999. Director: Selena Fox. Address: Circle Cemetery, Circle Sanctuary, P.O. Box 9, Barneveld, WI 53507. Phone: 608-924-2216. E-mail: circle@circlesanctuary.org.

Web site: www.circlesanctuary.org

Circle of the African Moon (CAM). A non-profit, national, religio-spiritual organization whose members are drawn from varying Pagan beliefs and practices. Established in 2002, the CAM Tradition recognizes the uniqueness and eclecticism of South African Wicca and "consequently draws heavily on the magickal inheritance and consciousness of South African Black/Tribal Paganisms." Potential candidates for training in the five-degree CAM tradition are required to complete a year-and-a-day postulancy to prepare them for entry into the tradition. Locating its role firmly in transformation in a post-apartheid South Africa, CAM has engaged with many forms of public information through various media, and through opening sabbat celebrations and the conducting of rites of passage for the public. Address: CAM, P.O. Box 1559, Durbanville 7551, Cape Town, South Africa. E-mail: darkwolf@netactive.co.za.

Web site: www.cam.za.net

Circle of Aradia/Temple of Diana in California. This is the California branch of Temple of Diana (see page 566), a national feminist Dianic Wiccan organization dedicated to celebrating Women's Magick and Mysteries. Letecia Layson is High Priestess of Diana, ordained by Ruth Barrett in 2000. Address: Circle of Aradia, P.O. Box 46130, Los Angeles, CA 90046. Phone: 323-650-1605. E-mail: letecia@seizethemagic.com.

Web site: www.circleofaradia.org

Circle of the Phoenix Spiritual Community (CotP). The Circle of the Phoenix has a long history of serving the local Twin Cities Wiccan community. CotP is an eclectic Alexandrian/Triskellion–based tradition with strong Greco/Egyptian influences. The mission of the organization is to serve the needs of its members by providing worship and celebration opportunities for members, students, and invited guests; to encourage personal and spiritual growth to all members; and to provide a broad-based education in the Craft and continuing education opportunities for advanced students. CotP stresses ethics in its teaching and its workings. In addition, CotP provides a series of five "seeker" classes designed as a basic introduction to the Craft for the curious, offered several times per year with the opportunity to continue on to the traditional year-and-a-day training. Address: CotP, 2944 Albert Street N, Roseville, MN 55113. E-mail: phoenix@circleofthephoenix.org.

Web site: www.circleofthephoenix.org

Community Seed—Earth-Spirit, Pagan Fellowship. Founded in 2000, Community Seed is a volunteer-based non-profit organization based in the Santa Cruz, California region, whose mission is to provide the local Pagan community with opportunities to create closer bonds of love and understanding through community service, publications, events, and ritual celebrations. Public rituals on the four major sabbats, monthly open circle, nature walks, beach clean-ups, charity work. Address: Community Seed, 849 Almar Avenue STE.C, PMB 217, Santa Cruz, CA 95060. Phone: 831-469-0336. E-mail: info@communityseed.org.

Web site and Community Forum: www.communityseed.org

Congregationalist Wiccan Association of British Columbia (CWA of BC). CWA of BC is a legal church and a provincial not-for-profit society, working toward charitable status. It is a Wiccan association of autonomous public congregations and temples, not an organization of covens or a pan-Pagan association. Its clergy all are trained and initiated Priestesses and Priests of Wicca. It takes a year of involvement to be a voting member and a minimum of a further year of training to be clergy. There are outer court public circles, as well as religious education, counseling, chaplancy in hospitals and prisons, and other public religious services (marriages, funerals, and other rites of passage). As of 2005, there were six congregations in the Vancouver area, Abbotsford, Venon, Penticton, Surrey, and Nanaimo. Address: Congregationalist Wiccan Association of British Columbia, upper floor, 5196 Moscrop Street, Burnaby, British Columbia, V5G 2G4 Canada. You can e-mail the Secretary/Summoner: samwagar@shaw.ca.

Web site: www.cwabc.org

Connecticut Wiccan & Pagan Network (CWPN, Inc). The CWPN is a not-for-profit educational and networking organization dedicated to meeting the spiritual needs of the greater Wiccan and Pagan community in Connecticut and surrounding areas. Established in December 1990, CWPN was the first organization of its kind in Connecticut. "Our goal has always been to help provide a forum for Wiccans and Pagans to meet others of 'like mind' and to come together and worship in a safe environment. Our hope has been to construct a sense of 'community' in which we can all share with and learn from one another." CWPN hosts monthly networking meetings throughout the state, as well as open Sabbat circles, a coven and study group referral service and an annual four-day Pagan festival called Harvest Home Gathering (see page 588). The Connecticut Wiccan and Pagan Network also publishes a quarterly newsletter, provides classes/workshops, various social events, and lectures with well-known members of the Pagan community. Address: CWPN, Inc., P.O. Box 1175, New Milford, CT 06776-1175. E-mail: info@cwpn.org.

Web site: www.cwpn.org

The Council of British Druid Orders (COBDO). An organization that brings together many Druid groups, formed in 1988 to facilitate the discussion and exchange of information of concern to members of Druid orders. A number of groups in other parts of the world are associates. Contact: Liz Murray (liaison officer), BM Oakgrove, London WCIN 3XX, U.K.

Council of Magickal Arts (CMA). A worldwide membership organization based in the state of Texas. A non-profit charitable organization, CMA's primary goal is to produce two festivals per year, Samhain (see page 587) and Beltane (see page 576), and to celebrate the sabbats. CMA holds programs and gatherings for members, and publishes a quarterly e-zine (*The Accord*) devoted to the magickal arts. CMA is open to adults of all traditions or religions who wish to celebrate nature, spirit, and community, and who are on or wish to explore a Pagan or magickal path. Membership is $33/year ($15 for each additional adult) and includes a subscription to the magazine *Accord*. Address: P.O. Box 8030, Ft. Worth, TX 76124-003. Phone: 361-865-9077. E-mail: cma@magickal-arts.org.

Web site: www.magickal-arts.org

Court of Earth Coven (Jordens Hov). An initiatory Wiccan coven in the Stockholm area, focusing mainly on the Celtic pantheon. Court of Earth is a daughter coven to Court of Joy and works in that tradition. Address: Court of Earth Coven, c/o Calle Dybedahl, Vasavägen 105 SE-177 32 Järfälla, Sweden, or Court of Earth Coven, c/o Jennifer Larsson, Lilla Nybacken, SE-195 93 Märsta, Sweden. E-mail: coe@faerywicca.se.

Court of Joy Coven. A group in Stockholm that works with Faery tradition and traditional Celtic Wicca. It also works with dragon energy, direct communication with the Gods, and with the Celtic Mysteries. Strongly inspired by the writings of R. J. Stewart and John and Caitlin Matthews. Address: Court of Joy Coven, c/o Thorbiörn Fritzon, Holmvägen 20, S-194 35 Stockholm, Sweden. Phone: 46 8 590 838 20.

Coven of the Mother Mountain Aerie (COMMA). Founded in 1986, COMMA is a woman-only group with Dianic tendencies, located in southern California. A collective effort of each of its priestesses, Coven of the Mother Mountain Aerie follows an eclectic spiritual path with a focus on woman-energy, goddess archetypes, and the Maid-Mother-Crone cycle, creating their own mythology and traditions where needed as they walk and weave their convoluted paths together. Although they hold very few public rituals, this group hosts open workshops or discussions at least four times a year on practical and esoteric topics useful and interesting to modern-day suburban Witches and seekers. Address: COMMA, P.O. Box 91803, Pasadena, CA 91109. Web site: www.mothermountain.org

Coven Oldenwilde. A non-profit religious organization dedicated to perpetuating the beauty, antiquity, and validity of Witchcraft. Founded October 31, 1994, and based in Asheville, North Carolina, this traditional Wiccan group teaches serious occult students of all ages British Gardnerian and Italian Strega magic. High Priestess Lady Passion and Diuvei are authors and social activists. They work to help Wiccans worldwide (Pagan prisoners, students, parents in custody battles, etc.), bless and de-ghost houses, marry and bury, and lecture on Craft topics at area universities. Coven Oldenwilde holds an elaborate, free, public Samhain rite each year. Address: 113 Clinton Avenue, Asheville, NC 28806. Phone: 828-251-0343. E-mail: oldenwilde@aol.com. Web site: www.oldenwilde.org

The Coven of the Wylde Rose. A Gardnerian Wiccan coven of the Whitecroft line, located in the greater Toronto area of Canada. The coven is dedicated to spiritual growth within the practices of the Old Religion. The coven offers invitation-only Sabbat Circles to friends of the coven and offers training to sincere seekers. Also performs legally recognized weddings and handfastings. The Coven of the Wylde Rose helps in networking with other Pagan and Wiccans within the greater Toronto area and internationally as well. E-mail: WyldeRose@rogers.com.

Web site: http://ca.geocities.com/torontopaganpubmoot@rogers.com/page18 .html

Covenant of Gaia Wiccan Church of Alberta. The Covenant of Gaia was legally constituted as a church in 1990. It offers membership to individuals of varying Pagan paths. Members share responsibility for regular celebrations of the Wheel of the Year. Address: Covenant of Gaia, P.O. Box 1742, Station M, Calgary, Alberta, Canada T2P 2L7. Phone: 403-283-5719. E-mail: info@cogcoa.ab.ca. Web site: www.cogcoa.ab.ca

Covenant of the Goddess. A cross-traditional federation of over one hundred covens, plus solitary elders and associates, who have joined together to win recognition for the Craft as a legitimate and legally recognized religion. The Covenant of the Goddess was organized in 1975 at Coeden Brith. It is incorporated as a non-profit religious organization in California, although it has grown to be a nationwide organization with members throughout the United Sates as well as some members in Canada and overseas. Decisions are made at an annual Grand Council or in local councils which may cover a city, state, or larger region. The Covenant publishes the *Covenant of the Goddess Newsletter* (see page 494) and sponsors the COG MerryMeet Festival (see page 583) and Grand Council each year. The festival is open to non-members. The Covenant makes ministerial credentials available to qualified members. It also publishes materials on the Craft and does a great deal of public education work with the media, law enforcement agencies, and interfaith groups. A coven can apply for membership if it is a cohesive, self-perpetuating group which has been meeting for six months or more; the group follows the code of ethics defined by COG; the coven has three or more members studying for the priesthood, one of whom is an Elder; and the focus of the group's ritual and thealogy is the worship of the Goddess and the Old Gods (or the Goddess alone). Address: COG, P.O. Box 1226, Berkeley, CA 94701. Web site: www.cog.org

Covenant of the Pentacle Wiccan Church—ATC. Founded in 1994, and led by Reverend Velvet Rieth, Covenant of the Pentacle Wiccan Church promotes Wicca throughout the Gulf South region. CPWC established the first Wiccan ministry for inmates in Louisiana. Reverend Rieth is an activist who works with women and native peoples, as well as on issues of choice, religious freedom, and gay rights. She also works with law enforcement agencies. Sabbats are open to the public; Esbats are by invitation. Classes on history, anthropology, circle protocol, and Wicca as it is practiced today. Classes open to new students every quarter. CPWC has satellite circles throughout Louisiana. Sponsors many events, including charitable food, clothing, and toy drives. Address: Covenant of the Pentacle Wiccan Church, P.O. Box 23033, New Orleans, LA 70183. Phone: 504-828-7169.

Web site: www.swampwitch.net

Covenant of Rhiannon: The Witches of Cape May. The community began in 1976 with Starlight Coven. The Coven was re-formed in 1981 and renamed Covenant of Rhiannon by Robert Bitting and Grace Kemelek. The Covenant of Rhiannon tradition is a blend of Victor Anderson's Feri Tradition and Sybil Leek's Horsa Tradition. It is one of the oldest continuously practicing covens in New Jersey. C.O.R. follows the traditional methods of teaching the Craft through mentoring/apprenticeship in a coven setting. An outgrowth of the Covenant of Rhiannon is the Church of Ravenstar, which was formed by Robert Bitting and William Wiggins in 2001 as a platform for Gay Men's Spirituality. Address: C.O.R., 10 Sunray Beach Road, Del Haven, NJ 08251. Phone: 609-889-3422.

Web sites: www.covenantofrhiannon.org; www.raven-star.org

Covenant of Unitarian Universalist Pagans (CUUPS). Over the last eighteen years, CUUPS has become one of the largest Pagan organizations in the world. It is unique in its connection to a mainstream church, being an interest group of the UUA and therefore giving Pagans full fellowship within the structure of the church without the necessity of changing, or hiding, their religion. CUUPS is a "revolving-door" resource, offering entry-level information on Paganism to people involved in Unitarian Universalism who are drawn to Earth-centered spirituality, and offering information on the beliefs and practices of Pagans to those within the UUA who are perhaps not interested in pursuing such a path but may be curious about it. CUUPS members and chapters have become active in local Pagan communities, offering a unique perspective and the resources of their host churches to further the cause of interfaith and intrafaith understanding among various kinds of Pagans and their non-Pagan communities. CUUPS has now more than eighty active chapters across the United States, as well as several hundred individual members in the United States, Canada, Great Britain, and other parts of Europe. The Covenant publishes a quarterly newsletter, provides Pagan and Earth-centered programming at the UUA General Assembly (GA), hosts a public Summer Solstice ritual at GA, as well as teaching workshops on Paganism, and is active in seeking to enrich UU worship using the resources of music, dance, and creative ritual. Cakes for the Queen of Heaven, the first formal program of Goddess studies in any mainstream church in America, celebrates its twentieth anniversary in 2006. Current membership rates are $35 for an individual membership; $30 for a chapter registration or renewal. Address: CUUPS, Inc., 8190 A Beechmont Avenue, Suite 334, Cincinnati, OH 45255-6117. E-mail: info@cuups.org.

Web site: www.cuups.org/content/support/membership.html

Crossroads Lyceum/Fellowship of Isis. The Crossroads Lyceum is a Mystery school within the Fellowship of Isis. It offers home-study programs, magi degrees, priesthood training, and initiate levels. Founded in 1993, the Lyceum has become one of the largest centers within the FOI. It provides an eclectic, self-directed course of study that honors all pantheons, traditions, and goddesses equally. It offers weekly attunements, group rituals, as well as the *Crossroads Torchlight*, a newsletter written by both staff and students. There is also a Crossroads Iseum, an FOI "hearth of the Goddess." Address: Crossroads Lyceum, P.O. Box 19152, Tucson, AZ 85731. E-mail: info@crlyceum.com.

Web site: www.crlyceum.com

Cultural Survival. An organization that works to promote and protect the rights of indigenous peoples and ethnic minorities around the globe. The organization has projects all over the world to work with and for indigenous people to help them secure land and political, social, economic, and basic human rights. It publishes *Cultural Survival Quarterly*, a magazine that focuses each issue around a central theme that is supported by articles, news briefs, and reports from the field on important issues facing indigenous peoples today. Membership is $45 or more ($25 for students) and includes a subscription to the quarterly. Address: Cultural Survival, 215 Prospect Street, Cambridge, MA 02139. Phone: 617-441-5400. E-mail: culturalsurvival@cs.org.

Web site: www.culturalsurvival.org

Daughters of the Goddess Womyn's Temple. This is a Dianic, Womyn-only Goddess Temple dedicated in the Spirit of Aloha to the preservation and perpetuation of Goddess culture, public ceremony, ritual, and Womyn's Mysteries. "We are not a coven but a dynamic community of like-minded womyn honoring Goddess in all Her incarnations. We are located in the Bay Area of Northern California and are led by our High Priestess, Leilani Birely, who was initiated by Z Budapest in 1998. We hold open public circles for all womyn, and one of our visions is to call as many of Her names as possible in this lifetime." Address: Daughters of the Goddess, 3527 Mt. Diablo Boulevard, #353, Lafayette, CA 94549. E-mail: Leilani@DaughtersoftheGoddess.com.

Web site: www.DaughtersoftheGoddess.com

Daughters of Kali. This is a teaching and training circle run by SHARANYA (see page 563), a non-profit religious organization based in San Francisco and India, whose core tradition is based on the tenets of the Craft and the Shakta Tantrick path of esoteric Hinduism. The circle is open to women and men, and participants can gain an understanding of Kali and other fierce goddesses (those who are powerful and often misrepresented) through ritual, myth, historical perspective, lecture, readings, discussion, and group work. In the spirit of the Sha'can tradition, classes require outside reading, participation, and commitment to exploring Eastern and Western practices. They offer a year-long course, which can lead to initiation, and can facilitate one's own mythic journey into and out of the underworld. "An opportunity for you to come together with others to learn, laugh and live the presence of the Divine." The

Daughters of Kali also teaches and supports those who wish to facilitate mentorship circles around rites of passage and coming of age for girls and boys. Address: (post only) Daughters of Kali, 859 36th Avenue, San Francisco, CA 94121. Phone: 415-505-6840. E-mail: DoK@sharanya.org.

Web site: www.sharanya.org

The Deep Root Community Lending Library. Founded in 2004 by a collective of Wiccans, Magicians, and other Pagan folk, the library is one of only a half dozen Pagan lending libraries in the country. It has a growing collection of more than 650 magical-metaphysical books, tapes, and videos. It is open to the public. A small membership fee or cash deposit is required to check out materials and helps maintain the library and replace lost items. The library trust welcomes donations of items from individuals, authors, and publishers and/or funds to purchase new titles. Address: Deep Root Community Lending Library, c/o Sekhet Bast Ra Oasis Temple, 2714 N. Pennsylvania Avenue, Oklahoma City, OK 73107. Phone: 405-816-5176. E-mail: info@sekhetbastra.org.

Web site: www.sekhetbastra.org

The Delaware Valley Pagan Network. A secular, non-profit organization founded in 1999 to support the Pagan community of the Delaware Valley (southeastern Pennsylvania, southern New Jersey, and the state of Delaware). DVPN provides networking opportunities in the form of gatherings such as the Crystal Ball and the Summer Social; online discussion forums, announcement lists, and an event calendar; and charitable works such as the Philadelphia AIDS walk, blood drives, and food collection for the homeless. Community outreach programs include sponsoring the local Pagan Pride Day and supporting creative and performing arts with the Pagan Arts Initiative. Address: DVPN, P.O. Box 34596, Philadelphia, PA 19101. E-mail: dvpn@dvpn.org.

Web site: www.dvpn.org.

Community Forum: http://groups.yahoo.com/group/dvpn-discuss

Diana's Grove. A spiritual community that welcomes men and women. "We honor the unknown, the unknowable, and the quest to discover. We have been welcoming people from all traditions since 1994. Our spiritual practice is dedicated to developing healthy communities and relationships. We offer a yearly Mystery School that invites you to step into a myth and take a journey of self-discovery in a community of seekers and spiritual adventurers. Using earth-centered practices and the magic of ritual, the work that we offer focuses on personal growth, community building and leadership development." Diana's grove has 102 acres of dedicated land, a monthly online magazine, and a large selection of gatherings, often with guest presenters. Housing and meals is included. Address: Diana's Grove, P.O. Box 159, Salem, MO 65560. Phone: 573-689-2400. E-mail: info@dianasgrove.com.

Web site: www.dianasgrove.com.

Dievturība. The reconstructionist Pagan tradition of Latvia. The name means bearer of the divine. It was established in 1925, but was suppressed during the Soviet period. The religion is based on ancient Latvian folklore, folk songs, and stories. It sings the dainas, ancient hymns believed to be the Baltic Vedas. It also celebrates the solar (solstices, change of seasons) and human ritual cycles, based on extant folkloric models. It publishes a journal called *Labietis*. Dievturība is legally recognized as a traditional religion in Latvia. It does not follow Western models and has avoided contact with Western Paganism. It is a member of the World Council of Ethnic Religions and does not consider itself to be Pagan. It reformed the ancient Latvian religious system, creating a monotheistic trinity of a God and two Goddesses. Since Latvia gained independence from the Soviet Union, the new generation of Dievturība members has opted for full Latvian polytheism, causing generational tension in the organization. In North America, there are local groups in Chicago, Minneapolis– St. Paul, Montreal, New York, Seattle, and Toronto. Address: Dievturība, c/o Alenes Janis, 3170 Sherbrook Street, Lachine, Quebec H8S 4G8 Canada.

The Druid Network (TDN). An international organization, TDN aims to be a source of inspiration and information about the Druid tradition, ancient and modern. Founded by Emma Restall Orr, it is definitely not an Order itself, instead bringing together Orders, Groves, and individuals, offering a forum for sharing skills and teachings, inspiration and experience, supporting environmental and community projects, camps and public rituals, encouraging the creative active expression of living Druidry in its many forms. The magical heart of the Network is the Druid Order of the Yew. Address: TDN, P.O. Box 3533, Whichford, Shipston on Stour, Warwickshire CV36 5YB, U.K. E-mail: office@druidnetwork.org.

Web site: http://druidnetwork.org

The Earth Conclave, Inc. A non-profit educational organization dedicated to bringing together people from many different paths and traditions to share ideas, work together, experiment, and bring results back to each of their home communities. "Some of our main interests are integrating the personal, political, and spiritual; creating, developing, and nurturing sustainable cultures of beauty, balance, and delight; and understanding our roles as co-creators of the multiverse along with all the other co-creators (all beings, animate and inanimate, physical and ethereal, etc.). We are committed to living as if these worlds of wonder were already here, alive and growing. We also have a deep dedication to fun, be it in our workshops, trances, magic, and meals at our twice-yearly events, the Spring Conclave and the Fall Conclave, or as we simply go about our daily lives." The Earth Conclave is based in the upper Mississippi Valley. Address: The Earth Conclave, Inc., P.O. Box 934, Kenosha, WI 53141-0934. E-mail: britanhugh@wi.rr.com.

Web site: http://danenet.danenet.org/conclave/

The Earth House Project, Inc. A tax-exempt, non-profit, volunteer community attempt to build a resource center in the Twin Cities area for people of all nature-reverent spiritual paths. Sponsors a bimonthly Coffee Cauldron in the Twin Cities area and provides service to other organizations. Address: The Earth House Project, P.O. Box 141251, Minneapolis, MN 55414-9998. E-mail: information@earthhousemn.org.

Web site: www.earthhousemn.org

Earth Religions Assistance List (ERAL). Dedicated to investigating and providing assistance to Earth Religionists facing legal problems associated with their religion. It is an international network of Earth Religion Rights activists on the Internet helping facilitate action through individuals and organizations in the real world. There are key members of most other Earth Religion rights organizations among its members. Most members are Earth Religionists, but helpful members of other faiths, such as attorneys, law students, or ordained clergy also belong. For further details, see ERAL's Web site: www.conjure.com/ERAL. There are also frequently updated topic-specific Web pages for finding help: http://members.aol.com/lcorncalen/helplink.htm. To subscribe, go to http://groups.yahoo.com/group/ERAL/.

EarthSpirit. A non-profit organization, founded in 1980, which provides services to an international network of Pagans and other followers of Earth-centered spiritual paths. EarthSpirit's mission is to promote Pagan spirituality, culture, and community by working to develop Pagan models and values for living in the present age, by encouraging communication and understanding among people of different traditions, by providing opportunities for shared spiritual experience, and by helping to educate the general public concerning Earth-centered spirituality. The organization sponsors workshops and classes, provides open moon circles and seasonal rituals, and helps to organize several wonderful and important festivals, including the annual Rites of Spring (see page 579), as well as A Feast of Lights (see page 575), Twilight Covening (see page 590), and Lunasdal (see page 583). Besides teaching, networking, and festivals, EarthSpirit participates in international interfaith work through a Parliament of the World's Religions. It also sponsors a ritual performance group, MotherTongue, which offers workshops, performances, recordings, and written materials for the public. Membership: $30/year; $40/year families. Address: EarthSpirit, P.O. Box 723, Williamsburg, MA 01096. Phone: 413-238-4240. E-mail: earthspirit@earthspirit.com.

Web site: www.earthspirit.com

Earth Spirit Pagans. A non-profit religious and cultural organization dedicated to the preservation and continued vitality of Pagan religions and cultures, founded in 1992 and based in Colorado Springs, Colorado. ESP membership is made up of individuals and families, not groups. It provides workshops, an online newsletter, Wicca 101 classes, public rituals and celebrations, and community service opportunities. It provides a caring religious and cultural environment for practitioners of different Pagan paths. Address: Earth Spirit Pagans, P.O. Box 1965, Colorado Springs, CO 80901-1965.

Web site: www.earthspiritpagans.org

Earth Spirituality and Education Center. This Center, in Ohio, was founded in 2005 by Bella Mahri and Sky Cat, HPS and HP of Lady of Sacred Grove and Stone Circle (L.S.G.S.C.), a coven founded in 1993, with a primarily Egyptian and Celtic orientation. The Center affords persons of Earth Spirituality religions a location to worship or commune with their deities privately in the Shrine Room. There is a growing no-loan library for research and classes are offered in many paths and religious topics. There are public rituals for most of the sabbats. Address: Earth Spirituality and Education Center, 118 E. Northern Avenue, Lima, OH 45801. E-mail: bellamahri@hotmail.com.

EarthTides Pagan Network (EPN). Founded in 1989 as a networking resource for Maine Pagans, this multigroup organization hosts an annual oceanfront Beltane celebration and offers an information table at the Common Ground Fair in September. Address: EarthTides Pagan Network, P.O. Box 161, East Winthrop, ME 04043.

Web site: www.earthtides.org.

Ecclesia Antinoi. Founded in 2002, the Ecclesia Antinoi (Gathered Believers in Antinous) is a group of people who are devoted to the modern restoration of the worship of Antinous. The Ecclesia are involved in reinterpreting and extending the worship and practices of the ancient Cult of Antinous into the very different circumstances of life in the twenty-first century. One of the essential tenets in the Ecclesia Antinoi is that a process of "self-deification" can take place "when one realizes the unity one has with divinity. Locating that individual aspect of the divine which has incarnated in one's life can allow it to be the best it can be, to be beautiful and active and reflective of timeless beauty and grace. One theme that runs through the lives of many in the Ecclesia Antinoi is the place of the homoerotic in whatever form that takes." E-mail: aediculaantinoi@hotmail.com.

Web site: www.liminalityland.com/aediculaantinoi.htm

Eldhrimnir Kindred. Practices and promotes the pre-Christian, indigenous religion of Northern Europe. "We honor the Gods, Goddesses, Landvaetter and Ancestors. We meet weekly for blot, rune study, lore study and seidhr. We are open to all who follow the Gods and Goddesses of the Aesir and Vanir and seek to educate ourselves and others about the many beautiful, deep and profound aspects of our religion." Address: Eldhrimnir Kindred, P.O. Box 60, Wanchese, NC 27981. E-mail: eldhrimnir@msn.com.

Web site: www.geocities.com/eldhrimnir

The Elf Queen's Daughters. "In the late 1960s, a doorway opened to the Realm of Faerie and the Elf Queen's Daughters was born. By the early 1970s the Tookes (Arwen and Elanor) began the Elven Magic Mail, which spun a network of about 60 Elven Vortices. Today, the EQD is smaller in number. We have grown toward a more experiential interweaving of magickal studies and activities, with the occasional Elf Letter. It is our dharma to ease the burden that has been placed on our Great Mother. It is our dharma to protect the Wild Places of Greenbase that still support the existence of what is left of Faerie. Tis Wild Magick that we work with our Hearts Desire to bring Love and Healing to all upon this Planet. The Fair Mothertongue—song and poetry unfold as we strive to act and to stir the Hearts and Visions into remembering the Beauty and Magick that once permeated all in existence." Address: Elf Queen's Daughters, P.O. Box 259244, Madison, WI 53725-9244. Phone: 608-288-8523.

ElvinHOME, inc. (formerly Elf Lore Family). The Elves of Lothlorien have been going strong since 1983. They maintain a nature sanctuary on 109 acres of land, a survival education center, and a woodland meeting ground. Their Lothlorien Nature Sanctuary runs on photovoltaics, has composting privies, solar showers, orchards, and herb and wild gardens. ElvinHOME operates by a consensus council circle. The Elves put on many activities and gatherings, including two large festivals: Wild Magick Gathering (see page 590) and Elf Fest (see page 577). They also run a children's program (Elf Scouts), and they publish a periodic newsletter, *Lothlorien Greenleaf.* Membership: $20/year. Address: ElvinHOME, P.O. Box 1082, Bloomington, IN 47402-1082. E-mail: elf@kiva.net.

Web site: www.elflore.org

The Federation of Circles and Solitaries (FOCAS). A non-profit organization for those who practice Earth-based faiths in southeast Michigan, based in the suburbs of Detroit. It is dedicated to healing the Earth and preserving wildlife, unifying the Pagan community through communication and networking, educating the community about Paganism, and increasing awareness and tolerance. Eight open circles a year, weekly chat nights, and park clean up projects. Address: Federation of Circles and Solitaries, P.O. Box 22, Wyandotte, MI 48192.

Web site: www.focasmi.org

Fellowship of Isis (FOI). An international multifaith organization that is dedicated to the Goddess in Her many forms. It was founded in 1976 by Lawrence, Pamela, and Olivia Durdin-Robertson at their family home, Clonegal Castle. The fellowship believes in the promotion of love, beauty, abundance, and reverence for all manifestations of life. There is reverence for God as well as Goddess. The rites exclude any form of sacrifice, whether actual or symbolic. A multicultural, multireligious, multiracial fellowship that is open to all regardless of religion, tradition, or race, it is dedicated to honoring the religion of *all* the Goddesses and pantheons throughout the planet. The Fellowship is organized on a democratic basis and all members have equal privileges within it. Membership is free, although there is a charge for publications. There are more than 25,000 members in 98 countries, and about 500 members of the priesthood. There are FOI Iseums and Lyceums around the world. Iseums are "Hearths of the Goddess" and offer celebratory rites, initiations, and fellowship. Lyceums are founded by a Hierophant and offer structured Magi Degree courses. The Web site lists publications, directories of centers, and events. The Fellowship of Isis also consists of sister organizations such as the Noble Order of Tara and the Druid Clan of Dana. They also publish *Isian News*. Address: Fellowship of Isis, Clonegal Castle, Enniscorthy, Eire, Ireland. E-mail: info@ fellowshipofisis.com.

Web site: www.fellowshipofisis.com

Feminist Spiritual Community. An open group that has been meeting and celebrating with women since 1980. There are weekly meetings every Monday night at the Friends Meeting House in Portland, Maine. Rituals vary and can celebrate life passages (birth, death, personal rebirth, Cronehood, and taking new names), or they can be seasonal (solstice and equinox rituals). Other rituals "explore ways of opening ourselves to the spirit of power, love, healing, and justice at work in the universe." There is also time for announcements and socializing. FSC has published two books about ritual: *Celebrating Ourselves* (about their beautiful Croning ritual) for $9 and *Keep Simple Ceremonies* for $15 (prepaid includes postage). Address: Feminist Spiritual Community, P.O. Box 3771, Portland, ME 04104. Phone: 207-774-2830.

Feraferia. (See Chapter 9.) Founded in 1967, Feraferia means Wilderness Sacrament. Feraferia is "a Paradisal Fellowship for the loving celebration of Wilderness Mysteries with Faerie style, courtly elegance, refinement and grace. The Great Work of Feraferia is the lyrical unification of Ecology, Artistry, Mythology and Liturgy." The vision of Fred McLaren Adams and Lady Svetlana, Feraferia flowered in the late 1960s and 1970s, but by the end of the 1990s only a small group of people followed these traditions. In 1999, Peter Tromp (Phaedrus), a Dutch artist trained in Wicca and other magical traditions, began a correspondence with Fred Adams and offered to put Feraferia on the Web as well as produce official versions of the core rituals. "The Nine Yearly Festivals of Feraferia" was produced in Dutch and English and the Web site has essays, rituals, and much of Fred Adams's splendid artwork. Phaedrus lives in Amsterdam, has his own Wiccan group, as well as being one of the two contact persons for Feraferia worldwide. E-mail: phaedrus@dds.nl.

Web site: www.phaedrus.dds.nl/fera.htm. Peter Tromp's personal Web site also features some Feraferia material: www.phaedrus.dds.nl. The other contact for Feraferia is Lady Selena Kareena. Address: Feraferian Paradisal Sanctuary, P.O. Box 21, Monticello, NM 87939. Phone: 505-743-2048. E-mail: selenakareena@ yahoo.com.

Web site: www.ancientartstudioproductions.com

Four Quarters: An InterFaith Sanctuary of Earth Religion. "A religious association of people, drawn to the Earth and its cycles, the natural world and its polarities; and seeing in them the manifest expression of spirit." Four Quarters is a church, a retreat camp, a monastery, and an interfaith organization for Earth Religions. Founded in 1995, in 1999 the Church purchased its first parcel of land, and by 2005, the Church had title to one hundred acres, including the main camp, the river, and the Stone Circle. By 2005, the Stone Circle had grown to thirty-two large standing stones, and half of the circle from East to West will soon be completed. A large, seven-fold labyrinth is also in construction. In 1999 Four Quarters began a monastic order, with three adults living under formal vows of poverty and working full time for the Church. Four Quarters maintains a large garden supplying much wintertime food, and has begun a permaculture program for the twenty-five acres of tillable farmland on the site. Four Quarters holds open Full and New Moon services, led by rotating Priestesses and Priests from their membership. Many use Wicca as a model, but members may lead services in other traditions. Four Quarters has approximately 400 dues-paying members and hosts eleven seasonal events in the camp, ranging from 50 to 500 people. They also publish a "Wheel of the Year" calendar, distributed free throughout the Mid-Atlantic region. They also host a Spiral Scouts group and a summer gathering for Spiral Scouts across the region. Four Quarters says the lesson they have learned from working with the Standing Stones is that it is important to be "in it for the long haul." Address: Four Quarters, 190 Walker Lane, Artemas, PA 17211. Phone: 814-784-3075/ fax -3999. E-mail: megalith@4qf.org.

Web site: www.4qf.org

Foxwood Temple of the Old Religion. A temple dedicated to the Old Gods, a legal church, and an educational institute founded in 1990 by Orion Foxwood, co-founder of the Alliance of the Old Religion, author of the book *The Faery Teachings,* and one of the mantle carriers for Lady Circe of Toledo, Ohio, Queen Mother of the line. The foundations of Foxwood teachings originate in the family folk-tradition passed down from the Lady Circe, inclusive of elements of Celtic, Strega, Faerie traditions, and Western magical traditions. The teachings are transmitted through structured training and initiations. Foxwood sponsors some international lecturers, open sabbat celebrations, and classes and spiritual counseling and hosts the Mountain Mayfest Gathering (see page 579). Address: Foxwood, P.O. Box 5128, Laurel, MD 20726. E-mail: L.orion@foxwood-temple.net.

Web site: www.Foxwood-temple.net

Free Spirit Alliance. A non-profit spiritual networking organization whose primary function is to provide administrative and technical support to members of the pantheist community in the practice of their faith. Founded in 1985, FSA sponsors both local and regional events in the Mid-Atlantic area—including workshops, rituals, and the promotion of communication, harmony, and goodwill between congregations and within the pantheist community. FSA runs Free Spirit Gathering (see page 577), a large national festival attracting people from as far as Hawaii, Canada, and Texas. FSA also runs a smaller Beltane festival, which it calls the only adult-only Sacred Sexuality Beltane festival in the country, as well as a number of other events and rituals in the D.C./Maryland area. Membership in the Alliance is $20/year and is open to anyone sharing the group's goals and objectives. Address: Free Spirit, P.O. Box 94, Lambertville, NJ 08530.

Web sites: www.free-spirit.org; www.FreeSpiritGathering.org

Gaea Retreat Center. Affectionately called Camp Gaea, the Gaea Retreat Center became a reality in February 1992, after a long search for land for a permanent home for the Hartland Pagan Festival. The Gaea Retreat Center is a 168-acre property in a rural setting within an hour's drive of the Kansas City metropolitan area. The center is owned and managed by Earth Rising, Inc., a volunteer, not-for-profit organization. The primary goal is to provide a private, natural retreat area for a variety of people of all spiritual traditions, and to promote a feeling of connection with the land and people on it. Gaea includes a twelve-acre lake with a sand swimming area. Many areas are available for tent camping and there are open areas for sports and other organized activities. Buildings include a large open pavilion with stage and folding chairs, an air-conditioned meeting hall, a dining hall and kitchen, and nine cabins. Flush facilities and heated showers are available. The cabins are equipped with bunk beds, and one cabin, for special health needs, is air-conditioned. Gardens and secluded areas provide quiet places for meditation or simple relaxation. Hiking and biking trails are maintained. Many groups call Gaea home, the largest still being the Heartland Pagan Festival (see page 578). Address: Earth Rising, Inc., P.O. Box 696, Tonganoxie, KS 66086. E-mail: info@campgaea.org.

Web site: www.campgaea.org

Gaia's Hearth. Formed to create a harmonious spiritual environment for Pagan families and friends in which to worship. People of all faiths and paths are welcome and members come from varied backgrounds and experiences. The only CUUPS (Covenant of Unitarian Universalist Pagans) group in Rhode Island, Gaia's Hearth follows the Wiccan Rede of "harm none," and holds strictly to UU Principles acknowledging the worth and dignity of each person. Gaia's Hearth follows the Wiccan Wheel of the Year and celebrates the eight sabbats, and all of its public celebrations are appropriate for families and children. Gaia's Hearth also holds regular workshops on a variety of magical and spiritual topics, both intellectual and practical, and holds beginner and advanced courses in the Cornerstones of Wicca. Gaia's Hearth is led by four women who share equal standing, and one of its foundational beliefs is in the concept of balance in all things. Gaia's Hearth is also involved in interfaith dialogue. One of its leaders, Lorna Buffum, is the coordinator for Pagan Pride in Rhode Island.

Web site: www.gaiashearth.com

Gaia's Womb. An interfaith spirituality organization that provides a place for those who embrace Nature-based spiritual paths to connect with the Divine Feminine. Gaia's Womb produces wonderful quality retreats for women twice a year with a number of smaller intensives more frequently. Additionally, Wheel of the Year celebrations for men and women are produced through Gaia's Womb Earth Traditions (the part of Gaia's Womb that includes men), and include Samhain, the Winter Solstice, Oimelc, the Spring Equinox, Beltaine, the Summer Solstice, Lughnassadh, and the Autumnal Equinox. Gaia's Womb events honor and draw upon ancient traditions and rituals in an effort to restore balance to the spiritual energy of the human psyche. Gaia's Womb is also involved in interfaith work and its director, Angie Buchanan, is on the Board of Trustees of the Council for A Parliament of the World's Religion, the first Pagan to hold that position. Address: Gaia's Womb, 2700 Wildwood Lane, Bannockburn, IL 60015. Phone: 847-405-0208. E-mail: Angie@GaiasWomb.com.

Web site: www.GaiasWomb.com

The Grandmother Council. Honors women elders and provides a unique forum for their wisdom to be shared for the healing and sustainable wellness of the people and the planet. The project was started in 2002 as a part of Living Earth Circle (see page 542), and has three parts: an annual public conference, ongoing open gatherings of women elders, and global community networking and support. The annual conference is held in April in Ashland, Oregon. It is open to everyone and features an Honoring Ceremony for Women Elders, a public Grandmother Council, and experiential workshops presented by women elders. Address: Living Earth Circle, c/o Lisa Pavati, 961 Harmony Lane, Ashland, OR 97520. Phone: 541-201-0372. E-mail: lisa@livingearthcircle.org.

Web site: www.livingearthcircle.org

The Green Faerie Grove. Founded on Yule of 1998, the Green Faerie Grove is the oldest continuously operating queer men's coven in Ohio. The tradition follows an eclectic path, with strong influences from Wicca and Druidry, bits of Greek and Roman mythos, Celtic Shamanism, men's Mysteries, and Radical Faerie thrown in for good measure. Solar sabbats and occasional full moons celebrated. Membership is open to queer men over eighteen years of age, and members come from a variety of spiritual backgrounds, including Witchcraft, Ceremonial Magick, Heathen, and Shamanist. Membership is through election. The coven is run by consensus within a framework of bylaws, with each member taking turns as facilitator. Members are active in the regional and national Pagan community. The coven's main public outreach project is the annual Between the Worlds Men's Gathering (see page 586). Address: Green Faerie Grove, 3000 B East Main Street, #240, Columbus, OH 43209. E-mail: witches@greenfaeriegrove.org.

Web site: www.greenfaeriegrove.org

GreenSong Grove (GSG). An eclectic non-profit Pagan church in St. Petersburg, Florida. GSG began in 1998, and incorporated with the state of Florida on June 14, 2001. "We formed to provide a place for Pagans and Wiccans to meet and improve communication in the magickal and mundane world, building a strong, connected community, and a safe place for new people to meet others of like mind." GSG provides a weekly online newsletter listing area events that are presented by local Covens and groups. GSG provides workshops, classes, healing circles, drum circles, and two festivals a year. It also hosts public sabbats and organizes community service projects. "We do not require anyone to follow any path, tradition or faith to attend our events, all who come with an open heart and mind are welcome." Address: GreenSong Grove, P.O. Box 55253, St. Petersburg, FL 33732-5253. Phone: 727-804-9370. E-mail: Council@greensonggrove.org.

Web site: www.greensonggrove.org

The Grey School of Wizardry. *"Omnia vivunt, omnia inter se conexa."* An online magickal school for students aged eleven to adult. The Grey School provides an extensive program of studies in all areas of Wizardry at an apprenticeship level. Graduates will be certified as "Journeyman Wizards." The basic textbooks are *Grimoire for the Apprentice Wizard* and *Companion for the Apprentice Wizard* by Oberon Zell-Ravenheart. There are sixteen departments: Wizardry, Nature Studies, Magickal Practice, Metapsychics, Healing, Wortcunning, Divination, Performance, Alchemy, Lifeways, Beast Mastery, Mathemagicks, Cosmology, Ceremonial Magick, Lore, and Dark Arts. The school really began in 2005, and there is a growing faculty. The Grey School is highly interactive, with four Elemental "Houses" for youths and "Lodges" for adults. There is also the Great Hall, where all students can communicate directly with each other. Headmaster: Oberon Zell-Ravenheart; Dean of Studies: Elizabeth Barrette. Address: Grey School of Wizardry, P.O. Box 758, Cotati, CA 94931.

Web site: www.GreySchool.com

Grok Fellowship: A Beloved Community of Waterkin. Founded October 15, 2004, the Grok Fellowship is a vessel combining water from the chalice of CAW and that of each individual member. "We came together for the purpose of continuing our tribal connections and helping each other in our journey of self-actualization. Our mission statement is: The sacred path of the Grok Fellowship is to promote and participate in the manifestation of our common values: Thou Art God/dess, Know Thyself, Grow Closer, All that Groks is God, Love Thy Neighbor, Love as Thou Wilt, and From Thy Heart, Laugh." The Grok Fellowship encourages the celebration of life, compassionate honesty, radical politeness, ultimate individual freedom, personal responsibility and the evolution of human potential. While there is not full agreement on the term "radical politeness," treating each person with courtesy and respect is very important to members of the fellowship. There are two levels of membership: full members and friends. Each requires two vouches from members/friends with no vetoes. E-mail: grokfellowship@gmail.com.

Web sites: http://groups.yahoo.com/group/grokfellowship/ (for group members) or http://groups.yahoo.com/group/GF_open/ (for interested non-members)

The Grove, South Africa. The Grove, formed in 1996, is a Pagan Mystery School dedicated to the exploration of Pagan gnosis and the practice of Neo-Paganism. The order is an initiatory tradition founded on the praxis of ancient and modern Pagan traditions. Year and a day degree courses are conducted by experienced facilitators who encourage personal spiritual growth and ethical community participation. Address: The Grove, P.O. Box 4238, Rivonia 2128, South Africa. Phone: (27-011) 789 7847. E-mail: info@sheermagic.co.za.

Web site: www.thegrove.za.net

Hearth & Grove Fellowship. A non-profit service organization serving southwest Michigan by providing local groups and individuals with opportunities for ecological service, book study groups, community sabbat celebrations, labyrinth walks, herb walks, classes about Pagan-related subjects such as Pagan traditions and paths, ethics, and magic, as well as practical skills such as making besoms, knitting, and growing herbs. The Fellowship feels strongly about continuing education for leaders who work in ministry capacities, and provides classes and workshops to further those skills. Hearth & Grove Fellowship has been fundraising to obtain property to create and maintain a Pagan community center with space set aside for a green cemetery. Address: Hearth & Grove Fellowship, P.O. Box 205, Kalamazoo, MI 49004. E-mail: Susannkae@yahoo.com.

Web site: http://groups.yahoo.com/group/HearthandGroveFellowship

Heartland Spiritual Alliance. A networking organization that sponsors Heartland Pagan Festival (see page 578), a five-day annual festival held over Memorial Day weekend. HSA is also a networking organization for new or transplanted Pagans. HSA sponsors an educational program, Spirit Circle, on the third Monday of the month. HSA publishes the newsletter *The Heartland Spirit* and sponsors fund-raising events during the year, with the money donated to local charitable organizations. Meetings occur on the second Sunday of each month and are open to the public. Please write for information. Address: Heartland Spiritual Alliance, P.O. Box 3407, Kansas City, KS 66103. Phone: 816-807-2472. E-mail: PR@kchsa.org.

Web site: www.kchsa.org

Hecate-Legba Coven. A Vancouver coven in the Pagans for Peace Tradition, a hybrid drawing from Feri, Alexandrian, Ceremonial Magick, "and just reading too many books." Skyclad, open to women and men of a variety of sexual persuasions. Initiatory with a three degree system. Address: Hecate-Legba Coven, upper floor, 5196 Moscrop Street, Burnaby, British Columbia, V5G 2G4 Canada. E-mail: samwagar@shaw.ca "and we can maybe go out for a coffee."

The Henge of Keltria. Keltrian Druidism was founded in 1985 by members of Ár nDraocht Féin who were looking for a Celtic-specific path. In doing so, they built an organization, the Henge of Keltria, a tradition honoring the ancestors, revering the spirits of nature, and worshipping the Gods and Goddesses of their Celtic heritage. The tradition uses a very specific ritual formula, and over the years has become mainly Irish/Scottish in focus. Keltrian Druids believe in divinity as it is manifest in the Celtic pantheons and that polytheism, pantheism, panentheism, animism, and pan-polytheism are all valid theistic perceptions of the pantheon. "We believe that Nature is the embodiment of the Gods, that natural law reflects the will of the Gods, that all life is sacred, that the spirit is immortal, and that our purpose is to gain wisdom through experience." Groves can be granted a charter by the Board of Trustees; there are also study groups and individuals who practice solitary. Most rituals are done around a sacred fire. In addition to the eight Neo-Pagan Feasts, the Henge of Keltria celebrates two lunar rites, the Mistletoe Rite and the Vervain Rite. E-mail addresses for all officers, elders, and groves are at: www.keltria.org/E-Mail.htm. Individual groves and study groups may be contacted via their Web site: www.keltria.org/ContactUs.htm.

Hof Guild Kindred. The focus of Hof Guild Kindrid is self-reliance and sustainable living. Based in Ohio, all kindred members must possess a skill or trade to contribute to the kindred and the growth of the Ásatrú community at large. Members include woodworkers, blacksmiths, brewers, and herbalists. Hof Guild Kindred is a member kindred of the Ásatrú Alliance, and some kindred members also belong to the Ásatrú Folk Assembly. A long-term goal of Hof Guild Kindred is acquisition of land for its members to create an intentional community. As of this publication, a kindred Web site is currently in progress and will be accessible through search engines. Address: Hof Guild Kindred, 2625 CR 12, Bellefontaine, OH 43311.

Holy Spring Heathen Fellowship. Serves the Denton/Dallas area of North Texas in offering ways to promote and practice Anglo-Saxon and Germanic early religion. With regular blessings both seasonal and deity specific and classes and activities for children, Holy Spring builds and sustains the Heathen community and fosters ties among Heathen folk. Phone: 972-625-RUNE: E-mail Rich at: rbculver@sbcglobal.net or Jennifer at: ferrrr@msn.com.

Web site: www.holyspring.org

The House of Ouroborus (HoO). Formally established in June 2002, the House of Ouroborus is South Africa's first "home-grown" Pagan tradition. The HoO was set up by a knowledgeable group of individuals who have expertise in many different Pagan paths, hence the combination of diverse elements of Neo-Paganism found in the Ouroborian tradition. From its inception the HoO clearly stated that "We do not claim long lost lineages, nor do we profess antiquity." All Ouroborian covens and groups act independently of each other, and yet subscribe to "a common vision of high quality Pagan training and responsible Pagan practices." Address: The House of Ouroborus, P.O. Box 462, Port Shepstone 4240, KwaZulu Natal, South Africa. E-mail: ariasafrika@ yahoo.com.

Web site: www.geocities.com/ariasafrika

Hrafnar Kindred. A Heathen group that was founded in 1988 in order to practice the native religion of the Germanic peoples (Ásatrú) and Norse shamanic skills such as oracular seidh—a form of trance working. "Hrafnar welcomes all who feel a spiritual affinity for the religious tradition of Northern Europe. We believe that all whom the gods have called to this path are our kin, regardless of gender, ethnic origin, or sexual orientation." Hrafnar meets monthly to honor the gods and goddesses. The Hrafnar community also includes special interest groups devoted to individual deities such as Odin, Frigga, Hella, and the Vanir, and a working group, "Seidhjallr," that presents oracular seidh as a service to the public. Address: Hrafnar Kindred, P.O. Box 5521, Berkeley, CA 94705.

Web site: www.hrafnar.org

Immanent Grove. An independent local church, Gnostic Pagan in concept, located in Maine. It meets primarily at Ironwood Circle, a dedicated outdoor ritual space. Visitors are welcome at open celebrations. Immanent Grove sponsors perhaps the longest-running Pagan athletic event in the U.S.: the Torch-race in Honor of Pan has been run seven times. Recently its venue has been changed to coincide with an open Beltane celebration at Popham Beach. Participation is free and open. One winner takes home a silver medallion. Details and past winners are online at: www.ctel.net/~applebooks/torch-race.htm. The Grove has also opened a savings account with the goal of purchasing Pagan Land to be open to Pagans in central Maine, and to create a legally sound church property. Address: Immanent Grove, 2328 Bog Road, Sidney, ME 04330. E- mail: grove@ctel.net.

Web site: www.ctel.net/~applebooks/ironwoodhollow.htm

The Index. A Pagan Network for the Greater San Francisco Bay Area, from

Big Sur to Sacramento and all points in between. Founded in 1987 by Constance De Binero and Brook Attic, the Index takes its name from the list the Papal Inquisition kept of accused heretics, including those accused of the heresy of Witchcraft (they have taken the name to honor Witches past and present). Its main purpose is to provide local event listings and networking for Wiccan, Pagan, Ásatrú, Umbanda, Druid, Shamanic, Thelema, Egyptian, and other Neo-Pagan traditions in California's Bay Area. E-mail: Index@cyprian.org. Web site: www.cyprian.org/Index

The Iowa Pagan Access Network (IPAN). IPAN is a newsletter, community education, and networking organization for people from Goddess-centered and/or Earth-based spiritual traditions. "Our goal is to provide a medium for building community and helping Pagans from all over Iowa and the surrounding states connect with each other." Monthly Craft circles, a free online newsletter, an online calendar of events, and a yearly symposium. Address: IPAN, P.O. Box 861, Iowa City, IA 52244-0861. E-mail: ipan@ipan.org. Web site: www.ipan.org

Isis Oasis Sanctuary. Founded in 1978 by Loreon Vigné, an artist and visionary who honors the teachings of the Goddess Isis, it is the home of the non-profit Isis Society for Inspirational Studies and of the Temple of Isis, a federally recognized church whose priestesses and priests are empowered to perform legal marriages, sacred unions, and other traditional and non-traditional clergy services. It is located in the Alexander Valley in the heart of the Sonoma County wine country in northern California. Its ten acres provide a refuge for an endangered species and a breeding program for ocelots, servals, and birds of many varieties. There is a meditation chapel, a stone labyrinth, an art gallery and studio, and many other sacred spaces. There are workshops, concerts, and Sunday services. The Temple of Isis hosts an annual Convocation in the fall. Fellowship of Isis founder Lady Olivia Robertson attends along with other well-known authors, priestesses, and priests. Address: Rev. Loreon Vigné, 20889 Geyserville Avenue, Geyserville CA 95441. Phone: 707-857-ISIS or 800-679-PETS. E-mail: isis@isisoasis.org. Web site: www.isisoasis.org

Kalamazoo Pagan Community Brunch. Formerly PINK (Pagan Individuals Near Kalamazoo) Brunch, it is held on the second Sunday of each month at the Blue Dolphin Restaurant, 502 S. Burdick, in Kalamazoo. The group meets in the banquet room at the rear of the restaurant from 11:00 a.m. until 1:00 p.m. Lively conversation and moderately priced, tasty food makes the brunch a favorite of Kalamazoo's Pagan community. Non-perishable food items are collected to support a local food pantry. Contact: Susannkae@yahoo.com.

The Kindred of Ravenswood. A non-racist, non-racialist, independent Ásatrú kindred founded in 1993 on the Feast of Vali. "Our mission is to rediscover, recreate, and revitalize the religion of the ancient Germanic peoples, especially as exemplified by the Vikings. Ravenswood honors the Aesir and the Vanir in our celebrations—and no other Gods. We remember our ancestors in the ancient rite of Sumble, and reverence the hidden wights that are our folk's lifeblood—the Disir and Alfar, Dvergar and Landvittar." Ravenswood meets every month for blot and sumble, and welcomes contact with other heathens of like mind and purpose. Their motto is "For Vali, For Vengeance, For Honor, For Kin." Address: The Kindred of Ravenswood P.O. Box 136, Zionsville, IN 46077. E-mail: chaviland@iquest.net.

Web site: http://members.iquest.net/~chaviland/Rindex.html

The Kindred of ShiEndra. Established in 1992 as a non-profit spiritual organization and temple in the United States after a petition was approved by the HaVlaEndra Council of Elders in Kemet, an ancient, enduring matriarchal society that is still in existence in present-day Egypt. Directly descended from the ancient Kemetic (pre-Egyptian) pantheon through a carefully safeguarded bloodline, "MaShiAat" (The Sacred Queen Mother) Oloya Philae, Ordained Priestess and Queen Mother of the HaVlaEndra tradition, formed the movement in the United States to fulfill the need for a broader and more balanced spectrum of spiritual practice that honors multiple philosophies, built on a solid foundation of the ancient Kemetic principles. "The Kindred of ShiEndra is an inclusive and unifying spiritual and cultural community dedicated to deepening our awareness and expressions of oneness/divinity; awakening of our personal and collective divine unity; activating our highest potential; and celebrating our many lineages through education, ritual, drumming, movement, and sacred play. We serve womin, children, men, allies, communities and villages of all cultures with our primary focus on working with underrepresented communities to end all forms of internalized oppression." Address: The Kindred of ShiEndra, 4100 Redwood Road #392, Oakland, CA 94619. Phone: 510-259-1239. E-mail: info@kindredofshiendra.org.

Web site: www.kindredofshiendra.org

Lady Liberty League (LLL). An international network of Pagan religious freedom and civil rights activists. Members work together to help Pagan individuals and groups who are being persecuted, discriminated against, or harassed because of their religion. The organization also works to help Nature religions get the same respect and protection under the law as "mainstream" religions do. Founded by Selena Fox in 1985, LLL is sponsored by Circle and is part of Circle Network. The Lady Liberty League Report is published in *CIRCLE Magazine* and online. Managing Director: Jerrie Hildebrand. Address: Lady Liberty League, Circle, P.O. Box 9, Barneveld, WI 53507. Phone: 609-924-2216. E-mail: liberty@circlesanctuary.org.

Web site: www.circlesanctuary.org/liberty

Lake View Covenant (LVC). A small Gardnerian coven in the Chicago area. Address: Hermes-Thoth, 835 Cornelia #2N, Chicago, IL 60657. E-mail: hermes-tothhp@Yahoo.com.

Living Earth Circle. Founded in 1999 in Ashland, Oregon, Living Earth Circle serves to "catalyze, support and celebrate sustainable wellness: personal, community and planetary. Through ceremony and sacred performance arts, workshops, conferences, literature, and global networking we honor all creation and promote active and co-creative responsibility for social and environmental well-being." Dynamic performance art and participatory ceremonies are offered at large festivals, conferences, and multicultural events. Experiential personal growth and intensive training programs are offered on Women's and Earth-based Spirituality, ceremonial facilitation, sacred dance and expressive arts, magical herbcraft, and wholistic health, as well as special events for children and community. LEC focalizes the Grandmother Council project (see page 535) and provides ceremonial and event coordination support for individuals and groups also serving the people and the planet. Founder and facilitator: Lisa Pavati. Address: Living Earth Circle, c/o Pavati, 961 Harmony Lane, Ashland, OR 97520. Phone: 541-201-0372. E-mail: lisa@livingearthcircle.org.

Web site: www.livingearthcircle.org

Loyal Arthurian Warband. A Druid order in the United Kingdom that has come to be known as Lawband, Clawband and Warband, led by King Arthur Pendragon. Members and others perform public rituals at Avebury on the Saturday closest to each Solstice and Equinox, at Primrose Hill, London, on the nearest Sunday to each Solstice and Equinox, and at Stonehenge on the dawn of the actual day (English Heritage and Wiltshire Constabulary permitting). The order and Arthur Pendragon are known to spend much time doing civil rights and environmental protest actions, challenging unjust laws and "the encroachment on our once green and pleasant land by developers." E-mail: pendragon@warband.org.

Web site: www.warband.org

Maetreum of Cybele. A reconstructionist revival of the ancient religion of the Great Mother Goddess Cybele founded in 1999. The Cybeline faith is served by a female Priesthood that includes transsexuals, intersexuals, and other gender-variant people. "The tradition follows a belief in the divine feminine principle of the universe—that all of us and all we see and experience are a part of Her and that since we are all part of Her, none are inferior or superior to others." The rituals of the Community are conducted by a priestess known as a Mellissa or Galla. "A Galla is a transsexual who combines her journey towards the unity of a female mind with a biologically female body with her journey towards closeness to the Goddess through the discovery of the Divine Feminine. The Gallae have been part of our community for at least eight millennia." There is also a living component to the Maetreum, the Phrygianum, dedicated to the Goddess Cybele. Celebrations of new and full moons and solar quarters (equinoxes and solstices) are open to all. Address: Maetreum of Cybele, P.O. Box 468, Palenville, NY 12453. E-mail: firstchurch@gallae.com. Web site: www.gallae.com

The Magaian Way. The Magaian Tradition is inspired by the ancient Magi who followed the path of the stars while gathering the sacred keys to wisdom. Magaians explore the path between the magical aspects of nature and the mysteries of the universe. Magaians work with unique and specific techniques of Alignment. The Magaian Training program is inclusive of a variety of traditions and religions and draws on myths from around the world. The first year Magaian Apprenticeship program learns the teachings of the sacred Gateways. Each gateway is a weekend workshop that focuses on specific skills, such as Ancestor work, Alter/Gridwork, mystical Tools, and Veils of the Mysteries and the Goddess. The second year program develops the personal strengths of each apprentice, who then builds in great detail the inner temple. The third year program helps the apprentice choose a path work for leadership. The leader of the Magaian apprenticeship program is Eclipse Fey, activist, author, ritual artist and co-founder of WomenCircles (see page 586.) Address: The Magaian Way, 183 Elmgrove Avenue, Providence, RI 02906. Phone: 401-521-0767. E-mail: eclipsfey@aol.com.

Magical Education Council (MEC) MEC (formerly known as MECAA) is a non-profit educational organization established in 1995 with the following mission statement: "This organization is established for the following purpose: To create community by promoting the sharing of knowledge, experience, and fellowship among people who follow mystical and esoteric traditions. In order to promote community, we do not include those paths or traditions whose doctrines advocate bigotry and/or violence against others on the basis of race, gender, sexual orientation, disability, or religion." MEC is the organizing body behind ConVocation every year and also presently is proud to be a sponsor of the following events: Pagan Coffee Night in Ferndale, the Pagan Picnic; the UnReal Witches Ball, and several fundraising events for the Tempest Smith Foundation. Address: MEC, P.O. Box 3190, Centerline, MI, 48015. E-mail: info@mec-mi.org.

Web site: www.mec-mi.org

Maine Pagan Clergy Association (MPCA). A network of self-identified Pagan clergy, which serves as a support resource for leaders with a ministry in Maine. Members meet quarterly for support and networking, and undertake projects of benefit to Maine's Pagan community. Also offers Maine's only legal Pagan clergy licensure. No dues. Address: MPCA, P.O. Box 731, Saco, ME 04072. E-mail: info@mainepaganclergy.org.

Web site: www.mainepaganclergy.org.

Mama Donna's Tea Garden & Healing Haven. A Ceremonial center run by Donna Henes, urban shaman and contemporary ceremonialist. Henes produces circles, ceremonies, and seminars, and offers four free public seasonal celebrations each year: Spring and Fall Equinox and Winter and Summer Solstice. She also publishes a quarterly journal, *Always in Season* (see page 492). Address: Mama Donna's Tea Garden & Healing Haven, P.O. Box 380403, Exotic Brooklyn, NY 11238-0403. Phone: 718-857-1343. E-mail: cityshaman@aol.com. Web site: www.DonnaHenes.net

MAMAROOTS: Ajama-Jebi Afrakan Sistahood. "A Spiritual Sistahood and *Afrakan* (Afrikan-womin-centered-self-loving) SpiraCultural community of Afrikan Diasporik wimmin, Wimmin of Color, and our allies, dedicated to Spiritual Awakening, Self-discovery and Self-development in Our unique *AfraKamaatik* TempleTradition. Founded in 1985 on the visionary work of artist, scholar, and Spiritual Philosopher AfraShe Asungi, Our MAMAROOTS' AfraKamaatik TempleTradition is a Modern *Afracentrik* (Black/Afrikan womin-centered as a positive and healthy norm) spiritual philosophy, rooted in the lost traditions of an *Ancient Afrikan matriarchal temple system.*" The Sistahood is open to all wimmin who earnestly seek to venerate "*Our Universal DivineShe* as Wholly Female and Afrikan in origin," and is committed in the effort to join with other seekers to restore and maintain productive balance and global peace. Workshops, classes, and liturgical services are held regularly throughout the year. Entrance into the Sistahood requires a written petition to join and regular attendance at any of the organization's public or online gatherings. Address: MAMAROOTS, P.O. Box 21066, Long Beach, CA 90804. Phone: 562-961-0900. E-mail: MAMAROOTS@aol.com or SistahMIND@yahoo.com. Web sites: www.MAMAROOTSweb.com; http://forums.delphiforums.com/SistahMIND

Military Pagan Network, Inc. Founded in 1992 and incorporated in 1997 by John Machate, MPN's threefold mission is to provide information, advocacy, and community support for U.S. military Pagans, including active duty, reservists, veterans/retirees, and dependents. MPN offers networking opportunities online and helps military Pagans find others in their area. MPN encourages military and government agencies to appropriately accommodate Neo-Pagans and assists service members who may be faced with harassment or discrimination. MPN also informs the general public and civilian Neo-Pagans about the unique challenges that Neo-Pagans encounter within the military. Finally, MPN helps military Pagans stay up-to-date on regulations and current events regarding religious accommodation in the U.S. military. Address: Military Pagan Network, Inc., P.O. Box 1225, Columbia, MD 21044. Web site: www.milpagan.org

Minnesota Heathens. Founded in 2002, Minnesota Heathens is an association of kindreds and individuals in Minnesota and the surrounding states. Soon to be a non-profit religious organization, Minnesota Heathens is currently an informal group of about two hundred individuals. Membership is open to all who are interested in the indigenous cultural, mystical, and spiritual traditions of the Scandinavian, German, Anglo-Saxon, Slavic, Baltic, and other Northern European peoples. "We only request that members try to keep an open mind about other alternative lifestyles, cultures, and religions." The purpose of Minnesota Heathens is to disseminate accurate knowledge about Heathen cultures, histories, beliefs, and practices, to serve the religious needs of its members, to promote and provide resources for the training of clergy and scholars for the practice and study of Heathen religions and to facilitate and promote cooperation and community among non-discriminatory groups and individuals practicing indigenous religions. Address: Minnesota Heathens, c/o Kent Escherich, P.O. Box 13075, Minneapolis, MN 55414. E-mail: Minnesota Heathens@yahoo.com.

Web site: www.minnesotaheathens.org; Minnesota Heathens' Yahoo Group: http://groups.yahoo.com/group/minnesota_heathens

Minoan Tradition. An initiatory Mystery tradition of Witchcraft that is based in Aegean and Ancient Near Eastern (particularly Cretan) mythology. The tradition comprises the single-sex lineages of the Minoan Brotherhood and Minoan Sisterhood. The Minoan Brotherhood was established in early 1977 in New York City by the late Edmund Buczynski (d. 1989) as a venue for gay/bisexual men to explore ritual Witchcraft. It has since spread throughout the United States and into Canada. The Minoan Sisterhood was established in New York unofficially in 1978 by Lady Rhea and Lady Miw-Sekhmet—based upon the work of Edmund Buczynski. The Sisterhood is open to any woman, and emphasizes Women's Mysteries and Magics. Both branches of the tradition offer a three-degree training structure, and follow an eight-sabbat wheel of the year tailored to the deities of the Cretan mythos. Minoan Sisterhood Address: The Magickal Realms, 409 East 189th Street, Bronx, NY 10458. E-mail: Magickal Realms@aol.com.

Web sites: www.minoantradition.org; www.minoan-brotherhood.org

Missionary Order of the Celtic Cross (MOCC). Founded in 1983, one of the "grandchildren" of the RDNA. Other than those Branches of Druidism composed primarily of solitaries, the MOCC is possibly one of the smallest Druid Orders in the United States and has a very broad variety of philosophies represented in its membership—from the Apollonian to the Dionysiac, from very stoic to the ecstatic, from city lovers to Nature kin. There are good cross sections of ages, genders, and economic/educational backgrounds. The basic teachings are put forward in a short list of fifteen tenets (these are usually recognized as generic, pan-Pagan beliefs). MOCC draws inspiration from both Reformed Druidism and from Wicca, and is an eclectic, decentralized Neo-Pagan path. There are also some alternative-minded Christians in the group, and everyone seems happy with the arrangement. As of 2005, there were groups in Oklahoma, Texas, Washington, Arizona, and a few other locations. Worship and study is held on the Full and New Moons and on the sabbats. There's an occasional newsletter. Contact: Thomas Lee Harris. E-mail: myrddinamaeglin@ yahoo.com.

Web site: http://groups.yahoo.com/group/moccgroveofthethreerays

Mother Earth Ministries-ATC (MEM). A Tucson, Arizona–based Neo-Pagan prison ministry. MEM's mission is to provide accurate information about Wicca and other Neo-Pagan faiths to interested inmates and prison staff, and to facilitate for Neo-Pagan prisoners the study and practice of their religions. Affiliated with the internationally recognized Aquarian Tabernacle Church, Mother Earth is very much a local group, founded by Carol Garr in the summer of 2000. Visiting clergy lead ritual for Pagan inmates in several Arizona facilities; corresponding clergy answer letters from Pagan inmates all over the country. MEM does *not* offer formal lessons or provide religious items, but does make introductory brochures about Wicca, the Wheel of the Year, Ásatrú, and Druidry available, along with flyers and pamphlets about various other aspects of Neo-Paganism. Address: MEM, P.O. Box 35906, Tucson, AZ, 85740-5906. E-mail: Scribe@MotherEarthMinistries.org.

Web site: www.MotherEarthMinistries.org

Neokoroi (The Temple Keepers). A group for Hellenic polytheists who feel called to a path of service and devotion to the gods. Neokoroi favors a Reconstructionist approach to Hellenismos (Greek Paganism), while recognizing the importance of personal experience and spiritual innovation. The group is especially dedicated to fostering "real life" worship through the formation of local groups, installation of religious advisors and diviners, and the building of shrines and eventually temples. They also publish a quarterly newsletter, *He Epistole,* in print and electronic formats. Address: Neokoroi, c/o Sarah Winter, 715 S. 20th Avenue #18, Bozeman, MT 59718. E-mail: info@neokoroi.org.

Web site: www.neokoroi.org

Neptune's Silver Web. A Wiccan coven and outer court that networks, teaches, and celebrates the sabbats. The background is primarily Alexandrian and Gardnerian, but the group also studies ceremonial magick and shamanism. Address: Neptune's Silver Web, P.O. Box 49187, Jacksonville Beach, FL 32240. E-mail: NeptsWeb@comcast.net.

The New Alexandrian Library. This is a project to create a modern, state of the art research and reference library where knowledge from many esoteric traditions can be accessed by scholars and serious seekers. Books, periodicals, special collections, music, media, digital data, etc., will all be carefully cataloged and cross-referenced to ease the work of research. Like the original Alexandrian Library in Egypt, it will be an interfaith crossroads and will collect materials from all spiritual traditions. The Library will work to restore and to preserve rare and damaged documents. In addition to creating a physical library, the New Alexandrian Library will have an Internet component with the idea that over time as much material as is possible, within the limits of logistics and legalities, will be available online. Land and architectural plans have been donated. Fundraising is proceeding and the projected date for the library is 2010. The library will be located in Southern Delaware, and will be under the aegis of the Assembly of the Sacred Wheel (see page 509). Address: Assembly of the Sacred Wheel, 14914 Deer Forest Road, Georgetown, DE 19947. Phone: 302-855-9422. E-mail: sacredwheel@sacredwheel.org.

Web site: www.sacredwheel.org/nal.html

New England Covens of Traditionalist Witches (N.E.C.T.W.). A center for Covens of Traditionalist origin, founded by Lady Gwen Thompson (1928–1986), a hereditary Witch from North Haven, Connecticut. It is a place for men and women to be trained as priests and priestesses of the Craft. Although formally named in 1972, this family tradition was brought into the public in the late 1960s. Gwen's family tradition originated in Somerset, England, and was brought to the United States by way of Nova Scotia. It was handed down through generations and blended with popular occultism to become the present form she named N.E.C.T.W. As not all who are born into a family tradition are destined to follow that path, Gwen feared her tradition would die out and fade into obscurity. This was the principal reason she decided to "foster" individuals outside her family bloodline in order to ensure that the Tradition would survive. Each Coven is completely autonomous and guided by its High Priestess and High Priest. The Council of Elders may decide upon matters between covens, or relating to the tradition. Gwen Thompson's teachings have had extensive influence on many other Craft Traditions in the United States, some of which are still active today: the New York Welsh Tradition, Blue Star Tradition (via New York Welsh Tradition), Georgian Tradition, Keepers of the Ancient Mysteries (K.A.M.), and the StarBorn Sothis Tradition. Address: N.E.C.T.W., P.O. Box 29182, Providence, RI 02909. E-mail: Theitic@cox.net (the historian and archivist for N.E.C.T.W.).

Web site: www.nectw.org

New Moon New York. An open, all-volunteer, not-for-profit Pagan networking organization that works to provide opportunities for members of the New York Pagan community to communicate with each other and exchange ideas in both social and ritual situations. It welcomes all people on life-affirming spiritual paths. It holds workshops and seasonal celebrations, including an annual Beltane celebration in Central Park that at least several hundred attend each year. Address: New Moon, NY, P.O. Box 1471, Madison Square Station, New York, NY 10159. Phone: 212-388-8288. E-mail: info@ newmoonny.org.

Web site: www.newmoonny.org

New Reformed Orthodox Order of the Golden Dawn (NROOGD). A Wiccan tradition that began in 1967 (see Chapter 7) with a student taking a class from filmmaker James Broughton at San Francisco State college. She was given an assignment to create and perform a ritual, and enlisted friends to create a Witches' sabbat based on the limited historical and liturgical sources available at the time, in particular Robert Graves, Margaret Murray, and Gerald Gardner. After repeating the ritual several times and feeling its effects, they decided to create NROOGD. The name is a play on the attitudes they had toward what they were doing and upon their spiritual antecedents. NROOGD is an initiatory, coven-based Mystery tradition, worshipping a threefold Goddess and various forms of the God stemming from non-Olympian Greek deities and British mythology. Covens are autonomous, recognize one another's initiates, and share a common liturgy notable for its poetic beauty. There are roughly fifteen covens active on the West Coast and in Michigan. Covens in the San Francisco area and elsewhere cooperate to host public sabbats. For information on public rituals, NROOGD's public e-list, covens, and study groups, visit their Web site: www.nroogd.org.

New Wiccan Church International (NWC). Founded in 1973, the New Wiccan Church is an international, professional association of individual members of various traditions of Wicca who are dedicated to preserving initiatory Witchcraft in an ethical manner. The NWC defines Wicca as the initiatory Priesthood of a Mystery religion with roots that originate in the British Isles. Members practice the ancient art of Witchcraft and recognize a belief in and a connection to the Old Gods of Nature—in particular the Goddess and her Consort, the Horned God. NWC membership is open only to initiated Witches who are in one or more of the following traditions: Kingstone, Silver Crescent, Daoine Coire (all derived from Central Valley Wicca, or CVW), Gardnerian, Alexandrian, Mohsian, and related traditions. All members agree to observe and uphold the bylaws of the New Wiccan Church, which were designed to implement a common-sense application of Craft tenets in accordance with the oaths taken at initiation. The NWC is not a church in the usual sense—it is not a public Pagan ministry—it does not provide "church services" or offer "correspondence courses." The focus of the NWC is to preserve and maintain the heritage of the member traditions as an initiatory Priesthood, as well as provide a communications and mutual aid network for British Traditional Wicca (BTW). The NWC networks with other Pagan and Wiccan organizations, and some of its members participate in Pagan festivals and interfaith efforts. The NWC provides referrals to BTW groups only. Address: NWC, P.O. Box 162046, Sacramento, CA 95816. SASE needed to ensure a reply. Overseas inquiries please send three International Reply Coupons. E-mail: NWCoutreach@yahoo.com.

Web site: www.newwiccanchurch.net

9 Mayans. A loose group of people in and around Cobán, Guatemala, who perform Mayan rituals, particularly the primicia, to invoke the 9 Mayan gods. Don Jeronimo's is an eco-hotel near Cobán which offers instruction in channeling and working with nature spirits, as well as hiking, tubing, swimming, and caving. Anyone coming to Guatemala who wants to invoke the 9 Mayan gods themselves at Tikal can get information at www.dearbrutus.com and www.dearbrutus.com/donjeronimo. E-mail: jeronimo@dearbrutus.com.

Nova Roma. A Roman history organization with a section devoted to ancient Roman religion. Active since 1998, with thousands of members worldwide, Nova Roma is currently raising money to restore a shrine of Magna Mater in Rome. "Tax" (dues) is $12/year, but it is possible to participate as a non-paying member. Address: Nova Roma, P.O. Box 1897, Wells, ME 04090. E-mail: senate@novaroma.org.

Web site: www.novaroma.org

Officers of Avalon, Inc. An organization representing Pagans in the emergency services (police, firefighters, paramedics) and related trades (physicians and nurses). Members come from all of the Neo-Pagan and Afro-Diasporan spiritual paths. It is incorporated in Nevada and is a 501(c)3 charity. It has members in the United States, Canada, the United Kingdom, and Australia. Officers of Avalon works to educate law enforcement organizations and the public about Pagan spiritual paths. Avalon Cares is a branch of Officers of Avalon set up to raise funds for disaster relief. Address: P.O. Box 22, Baraboo, WI 53913-0022.

Web sites: www.officersofavalon.com; www.avaloncares.com

The Open Hearth Foundation, Inc. (OHF). Established as a non-profit Pagan community center initiative in 1999, the mission of the OHF is to create gathering space and resources for Pagans of all paths. Primary programs of the OHF include a Pagan lending library, the Washington, D.C., Pagan Pride Week, the OHF Resource Guide, the D.C. Pagans' Night Out, Samhain Drumming at the Jefferson Memorial, the OHF Spring Ball, and an ongoing capital drive campaign for the creation of a dedicated Pagan community center in the D.C. region. Address: OHF, P.O. Box 76043, Washington, D.C. 20013-6043. E-mail: shea@openhearth.org.

Web site: www.openhearth.org

The Order of Bards Ovates & Druids (OBOD). A spiritual group dedicated to practicing, teaching, and developing Druidry as a valuable and inspiring spirituality. The Order was founded by Ross Nichols and a group of members of the Ancient Druid Order, including the writer Vera Chapman. The Ancient Druid Order was formed during the early years of the last century out of the Druid Revival that began about three hundred years ago. The ADO traces its origins to 1717. Membership of the Order is open to followers of all faiths and none, regardless of gender, sexual orientation, or ethnic origin, and there are currently over 8,000 members in 50 countries. Although most members practice Druidry on their own, there are over 90 groups around the world that offer the opportunity for members to meet and celebrate together. There are also OBOD gatherings, retreats, conferences and workshops. Address: OBOD, P.O. Box 1333, Lewes, East Sussex BN7 1DX, England. Phone from U.K.: 01273 470888; from abroad: 0044 1273 470888. E-mail: OBOD@ druidry.org. Web site: www.druidry.org

The Order of the Sacred Oaks & The Sacred Oak Grove. The Ancient and Honourable Order of the Sacred Oaks was founded on Winter Solstice, December 22, 1998, in Portland, Oregon, along traditional Druidic, Wiccan/ Arthurian lines. The Sacred Oak Grove was chartered the next day. According to the "Great Charter" of the Order, it exists "to revive and rediscover the Druidic mysteries, further the Druidic, Wiccan and Pagan communities and provide a safe and nurturing environment for its members." The Grove sponsors an annual Eisteddfod for the "bards" in the local Pagan community and conducts an open Summer Solstice ritual in Portland. Initiated members commit to a communal and individual path-seeking knowledge. The Order is a non-profit organization incorporated in the state of Oregon. Address: The Order of the Sacred Oaks (or The Sacred Oak Grove), 3352 SE Hawthorne Boulevard, Portland, OR 97214. Phone: 503-235-5774. E-mail: oakgrove@teleport.com. Web site: www.sacred-oak-grove.org

Order of the Whiteoak. The Order of the Whiteoak (Ord na Darach Gile) is a modern Druidic order which bases its beliefs and practices on what is known about the original faith and practices of the pagan Celts. It uses historical research and inspiration to build a viable tradition. Based on those studies, the order believes that the ancient Druids were philosophers, lawyers, judges, lore keepers and poets, as well as ritual leaders and teachers. Members of the order seek to achieve similar skills in these modern times. "We do not believe we are inheritors of the priesthood of Atlantis. We do not believe that Druidry was the sole province of men . . . We do not derive our traditions from medieval romances about Arthur and Merlin. We are not Wiccans or Witches of any sort, as witchcraft and Druidry have been separate though coexistent paths throughout their mutual histories. We do not believe we are the only true Druids." In 2006 the order split into three branches: the Order of the Whiteoak, a World Druid council. (e-mail: membership@whiteoakdruids.org; Web site: www.whiteoakdruids.org); the Order of the Whiteoak—European Continental (Web site: www.whiteoakgrove .de); the third group had not chosen a name when this book went to press.

Ordrine Scatere Stellae—Order of the Well of Stars: An Alexandrian Mystery Order. This is a magical group that traces its lineage to Alexander Sanders (Witch King of Hastings). It uses a seven-grade system that "takes Sanders's magick beyond the 3 tier level, yet preserves the integrity of Traditional Alexandrian Craft." Address: OSS, P.O. Box 653, Ulladulla 2539 N.S.W. Australia. Phone: +61 (02) 4455 3006. E-mail: alexandrianwiccans@ yahoo.com.au. E-group: http://groups.yahoo.com/group/Well_of_Stars

Web site: http://geocities.com/well_of_stars

Our Lady of the Earth and Sky (OLOTEAS). A non-denominational Pagan church serving the Seattle-area Pagan community. It conducts monthly free introductory classes on Wicca, Paganism, Magic, and community service efforts. Address: Our Lady of the Earth and Sky, P.O. Box 20032, Seattle, WA 98102. E-mail: oloteas@oloteas.org.

Web site: www.oloteas.org

Our Lady of Enchantment. A seminary of Wicca founded in 1978 by Lady Sabrina. The school offers home study courses and personal training in Wicca, magic, and metaphysics. It offers degrees and ministerial credentials. Workshops, library, and chapel are open to all students, as are sabbat celebrations and full moon rites. Beginners as well as seasoned practitioners welcome. Address: Our Lady of Enchantment, P.O. Box 355, Cobb, CA 95426. Phone: 707-928-0264. E-mail: LadyS1366@aol.com.

Web site: www.wiccaseminary.org

Our Lady of Spiritual Audacity. A networking organization co-founded by Lady Isadora and daughter Lady Andred for Pagans in open dialogue with people of other faiths. "We are inspired by such 'gender-bending' or 'uppity women' heroines of traditional male-dominated religion as Joan of Arc, the legendary Pope Joan, and medieval mystic abbess-composer Hildegard von Bingen. We're also intrigued by increasingly popular alternative ideas about Mary Magdalene in a priestess or goddess role, and we seek to promote public dialogue and awareness about the apparently Pagan roots of the legendary Jesus figure. Address: Our Lady of Spiritual Audacity, P.O. Box 41246, Des Moines, IA 50311. E-mail: olsa@ladyisadora.com.

Web site: www.ladyisadora.com/olsa.html

Our Lady of the Woods. A Wiccan coven and congregation whose missions are "Teaching Wicca, Healing the Earth." OLW provides priest/priestess training in the Ladywood Tradition established by Amber K. The coven offers a Wicca 101 course to the public on a periodic basis and accepts students into the coven by application. Honoring both the God and Goddess, this eclectic group also sponsors eight sabbat celebrations that are free and open to the public. Monthly lectures, workshops, or rituals may also be held. Announcements of events can be found on their Web site. The Web site also contains selected articles from *Lady Letter*, published by OLW from 1993 to 1999. Address: Our Lady of the Woods, P.O. Box 1107, Los Alamos, NM 87544.

Web site: www.ladywoods.org

Ouroborous Isis Gnosis (OBIG). Formed by Boneblossom, a Pagan missionary from Starhawk's Reclaiming coven in 1981, and still going strong today. "We are an Inanna based coven, taking Inanna's descent into the Underworld as our litany but we honor all gods and goddesses. Our ritual theme is Mirth and Reverence. We are an eclectic, non-hierarchical, consensus group spread across New England." A subgroup of Ouroborous (the Star Lodge), a ceremonial magickal group, practices a variant of Israel Regardie's Middle Pillar Meditation. E-mail: ouroborousig@gmail.com.

Ozark Avalon, Church of Nature. A Wiccan Church and Land Sanctuary located on 160 sacred acres near the Missouri River outside of Columbia, Missouri. "This is a magickal land with groves, woods, a lake, trails and natural and created shrines. Our mission is to steward and protect our land and offer it for outdoor worship and fellowship. We are open to all Earth Honoring persons of good intentions." Ozark Avalon is open for camping and personal retreats year round, as well as full moons and sabbat celebrations. Some limited indoor space is also available. There are family-oriented events as well as a few that are for adults only. Address: Ozark Avalon, 26213 Cumberland Church Road, Boonville, MO 65233. Phone: 660-882-6418 or 573-289-3657. E-mail: rosewise@socket.net.

Web site: www.ozarkavalon.net

Pagan Academic Network (PAN). An association of Pagan students, faculty, staff, and scholars in academia. Founded in 1992 and sponsored by Circle, members of the network share resources, perspectives, news, and support about the emerging field of Pagan studies and issues pertaining to Pagans on campuses in the United States and elsewhere. The Nature Religions Scholars Network, associated with the American Academy of Religion since 1995, was among the Pagan studies endeavors that emerged from this organization. PAN's annual meeting is held during the Pagan Spirit Gathering (see page 584). Director: Dennis Carpenter, Ph.D. Address: PAN, Circle Sanctuary, P.O. Box 9, Barneveld, WI 53507. 608-924-2216. E-mail: circle@circlesanctuary.org.

Web site: www.circlesanctuary.org/learn

Pagan Alliance. Founded in Australia in 1991 to provide a networking and information service to Pagans within Australia. Over a decade later it is still doing so, and also providing information about Pagan religions to official bodies, to the media, and any other interested parties that may require accurate advice or background information about Paganism. In 2000 the Pagan Alliance,

Inc. was formed and incorporated as a national body to produce the magazine *Pagan Times* (see page 500). The Pagan Alliance is structured as a network of connected State Bodies. Each State Admin team is independent but headed by a member-elected State Co-ordinator who sits on the National States Council, as a means of ensuring an overall National approach to both policy and any events requiring action by the Alliance, and providing a formal channel for national-level communication. E-mail: hiraeth@iprimus.com.au.

Web site: www.paganalliance.org.au

Pagan Alliance of Nurses (PAN). PAN strives to unite Pagan nurses for purposes of education, support, exchange of information, political action, and healing. "We seek these things for the overall benefit of ourselves, our religion, families, friends, communities and the world." PAN began in 2001 as an on-line discussion group. There is a periodic newsletter, workshops, educational and community projects, and a scholarship. The organization has been a source of information and support for many. "We have been able to ask our questions, to share knowledge, experience, even dreams. As members of a nature-centered religion we realize that all life is interconnected and that our actions as individuals and as a group can have a profound effect of the whole. By coming together as a coordinated force using our knowledge, skills and talents we enhance our effectiveness to facilitate and promote our goals." E-group site: health.groups.yahoo.com/group/PaganAllianceofNurses.

Web site: www.pagan-alliance-of-nurses.org

Pagan Community Council of Ohio. A network of Pagans in Ohio from many different traditions and paths. It sponsors meetings and four festivals: the Greening (Memorial Day weekend) (see page 578), Summerset (Labor Day weekend) (see page 586), as well as fall and winter festivals. It also lends support to various community organizations and Pagan Pride events. "We do not require members to follow any certain path, tradition or faith—all with an open mind are welcome." Address: Pagan Community Council of Ohio, P.O. Box 82089, Columbus, OH 43202-0089. To join the mailing list or inquire about membership, contact: pcco_secretary@yahoo.com or pcco_membership@yahoo.com.

Web site: www.thepcco.com

The Pagan Federation; The Pagan Federation (Scotland and Ireland). This is perhaps Europe's largest and most active Pagan organization. It was founded in 1971 as the Pagan Front, to provide information on Paganism and to counter misconceptions about the religion. The Pagan Federation works for the rights of Pagans to worship freely and without censure. Its membership is drawn from all Pagan paths, and while it seeks to advance the general interests of the Pagan community, it does not presume to represent all Pagans. All Pagans over the age of eighteen are welcome to join. The PF runs a growing number of annual, national, and regional conferences across Europe and is particularly active in anti-defamation work and civic advocacy, defending Paganism against abuse and misrepresentation and Pagans against discrimination. The PF handles hundreds of inquiries each year from radio, television, and newspapers, giving them accurate and authoritative information. The Pagan Federation provides pastoral care for Pagans in hospitals and prisons. It publishes a quarterly magazine, *Pagan Dawn* (see page 499). Address: The Pagan Federation, BM Box 7097, London WC1N 3XX, England, U.K. E-mail: Secretary@paganfed.demon.co.uk.

Web site: www.paganfed.org

Address: The Pagan Federation (Scotland and Ireland), P.O. Box 14251, Anstruther KY10 3YA, Scotland, U.K. E-mail: enquiries@scottishpf.org.

Web sites: www.scottishpf.org; www.pfireland.net

Pagan Federation/Fédération Païenne Canada (PFPC). A national association of Pagans in Canada founded in 1994 and federally incorporated in 1998. "Our purpose is to promote and protect the reputation of Pagans and Paganism in Canada. We do this through public education so our fellow Canadians know what we do and DON'T do, networking among Pagans in Canada so we get to know each other and help each other, a quarterly newsletter to members, a large and informative Web site, and an online discussion group for members." PFPC has in the past been contracted with the Federal Government (Corrections Canada) to provide Pagan chaplaincy in federal prisons in Ontario, and continues to do hospital visitation and mail or e-mail communication with federal prisons in other parts of the country. PFPC belongs to the Ontario Multifaith Council, a government-funded body that works on ensuring religious service for all faiths for people in Ontario hospitals, prisons, and long–term care facilities. Membership in the PFPC is open to people who are eighteen or older and adhere generally to these principles: 1. You feel love for and kinship with Nature. 2. You follow the ethic: If it harms none, do as you will. 3. You accept that if gender is attributed to the Divine, it can be masculine, feminine, or both. (These principles are held to be minimal and are not meant to restrict or invalidate anybody's spiritual beliefs.) Address: PEPC, P.O. Box 876, Station "B," Ottawa, ON, K1P 5P9, Canada. E-mail: info@pfpc.ca.

Web site: www.pfpc.ca

The Pagan Federation International. This is the international division of the organization listed above. The Pagan Federation International has branches all across the world, including Australia, Belgium, Canada, Scandinavia, Portugal, Italy, Germany, Turkey, South America, and the United States. PF is a membership organization and fees depend on the country. Membership includes a subscription to *Pagan Dawn*. Address: Pagan Federation International, Postbus 473, 3700 AL ZEIST, The Netherlands. E-mail: Morgana@paganfederation.org.

Web site: www.paganfederation.org

Pagan Federation of South Africa (PFSA). At winter solstice 1996, the

Pagan Federation of South Africa was born, making it the first formal Pagan organization in South Africa. It is a non-profit organization facilitating networking between all Pagans, providing contacts, Rites of Passage, public functions, festivals, and workshops across the full spectrum of Pagan activities. The organization strives to make Paganism accessible to everyone who genuinely seeks a nature-based spiritual path and subscribes to the principles of tolerance, both within the membership and without. It accordingly asserts its rights under the Constitution of South Africa in terms of protection against discrimination, freedom of association, freedom of movement, freedom of conscience, religion, thought, belief, and opinion. The PFSA has given rise to a variety of groups ideally suited to serve the Pagan community: The Temple of Athena, Hecate's Loom Training Coven, and Weaver's Web. Address: PFSA, Dairy Cottage, Riversands Farm, William Nicol Drive, Johannesburg 2000, South Africa. E-mail: President—scribe@eject.co.za, National Secretary—mynie@eject.co.za. Web sites: www.pfsa.org.za; http://pagan-home.net

PagaNet, Inc. Founded in 1995, PNI is a non-profit organization whose mission is to serve as an information, education, and networking resource for practitioners of alternative spirituality. Its slogan, "Non mihi, non tibi, sed nobis," which means "Not for me, not for you, but for us," embodies the goals behind the organization as a whole. Over the years, PNI has produced many events and resources, including the Pagan-specific newsprint publication PagaNet News, which has recently transitioned into more of an interfaith resource for practitioners of a wider variety of alternative faiths. The organization has also served as an information source for local police and cult crime investigators, and has frequently spoken at conferences and universities. PNI is governed by a board of directors and currently offers *If . . . Journal,* a very simple prison outreach program, a community library, occasional support for budding laypersons in the military, a women's retreat each fall, an annual medieval-themed fund-raiser weekend event, and an annual candlelight vigil for religious tolerance. Address: PagaNet, Inc., P.O. Box 61007, Virginia Beach, VA 23466. Phone: 757-539-4523. Fax: 757-539-6929. E-mail: pni@paganet.org. Web site: www.paganet.org

The Pagan Pride Project. The purpose of the Pagan Pride Project is the advancement of Paganism as a religion and the elimination of prejudice and discrimination. "Even today, there are Pagans in the United States and around the world who practice in secret out of fear of being ridiculed or even persecuted for their beliefs. Many non-Pagans do not understand the practices involved in Paganism, or that it is even an existing religious movement." Pagan Pride seeks to foster pride in Pagan identity through education, activism, charity, and community. The organizers believe that by taking the initiative in educating the public and by holding public and charitable events, Pagans will come to be accepted by the greater community. The Pagan Pride Project started with seventeen events in the United States and Canada and has grown to over one hundred events in the United States, Canada, Europe, and South America. The project held 112 events in 2005, attended by 40,495 people—10,000 at the New York City event alone. Collectively, the events raised more than 23,000 pounds of food and nearly $13,000 for local charities and disaster relief. Each year Pagan Pride gives more than a hundred interviews to the media discussing the Pagan religious faith. The local events and their Web sites also provide many written resources introducing Paganism to the world. The events distribute written literature, and they include open workshops on various Pagan topics and public rituals. E-mail: dagonet@paganpride.org.

Web site: www.paganpride.org

The Pagan Roundtable. A topical public discussion group that has been meeting since 1996 at the Mount Clemens Public Library in Mount Clemens, Michigan. It meets the first Tuesday of every month; topics vary and are selected by the membership every month. The library is located at 150 Cass Avenue, Mt. Clemens, MI. E-mail Arwen Starda at starend@aol.com; put "Pagan Roundtable" in the subject line.

Pagan Sanctum Recovery. Inspired by the twelve steps of Alcoholics Anonymous, the fellowship of Pagan Sanctum Recovery embraces Pagan beliefs, vocabulary, and ideologies in a program of dual recovery. PSR is a recovery alternative for today's growing membership of Goddess religions and other pre-Christian faiths, including Wicca, Witchcraft, Ásatrú, Odinism, Shamanism, Pantheism, Druidism, Native American paths, and many others. As in most twelve-step programs, there are no dues or fees. Each PSR group supports itself through its own contributions. "If you walk a Pagan path and have a substance abuse problem and/or have been diagnosed with a psychiatric or mood disorder, PSR provides a supportive group environment where you can freely discuss your faith without 'watching your pronouns,' or otherwise let something slip to a group that may or may not accept you unconditionally. If you're not certain you have an addiction problem, PSR can help you decide. Through meditation, magic and ritual, we discover our individual paths to recovery, and guide others to theirs." Buddhists and Hindus—and all others who wish to explore this alternative spirituality—are welcome. PSR helps all who come in need, and offers secular support to others in recovery, regardless of religion, spirituality, twelve-step program affiliation, or politics. PSR is not meant to replace other twelve-step programs, but to serve as a spiritual supplement for those needing to share their recovery-through-faith with others from similar backgrounds. Address: Pagan Sanctum Recovery, P.O. Box 657, Tulsa, OK 74101. E-mail: pagansanctum@cox.net.

Web site: www.pagansanctumrecovery.org

Pagan Unity Campaign (PUC). Founded in 2000 by Storm Bear Williams,

Pagan Unity Campaign is a political activism co-op that encourages Pagans to get involved with the political process by contacting their elected officials through e-mails, faxes, telephone calls, and postal mailings throughout each year during various PUC campaigns. PUC's annual Summer Solstice "I AM A PAGAN" postcard mailing campaign is a loud and proud religious diversity awareness message from Pagan Americans to government officials in Washington. PUC also runs an ongoing voter registration and voter education campaign called "SO VOTE IT BE." PUC's staff of volunteers now includes regional directors and state chairs representing all fifty states. The current PUC president is Ginger Strivelli. E-mail: Ginger@paganunitycampaign.org.

Web site: www.paganunitycampaign.org

Panthean Temple. The Panthean Temple (formerly known as the Pagan Community Church) is Connecticut's first open Pagan and Wiccan church, "In Celebration of the Old Religions since 1995." A growing community in the Naugatuck Valley and New Haven, Connecticut, the church is legally incorporated and its current home is the First Unitarian Universalist Society in New Haven. The church holds sabbat rituals, has a study group, drum circles, and workshops and hosts guest speakers—all open to the public—as well as a large Beltane festival (see page 576). Other rituals are open to members only. Members may apply to become students and attend classes. There is both an Outer Court and Inner Court, and ordination is available through acceptance and participation within the Inner Court. The temple is open to Pagans of all traditions who follow the ethics of harm none. The Panthean tradition has its roots in Odyssean, which is the tradition of the Wiccan Church of Canada. Address: Panthean Temple, 608 Whitney Avenue, New Haven, CT 06511. E-mail: PantheanTemple@aol.com.

Web site: www.pagancommunitychurch.org

Polyhymnia Coven. The coven is named for the Muse of Sacred Poetry and was founded in 1993. "A traditional Gardnerian coven, we focus on training our members as Wiccan clergy. Studies with Polyhymnia lead to initiation in the Gardnerian Tradition. We are non-sexist, non-racist, and non-homophobic, and expect our students to be also." Students wishing to investigate becoming part of Polyhymnia should send a letter or e-mail to Polyhymnia Coven, Box 726, Jackson Heights, NY 11370. E-mail: rwandel@pipeline.com.

Proteus Coven. A liberal Gardnerian coven located in northern New Jersey, near New York City. "We emphasize reverence for and service to Mother Earth, along with rigorous training and exuberant personal creativity. Entry into one of our pre-initiatory study groups requires certain specific ethical commitments." Proteus's Web site offers a collection of materials useful for mature Pagan seekers anywhere, and also contains contact information for seven covens descended from Proteus.

Web site: www.draknet.com/proteus

Radical Faeries. A "mainly" queer men's spiritual happening/movement. Harry Hay (d. 2002), John Burnside, Morris Knight, and others brought together several hundred like-minded queer men in New Mexico in 1979. This decentralized movement is mainly defined by its lack of authoritarian structure and its orientation toward a pro-humanist, pro-environment, pro-sex vision of the world that contrasts sharply with mainstream Western religious traditions. While not Pagan per se, the Radical Faeries count a large percentage of self-identified Pagans among their members. Gender blending is a hallmark of the Radical Faerie movement. "We're decentralized, and nobody's in charge—so every faerie who you ask will give a slightly different definition of 'Radical Faerie.' Generally, we tend to be Gay men who look for a spiritual dimension to our sexuality; many of us are healers of one kind or another. Our shared values include feminism, respect for the Earth, and individual responsibility rather than hierarchy. Many of us are Pagan." Several Radical Faerie groups have come together to form intentional communities/land projects. These include Short Mountain (TN), Ida (TN), Faerie Camp Destiny (VT), Camp Kawashaway (MN), Blue Heron Farm (NY), Zuni Mountain (NM), and Nomenus (OR). There is also a Radical Faerie sanctuary in eastern France called Folleterre. Many of the Radical Faerie communities have regular celebratory gatherings on the land throughout the year. The flagship publication of the movement is *RFD Magazine* (see page 501). While some Radical Faerie gatherings are spaces reserved primarily for queer men, others may include a mix of straight men, lesbians, straight women, and even children. More than forty groups are listed on the Web.

Web site: www.radfae.org

Reclaiming. An international community of women and men working to unify spirit and political action—magical activism. "Our vision is rooted in the religion and magic of the Goddess—the Immanent Life Force. We see our work as teaching and making magic—the art of empowering ourselves and each other." Reclaiming offers classes, public rituals, and/or Witch camps (weeklong intensives) in dozens of cities and regions in the United States, Canada, and Europe. Contacts are found in the magazine and Web site. Address: Reclaiming, P.O. Box 14404, San Francisco, CA 94114. Events line: 415-255-7623. E-mail: reclaiming@reclaiming.org.

Web site: www.reclaiming.org

Re-formed Congregation of the Goddess-International (RCG-I). A nonprofit religious organization incorporated in many states whose purpose is to foster positive spiritual growth among all women. "RCG-I is an international Goddess religion providing the recognition and benefits of organized religion to its members." RCG-I sponsors the Women's Thealogical Institute (see page

574), and, at the time of this listing (2006), had more than two thousand members. There are several RCG-I circles in Texas, several in Indiana, and circles in Wisconsin, Minnesota, North Carolina, and New Mexico, as well as ordained priestesses in a number of other states. RCG-I also puts on two annual festivals: Hallows Gathering in October (see page 588), and A Gathering of Priestesses in May (see page 577). Address: RCG-I, P.O. Box 6677, Madison, WI 53716. Phone: 608-226-9998. E-mail: rcgiorg@aol.com.

Web site: www.rcgi.org

The Reformed Druids of North America (RDNA). Founded in 1963 after some Carleton College students in Minnesota challenged a mandatory attendance of religious services by creating their own "religion/philosophy" as a test. The requirement was soon thereafter rescinded, but the RDNA joyfully continued and deepened. "The RDNA is the oldest and largest (yet also the most simple and eclectic) of the modern Druid movements in America. The RDNA believes that the observation and contemplation of Nature can assist members of every religion and / or philosophy in the world, and it encourages honestly reviewing one's own beliefs. An optional modest splash of Celtic terms and trappings completes the picture. Numerous groups have schismed or descended from the RDNA over the years (e.g., NRDNA, ADF, Keltria, etc.) and have enacted sensible by-laws, praiseworthy seminary programs, achieved tax-exempt status, narrowed their base-pool of traditions, labeled themselves as Neo-Pagan, and run busy responsible central offices; but the RDNA has proudly remained protean, dis-organized with strong local autonomy. The RDNA still has a trademarked sense of humor and is respectfully irreverent." After a downturn in the '80s, the RDNA is livelier than ever; as of 2006 there are about 51 groves and protogroves, with 450 grove-Druids and 3,300 solitary Druids in the United States, Canada, Japan, France, and beyond. Almost half of the RDNA have historically come from Carleton, but the Internet is now changing that. Overall RDNA membership is simple and free, although local groves may decide otherwise. Although the ancient Druids didn't write anything down, modern Druids love to write, and the RDNA has seven enormous online volumes of more than 3,526 dense pages of essays, stories, and liturgies. Its online magazine, *A Druid Missal-Any,* published eight times a year, is at http://druidmissal-any .tripod.com. Address: The Archdruid, c/o Carleton College, Northfield, MN 55057 (Include a SASE). E-mail: mikerdna@hotmail.com. RDNA's largest online conference is RDNAtalk: http://groups.yahoo.com/ RDNAtalk.

Web site: www.geocities.com/mikerdna

Religious Order of the Circle of Isis Rising (ROCIR). Founded in 1981 by writer and paranormal investigator Lady Nicole Everett, the coven is established in Miami, Florida. Based on Druidic principles to a point, the grove then goes eclectic. Also incorporated are Hermetic and Egyptian traditions. Membership is represented by people of all ages from diverse cultural and ethnic backgrounds. The Coven's focus is on religion and individual spiritual growth. Community service is also stressed, together with a respect for the environment and interpersonal relationships. Sabbat celebrations are open to all Kindred Spirits. The priests and priestesses offer legal handfastings, funeral rites, Wiccanings, healing events, and other services to the community. The ROCIR is legally recognized as a not-for-profit corporation. The goal is to establish a coven sanctuary that all Pagans can use for religious group and personal rites. Address: ROCIR, P.O. Box 83-1196, Miami, FL 33283-1196. Phone: 305-265-2228. E-mail: mysticalaamulet@earthlink.net.

Robin's Hood CommUNITY Center (RHCC). A Kentucky Pagan community center that helps the homeless. When temperatures dip below 20 degrees, RHCC stays open around the clock as a warming center. During the winter one can find anywhere between 80 and 150 people drinking coffee, scanning want ads, searching apartment listings, and staying warm. In the summer, the CommUNITY Center is a respite from the heat. During the winter holidays it serves complete meals and gives out gifts. It has helped many homeless people find jobs and get off the streets. RHCC also holds workshops and seminars. Address: Robin's Hood CommUNITY Center, 501 Madison Avenue, Covington, KY 41011. Phone: 859-743-6454. E-mail: rhccbonnie@yahoo.com. Web site: www.thefaerierealm.com/robin's_hood_community_center.htm

Romuva. Romuva is the reconstructionist Pagan tradition of Lithuania. Paganism was the state religion of Medieval Lithuania until 1387. Romuva was founded in 1967, but the Soviet Union suppressed it from 1969 to 1989. The name refers to a famous historical Old Prussian temple. Romuva celebrates the solar (the solstices and change of seasons), agrarian (the planting and harvest), and human (birth, naming, wedding, death) festival cycles that have survived to the present day, as well as fire rituals. It emphasizes the spiritual and religious nature of the ceremonies, discarding the Christian veneer and explanations that have been added. The rituals are unrelated to western Pagan models. A focal religious practice is singing dainas, ancient hymns that often have been called the Baltic Vedas. The religion reveres various goddesses, gods, and animistic spirits, many of which are anthropomorphic manifestations of nature, especially the heavens and flora, but not fauna. Some of the major deities are directly related to the Vedic gods of ancient India. Nature is sacred, and Romuva has a long-standing ecological commitment. Romuva avoids calling itself Pagan, and is a member of the World Council of Ethnic Religions. In North America, there are congregations in Chicago, Boston, Vancouver, and Toronto. Focusing on individuals of Lithuanian ancestry, they work in English. Romuva was incorporated in Wisconsin in 1992. Address: Romuva, c/o Kaze Kazlauskeine,

Spirit Thomes and Treasures, 810 Cedar Parkway, Schererville, IN 46375. Phone: 219-865-8986. E-mail: treasure@netnitco.net.

Web sites: www.romuva.lt; http://groups.yahoo.com/group/Romuva

The Rowan Tree Church. An Earth-focused network of communities and solitary practitioners founded by Paul Beyerl and dedicated to a Wiccan tradition called Lothlorien. It has been a legally recognized Wiccan Church since 1979 offering spiritual growth through publications, rituals, and formal pathworking. The Education division of the church is the Hermit's Grove, which offers classes, workshops, gardens and woodlands, facilities for research, and a stone circle for meditation. Address: The Rowan Tree Church, P.O. Box 0691, Kirkland, WA 98083. Phone: 425-828-4124.

Web sites: www.therowantreechurch.org; www.thehermitsgrove.org

The Sabaean Religious Order. The Sabaean Religious Order (see Chapter 9) was founded by Frederic M. De Arechaga (Odun). The philosophy of Sabaeanism is "one of action that states human beings should live in the present, identifying with those principles that are unchanging even in the face of death." Sabaeanism goes back to Egyptian and Babylonian sources. The Gods are called Am'n, a word said to mean the hidden, numberless point; it can be singular or plural, male or female, the source. Formerly located in Chicago, with a temple and store, the SRO moved to New Orleans. After Hurricane Katrina, the SRO moved to Denver, Colorado and the work of Sabaeanism continues. Sadly, Odun suffered a terrible stroke in 2005. As this book was going to press, he had still not recovered. Sabaeanism will continue. The priesthood of the Order will continue Odun's work, complete the books he was working on, and publish them in his name. E-mail: Odun@sabaean.org or SRO@sabaean.org.

Web site: www.sabaean.org

Sacre Radici (Sacred Roots—formerly La Federazione Pagana). Founded in 1992 and originally known as La Federazione Pagana, Sacre Radici is a national Italian Neo-Pagan network embracing all traditional Pagans: Greco-Roman, Celtic, shamanistic, etc. The founder of the group, Zoe Red Bear, considers herself very close to the California Reclaiming tradition. For Sacre Radici, polytheism represents honoring diversity in the fields of ecology, ethnicity, politics, religion, and sexuality. "Everything is sacred and everything is alive—the divine exists in all things." It is not to be confused with another Italian group called La Federazione Pagana, with which Sacre Radici has cordial relations. Address: Sacre Radici, c/o Roberto Fattore, Casella Postale 54— Forlì Centro 47100 Forlì, Italy. Although Sacre Radici doesn't have a Web site, there are several Italian Pagan Web sites listed at the end of this resource guide.

The Sacred Well Congregation: An International Wiccan Church and Fellowship. On Midsummer Day, 1994, in Hainin, Belgium, six Elders of the Greencraft Tradition of Wicca founded the Sacred Well Congregation. Greencraft is a branch of Traditional Craft Wicca that traces its lineage through the Alexandrian Tradition, although Greencraft Wicca has evolved to the point where it is recognizable as a distinct tradition of craft Wicca. In April 1996, Rev. David L. Oringderff, Ph.D., Rev. Tama L. Oringderff, and Rev. Dewey Oringderff incorporated the Sacred Well Congregation in the State of Texas as a non-profit organization and a legally recognized church. Headquartered in Converse, Texas, the SWC has some 1,200 members residing in 47 states and 19 foreign countries. Although the core leadership practices Greencraft Wicca, the SWC itself is universalistic in nature and embraces all spiritual paths into its membership. Membership is free and non-binding, and requires only that members acknowledge the Covenant of Five Tenets and request to affiliate with the Congregation. About half of the membership is either serving in, or affiliated with, the U.S. Armed Forces. The SWC provides Denominational Sponsorship and Leader Endorsement for some thirty Distinctive Faith Groups in all branches of service around the world. In 2002, the International Institute for Cultural and Religious Studies was incorporated as the educational, service, and outreach agency of the congregation. The Sacred Well Congregation has been a member agency of the Combined Federal Campaign since 2004. Address: The Sacred Well Congregation, P.O. Box 58, Converse, TX 78109. Phone: 210-658-9100. E-mail: staff@sacredwell.org.

Web site: www.sacredwell.org

The Sanctuary of the Crescent Moon. A Dianic Wiccan Temple and coven serving the Illiana areas of the greater Chicagoland and NW Indiana locations. As a mixed gender group, the Sanctuary honors the Lady Diana in her four aspects, through a Graeco-Roman tradition. The Temple hosts open sabbat rituals and social events, as well as conducting a devotee program (non-degree) for friends of the Temple, who wish to serve the Temple Gods in a more meaningful way. The Sancta Luna Coven offers a degree program for those who wish to be formally trained as Dianic Witches, as well as full moon rites and selected classes. The Temple is open to all women and men who wish to celebrate Wicca through the path of divine feminine empowerment. Phone: 219-308-3743. E-mail: Sanctaluna@hotmail.com.

Web site: www.Sanctamoon.8m.com

Sekhet Bast Ra, OTO. Founded in 1984, Sekhet Bast Ra is dedicated to the law of Thelema and promulgates that law by helping and encouraging those working toward their True Will, regardless of their affiliation—or non-affiliation—with Thelema. Sekhet Bast Ra's thelemic force is on the forefront of a magickal movement in Oklahoma and by becoming more involved in the community, they hope to promote peace, tolerance, and truth. Sekhet Bast Ra celebrates and encourages light, life, love, and liberty by performing the Gnostic Mass regularly, as well as providing a variety of classes, workshops, and discussion groups on various subjects, both publicly and privately. Sekhet Bast Ra has open public hours and is currently housing one of the few alternative belief lending libraries in the United States, Deep Root Community Lending Library (see page 527). Address: Sekhet Bast Ra, 2714 N. Pennsylvania Avenue, Oklahoma City, OK 73107. Phone: 405-816-5176, E-mail: info@sekhetbastra.org.

Web site: www.sekhetbastra.org

Sharanya. A non-profit religious organization and Devi Mandir (Goddess temple) founded in 1999 by scholar and activist Rashani Chandra Alexandre, Ph.D., and dedicated to an embodied and engaged spirituality that facilitates the life-affirming transformation of individuals, communities, and the world. The SHARANYA community consists of individuals from many backgrounds, but the core is a tradition based on the tenets of the Craft and the Shakta Tantrick path (Goddess-worshipping path of esoteric Hinduism). "We call this blend of authentic east-west tradition Sha'can. Based in San Francisco, with offices here and in India, we serve a diverse community worldwide and are committed to the work of spirit in action across lines of difference, such as age, religion, ethnicity, gender or other distinctions." The word SHARANYA is from Sanskrit, the ancient language of India, and means "refuge" or "sanctuary." The tradition and spiritual lineage of SHARANYA is dedicated to the mysteries of Kali, the Dark Goddess of India, who we celebrate as Great Mother, She Who Transforms, the Creatrix of the Three Worlds, the Churner of the Ocean of Milk. SHARANYA runs a teaching and training circle, Daughters of Kali, which offers a year-long course to men and women that can lead to initiation. They have offices in San Francisco and Puri, India. Address: SHARANYA, 859 36th Avenue, San Francisco, CA 94121. Phone: 415-505-6840. E-mail: info@sharanya.org.

Web site: www.sharanya.org

Silver Cauldron Coven. Silver Cauldron Coven is in the tradition of Circle of the Silver Cauldron, which was established at Samhain 1994, and honors the sanctity of life, growth, death, and rebirth through respectful example and activity to bring balance and equality into our world. "We are a mixed (female and male) group who meet to do magic and ritual. We look to the Celtic Wheel of the Year for our Solar Rituals and Magic, which are often open by invitation. We look to historical, feminist and other traditions for our lunar Rituals and Magic, which are celebrated only by the Coven." The coven is governed mostly by consensus. Each member of the coven is a priest or priestess and all are equals and share in the design and performance of magic and ritual. Members have given trainings, teachings and public service. Contact: Cynthia Jane Collins or Harry Spirito. Address: Silver Cauldron Coven, 86 High Street, Saco, ME 04072. Phone: 207-282-1491.

Silver Circle. A center for the Old Religion in the Netherlands, which represents the Gardnerian Craft in that country. They publish a quarterly magazine *Wiccan Rede* (see page 503) and a series of Dutch-language booklets about the Craft, produce a mail order course in Dutch, conduct other activities, and host a very lively Dutch-language forum for the initiatory traditions and Paganism in general. Address: Silver Circle, P.O. Box 473, 3705 AL, Zeist, The Netherlands.

Web site: www.silvercircle.org

The Sisterhood of Avalon (SOA). A fully incorporated, non-profit international Celtic Women's Mysteries organization that seeks to balance intuitive wisdom with scholastic achievement. Founded in 1995 by Jhenah Telyndru, and patterned after the all-female religious enclaves found throughout the Celtic lands, the SOA draws inspiration from the myths, legends, folklore, and tradition of the Celtic Britons or Cymry. Focusing on the concept of personal sovereignty, the pursuit of Awen, and connection with the Divine Feminine, the SOA seeks to empower women as they walk a path of wholeness and soul healing. The SOA sponsors the Avalonian Thealogical Seminary; facilitates training intensives; hosts spiritual pilgrimages to Wales, Glastonbury, and other Celtic Sacred Sites; organizes the International Avalonian Symposium for Celtic Women's Spirituality; supports a network of Avalonian Hearths and Learning Circles; publishes *The Tor Stone: A Quarterly Journal for Women's Mysteries*; and provides a variety of opportunities for learning and celebration. Address: The Sisterhood of Avalon, P.O. Box 842, Pagosa Springs, CO 81147. E-mail: BoardSecretary@sisterhoodofavalon.org.

Web site: www.sisterhoodofavalon.org

SisterSpirit. An eclectic women's spirituality group founded in 1985 and led by the Rev. Frodo Okulam. "Through female imagery we are transforming ourselves, building bridges between our traditions and the common ground we share with other traditions." Programs include weekly study groups, workshops, and monthly rituals, which focus on the sacredness of the female spirit. There are also classes, an annual Croning ceremony, some specialized workshops, and the annual Pagan Faire. Address: SisterSpirit, P.O. Box 9246, Portland, OR 97207. Phone: 503-736-3297. E-mail: sistersp@teleport.com.

Web site: www.sisterspirit-portland.com

Society of the Evening Star (S.O.T.E.S.). A non-profit cross-cultural organization founded in 1983 in Rhode Island, open to individuals who embrace the sameness in all cultures and religion. The mission of the Society of the Evening Star is to provide an educational facility, library, housing, and outdoor green space for the elder leaders of world faiths and minority religions to practice, to teach, and to mentor students who are searching for spiritual answers. S.O.T.E.S. maintains a library filled with culturally diverse materials; its healing circle, Hygeia, allows people from different faiths to explore healing techniques together. It sponsors lectures and classes and maintains a charitable organization, Acts of Kindness (A.O.K.). It also has a publishing arm, Olympian Press. Address: S.O.T.E.S., P.O. Box 29182, Providence, RI 02909. Phone: 401-331-8576.

Web site: www.sotes.org

South African Pagan Rights Alliance (SAPRA). Formed in 2004 in order to promote the constitutional liberties and freedoms enshrined in the Bill of Rights of the Constitution of the Republic of South Africa, SAPRA assists those South African Pagans whose constitutionally guaranteed rights and freedoms have been infringed upon due to unfair discrimination to obtain appropriate redress. In the execution of its mission statement, SAPRA welcomes the participation of all South African Pagan organizations, groups, religious affiliations, and individual South African Pagans without prejudice. Address: SAPRA, P.O. Box 184, Hoekwil 6538, South Africa. Phone: (044) 850 1297 E-mail: sapra@ananzi.co.za Forum: http://groups.yahoo.com/group/sapra.

Web site: www.geocities.com/paganrightsalliancesouthafrica

The Spiral Grove. The Spiral Grove, an Interfaith Church of Nature Spirituality, was founded in 1990 to support a diverse community of varied traditions. "We co-create rituals celebrating the nature holidays and moon phases in the Blue Ridge Mountains and Shenandoah Valley of Virginia, as far south as Madison County and as far north as Loudon County. We are interested in supporting the creation of non-hierarchal circles anywhere." The Spiral Grove provides open ceremonies, charity work, environmental activities such as Earth Day at Tasker Lake in Stephens City, and Shenandoah River clean-up days. A quarterly newsletter, *Close to Mother Earth*, has announcement lists, an event calendar, poems, readers' forum, and articles supporting issues important to earthy-spiritual community. There is also an Ordination Training Program, as well as workshops and individual mentoring. E-mail: the_spiral_grove@ yahoo.com.

Web site: www.spiralgrove.org

Summerland Grove, Inc. (SGPC). A Pagan Church and Networking Center, founded in 1994, designed to help Pagans and Wiccans in the mid-South to further evolve as a religious community. "Through meetings, classes and festivals, we hope to promote a positive image of Pagans/Wiccans in this community. We provide a United Front for groups, covens and solitairies in our community to rally behind as well as a great start in finding your own group or coven. We also wish to supply solitairies a place where they may worship and grow with others without the commitment involved with a group or coven." It is non-profit, tax-exempt church that has clergy to perform legal handfastings and other rites of passage, as well as a training program for becoming an ordained Priest/ess of the Church. The grove promotes involvement with other groups of like mind in the area, as well as national organizations. Address: Summerland Grove, P.O. Box 776, Memphis, TN 38088. E-mail: scribe@summerland.org.

Web site: www.summerland.org

Technicians of the Sacred. An organization formed in 1983 by Courtney Willis dedicated to the preservation and practice of Voudoun and other Neo-African religious systems, its art, magic, and culture. Technicians of the Sacred includes several magical and religious orders, including the Ordo Templi Orientis Antiqua and La Coulevre Noire—orders that began in Haiti in the 1920s and that combine Gnosticism, ceremonial magic, and Voudoun. They publish a journal, *Societe*. Address: Technicians of the Sacred, 1317 N. San Fernando Boulevard, Suite 310, Burbank, CA 91504.

Web site: www.techniciansofthesacred.com

Temple of Brigantia. A small local group offering open full moon rituals and occasional apprenticeship programs. The group has a focus on historical Celto-Roman deities and self-development through inner work. Address: Temple of Brigantia, P.O. Box 1897, Wells, ME 04090. E-mail: jane@janeraeburn.com.

Web site: www.janeraeburn.com/brigantia

Temple of Diana. A national feminist Dianic Wiccan organization dedicated to celebrating Women's Magick and Mysteries. Temple of Diana offers personal and public community rituals, classes, workshops, priestess training, and an annual conference, the Daughters of Diana Gathering. Temple of Diana was co-founded by Falcon River and Ruth Barrett, who was ordained as a High Priestess by Z Budapest in 1980. Address: Temple of Diana/Wisconsin, P.O. Box 6425, Monona, WI 53716-0425. Phone: 608-882-4655. E-mail: info@templeofdiana.org.

Web site: www.templeofdiana.org

Temple of the Feminine Divine and Iseum Musicum. Founded in 1998 by the late feminist musician Kay Gardner. In 1999, the first class of students entered the Iseum Musicum, a three-year ordination program chartered by the Fellowship of Isis. In November 2001, ten priestesses were ordained, and that year they opened the Temple of the Feminine Divine. The Iseum continues to accept students who want to deepen their spiritual lives and to serve others. The temple also offers classes to the public; subjects include music, reiki, spiritual counseling, bodywork, drumming, and Celtic art. It also has a lending library and a meditation space and offers rituals and other events. The Temple and Iseum are governed by a non-hierarchical decision-making process. Address: Temple of the Feminine Divine, Suite #203, 31 Central Street, Bangor, ME 04401. Phone: 207-941-0261. E-mail: TOFDBangor@aol.com.

The Temple of Goddess Spirituality Dedicated to Sekhmet. "Set in the

Mohave Desert of Nevada, the sand-colored stucco Temple embraces the elements of nature, with archways to the four directions and a roof that is open to the sky. In these serene and beautiful surroundings the Temple stands as a symbol of peace and the sacredness of giving." The Temple is a project of the Center for the Study of the Gift Economy under the direction of Genevieve Vaughan. Rituals are held at the Temple, and it is open for visitors. There is housing on site for women. Address: The Temple of Goddess Spirituality Dedicated to Sekhmet, P.O. Box 904, Indian Springs, NV 89018. Phone: 702-879-0872. Priestess: Anne Key; e-mail: annkey@direcway.com.

Web site: www.sekhmettemple.com

Temple of Nine Wells. A public Wiccan congregation currently administrated by Rev. H.P. Richard Pavish and Rev. H.P.s. Amy "Gypsie" Ravish, elders in British lineaged Wicca A/G/H/T. The TNC was founded in 1992 by Rev. Laurie Cabot, now H.P.s. Emeritas, to facilitate a multitraditional practice of the religion of Witchcraft and in order to serve the growing Wiccan community in Salem, Massachusetts. An affiliate of the Aquarian Tabernacle Church (see page 511), the Temple of Nine Wells offers open eclectic rites and ceremonies for the eight Sabbats. Hundreds of members and guests attend and there is always live music, singing, dancing, drumming, and merriment. The TNW provides a model for practice of the Wiccan religion, encouraging and fostering tolerance and interaction between members of Wicca and the many differing faiths of the world. The leadership of the TNW believes that religious diversity and freedom of thought are of benefit to all members of society. Services by TNW clergy are available for rites of passage, handfastings, and funerary rites. Address: The Temple of Nine Wells—ATC, P.O. Box 281, Salem, MA 01970. Phone: 978-745-8668. E-mail: tnwsale@tnw-salem.org.

Web site: www.tnw-salem.org

Thiasos Lusios. A group dedicated to the worship of the Greek god Dionysos. Based online, the Thiasos is a meeting place for devotees who are scattered across the globe—a forum in which to share experience and knowledge, and to bring Dionysian religion into everyday life. The Web site includes information on Dionysos, pictures of members, altars and rituals, a place to leave virtual offerings, and a modern festival calendar. E-mail: oenochoe@winterscapes.com.

Web site: www.winterscapes.com/thiasoslusios

Three Roads Community. A group that blends Druid Revival–style Druidry with Traditional Witchcraft (or Wicca). Druidry is polytheistic—believing in multiple Gods and Goddesses as separate Beings, and most Wiccan traditions believe that all Gods and Goddesses are aspects or facets of the God and the Goddess. "In our tradition, we recognize that being polytheistic or duo-theistic (or anything else) is a very personal decision, and we do not teach or believe that one is better than the other." The Three Roads Community was founded in 1998 and is now a member of the Ancient Order of Druids in America. Open worship services take place once a month and there are open celebrations of the eight Neo-Pagan sabbats. Legally ordained clergy are available for Rites of Passage ceremonies. Membership is open to anyone eighteen or older who wishes to honor and celebrate Nature and study the ways of Druids and Witches. Address: Three Roads Community, 3109 Sandalwood Avenue, Springfield, OH 45502. E-mail: tau.athanasios@gmail.com.

Web site: www.three-roads.org

The Toronto Pagan Pub Moot. The first and longest-running Pagan Pub Moot in Canada (founded February 1996) is an ongoing monthly gathering of Pagans, Wiccans, Druids, Ceremonial Magicians, etc. It is sponsored and hosted by Karwen and Evan and held on the third calendar Monday of every month at the Imperial Pub located at 54 Dundas Street East. A place to meet old friends, make new friends, and to relax with good food and drink. The Toronto Pagan Pub Moot has a Web site which includes all kind of links, including information on eleven other Canadian pub moots. Phone: 416-635-5981. E-mail: TorontoPaganPubMoot@rogers.com.

Web site: http://ca.geocities.com/torontopaganpubmoot@rogers.com

Tree of Thirteen Runes. A family-based Witch coven led by priestesses Lady Marne, daughter Lady Isadora, and granddaughter Lady Andred, incorporating decades of experience and practice. Its primary emphasis is Old English/Saxon, Scandinavian, and Celtic Pagan traditions, but also freely draws from other mythologies with which members have ancestral, past-life, or other spiritual kinships. Both Goddess and God are honored with music, poetry, dance, and other ritual artistry. There is a strong solar as well as lunar emphasis. "We are avid readers, but not by-the-book; positive-path, but not for the faint-hearted nor easily bent. We proudly practice passionate, dare-to-color-outside-the-lines Witchcraft, not the prim and PC 'Wicca' we've sometimes seen. As 'Iowa Stubborn' free-thinkers, we deeply prize individualism, and love rousing discourse and debate, pursuing reach-for-the-stars contemplation and study, and kick-up-your-heels good fun!" Address: Tree of Thirteen Runes Coven, P.O. Box 41246, Des Moines, IA 50311. E-mail: bluestocking@ladyisadora.com.

Web site: www.ladyisadora.com/13runes.html

The Troth. An international Heathen organization that promotes the practice of pre-Christian Germanic religion, collectively known as Heathenry. There are many variations, names, and practices within Heathenry, including Ásatrú, Theodish Belief, Irminism, Odinism, and Anglo-Saxon Heathenry. "What we all share is a defining personal loyalty to, or Troth with, the Gods and Goddesses of the Northlands, including Odin, Thor, Frigga, Frey, Freya, Tyr, Idunna, and many others; we also share a commitment to the moral principles followed by our predecessors. The Troth welcomes all who have heard the call of our Gods and would like to know more about Heathenry." The Troth publishes a quarterly journal, *Idunna* (see page 496), and a growing number of additional publications, including the two-volume compilation of Heathen lore and practice, *Our Troth*. The Troth also offers a clergy training program to its members, operates a number of e-mail lists on topics of interest to Heathens, and holds an annual gathering, *Trothmoot*, at a different location each year within the United States. Membership: $20/year for individuals and $30/year for families within the United States; $24/year for individuals and $34/year for families in other countries. Address: The Troth, P.O. Box 1369, Oldsmar, FL 34677. E-mail: troth-contact@thetroth.org.

Web site: www.thetroth.org

Tucson Area Wiccan-Pagan Network (TAWN). TAWN has been the public face of Neo-Paganism in Tucson since it was founded in 1988. TAWN's goals are communication, understanding, and goodwill among local Neo-Pagans and between the Pagan community and the general public. TAWN meetings are held once a month in Tucson's La Madera Park and are open to the public. There is a Moon School for members' and guests' children between the ages of four and thirteen. TAWN hosts twice-monthly adult public education classes on a variety of Pagan topics, facilitated by TAWN members on various paths. Open sabbat rituals are also presented by members, and the open Mabon rite is the centerpiece of TAWN's annual *Fall Festival and Faire*. There is also a quarterly newsletter, *Tapestry* (see page 502). Address: TAWN, P.O. Box 482, Tucson, AZ 85702-0482. E-mail: Board@TAWN.org.

Web site: www.TAWN.org

Two-Spirit Peoples. "Two-Spirit" is a modern phrase now being used by lesbian, gay, bisexual, and transgendered Native Americans to show a link to past cultures where some people possessed a balance of both feminine and masculine energies, making them inherently sacred people. Two-spirit often refers to the seers, the visionaries, the cultural keepers, and the peacekeepers of many Native American tribes. "The Two-Spirit tradition of old is being reborn into a new tradition for our age and time. Many gays and lesbians from all walks of life are now hearing the call of the Great Mystery and learning to reconnect with their gifts." E-mail: willrsf@netzero.com.

Web sites: Bay Area American Indian Two-Spirits: www.baaits.org; Oklahoma City Two-Spirit Society: www.aaip.com/programs/2spirit.html; Will Roscoe's home page: www.geocities.com/WestHollywood/Stonewall/3044

Warrior Circle. A networking and support circle for Pagans serving in the military and veterans, plus those involved in emergency and protective services, including police officers, firefighters, and medical personnel. Sponsored by Circle, members network with each other through an e-mail discussion list and through the Warrior Blessing Rite and other activities at the Pagan Spirit Gathering. Coordinator: Windwalker. Address: Warrior Circle, Circle Sanctuary, P.O. Box 9, Barneveld, WI 53507. Phone: 608-924-2216. E-mail: windwalker@circlesanctuary.org.

Web site: www.circlesanctuary.org/militarypagansupport

White Mare Sanctuary. The Sanctuary is a Dianic Sisterhood of the Goddess registered in the state of Michigan since 2002 that believes that the spiritual feminine power, when unleashed with controlled abandon, is true art. "We are free within the Circle to give full artistic and spiritual expression of the Goddess with unconditional love and acceptance of one another; it is a sacred breeding ground for our growth, peace, empowerment and strength." They meet every month for Full Moon Circles. Address: White Mare Sanctuary, 140 E. Hickory Grove Road, Bloomfield Hills, MI 48304. Phone: 248-593-8464.

Web site: http://hometown.aol.com/whitemaresanct/myhomepage/business.html

Wiccan Church of Canada. In 1979, the Wiccan Church of Canada became Canada's first Pagan organization whose services were entirely open to the public. "We are still the only group in Canada offering weekly services to our congregations in Toronto and Hamilton. Not all of our services are Wiccan. We encourage Ásatrú folk, Druids and other Pagans to visit and demonstrate their ways of worship to us. Why? We want Pagans in our area to know about all of their options of which Gods may speak to them." The Wiccan Church of Canada runs a weekly two-hour Wicca 101 class, on a one-year cycle. Address: Wiccan Church of Canada, 109 Vaughan Road, Toronto ON, M6C 2L9. E-mail: info@wcc.on.ca.

Web site: www.wcc.on.ca

Wiccan Church of Minnesota (WiCoM). A multitraditional Pagan organization made up of individuals and covens dedicated to the celebration of Pagan/Wiccan spirituality. The Church holds annual rituals for the eight sabbats as well as a memorial rite in October. In addition, it provides an annual conference, WiC*CoN, each spring, as well as providing referrals to seekers of various teaching groups/covens whose teachers are recognized by the church. It also publishes a newsletter for members as well as a public newsletter available at their Web site. A sample copy of the newsletter is $3.50. Address: WiCoM, P.O. Box 6715, Minnehaha Station, Minneapolis, MN 55406. E-mail: genrep@wiccanchurchmn.org.

Web site: www.wiccanchurchmn.org

Wiccan Religious Group, Iowa State Penitentiary. Founded in 2000 in order to provide a chance for inmates at the Iowa State Penitentiary to practice an Earth-based religion in a positive environment. Traditions currently being followed are Alexandrian, Gardnerian, and Teutonic Wicca. The group meets once a week. Sabbats and Esbats are celebrated, and there are initiations, dedications, and requiems. All must hold to the Wiccan Rede. Lawrence T. Gladson is the HP and group coordinator; Scott E. Howrey is the attending priest. All ritual items are made by hand. "Natural religions bring spiritual development, discipline, support and overall self realization." There is also a connected coven: the Coven of the Enchanted Dragon. The coven "follows the wisdom of the old ways," has inner and outer circles and holds open Wicca classes when an outsider wishes to visit. Address: Wiccan Religious Group, Iowa State Penitentiary (Attention Chaplain), P.O. Box 316, 31st Street, Avenue G, Fort Madison, IA 52627-0316. Phone: 319-372-5432, ext. 233. Fax: 319-372-6967.

Widsith. A Texas seidh group serving the soul-working and oracular Heathen needs of the Dallas area. Since its inception, Widsith has aimed to provide lore-based learning and practices of spae (divination) and seidh (soul-working) in service to the Heathen community. While not all of the members are Heathen, all of Widsith's workings are within the cosmology and ideology of the Heathen (Anglo-Saxon/Germanic) religion. Widsith members regularly meet to enhance skills, honor the deities who are traditionally associated with this work, observe seasonal holidays, and continue to explore the tradition. Beginner workshops are offered regularly. Phone: 972-625-RUNE. E-mail Jennifer at: ferrrr@ msn.com or wyrdteacher9@aol.com.

WindTree Ranch. Located in the southeast Arizona mountains and situated on more than 1,200 acres, WindTree Ranch is the home of Summerland Monastery (est. 1993), affiliated with the Aquarian Tabernacle Church (ATC). "We are a mortgage-free, off-grid (wind and solar power, water well), ecological research (alternative building and sustainable gardening) and healing retreat for tough pioneer spirits (tobacco and meat free). Our public outreach is the empowerment of minority, disabled youth who are living in poverty: serving them through education, including arts and drama." Contact a volunteer at WindTree Ranch, 4200 E. Summerland Road, Douglas, AZ 85607-5271. Phone: 520-364-4611. E-mail: summerlandmonastery@direcpc.com. Web site: www.summerlandmonastery.org

Wisteria. An intentional community dedicated to sustainable land stewardship, healthy lifestyles, and environmental education. Founded in 1996, Wisteria is situated on 620 rural acres in southeastern Ohio and supports a residential community, event campground, and nature preserve. Wisteria's event campground is operated by Wisteria Community members and offers private, natural space to alternative, spiritual, and progressive groups (20 to 1,000+ people). Facilities include a wetlands wastewater treatment system, residential solar power, and other progressive innovations. Wisteria is now home to the

Pagan Spirit Gathering (see page 584), one of the oldest and largest Pagan gatherings in the United States. Located near Athens, Ohio. Phone: 740-742-4302. E-mail: info@wisteria.org.

Web site: www.wisteria.org

The Witch & Famous Coven. Located in Tamarac, Florida, the Witch & Famous Coven was officially founded at Imbolc 1994 and follows the Celtic Pantheistic path. "We seek to keep alive the old ways, and to nurture our Spiritual selves in the worship of the old Gods and Goddesses. We are a teaching coven, and many of our initiates also feel the call to become teachers." Leaders are Lord Riekin and Lady Bridget, who is a singer and songwriter and has produced two Wiccan CDs. They are a member of the Covenant of the Goddess and Everglades Moon local council. Address: Witch & Famous Coven, P.O. Box 771273, Coral Springs, FL 33077. E-mail: ladybridget@comcast.net.

Web site: www.ladybridget.com

Witchcraft Education Network. Caters to Witches and would-be Witches living in Japan. They have published a highly successful booklet on the Craft and run an online Witchcraft study group. In the future they plan to publish more booklets and hold open rituals. WEN is Internet-based. E-mails should be in Japanese or English. E-mail: wiccaneducation@infoseek.jp

Web site: wiccaneducation.hp.infoseek.co.jp.

Witch Grass Coven. The coven was started in March of 2000 by a group of people connected by religion who also had children. Many covens require day care for children, but "We felt, if you can not have your children with you when you worship, then it is not a real religion. Witch Grass Coven was our answer. We do not require people to be parents to join this coven, but they must accept that this is what we are. We will not hide our children, nor hire child care to have a ritual; children's energy is the purest energy in the room!" The coven is based in NROOGD tradition but is eclectic and is as much a family as a coven. "We love to read, we all have children, we love to create, we love to have a good time."

Web site: http://members.tripod.com/witch_grass_coven-ivil/witchgrass coven/

Wolves' Wod Kindred. A Tribalist/Folkish Ásatrú Kindred founded in 1999 and serving the folks in Southwestern Indiana. "We unite as a tribe and family to celebrate and follow the Germanic religion of Ásatrú. We are a faith family devoted to our beliefs, toward learning, practice and kinship with the Aesir, Vanir, our ancestors and goodly wights. We are committed to resurrecting old customs and traditions—but we simultaneously strive to integrate our faith properly into our modern American lives." Wolves' Wod strives to serve local Ásatrú families, national organizations, and to serve as a positive example of Heathenry in the secular world. Kindred members facilitate rituals and rites of passage. They help create a learning environment, provide spiritual counseling, and foster community support. Address: Wolves' Wod Kindred, P.O. Box 13, Elberfeld, IN 47613. E-mail: contact@wolveswodkindred.com.

Web site: www.wolveswodkindred.com

Women in Conscious Creative Action (WICCA). WICCA was founded in 1983 to provide women with a place to call their own—a place where they could study and celebrate together. Women meet in small groups called Wings and come together for the eight holydays. Women who are not in Wings may also be members. "We hold retreats (called Forwards because we are not retreating for anyone), classes and a Summer Gathering in August of each year." Students can complete individual studies that can lead to ordination as Priestesses. WICCA held three Festivals of Women's Spirituality in 1985, 1986, and 1987 in Oregon. The organization has been working with women in Ghana, and with women, youth, and some men and who are incarcerated in the United States, holding classes and rituals within institutional walls. A newsletter, *On Wings*, is published six times a year, free samples are available. Priestess: Norma Joyce. Address: WICCA, P.O. Box 5296, Eugene, OR 97405. Phone: 541-485-3654. E-mail: normahp@iglide.net.

Web site: www.wiccawomen.com

Women of Wisdom Foundation: A non-profit organization for the empowerment of women through programs that offer healing, spiritual awareness, personal development, and community. WOW "celebrates the sacred feminine and is committed to creating a new paradigm through a circle structure of shared leadership." WOW has sponsored an annual conference for women every February since 1993, with lectures, concerts, ritual theater performances, and experiential workshops. This is a unique gathering for women to celebrate, share their stories, heal, and be validated to make positive changes in their lives. You can sign up for the WOW e-newsletter at their Web site: www.womenofwisdom.org. Address: Women of Wisdom Foundation, P.O. Box 30043, Seattle WA 98113. Phone: 206-782-3363. E-mail: wow@womenofwisdom.org.

Women's Spiritual Leadership Alliance (WSLA). An association of priestesses who meet regularly to support each other, to contribute to the life of the Pagan community in the Denver area, and to provide educational outreach to the public when needed or requested. WSLA has sponsored lectures, a leadership conference, and an introduction to Wicca classes. WSLA also does charitable work. Address: WSLA, Inc., 7482 East Providence Avenue, Denver, CO 80237.

Women's Spirituality Forum. The Women's Spirituality Forum really began in the late 1970s as a series of lectures; it was founded as a non-profit organization in 1986 by Zsuzsanna Budapest. The Forum is dedicated to bringing Goddess consciousness to mainstream awareness and to provide spirituality education for girls and women. In the past, it has produced a monthly lecture series in the Bay Area, spirituality retreats, Halloween Spiral Dances, and annual weeklong festivals for women and girls. In 2003, the Forum established an ongoing online course that facilitates education for women in the Dianic Tradition, the Dianic University Online. Address: Women's Spirituality Forum, Inc., P.O. Box 11363, Oakland, CA 94611.

Web site: www.zbudapest.com

Women's Thealogical Institute (WTI). The Women's Thealogical Institute is a seminary and multidimensional school for women who wish to further their understanding of the Goddess, women's spirituality, and/or Witchcraft. The Institute is run by The Re-formed Congregation of the Goddess-International (RCG-I— see page 558). There are three programs of self-directed spiritual development: the Cella Program, a course of study designed to assist women to explore, expand, and strengthen their practice of women's spirituality, to discover the inner mysteries of both themselves and women's religion; the Crone Program, for women over fifty-three, to build a future for the Crone years; and the Guardian Program, a course of spiritual development for women who identify with the Amazon archetype. The structure allows women to work at their own pace. Later they can choose a path or specialization. The Women's Thealogical Institute graduates and ordains priestesses of RCG-I. Address: RCG-I, P.O. Box 6677, Madison, WI 53716. Phone: 608-226-9998. E-mail: rcgiorg@aol.com.

Web site: www.rcgi.org

World Pagan Network (WPN). WPN is a free online service to Pagans seeking Pagans, and hopefully a spark for networking. WPN was founded in the spring of 1995 and has volunteers from across the country and around the world. WPN is not able to provide services to incarcerated individuals. "If you are looking for your local community, contacts, events or even the best part of town to live in, please visit our Web site." E-mail: Ceile@aol.com.

Web site: www.geocities.com/Athens/Aegean/8773/index.html

Y Tylwyth Teg. "A dynamic, active Mystery Tradition, founded in the Welsh Faerie Faith. Priestess led; seeking balance in all things; members bring a stronger connection to the Goddess and God into their daily lives through a closer bond with the natural world." There is a focus on Welsh deities revealed through Arthurian legend and historical texts. Whether celebrating the Wheel of the Year's eight festivals in the mountains of north Georgia, or in an urban circle, or meeting regularly for classes and sabbats, emphasis is placed on personal growth, ethics, and responsibility. Traditional and historical techniques are used to bring the seeker through nine levels of enlightenment. Neophyte classes are available, both in person and by correspondence. Open rituals are offered up to three times a year, as well as an annual open festival, CymryCon. Address: Lady Cerridwen, 3075 Mary Drive, Marietta, GA 30066, E-mail: Cerridwen@ytylwythteg.org.

Web site: www.ytylwythteg.org

FESTIVALS AND GATHERINGS

There are more than 350 annual Pagan festivals. About seventy of them are listed here. Some are large—Pagan Spirit Gathering PantheaCon, Starwood, Heartland, and a few others recently have had between 900 and 1,200 attendees. The Michigan Womyn's Music Festival has at least six times that many. Other gatherings are small and intimate. Some are totally rustic camping affairs; others are held in hotels and retreat centers. Some festivals have been around for thirty years; others are relatively new. Many have Web sites with descriptions of activities and pictures of previous gatherings.

WINTER

Con Vocation. ConVocation is "the largest indoor Pagan event in the midwest." Founded in 1995, it is held annually in February in the metro Detroit area. ConVocation is a four-day event running Thursday through Sunday which hosts the largest indoor drum circle in the region and offers over one hundred classes following a variety of spiritual paths, including Wiccan, Shamanic, Druidic, Buddhist, Ceremonial Magick, and many more. ConVocation is put on by MEC (see page 543). Address: ConVocation, P.O. Box 3190, Centerline, MI 48015. E-mail: info@convocation.org.

Web site: www.convocation.org

A Feast of Lights. A weekend gathering at the end of January sponsored by EarthSpirit (see page 529). In a hotel setting in western Massachusetts, this gathering has a focus on traditional bardic wintertime themes of story, song, the arts, and community. There are workshops, music, rituals, storytelling, and other activities for adults and children as well as a ritual costume ball, the Stag King's Masque. There are hotel accommodations, an indoor pool, and food available. Address: EarthSpirit, P.O. Box 723, Williamsburg, MA 01096. Phone: 413-238-4240. E-mail: earthspirit@earthspirit.com.

Web site: www.earthspirit.com

Festival of Lights. An annual winter festival celebrating St. Lucia's Day, Our Lady of Guadalupe, Solstice, Hanukah, Kwanzaa, and Christmas on an evening in the middle of December. Sponsored by SisterSpirit (see page 564). Address: SisterSpirit, P.O. Box 9246, Portland, OR 97207. Phone: 503-736-3297.

PantheaCon. Sponsored by Ancient Ways and held every President's Day weekend at a hotel in San Jose, California. Founded in 1995, this Pagan convention (of over 1,700 attendees in 2004) includes workshops and panels from many spiritual traditions, scholarly papers, rituals, music, a Masquerade Ball, and many "featured guests" like R. J. Stewart, Isaac Bonewits, Luisah Teish, Z Budapest, Amber K, Don Craig, Raven Grimassi, Lon DuQuette, T. Thorn Coyle, Christopher Penczak, and Phillip Heselton. Program tracks include Neo-

Pagan topics, Goddesses, Norse and Celtic, Egyptian and African, Body Spirit, healing and psychic development, magic, tarot, and divination. Address: Ancient Ways, 4075 Telegraph Avenue, Oakland, CA 94609. Phone: 510-653-3244. E-mail: pantheacon@ancientways.com.

Web site: www.ancientways.com

Winterfire. A three-day gathering sponsored by the Pagan Community Council of Ohio (see page 553). Held on a fluctuating date between Imbolc and Ostara at a central Ohio camp, there are workshops, rituals, vendors, and a bardic circle. It focuses on the turning of the wheel and spring bringing new life to the earth. This is cabin camping—please bring your own linens.

Web site: www.thepcco.com

The WinterStar Symposium. A four-day festival held in or around February at a resort in central Ohio sponsored by ACE, the Association for Consciousness Exploration (see page 514). There are seminars on magical, spiritual, social and religious topics, as well as consciousness exploration, health, alternative lifestyles, and political issues. It also has drumming, rituals, films, parties, dancing, chanting, and musical performances. Considered by some to be the cushiest festival in the Magical Movement, the site has fully-appointed hotel rooms, a restaurant and lounge, large seminar spaces and merchants' areas, pool, sauna, hot tub, and exercise and game rooms. It also features seventeen four-bedroom heated cottages with two bathrooms and full kitchens. Mailing address: ACE, 1643 Lee Road #9, Cleveland Hts., OH 44118. E-mail: ace@rosencomet.com.

Web site: www.rosencomet.com

SPRING

Beltaine: A Pagan Odyssey. A weekend campout festival put on by the Panthean Temple in Connecticut (see page 557), with many other groups participating from all over the Northeast. The festival takes place at Schrieber's Farm in Oxford, Connecticut, and is a fund-raising event for the church's land fund. Events include rituals, bardic circles, drumming and bonfires, workshops, classes, children's activities, and more.

Web site: www.PaganOdyssey.org

CMA—Beltane Festival. A campout festival in Texas sponsored by the Council of Magickal Arts (CMA) (see page 522). Several hundred CMA members gather for a weekend-long gathering to celebrate the turning of the Wheel of the Year. Events include rituals presented by some of the different CMA member traditions, workshops, drumming, children's and teens' activities, and much more. CMA encompasses members from around the world who attend CMA festivals from a multitude of paths. Attendance at festivals requires membership in CMA. Address: CMA, P.O. Box 8030, Fort Worth, TX 76124-0030. Phone: 361-865-9077. E-mail: cma@magical-arts.org.

Web site: www.magickal-arts.org

Elf Fest. An annual fertile earth gathering and camping festival held over Memorial Day weekend at Lothlorien Nature Sanctuary near Needmore, Indiana, and sponsored by ElvinHOME, inc., formerly the Elf Lore Family (see page 531). There are workshops, music, drumming, networking, rituals, circle dances, alternative technologies, and activities for children. All spiritual paths are welcome. Address: Lothlorien Nature Sanctuary, P.O. Box 1082, Bloomington, IN 47402-1082. E-mail: elf@kiva.net.

Web site: www.elflore.org

Florida Pagan Gathering—Beltane. (Also held at Samhain.) Founded in 1995, and once called Freedom Fest, this is a large regional festival held south of St. Petersburg in a nature preserve called Boyd Hill. Camping, cabins, and a meal plan are available. Activities include music, ritual, drumming, Celtic games, bardic circles, authors, and special guests. The fesitival is now run by Temple of the Earth Gathering. E-mail: coordinator1@flapagan.org.

Web site: www.flapagan.org

Free Spirit Gathering. A five and a half day (Tuesday through Sunday) festival held in mid-June the week before Father's Day. Approximately six hundred to one thousand people attend. FSG is held at a private campground in Darlington, Maryland (http://ramblewood.com). Cabins, hot showers, optional meal plans, and a canteen are available. Tents are welcome. Clothing optional, garb welcome. Workshops, sweat lodges, rituals, dancing and drumming, children's programming. Address: Free Spirit, P.O. Box 94, Lambertville, NJ 08530.

Web site: www.FreeSpiritGathering.org

Gaia Gathering—Canadian National Pagan Conference. A gathering of Canadian Pagan academics, leaders of groups, and serious activists that takes place in late May (over the Victoria Day weekend) to talk about Canada's Pagan communities, activities, history, and challenges. It changes venues to a different part of Canada each year. Strong emphasis on presentation of academic papers and networking across Canada. Address: Gaia Gathering, P.O. Box 1937, Station Main, Kingston, Ontario, K7L 5J7, Canada. E-mail: info@gaiagathering.ca.

Web site: www.gaiagathering.ca

A Gathering of Priestesses and Goddess Women. Held the third weekend in May, this annual gathering is sponsored by the Re-formed Congregation of the Goddess-International (RCG-I) (see page 558). The festival takes place in Wisconsin Dell, Wisconsin, at a retreat center with heated cabins, lodge, and meals. There is an opportunity to network with women leaders in Wicca and women's spirituality from around the country. Women-centered and Dianic paths are represented. You do not have to be a priestess to attend. There are rituals, workshops, and affinity groups on ritual, healing Earth magic, scholarship, the arts, and organizing. Address: RCG-I, P.O. Box 6677, Madison, WI 53716. Phone: 608-226-9998. E-mail: rcgiorg@aol.com.

Web site: www.rcgi.org

The Gathering of the Tribes. A festival held in the Blue Ridge Mountains of North Georgia near Beltane since 1971. Sponsored by the Church and coven of Dynion Mwyn. The gathering is an opportunity to express religious freedom of choice and to honor the Old Ways of Spirit and Nature. Includes rituals, workshops by Pagan leaders, bardic and nightly drum circles, live music, dancing, and opportunities to enjoy nature and share what is sacred in your life. Cabins, tent camping, and RV spaces available. E-mail: dynionmwyn23@ hotmail.com or moonpanther2004@yahoo.com.

Web site: www.tylwythteg.com

Greening. A four-day gathering held over Memorial Day weekend at a campground in central Ohio, sponsored by the Pagan Community Council of Ohio (see page 553). The festival focuses on Neo-Paganism, Wicca, and Nature spirituality. There are vendors, workshops, rituals, music, entertainment, and activities for children. This is a camping festival; tents are required.

Web site: www.thepcco.com

Heartland Pagan Festival. A five-day festival held over Memorial Day weekend, sponsored by the Heartland Spiritual Alliance (see page 537). Founded in 1986 and open to men, women, children, even pets. The festival features guest speakers, concerts, workshops, rituals of many traditions and styles, bonfires, a bardic circle, children's activities, and a large eclectic merchant circle. Currently held on a 168-acre property, Camp Gaea (www.campgaea.org), forty minutes west of Kansas City, Missouri. The festival averages one thousand people a year. Address: Heartland Spiritual Alliance, P.O. Box 3407, Kansas City, KS 66103. Phone: 816-807-2472.

Web site: www.kchsa.org

The Mid-Atlantic Men's Gathering—Spring Gathering. The Mid-Atlantic Men's gathering happens on two weekends—one in the spring, and one in the fall. It is a camping retreat held at Four Quarters Farm in Pennsylvania (see page 533). "The gathering is for queer, gay, bisexual, straight, transgender, questioning and intersexual men who wish to promote a safe, supportive space in which men of different sexual orientations, faiths, heritages, ages, and occupations can come together, challenge themselves, and grow. It is an opportunity to explore male notions of spirituality, sexuality, intimacy, aging and gender expression." Tents and sleeping bags are essential. Activities include Circles, workshops, fire circles, and drumming. This gathering has been around for almost twenty years.

Web site: www.themensgathering.org

Mid-Atlantic Pagan Alliance's Annual Beltane. A three-day celebration held on the last full weekend of April. The gathering takes place in the Brendan T. Byrne State Forest of south-central New Jersey. The MPA's Beltane offers an eclectic mix of workshops ranging from beginner 101-type topics to more advanced subjects. Includes rituals, sweat lodges, bonfires, vendors, drumming, and a well thought out kids' track. Fun events as well, including a recent Pagan Idol talent contest. A very family-friendly event. Address: MPA, P.O. Box 122, Beachwood, NJ 08722. Phone: 732-684-3950. E-mail: Info@midatlanticpaganalliance.org. Web site: www.midatlanticpaganalliance.org

Moondance. A Pagan festival at Dragon Hills in Georgia held over Memorial Day weekend since 1991. Primitive camping. Includes rituals, music, classes, drumming, bonfires. Run by Linda Kerr. E-mail: murgen@faeriefaith.net. Web site: www.faeriefaith.net/Moondance.html

Mountain Mayfest. A Beltane festival held the last weekend in April in Charlestown, West Virginia. The central theme of the gathering is the MayFest Village, an intentional community bound together in celebration of the Old Ways. There is a Maypole Dance, Balefire celebration, baby blessings, workshops, community feasts, and handfastings. The emphasis is on living the teachings of the Old Religion in a community context, Faery Magick, and working with the land. Accommodations include camping or rooms, hot showers, and meal options. The Festival has 150 to 200 attendees. Address: MayFest, c/o Foxwood, P.O. Box 5128, Laurel, MD 20726. Web site: www.Foxwood-temple.net

PaganFaire. An annual daylong spring equinox festival sponsored by Sister-Spirit (see page 564) with crafts, workshops, a raffle, musical entertainment, and rituals. Address: SisterSpirit, P.O. Box 9246, Portland, OR 97207. Phone: 503-736-3297. Web sites: www.paganfaire.org; www.sisterspirit-portland.com

Paganstock. A music festival held every June in rural southwestern Michigan to support Pagan bands and artists. Pagan musicians, including Kellianna, Scott Helland, and Thirteen Winters have performed. There are Vendors, camping, and rituals for all ages to enjoy. "Open your heart and your mind and feel the magic of Paganstock." Ethan Pulka is the festival organizer. Address: Paganstock, 41261 County Road 681, Bangor, MI 49013. Phone: 269-427-7470. E-mail: Paganbeergod@gmail.com. Web site: www.paganstock.com

Rites of Spring. One of the oldest and largest Pagan festivals in the country, sponsored by EarthSpirit (see page 529) and held (since 1979) during the week leading up to and including Memorial Day weekend on a private lake in western Massachusetts. Rites of Spring is an extended community of Pagans from all parts of the country and abroad, gathered to create and renew connections with each other and the Earth. This is a fabulous festival with rituals from many traditions, workshops, drumming, bonfires, music, discussions, rites of passage, and many activities for both adults and children. It is a beautiful site with cabins and many facilities, including swimming, boating, and hiking. A meal plan is available. Open to all Pagan paths as well as kindred spirits from other traditions. Send SASE to: EarthSpirit, P.O. Box 723, Williamsburg, MA 01096. Phone: 413-238-4240. E-mail: earthspirit@earthspirit.com. Web site: www.earthspirit.com

Spring Mysteries Festival. For more than twenty years, the Aquarian Tabernacle Church (see page 511) has sponsored this four-day re-creation of the Eleusinian Mysteries over Easter week (Thursday through Sunday), the ancient initiatory rites of classical Greek Paganism which were conducted in secrecy for over two thousand years. It takes place in a seaside setting. Rituals include a purification parade to the Sea, Lesser Mysteries Initiation, Greater Mysteries Initiation for those who have gone through the Lesser Mysteries in a prior year, and Rites of Passage for youngsters coming into adulthood. There are also discussions, workshops, classes, arts, crafts, networking, music, drumming, bardic circles, family activities, and a Pagan talent show. Heated dorms, showers, and meals. Send a SASE to: Aquarian Tabernacle Church—SMF, P.O. Box 409, Index, WA 98256. Phone: 360-793-1945. E-mail: atc@AquaTabCh.org. Web site: www.AquaTabCh.org

The Weaving Community Symposium. A daylong educational, spiritual, and networking event hosted yearly by the Iowa Pagan Access Network (IPAN) in the early spring. Includes workshops, discussions, rituals, drumming, vendors. The hope is for everyone to reach out beyond their covens and circles and local groups, beyond their traditions and paths to come together, weaving a picture of the community as a whole. Address: IPAN, P.O. Box 861, Iowa City, IA 52244-0861. E-mail: ipman@ipan.org. Web site: www.ipan.org

Wic-Can Fest. Canada's oldest Pagan festival. The gathering usually takes place the six days ending on the second Sunday in June, and is attended by 250+ people. Programming is eclectic, following the needs of Pagans in southwestern Ontario. The current site is the Mansfield Outdoor Center, about fifteen minutes closer to Toronto than the old site. Includes workshops, rituals, family events, and a meal plan. Camping and cabins are available. Address: Wic-Can Fest, 19 Elizabeth Street, P.O. Box 111, Coboconk, ON, L0M 1K0 Canada. E-mail: greymoonlake@yahoo.ca. Web site: www.wiccanfest.on.ca

SUMMER

The Ancient Ways Festival. The festival is held around the third weekend of June (Wednesday through Sunday) at Harbin Hot Springs in Middletown, California, near the Clear Lake area above the Napa Valley. Founded in 1983, the Ancient Ways Festival is a relaxed gathering with rituals every night, along with some kind of musical jamming or bardic circle. Wiccan, Neo-Pagan, Umbanda, ceremonial magic, and eclectic paths are included. During the day there are two to four tracks of workshops. Harbin is a clothing-optional site with warm, hot, and cold pools and a fair amount of shade. There is both a campground and hotel rooms. Contact: Ancient Ways, 4075 Telegraph Avenue, Oakland, CA 94609. Phone: 510-653-3244. E-mail: festival@ancientways.com. Web site: www.ancientways.com

Call of the Crow (COTC). Founded in 2002, Call of the Crow is an annual gathering intended for networking and education of the Pagan community (though anyone with an open mind is welcome). It is a one-week-long rustic camping event, held on a private, family-owned 240 acres in the heart of Michigan, near Lansing. The date of the event is June 18–25 every year. Different traditions perform their own rituals. Cost is $10 and no money is exchanged on the property; vendors can only exchange by barter. Address: Call of the Crow, c/o Stacey Knerr, 4254 Braden Road, Byron, MI 48418. E-mail: callofthecrow@gmail.com.

Chesapeake Pagan Summer Gathering. A three-day gathering held in Maryland during the late summer. It's a small, highly focused gathering for a little over one hundred people. The gathering is held at a secluded, partly wooded private campground with a pool, cabins, hot showers, playground equipment, and optional meal plans. Includes workshops, music, firedancing, drumming, rituals, and sweat lodge. Tents welcome. Family friendly, with activities for children. Address: Gathering Registrar, Chesapeake Pagan Community, P.O. Box 25242, Baltimore, MD 21229. Web site: www.chesapeakepagans.org

Daughters of Diana Gathering. A Dianic conference for all Goddess women produced by Temple of Diana (see page 566) that takes place in mid-September in south-central Wisconsin. "Three days of ritual, music, art, dance, Amazon skills (including archery), vendors, and presentations by Goddess scholars." Comfortable and fully accessible lodging and great food. Address: Temple of Diana, P.O. Box 6425, Monona, WI 53716-0425. Phone: 608-882-4655. E-mail: info@templeofdiana.org. Web site: www.templeofdiana.org

Earth and Sky Summer Creation Festival. A weekend gathering in the Oregon Coast Range, which generally takes place in August. It's sponsored by

Aerious (see page 508), an educational center that focuses on metaphysics, permaculture, and wholistic healing. There are workshops in astrology, herbs, healing, yoga, dance, drumming, and dream journeying. The gathering is mostly camping with some indoor sleeping. Address: Aerious, c/o Mark McNutt, 93640 Deadwood Creek Road, Deadwood, OR 97430. Phone: 541-964-5341.

Web site: www.aerious.org

Elderflower WomenSpirit Festival (EWF). A participatory four-day festival that takes place every August in the Mendocino Woodlands of northern California. "Our focus is earth-based spirituality and honoring the feminine through Goddess. We celebrate our diverse spirituality by sharing knowledge, music, arts, and ritual. EWF is open to all women and girls age eleven and over. We are committed to providing a welcoming and empowering environment for all women including older women, women of color and from all cultures, women of all sexual orientations, differently-abled women, women in recovery, and limited income women. We are run entirely by volunteers." E-mail: info@ elderflower.org.

Web site: www.elderflower.org

Firedance Festival. A magical celebration of drum, dance, and song. Founded in 2000 and blending many traditions, Firedance has its roots in a style of fire circle celebration that evolved over the last two decades at magical drum and dance events held in the Northeast. "We join together in community in the beautiful Santa Cruz, California, Mountains amongst the Redwoods. Together we create a sacred place for deep play. Each night we join together in spiritual community to drum and dance the fire circle until the rising sun—connecting nature, our bodies, our voices and our selves with the magic of the fire and the spirit in each of us. Each day we explore ancient and modern mysteries through experiential playshops on drumming, sacred dance, chanting, exploring sacred space, and community rituals." There are many accomplished artists and teachers, affinity groups, community rituals, and an opportunity to study drumming, dance, and magical arts. This is a camping festival, family friendly with children's programs and some partial child care available. E-mail: info@firedance.org.

Web site: www.firedance.org

Gathering for Life on Earth. A regional, family-friendly festival that takes place every year in August near Vancouver. It began in 1991 and is considered by many to be the premier event of the Vancouver Pagan calendar. It's a mixture of party-hearty activity, rituals, workshops, marketplace, Aphrodite's Temple, and an excellent children's program. There's good food, cabins, and tenting space available. Address: Gathering for Life on Earth, P.O. Box 47568, 1-1020 Austin Avenue, Coquitlam, BC V3K 6T3 Canada. E-mail: gathering@gatheringforlife.org.

Web site: www.gatheringforlife.org

Harvest Gathering. A camping festival held over Labor Day weekend at Ozark Avalon, a Wiccan Church and Land Sanctuary near Columbia, Missouri (see page 552). There are workshops on various sacred arts and magical subjects, drumming, chanting, rituals, swimming, a sweat lodge, community meals, and fellowship. Address: Ozark Avalon, 26213 Cumberland Church Road, Boonville, MO 65233 Phone: 660-882-6418 or 573-289-3657. E-mail rosewise@socket.net.

Kaleidoscope Gathering. Canada's largest Pagan gathering, which takes place on the weekend ending in the first Monday of August at Whispering Pines campground about forty-five minutes east of Ottawa. More than four hundred people attend. Kaleidoscope is in a part of English-speaking Canada, where the dominant language locally is French, bringing together Pagans from both cultures. Since it happens during Lughnasadh, there is a strong Celtic flavor. For more information, visit the Web site: www.kaleidoscope-gathering.com.

Lunasdal. A celebration of summer and community building held at the end of July in western Massachusetts, including rituals, sharing of stories and chants, drumming, dancing, music, and other activities for both adults and children. Tenting only. Sponsored by EarthSpirit (see page 529). Address: EarthSpirit, P.O. Box 723, Williamsburg, MA 01096. Phone: 413-238-4240. E-mail: earthspirit@earthspirit.com.

Web site: www.earthspirit.com

MerryMeet. This is the Covenant of the Goddess's (see page 524) annual festival held in conjunction with the Grand Council, COG's annual business meeting. It is held on Labor Day weekend or the weekend before in a different region of the United States each year. The event is usually held at a secluded campground or hotel. Meals are provided. Includes workshops, rituals, bardic circles, concerts, talent shows, and Pagan artisans. An optional leadership institute often takes place on the first day (Thursday). Address: COG, P.O. Box 1226, Berkeley, CA 94701. E-mail: merrymeet@cog.org.

Web site: www.cog.org

Michigan Womyn's Music Festival. For more than thirty years this has been the preeminent women's music festival, bringing thousands of women from every state and every continent for a week of music and camping out on 650 acres of private land in Michigan. It usually takes place during the second week of August. There are also workshops and rituals. Women only; very lesbian identified. There is fabulous access for disabled women. It is very political and intense; issues of racism and sexuality come up often. Truly an experience of living in an alternate world. Address: WWTMC, Box 22, Walhalla, MI 49458. Send SASE. Phone: 217-757-4766.

Web site: www.michfest.com

MidSummer Gather Festival. An eight-day/seven-night festival held over Midsummer, sponsored by the Earth House Project of Minnesota. Founded in

2001, it's a week of celebration, of sharing, of learning and of honoring one another's unique rituals. "Meet new people, learn new ways, and play like Pagans!" The festival features rituals and workshops, music and drumming, late-night community fires, and several community feasts. Open to Pagans everywhere, with child rates available; there is no additional fee for merchanting. Held currently at Eagle Cave Campgrounds (the old PSG site) in the heart of Wisconsin. Address: EHP Midsummer Gather, P.O. Box 141251, Minneapolis, MN 55414-9998. Phone: 877-538-4121.

Web site: www.earthhousemn.org

National Women's Music Festival–Spirituality Conference. A four-day national gathering held in June or July at a midwestern college campus. This is a big music festival that also has a spirituality track of workshops and also a writer's track. Housing and meals are provided in dorms and cafeterias. Sponsored by Women in the Arts, P.O. Box 1427, Indianapolis, IN 46206.

Web site: www.WIAonline.org

Pagan Spirit Gathering (PSG). One of Paganism's oldest and largest gatherings, PSG is a week-long festival that has been going strong since 1980. It brings together Pagans from many paths from across the United States and several other countries to create community, develop Pagan culture, and celebrate Summer Solstice. Participants create and live cooperatively in a tribal Pagan village in a scenic setting. Many pitch tents; some lodge in camping vehicles. The gathering is open to women, men, and children, and includes rituals from different traditions, workshops, discussions, sweat lodges, concerts, a marketplace, youth programs, a leadership institute, women's rituals, men's rituals, chant sharing, ecstatic dancing, drumming, and more. Sponsored by Circle (see page 519) PSG takes place each June during the week of Summer Solstice, and since 1997 has been held at Wisteria campground and Nature Preserve in Ohio. Pre-registration is required. Articles, photos, and more details are online. Managing Director: MoonFeather. Address: PSG, Circle Sanctuary, P.O. Box 9, Barneveld, WI 53507. 608-924-2216. E-mail: psg@circlesanctuary.org.

Web site: www.circlesanctuary.org/psg

Pan Fest. Pan Fest is Alberta's Pagan festival. The gathering usually takes place the weekend ending on the first Monday of August, and is attended by about 150 people. Includes rituals, workshops, music, and a marketplace. For more information, visit the Web site: www.panfest.net.

Pan Pagan Festival. Founded in 1976, making it possibly the oldest national annual outdoor Pagan gathering anywhere. The Midwest Pagan Council puts on this five-day festival (Wednesday to Sunday), which is held in August. It's an outdoor camping festival—mostly tents, although there are a limited number of RV hookups available for an additional charge. The campground is located about twelve miles outside of Knox, Indiana, on the Tippacanoe River, and offers canoe trips and inner tube rafting down the river for a reasonable charge. The campground also has a well-stocked store and a swimming pool. Includes rituals, workshops, feasts, follies, and children's workshops and activities. Address: M.P.C., P.O. Box 160, Western Springs, IL 60558.

Web site: www.midwestpagancouncil.org

Ravenwood Gathering. An annual gathering (since 1990) held the first or second weekend in July with a Northern European Tradition(s) focus. There are workshops, music and merriment, Viking games, a feast, and vendors. The event is limited to seventy-five campers ("no electricity—just like the 'good old days'"). Held on top of Mt. Tamalpais (the Sleeping Lady) in the Redwoods just north of San Francisco. Address: Freya's Folk, PMB 165, 537 Jones Street, San Francisco, CA 94102-2007.

Web site: www.freyasfolk.org

Sirius Rising. An eclectic weeklong festival that nurtures creative and spiritual potential by bringing together, involving, and teaching the community. The festival takes place at Brushwood Folklore Center, a secluded 180-acre clothing-optional campsite in western New York state. Brushwood is also the site of the Starwood festival. Workshops, drumming, dancing, rituals, eclectic music, and nightly bonfires. Address: Brushwood Folklore Center, 8881 Bailey Hill Road, Sherman, NY 14781. Phone: 716-761-6750. E-mail: camp@brushwood.com.

Web site: www.brushwood.com

Spirits of the Earth Festival. Founded in 2003, Spirit of the Earth Festival is a one-week Pagan gathering in Ontario, Canada, that is held annually in July. The festival consists of workshops for both adults and children, nightly entertainment, access to specialized vendors, and meet and greets with Pagan authors. "Come and join in our nightly drum circle and revel fires." Day, weekend, and week-long passes are available.

Contact: Tameika and Fox. Address: RR3 Iona Station, ON N0L 1P0, Ontario, Canada. Phone: 519-762-2000. E-mail: info@spiritsfest.com.

Web site: www.spiritsfest.com

The Starwood Festival. A large six-day festival held in western New York State in the third or forth week of July, sponsored by ACE, the Association for Consciousness Exploration. For over twenty-five years Starwood has been a celebration of diversity, combining elements of Neo-Paganism, mind-sciences, environmentalism, new technologies, holistic healing, alternate lifestyles, and much more. Starwood has become one of the biggest festivals of this movement, with over 1,500 participants, hosting world-renown speakers and performers (including some Grammy winners). It is held at Brushwood Folklore Center, a clothing-optional campground with fields and woods, hot showers, a pool and hot tub, and a food court with bar and coffee shop. There are over

150 workshops, about 15 concerts with full sound system and video support, rituals from many cultures, theater, comedy, fireworks and multimedia presentations, drumming classes and all-night circles, an on-site radio station, an inflatable dance party dome, day care and children's programs, ecstatic dancing, and an immense bonfire. Address: Association for Consciousness Exploration, 1643 Lee Road #9, Cleveland Hts., OH 44118. E-mail: ace@rosencomet.com. Web site: www.rosencomet.com

Summerset. A four-day gathering held over Labor Day weekend at a campground near Columbus, Ohio, sponsored by the Pagan Community Council of Ohio (see page 553). This is their pre-Mabon gathering, which focuses on Neo-Paganism, Wicca, and Nature spirituality. There are workshops, rituals, music, entertainment, and activities for children. This is a camping festival; tents are required. Web site: www.thepcco.com

WomenCircles. WomenCircles has been in existence for over thirty years. For five days and nights in late August, women gather in a place where women's spirits are honored, nurtured, and celebrated in the name of the Goddess. "Each year one goddess is chosen to explore—and through a carefully designed program, lead by a team of powerful women, participants learn ways to claim their healing powers for their own and to commit to their healing work. WomenCircles is similar to an ancient mystery school. The Goddess is recognized through many traditions and many disciplines. Throughout the week, women go deeper into the mysteries and expand their knowledge of self, gentleness and earth blessing. Women gather in ceremonies to greet their lyrical, poetic, drumming, dancing, mystical, and wise selves. There are daily events and workshops and evening rituals that honor the goddess in all her magnitude." The event takes place at a beautiful Unitarian retreat center in the Berkshires. Directors: Eclipse Fey and Felicity Pickett. Address: Rowe Camp and Conference Center, P.O. Box 273, Rowe, MA 01367. Phone: 413-339-4954. Web site: www.rowecenter.org/schedule/camps/WomenCircles.html

FALL

Between the Worlds Men's Gathering. Since 2002, the Between the Worlds (BTW) Men's Gathering has provided a safe place for men who love men to explore spiritual practices such as Pagan and Earth-centered paths. The focus of BTW is to promote spiritual networking and understanding on a national level within the gay community. BTW comes together each Autumnal Equinox to form a community of Pagan brotherhood among the forested hills of southeastern Ohio. The event offers rituals, workshops, drumming, dancing, performances, social events, and a marketplace. It's a place for queer men to learn, worship, network, and explore. Past keynote speakers have included Drake Spaeth of Circle Sanctuary, author and teacher Christopher Penczak, and Toby Johnson, author and contributing editor to *White Crane Journal*. Address: Between the Worlds Men's Gathering, c/o The Green Faerie Grove, 3000 B East Main Street, #240, Columbus, OH 43209. E-mail: garandu@betweentheworlds.org and ea@betweentheworlds.org.

Web site: www.betweentheworlds.org

CMA-Samhain Festival. A weekend campout festival held in Central Texas and sponsored by the Council of Magickal Arts (CMA) (see page 522). Events include rituals presented by some of the different CMA member traditions, workshops, drumming, children's and teens' activities, and much more. Attendance at festivals requires membership in CMA. Members from around the world attend CMA festivals from a multitude of paths. Address: CMA, P.O. Box 8030, Fort Worth, TX 76124-0030. Phone: 361-865-9077. E-mail: cma@magical-arts.org.

Web site: www.magickal-arts.org

CymryCon. An annual festival held each fall in northern Georgia, sponsored by Y Tylwyth Teg (see page 574). This four-day, family-oriented camping gathering features guest speakers such as Caitlyn Matthews, Ann Moura, Edain McCoy, as well as contemporary Pagan musicians and artists. Drumming and bardic circles are held each evening under the stars. An open ritual is held in celebration of the Goddesses and Gods of Nature and Spirit. Workshops are offered on a variety of contemporary and traditional topics. All Pagan or Earth-based traditions are invited to attend and present workshops on their practices and beliefs. Open forum discussions are encouraged. Address: Lady Cerridwen, 3075 Mary Drive, Marietta, GA 30066. E-mail: Cerridwen@ytylwythteg.org.

Web site: www.ytylwythteg.org

Elysium Gathering. Founded by Three Roads Community of Springfield, Ohio (see page 567), as a way to foster community between people of various Pagan paths. Elysium is a four-day festival held in the fall in Yellow Springs, Ohio. The campsite offers cabins, showers, and flush toilets, as well as lots of space for tent camping. There are workshops on Wicca, Druidry, Ceremonial Magick, Pagan Reconstructionism, and many others and diverse rituals from many paths, ranging from a sunrise Rites of Offering in traditional Roman style, to a Hindu-influenced puja. Includes drumming, dancing, bardic circles, fine arts, feasting, and on-site food vending. Address: Three Roads Community, ATTN: Elysium Gathering, 3109 Sandalwood Avenue, Springfield, OH 45502. E-mail: ladyoceanstar@gmail.com.

Web site: www.three-roads.org/elysium.html

FallFling. A Pagan festival at Dragon Hills in Georgia, usually held in October, which started in 1994. Primitive camping. Includes dancing, live music, rituals, classes, and a potluck feast. Run by Linda Kerr. E-mail: murgen@ faeriefaith.net.

Web site: www.faeriefaith.net/FallFling.html

Feast of Einharjar (Heroes in Heaven). Fixed holiday celebrated every November 11 at 5:00 P.M. at the Wave Organ in San Francisco, California (since 1988). Freya's Folk celebrates a Sumbel (ritualized form of drinking) for the Dead in three rounds at sunset. Starts promptly. Contact: prudence@ freyasfolk.org.

Florida Pagan Gathering—Samhain. See the FPG Beltane listing, page 577.

Web site: www.flapagan.org

Hallows Gathering. A celebration of Hallows/Samhain for women, sponsored by the Re-formed Congregation of the Goddess-International (RCG-I) (see page 558). Takes place on a weekend in October, with rituals, workshops, singing, drumming, dancing, artists, and craftswomen. Paths represented are women-centered, especially Dianic. Held in a wooded and accessible retreat center in Wisconsin Dells, Wisconsin, with a lodge, heated cabins, and meals. Contact: RCG-I, P.O. Box 6677, Madison, WI 53716. Phone: 608-226-9998. E-mail: rcgiorg@aol.com.

Web site: www.rcgi.org

Harvest Home Gathering. A four-day Pagan festival that takes place in Connecticut in mid-September. Harvest Home Gathering is an indoor/outdoor event, which promotes celebration, knowledge, spirituality, family, and fellowship. "By virtue of its very name, we embrace the collective spirit of our kindred. We work together in harmony and compassion to achieve that which is sacred. Together we plant the seeds of our future and together we shall enjoy the fruitful harvest of our collective efforts." There are workshops, classes with world renowned authors, rituals, an all-night bonfire with drumming and dancing, a large vending area, a dance with a D.J., a live concert, and more. E-mail John Boye at: johnboye777@yahoo.com or Liz Guerra at jasmine@sevensages.com.

Web site: www.cwpn.org/hhg

Hekatee's Sickle Festival. An annual retreat for introspection, self-examination, and adult rites of passage sponsored by the Aquarian Tabernacle Church (see page 511). The festival was founded in 1990. "It's a time to look at your intentions, accomplishments and future." Held the first full weekend in November. There are heated cabins, showers, and meals. Send a SASE to: Aquarian Tabernacle Church—HSF, P.O. Box 409, Index, WA 98256. Phone: 360-793-1945. E-mail: atc@AquaTabCh.org.

Web site: www.AquaTabCh.org

Isis Oasis Convocation. A four-day festival held each October at the Isis Oasis Sanctuary (see page 540) in the heart of the Alexander Valley wine country. Events usually include a special meditation led by Olivia Robertson, Fellowship of Isis co-founder, sacred dancing, a mystery play written by Isis Oasis founder Loreon Vigné, and more than a dozen workshops and presentations by authors and Isian clergy. Past presenters have included Isadora Forrest (*Isis Magic*), Leonard Shain (*The Alphabet and the Goddess*), and deTraci Regula (*Mysteries of Isis*). Food and lodging in Egyptian-themed rooms is included; there is also a bazaar. Address: Isis Oasis Convocation, c/o Rev. Loreon Vigné, 20889 Geyserville Avenue, Geyserville, CA 95441. Phone: 707-857-ISIS or 800-679-PETS. E-mail: isis@isisoasis.org.

Web site: www.isisoasis.org

Magickal Mountain Mabon. A festival at or near the weekend of the Fall Equinox (Thursday to Sunday) sponsored by the Chamisa Local Council of COG (see page 524). It takes place at a campground near Albuquerque, New Mexico. Activities include workshops, rituals, drumming and bardic circles, and usually nationally and locally known authors and special guests. Campers provide their own food and fees are low. Families and children are welcome. Contact: www.ladywoods.org, usually after Summer Solstice. Address: MMM, Chamisa Local Council, P.O. Box 892, Tijeras, NM 87059. E-mail: chamisa@cog.org.

The Mid-Atlantic Men's Gathering—Fall Gathering. See the listing for spring, page 578.

Web site: www.themensgathering.org

Mt. Franklin Annual Pagan Gathering. Held since 1981, this gathering, which takes place on the last weekend of October, is the longest running Pagan festival in Australia. Mt. Franklin is a dormant volcano located in Central Victoria. The gathering takes place in the crater, a garden of great beauty, with outdoor barbecue facilities, tap water, and toilets. This is a camping festival, so bring tents, cooking gear, and food to share. This is a Beltane festival with a bonfire and a Maypole dance. (Spring in Australia is fall in the United States.) Address: "October Gathering," P.O. Box 54, Castlemaine, Victoria 3450, Australia. E-mail: lindamarold@yahoo.com.au (but they live off the grid so regular mail is just as fast).

Shadowmas. A three-day gathering sponsored by the Pagan Community Council of Ohio (see page 553) held in October, before Samhain, at a central Ohio camp. There are workshops, rituals, vendors, and a bardic circle. It focuses on honoring ancestors who have passed on and the wisdom they have given, as well as the reverence for nature's cycles. This is cabin camping; bring your own linens.

Web site: www.thepcco.com

The Spiral Dance. An annual public ritual put on near Samhain (Halloween) by San Francisco Reclaiming groups. Reclaiming (see page 558), an international community of women and men working to unify spirit and political action (magical activism), began at the 1979 Spiral Dance ritual. Address: Reclaiming, P.O. Box 14404, San Francisco, CA 94114. Events line: 415-255-7623. E-mail: reclaiming@reclaiming.org.
   Web site: www.reclaiming.org

Twilight Covening. A long weekend of concentrated spiritual experience focused on the "twilight" of the year, the time of harvest and turning inward—a time for reflection, dreaming, seeking visions, and sharing. Twilight Covening takes place in western Massachusetts over the Columbus Day weekend, and is for adults only. It is a highly structured gathering, with participants divided into clans focusing on a single theme, such as drumming, dreams, tarot, meditation, or healing. All clans meet separately but come together for daily circles, meals, and the main Visioning Ritual. Clans also work together to provide meals, tend the fire, and do other work necessary for community living. It is a remote site with cabins, hot showers, and meals. Sponsored by EarthSpirit (see page 529). Address: EarthSpirit, P.O. Box 723, Williamsburg, MA 01096. Phone: 413-238-4240. E-mail: earthspirit@earthspirit.com.
   Web site: www.earthspirit.com

Valhallapalooza. A festival that showcases the richness and variety of Northern European music, religion, and culture. The annual September gathering emerged from Ancient Pathways: Loot for the Moot!, which was envisioned as a series of fund-raisers sponsored by Blood Eagle Kindred of the Ásatrú Alliance in order to foster the strength and growth of Odin's Nation. Loot for the Moot! featured talks and workshops with American Heathen elders, authors, poets, brewers, herbalists, folklorists, and showcased local ethnic fusion bellydancers. Valhallapalooza became the second fund-raiser in the series. The non-profit *Odin LIVES!* radio program brought powerful musical muscle to the mix and increased the scope and breadth of the festival.
   Web site: www.valhallapalooza.org

Wild Magick Gathering. A four-day camping festival held near the Autumn Equinox, sponsored by ElvinHOME, inc., formerly the Elf Lore Family (see page 531), at their nature sanctuary, Lothlorien. Many different magical and spiritual paths are represented. There are workshops, ceremonies, discussion circles, song swapping, drumming, and activities for children. Address: Lothlorien Nature Sanctuary, P.O. Box 1082, Bloomington, IN 47402-1082. E-mail: elf@kiva.net.
   Web site: www.elflore.org

SOME INTERESTING ADDITIONAL WEB SITES

www.godchecker.com. It calls itself "your guide to the gods," and has almost every pantheon you can think of, information on almost 2,500 different gods. Done with a sense of humor but contains some fun information. They have a God shop with items to sell, and a god-a-day feed for your Web site.

www.aradiagoddess.com. A Web site devoted to the Goddess Aradia, with spells, rituals, folklore, stories, and mythology.

www.istillworshipzeus.com. The Web site of a film that explores the revival of Paganism in Greece, which just won its fight for legality. You can watch the movie trailer for free, and there are links to various Greek Pagan Web sites and anti-discrimination organizations.

www.branwenscauldron.com/resources/student.html. This site lists the Web sites of more than twenty-five Pagan student associations, most of them at colleges and universities.

www.paganwiki.org/wiki/index.php?title=Main_Page. The PaganWiki project has been created in the hope that it will become the most comprehensive resource on Paganism. Like Wikipedia, anyone can contribute.

www.journey1.org. A Web site dedicated to living with joy and happiness, harming as little possible while living in harmony with Mother Earth. The Web site includes the Virtual Candle, at www.virtual-candle.org. Since 2000, people may light a candle choosing from a variety of colors and leave a personal message or prayer; there is also a forum and a blog. As of 2005, there are over forty thousand messages in the archives. The Virtual Candle site has become a worldwide community of many religions existing peacefully together, with well over one hundred countries being heard from so far.

www.wiccanrede.dreamhost.com. A fascinating Web site that focuses on the Wiccan Rede, Wicca's most basic and important statement of ethics. It looks at the history, different forms of the rede, the history of redes in general, and many alternate versions of the Wiccan Rede.

www.serpentinemusic.com. Although we have not listed stores or personal services in this guide, this particular catalogue lists almost everything in Pagan music. A related site, www.circleround.com, with many articles, songs, and more, comes out of the wonderful songbook *Circle Round: Raising Children in Goddess Traditions.*

www.monicasjoo.com. Monica Sjoo died in 2005, but her artwork and books, particularly *The Great Cosmic Mother of us all,* contributed much to the Goddess Spirituality movement. This Web site allows her work to be shared by everyone, and includes many paintings and some writing.

www.circlesanctuary.org/liberty/pagancharitywork.html. A good list of Pagan charity organizations put out by Circle.

http://members.aol.com/oldenwilde/gen_info/paganco.html. A Web site for Pagans seeking conscientious objector status.

DISCORDIAN WEB SITES

http://jubal.westnet.com/hyperdiscordia/
www.rawilson.com
www.principiadiscordia.com
www.23ae.com/
www.livejournal.com/community/discord_society
www.livejournal.com/community/haileris
www.poee.co.uk
www.discordian.com
www.theoi.com/Daimon/Eris.html (real information about Eris).
http://k.webring.com/hub?ring=discordia. A webring dedicated to the worship of Eris, Goddess of Confusion, and to the kind of seemingly insane concepts, which, though often long hidden or derided, actually underpin the universe. This site will lead you to a score of Discordian Web sites and groups.

WEB SITES FOR SOME PAGAN TRADITIONS

www.witchvox.com/_x.html?c=trads. *The Witches' Voice* has more than fifty articles on different Pagan traditions and is a good place to start if you want information.

www.geraldgardner.com. A fascinating Web site created by Morgan Davis filled with documents relating to Gerald Gardner as well as links to many fascinating essays by scholars on related issues.

www.metista.com. Information on the 1734 tradition. This Web site, co-authored by Joe Wilson, who introduced the 1734 tradition to North America, includes a history of 1734 in America and copies of the Robert Cochrane letters, as well as information on Metista, a new shamanic tradition influenced by Cochrane's Witchcraft and Native American teachings.

www.cyberwitch.com/bowers. A Web site with articles by Robert Cochrane and some of his letters.

http://traditionalgeorgians.net. This Web site is devoted to covens from three lines of George Patterson's Georgian Tradition of Wicca—all consider themselves traditionalist, and a part of British Traditional Wicca. There are other Georgians that follow a more eclectic or Dianic path.

www.druidnetwork.org/directory/index.html.
www.geocities.com/mikerdna/drulinks.html. These Web sites give information and links to Druid groups in the United States and around the world.

www.thetroth.org/links/#orgs.

www.thetroth.org/links/people.html. These Web sites from the Troth list Heathen kindreds, groups, and more scholarly organizations.

www.cesnur.org/religioni_italia/n/neo_paganesimo_01.htm.
www.cesnur.org/religioni_italia/n/neo_paganesimo_06.htm.
www.federazionepagana.com. These Web sites give information about Neo-Paganism, Neo-Shamanism, and Wicca in Italy.

RESOURCE GUIDE BY LOCATION

This section organizes the resource guide—publications, groups, and festivals—according to location and address. However, note that some organizations have groups in many different states and others only give Web sites—but often those Web sites show where local groups can be found. The festivals are listed in the state where the festivals most often take place—not where the organizations that sponsor the festivals are located. Groups, publications, and festivals listed here represent 39 states plus D.C. and eleven countries.

Arizona

Publications: *Earth First! Journal, Oak Leaves, Tapestry*

Groups: Ár nDraíocht Féin, The Ásatrú Alliance, Crossroads Lyceum, Mother Earth Ministries-ATC, Tucson Area Wiccan-Pagan Network, WindTree Ranch

California

Publications: *AFA Update, Awakened Woman, The Blessed Bee, Covenant of the Goddess Newsletter, Faces of the Goddess, MAMAROOTS Forum, Metaformia, newWitch, PanGaia, Reclaiming Quarterly, SageWoman, Societe, The Wise Woman, Witch Eye, Yggdrasil*

Groups: American Vinland Association, The Ancient Keltic Church, Ancient Ways, Annwfn/Forever Forests, The Ásatrú Folk Assembly, Bay Area Pagan Assemblies, California Utlandr Alliance, The Celtic Witan Church, Church of All Worlds, Church of the Eternal Source, Circle of Aradia, Community Seed, Coven of the Mother Mountain Aerie, Covenant of the Goddess, Daughters of the Goddess, Daughters of Kali, The Grey School of Wizardry, Hrafnar Kindred, Index, Isis Oasis Sanctuary, The Kindred of ShiEndra, MAMAROOTS, New Reformed Orthodox Order of the Golden Dawn, New Wiccan Church International, Our Lady of Enchantment, Reclaiming, SHARANYA, Technicians of the Sacred, Women's Spirituality Forum

Festivals: The Ancient Ways Festival, Elderflower, Feast of Einharjar, Firedance Festival, Isis Oasis Convocation, PantheaCon, Ravenwood Gathering, The Spiral Dance, WomenSpirit Festival

Colorado

Publications: *The Pomegranate (subscriptions—England)*
Groups: Earth Spirit Pagans, The Sabaean Religious Order, The Sisterhood of Avalon, Women's Spiritual Leadership Alliance

Connecticut

Groups: Connecticut Wiccan and Pagan Network, The Panthean Temple
Festivals: Beltaine: A Pagan Odyssey, Harvest Home Gathering

Delaware

Groups: Assembly of the Sacred Wheel, The New Alexandrian Library

District of Columbia

Groups: The Open Hearth Foundation, Inc.

Florida

Publications: *Goddessing, Idunna*
Groups: The Church of Iron Oak, GreenSong Grove, Neptune's Silver Web, Religious Order of the Circle of Isis Rising, The Troth, The Witch & Famous Coven
Festivals: Florida Pagan Gathering (Beltane and Samhain)

Georgia

Groups: Church of the Spiral Tree, Y Tylwyth Teg
Festivals: CymryCon, FallFling, The Gathering of the Tribes, Moondance

Idaho

Groups: Church of the Eternal Source

Illinois

Groups: Gaia's Womb, Lake View Covenant, The Sanctuary of the Crescent Moon

Indiana

Groups: ElvinHOME, inc. (formerly Elf Lore Family), The Kindred of Ravenswood, Romuva, Wolves' Wod Kindred
Festivals: Elf Fest, National Women's Music Festival, Pan Pagan Festival, Wild Magick Gathering

Iowa

Publications: *Weavings*
Groups: The Black Witch-Hat Society, The Iowa Pagan Access Network, Our Lady of Spiritual Audacity, Tree of Thirteen Runes, Wiccan Religious Group, Iowa State Penitentiary
Festivals: The Weaving Community Symposium

Kansas
Groups: Gaea Retreat Center, Heartland Spiritual Alliance

Kentucky
Groups: Alternative Religions Educational Network, Robin's Hood CommUnity Center

Louisiana
Groups: Covenant of the Pentacle Wiccan Church

Maine
Groups: EarthTides Pagan Network, Feminist Spiritual Community, Immanent Grove, Maine Pagan Clergy Association, Nova Roma, Silver Cauldron Coven, Temple of Brigantia, Temple of the Feminine Divine and Iseum Musicum

Maryland
Publications: *The Mystics Wheel of the Year Calendar*
Groups: Chesapeake Pagan Community, Foxwood Temple of the Old Religion, Military Pagan Network
Festivals: Chesapeake Pagan Summer Gathering

Massachusetts
Publications: *The Lunar Calandar*
Groups: Cultural Survival, EarthSpirit, Temple of Nine Wells
Festivals: A Feast of Lights, Lunasdal, Rites of Spring, Twilight Covening, WomenCircles

Michigan
Publications: *The Fifth Estate, Northwood Journal*
Groups: Caer na Donia y Llew, The Federation of Circles and Solitaries, Hearth & Grove Fellowship, Kalamazoo Pagan Community Brunch, Magical Education Council, New Reformed Orthodox Order of the Golden Dawn, The Pagan Roundtable, White Mare Sanctuary
Festivals: Call of the Crow, ConVocation, Michigan Womyn's Music Festival, Paganstock

Minnesota
Groups: Circle of the Phoenix Spiritual Community, The Earth House Project, Minnesota Heathens, The Reformed Druids of North America, Wiccan Church of Minnesota

Mississippi
Groups: Camp Sister Spirit Folk School

Missouri
Groups: Diana's Grove, Ozark Avalon
Festivals: Harvest Gathering, Heartland Pagan Festival

Montana
Groups: Neokoroi (The Temple Keepers)

Nevada
Groups: The Temple of Goddess Spirituality Dedicated to Sekhmet

New Jersey
Groups: Covenant of Rhiannon, Free Spirit Alliance, Proteus Coven
Festivals: Free Spirit Gathering, Mid-Atlantic Pagan Alliance's Annual Beltane.

New Mexico
Groups: Ardantane, Feraferia, Our Lady of the Woods
Festivals: Magickal Mountain Mabon

New York
Publications: *Always in Season, Enchante, White Crane Journal*
Groups: Branching, Maetreum of Cybele, Mama Donna's Tea Garden & Healing Haven, Minoan Sisterhood, New Moon New York, Polyhymnia Coven
Festivals: Sirius Rising, The Starwood Festival

North Carolina
Publications: *Communities Magazine*
Groups: Appalachian Pagan Alliance, Coven Oldenwilde, Eldhrimnir Kindred

Ohio
Publications: *The Oak Leaf, Odin LIVES!* (radio show)
Groups: Association for Consciousness Exploration, The Chameleon Club, The Church of Spiral Oak, Covenant of Unitarian Universalist Pagans, Earth Spirituality and Education Center, The Green Faerie Grove, Hof Guild Kindred, Pagan Community Council of Ohio, Three Roads Community, Wisteria
Festivals: Between the Worlds Men's Gathering, Elysium Gathering, Greening, Pagan Spirit Gathering, Shadowmas, Summerset, Winterfire, The WinterStar Symposium

Oklahoma
Groups: Deep Root Community Lending Library, Pagan Sanctum Recovery, Sekhet Bast Ra, OTO

Oregon
Publications: *Spirited Woman, WomenSpirit*
Groups: Aerious, Ancient Order of Druids in America, The Grandmother Council, Living Earth Circle, The Order of the Sacred Oaks & The Sacred Oak Grove, SisterSpirit, Women in Conscious Creative Action
Festivals: Earth and Sky Summer Creation Festival, Festival of Lights, Pagan Faire

Pennsylvania
Groups: Delaware Valley Pagan Network, Four Quarters
Festivals: The Mid-Atlantic Men's Gathering (Spring and Fall)

Rhode Island
Groups: Blood Eagle Kindred, Gaia's Hearth, The Magaian Way, New England Covens of Traditionalist Witches, Society of the Evening Star
Festivals: Valhallapalooza

Tennesse
Publications: *RFD Magazine*
Groups: Summerland Grove, Inc.

Texas
Publications: *The Accord*
Groups: Council of the Magickal Arts, Holy Spring Heathen Fellowship, The Sacred Well Congregation, Widsith
Festivals: CMA Festival (Beltaine and Samhain)

Vermont
Groups: Cherry Hill Seminary, Church of the Sacred Earth

Virginia
Publications: *If . . . Journal*
Groups: PagaNet, Inc., The Spiral Grove

Washington
Publications: *The Beltane Papers, The Hermit's Lantern, Panegyria, The Unicorn*
Groups: Aquarian Tabernacle Church, Our Lady of the Earth and Sky, The Rowan Tree Church, Women of Wisdom Foundation
Festivals: Hekatee's Sickle Festival, Spring Mysteries Festival

West Virginia
Publications: *Survival*
Groups: Church and School of Wicca
Festivals: Mountain Mayfest

Wisconsin
Publications: *Circle Guide to Pagan Groups, Circle Magazine*
Groups: The Black Earth Institute, Circle, Circle Cemetery, The Earth Conclave, Elf Queen's Daughters, Lady Liberty League, Officers of Avalon, Pagan Academic Network, The Re-formed Congregation of the Goddess-International, Temple of Diana, Warrior Circle, Women's Thealogical Institute
Festivals: Daughters of Diana Gathering, A Gathering of Priestesses and Goddess Women, Hallows Gathering, MidSummer Gather Festival

OTHER COUNTRIES

Australia
Publications: *Pagan Times*
Groups: Alexandrian Wicca Incorporated, Australian Pagan Information Center, Ordrine Scatere Stellae—Order of the Well of Stars, Pagan Alliance
Festivals: Mt. Franklin Annual Pagan Gathering

Canada
Groups: Congregationalist Wiccan Association of British Columbia, The Coven of the Wylde Rose, The Covenant of Gaia Wiccan Church of Alberta, Dievturība, Hecate-Legba Coven, The Pagan Federation/Fédération Païenne Canada, The Toronto Pagan Pub Moot, Wiccan Church of Canada
Festivals: Gaia Gathering—Canadian National Pagan Conference, Wic-Can Fest, Gathering for Life on Earth, Kaleidoscope Gathering, Pan Fest, Spirits of the Earth Festival

Guatamala
Groups: 9 Mayans

Ireland
Groups: Fellowship of Isis, The Pagan Federation (Scotland and Ireland)

Italy
Groups: Sacre Radici

Japan
Groups: Witchcraft Education Network

The Netherlands
Publications: *Wiccan Rede*
Groups: Feraferia, The Pagan Federation International, Silver Circle

South Africa
Groups: Circle of the African Moon, The Grove, The House of Ouroborus, The Pagan Federation of South Africa, South African Pagan Rights Alliance

Sweden
Groups: Court of Earth Coven, Court of Joy Coven

United Kingdom
Publications: *The Cauldron, Goddess Alive!, Meyn Mamvro, Pagan Dawn, The Pomegranate, Quest, Touchwood*
Groups: Albion Conclave, The Council of British Druid Orders, The Druid Network, Loyal Arthurian Warband, The Order of Bards Ovates & Druids, The Pagan Federation, The Pagan Federation (Scotland and Ireland)

No Address or Cyber Address Only
Publications: *Cup of Wonder, MatriFocus Cross-Quarterly, Waxing & Waning, WiccanPagan Times, The Witches' Almanac, The Witches Voice, Inc.*
Groups: Ancient Riders, Earth Religions Assistance List, Ecclesia Antinoi, Grok Fellowship, The Henge of Keltria, Minoan Tradition, Missionary Order of the Celtic Cross, Order of the WhiteOak, Ouroborous Isis Gnosis, Pagan Alliance of Nurses, The Pagan Pride Project, Pagan Unity Campaign, Radical Faeries, Thiasos Lusios, Two-Spirit Peoples, Witch Grass Coven, World Pagan Network
Festivals: MerryMeet (rotates between different parts of the country)

Notes

Chapter 1: PAGANISM AND PREJUDICE

1. Craft/Pagan publications (either currently being published or appearing within the last thirty-five years) include: *The Crystal Well, The Waxing Moon, Nemeton, Green Egg, Korythalia, The New Broom, The Hidden Path, Medicine Wheel, Earth Religion News, The Witches Broomstick, Wica Newsletter, The Witches' Trine, Star-Child, Insight, Quest, Revival, The Wiccan, Florida Aquarian, Northwind News, The Black Lite, Survival, Iris, Julian Review, The Harp, Witchcraft Digest, Psychic Eye, Seax Wica Voys, Word to the Wise, Gnostica, The Enchanted Cauldron, Khepera, Esbat, Moon Rise, Wicca Times, Georgian Newsletter, Runestone, Women's Coven Newsletter, Druid Chronicler, Castle Rising, Caveat Emptor, Pagan Renaissance, The Coming Age, The Cauldron, The Covenstead, The Unicorn Speaks, The Summoner, The Sword of Dyrnwyn, Old Gods and New Devils, The Heathen, Raven Banner, Shrew, The Pagan Way.*

2. "Neo-sacral" was used, for example, by Andrew M. Greeley in "Implications for the Sociology of Religion of Occult Behavior in the Youth Culture," in *On the Margin of the Visible: Sociology, the Esoteric and the Occult,* ed. Edward A. Tiryakian (New York: John Wiley & Sons, 1974), p. 295. First presented as a paper at the 1970 annual meeting of the American Sociological Association; "Neo-transcendentalist" was used, for example, by psychiatrist Raymond Prince in "Cocoon Work: An Interpretation of the Concern of Contemporary Youth with the Mystical," in *Religious Movements in Contemporary America,* ed. Irving Zaretsky and Mark Leone (Princeton: Princeton University Press, 1974), p. 263.

3. Most Neo-Pagan groups meet in *groves, circles,* or *covens.* The word *nests* is used to describe groups within the Church of All Worlds. The word *vortices* has been used by the Elf Queen's Daughters.

4. Originally called Craftcast Farm, it became The Holy Order of St. Brigit in 1977.

5. Aleister Crowley, *Magick in Theory and Practice,* privately published in Paris in 1929. Recently published in *Magick,* ed. John Symonds and Kenneth Grant (London: Routledge Kegan Paul, Ltd., 1973), p. 131. Crowley spells magic with a *k* to distinguish it from stage magic. Many magical practitioners do likewise. I do not.

6. Bonewits's definition of magic is not simply "folk parapsychology," a phrase he has used effectively in TV interviews, etc. Bonewits considers magic "an art as well as a science that has to do with the methods people have developed over the centuries for getting their psychic talents to do what they want them to do" (taped letter, winter 1978). My own tendency is to smudge the line between the psychological and the psychic. Bonewits disagrees: "It's true that it is often hard to make a fine line between where the psychic starts

and the psychological ends, but it is a distinction that still has to be made from time to time. Most people who have a sloppy definition of magic (or a definition that makes it impossible to distinguish it from art or psychology) are usually not very good occultists who don't have much in the way of psychic talent."

7. Edward Gibbon, *The Decline and Fall of the Roman Empire* (New York: Modern Library, 1932), I, 725–26. In a footnote (Chapter XXI, note 174), Gibbon writes that *pagan* derives from the Greek παγή, signifying fountain and the rural neighborhood surrounding it. It became synonymous with "rural" in Rome and came to mean *rustic* or *peasant*. With the rise of the Roman military, *pagan* became a contemptuous epithet meaning *nonsoldier.* The Christians considered themselves soldiers of Christ and those who refused the sacrament of baptism were reproached with the term *pagan* as early as the reign of Emperor Valentinian (365 C.E.) and the word was introduced into Imperial law in the Theodosian Code. After Christianity became the official religion of the Roman Empire, the ancient religion lived on in obscure places and, writes Gibbon, "the word pagans, with its new signification, reverted to its primitive origin." It was then applied to all polytheists in the old and new world. It was used by Christians against the Mohammedans, the Unitarians, etc.

8. Gore Vidal, *Julian* (Boston: Little, Brown and Company, 1964), p. 497.

9. *The Julian Review* was published by the Delphic Fellowship, a Neo-Pagan group, now defunct. *The Julian Review* was founded in 1967 by Don Harrison. Shortly thereafter, Harrison met Michael Kinghorn and together they founded the Delphic Fellowship, which considered itself to be the voice of resurgent Greek Paganism. Today, Harrison is a priest in the Church of the Eternal Source (see Chapter 9).

10. "The First Epistle of Isaac," *The Druid Chronicles (evolved)* (Berkeley: Berkeley Drunemeton Press, 1976), 2:4.

11. The first quote is from an undated Church of All Worlds tract, "An Old Religion for a New Age: Neo-Paganism." The second quote appears in Bonewits's "The First Epistle of Isaac," 2:2.

12. The *Oxford English Dictionary* observes that the etymology of *religion* is doubtful but that one view connects it with *religáre*—to bind. The *American Heritage Dictionary* observes that *religion*, from the Latin *religió,* is "perhaps from religáre, to bind back: re-, back and ligáre, to bind, fasten."

13. Harriet Whitehead, "Reasonably Fantastic: Some Perspectives on Scientology, Science Fiction and Occultism," *Religious Movements in Contemporary America,* pp. 547–87. The original quote from William James ("His contentment with the finite incases him like a lobstershell") appears in William James, *The Varieties of Religious Experience: A Study in Human Nature,* being the Gifford Lectures on natural religion delivered at Edinburgh in 1901–1902 (New York: Longmans, Green, and Co., Ltd., 1903), p. 93.

Chapter 2: A RELIGION WITHOUT CONVERTS

1. Among those books influencing my childhood were: Caroline Dale Snedeker, *The Spartan* (or *The Coward of Thermopylae*) (New York: Doubleday, 1911) and *The Perilous Seat* (New York: Doubleday, 1923); Mary Renault, *The King Must Die* (New York: Pantheon, 1958).

2. For an understanding of *Star Trek* literature, see J. Lichtenberg, S. Marshak, and J. Winston, *Star Trek Lives* (New York: Bantam, 1975); see also spin-off *Star Trek* myths

written by fans in Jacquelin Lichtenberg, *Kraith Collected*, Vol. I, and issues of *Babel*, a "Trekkie" fan magazine.

3. The famous "opium of the people" quote is almost never given in full. My favorite translation is in Christopher Caudwell, *Further Studies in a Dying Culture* (London: The Bodley Head, 1949), pp. 75–76: "Religious misery is at once the expression of real misery and a protest against that misery. Religion is the sigh of the hard pressed creature, the heart of a heartless world, the spirit of unspiritual conditions. It is the opium of the people." For a more accessible version, see Karl Marx, *Selected Writings in Sociology and Social Philosophy*, trans. T. B. Bottomore (New York: McGraw-Hill, 1964), p. 27.

4. John McPhee, *Encounters with the Archdruid* (New York: Farrar, Straus and Giroux, 1971), pp. 84, 95.

5. Arnold Toynbee, "The Religious Background of the Present Environmental Crisis," *International Journal of Environmental Studies*, Vol. III, 1972. Also published under the title "The Genesis of Pollution," in *Horizon*, Vol. XV, No. 3 (Summer 1973), pp. 4–9.

6. Lynn White, Jr., "The Historical Roots of Our Ecologic Crisis," *Science*, Vol. 155 (March 10, 1967), 1203–07. Also in *The Environmental Handbook*, ed. Garrett de Bell (New York: Ballantine, 1970), pp. 12–26. Quotations on pp. 19 and 20.

7. See "An Interview with Doris and Sylvester [Vic] Stuart," *Earth Religion News*, Vol. 1, No. 4 (1974), 23–25.

8. Published versions of this ritual—often called "The Charge of the Goddess"—can be found in *The Grimoire of Lady Sheba* (St. Paul: Llewellyn, 1972), pp. 145–47, and in Stewart Farrar, *What Witches Do* (New York: Coward, McCann & Geoghegan, 1971), pp. 193–94. The version on the Stuarts' tape that I heard was written by Neo-Pagan writer Ed Fitch.

9. This attitude toward *belief* is actually not uncommon among writers who treat "occult" subjects. For example, D. Arthur Kelly writes in "Theories of Knowledge and the I Ching," "I cannot say that I 'believe' in the I Ching; rather, I would say that I have learnt a great deal about life and the universe from a contemplation of its 'teachings'" (*Gnostica*, Vol. IV, No. 5 [January 1975], 33).

10. Robert S. Ellwood, Jr., *Religious and Spiritual Groups in Modern America* (Englewood Cliffs, NJ: Prentice-Hall, 1973), p. 189.

11. In "An Interview with Doris and Sylvester Stuart," p. 24, Sylvester Stuart observes, "I see Wicca as the only hope of the survivors of mankind after there has been a complete breakdown in our present type of society, a breakdown which I see coming in the foreseeable future." Stuart said he saw the Craft as a repository for survival skills.

Chapter 3: THE PAGAN WORLD VIEW

1. R. H. Barrow, trans., *Prefect and Emperor, the Relationes of Symmachus A.D. 384* (London: Oxford University Press, 1973), pp. 40–41. From an address to Valentinian, Theodosius, and Arcadius. In Latin: "Eadem spectamus astra, commune caelum est, idem nos mundus involvit: Quid interest, qua quisque prudentia verum requirat? Uno itinere non potest perveniri ad tam grande secretum."

2. James Henry Breasted, *Development of Religion and Thought in Ancient Egypt* (New York: Charles Scribner's Sons, 1912), p. 315.

3. Dagobert D. Runes, *Dictionary of Philosophy* (New York: Philosophical Library, 1942), p. 242.

4. *Whole Earth Catalog* (Menlo Park, CA: Portola Institute, 1969).

5. Isaac Bonewits, "The Second Epistle of Isaac," *The Druid Chronicles (evolved)* (Berkeley: Berkeley Drunemeton Press, 1976), 2:13.

6. David Hume, "The Natural History of Religion," *Essays and Treatises on Several Subjects* (Edinburgh: Bell & Bradfute, 1825), II, 384–422. Quotations are on pp. 386 and 395.

7. Paul Radin, *Monotheism Among Primitive Peoples* (Basel: Bollingen Foundation, Special Publication No. 4, 1954). Quotations are on pp. 24, 29, 30, and 25.

8. Harold Moss, *Green Egg,* Vol. V, No. 51 (December 21, 1972), Forum section, p. 5.

9. Theodore Roszak, *Where the Wasteland Ends: Politics and Transcendence in Postindustrial Society* (New York: Anchor Books, 1973), pp. 108–09.

10. David Miller, *The New Polytheism* (New York: Harper & Row, 1974), p. 4. Other quotations from Miller are on pp. 5–6, 59–60, vii–viii, ix, and 24.

11. For example, in noting the controversial monotheistic Witchcraft system of Gavin and Yvonne Frost's School of Wicca, Harold Moss of the Church of the Eternal Source observed, "In the discussions with the Frosts, we should remember that polytheism can contain monotheism, but not the other way around. When we say that Witches are polytheists, we are admitting that some of them were and are monotheists. [The Frosts are] monotheist(s) in a polytheistic religion . . . which is perfectly OK!" (*Earth Religion News,* Vol. I, No. 4 [1974], 3–4).

12. James Hillman, "Psychology: Monotheistic or Polytheistic," *Spring 1971* (New York: Spring Publications, 1971), pp. 197, 199–200.

13. Miller, *The New Polytheism,* p. 55.

14. Hillman, "Psychology: Monotheistic or Polytheistic," p. 206. Hillman considers a revival of Paganism a "danger" because it would bring "along its accoutrements of popular soothsaying, quick priesthoods, astrological divination, extravagant practices and the erosion of psychic differentiations through delusional enthusiasms" (p. 206).

15. Miller, *The New Polytheism,* p. 81.

16. Harold Moss, *Green Egg,* Vol. VII, No. 63 (June 21, 1974), p. 28.

17. Robert Ellwood, Jr., "Polytheism: Establishment or Liberation Religion?", *Journal of the American Academy of Religion,* Vol. XLII, No. 2 (1974), 344–49.

18. The next few quotations were culled from answers to a questionnaire sent out in the mail to various Neo-Pagans during the winter and spring of 1976. The questionnaire appeared in *Green Egg,* Vol. VIII, No. 76 (February 2, 1976), 32–36.

19. Isaac Bonewits, first quote from interview; second from "The Second Epistle of Isaac," *The Druid Chronicles (evolved)* (Berkeley: Berkeley Drunemeton Press, 1976) 1:12. In an editorial in *Gnostica,* Vol. IV, No. 6 (February 1975), 2, Bonewits, with typical humor, added that "monotheistic religions inevitably promote bigotry and chauvinism of all sorts, but let us not forget that polytheistic cultures have also produced chauvinistic behavior. . . . However, while monotheists are *required* to be bigots, for polytheists, bigotry is merely an exciting option."

20. Harold Moss, *Green Egg,* Vol. VIII, No. 70 (May 1, 1975), 38.

21. Apropos Neo-Pagans as an elite, Bonewits, in an editorial in *Gnostica,* Vol. IV, No. 9 (July 1975), 2, writes that Neo-Pagans are part of the *andermenschen*—the *other people*—as opposed to *übermenschen* or *untermenschen:* "We have always had the *ander-*

menschen—the odd ones, the different people. We have always had the *andermenschen*, in every society on our planet; they are our painters and poets, our composers and musicians, our dancers and story-tellers, our witches and mediums, our mystics and shamans, our magicians and psychics. These are the strange ones, the people who have dipped their toes into the otherworld and come back raving and enchanting, healing and prophesying, always trying desperately to point toward the new and the inexplicable as the only source of salvation for our poor, confused species."

22. See www.adherents.com.

Chapter 4: THE WICCAN REVIVAL

1. Ann Belford Ulanov, "The Witch Archetype," a lecture given to the Analytical Psychology Club of New York on November 17, 1976. Printed in *Quadrant*, Vol. X, No. 1 (1977), 5–22.

2. Elliot Rose, *A Razor for a Goat* (Toronto: University of Toronto Press, 1962), p. 3.

3. Isaac Bonewits, "Witchcraft: Classical, Gothic and Neopagan (Part I)," *Green Egg*, Vol. IX, No. 77 (March 20, 1976), 15. Bonewits's etymological excursion through the word *witch* appears on pp. 15–17.

4. "Witchcraft in Wichita," *The Waxing Moon* (British edition), New Series No. 1 (Samhain 1970), p. 5. *The Waxing Moon* was the journal of the Pagan Movement in Britain and Ireland.

5. Robert Graves, *The White Goddess,* amended and enlarged ed. (New York: Farrar, Straus and Giroux, 1966), p. 14.

6. For a summary of this myth see Raymond Buckland, *Witchcraft from the Inside* (St. Paul: Llewellyn, 1971).

7. Elliot Rose, *A Razor for a Goat*, pp. 8–10. Actually Rose, in humor, puts forth four schools: Bluff, Knowing, Anti-Sadducee, and Murrayite.

8. Margaret A. Murray, *The Witch-Cult in Western Europe* (Oxford: Oxford University Press, 1921), pp. 12, 233, and 236.

9. Margaret A. Murray, *The God of the Witches* (London: Sampson Low, Marston & Co., Ltd., 1933); *The Divine King in England* (London: Faber & Faber Ltd., 1954); *My First Hundred Years* (London: William Kimber and Co., Ltd., 1963).

10. Norman Cohn, *Europe's Inner Demons* (New York: Basic Books, 1975), p. 125. Other quotations are on pp. 104–09, 124, and 258–61. The reference to the Witches International Craft Association refers to New York Witch Leo Martello whose civil-rights activities on behalf of Witches can be read about in his book, *Witchcraft: The Old Religion* (Secaucus, NJ: University Books, 1973).

11. Mircea Eliade, "Some Observations on European Witchcraft," in *Occultism, Witchcraft and Cultural Fashions* (Chicago: University of Chicago Press, 1976), p. 71.

12. Ibid., p. 85. Other quotations are on pp. 75–78 and 81.

13. Geoffrey Scarre and John Callow, *Witchcraft and Magic in Sixteen- and Seventeenth-Century Europe* (Hampshire, UK: Palgrave, 2001) pp. 1–2.

14. Ibid., p. 25.

15. H. R. Trevor-Roper, "The European Witch-Craze and Social Change," in *Witchcraft and Sorcery,* ed. Max Marwick (Harmondsworth, UK: Penguin Books, 1970), pp. 121–23, 127–28, 131–32, 136, and 146.

16. Scarre and Callow, *Witchcraft and Magic in Sixteen- and Seventeenth-Century Europe*, p. 44.

17. Starhawk, "The Burning Times: Notes on a Critical Period of History," in *Dreaming the Dark, Magic, Sex and Politics* (Boston: Beacon Press, 1982, 1997), pp. 183–219.

18. Ronald Hutton, e-mail: October 28, 2005.

19. Lucius Apuleius, *The Golden Ass,* trans. Robert Graves (New York: Farrar, Straus & Young, 1951); also W. Adlington trans. of 1566 (Cambridge: Harvard University Press, 1965).

20. Charles Godfrey Leland, *Aradia, or the Gospel of the Witches* (London: David Nutt, 1899); reprinted (New York: Samuel Weiser, 1974).

21. Jeffrey Burton Russell, *Witchcraft in the Middle Ages* (Ithaca: Cornell University Press, 1972), p. 298.

22. Leo Martello, *Witchcraft: The Old Religion* (Secaucus, NJ: University Books, 1973), pp. 45–68. See also Ronald Hutton, *The Triumph of the Moon: A History of Modern Pagan Witchcraft* (Oxford: Oxford University Press, 1999), pp. 141–148.

23. Charles Godfrey Leland, *Etruscan Roman Remains* (London: T. Fisher Unwin, 1892).

24. Rose, *A Razor for a Goat,* p. 218.

25. Leland, *Aradia,* pp. 5–7.

26. Jessie Wicker Bell, *The Grimoire of Lady Sheba* (St. Paul: Llewellyn, 1972), p. 145.

27. T. C. Lethbridge, *Witches* (New York: Citadel Press, 1968), p. 9.

28. Buckland, *Witchcraft from the Inside,* p. 50.

29. Doreen Valiente, *An ABC of Witchcraft Past & Present* (New York: St. Martin's Press, 1973), p. 12.

30. Leland, *Aradia,* pp. 104–06 and 111.

31. Aidan Kelly, "The Rebirth of Witchcraft: Tradition and Creativity in the Gardnerian Reform" (unpublished Ms., 1977), p. 274.

32. Graves, *The White Goddess,* p. 488. This is one area where Isaac Bonewits and Aidan Kelly are in disagreement. Aidan wrote to me in the spring of 1978: "Graves says many times in *The White Goddess* that it is a poetic work, and specifically disclaims it as scholarship in the usual sense. Certainly many in the Craft who wouldn't know scholarship from a raven have blithely overlooked this point—but Graves can't be blamed for that."

33. Robert Graves, "Witches in 1964," *The Virginia Quarterly Review,* Vol. XL, No. 4 (1964), 550–59.

34. Patricia Crowther, *Witch Blood!* (New York: House of Collectibles, 1974); Stewart Farrar, *What Witches Do* (New York: Coward, McCann & Geoghegan, 1971); Buckland, *Witchcraft from the Inside.*

35. Valiente, *An ABC of Witchcraft,* p. 153.

36. J. L. Bracelin, *Gerald Gardner: Witch* (London: Octagon Press, 1960), pp. 164–65.

37. Valiente, *An ABC of Witchcraft,* p. 153.

38. Janet and Stewart Farrar, *The Witches' Way.* First published in the United States as *A Witches Bible,* Vol. I, II (New York: Magickal Childe Publications, 1984), Vol. II, pp. 283–93.

39. Hutton, *The Triumph of the Moon,* pp. 207–214.

40. Bracelin, *Gerald Gardner: Witch,* p. 165.

41. Gerald B. Gardner, *High Magic's Aid* (London: Michael Houghton, 1949). The main god mentioned is Janicot. There are indirect references to Isis (p. 172) and "kerwiddeon" (p. 205), and the idea of the priestess representing the "divine spirit of Creation" (p. 120).

42. Valiente, *An ABC of Witchcraft,* pp. 154–55.
43. Gerald B. Gardner, *Witchcraft Today* (New York: The Citadel Press, 1955). First published in 1954 in England by Rider & Company.
44. Valiente, *An ABC of Witchcraft,* pp. 155–57. Many have observed that those portions of the Gardnerian rituals that have been published contain phrases from Ovid, Kipling, Leland, Crowley, and the *Key of Solomon.*
45. Francis King, *The Rites of Modern Occult Magic* (New York: Macmillan, 1970), pp. 176 and 179–80.
46. Rose, *A Razor for a Goat,* p. 230. Other quotations are on pp. 200–1, 204, 206, 210, 217, and 220.
47. *Pentagram,* No. 2 (November 1964), pp. 5, 7.
48. Valiente, letter in *Pentagram,* No. 1 (August 1964), p. 1.
49. Isaac Bonewits, "Witchcult: Fact or Fancy?" *Gnostica,* Vol. III, No. 4 (November 21, 1973), 5.
50. Isaac Bonewits, *Real Magic* (New York: Berkley Publishing Corp., 1972), pp. 129–30.
51. Isaac Bonewits, "Witchcraft," Pt. I, pp. 17–18. See also Bonewits, *Bonewits' Essential Guide to Witchcraft and Wicca* (New York: Citidel Press, 2006), appendix 3.
52. Ibid., Pt. II, *Green Egg,* Vol. IX, No. 78 (May 1, 1976), 13–17.
53. Ibid., Pt. III, *Green Egg,* Vol. IX, No. 79 (June 21, 1976), 10.
54. Ibid., p. 7.
55. Ibid., Pt. II, pp. 15–16.
56. Ibid., Pt. III, pp. 5–6.
57. Victor Anderson, *Thorns of the Blood Rose* (privately published by Cora Anderson, San Leandro, CA, 1970).
58. Aidan Kelly, op. cit., p. 4.
59. Ibid., p. 18. Other quotations are on pp. 1, 5, and 274.
60. Gertrude Rachel Levy, *The Gate of Horn* (London: Faber and Faber, 1963). Originally published in 1948.
61. Kelly, "The Rebirth of Witchcraft," p. 274. Aidan's summary of the history of Goddess worship is on pp. 281–94.
62. *Iron Mountain* (Summer 1984), 19–29.
63. *Iron Mountain* (Fall 1985), 3–6.
64. Letters from Doreen Valiente, September 12, 18, and November 14, 1985.
65. Donald H. Frew, "Harran: Last Refuge of Classical Paganism," *The Pomegranate,* issue 9, Lammas, 1999.
66. Bonewits, "Witchcraft," Pt. III, p. 10. Bonewits's arguments may have played a large role in changing the attitudes of many Wiccans on this issue.
67. Hans Holzer, *The Witchcraft Report* (New York: Ace Books, 1973), pp. 135–45.
68. Marcello Truzzi, "Toward a Sociology of the Occult: Notes on Modern Witchcraft," in *Religious Movements in Contemporary America,* ed. Irving Zaretsky and Mark Leone (Princeton: Princeton University Press, 1974), p. 636.
69. Buckland, *Witchcraft from the Inside,* pp. 79–80.
70. Buckland, *Earth Religion News,* Vol. 1, No. 1 (Yule 1973), p. 1.
71. Buckland, *The Tree: The Complete Book of Saxon Witchcraft* (New York: Samuel Weiser, 1974), p. 4.
72. Buckland, *Earth Religion News.*

Chapter 5: THE CRAFT TODAY

1. Joseph Wilson, *Gnostica*, Vol. III, No. 11 (June 21, 1974), 17.

2. June Johns, *King of the Witches: The World of Alex Sanders* (London: Peter Davies, 1969), pp. 10–21; Stewart Farrar, *What Witches Do* (New York: Coward, McCann & Geoghegan, 1971), pp. 1–2.

3. Leo Martello, *Wica Newsletter*, No. 15 (1972), p. 1.

4. *Gnostica*, Vol. II, No. 8 (June 21, 1973), 19.

5. Phoenix, "Gardnerian Aspects," *Green Egg*, Vol. VII, No. 63 (June 21, 1974), 18.

6. Carl Weschcke, "Spirit of the Witchmeet," *Touchstone—Witch's Love Letter* (April 11, 1974), 1. This newsletter, edited by Weschcke, was published for the Council of American Witches by the First Wiccan Church of Minnesota, 476 Summit Ave., St. Paul, MN 55102.

7. Ibid., February 1974, 5–6, 9.

8. Ibid., Spring Equinox 1974, 3.

9. Ibid., February 1974, 5–6.

10. "Principles of Wiccan Belief," *Green Egg*, Vol. VII, No. 64 (August 1, 1974), 32. Adopted by the Council of American Witches during its spring Witchmeet, April 11–14, 1974, in Minneapolis.

11. *The Witches Trine*, Vol. IV, No. 2 (Lughnasadh, 1974), 7.

12. Sybil Leek, *The Complete Art of Witchcraft* (New York: New American Library, 1973), p. 15.

13. Marcello Truzzi, "Toward a Sociology of the Occult: Notes on Modern Witchcraft," in *Religious Movements in Contemporary America*, ed. Irving Zaretsky and Mark Leone (Princeton: Princeton University Press, 1974), p. 637.

14. Susan Roberts, *Witches, U.S.A.* (New York: Dell, 1971), p. 17.

15. In a few traditions, the sword represents fire and the wand air.

16. Helica, letter (New York, November 1977).

17. Farrar, *What Witches Do*, p. 190. Other quotations are on pp. 4 and 22.

18. Doreen Valiente, *An ABC of Witchcraft Past & Present* (St. Martin's Press, 1973), p. xiii.

19. In England the covens that descend from Gardner do not call themselves "Gardnerian."

20. C. A. Burland, *The Magical Arts* (London: Arthur Barker Ltd., 1966), p. 175.

21. "Family of covens" was a term used by a Gardnerian journal that was published from 1974 to 1976 in Louisville, Kentucky.

22. Gerald B. Gardner, *High Magic's Aid* (London: Michael Houghton, 1949); also published in New York by Samuel Weiser (1975); *Witchcraft Today* (New York: The Citadel Press, 1955); *The Meaning of Witchcraft* (London: Aquarian Press, 1959); and Janet and Stewart Farrar, *The Witches' Way* (London: Robert Hale, Ltd., 1981), published in the United States as *A Witches' Bible*, Vol. I, II (New York: Magickal Childe Publications, 1985).

23. Ronald Hutton, *The Triumph of the Moon: A History of Modern Pagan Witchcraft*, (Oxford: Oxford University Press, 1999), p. 321.

24. Chas S. Clifton, "The '1734' Tradition in North America," published in *The Witches' Voice*, March 18, 2001. Article ID: 3356: www.witchvox.com/va/dt_va.html?a=usco&c=trads&id=3356.

25. Ibid.

26. See Joseph Wilson, "Flags, Flax, and Fodder—The Secrets of 1734 Revealed," available at www.1734.us/riddles.html.

27. Letter from Robert Cochrane to Joseph Wilson, 1966, available at www.cyberwitch.com/bowers.

28. Steve Hewell, "The Feri Tradition," published in *The Witches' Voice*, January 1, 2002. Article ID 3785: www.witchvox.com/va/dt_va.html?a=usga&c=trade&id=3785.

29. M. Macha NightMare and Vibra Willow, "Reclaiming Tradition Witchcraft," published 1999, 2000: www.reclaiming.org/about/origins/rectrad-craft.html.

30. Ruth Barrett, *Women's Rites, Women's Mysteries* (Bloomington: AuthorHouse, 2004), p. 420.

31. Ibid, pp. 421–22.

32. Ibid, p. 422.

33. Mark Roberts, "An Introduction to Dianic Witchcraft," unpublished Ms., Chap. VI, pp. 1–2.

34. Mark Roberts, "The Dianic Aspects," *The New Broom,* Vol. I, No. 2 (Candlemas, 1973), 17.

35. Gavin and Yvonne Frost, *The Witch's Bible* (New York: Berkley, 1975).

36. *Touchstone—Witch's Love Letter* (February 1974), p. 9.

37. Roberta Ann Kennedy, *Green Egg,* Vol. V, No. 51 (December 17, 1972), Forum section, 14.

38. Diana Demdike, "Don't Let Witchcraft Die!" in *Quest,* No. 15 (September 1973), 6. This is the British Witchcraft journal and should not be confused with the U.S. feminist journal of the same name.

39. On the death of Robert Williams see *Green Egg,* Vol. VIII, No. 74 (November 1975), 11; also Vol. VII, No. 65 (September 1974), 3, 37; also No. 66 (November 1974), 39–42.

40. Leo Martello, *Witchcraft: The Old Religion* (Secaucus, NJ: University Books, 1973), pp. 23–27.

41. Isaac Bonewits, "Witchburning . . . Now & Then," *Gnostica,* Vol. III, No. 6 (January 21, 1974), 5–6, 8, 10, 16.

42. Ibid., p. 6.

43. C. A. Burland, *Echoes of Magic* (Totowa, NJ: Rowman and Littlefield, 1972), pp. 117–18, 132.

44. Letter (name withheld by request), Long Beach, CA, summer 1977.

Chapter 7: MAGIC AND RITUAL

1. Dr. Timothy Leary, quoted in "Neurologic, Immortality & All That," by Robert A. Wilson in *Green Egg,* Vol. VIII, No. 72 (August 1, 1975), 9.

2. "Magick" by the Abbey of Thelema, *Green Egg,* Vol. VIII, No. 75 (December 21, 1975), 19.

3. Isaac Bonewits, "The Second Epistle of Isaac," in *The Druid Chronicles (evolved),* ed. Isaac Bonewits (Berkeley: Berkeley Drunemeton Press, 1976), 1:7.

4. "An Interview with Robert Anton Wilson," by Neal Wilgus, *Science Fiction Review,* Vol. 5, No. 2 (May 1976), 32.

5. Leo Martello, *Witchcraft: The Old Religion* (Secaucus, NJ: University Books, 1973), p. 12.

6. See "The First Epistle of Isaac," *The Druid Chronicles (evolved),* 3:1.

7. Isaac Bonewits, *Real Magic* (New York: Berkley Publishing Corp., 1972), pp. 209, 53.

8. Doreen Valiente, *Natural Magic* (New York: St. Martin's Press, 1975), p. 13.

9. Jacob Needleman, *A Sense of the Cosmos: The Encounter of Modern Science and Ancient Truth* (New York: Doubleday & Co., 1975).

10. Colin Wilson, *The Occult* (London: Hodder and Stoughton, 1971), p. 59.

11. Valiente, *Natural Magic,* p. 33.

12. Dianic Grove training material of the Covenstead of Morrigana in Dallas, Texas, Lesson No. 1.

13. See Bonewits, Real Magic, pp. 91–112 and 163–76; "Second Epistle of Isaac," Chap. 6, "The Tools of Ritual."

14. Robert Anton Wilson, "All Hail the Goddess Eris!" *Gnostica,* Vol. 4, No. 11 (September–October 1975), 11.

15. Jane Ellen Harrison, *Epilegomena to the Study of Greek Religion* (New Hyde Park, NY: University Books, 1962), pp. xliv–xlvi.

16. Robert Anton Wilson, "The Origins of Magick," Green Egg, Vol. VII, No. 63 (June 21, 1974), 7.

17. Sam'l Bassett ("The Inquisitor"), "An Essay in Divination," *The Witches' Trine,* Vol. 5, No. 2 (Litha, 1976), 7–8.

18. Aidan Kelly, "Aporrheton No. 1, To the New Witch," March, 1973, p. 5. This was part of materials given to new members of NROOGD. A copy of these materials, as well as NROOGD's journal, *The Witches' Trine,* is on file with the library of the Graduate Theological Union in Berkeley, California.

19. Isaac Bonewits, taped letter from Berkeley, winter 1978.

20. Bonewits, "Second Epistle of Isaac," 5:5–6.

21. Bonewits, *Real Magic,* p. 175.

22. *The Witches' Trine,* Vol. 1, No. 6 (Winter Solstice 1972), 2.

23. Ibid., Vol. 3, No. 4 (Lughnasadh 1974), 11.

24. Ibid., "How We Happened to Get the NROOGD Together (Part I)," 9, 10, 12; Vol. 3, No. 5 (Samhain 1974), "How We Happened to Get the NROOGD Together (Part II)," 18, 19, 21–22.

25. Aidan Kelly, "Why a Craft Ritual Works," Gnostica, Vol. 4, No. 7 (March–April–May 1975), 33.

26. I. M. Lewis, *Ecstatic Religion* (Harmondsworth, UK: Penguin Books, 1971), p. 205.

27. Kelly, "Why a Craft Ritual Works."

28. Ibid.

29. Ibid.

30. Aidan Kelly, Diary entry, July 6, 1972.

31. Kelly, "Why a Craft Ritual Works," p. 5.

32. Aidan Kelly, "O, That Vexed Question: Is the Craft a Survival, a Revival, or What?" *Nemeton,* Vol. 1, No. 1 (Samhain 1972), 19.

33. Kelly, "Aporrheton No. 1," p. 2.

34. Most of these arguments appear in Aidan Kelly, "Palengenesia," *Gnostica,* Vol. 4, No. 9 (July 1975), 7, 40, 41. Any additions come from interviews.

35. Kelly, "Aporrheton No. 1," p. 1.

36. Kelly, "Aporrheton No. 5, The Craft Laws," April 1973, p. 1.

37. Kelly, "O, That Vexed Question," p. 20.

Chapter 8: WOMEN, FEMINISM, AND THE CRAFT

1. The poem appeared in *WomanSpirit*, Vol. 1, No. 3 (Spring Equinox 1975), back cover.

2. Where did feminist Witches get Laverna from, you may ask? From Charles Godfrey Leland's *Aradia, or the Gospel of the Witches* (London: David Nutt, 1899), reprinted (New York: Samuel Weiser, 1974), pp. 89–98: Leland writes that Laverna is mentioned in Horace, *Epistles,* I, xvi, 59–62.

3. Two examples of conferences on feminist spirituality: Through the Looking Glass, a Gynergenetic Experience, in Boston, April 23–25, 1976; A Celebration of the Beguines, in New York City, October 30–31, 1976.

4. I originally saw this manifesto in mimeographed form, but it has been published, thanks to Robin Morgan, in *Sisterhood Is Powerful,* ed. Robin Morgan (New York: Random House, 1970), pp. 539–43. Quotation on p. 539.

5. Kirsten Grimstad and Susan Rennie, eds., *The New Woman's Survival Sourcebook* (New York: Alfred A. Knopf, 1975).

6. Kirsten Grimstad and Susan Rennie, "Spiritual Explorations Cross-country," *Quest,* Vol. 1, No. 4 (Spring 1975), 49–51.

7. *Country Women* (April 1974), 1. Available: Box 51, Albion, Cal. 95410.

8. Judy Davis and Juanita Weaver, "Dimensions of Spirituality," *Quest,* Vol. 1, No. 4 (Spring 1975), 6.

9. Z Budapest, *The Feminist Book of Lights and Shadows* (Venice, CA: Luna Publications, 1976), p. 1. Available from The Feminist Wicca, 442 Lincoln Blvd., Venice, CA 90291. Z's spelling of woman as *womon* and women as *wimmin* is intended to take the *man* out of woman.

10. Sally Gearhart, "Womanpower: Energy Re-sourcement," *WomanSpirit,* Vol. 2, No. 7 (Spring Equinox 1976), 19–23.

11. Z Budapest, *Feminist Book of Lights and Shadows,* pp. 1–2.

12. Ibid, pp. 3–4.

13. Friedrich Engels, *The Origin of the Family, Private Property, and the State* (New York: International Publishers, 1967); Evelyn Reed, *Woman's Evolution* (New York: Pathfinder Press, 1975); J. J. Bachofen, *Myth, Religion and Mother Right* (Princeton: Princeton University Press—Bollingen Series LXXXIV, 1973); Helen Diner, *Mothers and Amazons* (New York: Anchor Books, 1973); Erich Neumann, *The Great Mother: An Analysis of the Archetype* (Princeton: Princeton University Press—Bollingen Series XLVII, 1963).

14. Sarah B. Pomeroy, *Goddesses, Whores, Wives, and Slaves* (New York: Schocken Books, 1975).

15. Elizabeth Gould Davis, *The First Sex* (New York: G. P. Putnam's Sons, 1971).

16. Monique Wittig, *Les Guérillères* (Boston: Beacon Press, 1985), p. 89.

17. Paula Webster and Esther Newton, "Matriarchy: Puzzle and Paradigm," presented at the 71st Annual Meeting of the American Anthropological Association, Toronto, 1972. This paper was later published in *APHRA—A Feminist Literary Magazine* (Spring/Summer 1973) as "Matriarchy: As Women See It." A revised version, *Matriarchy: A Vision of Power* by Paula Webster appears in *Toward an Anthropology of Women,* ed. Rayna Reiter (New York: Monthly Review Press, 1975), pp. 141–56.

18. Joanna Russ, *The Female Man* (Boston: Beacon Press, 1986); *We Who Are About To . . .* (New York: Dell, 1975); *The Two of Them* (New York: Berkley Publishing Corp., 1978), among others.

19. Gordon Rattray Taylor, *Sex in History* (New York: The Vanguard Press, 1954).

20. Jean Markale, *Women of the Celts* (London: Gordon Cremonesi, 1975). First published as *La Femme Celte,* Editions Payot, Paris, 1972.

21. Adrienne Rich, "The Kingdom of the Fathers," *Partisan Review,* Vol. XLIII, No. 1 (1976), 29–30, 26.

22. Philip Zabriskie, "Goddesses in Our Midst," *Quadrant,* No. 17 (Fall 1974), 34–45.

23. Robert Graves, *The White Goddess,* amended and enlarged ed. (New York: Farrar, Straus and Giroux, 1966), pp. 484–86.

24. Ruth Mountaingrove, "Clues to Our Women's Culture," *WomanSpirit,* Vol. 2, No. 6 (Fall Equinox 1975), 45.

25. Jude Michaels, "Eve & Us," *WomanSpirit,* Vol. 1, No. 1 (Autumn Equinox 1974), 5–6. In connection with this, I am reminded of the words of the fourth-century Emperor Julian, who observed that the doctrine of Adam and Eve was unfit for any enlightened mind: "What could be more foolish than a being unable to distinguish good from bad? . . . In short, God refused to let man taste of wisdom, than which there could be nothing of more value . . . so that the serpent was a benefactor rather than a destroyer of the human race." *The Works of the Emperor Julian,* trans. Wilmer Cave Wright, 3 vols. (Cambridge: Harvard University Press, 1961), III, 327.

26. "Voices," *WomanSpirit,* Vol. 1, No. 1 (Autumn Equinox 1974), 38.

27. Carol, Patti, and Billie, "Moon Over the Mountain: Creating Our Own Rituals," *WomanSpirit,* Vol. 1, No. 1 (Autumn Equinox 1974), 30. Robin Morgan's poem appears in *Monster* (New York: Vintage Books, 1972), pp. 81–86.

28. W. Holman Keith, *Divinity as the Eternal Feminine* (New York: Pageant Press, 1960), p. 14.

29. Mary Daly, *Beyond God the Father* (Boston: Beacon Press, 1973), pp. 16–19.

30. Records: Alix Dobkin, Kay Gardner, et al., "Her Precious Love," on *Lavender Jane Loves Women* (1975), Alix Dobkin Project 1, 210 W. 10 St., New York, N.Y. 10014; Cassie Culver, "Good Old Dora," on *3 Gypsies* (1976), Urana Records—ST-WWE-81; Kay Gardner, *Mooncircles* (1975), Urana Records, a division of Wise Women Enterprises, Inc., P.O. Box 297, Village Station, New York, NY 10014—ST-WWE-80.

31. Fran Winnant, "Our Religious Heritage," *WomanSpirit,* Vol. 1, No. 3 (Spring Equinox 1975), 51.

32. Monica, letter to *WomanSpirit,* Vol. 2, No. 7 (Spring Equinox 1976), 62.

33. *WomanSpirit,* Vol. 2, No. 6 (Fall Equinox 1975), 64.

34. Fran Rominsky, "goddess with a small g," *WomanSpirit,* Vol. 1, No. 1 (Autumn Equinox 1974), 48.

35. WITCH documents, in Morgan, *Sisterhood Is Powerful,* p. 546. Other quotations are on pp. 541–43 and 540.

36. Graves, *The White Goddess,* p. 458.

37. Robert Graves, "Real Women," in *Masculine/Feminine,* eds. Betty Roszak and Theodore Roszak (New York: Harper Colophon Books, 1969), pp. 35–36.

38. Keith, *Divinity as Eternal Feminine,* p. 4.

39. W. Holman Keith, "The Garden of Venus," *Green Egg,* Vol. IV, No. 38 (May 7, 1971); *Divinity as Eternal Feminine,* p. 192. See also "The Priestess," *Green Egg,* Vol. VI, No. 60 (February 1, 1974), 28, and "Venus Proserpina," *Green Egg,* Vol. VI, No. 55 (June 21, 1978), 8.

40. Morning Glory Zell, in *Green Egg,* Vol. VII, No. 68 (February 1, 1975), 43.

41. Gearhart, "Womanpower," p. 20.

42. "Woman, Priestess, Witch," *The Waxing Moon,* Vol. 7, No. 2 (Summer Solstice 1971), 3. This Neo-Pagan journal soon changed its name to *The Crystal Well* and was published for many years out of Philadelphia. *The Crystal Well* was later published (in a different format) out of California.

43. Ravenwolf, "In Defense of Men and Gods," *Earth Religion News,* Vol. 3, Issues 1, 2, 3 combined (1976), 140.

44. Letter from Julie Jay, ibid., p. 11.

45. Morning Glory Zell, *Green Egg,* Vol. VIII, No. 72 (August 1, 1975), 43.

46. Isaac Bonewits, *Gnostica,* Vol. 4, No. 5 (January 1975), pp. 2, 34, 38.

47. Leo Martello, "Witchcraft: A Way of Life," *Witchcraft Digest,* No. 1 (1971), 3. Publication of the Witches International Craft Associates (WICA), Suite 1B, 153 W. 80 St., New York, N.Y. 10024.

48. Margo and Lee, "The Liberated Witch," *The New Broom,* Vol. 1, No. 2 (Candlemas 1973), 10.

49. I. M. Lewis, *Ecstatic Religion* (Harmondsworth, UK: Penguin Books, 1971), pp. 31, 117.

50. *The New Broom,* Vol. 1, No. 3 (Lammas 1973), 21, 28.

51. *The New Broom,* Vol. 1, No. 1 (Samhain 1972), 10–11.

52. *Nemeton,* Vol. 1, No. 1 (Samhain 1972), 12.

53. *The New Broom,* Vol. 1, No. 4 (undated), 9.

54. Deborah Bender, "Raising Power in a Single-Sex Coven," *The Witches' Trine,* Vol. 5, No. 2 (Litha 1976), 5–6.

55. Barbara Starrett, "I Dream in Female: The Metaphors of Evolution," *Amazon Quarterly,* Vol. 3, No. 1 (November 1974), 24–25. Other quotation on p. 20.

56. Bender, "Raising Power," 5–6.

57. Deborah Bender, letter, summer 1976, Oakland, CA.

58. *Women's Coven Newsletter.* Available to feminist Witches from 5756 Vicente St., Oakland, CA 94609.

59. Leland, *Aradia,* pp. 4, 6–7.

60. E-mail: December 1, 2005.

61. E-mail: November 15, 2005.

62. E-mail: September 20, 2005.

63. E-mail: November 29, 2005.

64. E-mail: September 15, 2005.

65. E-mail: September 20, 2005.

66. Jenny Gibbons, "Recent Developments in the Study of the Great European Witch Hunt," *The Pomegranate,* Issue no. 5 (August 1998), pp. 3–16. Also see Geoffrey Scarre and John Callow, *Witchcraft and Magic in Sixteenth- and Seventeenth-Century Europe,* 2nd edition (Hampshire, UK: Palgrave, 2001).

67. Max Dashu, "Another View of the Witch Hunts," *The Pomegranate,* Issue no. 9 (August 1999), pp. 30–43.

68. E-mail: December 1, 2005.

69. Sabina Magliocco, *Witching Culture* (Philadelphia: University of Pennsylvania Press, 2004), p. 204.

70. Ronald Hutton, *The Triumph of the Moon* (Oxford, UK: Oxford University Press, 1999), p. 356.

71. E-mail: December 1, 2005.

72. *The Pomegranate,* Issue no. 10 (November 1999) pp. 55–56.

73. Lisa Jervis, "If Women Ruled the World, Nothing Would Be Different," in *LiP* magazine, September 15, 2005 (www.lipmagazine.org).

Chapter 9: RELIGIONS FROM THE PAST—THE PAGAN RECONSTRUCTIONISTS

1. Gleb Botkin, *The Woman Who Rose Again* (New York: Fleming H. Revell, 1937); *Immortal Woman* (New York: The Macaulay Co., 1933); *The God Who Didn't Laugh* (New York: Payson & Clarke, 1929); *Her Wanton Majesty* (New York: The Macaulay Co., 1933).

2. Botkin, *Immortal Woman,* p. 184.

3. Botkin, *The God Who Didn't Laugh,* p. 250. Botkin himself at one time studied for the priesthood in the Greek Catholic Church in Russia: see William Seabrook, *Witchcraft: Its Power in the World Today* (New York: Harcourt, Brace and Company, 1940), p. 343, and the November 15, 1939, edition of the *New York World-Telegram.* When *The God Who Didn't Laugh* and *Immortal Woman* appeared, reviewers did not emphasize the Aphrodisian aspects of the books: see the 25th and 29th annual cumulation of *The Book Review Digest* (New York: H. W. Wilson Co., 1930 and 1934), pp. 105 and 102, respectively.

4. Quoted by Seabrook, in *Witchcraft,* pp. 343–44. See also *Newsweek,* November 27, 1939, p. 32; *Life,* December 4, 1939, p. 101.

5. Seabrook, *Witchcraft,* p. 342. The beginning of the creed goes as follows: "I believe in Aphrodite, the flower-faced sweetly-smelling, laughter-loving goddess of Love and Beauty; the self-existing, eternal and only Supreme Deity; creator and mother of the Cosmos; the Universal Cause; the Universal Mind; the source of all life and all positive creative forces of nature; the Fountain Head of all happiness and joy. . . ."

6. W. Holman Keith, "Obituary for a Neo-Pagan Pioneer," *Green Egg,* Vol. IV, No. 45 (February 3, 1972), 9. Also see Botkin's obituary in *The New York Times,* December 30, 1969, p. 33.

7. Keith, "Obituary."

8. Robert Graves, *Watch the North Wind Rise* (New York: Creative Age Press, 1949), p. 155.

9. Alvin Toffler uses this same idea in *Future Shock* (New York: Bantam, 1971), pp. 390–92. He suggests that the purpose of enclaves such as the Amish communities and preserved sites like Williamsburg, Virginia, is twofold: to provide a place where the rate of change is slower and "future shock" can be escaped, and to provide safety if a technological catastrophe occurs in the larger society.

10. Graves, *Watch the North Wind Rise,* p. 43.

11. Feraferian literature has also said that the name means "wilderness sacrament," "wild festival," and the union of Wilderness and Dream to yield a Life of Eternal Celebration. *Feraferia* (newspaper), Vol. 1, No. 1 (Autumn 1967), 1.

12. Robert S. Ellwood, Jr., *Religious and Spiritual Groups in Modern America* (Englewood Cliffs, NJ: Prentice-Hall, 1973), pp. 196–97.

13. *Earth Religion News,* Vol. 1, No. 5, 49.

14. William Morris, *News from Nowhere, or An Epoch of Rest* (New York: Monthly Review Press, 1966), first published in Great Britain in 1890; Robert Graves, see note 8; William Hudson, *A Crystal Age* (New York: Dutton, 1906).

15. Henry Bailey Stevens, *The Recovery of Culture* (New York: Harper & Brothers, 1953), p. 168. Originally published in 1949. Other quotations are on p. 86; the story of Cain and Abel is on pp. 66–67 and 176; the story of Adam and Eve on pp. 82–87.

16. Ibid., pp. 206–8.

17. Frederick C. Adams, "Hesperian Life and the Maiden Way." This paper was originally issued in 1957 and revised in 1970. It is privately published and is available through Feraferia (see Resources). Quotations taken from pp. 1–7.

18. On jargon, see, for example, *Earth Religion News*, Vol. 3, issues 1, 2, 3 combined, 186: "The Individual Personal: Psycho-Analytic encounter; the individuation process and all inner fantasy production," etc.

19. Frederick Adams, "Feraferia for Beginners," *Earth Religion News*, Vol. 1, No. 5 (August Eve 1974), 51.

20. Frederick Adams, "The Korê," privately published by Feraferia in 1969. Also appears in Robert Ellwood, "Notes on a Neopagan Religious Group," in *History of Religions*, Vol. XI, No. 1 (Chicago: University of Chicago Press, August 1971), 134.

21. Adams, "Hersperian Life," pp. 11, 13–16.

22. Frederick Adams, poem published in *The Pagan*, No. 1 (November 1, 1970), 7. *The Pagan* had two issues and was published out of St. Louis, Missouri. Adams's poem originally appeared in a privately published article of Feraferia: "Topocosmic Mandala of the Sacred Land Sky Love Year" (1969).

23. From Feraferia's statement, which appears on the inside cover of its journal, *Korythalia*.

24. *Feraferia* (newspaper), Vol. 1, No. 1 (Autumn 1967), 1.

25. Frederick Adams, "The Henge: Land Sky Love Temple," *Earth Religion News*, Vol. 3, Issues 1, 2, 3, combined (1976), 182.

26. Adams, "Feraferia for Beginners," p. 51.

27. Ellwood, "Notes on a Neopagan Religious Group in America," 137.

28. Ellwood, *Religious and Spiritual Groups in Modern America*, p. 198.

29. *Iris*, Vol. 3, No. 1 (August 18, 1974), 1, 3.

30. "The Am'n," *Iris*, Vol. 3, No. 3 (February 1975), 1–2.

31. Ibid., p. 2.

32. For another description of this myth, see Robert Graves, *The Greek Myths* (Baltimore: Penguin, 1955), I, p. 27.

33. The stories of Jim Kemble, Don Harrison, and Harold Moss appeared in the Church of the Eternal Source's members' newsletter, No. 2 (September 5, 1973), 7–12. CES address: P.O. Box 7091, Burbank, CA.

34. Harold Moss, taped letter, spring 1977.

35. *Green Egg*, Vol. VI, No. 55 (June 21, 1973), 17.

36. Introductory leaflet from the Church of the Eternal Source.

37. Letter from Harold Moss to Reverend Gordon Melton, September 18, 1972.

38. "Our Modern Practice of the Ancient Egyptian Religion," a CES pamphlet published in 1974, p. 4.

39. Harold Moss, taped letter, spring 1977.

40. "Modern Practice of Ancient Egyptian Religion," p. 3.

41. Henri Frankfort, *Ancient Egyptian Religion* (New York: Columbia University Press, 1948), p. 4. The other quotation is on p. 13. A good summary of Frankfort appears in the CES pamphlet, "Modern Practice of Ancient Egyptian Religion," p. 8.

42. "Modern Practice of Ancient Egyptian Religion," pp. 2–5.

43. Moss, taped letter, spring 1977.

44. The first paragraph of this quotation comes from a letter by Harold Moss published in *Green Egg*, Vol. V, No. 52 (February 1973), Forum section, 4–7. The second paragraph comes from *Khepera*, No. 1, in *Green Egg*, Vol. VI, No. 56 (August 1, 1973), 24.

45. From a pamphlet, "What Is Asatru," published by the Asatru Free Assembly, p. 3.

46. "Ancestry Is Better Than Universalism," *The Runestone*, No. 50 (Winter 1984), 11.

47. *The Odinist*, No. 92, p. 2. There are other more extreme Odinist Pagan groups. Here are some quotes from a publication called *Quarterstaff*, edited by a Canadian, Jack Leavy. "If we didn't have to worry about Judeo-Christianity and watch our Race being mongrelized, our Celtic culture dissipated, we would still have to contend with the Masons and those who seek One World Government"; "When North American 'Indians' start making incredible land claims, demands for compensation and the right to self-government—including their own courts—we say, 'Wait just a minute!' It's not bad enough that a 'Jew' is credited with (re)discovering America, our People have been on this Continent for at least as long as any of the indigenous Aboriginals. And, an integral body of Celts should be able to make the same demands for recognition etc., from the U.S. and Canadian governments." These quotes came from an analysis of *Quarterstaff* in *The Magickal Unicorn Messenger*, Vol. 5, Issue 2.

48. "Joy Is Better Than Guilt," *The Runestone*, No. 51 (Spring 1985), 11.

49. "The Jesus Flag," *The Runestone*, No. 50 (Winter 1984), 9.

50. "How to Live," *The Runestone*, No. 50 (Winter 1984), 1.

51. Waggoner suggests that there are better categories than *folkish, tribalist,* and *universalist,* and suggests an article written by Jarnsaxa Thorskona, "Scale of Racial and Cultural Tolerances in Asatrú," available on the Web at http://marklander.ravenbanner.com/jarnsaxa%20scale.html. Another interesting article on "Folkish Universalism" is by Dave Haxton: http://www.haxton.org/weblog/Asatru/folkishUniversalism.html.

52. Diana Paxson, "The Return of the Völva: Recovering the Practice of Seidh," originally published in *Mountain Thunder,* Summer, 1993, but now available on the Web at: www.seidh.org, Diana Paxson's site. Also see Jenny Blain, "On the knife-edge: Seidr-working and the Anthropologist," available on the Web at www.geocities.com/SoHo/Lofts/2171/seidhr_account.html.

53. Devyn Gillette and Lewis Stead, "The Pentagram and the Hammer," written in 1994, and available on the Web at: www.webcom.com/~lstead/wicatru.html.

Chapter 10: A RELIGION FROM THE FUTURE—THE CHURCH OF ALL WORLDS

1. Mircea Eliade, "The Occult and the Modern World," a paper delivered at the 21st Annual Freud Memorial Lecture, held in Philadelphia on May 24, 1974. Published in *Occultism, Witchcraft and Cultural Fashions* (Chicago: University of Chicago Press, 1976), p. 62.

2. Hans Holzer, *The Witchcraft Report* (New York: Ace Books, 1973), p. 179. See also Holzer, *The New Pagans* (New York: Doubleday & Co., 1972), p. 120, and *The Directory of the Occult* (Chicago: Henry Regnery Co., 1974), p. 176. Many of the people quoted in this book do not consider Hans Holzer to be friendly to Neo-Paganism. Holzer might have been able to understand CAW a bit better if he had realized that almost all

Neo-Pagan groups are based on the creative and artistic efforts of their members rather than on "ancient tradition." The traditions are fragments; creativity is the glue; and CAW has been as inventive as anyone else.

3. See Ursula K. Le Guin, *The Left Hand of Darkness* (New York: Walker and Co., 1969); *The Dispossessed* (New York: Harper & Row, 1974); *A Wizard of Earthsea* (Berkeley: Parnassus Press, 1968); *Planet of Exile* (New York: Ace Books, 1966); Joanna Russ, *The Female Man* (New York: Bantam, 1975); *We Who Are About To . . .* (New York: Dell, 1975); *The Two of Them* (New York: Berkley Publishing Corp., 1978); Vonda McIntyre, *Dreamsnake* (Boston: Houghton Mifflin Co., 1978). Of Le Guin, Robert Scholes, in *Structural Fabulation* (Notre Dame, IN: University of Notre Dame Press, 1975), p. 82, writes that her perspective

is broader than the Christian perspective—because finally it takes the world more seriously than the Judeo-Christian tradition has ever allowed it to be taken.

What *Earthsea* represents, through its world of islands and waterways, is the universe as a dynamic, balanced system, not subject to the capricious miracles of any deity, but only to the natural laws of its own working, which include a role for magic and powers other than human, but only as aspects of the great Balance or Equilibrium, which is the order of the cosmos. . . . Ursula Le Guin works not with a theology but with an ecology, a cosmology, a reverence for the universe as a self-regulating structure . . . it is a deeper view, closer to the great pre-Christian mythologies of this world and also closer to what three centuries of science have been able to discover about the nature of the universe.

4. Eliade, "The Occult and the Modern World," pp. 67–68.
5. Scholes, *Structural Fabulation,* p. 75, 38.
6. Tom Williams, "Science-Fiction/Fantasy: A Contemporary Mythology," *Green Egg,* Vol. VIII, No. 69 (March 21, 1975), 5–6.
7. This statement was attributed to Hans Holzer by Carroll Runyon, Jr., head of the OTA, in a letter to Tim and Julie Zell on April 26, 1972. This letter appeared in Zell's "Open Communiqué" to all members of the Council of Themis, May 27, 1972.
8. Jerome Tuccille, *It Usually Begins with Ayn Rand* (New York: Stein and Day, 1972), pp. 14–17.
9. See ibid., pp. 32, 175; also, National Public Radio broadcast of April 18, 1976, as reported in *Akwesasne Notes* (Early Summer 1976), p. 44. Rand's attitudes toward technology and environment are also pretty clearly stated in *Atlas Shrugged* (New York: New American Library, 1959).
10. Lance Christie, "The Origin of Atl," *Atlan Logbook,* p. 23.
11. Abraham H. Maslow, *Motivation and Personality,* 2nd ed. (New York: Harper & Row, 1970), pp. 149–80. Quotation appears on p. 166. It also appears as a selection in the *Atlan Logbook,* p. 64.
12. Christie, "Origin of Atl."
13. Ibid., pp. 23–24.
14. Robert A. Heinlein, *Stranger in a Strange Land* (New York: G. P. Putnam's Sons, 1961; Avon Books, 1962).
15. Robert S. Ellwood, Jr., *Religious and Spiritual Groups in Modern America* (Englewood Cliffs, NJ: Prentice-Hall, 1973), pp. 200–4.

16. All quotes from *Atlan Logbook,* pp. 1, 14, 17–18 and 23–24.

17. *Atlan Annals,* Vol. 1, No. 1, 5.

18. Political statements of Dagny, Prometheus, Thor, and Adonai in *Atlan Logbook,* individual statements section.

19. Lance Christie, *Atlan Annals,* Vol. IV, No. 2, 6.

20. Ibid., Vol. IV, No. 1, 4, 7. Also, Vol. III, No. 10, 23.

21. First statement, Tim Zell, "Ideals and Principles of Atl," *Atlan Logbook,* p. 11; also appears in *Green Egg,* Vol. 1, No. 2 (March 1968). Second statement is CAW's statement of purpose, which appeared in every issue of the *Green Egg.*

22. *Green Egg,* Vol. 1, No. 1 (March 20, 1968). Zell also described himself as a Pagan in the *Atlan Logbook,* saying, "I am a pagan, considering Atl to be in the vanguard of the new pagan resurgence" (individual statements section).

23. Young Omar, "Kerista's Erotic Ethic and Etcs." (September 4, 1966), reprinted in *Atlan Logbook,* pp. 40–42. Originally published by Kerista Press, Box 34708, Los Angeles, CA 90034. Actually, Young Omar paraphrases Goldberg. Goldberg's quote goes as follows: "What was forbidden in ordinary life was allowed in the life of religion. Bonds were broken and taboos raised, once people entered into the temple of the gods." B. Z. Goldberg, *The Sacred Fire* (New York: Horace Liveright, 1930), pp. 36–37.

24. Young Omar, "Kerista's Erotic Ethic."

25. See address by Doreen Valiente, *Pentagram,* No. 2 (November 1964), 5.

26. *Green Egg,* Vol. III, No. 20 (December 29, 1969), 1.

27. *Green Egg,* Vol. III, No. 23 (March 18, 1970), 1. The phrase "the Green Hills of Earth" comes from a story by C. L. Moore (Mrs. Henry Kuttner), and Heinlein used it with her permission in *The Green Hills of Earth* (Chicago: Shasta, 1951).

28. Tim Zell, "Theagenesis: The Birth of the Goddess," *Green Egg,* Vol. IV, No. 40 (July 1, 1971), 7–10. Also published in *The Witch's Broomstick,* Vol. 1, No. 1 (Candlemas 1972), 19–25. Excerpts appeared in Leo Martello, *Witchcraft: The Old Religion* (Secaucus, NJ: University Books, 1973), pp. 102–7. Martello also refers to it in *Black Magic, Satanism and Voodoo* (New York: HC Publishers, 1973), pp. 135.

29. Tim Zell, "The Gods of Nature, the Nature of Gods (Part I)," *Green Egg,* Vol. VII, No. 66 (November 1, 1974), 12.

30. Zell, "Theagenesis," p. 10.

31. Zell, "The Gods of Nature," p. 14.

32. Tim Zell, "Biotheology: The Neo-Pagan Mission," *Green Egg,* Vol. IV, No. 41 (August 4, 1971), pp. 7–8.

33. Lance Christie, *Green Egg,* Vol. IV, No. 42 (September 27, 1971), Forum section, 9.

34. *Newsweek,* March 10, 1975, p. 49.

35. From a CAW tract, "Neo-Paganism and the Church of All Worlds," undated.

36. From a CAW tract, "An Old Religion for a New Age, Neo-Paganism," undated.

37. Lewis Shieber, "The CAW and Tribalism," *Green Egg,* Vol. VIII, No. 75 (December 21, 1975), 5–6.

38. Council of Themis statement on the "Common Themes of Neo-Pagan Religious Orientation," *Green Egg,* Vol. IV, No. 43 (December 3, 1971), 11.

39. Tom Williams, "Science: A Mutable Metaphor," *Green Egg,* Vol. VIII, No. 73 (September 21, 1975), 9.

40. Lance Christie, *Green Egg,* Vol. VI, No. 58 (November 1, 1973), 50.

41. Ellwood, *Religious Groups in Modern America,* p. 203.

42. Tim Zell, "Neo-Paganism and the Church of All Worlds: Some Questions and Answers," a CAW tract, undated.

43. *Springfield* (Oregon) *News* (October 27, 1976), p. 3A. See also *Eugene Register-Guard* (October 30, 1976), p. 3B.

Chapter 11: RELIGIONS OF PARADOX AND PLAY

1. "Trapped!" (a tract from the First Arachnid Church), *Green Egg,* Vol. VII, No. 66 (November 1, 1974), 21–22.

2. Robert Shea and Robert Anton Wilson, *Illuminatus:* Part I *(The Eye in the Pyramid);* Part II *(The Golden Apple);* Part III *(Leviathan)* (New York: Dell, 1975).

3. Harvey Cox, *The Feast of Fools* (Cambridge: Harvard University Press, 1969); "Religion in the Age of Aquarius: A Conversation with Harvey Cox and T. George Harris," *Psychology Today,* Vol. 3, No. 11 (April 1970), 63.

4. Johan Huizinga, *Homo Ludens* (Boston: Beacon Press, 1968), 12. Other quotations on pp. 1, 3, 4, and 5.

5. *The Druid Chronicles (evolved),* ed. Isaac Bonewits (Berkeley: Berkeley Drunemeton Press, 1976), Introduction, p. 1.

6. Ibid., "The Book of the Law," p. 4.

7. Ibid., "Later Chronicles—Chapter the Tenth," p. 12.

8. "Part V: The Great Druish Books, *Druid Chronicles."*

9. "The First Epistle of Isaac," 2:12, *Druid Chronicles (evolved).*

10. Isaac Bonewits, "What & Why Is Reformed Druidism in the 1970's," *Green Egg,* Vol. VII, No. 75 (December 21, 1975), 15–17.

11. *The Druids' Progress,* No. 1, p. 10.

12. These two quotations come from the inside cover of the third and fourth editions of *Principia Discordia, or How I Found Goddess and What I Did to Her When I Found Her,* privately published.

13. Robert Anton Wilson, "All Hail the Goddess Eris," *Gnostica,* Vol. 3, No. 12 (July 21, 1974), 19.

14. *Principia Discordia,* 4th ed., pp. 7–10.

15. "An Interview with Robert Anton Wilson," by Neal Wilgus, *Science Fiction Review,* Vol. 5, No. 2 (May 1976), 32.

16. Thomas J. Walsh, *Beyond the Barrier,* Issue 1, p. 1. Published irregularly out of Irvington, New Jersey. A previous publication was *Patterns of Form,* published by the Morgan Delt cabal.

17. "Erisianism: A Neo-Pagan Path," *Green Egg,* Vol. IX, No. 78 (May 1, 1976), 10.

18. *Principia Discordia,* 4th ed., pp. 42, 63.

19. Robert Anton Wilson, "All Hail the Goddess Eris!" *Gnostica,* Vol. 4, No. 9 (July 1975), 27.

Chapter 12: RADICAL FAERIES AND THE GROWTH OF MEN'S SPIRITUALITY

1. "A Light in the Darkness," *Brothers of the Earth Newsletter,* No. 3 (Yule 1983), 7–9.

2. See "What Men Really Want," an interview with Robert Bly by Keith Thompson, *New*

Age (May 1982). See also *Brothers of the Earth Newsletter,* Cycle 2, Issue 5 (Summer Solstice 1984), 9–19.

3. Shepard Bliss, "Bound for Glory," *UTNE Reader,* No. 15 (April–May 1986).

4. *RFD,* No. 22 (Winter Solstice 1979), 59.

5. *RFD,* No. 22, p. 61.

6. *RFD,* No. 22, p. 50.

7. *RFD,* No. 22, p. 29.

8. *RFD,* No. 22, p. 38.

9. *RFD,* No. 22, pp. 62–63.

10. Don Kilhefner, "A Sprinkling of Radical Faerie Dust," *RFD,* No. 24 (Summer 1980), 25–27.

11. Stanley Johnson, "On the Banks of the River Time Looking Inland," *RFD,* No. 43 (Summer 1985), 63.

12. J. Michael Clark, "The Native American Berdache," *RFD,* No. 40 (Fall 1984), 22–30.

13. Mitch Walker and Friends, *Visionary Love: A Spirit Book of Gay Mythology and Trans-Mutational Faerie* (San Francisco: Treeroots Press, 1980).

14. Will Roscoe, "A Call for Dialogue," *RFD,* No. 34 (Spring 1983), 14.

15. *Pagan Spirit Journal,* No. 2 (1983), 41.

Chapter 13: LIVING ON THE EARTH

1. *Green Egg,* Vol. VIII, No. 76 (February 2, 1976), 32–36.

2. Stanley Diamond, *In Search of the Primitive* (New Brunswick, NJ: Transaction, 1974), pp. xv, 10, 122, 129.

3. E. R. Dodds, *Pagan and Christian in an Age of Anxiety* (New York: W. W. Norton, 1970), p. 29.

4. Interview with Rarihokwats, conducted by Natasha A. Friar, July 30, 1975.

5. Ibid.

6. *Akwesasne Notes,* Vol. IX, No. 3 (Summer 1977), 3. (c/o Mohawk Nation, via Rooseveltown, NY 13683.)

7. Fiftieth Anniversary Editorial, *Akwesasne Notes,* Vol. VIII, No. 2 (Early Summer 1976), 4.

8. José Barreiro, "The Damage Close to Us," *Akwesasne Notes,* Vol. IX, No. 3 (Summer 1977), 8.

9. Jonny Lerner, "A Patch of Poison Cabbage," *Akwesasne Notes,* Vol. IX, No. 3 (Summer 1977), 11.

10. Interview with Rarihokwats conducted by Friar. In 1977, Rarihokwats left *Akwesasne Notes* after a complicated political dispute. He subsequently worked with Four Arrows: A Communications Group of Native People of the Americas, PO Box 496, Tesque, NM 87574.

11. Dr. Jack D. Forbes, "Americanism Is the Answer," *Akwesasne Notes,* Vol. VI, No. 1 (Early Spring 1974), 37.

12. Gayle High Pine, "The Non-progressive Great Spirit," *Akwesasne Notes,* Vol. V, No. 6 (Early Winter 1973), 38.

13. See Sotsisowah, "The Sovereignty Which Is Sought Can be Real," *Akwesasne Notes,* Vol. VII, No. 4 (Early Autumn 1975), pp. 34–35.

14. Susan Roberts, *Witches, U.S.A.* (New York: Dell, 1971), pp. 5. 7, 17, 18.
15. See *The New York Times,* September 3, 1975, p. 1; September 11, 1975, p. 40; September 7, 1975, IV, p. 7.
16. In particular, Hans Holzer, *The Witchcraft Report* (New York: Ace Books, 1973), pp. 182–88.
17. Excerpts from these letters appeared in an open communiqué to all members of the Council of Themis from CAW, May 27, 1972.
18. Penny Novack, "Pagan Way—Where Now?" *Earth Religion News,* Vol. I, No. 4 (1974), 35–36.
19. "Why the Indians Weren't Ecologists," *Akwesasne Notes,* Vol. III, No. 9 (December 1971); also reprinted in *Green Egg,* Vol. V, No. 49 (August 11, 1972), 19.
20. Carol Maddox, "The Neo-Pagan Alternative," *Green Egg,* Vol. VIII, No. 70 (May 1, 1975), 17. Also in *Green Egg,* Vol. IV, No. 39.
21. Murray Bookchin, *Our Synthetic Environment* (rev. ed.) (New York: Harper & Row, 1974), pp. xv, lxxii, 242. Originally published in 1962.
22. Ernest Callenbach, *Ecotopia* (Berkeley: Banyan Tree Books, 1975).
23. Regina Smith Oboler, "Nature Religion as a Cultural System: Sources of Environmental Rhetoric in a contemporary Pagan Community," *The Pomegranate* 6:1 (May 2004), pp. 86–106.
24. Judy Harrow, "If You Love Her, Why Not Serve Her? Nature Spirituality, Environmental Service and Pagan Religion," in *Paganism and Ecology* (Lanham, MD: AltaMira Press, 2007).
25. *Red Garters,* April 1985, p. 4.
26. *Congressional Record—Senate,* September 26, 1985, p. S12174.
27. Chas Clifton, *Witchcraft Today: Witchcraft and Shamanism* (St. Paul, MN: Llewellyn, 1994).
28. Ibid., p. 3.
29. *Circle Network News,* Winter 1984.
30. *Georgian Newsletter,* August 1985, p. 28.
31. William F. Schultz, "What the Women and Religion Resolutions Mean to Me," a paper issued February 1985.
32. *Pagan Spirit Journal #1* (Madison, WI: Circle Publications, 1982).
33. Ibid., p. 8.
34. Ibid., p. 33.
35. Ibid., p. 32. *Circle Network News,* Vol. 6, No. 4 (Winter 1984).
36. *Pagan Spirit Journal #2* (Madison, WI: Circle Publications, 1983), p. 54.
37. Ibid., p. 55.

Epilogue

1. Mircea Eliade, "The Occult and the Modern World," in *Occultism, Witchcraft and Cultural Fashions* (Chicago: University of Chicago Press, 1976), p. 64.
2. *The Odes of Pindar,* trans. Sir John Sandys (Cambridge: Harvard University Press, 1968), Fragment 137, pp. 592–95.
3. George Mylonas, *Eleusis and the Elusinean Mysteries* (Princeton: Princeton University Press, 1961), p. 281.

4. Karl Kerényi, *Eleusis*, trans. Ralph Manheim (New York: Bollingen Foundation, 1967), pp. 105–74.

5. Statement for beginning a coven by Lyr ab Govannon, spring 1976.

6. Aidan Kelly, "Palingenesia," *Gnostica*, Vol. 4, No. 9 (July 1975), 40. In *Nemeton*, Vol. 1, No. 1 (Samhain 1972), 19, Aidan wrote that one can define the "essence of the Craft as worship of the Goddess."

7. Aidan Kelly, "Why a Craft Ritual Works," *Gnostica*, Vol. 4, No. 7 (May 1975), 32. Aidan has said that he was really paraphrasing Kerényi, *Eleusis*, pp. 24–25.

8. Penny Novack and Michael Novack, *The New Broom*, Vol. 1, No. 4, 25.

Appendix I: SCHOLARS, WRITERS, JOURNALISTS, AND THE OCCULT

1. *Principia Discordia, or How I Found Goddess and What I Did To Her When I Found Her*, 4th ed., p. 40.

2. Marcello Truzzi, "Definition and Dimensions of the Occult: Toward a Sociological Perspective," in *On The Margin of the Visible: Sociology, the Esoteric, and the Occult*, ed. Edward A. Tiryakian (New York: John Wiley & Sons, 1974), p. 252. Originally published in *Journal of Popular Culture*, Vol. V, No. 3 (Winter 1971), 635/7–646/18.

3. Egon Larsen, *Strange Sects and Cults* (London: Arthur Barker, 1971), p. 2.

4. Richard Cavendish, *The Black Arts* (New York: Capricorn Books, 1967), p. 3.

5. J. Gordon Melton, *A Dictionary of Religious Bodies in the United States* (New York: Garland, 1967), p. 267. "Manipulation and a manipulative world view is of the essence of magical existence."

6. Susan Roberts, *Witches, U.S.A.* (New York: Dell, 1971), pp. 17–24.

7. Edward A. Tiryakian, "Toward the Sociology of Esoteric Culture," *American Journal of Sociology*, No. 78 (November 1972), 491–512. Also in *On the Margin of the Visible*, pp. 257–80. "Occult" is defined on p. 265.

8. Andrew M. Greeley and William C. McCready, "Some Notes on the Sociological Study of Mysticism," in *On the Margin of the Visible*, p. 304.

9. Raymond Prince and Charles Savage, "Mystical States and the Concept of Regression," *Psychedelic Review*, No. 8 (1966), 59–75.

10. Raymond Prince, "Cocoon Work: An Interpretation of the Concern of Contemporary Youth with the Mystical," in *Religious Movements in Contemporary America*, ed. Irving Zaretsky and Mark Leone (Princeton: Princeton University Press, 1974), pp. 255–71.

11. A. L. Kroeber, "Psychosis or Social Sanction" (1940), in *The Nature of Culture* (Chicago: University of Chicago Press, 1952), pp. 309–10.

12. E. Fuller Torrey, "Spiritualists and Shamans as Psychotherapists: An Account of Original Anthropological Sin," in *Religious Movements in Contemporary America*, pp. 330–37. Quotations on p. 331.

13. Mircea Eliade, *Myths, Dreams, and Mysteries* (New York: Harper & Row, 1967), p. 71.

14. Greeley and McCready, "Notes on Study of Mysticism," p. 310.

15. Marvin Harris, *Cows, Pigs, Wars and Witches* (New York: Vintage, 1975), pp. 251, 255, 257–58, 263.

16. Edwin Schur, *The Awareness Trap: Self-Absorption Instead of Social Change* (New York: Quadrangle, 1976).

17. Christopher Lasch, "The Narcissist Society," *The New York Review of Books* Vol. XXIII,

No. 15 (September 30, 1976), 5, 8, 12; also, "The Narcissistic Personality of Our Time," *Partisan Review,* Vol. XLIV, No. 1 (1977), 9–19.

18. Tiryakian, "Sociology of Esoteric Culture," p. 271.

19. Mircea Eliade, "The Occult and the Modern World," in *Occultism, Witchcraft, and Cultural Fashions* (Chicago: University of Chicago Press, 1976), pp. 52–53.

20. Nathan Adler, "Ritual, Release, and Orientation: Maintenance of the Self in the Antinomian Personality," in *Religious Movements in Contemporary America,* p. 285.

21. Edward A. Tiryakian, "Preliminary Considerations," in *On the Margin of the Visible,* p. 3.

22. Theodore Roszak, ed., *Sources* (New York: Harper & Row, 1972), p. 419.

23. Harriet Whitehead, "Reasonably Fantastic: Some Perspectives on Scientology, Science Fiction, and Occultism," in *Religious Movements in Contemporary America,* pp. 547–87.

24. Louis Pauwels and Jacques Bergier, *The Morning of the Magicians,* trans. Rollo Myers (New York: Avon, 1968). Originally published in France in 1960 as *Le Matins des Magiciens* by Éditions Gallimard.

25. Mircea Eliade, "Cultural Fashions and History of Religions," in *Occultism, Witchcraft, and Cultural Fashions,* pp. 10, 13, 16.

26. Mircea Eliade, "The Occult and the Modern World," in *Occultism, Witchcraft, and Cultural Fashions,* pp. 52–53, 57–58, 64–65.

27. Edward J. Moody, "Magical Therapy: An Anthropological Investigation of Contemporary Satanism," in *Religious Movements in Contemporary America,* pp. 380–82.

28. Edward J. Moody, "Urban Witches," in *On the Margin of the Visible,* p. 233.

29. Marcello Truzzi, "The Occult Revival as Popular Culture: Some Random Observations on the Old and Nouveau Witch," *Sociological Quarterly,* No. 13 (Winter 1972), 29.

30. Marcello Truzzi, "Toward a Sociology of the Occult: Notes on Modern Witchcraft," in *Religious Movements in Contemporary America,* pp. 629, 635–36.

Bibliography

When I originally put together this bibliography, I described it as personal and eclectic, with no attempt to be complete. This is even more so today, given the explosion of publications on Wicca and Paganism. But it is a rough guide—particularly for a newcomer—to some of the better books on modern Neo-Paganism, Wicca, and Goddess spirituality. Many of the books footnoted in *Drawing Down the Moon* are not listed here. This list includes some of the standard works and a number of my personal favorites. It was put together with the notion that someone new to Earth-centered spirituality might like a guide to some of the choices available for further exploration.

Adair, Margo. *Working Inside Out: Tools for Change* (Berkeley, CA: Wingbow Press, 1984). A book that focuses on applied meditations, affirmations, and pathworking by an author who has been involved in political struggles for many years.

Anonymous. *A Book of Pagan Rituals.* (York Beach, ME: Samuel Weiser, 1978). Authors include Ed Fitch and Donna Cole-Schultz. Many of the Pagan Way rituals that provided entry points into Wicca are published here. A very good basic group of entry-level seasonal and passage ceremonies.

Apuleius, Lucius. *The Golden Ass.* Many different translations exist. Apuleius was an initiate of Isis, and the book was written in the second century C.E., so this is either the first Goddess novel or the oldest one still in print. The vision of Isis near the end of the book is poetic and inspired.

Bado-Fralick, Nikki. *Coming to the Edge of the Circle: A Wiccan Initiation Ritual* (New York: Oxford University Press, 2005). Perhaps the first book to look deeply at Wiccan ritual, and initiation in particular.

Bardon, Franz. *Initiation into Hermetics* (Wuppertal, Germany: Dieter Ruggeberg, 1971). A well known magical training system that many Wiccan and Pagan groups have used.

Barin, Anne, and Jules Cashford. *The Myth of the Goddess: Evolution of an Image* (London: Penguin, 1993). A scholarly work on the Goddess from ancient times up until Christianity.

Barrett, Ruth. *Women's Rites, Women's Mysteries: Creating Ritual in the Dianic Wiccan Tradition* (Bloomington: AuthorHouse, 2004). A primer for Dianics that comes out of Z Budapest's Dianic tradition.

Berger, Helen. *A Community of Witches: Contemporary Neo-Paganism and Witchcraft in the United States* (Columbia: University of South Carolina Press, 1999). A good study of modern Paganism. Most of the emphasis is on Wicca. The book examines the coven, conceptions of community, children, and sexuality, among other issues.

Blain, Jenny, Douglas Ezzy, and Graham Harvey. *Researching Paganisms* (Walnut Creek, CA: AltaMira Press, 2004). A very good and fascinating selection of papers in Pagan studies.

Bolen, Jean. *Goddesses in Everywoman, A New Psychology of Women* (San Francisco: Harper & Row, 1984). A Jungian therapist looks at the archetypal images of the Greek goddesses, including Athena, Hera, Hesia, Artemis, Demeter, and Persephone as a method of personal exploration and growth.

Bonewits, Isaac. *Bonewits's Essential Guide to Witchcraft and Wicca* (New York: Citadel Press, 2006). Like all of Bonewits's work, a down-to-earth guide, slightly irreverent at times, and very good.

————. *Real Magic* (Berkeley, CA: Creative Arts Book Company, 1979; New York: Samuel Weiser, 1989). A no-nonsense guide to magic and psychic reality by a feisty, opinionated practitioner.

Bracelin, J. L. *Gerald Gardner: Witch* (London: Octagon Press, 1960). This is the only biography of Gerald Gardner. Actually written by Idries Shah. Somewhat of an apology, and not great literature, but contains wonderful anecdotes about Gardner's life.

Bradley, Marion Zimmer. *The Mists of Avalon* (New York: Knopf, 1983). One of the only books with a Pagan theme to make *The New York Times* best-seller list. A powerful retelling of the Arthurian legend from a feminist and Pagan point of view.

Cameron, Anne. *Daughters of Copper Woman* (Vancouver, British Columbia: Press Gang Publishers, 1981). Matriarchal legends from the indigenous peoples of Vancouver Island, beautifully written.

Campanelli, Dan and Pauline. *Ancient Ways: Reclaiming Pagan Traditions* (St. Paul, MN: Llewellyn Publications, 1991).

————. *Circles, Groves, and Sanctuaries* (St. Paul, MN: Llewellyn Publications, 1992). The ways Pagans worship and the places where worship takes place.

Christ, Carol P. *Diving Deep and Surfacing: Woman Writers on Spiritual Quest* (Boston: Beacon Press, 1980). An excellent introduction to women's spirituality.

Christ, Carol P., and Judith Plaskow. *Womenspirit Rising, a Feminist Reader in Religion* (San Francisco: Harper & Row, 1979). An early but excellent sourcebook in feminist theology, including selections from Mary Daly, Merlin Stone, Starhawk, Rosemary Radford Ruether, and many others.

Clifton, Chas. S. *Witchcraft Today: The Modern Craft Movement* (St. Paul, MN: Llewellyn Publications, 1992). Clifton gives a brief history of Wicca and then a group of very experienced Wiccan practitioners provide articles on seasonal festivals, healing, men and women, sex magic, Witchcraft and the law, and more.

————. *Witchcraft Today: Modern Rites of Passage* (St. Paul, MN: Llewellyn Publications, 1993). This is book two of the series. It has articles by noted practitioners on rites of passage: handfastings, puberty rites, initiation, rites of dying, as well as sections on military Pagans, raising a Pagan child, and more.

————. *Witchcraft Today: Witchcraft and Shamanism* (St. Paul, MN: Llewellyn Publications, 1994). This is book three of the series. Articles explore the complex connection between shamanism and Paganism.

Crowley, Vivianne. *Wicca: The Old Religion in the New Age* (Wellingborough, UK: Aquarian Press, 1989). An English Wiccan and Jungian therapist talks about the theory of Wicca. Beautifully and poetically written.

————. *Phoenix from the Flame: Pagan Spirituality in the Western World* (London: Aquarian, 1994). A lovely treatise on modern Paganism as a pluralistic and joyous religion.

Cunningham, Scott. *Living Wicca* (St. Paul, MN: Llewellyn Publications, 1993).

————. *Wicca for the Solitary Practitioner* (St. Paul, MN: Llewellyn Publications, 1988). These are simple and quite lovely books for people encountering Wicca for the first time.

Downing, Christine. *The Goddess: Mythological Images of the Feminine* (New York: Crossroad Publishing Co., 1981). A Jungian therapist and professor of religious studies explores the relationship of the classical Greek goddesses to who we are and who we might become.

Eclipse. *The Moon in Hand: A Mystical Passage* (Portland, ME: Astarte Shell Press, 1991). The wheel of life through the elements and directions with poetry, stories, and visualizations.

Ehrenreich, Barbara, and Dierdre English. *Witches, Midwives and Nurses* (New York: Feminist Press, 1963). An early feminist classic. Although later scholarship has questioned some of the premises, it's a groundbreaking small booklet linking the persecution of women, the persecution of Witches, and the rise of the medical profession.

Eisler, Riane. *The Chalice and the Blade* (San Francisco: Harper & Row, 1988). A provocative, controversial feminist reinterpretation of history.

Eliade, Mircea. *Occultism, Witchcraft and Cultural Fashions* (Chicago: University of Chicago Press, 1976). Intelligent and perceptive essays on occultism and Witchcraft. Check out his other writings as well, including his *History of Religious Ideas, Volumes I, II, III* (Chicago: University of Chicago Press, 1982).

————. *Shamanism: Archaic Techniques of Ecstasy* (London: Penguin Arkana, 1989). A monumental study originally published in 1964.

Eller, Cynthia. *Living in the Lap of the Goddess: New Feminist Spiritual Movements* (Boston: Beacon Press, 1995). A very interesting survey of feminist spirituality.

Evans, Arthur. *Witchcraft and the Gay Counterculture* (Boston: Fag Rag Books, 1978). A classic work that helped lead to the Radical Faery movement among gays. The book attempts to find, understand, and reclaim gay history and to uncover its links to pre-Christian spiritual traditions.

Farrar, Janet and Stewart. *The Witches Way* (London: Robert Hale, Ltd., 1984). Published in the United States as *A Witches Bible, Volumes I and II* (New York: Magickal Childe, 1985). The rituals used by Gardnerians and Alexandrians, as well as chapters on the history and practice of Wicca. The late Stewart Farrar was a former journalist who became an initiate of Alex and Maxine Sanders. He also wrote *What Witches Do,* one of the better early books on Wicca.

Fitch, Ed, and Janine Renee. *Magical Rites from the Crystal Well* (St. Paul, MN: Llewellyn Publications, 1984). For years, entry-level Pagans were doing many of these lovely rituals without knowing where they came from.

Forfreedom, Ann, and Julie Ann. *The Book of the Goddess* (1980). Available from Ann Forfreedom, 2441 Cordova Street, Oakland, CA 94602. Personal experiences of the Goddess, poetry, and illustrations.

Fortune, Dion. *The Sea Priestess* (New York: Samuel Weiser, 1978). Dion Fortune wrote many novels as well as books on practical occultism. Within the novels, Pagan initiatory themes are dominant; in her nonfiction, they are not. All the Pagan novels, including *Moon Magic* and *The Goat Foot God,* are interesting, but *The Sea Priestess* is very special, portraying the power of ritual and initiatory experience in a way that words are seldom able to express. None of these novels work *as novels,* but *The Sea Priestess* works despite its structural flaws. Students at the beginning of a Pagan spiritual search should find this novel particularly powerful.

Fox, Selena. *Circle Guide to Pagan Resources* (Madison, WI: Circle Publications, 2003). By the time you read this, there may be a later edition. The absolute best guide to groups, gatherings, journals, and Web resources. Goes state by state, country by country, and probably has three times the number of groups listed in this resource guide.

Foxwood, Orion. *The Faery Teachings* (Coral Springs, FL: Muse Press, 2003). Lessons from an Elder trained in Celtic, Alexandrian, and Faery traditions of the Craft.

Gardner, Gerald B. *Witchcraft Today* (New York: Citadel Press, 1955). One of the books that started the Wiccan revival. It was first published in 1954 after the repeal of the last Witchcraft Acts in Britain. There is some questionable scholarship here, but if it weren't for Gardner, *Drawing Down the Moon* would never have been written, and more importantly, the Wiccan revival might not have taken place.

————. *The Meaning of Witchcraft* (New York: Samuel Weiser, 1959). A much more comprehensive book than *Witchcraft Today,* and a further expansion of Gardner's views. Gardner also wrote an early Witchcraft novel, *High Magic's Aid.*

Gimbutas, Marija. *Goddesses and Gods of Old Europe, 6500–3500 B.C.* (Berkeley, CA: University of California Press, 1982).

————. *The Language of the Goddess: Unearthing the Hidden Symbolism of Western Civilization* (San Francisco: Harper & Row, 1989).

————. *The Civilization of the Goddess: The World of Old Europe* (San Francisco: Harper & Row, 1991). Controversial, contested, and pioneering works by an archeologist who delved into the pre-patriarchal cultures of Old Europe.

Glass, Justice. *Witchcraft, the Sixth Sense* (North Hollywood, CA: Wilshire Book Company, 1970). When this book came out, it was one of the only good books on the modern Craft. This is one of the earliest guides to Wicca, and still a sensible, sensitive, well-written introduction to the Craft.

Goldenberg, Naomi. *Changing of the Gods: Feminism and the End of Traditional Religions* (Boston: Beacon Press, 1979). A study of the rise of women's spirituality and the problems patriarchal religions have failed to address.

Goodrich, Norma Lorre. *Priestesses* (New York: HarperCollins, 1989). A study of priestesses from the Hittites through the Roman Empire.

Graves, Robert. *The White Goddess* (New York: Farrar, Straus & Giroux, 1966). This is a great work of poetic prose often confused for scholarship. A massive, mythic framework for the Great Goddess in hope of her re-emergence. An important book in the history of the revival of Wicca and Goddess spirituality.

Griffin, Susan. *Woman and Nature: The Roaring Inside Her* (New York: Harper & Row, 1978). A deep, dark, and powerful work that argues, among other things, that there is a connection between the "age of enlightenment" and the persecution of Witches.

Guiley, Rosemary Ellen. *The Encyclopedia of Witches and Witchcraft* (New York: Facts on File, 1989).

————. *The Encyclopedia of Witches and Witchcraft* (New York: Facts on File, 2nd Ed., 1999). Many of the leaders of the Wiccan and Pagan revival are in this encyclopedia. Fun to peruse.

Harner, Michael. *The Way of the Shaman* (San Francisco: HarperCollins, 1982). Harner writes about and promotes "core shamanism," a way of using shamanic techniques that can be applied to any group and culture.

Harrow, Judy. *Spiritual Mentoring* (Toronto: ECW Press, 2002). An excellent book on mentoring and pastoral counseling from a Pagan and Wiccan point of view.

————. *Devoted to You: Honoring Deity in Wiccan Practice* (New York: Citidel Press, 2003). Insights from working with various deities.

Hopman, Ellen Evert, and Lawrence Bond. *People of the Earth* (Rochester, VT: Destiny Books, 1996). A great supplement to *Drawing Down the Moon*. Contains long interviews with Pagans and Wiccans from all across the country and Canada.

Hutton, Ronald. *The Triumph of the Moon: A History of Modern Pagan Witchcraft* (Oxford: Oxford University Press, 1999). This is an utterly brilliant book written by an English historian.

James, William. *The Varieties of Religious Experience* (London: Collins, 1982, reprinted from 1902). The classic treatise on religious experience, still worth reading one hundred years later.

Jong, Erica. *Fanny* (New York: New American Library, 1980). There have been very few best-sellers that feature a priestess of the Goddess or a Witch from a Wiccan perspective. This is one of the few. Fanny is a feisty, bawdy character.

Kelly, Aidan. *Crafting the Art of Magic* (St. Paul, MN: Llewellyn, 1991). Some of Kelly's work on Gerald Gardner. Kelly was the first to note that Gardner's manuscript "Ye Bok of ye Art Magical" was the earliest version of the Gardnerian Book of Shadows.

Lamond, Frederick. *Religion without Beliefs: Essays in Pantheist Theology, Comparative Religion and Ethics* (London: Janus, 1997). A fascinating book by a former member of Gardner's coven on Wicca as a practical religion without dogma, based on direct personal experience.

Luhrman, T. M. *Persuasions of the Witch's Craft* (Cambridge, MA: Harvard University Press, 1989). A fascinating survey of Witches and magical groups in England. This was Luhrman's doctoral thesis; she might have been more forthcoming if she didn't have to play academic politics, but she was more a participant than she lets on.

Magliocco, Sabina. *Witching Culture: Folklore and Neo-Paganism in America* (Philadelphia: University of Pennsylvania Press, 2004). A truly excellent study of Wicca and Paganism and their relationship to folklore and anthropology.

Mariechild, Diane. *Mother Wit: A Feminist Guide to Psychic Development* (Trumansburg, NY: The Crossing Press, 1981). One of the early feminist guides to psychic work; the exercises and affirmations are done with a poetic sensibility and great sensitivity.

Markale, Jean. *Women of the Celts* (London: Gordon Cremonesi, 1975). A fascinating study of women in Celtic society.

Melton, J. Gordon. *Encyclopedia of American Religions*, 2nd ed. (Detroit: Gale Research, 1987).

————. *Magic, Witchcraft, and Paganism in America: A Bibliography* (New York: Garland Publishing, 1982). Melton is important as one of the first outsiders to study Paganism and Wicca respectfully.

Merchant, Carolyn. *The Death of Nature: Women, Ecology and the Scientific Revolution* (San Francisco: Harper & Row, 1980). A more scholarly and less poetic exploration of some of the same issues explored by Susan Griffin in *Woman and Nature*.

Miller, David. *The New Polytheism, Rebirth of the Gods and Goddesses* (New York: Harper & Row, 1974). In this early and groundbreaking book, Miller used the Greek gods and goddesses as archetypal images to discover a new world of multiple values. While his reliance on classical Greek imagery is limiting, his political and philosophical insights on the relationship of polytheism to politics and society is illuminating and liberating.

Murray, Margaret A. *The Witch-Cult in Western Europe* (London: Oxford University Press, 1962). Much of her scholarship is now considered questionable. Other parts are valuable, including much of the history of folk traditions and the continuation of Pagan customs. Her books, like those of Gardner, are important because they provided a springboard for the Wiccan revival.

———. *My First Hundred Years* (London: William Kimber, 1963). She did live to be one hundred, and for all the controversy surrounding her scholarship, was an extraordinary woman.

Patai, Raphael. *The Hebrew Goddess* (Philadelphia: Ktav Publications, 1967). Patai asserts that the Hebrews continued to worship the Canaanite goddesses of old. Patai looks at the place of the Shekinah, of Lilith, and explores the battles between patriarchal and matriarchal forces within Jewish history and tradition.

Piggott, Stuart. *The Druids* (New York: Thames and Hudson, 1986). Although there is more recent scholarship, this is a classic study of the Druids that separates fact from fiction.

Pike, Sarah M. *Earthly Bodies, Magical Selves: Contemporary Pagans and the Search for Community* (Berkeley: University of California Press, 2001). A fascinating study of the Pagan festival movement.

———. *New Age and Neopagan Religions in America* (Columbia Contemporary American Religion Series) (New York: Columbia University Press, 2004). A complicated study that tries to cover both New Age and Neo-Pagan religions and place them in historical context.

Rabinovitch, Shelly, and James Lewis. *The Encyclopedia of Modern Witchcraft and Neo-Paganism* (New York: Citadel Press, 2002). A really excellent encyclopedia that tackles most of the important issues and controversies surrounding Wicca and Paganism.

Robinson, James, ed. *The Nag Hammadi Library* (San Francisco: Harper & Row, 1977). The Gnostic writings unearthed at Nag Hammadi. An important series of documents, especially for women interested in finding sources for goddesses in religion. For example, The Thunder, Perfect Mind is one of the most amazing invocations of the feminine, and it dates back at least to the second century.

Ruether, Rosemary Radford. *Gaia & God: An Ecofeminist Theology of Earth Healing* (New York: HarperCollins, 1992). A Christian feminist theologian explores issues relating to women, nature, and patriarchy, and creates new theology.

Sallustius. *Concerning the Gods and the Universe*; edited with prolegomena and translation by Arthur Darby Nock (Cambridge: The University Press, 1926). A short, forty-seven-page work by a Neoplatanist and friend of the Pagan Emperor Julian that Gerald Gardner thought similar to the theology of the Craft.

Scarre, Geoffrey, and John Callow. *Witchcraft and Magic in Sixteenth- and Seventeenth-Century Europe,* 2nd ed. (Hampshire, UK: Palgrave, 2001). An excellent summation of recent scholarship on the issue of the Witchcraft persecutions in Europe.

Sjoo, Monica, and Barbara Mor. *The Great Cosmic Mother: Rediscovering the Religion of the Earth* (San Francisco: Harper & Row, 1987). The late Monica Sjoo was an artist, a writer, and an activist. Scholars may quibble, but it's a powerful, passionate, feminist exploration of the Goddess.

Sky, Michael. *Sexual Peace: Beyond the Dominator Virus* (Santa Fe, NM: Bear & Company, 1993). A basic and very eloquent primer on the problems of patriarchy, uniquely and personally told from a male point of view.

Spretnak, Charlene. *The Politics of Women's Spirituality* (Garden City, NY: Anchor Press, 1982). Almost six hundred pages of essays charting the rise of the Feminist Spirituality Movement. A sourcebook filled with scholarship and controversy. Also contains poetry, prose, and an excellent bibliography.

Starhawk. *Dreaming the Dark: Magic, Sex and Politics* (Boston: Beacon Press, 1982). This book joins the insights of the direct action non-violent peace movements with the insights of the Wicca coven. Starhawk draws on her own experiences with groups, doing rituals, protest actions, and spending time in jail, and provides a primer for working with groups. Parts of the appendix on the history of the "Burning Times" would be contested by most scholars today, but her analysis of the loss of the commons, which combines the insights of feminist writers with English labor historians like Christopher Hill, is fascinating.

———. *The Spiral Dance, A Rebirth of the Ancient Religion of the Great Goddess* (San Francisco: Harper & Row, 1979). This book came out the same day as *Drawing Down the Moon*. It remains one of the best books on modern Wicca, filled with theory, practice, rituals, and exercises. As with all of Starhawk's work, a beautiful interweaving of spiritual and social concerns.

———. *Truth and Dare* (San Francisco: Harper & Row, 1987). A psychology of liberation.

———. *The Fifth Sacred Thing* (New York: Bantam, 1993). The first of several novels. A future imperfect utopia struggles to maintain its integrity in the face of war, violence, and other struggles.

Stone, Merlin. *Ancient Mirrors of Womanhood, Volumes I, II* (New York: Sibylline Books, 1979). Another controversial feminist classic. A collection of Goddess legends from all over the world, with a feminist point of view, and arranged culture by culture. Includes a lot of source material.

Sulak, John, and V. Vale. *Modern Pagans: An Investigation of Contemporary Pagan Practices* (San Fransicso: RE/Search Publications, 2001). Interviews with modern Pagans, and others, including Oberon Zell, Starhawk, Matthew Fox, Patricia Monaghan, Diane di Prima, and me. A few interviews explore some of the edgier issues, including polyamory and sacred prostitutes.

Teish, Luisah. *Jambalaya, The Natural Woman's Book of Personal Charms and Practical Ritual* (San Francisco: Harper & Row, 1985). A book by a publicly avowed Voudoun priestess, which lays to rest various stereotypes and gives information on Yoruba goddesses and ritual workings.

Turner, Kay. *Beautiful Necessity: The Art and Meaning of Women's Altars* (London: Thames and Hudson, 1999). For many years I listed Kay Turner's wonderful journal, *Lady Unique Inclination of the Night*, and her special issue on altars in the resource guide. Now that issue has morphed into something larger—a beautiful book.

Valiente, Doreen. *An ABC of Witchcraft: Past and Present* (New York: St. Martin's Press, 1973).

———. *The Rebirth of Witchcraft* (London: Robert Hale, 1989).

———. *Witchcraft for Tomorrow* (Custer, WA: Phoenix Publishing, 1985). A priestess who worked with Gerald Gardner, was a good writer, and had loads of common sense. All her books are lucid and well written. Many of the rituals in the Gardnerian tradition of

Wicca bear her stamp. And for all those priestesses who are full of themselves, it's good to remember that she once said: "The only queen I bow to is the Queen of England."

Walker, Mitch, and Friends. *Visionary Love: A Spirit Book of Gay Mythology and Trans-Mutational Faerie* (San Francisco: Treeroots Press, 1980). An early introduction to Radical Faery spirituality. Also take a look at *The Faggots and Their Friends Between Revolutions* by Larry Mitchell (New York: Calamus Books, 1977).

Weinstein, Marion. *Positive Magic: Occult Self-Help* (Custer, WA: Phoenix Publishing Company, 1981). A very good introductory book on magical working from a totally non-manipulative point of view. Includes everything from Astrology to I Ching to Wicca. Chapter 8, "Words of Power, the World of Self-Transformation," is very valuable and worth the price of the book. Techniques of affirmation are clear and beautifully described. Some people will find Weinstein's approach too saccharine, with almost no acknowledgment of the darker side of life, but the book is a great ethical antidote to the thousands of worthless pages published every day promising readers power, money, love, and glory through the control of others.

————. *Earth Magic: A Dianic Book of Shadows* (Custer, WA: Phoenix Publishing Company, 1986).

Zaretsky, Irving I., and Mark P. Leone. *Religious Movements in Contemporary America* (Princeton, NJ: Princeton University Press, 1974). This is a fascinating collection of essays on new religions in America, and includes such gems as "Reasonably Fantastic: Some Perspectives on Scientology, Science Fiction and Occultism" by Harriet Whitehead.

Zell-Ravenheart, Oberon. *Grimoire for the Apprentice Wizard* (Franklin Lakes, NJ: New Page, 2004). Oberon likens this to the *Boy Scouts Handbook* for wizards, and it is a mix of life skills, nature craft, and occult study.

Index